LISP Network Deploy... and Troubleshooting

The Complete Guide to LISP Implementation on IOS-XE, IOS-XR, and NX-OS

Tarique Shakil, CCIE No. 37319

Vinit Jain, CCIE No. 22854

Yves Louis

Cisco Press

LISP Network Deployment and Troubleshooting

The Complete Guide to LISP Implementation on IOS-XE, IOS-XR, and NX-OS

Tarique Shakil, Vinit Jain, Yves Louis

Published by:
Cisco Press

Library of Congress Control Number: 2019910829

ISBN-13: 978-1-58714-506-3
ISBN-10: 1-58714-506-5

Warning and Disclaimer

Trademark Acknowledgments

Special Sales

For information about buying this title in bulk quantities, or for special sales opportunities (which may include electronic versions; custom cover designs; and content particular to your business, training goals, marketing focus, or branding interests), please contact our corporate sales department at corpsales@pearsoned.com or (800) 382-3419.

For government sales inquiries, please contact governmentsales@pearsoned.com.

For questions about sales outside the U.S., please contact intlcs@pearson.com.

Feedback Information

At Cisco Press, our goal is to create in-depth technical books of the highest quality and value. Each book is crafted with care and precision, undergoing rigorous development that involves the unique expertise of members from the professional technical community.

Readers' feedback is a natural continuation of this process. If you have any comments regarding how we could improve the quality of this book, or otherwise alter it to better suit your needs, you can contact us through email at feedback@ciscopress.com. Please make sure to include the book title and ISBN in your message.

We greatly appreciate your assistance.

Editor-in-Chief: Mark Taub

Alliances Manager, Cisco Press: Arezou Gol

Director, Product Management: Brett Bartow

Managing Editor: Sandra Schroeder

Development Editor: Marianne Bartow

Project Editor: Mandie Frank

Copy Editor: Kitty Wilson

Technical Editors: Richard Furr
Max Ardica

Editorial Assistant: Cindy Teeters

Designer: Chuti Prasertsith

Composition: codeMantra

Indexer: Erika Millen

Proofreader: Charlotte Kughen

Credits

Figure 5-4   Screenshot of LISP encapsulated traffic using the Wireshark © Wireshark

Figure 5-7   Screenshot of LISP IPv6 multicast packet using the Wireshark © Wireshark

Figure 10-6   Screenshot of Packet Capture showing ICMP using the Wireshark © Wireshark

ı|ı.ı|ı.
CISCO.

Americas Headquarters
Cisco Systems, Inc.
San Jose, CA

Asia Pacific Headquarters
Cisco Systems (USA) Pte. Ltd.
Singapore

Europe Headquarters
Cisco Systems International BV Amsterdam,
The Netherlands

Cisco has more than 200 offices worldwide. Addresses, phone numbers, and fax numbers are listed on the Cisco Website at www.cisco.com/go/offices.

Cisco and the Cisco logo are trademarks or registered trademarks of Cisco and/or its affiliates in the U.S. and other countries. To view a list of Cisco trademarks, go to this URL: www.cisco.com/go/trademarks. Third party trademarks mentioned are the property of their respective owners. The use of the word partner does not imply a partnership relationship between Cisco and any other company. (1110R)

About the Authors

Tarique Shakil, CCIE No. 37319 (Service Provider, Data Center, and Security), CCSI #32545, CISSP (ISC2), CCSP (ISC2), VCP-DCV, is an Architect with the Cisco Customer Experience (CX) Data Center New Product Management team, specializing in software-defined networking (SDN) and cloud technologies. His previous experience with Cisco includes working as a high touch technical support engineer supporting Cisco premium customers for enterprise routing and service provider technologies. In his current role, Tarique leads the incubation of the latest SDN and cloud solutions, which includes working closely with engineering. Tarique has been involved in products such as Application Centric Infrastructure (ACI), Data Center Network Manager, and Virtual Topology Systems (VTS). He was also part of a startup, Candid Systems, that brought the Network Assurance Engine (NAE) to market. His areas of interest and expertise include data center virtualization, programmable fabric, network assurance, cloud data center security, and SDN. He holds a bachelor's degree in telecommunications engineering. Tarique can be found on LinkedIn at www.linkedin.com/in/tarique-shakil-cisco.

Vinit Jain, CCIE No. 22854 (R&S, Service Provider, Security, and Data Center), is a technical leader with the Cisco Customer Experience (CX), supporting customers and TAC teams around the world. For the past 10 years, Vinit has worked for the Cisco TAC and High Touch Technical Support (HTTS) organizations, supporting several customers in enterprise, service provider, and data center environments. Vinit has been a speaker at various global networking forums, including Cisco Live events. Vinit has also authored other Cisco Press books, including *Troubleshooting BGP* and *Troubleshooting Cisco Nexus Switches and NX-OS*, and he has worked on the *NX-OS and BGP Troubleshooting Live Lesson* series. Prior to Joining Cisco, Vinit worked as a CCIE trainer and as a network consultant. In addition to his CCIEs, Vinit holds multiple certifications related to programming and databases. Vinit studied mathematics at Delhi University and received a master's in information technology from Kuvempu University in India. Vinit can be found on Twitter at @VinuGenie.

Yves Louis attended the Control Data Institute in Paris (*Diplôme d'Ingénieur*), where he majored in computing. Yves is a pre-sales engineer covering data center networking as a technical solution architect at Cisco Systems. Yves focuses on fabric design and the architecture of modern data center network–based VXLAN EVPN transport and the Application Centric Infrastructure (ACI) technology. Yves also supports the Data Center Network Manager (DCNM) software framework for the next generation of data centers that rely on VXLAN EVPN for visibility, control, and fabric automation, including VXLAN EVPN Multi-site infrastructures. He also works with the Network Assurance Engine (NAE) solution, deployed in conjunction with the ACI architecture. Yves is an expert on data center interconnection solutions and has written several public technical articles at Cisco and in his personal blog related to business continuity which you can find at, http://yves-louis.com/DCI/.

About the Technical Reviewers

Richard Furr, CCIE No. 9173 (R&S and Service Provider), is a technical leader with Cisco's Customer Experience (CX), supporting customers and TAC teams around the world. For the past 19 years, Richard has worked for the Cisco TAC and High Touch Technical Support (HTTS) organizations, supporting service provider, enterprise, and data center environments. Richard specializes in resolving complex problems related to routing protocols, MPLS, multicast, and network overlay technologies. Richard co-authored the Cisco Press book *Troubleshooting Cisco Nexus Switches and NX-OS*, and has reviewed for several other books.

Max Ardica is a principal engineer with the Cisco Data Center Networking Business Unit (DCNBU), focusing on data center virtualization, automation, compute, storage, and switching architectures. Prior to the current position, Max covered during the last 20 years different roles inside Cisco ranging from SW development to product management. Before joining the DCBNU team, was part of the Server and Access Virtualization Technology Group at Cisco Systems, working on evolving protocol standards, their impact on LAN and SAN design, and the integration of Nexus and UCS as components in data center architectures.

Dedications

My late father, Shakil Ahmad, entered this world as an orphan with all odds against his success. Books helped him escape poverty. This book is dedicated to my father, whose only instrument in this world to succeed was knowledge through books. In addition, my beloved mother, Azima Shakil, always stood by all her five children, day and night, to make sure we had all that we needed to succeed in this world. Her love and prayers were always a source of hope and motivation. I dedicate this book to my mother. Last but not least, I dedicate this book to my dear wife, Shaifali, for always being by my side through good and bad times. Thank you for always patiently supporting me in all my challenges and endeavors in life. This book and many things I have accomplished would have not been possible without your support.

—*Tarique*

I would like to dedicate this book to my late sister-in-law, Kusum Sethia. The time I spent with you in Calcutta (Kolkata) was one of the most important learning phases of my life. I got to learn so much from you and, most importantly, how to handle success, failure, and pain with patience. I still remember the days we spent at the balcony, talking about different things in life. You were and will always be like a mother to me and will always remain in my thoughts and in my heart. This book is a small token of my love and gratitude for you. May you rest in peace as the memories of you live on.

—*Vinit*

I would like to dedicate this book to my wife, Pascale, and my daughter, Nina, who always supported my drive and my ambition as i was writing some chapters of this book. Thank you for being so patient and for supporting me during long evening and weekends, so I could focus on this book.

—*Yves*

Acknowledgments

Tarique Shakil:

A sincere thanks to my friends and co-authors, Vinit Jain and Yves Louis. You both are among the best experts in Cisco in your field of work. You have done great work in the field, and bringing your field experience to a book was something that had to be done. Each of you brought unique experience and knowledge to this project. Thank you for the opportunity to work with you both.

Brett and Marianne, you both have supported us with a lot of patience. My sincere gratitude for supporting us through this challenging project.

Richard Furr, thank you for reviewing the content and making sure we delivered our best. I have learned tremendously from your honest and valuable input.

Saad Hasan, you have not only been a manager but a mentor, guiding me in how I can improve myself. Thank you for supporting me in this project and my work at Cisco.

Last but not least, I would like to thank Victor Moreno and Dino Farinacci for their encouragement and guidance during my journey in authoring this book. I hope I have done some justice to the tremendous work you guys have done on LISP.

Vinit Jain:

A special thank you goes to Brett Bartow and Marianne Bartow for their wonderful support and patience on this project. This project wouldn't have been possible without your support.

Tarique, thanks for asking me to co-author this book with you. I would like to thank you and Yves for such an amazing collaboration on this project. I learned a lot from both of you guys. I look forward to working with both of you in the future.

I wouldn't have been able to complete the milestone without support from my manager, Mike Stallings. Thank you for enabling me with so many resources as well as being flexible and making an environment that is full of opportunities.

Last but not the least, I would like to thank our technical editors, Richard and Yves, for your in-depth verification of the content and insightful input to make this project a successful one.

Yves Louis:

Writing a book is harder than I thought, but I learned a lot, from LISP technology itself and especially from the close relationship established when people bring their unique and personal values.

I would like to thank Tarique and Vinit for asking me to co-author this book. It is a great honor to have been able to work with you on this technology, which covers so many different areas of interest for many diverse companies.

I am definitely grateful to Marianne Bartow and Brett Bartow for their great support and enormous tolerance during this long period of testing, writing, and reviewing.

The section on LISP Mobility deployment with modern data center fabrics could not have been completed without the amazing support of my colleague and friend Max Ardica. Max, thank you so much for being always available to exchange and share technical points of view on this network transport, as well as for the delightful in-depth technical review you provided. You rock, as usual! Finally, I would like to thank Victor Moreno and Marc Portoles Comeras for their invaluable help with LISP IP Mobility. Your constant support, always well-organized and precise, allowed us to realize the section on LISP IP Mobility.

Contents at a Glance

Reader Services

Register your copy at www.ciscopress.com/title/ISBN for convenient access to downloads, updates, and corrections as they become available. To start the registration process, go to www.ciscopress.com/register and log in or create an account*. Enter the product ISBN 9781587145063 and click Submit. When the process is complete, you will find any available bonus content under Registered Products.

*Be sure to check the box that you would like to hear from us to receive exclusive discounts on future editions of this product.

Contents

Icons Used in This Book

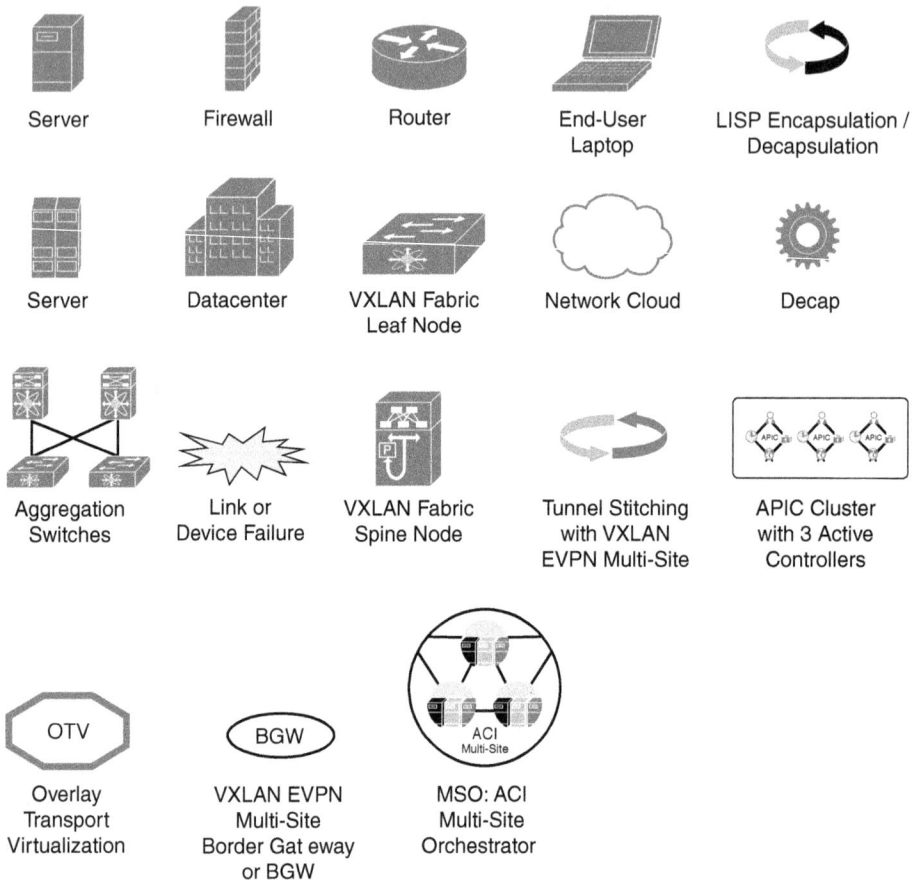

Server	Firewall	Router	End-User Laptop	LISP Encapsulation / Decapsulation

Server	Datacenter	VXLAN Fabric Leaf Node	Network Cloud	Decap

Aggregation Switches	Link or Device Failure	VXLAN Fabric Spine Node	Tunnel Stitching with VXLAN EVPN Multi-Site	APIC Cluster with 3 Active Controllers

OTV	BGW	ACI Multi-Site
Overlay Transport Virtualization	VXLAN EVPN Multi-Site Border Gat eway or BGW	MSO: ACI Multi-Site Orchestrator

Command Syntax Conventions

The conventions used to present command syntax in this book are the same conventions used in the IOS Command Reference. The Command Reference describes these conventions as follows:

- **Boldface** indicates commands and keywords that are entered literally as shown. In actual configuration examples and output (not general command syntax), boldface indicates commands that are manually input by the user (such as a **show** command).

- *Italic* indicates arguments for which you supply actual values.

- Vertical bars (|) separate alternative, mutually exclusive elements.

- Square brackets ([ ]) indicate an optional element.

- Braces ({ }) indicate a required choice.

- Braces within brackets ([{ }]) indicate a required choice within an optional element.

Introduction

Over the past few years, the networking industry has witnessed an explosion in cloud services, virtualization, and now the next wave of the Internet, with Internet of Things (IoT) information and resources that need to be accessible any time and from any place. People, information, and devices are mobile. Connectivity to devices and workloads must be seamless, even when those devices and workloads move. Thus, location has to be independent of the identity of a device. Locator/ID Separation Protocol (LISP) is an overlay protocol that has been designed to support the implementation of various applications for an open and scalable Internet.

LISP is a routing protocol that is easy to deploy and non-disruptive, and it has a variety of use cases in enterprise and service provider networks. IPv4 addresses are now near exhaustion, and IoT IPv6 networks are being deployed around the world at exponential rates. LISP enables the smooth transition from IPv4 to IPv6, with investment protection for the service providers and enterprise networks. LISP is protocol agnostic, so it can encapsulate any protocol within another and provide routing across any type of network.

LISP applications include network virtualization and virtual machine mobility in multi-tenant data centers, LISP device mobility in the mobile network, and LISP for IPv6 transitions. Every single application of LISP assists organizations in smoothly modernizing their networks for the cloud and IoT. The potential for LISP is huge, and thus it has drawn a lot of attention from both private and government organizations.

To use the various applications that LISP provides, network engineers require in-depth knowledge and understanding of how LISP works and how it can be configured in various deployment scenarios. This book describes the knowledge and techniques not only to configure and understand the working behavior of LISP but also to troubleshoot existing deployments in data center and SDN environments.

What This Book Covers

This book is the single source for understanding, configuring, and troubleshooting LISP on Cisco IOS, IOS XR, and NX-OS platforms. This book explains in great detail how LISP works, the architecture on various Cisco platforms, and configuration and troubleshooting techniques for LISP-related problems.

This book provides various LISP design and deployment scenarios from real production environments. This book also covers various scalability and convergence issues that are common in most networks and lead to outages; it explains how to troubleshoot them from a LISP perspective. The book also provides guidance in deploying LISP according to industry best practices.

The book contains the following chapters and topics:

- **Chapter 1, "LISP Introduction":** This chapter discusses the problems that the designers of LISP were initially trying to address. It covers existing use cases and upcoming future applications, as well as various LISP standards.

- **Chapter 2, "LISP Architecture":** This chapter focuses on building a fundamental understanding of the control plane and data plane layers of LISP. It provides a thorough explanation of LISP packets, messages, and communication processes; describes the LISP mapping system and infrastructure devices; and explains the LISP protocol design on various Cisco platforms.

■ **Chapter 3, "LISP IPv4 Unicast Routing":** This chapter provides a detailed explanation of unicast packet forwarding between LISP sites. It discusses internetworking between LISP and non-LISP sites and configuration and troubleshooting of unicast forwarding scenarios.

■ **Chapter 4, "LISP IPv6 Unicast Routing":** This chapter discusses existing IPv6 transition methods related to LISP. It provides details about LISP as an IPv6 transition method and analyzes several use cases for interconnecting IPv6 networks using LISP. Finally, this chapter covers troubleshooting of IPv6 networks with LISP overlays.

■ **Chapter 5, "LISP Multicast Routing Fundamentals":** This chapter covers multicast control plane concepts, including multicast packet walk and implementation and troubleshooting of LISP IP Multicast.

■ **Chapter 6, "LISP IP Mobility in Traditional Data Center Network":** Understanding the current data center workload types and how LISP helps achieve the workload requirements such as mobility. An in-depth look at how LISP helps achieve ingress route optimization in a multi-site 3-tier data center networks as workloads move across from one site to the other within a subnet or across subnets. Designing and Implementing LISP in virtualized cloud data centers with mobile workloads in traditional data centers.

■ **Chapter 7, "LISP IP Mobility in Modern Data Center Fabrics":** This chapter describes how LISP and modern data center fabrics integrate together to provide end-to-end optimized routing from the WAN to multi-site data centers. It provides a primer on VXLAN EVPN fabric and how it operates in stand-alone NX-OS deployments and with Cisco Application Centric Infrastructure (ACI) fabric in SDN-based deployments.

■ **Chapter 8, "LISP Network Virtualization/Multi-Tenancy":** This chapter describes various techniques for virtualizing enterprise and service networks to support multiple tenants using LISP virtualization models such as shared and parallel models. It also covers implementation and troubleshooting of LISP virtual private networks (VPNs) and provides examples.

■ **Chapter 9, "LISP in the Enterprise Multihome Internet/WAN Edge":** This chapter discusses and explains various challenges with BGP multihoming and load-balancing techniques deployed in enterprise networks. It explains LISP's versatility as a practical solution for multihoming at the Internet/WAN edge. This chapter describes various use cases of LISP deployments at Internet edge and discusses configuration and troubleshooting of LISP on Internet/WAN edge routers. Finally, this chapter explains LISP traffic engineering using re-encapsulating tunneling routers and disjoint RLOC domains.

■ **Chapter 10, "LISP Security":** This chapter discusses and explains various features that help secure the control plane and data plane of a LISP network. It also discusses configuration and troubleshooting related to securing LISP data packets and mapping systems.

Chapter 1

LISP Introduction

Every technology has a beginning that involves trying to solve a problem. The problem might be to invent a new concept, device, or system. Or the technology might be an effort to improve an existing system. Understanding the problem a particular technology is trying to solve helps you understand its possible function and applications. This book provides an understanding of some of the challenges—many of which still exist today—that the vendors and network operators faced as the Internet grew exponentially starting in the 1990s, when the Internet became commercialized. A new approach was required to address the various challenges caused by the unscalable exponential growth of the Internet and Internet application requirements such as host mobility and traffic engineering. Locator/ID Separation Protocol (LISP) is a solution that addresses a lot of the fundamental problems facing the Internet.

This chapter covers the following topics:

- The problems of routing scalability on the Internet and how LISP addresses them

- The various applications of LISP, including multihoming at the edges of networks, workload mobility in modern data center fabrics, network virtualization through LISP multi-tenant capabilities, and traffic engineering

- The standards of LISP in the industry

LISP and the Internet

On October 24, 1995, the Federal Networking Council (FNC) passed a resolution defining the term *Internet*. In the same year, the National Science Foundation Network (NSFNET) was decommissioned, removing the last restriction for the full commercialization of the Internet. In 1996, the size of the Internet routing table was around 50,000 networks. Ten years later, in 2006, the Internet routing table held around 200,000 prefixes. Today, in June 2019, the number of Internet Protocol version 4 (IPv4) prefixes is more than 785,000, and the IPv4 Internet autonomous system (AS) count has surpassed 64,000, as shown in Figure 1-1.

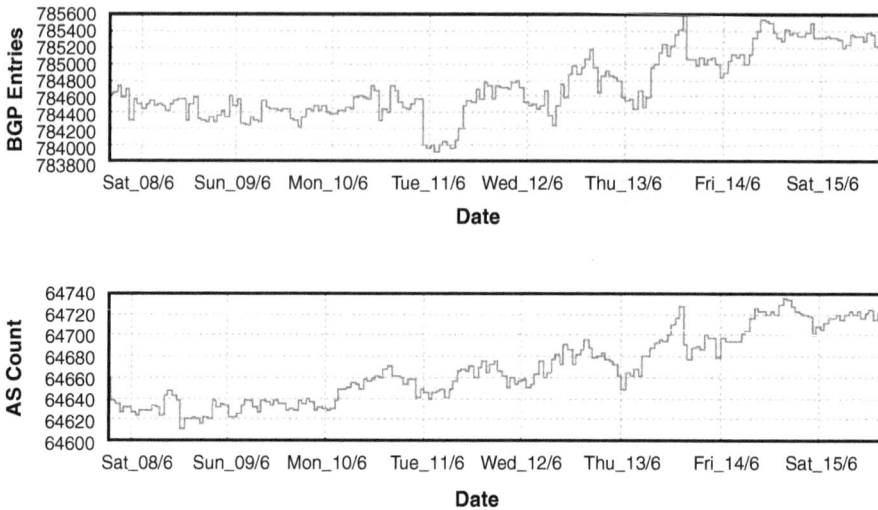

Figure 1-1   *IPv4 Internet Routing Table Size from cidr-report.org*

The current Internet Protocol version 6 (IPv6) Border Gateway Protocol (BGP) Internet routing table size is larger than 73,000 entries, and it continues to grow rapidly. Figure 1-2 shows the growth of the Internet BGP table from 1994 until 2018.

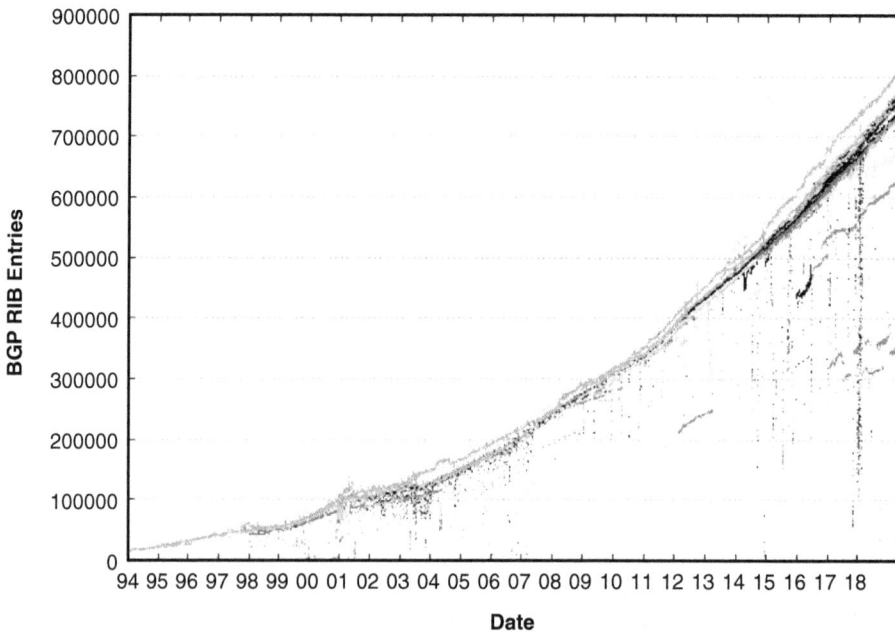

Figure 1-2   *BGP Internet Routing Table Size Trend from cidr-report.org*

In October 2006, network operators and vendors came together for the Routing and Addressing Workshop sponsored by the Internet Architecture Board (IAB) to discuss and provide recommendations to address the pressing problem of the scalability of the Internet. The complete report from the workshop is documented in RFC 4984. The key goal of the workshop was to devise a scalable routing and addressing system. RFC 4984 identified two key problems that urgently needed to be addressed:

- The scalability of the Internet routing system
- The overloading of IP address semantics

The continuous injection of new routes into the Internet routing table increases the size of the routing table. The main sources of the routes into the Internet routing table were identified as being due to multihoming, traffic engineering, non-aggregable address allocations, mergers, and acquisitions. IPv6 was also seen as a major factor in the increasing size of the Internet routing table mainly due to the foreseeable depletion of IPv4 prefixes in the near future and the much larger address space provided by IPv6. The IPv6 network prefix is 128 bits, compared to 32 bits for the IPv4 prefix. More recent trends such as mobility and the Internet of Things (IoT) are further causing the Internet routing table to grow at an accelerating rate.

The large Internet routing table size causes routing convergence to be slow and increases BGP churns. To keep up with the performance requirements, network operators have had to invest in more hardware to support the scale and have faced increasing resource requirements in terms of central processing unit (CPU), memory, heat, and power on the routing systems. To improve performance of routing systems, dedicated application-specific integrated circuits (ASICs) were designed to achieve high-rate packet switching by including forwarding information programmed into specialized hardware for switching. Specialized high-performance hardware from vendors increased capital and operational expenditures for network operators as they tried to catch up to the demand for more Internet services for their customers.

An Internet Protocol (IPv4 or IPv6) address contains bits that identify the network in which an endpoint exists and bits that uniquely identify the host within the network. The subnet mask indicates the number of bits allocated for the network in an IP address, and the remaining bits are for the host. The IP address assigned to the host puts that host in a specific network and identifies its location, answering the question "Where is the host?" The IP address assigned to an end host also uniquely identifies the host within the network, answering the question "Who is the host?" If an endpoint—for example, a laptop—moves from one network to another network, it has to change its network, which means its identity also changes because network and identity are coupled together as part of the structure of an IP address. Changing the IP address of an endpoint breaks communication because the identity changes, so the communication protocol stack and application see the endpoint as being a different endpoint. This design flaw in the IP semantics is a challenge to seamless mobility of endpoints. Figure 1-3 further illustrates this challenge.

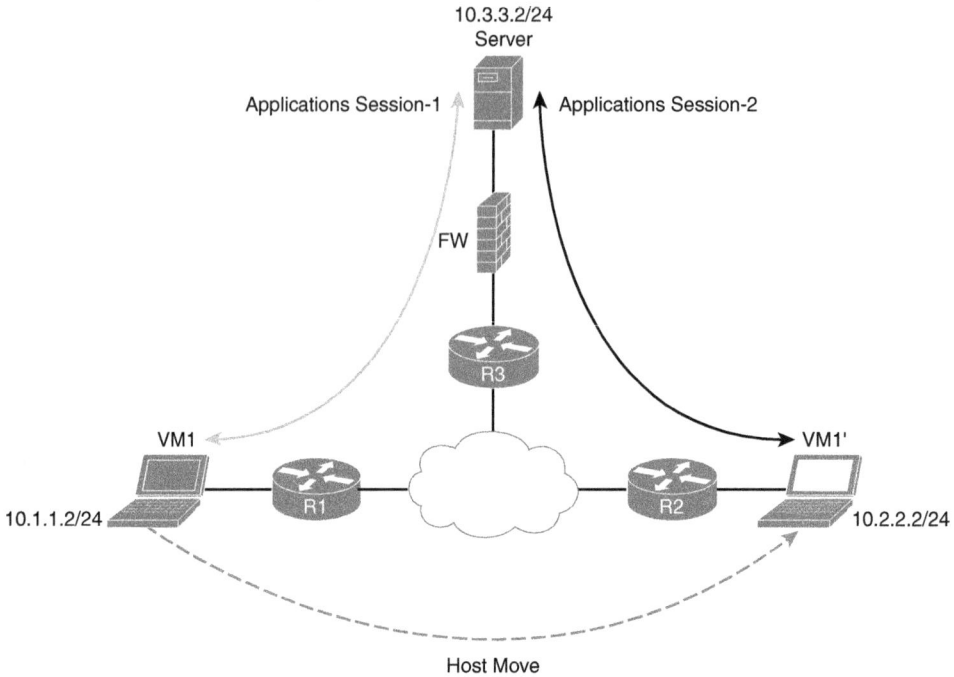

Figure 1-3 *Location and Identity in a Single IP Address Space*

In the network shown in Figure 1-3, a host machine initially exists in the network 10.1.1.0/24 on router R1, and it has the IP address 10.1.1.2/24. The 10.1.1.2/24 IP address includes the network the host exists in, which is derived from the subnet mask of the IP address, /24. The remaining 8 bits are the host bits; of these, one of the binary combinations of the host bits with decimal value 2 is assigned to the host. The 24 bits of the network plus the 8 bits of the host concatenated becomes a single address assigned to a single interface, coupling identity and location into one address. The host has an active application session, with the server hosting a particular service such as a web service or Voice over IP (VoIP). As the host moves from the router R1 location to the router R2 location, the host connects to the network 10.2.2.0/24 attached to R2, and therefore it must receive a new IP address, 10.2.2.2/24, within the same network to use R2 as a gateway for network connectivity. The host now has a new IP address, which causes the previous session to time out and disconnect, so the host must now initiate a new application session (2) with its new IP address. The firewall rules filtering traffic between the clients and the server also have to include all the combinations of application flows because addresses keep changing as hosts hop locations; this leads to an explosion in the number of rules. With the rapid adoption of mobile devices and evolution of hot live migration offered with virtual machines, clearly this is not a desirable behavior. Any sort of movement of a host from one location to another—either due to smartphone roaming or a virtual machine migrating from the primary data center to a disaster recovery site—should be seamless and scalable operationally. In a LISP network, as a host changes locations, its IP address remains the same; therefore, LISP prevents application sessions from terminating due to changing IP addresses.

An enterprise connecting to the Internet through a service provider has the option of having its own provider-independent (PI) IP address or provider-assigned (PA) network address. A PA address is a subnet under the major network of the provider, while a PI address does not fall under the major network of the provider and therefore is not aggregable by the provider to the Internet. If an enterprise is multihomed to two service providers, the preference is always to have a PI network address. A PI address provides the enterprise with more flexibility in traffic engineering and routing policy design by simply taking advantage of the longest prefix match rule of routing systems. A longer prefix is always preferred as the optimal path, regardless of the administrative distance or metric of a route. Plus, when an enterprise changes service providers, there is never a need to do IP reassignments of its network. IP address reassignment has severe impacts on network infrastructure and applications. The more PI address space in the Internet, the more the Internet table size continues to grow since the addresses are non-aggregable by the service providers with which the enterprise networks are peering. As a provider's Internet routing table size grows, the cost of maintaining the network grows. As enterprises manipulate routing policy (by adjusting the number of prefixes advertised and the prefix length) to optimize inbound and outbound network traffic, service providers must adjust capacity to meet traffic demands on links.

The IAB workshop report emphasized finding a solution that separates the Internet addressing semantics into two separate namespaces: one namespace that tells the location and a separate namespace that tells the identity. Although this concept is simple, its impact is enormous. Imagine that a tree has a trunk (the Internet backbone) and branches (service providers) spreading outward. Attached to each branch are leaves. The branches and trunks represent the Internet transport network, and the leaves are the enterprise or endpoints connecting to the Internet. The leaves are detachable and can be placed anywhere on the branches of the tree and still be reached with the same properties (addresses) that identify the individual leaves. The Internet or the branches do not have to change properties; a leaf simply changes its location to another branch, and its relationship to the tree as a whole is a new location that it attaches to. You can continue to add more leaves (enterprises) and attach them to the various branches (Internet service providers [ISPs]), and the structure of the tree remains relatively the same in terms of scale because the tree grows only when you add more branches, not when you add leaves. Branches grow at a much slower rate than do leaves. The IAB workshop attendees aspired to achieve a scalable Internet that limits the impact on the Internet routing system as more users connect to the Internet. The means to achieve the stability and scalability is to separate how we address the leaves from how we address the branches; the goal was to separate the namespace that the ISPs and the enterprises or endpoints exist in. The ISPs define the locations on the Internet where the endpoints and enterprises will attach. LISP is the solution that came out of the specific recommendations from the IAB workshop report.

LISP is an IP overlay solution that retains the same semantics for IPv4 and IPv6 packet headers but uses two separate namespaces: one to specify the location and the other to specify the identity, as shown in Figure 1-4.

Outer Header	UDP	LISP Header	Inner IP Header	IP Payload
Source and Destination Routing Locator RLOCs "where"	UDP	LISP	Original Source and Destination Endpoints IDs "who"	User Data

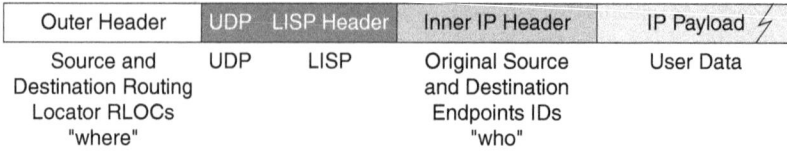

Figure 1-4   *LISP Packet High-Level Header Format*

A LISP packet has an inner IP header, which, like the headers of traditional IP packets, is for communicating endpoint to endpoint, from a particular source to a destination address. The outer IP header provides the location the endpoint attaches to. The outer IP headers are also IP addresses. Therefore, if an endpoint changes location, its endpoint IP address remains the same. It is the outer header that always gets the packet to the location of the endpoint. The endpoint identifier (EID) address is mapped to a router that the endpoint sits behind, which is known as the routing locator (RLOC) in LISP terminology. So how does a router know where the endpoint is currently located or which EID maps to which RLOC?

The LISP network consists of a mapping system that contains a global database of RLOC-EID mapping entries. The mapping system is the control plane of the LISP network decoupled from the data plane. The mapping system is address family agnostic— that is, the EID can be IPv4 address mapped to an RLOC IPv6 address and vice versa. Or the EID may be a Virtual Extensible LAN (VXLAN) Layer 2 virtual network identifier (L2VNI) mapped to a VXLAN tunnel endpoint (VTEP) address functioning as an RLOC IP address.

The separation of the control plane from the data plane provides the flexibility to introduce many new applications across various network environments. Enhanced Interior Gateway Routing Protocol (EIGRP) over the top uses EIGRP as the control plane and LISP as the data plane encapsulation to route over a wide area network (WAN). A very hot upcoming application of LISP is Cisco Software Defined Access (SD-Access) in the enterprise network, which uses LISP as the control plane and VXLAN as the data plane encapsulation protocol.

Use Cases for LISP

The separation of location and identity sounds like a very simple concept, but it is very powerful in terms of application. This simple solution does address the challenges around improving the scalability of the Internet, but it also has many other applications. The list of applications keeps growing mainly due to the fundamental characteristics of the LISP protocol:

- **Identity and location address separation:** This separation allows endpoint mobility to be achieved using a scalable approach. The *where* and *who* addresses are in separate address spaces, as explained earlier. The *who* part can move anywhere without changing who it is, and the *who* can be a single mobile device or an entire enterprise network site attaching to a service provider, depending on the use case.

■ **Decoupling of the data plane from the control plane:** LISP is not a routing protocol. LISP does not learn routes, and LISP does not calculate the best path by using metrics such as cost and then push routing information to its neighboring routers. LISP does not form any sort of control plane sessions with any other neighbor, as BGP does, and it does not form neighbor relationships within a router, as the Open Shortest Path First (OSPF) routing protocol process does. Every single LISP router learns forwarding information through a pull mechanism from an external mapping system database using LISP control plane messages. LISP routers push or register locally attached network information to the mapping system using LISP control plane messages. The mapping system can store any sort of addressing or route attributes, such as security tags or virtual routing and forwarding (VRF), for the purpose of packet encapsulation and forwarding. LISP may be used purely as a control plane protocol to map and learn certain destination endpoint attributes prior to encapsulation of the packet for forwarding. The data plane encapsulation of the packet may append a LISP header if the node is a LISP router in a LISP network or a VXLAN header if the node is a VTEP in a Layer 3 VXLAN fabric. Depending on the use case, LISP may be used purely as a control plane protocol to provide mapping service without using LISP for data packet encapsulation. This is possible only because the decoupling of the control plane from the data plane.

■ **Address family versatility:** LISP can encapsulate and map IPv4 or IPv6 packets. The packets may be unicast or multicast, both in the location and in the identifier namespace. This characteristic complements the location and identity separation characteristic because the identity namespace may be of one address family and the location namespace of another. These are identified as two separate characteristics because address family versatility may not necessarily be applied, but the namespace separation is always applied in any LISP use case.

Based on these three characteristics of LISP, imagine the various applications LISP can be used for where various address family support, traffic engineering, network virtualization, and overlays are required. At the time of this writing, these are some of the common applications of LISP:

■ **Enterprise edge multihoming:** An enterprise can exist in its own EID address namespace while peering with two separate ISPs, each in its own RLOC namespace on the Internet. Because an enterprise can now exist in its own namespace but be reachable through a different provider RLOC namespace, the enterprise no longer depends on a single specific SP for IP address space, eliminating the challenges of PI and PA design requirements for multihoming implementations. LISP simplifies the routing and traffic engineering implementation sites by removing the complexities of BGP routing policy design. Anyone with experience in BGP knows that ingress and egress traffic engineering design and implementation in multihomed BGP sites can get very complexed in largescale environments.

■ **Data center workload mobility:** Multi-tenant cloud data centers with virtualized workloads provide data center administrators the ability to spawn virtual machines with a click of a few buttons and provision applications to meet the immediate demands of business. To maintain 99.999% (five 9s) uptime, virtual machines at times get migrated from one host to another to meet demand or to ensure continuous service as a host in which the virtual machine lives may experience resource shortages and system or hardware failures. LISP ensures that in such environments, virtual machines can move across the host attached to separate top-of-rack (ToR) switches within the same data center or across different data centers. The migrations can be within the same subnet or across subnets within the same data center or across different data centers; in any case, a virtual machine maintains its original IP address and is still reachable regardless of its location. LISP ensures that inbound and outbound traffic takes optimal paths as workloads are migrated. The two modes are known as Extended Subnet Mode (ESM), which works in conjunction with the extension of the VLANs of interest (Layer 2 DCI), and Across Subnet Mode (ASM), which offers mobility across a routed network (Layer 3 DCI).

■ **IP mobility:** Mobile devices connected to wireless or cellular networks were designed to allow endpoints to move across rooms, campuses, metro areas, countries, and even the whole world, via international roaming. Today it is possible to make phone calls from mobile phones while on a flight 35,000 feet in the sky. In addition, Internet access is available with most major international carriers as you travel across seas from one country to another. Your position is continuously changing, yet the expectation is to have seamless access to the network for data, voice, or both. Seamless connectivity is achieved only if the same connectivity is always maintained. The same connectivity is always maintained if the endpoint device information is consistent as the endpoint moves. LISP provides this fundamental requirement to achieve IP mobility. LISP provides optimal reachability to endpoints as they move, regardless of the address family. Other IP mobility solutions had caveats such as suboptimal routing or support for only IPv4 or IPv6.

■ **IPv6 enablement and transition:** With the exhaustion of IPv4 addresses and the growth of the cloud, mobile devices, and now the Internet of Things (IoT), billions of addresses will be needed in the coming years as more organizations, governments, and people connect to the Internet. Cars, airplanes, home appliances, traffic lights, public transport system, manufacturing machines, and industrial sensors all are connecting to the Internet. IPv6 address space will supply the addresses required to connect the billions of devices in the coming years. IPv4 networks will also exist in the years to come. It is not possible for any organization to turn off IPv4 overnight. The migration to IPv6 must be hitless, and IPv4 and IPv6 must be allowed to coexist for some time. LISP address family versatility smooths the transition to IPv6 and allows the successful enablement of IPv6.

■ **Network virtualization:** In the data center fabric or the service provider network, the infrastructure is shared among various tenants or customers. The segmentation of the control plane and data plane forwarding information is imperative to provide security and isolation of the traffic from the various individual consumers of the network. Network virtualization technologies such as VLANs and VRF were traditionally used to segment the network at Layer 2 and Layer 3. Routing protocols also create multiple routing context mapping to each VRF network created.

LISP segments the data plane and control plane mapping using a 24-bit instance ID field in the LISP packet header. LISP provides transport-independent network virtualization through a highly scalable overlay-based solution.

■ **Software Defined Access (SD-Access):** Cisco Digital Network Architecture (DNA) provides an architectural model and framework to implement network automation, assurance, and security in the enterprise WAN, campus, and edge networks. The Cisco DNA architecture for the enterprise campus introduces Layer 3 programmable fabric using VXLAN as the data plane, LISP as the control plane, and TrustSec as the policy plane. SD-Access fabric is an example of LISP being used purely as a control plane protocol to provide mapping function of the endpoints and location address in the fabric with some policy attributes for each endpoint. This is possible because of the decoupling of the LISP control plane and data plane function.

Some of the applications mentioned here are discussed in detail later in this book.

Standards of LISP

Cisco created LISP, but the protocol has been an open standard protocol from the beginning. An IETF LISP Working Group created in spring 2009 was dedicated to the open standardization of LISP. Today more than 20 Internet Drafts and Requests for Comments (RFCs) exist for LISP.

Note Refer to the LISP Working Group website for access to the LISP RFCs: https://datatracker.ietf.org/wg/lisp/charter/.

LISP is supported across all of Cisco's operating systems, including Cisco IOS, IOS-XE, NX-OS, and IOS-XR. For certain operating systems, specific licenses and packages must be installed to configure LISP. For example, Cisco Internetwork Operating System (IOS) requires a datak9 license, and the Nexus operating system requires a transport license. It is important to confirm platform support for LISP. In addition, the modular line card model or ASIC generation also must be considered when deploying LISP on certain platforms.

Note To confirm hardware and software requirements to run LISP on Cisco enterprise, service provider, and data center platforms, refer to http://lisp.cisco.com/lisp_hwsw.html#HW. The following chapters explain Cisco platform-specific LISP architecture and configuration in detail.

In meeting the demands of SDN/NFV infrastructures, Cisco has built virtualized appliances for some of its routing and switching platforms, including NX-OSv, IOSv, Cloud Services Router (CSR1000V), and XRv. Refer to the release notes for supported features. CSR1000V is a virtualized implementation of the IOS-XE operating system that has become popular in cloud data centers deploying LISP as an overlay solution.

The OpenLISP Project is an open source implementation of LISP that runs on the FreeBSD operating system. The data plane functions, such as caching, encapsulation, and de-encapsulation, run on the kernel space; the control plane is meant to run on the user space.

LISP Open Overlay Router (OOR), which was initially called LISPMob, is an open implementation of LISP available for Android, OpenWrt, and Linux. OOR has evolved into a data plane and control plane protocol that integrates with the OpenDaylight controller's LISP Flow Mapping module to provision overlays. OOR supports various overlay encapsulation standards, such as VXLAN-GPE and LISP. NETCONF/YANG and the LISP control plane are both supported with OOR. OOR runs on the user space of the Linux systems.

Other implementations of LISP include AVM/Fritz!Box and Aless. A few third-party vendors also provide LISP support on their platforms.

Summary

This chapter covers the genesis of LISP and describes the benefits and application of LISP. LISP is a Layer 3 overlay protocol that is addressing the challenges of the scalability of the Internet and mobility through separation of the identity and location namespaces, decoupling of the control plane and data plane, and address family versatility. The LISP protocol from its inception has been an open standard protocol that interoperates across various platforms and is incrementally deployable on top of any type of transport. LISP's flexibility has led to its application in every part of today's modern network, from the data center to the enterprise WAN to the enterprise campus to the service provider edge and to the core.

References

The following references provide more details on the topics discussed in this chapter:

RFC 4984, "Report from the IAB Workshop on Routing and Addressing"

RFC 6830, "The Locator/ID Separation Protocol (LISP)" (updated by RFC 8113)

RFC 6831, "Locator/ID Separation Protocol for Multicast Environments"

RFC 6832, "Locator/ID Separation Protocol and Non-LISP Sites"

RFC 6833, "Locator/ID Separation Protocol Map-Server Interface"

RFC 6834, "Locator/ID Separation Protocol Map-Versioning"

RFC 6835, "Locator/ID Separation Protocol Internet Groper (LIG)"

RFC 6836, "Locator/ID Separation Protocol Alternative Logical Topology (LISP+ALT)"

RFC 7052, "Locator/ID Separation Protocol MIB"

RFC 7215, "Locator/ID Separation Protocol Network Element Deployment Considerations"

RFC 7835, "Locator/ID Separation Protocol Threat Analysis"

RFC 7934, "Locator/ID Separation Protocol Impact"

RFC 7954, "Locator/ID Separation Protocol Endpoint Identifier (EID) Block"

RFC 7955, "Mgmt Guide for Locator/ID Separation Protocol Endpoint Identifier Block"

RFC 8060, "Locator/ID Separation Protocol Canonical Address Format (LCAF)"

RFC 8061, "Locator/ID Separation Protocol Data-Plane Confidentiality"

RFC 8111, "Locator/ID Separation Protocol Delegated Database Tree (LISP-DDT)"

RFC 8113, "LISP Shared Extension Message & IANA Registry for Packet Type Allocations"

RFC 8373, "Locator/ID Separation Protocol Multicast"

Internet Draft, "An Architectural Introduction to the Locator/ID Separation Protocol (LISP)"

https://www.lispers.net

## Chapter 2

LISP Architecture

Locator/ID Separation Protocol (LISP) architecture is a feature-rich architecture that not only does the separation of device identity and location but also brings down operational expenses (opex), provides a Border Gateway Protocol (BGP)–free multihoming network, enables multi address-family (AF) support, provides a highly scalable virtual private network (VPN) solution, enables host mobility in data centers, and much more. To understand how all these functionalities and benefits are achieved, it is important to know the underlying architectural components of LISP and also understand how LISP works. This chapter explores the details of the architecture of LISP.

This chapter covers the following topics:

- LISP architecture
- LISP Canonical Address Format (LCAF)
- LISP packet headers
- LISP control plane messages
- LISP Database Architecture: LISP-DDT
- LISP architecture on Cisco platforms

LISP Architecture

LISP, defined in RFC 6830, is a routing and addressing architecture of the Internet Protocol. The LISP routing architecture was designed to solve issues related to scaling, multihoming, inter-site traffic engineering, and mobility. An address on the Internet today combines location (how the device is attached to the network) and identity semantics in a single 32-bit (IPv4 address) or 128-bit (IPv6 address) number. The purpose of LISP is to separate the location from the identity. In simple words, with LISP, *where* you are (the network layer locator) in a network that can change, but *who* you are (the network layer identifier) in the network remains the same. LISP separates the end user device identifiers from the routing locators used by others to reach them. The LISP routing architecture design creates a new paradigm, splitting the device identity—that is, the *endpoint identifier (EID)*—from its location—that is, the *routing locator (RLOC)*.

In order to further understand how LISP does the locator/ID separation, it is important to first learn about the architectural components of LISP. The following are some of the functions or components that form the LISP architecture:

- **Ingress tunnel router (ITR):** The ITR receives the packets from the site-facing interfaces and encapsulates them to the remote LISP site or natively forwards the packets to a non-LISP site.

- **Egress tunnel router (ETR):** The ETR receives the packets from core-facing interfaces and de-encapsulates them to deliver them to local EIDs at the site.

- **Proxy ingress tunnel router (PITR):** A PITR is an infrastructure LISP network entity that receives packets from non-LISP sites and encapsulates the packets to LISP sites or natively forwards them to non-LISP sites.

- **Proxy egress tunnel router (PETR):** A PETR is an infrastructure LISP network entity that de-encapsulates packets from LISP sites to deliver them to non-LISP sites.

- **Map server (MS):** An MS configures LISP site policy to authenticate when LISP sites try to register to the MS. It also performs the following functions:

  - Provides a service interface to the ALT router and injects routes in the ALT BGP when the site registers.

  - Receives MAP requests over the ALT router and encapsulates them to registered ETRs.

- **Map resolver (MR):** The MR performs the following functions:

  - Receives MAP requests, which are encapsulated by ITRs.

  - Provides a service interface to the ALT router, de-encapsulates MAP requests, and forwards on the ALT topology.

  - Sends negative MAP replies in response to MAP requests for non-LISP sites.

- **ALT router (ALT):** An ALT router is a router that runs External Border Gateway Protocol (eBGP) over an alternate Generic Routing Encapsulation (GRE) tunnel topology. It is an off-the-shelf router that does not run LISP. The ALT router simply forwards MAP requests according to the BGP Routing Information Base (RIB). ALT routers are used to aggregate BGP connections and to summarize EID prefix routes.

- **LISP Delegated Database Tree (LISP-DDT):** LISP-DDT is a hierarchical distributed database authority that provides EID-to-RLOC mappings. It is statically populated with the EID namespace and other nodes, called *DDT nodes*. Each DDT node is authoritative for one or more EID prefixes, or "child" DDT nodes, for more specific EID prefixes addressed by an authoritative DDT node.

The following sections discuss these components and features in detail.

Routing Locators and Endpoint Identifiers

The IPv4 or IPv6 address of a device represents its identity and location. In the present-day Internet, when a host moves from one location to another location, it is assigned a different IPv4 or IPv6 address, which overloads the location/identity semantic. LISP separates the location and identity of a device through the RLOC and EID. The RLOC represents the IP address of the egress tunnel router (ETR) the host is attached to, and the EID represents the IP address assigned to the host. With LISP, the change in location of a device does not result in a change in its identity. In other words, when the device moves from one location to another, it still retains its IPv4 or IPv6 address; however, the site tunnel router (xTR) is dynamically updated. Ensuring that the identity does not change for the host even with the change in location requires a mapping system. LISP provides the distributed architecture *EID-to-RLOC mapping* that maps EIDs to RLOCs. Figure 2-1 displays the location and identity separation in a network with EIDs and RLOCs.

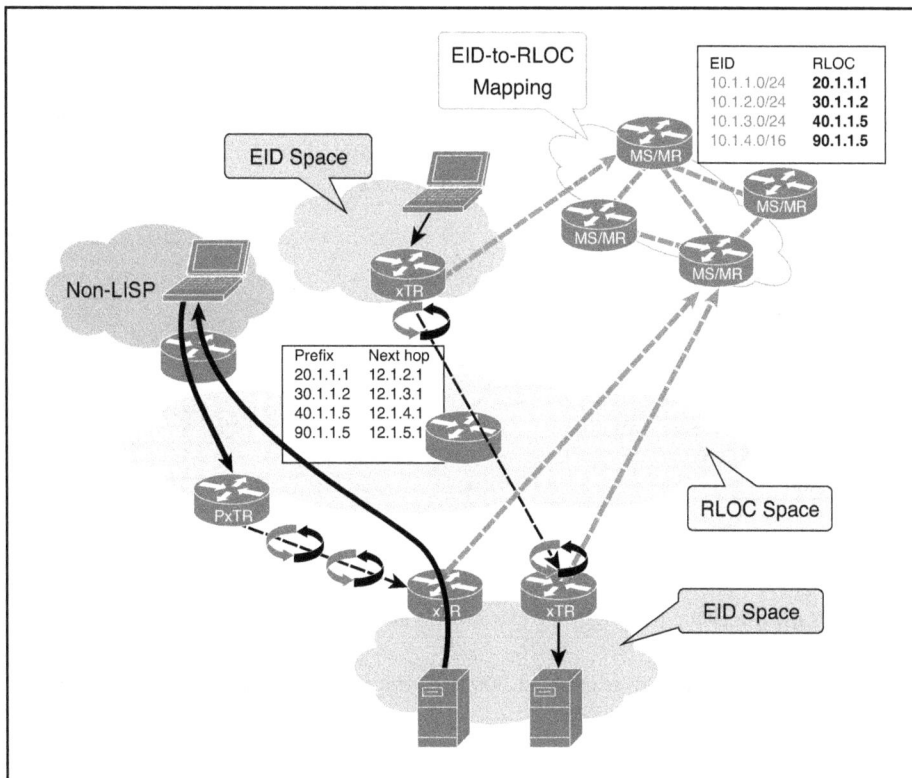

Figure 2-1 *Using EIDs and RLOCs for Location/ID Separation*

Ingress/Egress Tunnel Routers (xTRs)

Both the ITRs and ETRs are also referred to as xTRs. The ITRs and ETRs play a vital role in packet forwarding in the LISP architecture.

An ITR is a router that performs the following tasks:

- Accepts an IP packet from a host and treats the IP destination as an EID

- Performs an EID-to-RLOC mapping lookup in its local map caches or remote map resolver in the event of a missed hit

- Prepends the packet with a LISP header, with the RLOC as the destination IP address

- Forwards the packet to the ETR that is hosting the RLOC

An ETR is a router that performs the following tasks:

- Accepts an IP packet with a LISP header, where the destination IP address is hosted by the router

- Strips the LISP header and forwards the packet based on the next IP header found on the packet

To further understand the functioning of the ITR and ETR routers, examine the topology shown in Figure 2-2. In this topology, there are two LISP sites, Site1 and Site2, with hosts in subnets 100.1.1.0/24 and 200.1.1.0/24. The Internet cloud has four ISP networks, with the subnets 10.0.0.0/8, 20.0.0.0/8, 30.0.0.0/8, and 40.0.0.0/8.

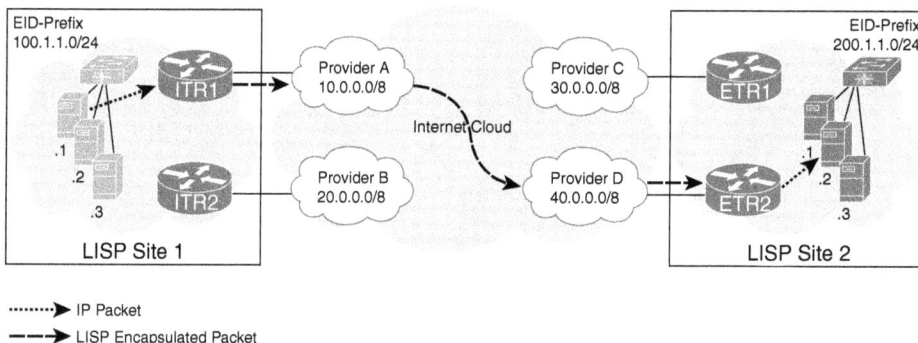

········▶ IP Packet
── ─ ▶ LISP Encapsulated Packet

Figure 2-2 *LISP-Enabled Topology*

If the host 100.1.1.1 wants to reach host 200.1.1.2, the following control plane lookups happen in a LISP-enabled network:

Step 1.   Host S1 with IP address 100.1.1.1 performs a DNS lookup for destination host D1 with IP address 200.1.1.2.

Step 2.   After the DNS lookup is performed, the host forwards the packet to one of the ITRs, based on the routing and forwarding preference. In this case, the packet is sent to ITR1.

Step 3.   ITR1 receives the packet and checks the IP headers and does not find a relevant next-hop entry for forwarding the received packet with source IP address 100.1.1.1 and destination IP address 200.1.1.2. The ITR then thinks that it might be a potential packet for LISP encapsulation. It performs a lookup in the map cache entry and finds two locator sets for the destination 200.1.1.0/24 subnet.

Step 4.   The ITR creates an overlay from ITR to ETR with LISP encapsulation. The encapsulation of the IP packet happens on the ITR, and the de-encapsulation happens on the ETR.

Step 5.   The ETR forwards the IP packet to the destination host.

Map Servers (MSs) and Map Resolvers (MRs)

The fundamental behavior of LISP is to separate the EID from the RLOC, which allows the host to retain its identity even with a change in location. But the seamless mobility is achieved using the EID-to-RLOC mapping, which is maintained in the distributed database. The *map server* (MS) learns EID-to-RLOC mapping entries from the ETRs and publishes these mappings to the distributed mapping database. To publish its EID prefixes, an ETR periodically sends its mapping entries to the MS. The MS also receives the map requests via the mapping system and forwards them to the registered ETRs.

The *map resolver* (MR), on the other hand, accepts LISP encapsulated map requests from an ITR. Based on a map request, two things may happen.

▪ If the destination IP address is part of the EID namespace, the MR finds the appropriate EID-to-RLOC mapping by consulting the distributed mapping database system.

▪ If the destination is not found in the EID namespace, then a negative map reply is sent to the ITR. This means that if the MR receives a map request for a non-LISP site, the MR sends a negative map reply in response.

To understand the functioning of MR/MS routers, examine the topology shown in Figure 2-3.

In this topology, when host S1 with IP address 100.1.1.1 tries to reach host D2 with IP address 200.1.1.2, it sends the packet to one of the local ITRs at the site. Then, if the ITR does not have an entry in its map cache table, the ITR creates a map request looking for the host 200.1.1.2 and sends it to the map resolver (MR). The map request is also LISP encapsulated where the outer header has the source IP address of 20.0.0.2 and destination IP address of 50.0.0.2. Based on the request, the MR forwards the map request to the map server (MS). The MS redirects the packet to the ETR, which has the information about the host prefix/subnet. One important thing to notice in this map request/map reply is that the map request comes toward the mapping system, but the mapping system does not send the reply. The ETR sends the map reply directly to the ITR that raised the map request. This significantly reduces the load on the MR/MS and at the same time helps validate the path between the ETR and the ITR. The map reply contain the mapping entries of the ETRs that hold the destination EIDs.

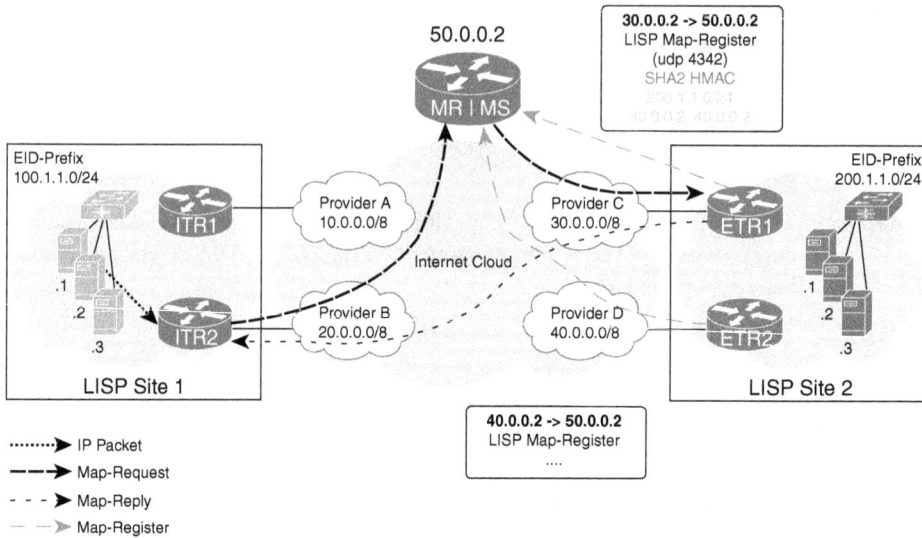

Figure 2-3   *LISP Map Request and Map Reply*

Figure 2-4 illustrates an example of an ITR sending a map request for a prefix in a non-LISP site.

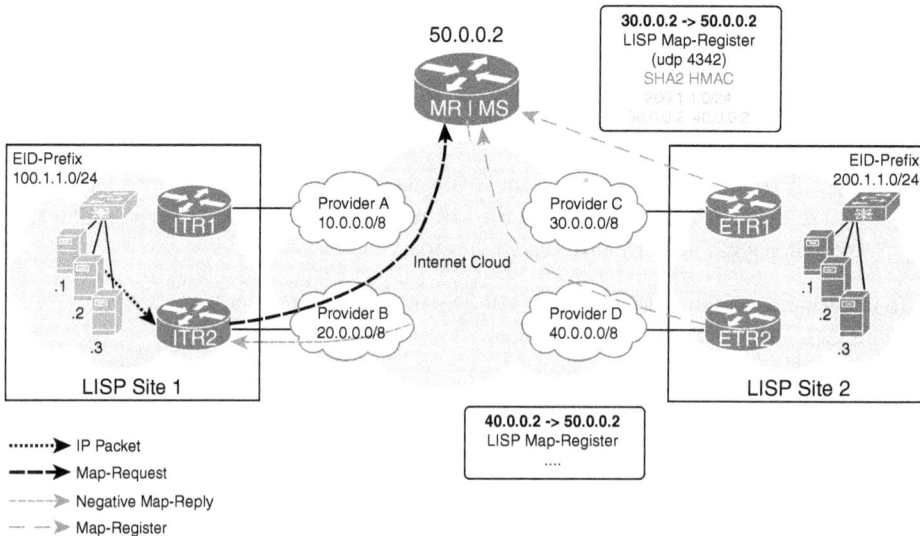

Figure 2-4   *LISP Map Request and Negative Map Reply*

In this scenario, if a host connected to the ITR tries to reach a destination that is on a non-LISP site, the ITR (as in the previous scenario) creates a map request and sends it to the MR. The MS performs a lookup to see whether the EID is present in its mapping database. If the MS cannot find a matching entry, it sends a negative map reply back to the originating ITR. On receiving the negative reply, the ITR updates its map cache entry with the tag *forward-native*, which means that the destination is part of a non-LISP site.

Proxy Ingress/Egress Tunnel Router (PxTR)

Sites cannot all be LISP enabled immediately, and not all segments of the network are not capable of running LISP from day 1. With the gradual migration from non-LISP-enabled sites to LISP-enabled sites, network operators still require that the non-LISP-capable sites be able to send traffic destined to LISP-enabled sites. This is where *proxy ingress/egress tunnel routers* (*PxTRs*) come into play.

Proxy ingress tunnel routers (*PITRs*) allow for non-LISP sites to send packets to LISP sites. A PITR is a new network element that shares many characteristics with a LISP ITR. A PITR allows non-LISP sites to send packets to LISP sites without requiring changes in the protocol or devices at the non-LISP sites. PITRs perform two primary functions:

- **Originating EID advertisements:** PITRs advertise highly aggregated EID-prefix space on behalf of LISP sites to the non-LISP sites so that the non-LISP sites can reach them.

- **Encapsulating legacy Internet traffic:** PITRs encapsulate non-LISP Internet traffic into LISP packets and route them toward their destination RLOCs.

Proxy egress tunnel routers (*PETRs*) are used to allow traffic from LISP sites to non-LISP sites. A PETR acts as an ETR for traffic sourced from LISP sites and destined to non-LISP sites. PETRs are useful in the following cases:

- **Avoiding strict uRPF failures:** Some providers' access networks require the source of a packet to be within the address scope of the access networks. PETRs allow for LISP sites to send packets to non-LISP sites in cases where the access network does not allow for the LISP site to send packets with the source address of the site's EIDs.

- **Traversing a different IP protocol:** The transit path network between LISP sites and non-LISP sites may not be IPv4 or IPv6 enabled. LISP support for mixed protocol encapsulation allows PETRs to hop over such networks in order to route the traffic between the LISP and non-LISP sites.

Note   PITRs and PETRs are the same physical devices. As with xTRs, the distinction is based on the direction of the flow with functions of de-encapsulation or encapsulation.

The LISP ALT System

The LISP *Alternative Logical Topology* (*ALT*) system is defined in RFC 6836. The LISP ALT system is a simple distributed index system that assists the ITR or MR in finding the ETR that holds the RLOC mapping information for a particular EID. ALT is a topology formed using GRE tunnels via which EIDs are routable. It is used to propagate mapping entries to the ITR. The purpose of the ALT system is to advertise EID prefixes in BGP on an alternative topology. The ALT system thus allows for incremental deployment of LISP. Figure 2-5 shows a LISP-enabled topology with ALT routers in the network.

192.168.1.1

ITR

(1)

192.168.1.1 -> 192.168.10.10
LISP Packet
UDP 4341

192.168.1.1 -> 10.1.1.1
Map-Request
UDP 4342

192.168.10.10

Map-Resolver

LISP-ALT — LISP-ALT   Transit   (2)

(3)

192.168.1.1 -> 10.1.1.1
Map-Request
UDP 4342

LISP-ALT — LISP-ALT   Transit   (4)

Map-Server

192.168.20.20

(5)

192.168.20.20 -> 192.168.2.2
LIST-Packet
UDP 4341

192.168.1.1 -> 10.1.1.1
Map-Request
UDP 4342

192.168.2.2

192.168.2.2 -> 192.168.1.1
Map-Reply
UDP 4342

(6)

ETR

10.1.0.0/24

Legend:
EIDs -> Green
Locators -> Red
BGP-over-GRE___
Physical Link ▬
Map-Request Path ▬▬
  ••••

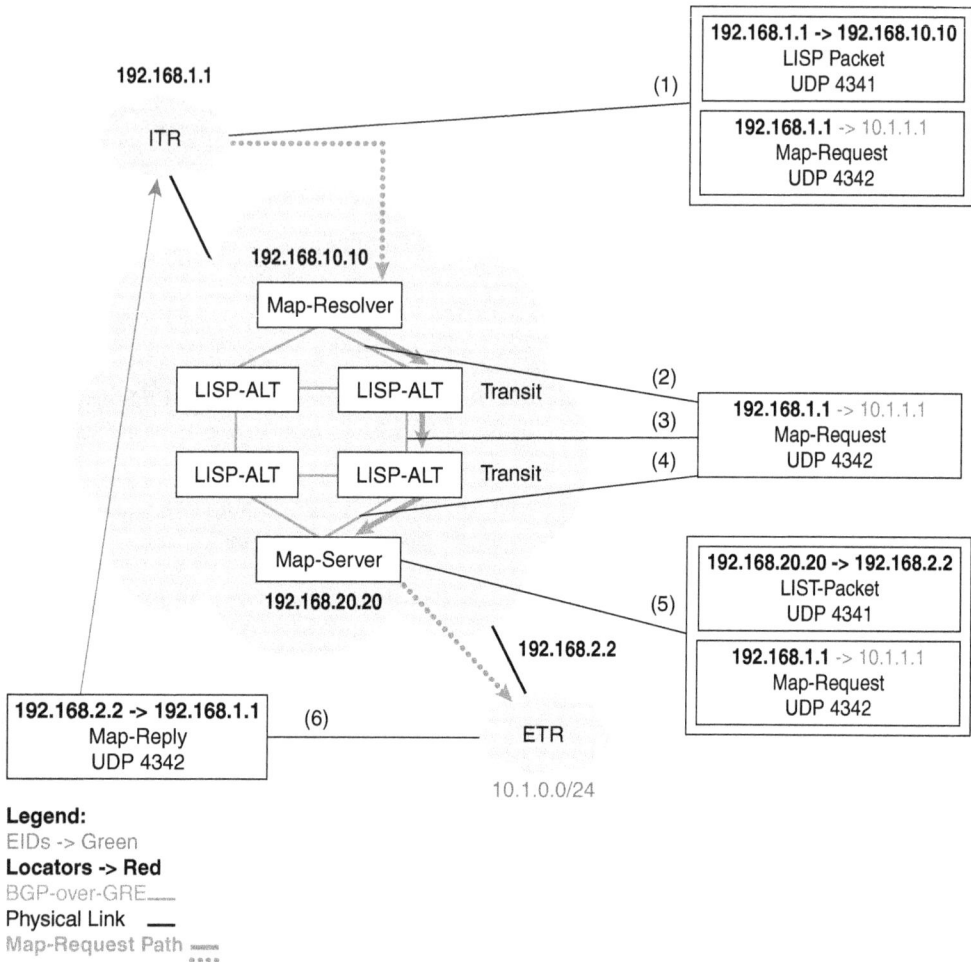

Figure 2-5 *LISP ALT*

An ALT-only device can be off-the-shelf gear that can be configured on router hardware or even on a Linux host. The device just needs to be BGP and GRE capable. Often users confuse the functionality of LISP ALT system. The ALT system does not distribute the actual EID-to-RLOC mappings but provides a forwarding path from an ITR or MR to an ETR that holds the mapping for a particular EID prefix.

LISP Canonical Address Format (LCAF)

There are two primary numbering spaces in the LISP architecture: EIDs and RLOCs. These addresses are either 32-bit for IPv4 or 128-bit for IPv6 and are encoded inside a LISP control message. Current deployment of LISP allows for only IPv4 and IPv6 AFI encodings, but other arbitrary address family identifier (AFI) values may need encodings for LISP to support them. To support such arbitrary AFIs, LISP introduced *LISP*

Canonical Address Format (LCAF), defined in RFC 8060. IANA has assigned the AFI value 0x4003 (16387) to the LCAF.

The LCAF information gets encoded inside the LISP header. The initial 6 bytes of the canonical address are as follows (see Figure 2-6):

- **2-byte AFI field:** Set to 16387.
- **1-byte Rsvd1 field:** Reserved for future use. Set to 0.
- **1-byte Flags field:** For future use. Set to 0.
- **1-byte Type field:** Canonical Address Format encodings.
- **1-byte Rsvd2 field:** Reserved for future use. Set to 0.

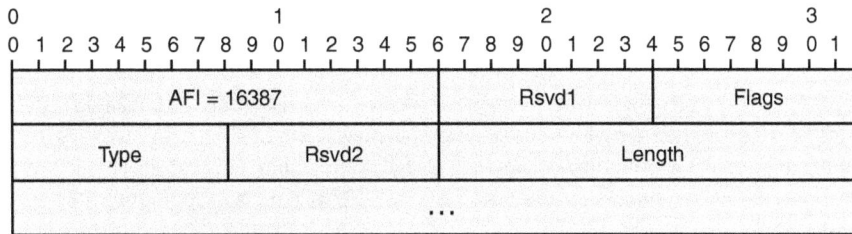

```
 0                   1                   2                   3
 0 1 2 3 4 5 6 7 8 9 0 1 2 3 4 5 6 7 8 9 0 1 2 3 4 5 6 7 8 9 0 1
+-+-+-+-+-+-+-+-+-+-+-+-+-+-+-+-+-+-+-+-+-+-+-+-+-+-+-+-+-+-+-+-+
|              AFI = 16387              |      Rsvd1      |      Flags      |
+---------------------------------------+-----------------+-----------------+
|      Type       |      Rsvd2      |                 Length                  |
+-----------------+-----------------+-----------------------------------------+
|                              . . .                                          |
+-----------------------------------------------------------------------------+
```

Figure 2-6   *Canonical Address Header*

The Length field is a 2-byte field that holds the value, in bytes. The value of this field represents canonical address payload starting with and including the byte after the Length field.

The Type field can contain various values that represent the kinds of information encoded in the LISP canonical address. The various approved and unapproved values and their use cases are as follows:

- **Type 0 (null body):** In this case, the size of the Length field is set to 0 (that is, no other fields are part of the LCA payload). If the Length field is set to 0, the minimum length of the LCAF-encoded address will be either 8 bytes or 6 bytes, based on whether the AFI value is encoded as part of the LCA.
- **Type 1 (AFI list):** The AFI List LCAF type is used in DNS names or URIs as ASCII strings when such information is part of the mapping database system.
- **Type 2 (instance ID):** The instance IDs can be useful for creating multi-segmented VPNs within a LISP site. When the organizations inside LISP sites are using private addressing, the instance ID can help segregate those addresses.
- **Type 3 (AS number):** Type 3 is used to encode the AS number in the canonical address when the AS number is stored in the mapping database.
- **Type 4 (application data):** This type is unapproved.
- **Type 5 (geo-coordinates):** If the RLOCs are geographically displaced, an ETR may want to send the geographic location in the map reply. In such cases, the ETR sends the LCAF Type 5 with the RLOC's physical location (latitude and longitude) in its locator set. Figure 2-7 shows a geo-coordinates LCAF.

0										1										2										3	

```
 0 1 2 3 4 5 6 7 8 9 0 1 2 3 4 5 6 7 8 9 0 1 2 3 4 5 6 7 8 9 0 1
```

AFI = 16387		Rsvd1	Flags
Type = 5	Rsvd2	Length	
N	Latitude Degrees	Minutes	Seconds
E	Longitude Degrees	Minutes	Seconds
Altitude			
AFI = x		Address ...	

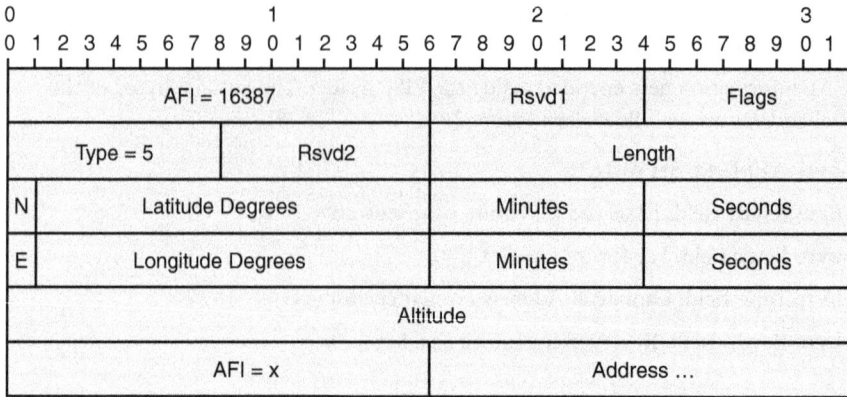

Figure 2-7   *Geo-Coordinates LCAF*

■ **Type 7 (NAT traversal):** Usually enterprises deploy network address translation (NAT) devices in their networks for security purposes. If a LISP system traverses a NAT device, it is required to convey the global address and mapped port information. In such instances, the NAT traversal LCAF type is used. Figure 2-8 shows a NAT traversal LCAF.

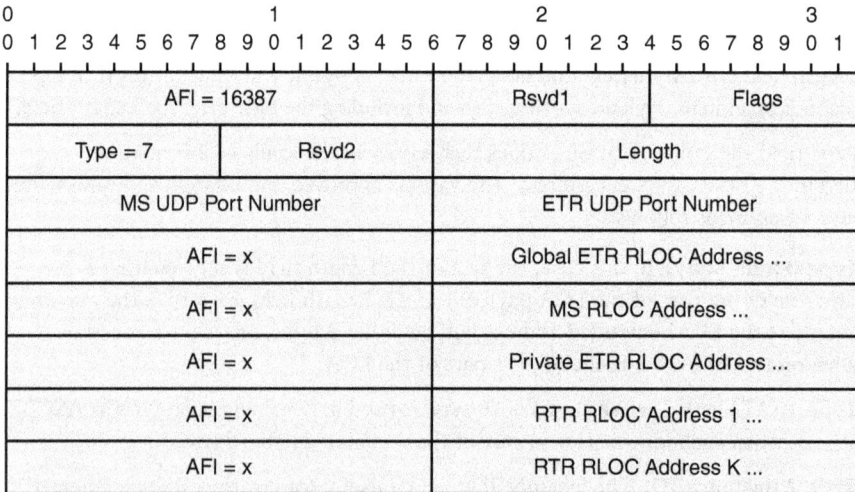

```
 0                   1                   2                   3
 0 1 2 3 4 5 6 7 8 9 0 1 2 3 4 5 6 7 8 9 0 1 2 3 4 5 6 7 8 9 0 1
```

AFI = 16387		Rsvd1	Flags
Type = 7	Rsvd2	Length	
MS UDP Port Number		ETR UDP Port Number	
AFI = x		Global ETR RLOC Address ...	
AFI = x		MS RLOC Address ...	
AFI = x		Private ETR RLOC Address ...	
AFI = x		RTR RLOC Address 1 ...	
AFI = x		RTR RLOC Address K ...	

Figure 2-8   *NAT Traversal LCAF*

Note   The xTR and MS use encoding in info request and info reply messages to convey private and public addresses information. This information is not part of the map request or map reply since the MS does not store this information.

■ **Type 9 (multicast info):** The distributed mapping database holds multicast group information. If an ITR requests an information on a multicast group address EID, the MS may return a replication list of RLOC group addresses or RLOC unicast addresses. A multicast info LCAF allows for encoding of multicast group information for a given VPN as well. For a given VPN, the mapping database holds the three-tuple entry (Instance ID, S-Prefix, G-prefix), where S-Prefix represents the source EID and G-Prefix represents the group EID.

■ **Type 10 (explicit locator path):** *Traffic engineering* (*TE*) is the key to ensuring proper network and link utilization. The LISP control messages can be encoded with the *explicit locator path* (*ELP*) LCAF type to provide explicit re-encapsulation paths for a given EID prefix lookup in the mapping database to ensure that certain hops are traversed in order to reach a particular destination host. Figure 2-9 shows the ELP LCAF.

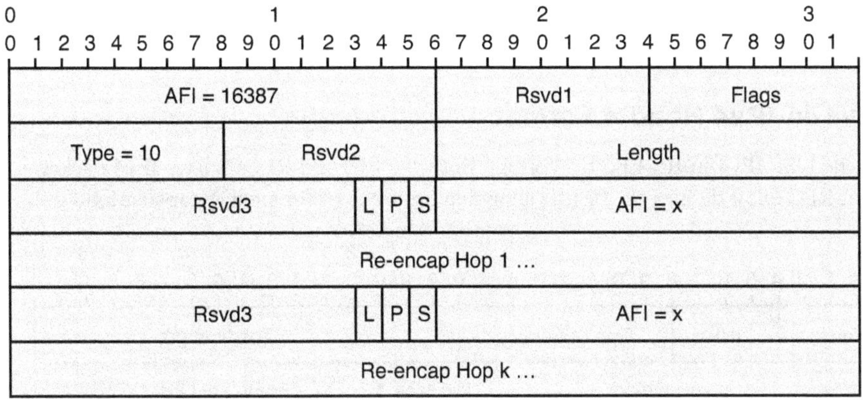

Figure 2-9 *Explicit Locator Path LCAF*

Note It is not required for the mapping database to understand this encoding because the ELP LCAF type is not a lookup key.

■ **Type 11 (security key):** When a locator has a security key associated with it, it needs to be securely transmitted across the LISP system and over the Internet. The security key LCAF is used to encode the key material of the security key.

■ **Type 12 (source/dest key):** Usually all the mapping database lookups are based on the destination EID prefix. But if the xTR requires a lookup based on a particular flow (for example, based on two-tuple entry of a source/destination pair), this LCAF type is used in the LISP control messages.

■ **Type 13 (replication list entry):** The replication list entry LCAF encodes the locator being used for the unicast replication for multicast forwarding, as pointed by the multicast info LCAF. This locator entry is registered by the re-encapsulating tunnel routers that are participating in the overlay distribution tree.

Note A few LCAF types are unapproved per RFC 8060, and they are not discussed in this chapter. To see the unapproved LCAF types, refer to RFC 8060.

LISP Packet Headers

When an xTR at one site knows about the mapping of the destination EID and the destination RLOC, the data packets from the client are encapsulated with the LISP header and sent to the destination site through the selected path. The xTR at the destination site strips off the LISP header and then forwards the packets to the destination host. LISP supports all four different encapsulations:

■ IPv4-in-IPv4 encapsulation

■ IPv6-in-IPv4 encapsulation

■ IPv4-in-IPv6 encapsulation

■ IPv6-in-IPv6 encapsulation

LISP IPv4-in-IPv4 Header Format

With the LISP IPv4-in-IPv4 header format, both the EID and RLOCs have IPv4 packet format. RFC 6830 defines the header shown in Figure 2-10 for such encapsulation.

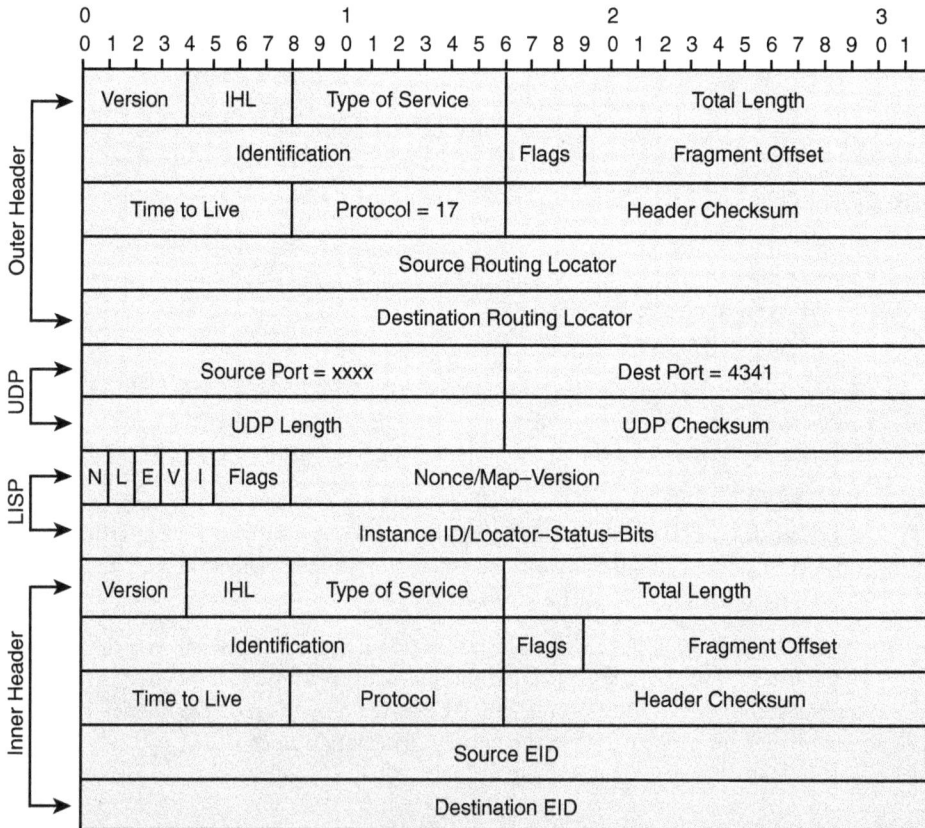

Figure 2-10 *LISP IPv4-in-IPv4 Packet Format*

In this format, the first 20 bytes are the outer header, which is an IPv4 header for the RLOC. It consists the information about the source and the destination RLOC. The outer header is followed by the UDP header, with the destination port 4341. Then comes the LISP header. The LISP header contains five different bits:

■ **N (nonce present bit):** When this bit is set, the lower 24 bits of the initial 32 bits contain a nonce.

■ **L (locator status bits):** When this bit is set to 1, the *locator status bits* (*LSBs*) in the next 32 bits inside the LISP header are in use. ITRs use LSBs to inform ETRs about the status (up/down) of all ETRs at the local site. These bits are used as a hint to convey router status (up/down) and not path reachability status.

■ **E (echo nonce request bit):** This bit is set to 0 if the N bit is set to 0. It can be set to 1 only when the N bit is set to 1. This is useful when an ITR is also an ETR and the ITR is requesting the nonce to be echoed back to it in the LISP-encapsulated packets.

■ **V (map version bit):** When this bit is set, the N bit is set to 0. With this bit set to 1, the lower 24 bits of the initial 32 bits of the LISP header are encoded with the map version. With the V bit set, the LISP header is encoded as shown in Figure 2-11.

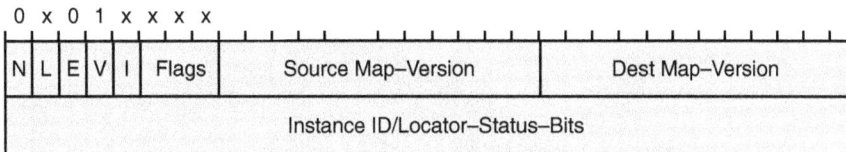

```
0  x  0  1  x  x  x  x
┌─┬─┬─┬─┬─┬──────┬─────────────────────┬──────────────────┐
│N│L│E│V│I│ Flags│  Source Map–Version │ Dest Map–Version │
├─┴─┴─┴─┴─┴──────┴─────────────────────┴──────────────────┤
│            Instance ID/Locator–Status–Bits              │
└─────────────────────────────────────────────────────────┘
```

Figure 2-11 *LISP Header*

■ **I (instance ID bit):** When this bit is set, the LSBs are reduced from 32 bits to 8 bits, and the higher-order 24 bits are used for the instance ID.

After the LISP header, the next 20 bytes account for the inner IP header, which represents the source and destination EIDs.

LISP IPv6-in-IPv6 Header Format

With the LISP IPv6-in-IPv6 header format, both the EID and the RLOC are IPv6 based. Figure 2-12 shows the LISP IPv6-in-IPv6 header format, as defined in RFC 6830.

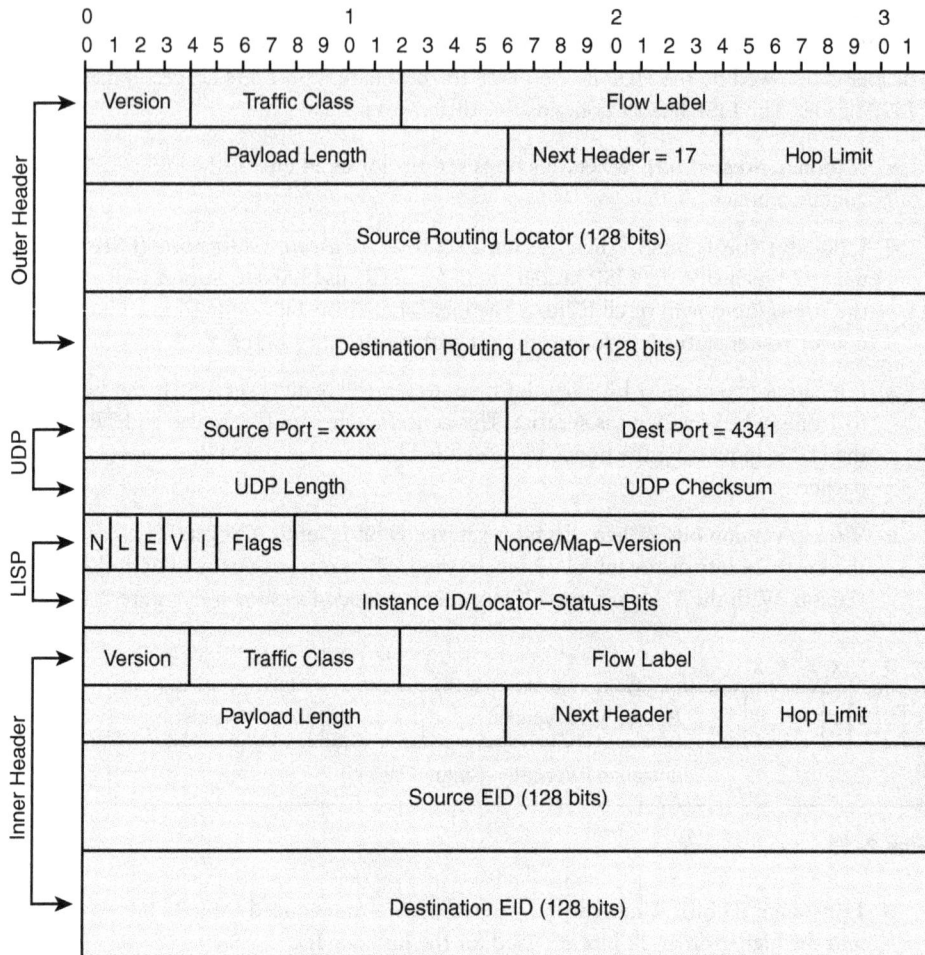

Figure 2-12   *LISP IPv6-in-IPv6 Packet Format*

In this case, the outer header is a 40-byte IPv6 header containing information about the source and the destination RLOCs. The UDP header and the LISP header remain the same as described earlier. The inner header in this format is again a 40-byte IPv6 header with the information about the source and destination EIDs.

Note   When deploying LISP, ensure that the extra header bytes are accounted for in the MTU settings. This is achieved by setting the internal network MTU to be lower and by setting TCP adjust-mss on internal interfaces so that the encapsulated TCP traffic does not require fragmentation. Typically, only 1500 bytes are guaranteed over the Internet. Thus, it is vital to ensure that the encapsulated frames along with LISP headers are less than or equal to 1500 bytes.

LISP Control Plane Messages

A LISP control plane message is a User Datagram Protocol (UDP) message with either a source or destination UDP port of 4342. The control plane packet is either in IPv4 or IPv6 format. Figure 2-13 shows the IPv4 control plane message format, and Figure 2-14 shows the IPv6 control plane message format. From the packet headers shown in Figures 2-13 and 2-14, notice that LISP message formats are similar to the previously discussed packet headers; however, in place of the LISP header, there is a LISP message, and there is no header for the EID.

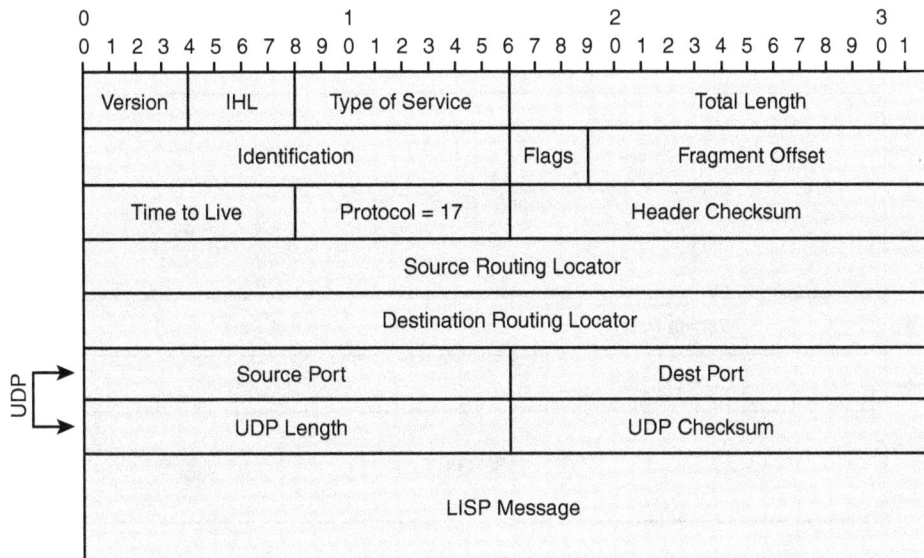

Figure 2-13   *LISP IPv4 Message Format*

These are the various LISP control plane messages, as defined in RFC 6830:

- **Type 0:** Reserved
- **Type 1:** LISP map request
- **Type 2:** LISP map reply
- **Type 3:** LISP map register
- **Type 4:** LISP map notify
- **Type 8:** LISP encapsulated control message

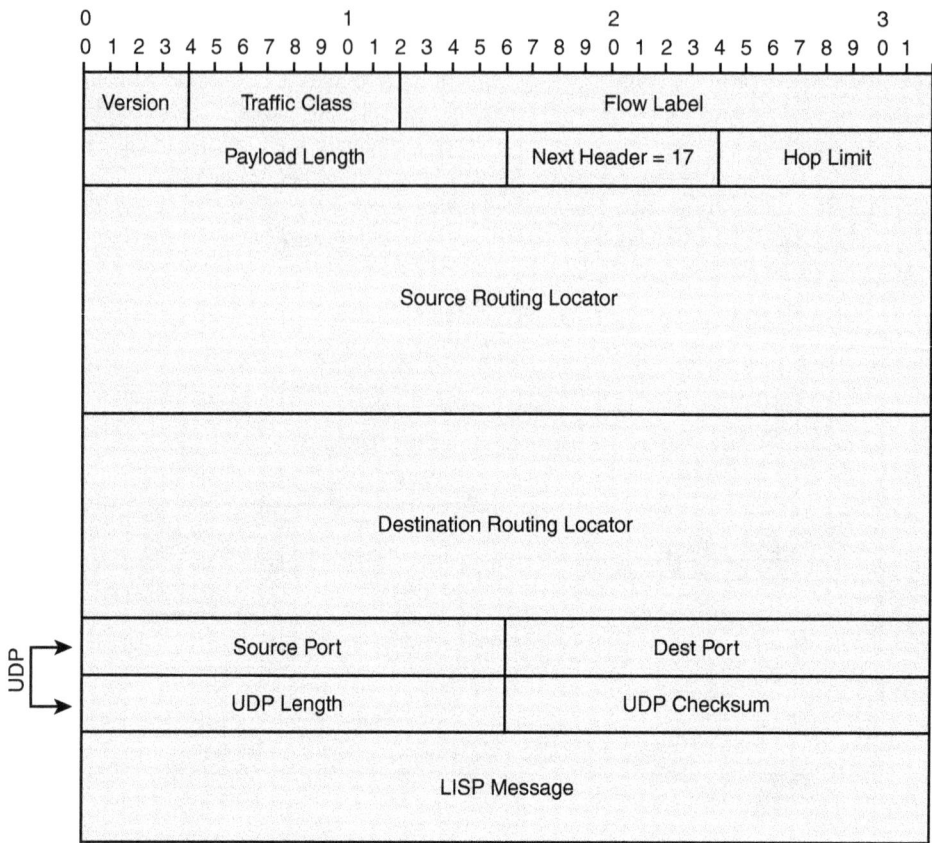

Figure 2-14 *LISP IPv6 Message Format*

LISP Map Request

As defined in RFC 6830, a map request is initiated by the ITR and sent to the ETR of interest by the map server. A map request is initiated by an xTR when

- It needs a mapping for an EID.

- It wants to test an RLOC for reachability.

- It wants to refresh a mapping before TTL expiration.

- It receives from the ETR a solicitation for a map request (SMR) in case of a virtual host move.

As stated earlier, map requests can also be LISP encapsulated with a LISP type value set to encapsulated control message when sent from an ITR to an MR. In addition, map requests are LISP encapsulated the same way from an MS to an ETR. When a map request is sent, the source UDP port is chosen by the xTR (sender), but the destination UDP port is always 4342.

Figure 2-15 shows the map request message format. The map request contains information about the EID prefix, EID prefix length, and AFI that it belongs to, the ITR-RLOC address, and the ITR-RLOC AFI to which the ITR-RLOC address belongs. Note that at the end of the map request message, there is a map reply record. This field is useful when the M bit (the map data present bit) is set and can be used by an ETR to update its map cache entry for the EID-to-RLOC mapping for the source EID. When the M bit is set, it indicates that the map reply record segment is included in the map request.

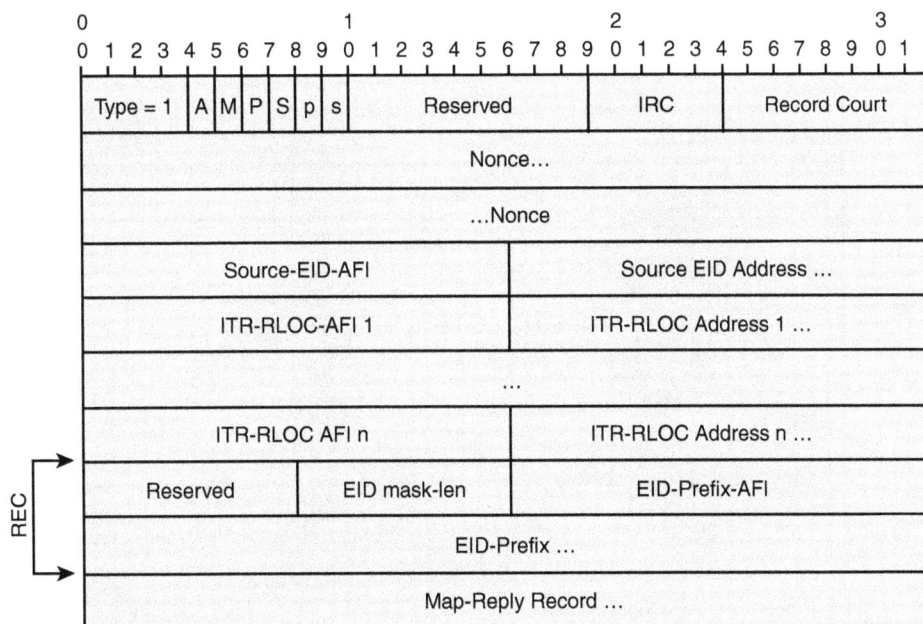

Figure 2-15 *LISP Map Request Message Format*

LISP Map Reply

In response to a map request, the ETR sends a map reply with the EID-to-RLOC mapping information that is requested either in the destination field of the IP header of a data probe or the EID record of a map request. The RLOCs are globally routable IP addresses of all ETRs for the LISP site. In a map reply message for the map request message, the destination address is copied from the source address of the data probe message. The map reply can have an empty locator set. This kind of reply message is called a *negative map reply* message. The map reply is sent with the source UDP port number 4342, and the destination UDP port number is copied from the source port of either the map request or the invoking data packet.

Figure 2-16 shows the map reply message format. In the map reply, the record consists of information about the EID and the locator along with the respective AFI. It also contains a record time-to-live (TTL) field. The value of this field is the time, in minutes, the recipient of the map reply stores the mapping. If the TTL value is set to 0, the entry is removed from the cache immediately. If the value is set to 0xffffffff, the recipient decides locally how long it wants to save the entry in the map cache. Note that in Cisco's implementation, when there is just 1 minute left for the map cache entry to expire, the xTR initiates another map request to update its map cache before the entry expires.

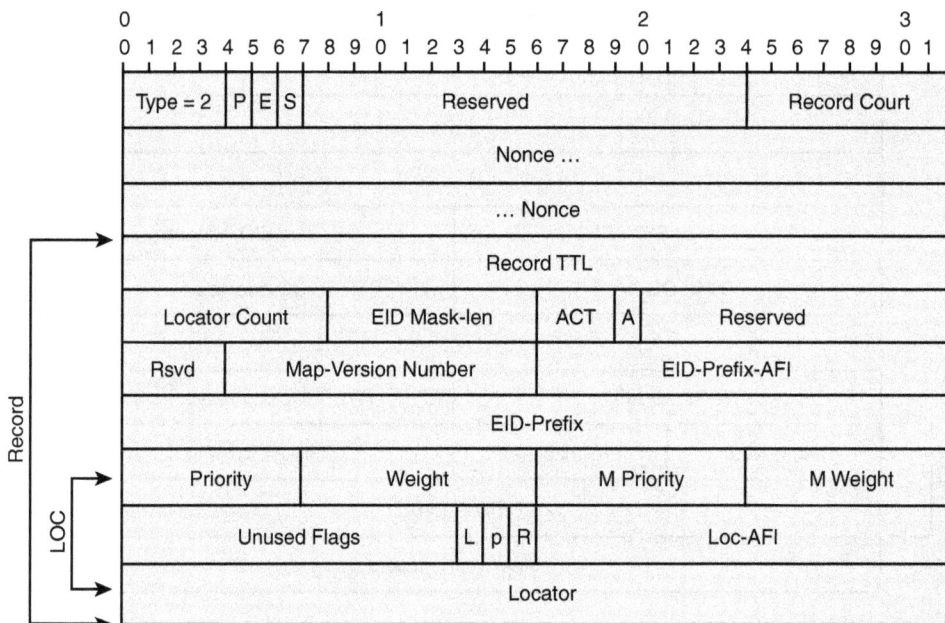

Figure 2-16   *LISP Map Reply Message Format*

LISP Map Register Message

As explained in RFC 6833, an xTR sends a map register message to an MS to register its associated EID prefixes and also includes one or more RLOCs to be used by the MS when forwarding map requests. An MS can send a map reply in response to a map request on behalf of the xTR upon request. It is done by setting the P bit (the proxy map replay bit) in the map register message. The map register message is sent with the destination UDP port number 4342 and a random source UDP port. Figure 2-17 shows the map register message format. The map register message format is similar to the map reply message format, except that there are a few extra bits in a map reply message, and have an additional 8 bytes of key ID, authentication data length, and authentication data.

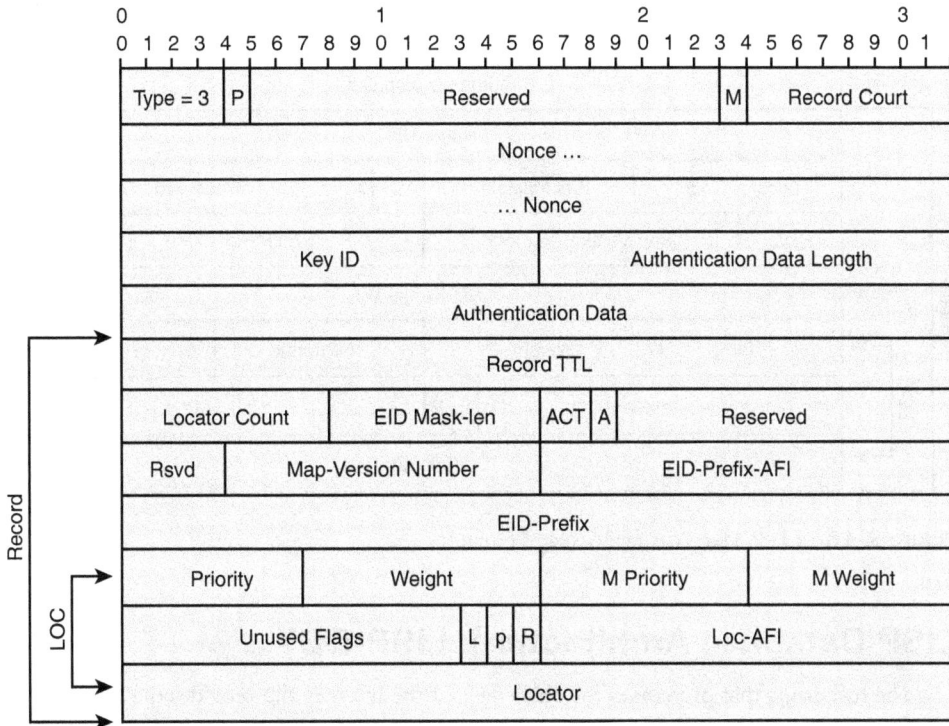

Figure 2-17 *LISP Map Register Message Format*

LISP Map Notify Message

An MS sends a map notify message to an xTR to confirm that the map register message was received and processed. An xTR requests that a map notify be returned by setting the M bit in the map register message. The map notify uses 4342 as both the source and destination UDP port number. Figure 2-18 shows the map notify message format.

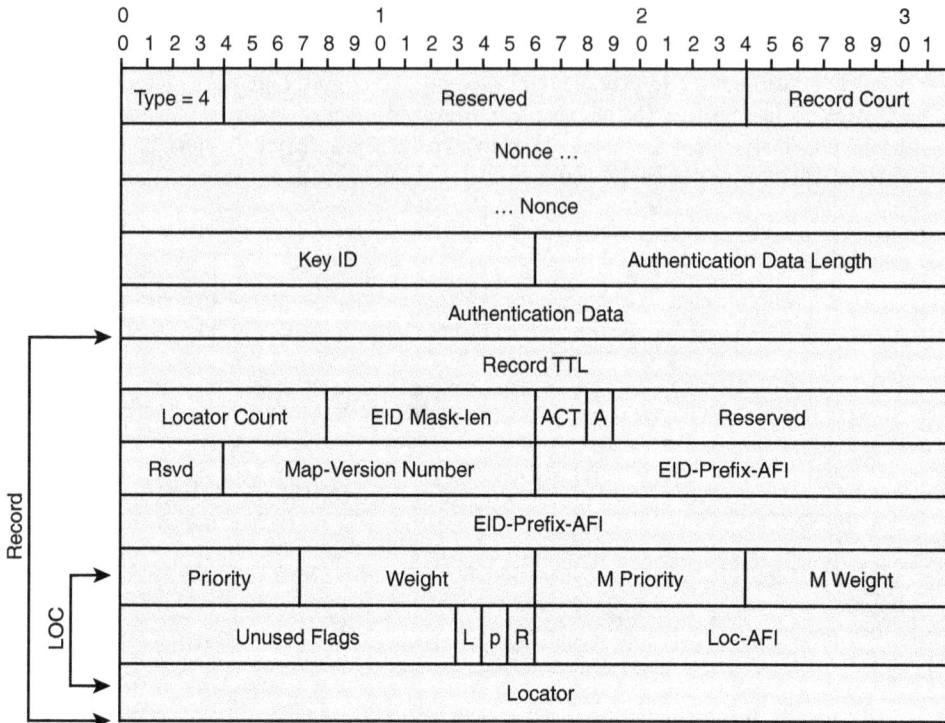

Figure 2-18 *LISP Map Notify Message Format*

LISP Database Architecture: LISP-DDT

The real magic that overcomes the challenges of the Internet and provides the LISP functionality is the mapping database. The mapping database contains the EID-to-RLOC mappings, which make it possible to identify which EIDs map to what locators. This mapping database allows support for millions of sites and changes happening across the sites. You can deploy multiple stand-alone MRs and MSs, but for a truly globally scaled MS, a hierarchical mapping system is required. In addition, a scaled and resilient mapping system needs to have an interface to the mapping system. LISP Delegated Database Tree (LISP-DDT) is one such mapping system that provides scalability and resiliency in a LISP-enabled network.

LISP-DDT provides a hierarchy for instance IDs and EID prefixes. LISP-DDT defines a new device type called a *DDT node*. DDT nodes are preconfigured with delegations that are based on static and secure delegation hierarchy, much like DNS. The parent DDT node is configured with a set of more specific sub-prefixes that are further delegated to other DDT nodes lower in the hierarchy. The DDT map resolvers send map requests to a preconfigured DDT node RLOC. The DDT nodes return map referral messages in response to the map request messages. The map referral message is a new LISP message type that assists with traversing the database tree. When the DDT node responds with a map referral message, it indicates either of the following:

- It is able to or will be able to find the requested mapping.

- Another DDT node is queried for more specific information.

Before discussing what different map referral messages mean, it's vital to understand the *extended EID prefix* (*XEID prefix*). In order to have uniquely identifying prefixes in the mapping database, a unique database index key is created. This index key is formed by logically prepending and appending several fields to the EID prefix. These fields include a 16-bit database ID (DBID) field, a 32-bit instance ID (IID) field, a 16-bit AFI field, and a variable-length EID prefix field. The resulting concatenation of these fields is called an *XEID prefix*. All the EID prefixes in DDT are DDT clients and are referred to as *XEID prefixes*.

A map referral message can indicate two kinds of responses:

- **Positive referrals:** These responses are used to discover a DDT node's RLOC for a given EID prefix:

    - **Type 0 (NODE-REFERRAL):** This type indicates that the replying DDT node delegated an XEID prefix that matches the requested XEID to one or more other DDT nodes. The map referral message contains a map record with additional information, most significantly the set of RLOCs to which the prefix was delegated.

    - **Type 1 (MS-REFERRAL):** This type indicates that the replying DDT node delegated an XEID prefix that matches the requested XEID to one or more DDT map servers.

    - **Type 2 (MS-ACK):** This type indicates that a replying DDT map server received a DDT map request that matches an authoritative XEID prefix for which it has one or more registered ETRs. This means that the request can be forwarded to one of those ETRs to provide an answer to the querying ITR.

- **Negative referrals:** These responses are used to indicate the following actions:

    - **Type 3 (MS-NOT-REGISTERED):** This type indicates that the replying DDT map server received a map request for one of its configured XEID prefixes that has no ETRs registered.

    - **Type 4 (DELEGATION-HOLE):** This type indicates that the requested XEID matches a non-delegated sub-prefix of the XEID space. This is a non-LISP "hole" that was not delegated to any DDT map server or ETR.

    - **Type 5 (NOT-AUTHORITATIVE):** This type indicates that the replying DDT node received a map request for an XEID request for which it is not authoritative. This occur if a cached referral becomes invalid due to a change in the database hierarchy.

Figure 2-19 shows a global LISP mapping system using LISP DDT. It is clear from this figure that there are primarily three different LISP nodes:

■ DDT root nodes

■ DDT map resolver nodes

■ DDT map server nodes

LISP Delegated Database Tree

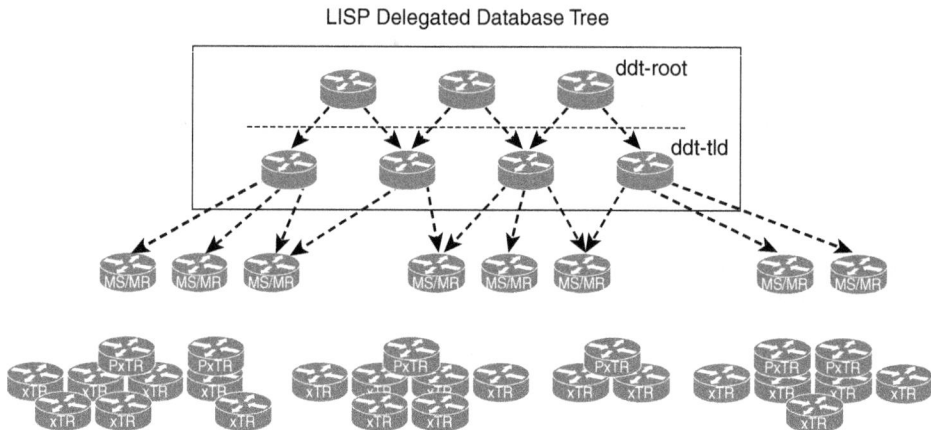

Figure 2-19   *Global LISP Mapping System Using LISP-DDT*

The DDT root node forms the logical top of the database hierarchy. It is configured to be authoritative for all IIDs, AFIs, and EIDs included in the DDT hierarchy. The root node also delegates IIDs, AFIs, and EIDs to the lower-level DDT nodes that are authoritative for their piece of hierarchy. DDT root nodes perform the following functions:

■ Accept map requests (from DDT map resolvers)

■ Compute and return map referral Type 0 messages (positive)

■ Compute and return map referral Type 4 messages (negative)

The DDT map resolvers performs the following functions:

■ Accept and cache map requests from ITRs and PITRs

■ Forward map requests to DDT root nodes

■ Accept and follow map referral messages iteratively to query the DDT hierarchy

■ Resolve the location of the DDT map server (map referral MS-ACK)

■ Detect loops/delegation errors

■ Send negative map reply (NMR) messages to ITRs and PITRs

The DDT map server nodes performs the following functions:

- Forward map requests to registered ETRs
- Return proxy map replies to ITRs
- Compute and return map referral DELEGATION-HOLE messages
- Compute and return map referral MS-NOT-REGISTERED messages

LISP-DDT Operations

To understand the LISP-DDT operations, examine the topology shown in Figure 2-20. In this topology, nodes Root-N1, DDT-N2, DDT-N3, and MS are configured with child prefixes and authoritative prefixes. Here are some instances:

- Root-N1 is configured as root for *
- Root-N1 delegates IID=0, 10.0.0.0/8 to DDT-N2
- DDT-N2 delegates IID=0, 10.0.0.0/16 to DDT-N3
- DDT-N3 delegates IID=0, 10.0.0.0/17 to MS

The topology also consists of MR, ITR1 and ITR2, and an ETR1 node. In this topology, MR is configured to point to the DDT root RLOC. The ETR1 node registers its prefix with MS, where the ETR prefix is within the delegation range of the MS node.

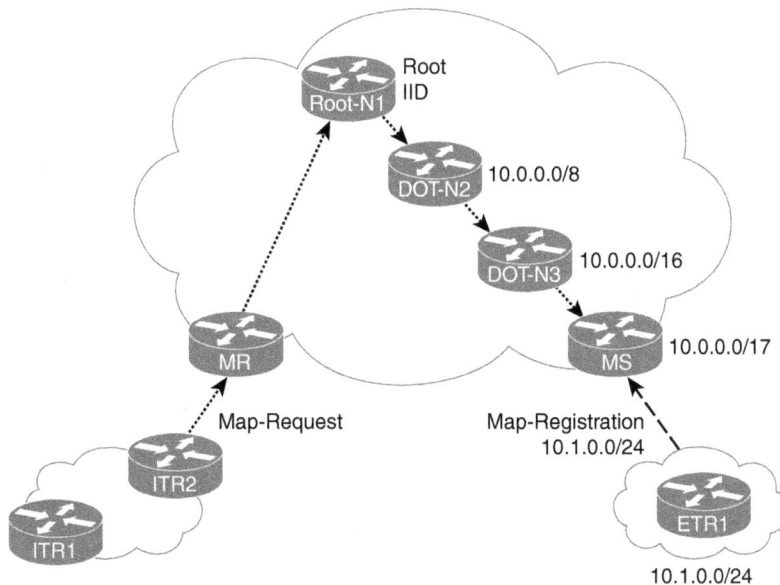

Figure 2-20   *Topology with LISP-DDT*

When the ITR sends a first map request message to the MR, the MR caches the map request and queues the pending requests. It then checks the referral cache, where it finds no entry. It then forwards the map request to its statically configured DDT root, which is the Root-N1 node in this case. Root-N1 then sends the map referral to the MR. In the map referral, Root-N1 tells the MR which node to try next, which in this case is the DDT-N2 node. This process keeps on happening until the map-request reaches the MS device that has the EID delegation. On receiving the map request, the MS node processes the map request and sends a map referral/MS-ACK to the MR, which then dequeues the pending request and caches the map referral. The MS node also forwards the map request to the ETR. Finally, the ETR sends a map reply to the ITR.

If the MR, on receiving the map request, finds an entry in the referral cache, it sends the map request to the cached referral MS. The MS node receives and processes the map request and sends the map referral/MS-ACK to the MR, which dequeues the pending request and forwards the map request to the ETR. The ETR then sends the map reply to the ITR.

The scenario and operational flow just described occur when the ETR EID prefix is registered with the MS, but imagine what happens when the EID prefix is not registered with the MS node. In such a scenario, the MS node, on receiving the map request, computes the DELEGATION-HOLE and sends a map referral/DELEGATION-HOLE (Type 4, negative referral, message) to the MR. The MR, on receiving the negative map referral, dequeues the pending request and caches the map referral. The MR then sends a negative map reply with the TTL value 15 minutes for the DELEGATION-HOLE to the ITR. The DELEGATION-HOLE set in the ACT (Action) field of the map referral message indicates that the XEID is not a LISP destination.

LISP Architecture on Cisco Platforms

LISP is supported on various Cisco platforms, but primarily the Cisco platforms are characterized based on the operating system software running on them. Cisco platforms support LISP on IOS/IOS-XE, IOS-XR, and NX-OS software. LISP offers a number of distinct functions and features, including xTR/MS/MR, IGP Assist, and ESM/ASM Multi-hop. Not all hardware supports all functions or features. Users should validate that a particular platform supports key features before implementing it.

Note   For information on LISP features and hardware and software support, see http://lisp.cisco.com/lisp_hwsw.html#HW.

The Cisco IOS/IOS-XE software does not have a distributed architecture similar to that of IOS-XR or NX-OS. On IOS/IOS-XE platforms, the LISP control plane functionality is maintained by the *LISP control* process, which works in conjunction with RIB and Cisco Express Forwarding (CEF) to provide the forwarding architecture for LISP. This section focuses on the LISP architecture on IOS-XR and NX-OS platforms as there are various software components that work together to provide the LISP functionality.

LISP Software Architecture on NX-OS

The LISP control plane software is a conditional feature running on NX-OS. The process is enabled when the user enables the LISP feature and configures LISP functions. To enable LISP and its functions on NX-OS, a user must configure **feature lisp.** When LISP is configured, LISP interacts with various software components on the NX-OS platform to exchange the control plane information and program the hardware to forward LISP-encapsulated packets. Figure 2-21 shows the software architecture of LISP on NX-OS platform.

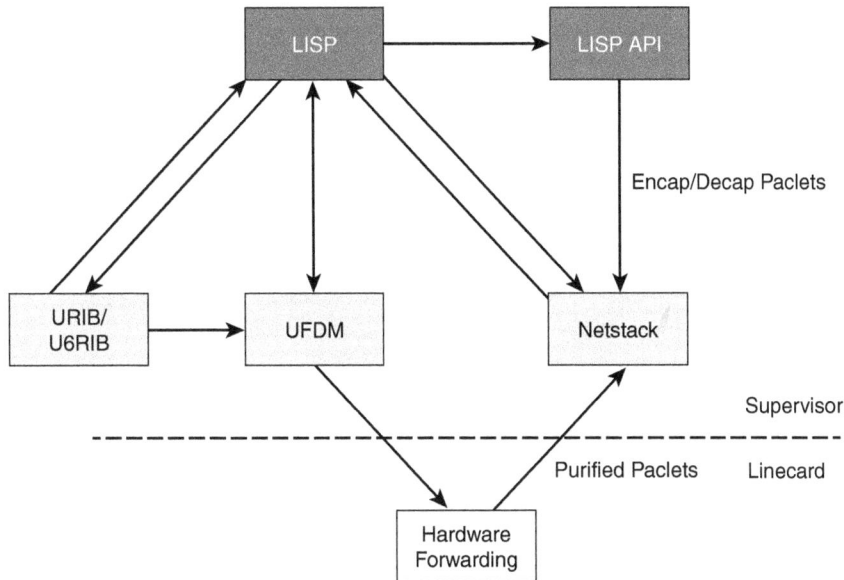

Figure 2-21   *Software Architecture of LISP on NX-OS*

A number of software interactions take place on the NX-OS platform:

- The map cache entries are equivalent to the routing entries on the NX-OS platform. They are managed by the Unicast Routing Information Base (URIB)/Unicast IPv6 RIB (U6RIB) process on NX-OS.

- As with other routing protocols, with LISP the map cache entries are pushed down the forwarding plane using the application programming interfaces (APIs) provided by the Unicast Forwarding Distribution Manager (UFDM) process. The LISP process interacts with the UFDM process via Message Transaction Service (MTS), which provides the feature of inter-process communication on NX-OS.

- The software forwarding takes place in the *netstack* process. LISP publish the map cache entries in the shared database. A library (LISP API) is provided to access the shared database and also do the LISP encapsulation/decapsulation of the data packets.

- Netstack can request an update from the shared database by sending MTS messages to LISP. The LISP API provides the interface to send these messages.

The information is passed on to UFDM, which then presents the information to hardware to form the adjacencies. This allows for programming the Forwarding Information Base (FIB) and performing hardware-based forwarding. This is very similar to how IPv4 or IPv6 unicast routes are programmed in the hardware.

LISP Software Architecture on IOS-XR

On IOS-XR, no separate feature package information envelope (PIE) is required to enable LISP. The LISP software architecture is somewhat similar to that on NX-OS, except that the process names are different between the two platforms. Figure 2-22 shows the software architecture of the LISP control plane on the IOS-XR platform. On IOS-XR, the LISP process handles the core logic of the LISP control plane and interacts with other system components to provide the complete LISP functionality.

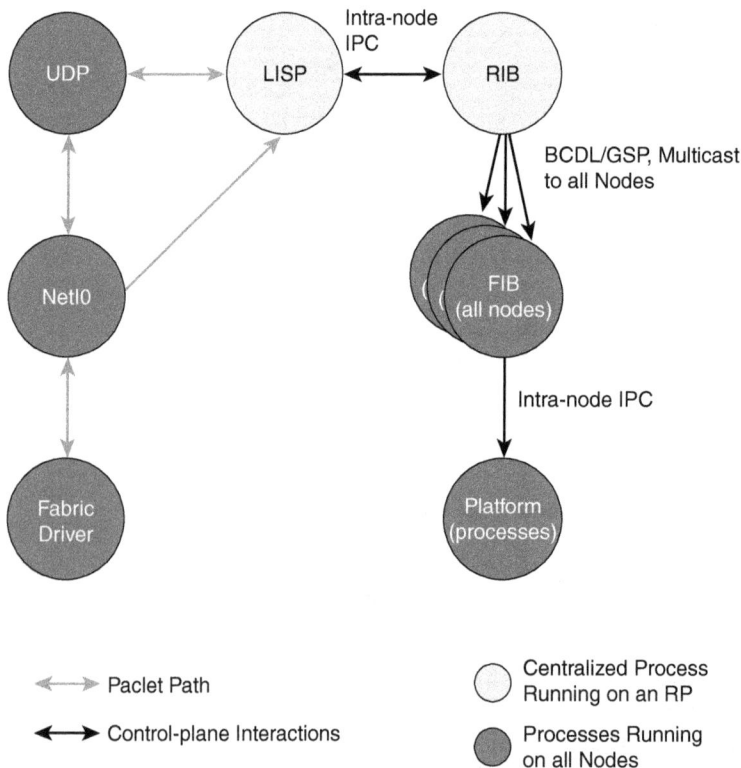

Figure 2-22   *LISP Software Architecture on IOS-XR*

The LISP process collaborates with the IPv4/IPv6 RIB, UDP, and NetIO processes, as shown in Figure 2-21. Also, the LISP process interacts with the sysdb process for learning configuration and providing the output for the **show** commands, the RSI agent for learning VRF configuration, the ifmgr process for learning about interfaces, and other processes that are not shown in the Figure 2-21. The threading model of IOS-XR software for LISP process allows for processing of different packets to be handled by separate threads. While various threads interact with NetIO and UDP processes, the main thread runs the LISP finite state machine (FSM).

The LISP process creates a UDP socket on port 4342 for sending/receiving the map request, map register, and map reply messages. When the socket is created, a corresponding binding entry is created in *Local Packet Transport Service* (*LPTS*) and gets programmed in line card ternary content-addressable memory (TCAM). The LPTS is a system-level protocol policer, and the system accounts for LISP features when enabled by creating an entry in LPTS. If the hardware is not programmed, the LISP process needs to add an LPTS entry for UDP port 4341 on the *route processor* (*RP*) by directly interacting with the LPTS infrastructure.

NetIO is used for servicing the control plane packets on the IOS-XR platform. NetIO is a slow-path switching engine that comes into play when the hardware is not programmed to forward LISP-encapsulated packets and software-based forwarding is done by the system. Normally, all data plane packets should be hardware switched and not software switched. The main functions of NetIO from a LISP functionality perspective are as follows:

- It facilitates the rx/tx of LISP control plane messages on UDP port 4342.

- If hardware forwarding is not programmed, the NetIO process de-encapsulates the received LISP-encapsulated messages on UDP port 4341 and switches them out on the inner IP header.

- If hardware forwarding is not programmed, NetIO encapsulates the LISP-eligible packets by performing a lookup in the map cache table in the FIB shared memory and then switches them out on the outer IP.

- If the match for a packet is not found in the unicast routing table or map cache table, it is punted to the LISP process to trigger a map request. This punt action is also performed by the NetIO process.

- The NetIO process punts the packets containing updates to the RLOC status bits. The LISP process initiates the RLOC probing to learn the new and correct status bits.

Note   It is expected that all data plane traffic is handled in hardware. If NetIO is handing the data plane packets, then it is an exception to normal traffic forwarding, and thus the packets are subjected to LPTS policing.

RIB is actually a set of two processes: ipv4_rib and ipv6_rib. The map cache and map db (mapping database) are pushed into the FIB via RIB to take advantage of the existing point-to-multipoint distribution mechanism between the centralized RIB and all the FIB instances running on various nodes (for example, RPs, line cards, service cards). A LISP process also registers with RIB to get notified about the up/down changes to the RLOCs of an ETR's database mapping. When it is notified of any such changes, it recomputes the RLOC status bits and reprograms FIB via RIB.

Summary

This chapter describes the LISP core architecture and components. As discussed in this chapter, various LISP nodes play important roles in LISP. This chapter discusses details of the roles and functionality of xTRs, PxTRs, MR/MS, and ALT. This chapter also describes the various packet formats in exchanging LISP control plane messages. It is important to understand the purpose of various LISP control plane messages and when and from where they are triggered. This chapter also covers how to scale a LISP deployment for the global Internet by using LISP-DDT. The chapter concludes by examining the LISP software architecture on various Cisco platforms.

References

RFC 8060, "LISP Canonical Address Format (LCAF)"

RFC 6830, "The Locator/ID Separation Protocol (LISP)"

## Chapter 3

LISP IPv4 Unicast Routing

This chapter focuses on IPv4 unicast packet handling fundamentals in LISP networks. It begins with an in-depth look at a packet walk between LISP sites followed by a configuration and troubleshooting example.

This chapter covers the following topics:

- Communication between LISP and non-LISP sites

- How LISP interconnects LISP networks from different routing domains

- Unicast packet forwarding, which between LISP and non-LISP sites in the following combinations:

  - LISP site to LISP site

  - LISP site to non-LISP site

  - Non-LISP site to LISP site

  - Non-LISP site to non-LISP site

The current traditional Internet architecture involves packet forwarding from non-LISP site to non-LISP site, with destination-based routing with single namespace encompassing both the location and identifier in one address; this is a well understood scenario and not the focus of this book. This chapter focuses on how IPv4 unicast packet forwarding happens between LISP sites. Chapter 4, "LISP IPv6 Unicast Routing," cover IPv6 unicast packet forwarding.

LISP IPv4 Unicast Routing Concepts

The separation of namespaces for location and identifier, as explained in Chapter 2, "LISP Architecture," uses the endpoint ID (EID) space for identification of end stations and the routing locator (RLOC) space for forwarding of traffic. The EID and RLOC are generally in IPv4 or IPv6 address format. The address structures for both the IPv4 and IPv6 address families in the source and destination addresses for the EID and RLOC are used without alteration in LISP. The scope and purpose of the EID and RLOC are different: The EID identifies who the endpoint is, and the RLOC tells where the endpoint is.

Note   LISP architecture allows non-IPv4/IPv6 EIDs such as MAC addresses. As explained in Chapter 1, "LISP Introduction," LISP is multiprotocol and address family agnostic.

LISP tries to establish communication among endpoint devices. In an IP network, endpoints are commonly known as *IP hosts*, and these hosts are normally not LISP enabled; therefore, each endpoint originates packets to another endpoint with a single IPv4 or IPv6 header. Endpoints include servers (physical or virtual), workstations, tablets, smartphones, printers, IP phones, and telepresence devices. The addresses assigned to endpoints are referred to as EIDs in LISP.

Like other IP addresses, EIDs must be globally unique when communicating on the Internet. If private addresses are used for EIDs outside a private network, they must be translated to global addresses through network address translation (NAT) to be reachable from the public IP space. The global LISP mapping database, like any other routing database on the Internet, cannot be populated with private addresses. However, the global LISP mapping database can identify entries in its database as members of different virtual private networks (VPNs). BGP/MPLS Internet Protocol (IP) VPN network routers have separate virtual routing and forwarding (VRF) tables for each VPN; similarly, it is possible to create private networks in LISP and have an Internet router with separate routing tables (VRFs) for Internet routes and private addresses. Alternatively, a dedicated private LISP mapping database may be used to exclusively handle private EID addresses, which in many cases may not even need to be routable in the public Internet. These private networks may leverage the public Internet for transport, and the overlay nature of LISP enables private deployments that may use the Internet as their underlay to create VPNs.

EIDs are assigned from an EID prefix block. In the IP namespace, an EID prefix is a power-of-two block of IP addresses. This is no different from the assignment of IP addresses to IP hosts in a traditional network except that EID prefixes are handled as EIDs in a LISP network. The EID prefixes assigned to a LISP site may be hierarchically designed for efficient routing within a site. This type of hierarchical design is currently used in non-LISP networks, where the hierarchy may be quickly lost when use cases such as mobility are implemented. One interesting characteristic of the LISP system is that it decouples the organization of the EID namespace from its topological distribution; this allows the EID space to be organized hierarchically in the mapping system even if the distribution of EID prefixes does not follow the structure of the topology and sites. The implication is that the EID space can be structured in a way that allows summarization and the corresponding scale benefits of such summarization, regardless of how EIDs are distributed across sites. This allows for handling of host routing (which is necessary to achieve mobility) without affecting scale because the EID space remains hierarchically structured as the entropy of the EID space increases.

A public EID prefix on the Internet can either be provider independent or provider assigned. A provider-independent address is a block of IP addresses assigned by a regional Internet registry (RIR) to the end-user organization that is independent from the addressing used by the service provider the end-user organization peers with to connect to the Internet. The service provider peering with the end-user organization cannot aggregate the provider-independent addresses of its customer. Provider-independent addresses allow an organization to change service providers easily.

A provider-assigned address is a sub-block of the block of addresses assigned to the service provider by an RIR. If an organization changes its upstream provider, it has to change its addressing to fit within the address block of the new provider. Imagine an enterprise peering with service provider A and deciding to move to a different service provider due to lack of satisfaction with service provider A's commitment to delivering good quality service. When searching for a new service provider, the enterprise learns of another provider, service provider B. At this point, the enterprise might choose to change providers, which means its IP addresses must change for the enterprise routers peering with the new service provider B; this would cause operational overhead and possibly downtime. Because LISP separates the addressing namespace into two, an organization may be able to change providers by only changing its RLOC addresses and maintain its original EID space untouched. When provider-assigned addresses are used, they remain the property of the original upstream provider and are generally only reachable from the Internet through the original upstream provider. So, although LISP enables a certain level of provider independence, caution must be exercised when provider-assigned addresses are used for the EID space.

The EID forwarding namespace is independent from the RLOC address. On the Internet, EIDs are globally unique but routable within a LISP site, whereas RLOCs are globally unique and globally routable. For the purposes of providing interoperability between LISP networks and non-LISP networks, EIDs can be globally routable through proxy ITRs. This is seen in transition or interoperability scenarios where all sites have not migrated to LISP. To enable communication between LISP and non-LISP sites, EIDs may need to be routable outside the LISP network, and the proxy ITRs might need to function as devices advertising the EID prefixes into the non-LISP network and also act as gateway devices between LISP and non-LISP networks. (This is discussed further in the section "Internetworking LISP and Non-LISP Sites," later in this chapter.)

The RLOC address is a globally visible IPv4 or IPv6 address in a LISP mapping system that is assigned to an egress tunnel router (ETR) for the purpose of LISP site reachability. The reachability of EIDs in a LISP site is possible through the mapping of the EID prefixes in a LISP site to the ETR RLOC addresses of the same LISP site. A LISP site may have multiple ETRs. Each ETR advertises its attached EID prefixes to the LISP mapping system. An ETR may have multiple RLOC addresses.

Each ingress tunnel router (ITR) learns which RLOCs map to a particular EID prefix to send traffic from an EID locally attached to a remote EID attached to an ETR router. The RLOC is resolved through an EID-to-RLOC mapping lookup, as discussed in Chapter 2, that is initiated by the ITR sending a map request message to the mapping system. The information on where to route a map request within the LISP mapping system resides in the map server (MS) or in the caching map resolvers (MRs) running LISP Delegated Database Tree (DDT). As explained in Chapter 2, the MS learns the EID-to-RLOC mapping from ETRs and can route map requests to the right ETRs based on this information. The map resolver (MR) accepts map requests from ITRs and forwards them through the mapping system to have the authoritative ETR (or map server, when proxy replies are enabled) resolve the EID-to-RLOC mapping and reply directly to the ITR. The control plane signaling is broken into two main parts:

- The ETR registration of its attached EID to the MS

- The ITR resolution of EID-to-RLOC mapping

Each ETR attached to a LISP site uses the map register message to publish its EID prefix to the MS. The MS may respond with a map notify message to acknowledge receipt of registration information from the ETR if the map request message sent from ETR has the M-bit (the want map notify bit) flag set. The ETR may also signal to the MS to respond on its behalf to map request messages to the ITRs by setting the P-bit (the proxy map reply bit) in the map register message. The MS and ETR share a key for authentication to prevent rogue ETRs from issuing registrations to the MS. In addition, the MS is configured with a list of EID prefix-to-RLOC (ETR) entries as a way to protect against spoofed map register messages or misconfigured ETRs. The ETR registers its EID at 60-second intervals on Cisco routers. The MS does not push the registered EID to the remaining xTRs.

When the MS learns EID prefixes from the ETRs, you have a source of information to which ITRs can be directed when you need to resolve EID-to-RLOC mappings. When a packet arrives at an ITR from an attached EID, the ITR first verifies (by searching in its locally configured database mapping list of entries) whether the source IP address is an EID address. The locally configured database mapping is an aggregate prefix list that identifies all the EID IP subnets deployed on the ITR. If the source address is not an EID address, a routing lookup is performed on the IP routing table. However, if the source address is identified as an EID address, the ITR refers to the LISP map cache to route the packet. If a mapping entry is not found for the destination EID in the LISP map cache (a situation referred to as a *LISP map cache miss*), the ITR must consult the mapping system. In order to obtain the required mapping, the ITR sends a map request message to the MR, asking for the mapping corresponding to the destination EID. The MR searches in its internal database for an entry that matches the EID requested. The MR then forwards a re-encapsulated map request with the original ITR as the source RLOC in the payload toward the MS. The MS verifies that the destination EID matches the configured EID prefix in its mapping database and determines whether any ETR is registered with the matching EID prefix. If the EID matches an EID prefix in the MS, the following responses can occur:

- If ETRs requested proxy service from the MS, the MS responds directly to the ITR with the EID-to-RLOC mapping details in a map reply message.

- If the ETRs did not request proxy service from the MS, the MS forwards the encapsulated map request to the registered ETR for the matched EID prefix. The ETR responds directly to the source of the map request, the ITR node that initiated the map request.

When the ITR learns the EID-to-RLOC mapping from the exchanges of map request and map reply messages just described, it finally encapsulates the LISP unicast packet for forwarding out the interface as per the path to reach the RLOC address in the routing table mapped to the destination EID. What if the MS has no EID-to-RLOC mapping entry? The MS returns a negative map reply message with action code "Natively Forward." To understand further how this mapping information is used, let's look at several scenarios of unicast packet forwarding in a LISP network.

In Figure 3-1, notice how the communication flows between an endpoint in one LISP site and an endpoint in another LISP site.

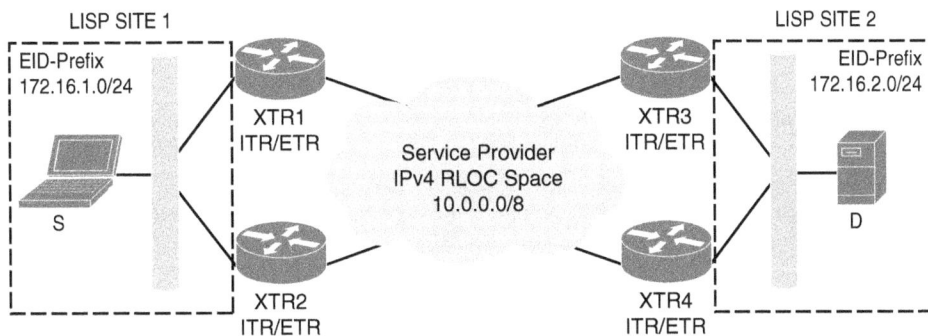

Figure 3-1   *Unicast Packet Forwarding Between LISP Sites*

The client S represents the source EID with IP address 172.16.1.1 that is sending packets to the destination EID server D with IP address 172.16.2.1 on the right. The client and server each exist in a LISP site separated by service provider networks in between. Each LISP site is multihomed to its service provider. The ITRs and ETRs are customer edge routers peering with the provider edge routers. The LISP site sits behind the ITRs and ETRs. The customer edge routers play the role of ITR and ETR because the customer edge routers are encapsulating LISP packets when sending out of the LISP site toward the provider and de-encapsulating LISP packets when receiving packets from the provider destined to the EID attached to it.

Let's analyze the packet processing hop by hop when client S wants to connect to a web application hosted on server D with hostname D.abc.com, as shown in the following steps:

Step 1.   Client S resolves the EID IP address of server D through a Domain Name System (DNS) resolution of server D hostname D.abc.com. An A record is returned because the address being resolved is an IPv4 address. The packet is encapsulated as an IPv4 packet and routed toward the LISP ITR router with the source EID as client S with IP address 172.16.1.1 and the destination EID as server D with IP address 172.16.2.1. The packet is routed toward the ITR based on the optimal path toward the nearest ITR, as determined by the routing protocol within the LISP site. The ITRs that are also acting as customer edge routers learn default routes from the provider edge routers and advertise them down toward the customer edge router into the LISP site, and thus all packets destined outside the local LISP site next-hop devices become ITR routers. The administrator should design the intra-site routing with the objective of ensuring that the packets reach the ITR through an optimal path.

Step 2.   The packet is now at the LISP ITR. The ITR first refers to its local underlay routing table to look for a route to the destination EID. The destination EID, by definition, should not have a route in the underlying routing table, and therefore the ITR should not find a route to the destination EID. Upon the miss in the routing table, the router refers to the LISP map cache. The ITR also verifies whether the source EID is part of a configured EID prefix. If the ITR has a match for the destination EID in the local map cache, the packet is encapsulated as a LISP packet with the RLOC addresses of the ETRs in the outer IP header and EID addresses in the inner IP header. In the absence of a LISP map cache entry, the ITR must request the mapping that contains the RLOC addresses of the valid ETRs to reach the destination EID. The ITR sends a LISP map request control message to the mapping system with the EID of server D as the lookup key. The map request routes through the mapping system and arrives at one of the ETRs attached to the destination EID site.

Step 3.   If the map request is for an EID that was registered with the mapping system, the map request is forwarded to the authoritative ETR that registered the requested EID. If the EID was not registered, the map resolver replies to the requesting ITR with a negative map reply, indicating that the requested destination is not a LISP destination. If the destination is a registered EID, the LISP map request should have been forwarded to the ETR at this point. The ETR is configured with the EID-to-RLOC mapping entries for the locally attached LISP EID prefixes; this information is part of the LISP mapping database. A map reply message is returned directly from the ETR to the ITR, and it contains the following information:

   ■ A list of locators (XTR3 and XTR4)

   ■ Priority and weight values for traffic engineering policy

Step 4.   The ITR receives the map reply and ensures that the message is received with proper format; then it caches the mapping information learned from the map reply message. This caching speeds up the forwarding lookup for any future packets destined to the same EID. The record time-to-live (TTL) field in the map reply defines how long, in minutes, the ITR will store the mapping information. Therefore, for any future packets from client S to server D, the ITR prepends the ETR's RLOC address as populated in the local cache, considering the traffic engineering policies defined in the weight and priority parameters. The priority and weight influence the selection of the destination RLOC by being included in a forwarding hash along with the EID header Layer 2 through Layer 4 parameters. At this point, the ITR encapsulates the traffic and tunnels it to the ETR.

Step 5.   The ETRs XTR3 and XTR4 receive all LISP data packets directly from the ITRs attached to client S, and the ETRs de-encapsulate the traffic and forward packets to the attached destination host server D. XTR3 and XTR4 also function as ITRs for packets sent from server D in response to client S packets. As a possible optimization based on implementation, XTR3 and XTR4 can glean into the LISP packets received, take note of the source RLOC and source EID of the packet, and cache the information. The gleaned mapping provides only single EID-to-RLOC information for the packet received. For complete information about remaining RLOCs, XTR3 and XTR4 have to also send LISP map requests to learn the remaining RLOCs for the EID—in this case the RLOCs for XTR1 and XTR2 attached to client S (using the same process described in steps 1 through 4).

RLOC Reachability

RLOC addresses may become unreachable due to the interface with the RLOC IP address going down on the ITR/ETR nodes. Interfaces can go down for many reasons, such as an administrator shutting down an interface intentionally during a late-night maintenance window or accidently fat fingering at 2:00 a.m. while troubleshooting a network incident. Or a software process crash in the operating system of the node might cause interfaces to reset. Of course, it is also possible for hardware failures to cause nodes to fail. Whatever the cause of the interface failure with the RLOC address, the LISP nodes all must have up-to-date reachability information for the various RLOCs. Should the availability of the RLOC be confirmed through a data plane or control plane mechanism? The LISP RFCs provided several options. Let's go over some of them briefly.

Let's start with the control plane mechanisms. On the Internet, the RLOC address is reachable in the global routing system through BGP. Therefore, when the RLOC address is no longer reachable, the BGP routing system propagates a withdrawal message across the global routing system for the RLOC address. The dependency on the BGP routing protocol failure detection and convergence time determines the reliability of the information available on the reachability of the RLOC IP address. There are ways to optimize the convergence times of these protocols to help determine the availability of the RLOC IP address more quickly. (That topic could fill a book on its own.)

The classic tool used to test connectivity is the Internet Control Message Protocol (ICMP) **ping** command, which can also be used to verify the reachability of the RLOC address from one LISP ITR node to an ETR node. The issue with this is that most service providers block ICMP **ping** in the core and edge of the infrastructure for security reasons. This is common practice, particularly in the service provider space. In addition, **ping** confirms that the remote IP address is reachable but does not confirm whether the remote node was correctly configured as an RLOC for a particular EID prefix. Furthermore, underlay reachability is not representative of the ability of the ETR to actually reach the destination EID; the ETR may be perfectly reachable yet not be able to get to the destination EID, which can lead to black-holing of traffic in scenarios in which a perfectly healthy alternative path actually may exist. It is preferable to have a mechanism within LISP that validates a node as an ETR and its ability to reach an EID prefix to essentially keep track of the locator status.

The algorithms to determine locator status on Cisco platforms are called *locator reachability algorithms*. Three possible algorithms exist for keeping track of locator status: count-tcp, echo-nonce, and rloc-probing. echo-nonce is the only data plane mechanism of these three algorithms.

Note　Refer to the software configuration guides for specific platforms to confirm which locator algorithms are supported. At the time of the writing of this book, NX-OS on the Nexus 7000 platform is the only operating system that supports all three locator reachability algorithms.

If the count-tcp algorithm is configured on a LISP node, the LISP node sends Transmission Control Protocol (TCP) SYN packets to each locator known in its LISP cache and counts how many ACKs it receives back from the locator every minute. If the SYN count is non-zero and the ACK count is zero, the LISP node assumes that the locator is down and marks it as down. The LISP node then sends LISP-encapsulated packets to another locator for a specific EID prefix, if available. After 3 minutes, the LISP node enables the status of the locator it previously marked down as up and performs the same count-tcp locator reachability test. The count-tcp algorithm is most useful when the traffic pattern is asymmetric between LISP sites, but it can also be used in symmetric traffic patterns. count-tcp is configured on ITR or proxy ingress tunnel router (PITR) nodes.

The echo-nonce algorithm is useful when LISP-encapsulated traffic flows bidirectionally between the ITR and ETR. The nonce is a 24-bit value that is randomly generated by the ITR when encapsulating a LISP packet to an ETR and expecting the ETR to encapsulate the same nonce value in the return traffic back to the ITR. The ITR signals to ETR the expectation of the nonce value in its response by turning on the N-bit and E-bit on the LISP headers of the data packets. The N-bit is the nonce present bit, and the E-bit is the echo nonce request bit. Considering that echo-nonce expects LISP packet bidirectionally between two LISP nodes, PITRs would not be nodes where you implement echo-nonce algorithms. An ITR should enable the E-bit in LISP data packets only when the ETR is also configured with the echo-nonce algorithm.

RLOC probing is LISP's control plane method of verifying the RLOC reachability for map cache entries. With the probe bit set, the ITR/PITR nodes send map request messages directly to locators in the EID-to-RLOC cache at regular intervals. Since the intention is to send a map request packet as a probe packet, map request packets with the P-bit set are not sent to the map server or to any mapping system. The map request is forwarded to the ETR, which verifies underlay connectivity to the ETR; the response to the probe is successful only if the ETR actually has a viable route in its routing table to the EID for which the ITR probed. This provides visibility of the health of the ETR beyond just its core/underlay facing interfaces.

LISP Ingress Traffic Engineering

Traffic Engineering (TE) basically involves distributing traffic across multiple paths based on application or business requirements. Other applications exist, such as establishing pre-signaled protected or fast re-route backup paths that are specific to MPLS Traffic Engineering. In Traffic Engineering, the packet's path is always defined at the beginning or ingress of the TE path. The packet is then steered from the ingress point to the egress point of the path, based on some requirements or constraints of the ingress node. The egress node or nodes accept the packet and forward it on to the destination. What if you have two egress nodes located at a site and you want to influence the ingress nodes in preferring one egress node over the other or to equally send traffic to the different egress nodes? This is possible through LISP ingress Traffic Engineering. The ETRs signal to the ITRs the preferred ETRs to ingress into the LISP site hosted behind the ETRs. An airport air traffic control tower comes to mind. This tower signals to the planes entering the airport which runway to land on. The airport traffic control tower is analogous to a LISP process running on ETR nodes. The ETR nodes are the runways, the entry points into the network/airport. The ITRs are the airplanes. The air traffic control tower distributes air traffic based on various factors, such as runway size, directing larger planes (such as Boeing 787 or Airbus 380) to land using the large runways. The larger runways are able to accommodate the larger traffic. Air traffic control telling airplanes which runway to use to enter the airport is similar to LISP ETR nodes telling ITR routers on which ETR node to ingress the LISP site.

Let's look into how the LISP ingress Traffic Engineering mechanism works. The packet forwarding between LISP sites is based on the outer IP header of the LISP packet, which consists of the ITR source RLOC and ETR destination RLOC addresses. The routing protocol in the core network determines the best path from ITR to ETR, based on the best metric. The RLOC address is determined by resolving the EID-to-RLOC mapping from the mapping system. The RLOC is the address of the ETR device attached to the EID prefix. Every ETR registers with the mapping system its RLOC address, its attached EID prefixes, and the priority and weight values. The priority and weight values are administratively defined. Each RLOC has a priority value; lower values are preferred. A priority value of 255 excludes an RLOC from being used to reach an EID prefix. If the priority values across multiple RLOCs in a locator set are equal, the weight is then referenced to determine the distribution of traffic. Say that there are four RLOCs mapped to a single EID prefix, with the weight values 25:25:40:10. In this case, the first RLOC receives 25% of the traffic, the second RLOC 25% of the traffic, the third RLOC 40% of the traffic, and last RLOC 10% of the traffic. A hashing mechanism is used to distribute the traffic across the locator set. If priorities and weights are equal for all RLOCs, the hash should render a fairly equal distribution. The hash used in LISP is an augmentation of the traditional five-tuple hash used in IP routing. The hash includes the LISP priorities and weights, effectively resulting in a seven-tuple hash, which includes the following:

- Source and destination IP address

- Source and destination Layer 4 TCP, User Datagram Protocol (UDP), or Stream Control Transmission Protocol (SCTP) port numbers

- IP protocol number field or IPv6 next-protocol fields of a packet that a host originates from within a LISP site

- RLOC priority value

- RLOC weight value

If a packet is not a TCP, UDP, or SCTP packet, the source and destination addresses from the header are only used to calculate the hash. Different vendors may use different hashing mechanisms. In Figure 3-1, the map cache has two RLOCs with equal weight values of 50 and priority equal to 1. Thus, in that case, any packets sent from the ITR from LISP site 1 to LISP site 2 get distributed evenly across both ETR RLOCs attached to LISP site 2.

The direction of traffic is steered or engineered based on the priority and weight value assigned to each RLOC-to-EID mapping for an ETR advertising its attached EID prefixes to the mapping system. ETR thus uses the map reply message to control which ETR is the preferred entry point into the LISP site. The exit point out of the LISP site is, of course, defined by the routing protocol best-path decision process within the LISP site. You look at an ITR as the head end of a routing path and the ETR as the tail end; this is analogous to MPLS Traffic Engineering (TE) tunnels. In MPLS TE, the head end calculates the path through the network dynamically or explicitly. In explicit calculation, the next-hop nodes from head end to tail end are manually defined through the explicit route object (ERO) field in the packet. The explicit path calculation using the explicit locator path (ELP) field in LISP is covered in Chapter 9, "LISP in the Enterprise Multihome Internet/WAN Edge."

A fundamental difference between MPLS TE and LISP ingress Traffic Engineering is that in MPLS TE, the head end or ingress node of the label switch path determines the tail end at which the tunnel terminates. In LISP the ETR or tail end determines which RLOC the ITR uses, and therefore it determines the preferred RLOC at which the LISP overlay tunnel should terminate.

MTU Handling

As explained in Chapter 2, a LISP packet contains an outer IP header, a UDP header, a LISP header, and an inner IP header, which can add up to 36 bytes of overhead for IPv4 and 56 bytes of overhead for IPv6. Assuming the default maximum transmission unit (MTU) of 1500 bytes in a network, any LISP packet transmitted out interfaces with 1500 bytes MTU would be dropped due to the need for fragmentation. To prevent packets from being dropped in the path between the ITR and ETR, the network must be implemented to address packets exceeding MTU in the paths between the ITR and the ETR. There are two common methods to handle packet path MTU:

- **Stateless:** The fragmentation of LISP packets is the responsibility of the ITR, and the reassembly is performed at the destination host with the destination EID address. In Figure 3-1, if client S sends packets exceeding the path MTU between the service providers, XTR1 and XTR2 fragment the LISP packet, and destination server D reassembles the packet on reception. If the ITRs receive the packet with the don't fragment bit set (IPv4 or IPv6 header DF=1), the ITRs drop the packet and reply with an ICMP too big message back to the source.

▪ **Stateful:** The ITR keeps track of the MTU for the paths toward the ETR through a mechanism such as path MTU discovery (PMTUD). With PMTUD, the ITR sends out discovery packets. The IP packets sent out have the don't fragment (DF=1) bit set. When a packet encounters a router in the path toward the ETR that cannot forward the packet without fragmenting it, the router notices that the DF bit is set to 1, drops the packet, and sends the ICMP error message "Fragmentation needed and do not fragment bit set" (ICMP type 3, code 4) back to the ITR. The ITR then lowers the size of the packet and retransmits the packet until no ICMP message is received for the packet. The size of the last IP packet successfully sent is then used as the maximum packet size for all subsequent IP traffic between the ITR and ETR. As a result, the destination host does not have to reassemble packets. It is important to note that many providers disable ICMP on their routers, and when this is the case, the transmitting routers cannot send necessary ICMP messaging back to the ITR; in such situations, PMTUD is not an option.

LISP IPv4 Unicast Routing Configuration

The scenario shown in Figure 3-2 is a simple IPv4-only LISP network with three sites, each with a single XTR node and client router. The XTR node functions both as an ITR LISP router and as an ETR LISP router. In the topology, notice that each XTR has a different icon because each node requires a different Cisco operating system (OS). The XTR1 router is running the Cisco IOS-XE OS, XTR2 is running IOS-XR OS, and XTR3 is running the Nexus OS (NX-OS). The LISP sites connect to each other through a backbone network. The backbone network has two core routers with hostnames based on the ISP, each with single MS-MR attaching to it. The core routers ISP1 and ISP2 are both running IOS-XE OS. The MS-MR1 router is also an IOS-XE router, and the MS-MR2 is an IOS-XR node.

The client routers CE1 through CE3 represent clients in a LISP site, each in its own EID namespace. Each client router is peering OSPF with its local XTR router. The backbone network is a BGP network where each of the routers is in its individual autonomous system (AS), with Exterior Border Gateway Protocol (eBGP) neighbor relationships between the xTRs and both ISP routers. Routing between MS-MRs and ISP routers simply involves static routing.

Implementing LISP in the scenario presented in Figure 3-2 requires configuration of two LISP components: the xTRs and the MS-MR nodes. The remaining nodes do not require any LISP-related configuration but only standard routing configuration, such as OSPF on the customer edge (CE) nodes at each LISP site and BGP routing configuration on the ISP nodes. (This book assumes that you have a background in configuring routing protocols. The focus of all the examples is on the LISP-related configurations.)

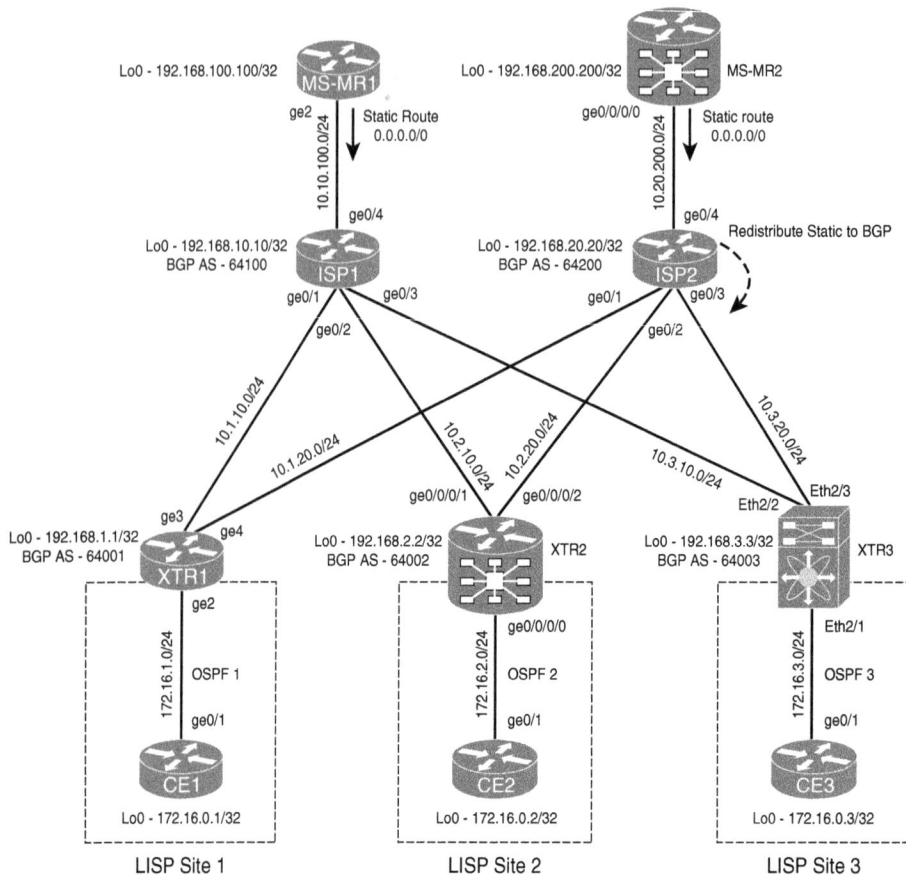

Figure 3-2   *IPv4 Routing Between LISP Sites Topology*

Note   With IOS-XE version 16.6.1, the new CLI model for LISP configuration was redesigned with improvements to the structure and flow of the commands as part of the development effort around the campus fabric solution that later evolved into Software Defined Access (SDA). Most LISP-specific configuration guides still adhere to old LISP CLI structure. The old and common CLI structure is followed in this book. Please reference the "IOS-XE Campus Fabric Guide" or "SDA Configuration Guide" for more details on the new LISP CLI structure. Current versions of IOS-XE support both CLI structures.

The following are the general steps to configure XTR nodes:

Step 1.   Enable the LISP process.

Step 2.   Enable the LISP ITR/ETR functionality.

Step 3.   Configure the map server and the map resolver.

Step 4.   Configure an EID-to-RLOC mapping database.

The syntax across the various Cisco platforms is similar, but there are a few subtle differences, so this chapter provides examples for the various platforms, starting with the XTR1 node running an IOS-XE image.

These are the steps to configure LISP XTR on IOS and IOS-XE:

Step 1.   **Enable the LISP process.** The command **router lisp** takes you to the router configuration mode (config-router) to configure the LISP process. All LISP-related configuration commands are executed under the router configuration mode on both the IOS and IOS-XE platforms.

Step 2.   **Enable the LISP ITR/ETR functionality.** Under the router configuration mode, the command **ipv4 itr** configures the device as an ITR node, and the command **ipv4 etr** configures the device as an ETR node. In this example, XTR1 performs the function of both ITR and ETR, so you need to apply both commands.

Step 3.   **Configure the map server and the map resolver.** The command to specify which map server an ETR will register to is **ipv4 etr map-server** *map-server-address* **key** *key-type authentication-key*. To prevent rogue ETRs from registering spoofed prefixes, an ETR has to have a matching authentication key to register EID prefixes to its map server. The map server accepts register messages only from ETRs that have matching keys. The map server address specified in the command must be a reachable locator address. The command to specify which map resolver the ITR sends map request messages for resolving IPv4 EID to RLOC is **ipv4 itr map-resolver** *map-resolver-address*. The map resolver address specified in the command must be a reachable locator address. There is no requirement to configure an authentication key to the map resolver. A maximum of two MRs and MSs are configurable.

Step 4.   **Configure an EID-to-RLOC mapping database.** Every ETR must populate its local LISP mapping database with entries that specify the locally connected EID prefix and RLOC address of the ETR. The entries are manually populated, similar to how prefixes are manually injected into a BGP table with the **network** command. The commands to create the EID-to-RLOC entries are **database-mapping** *EID-prefix/prefix-length locator* **priority** *priority* **weight** *weight* and **database-mapping** *EID-prefix/prefix-length* **ipv4-interface** *locator* **priority** *priority* **weight** *weight*. The first variation of the command allows you to manually specify the RLOC IP address, and the second variation allows you to specify the interface that the RLOC address will map to. The priority and weight options are LISP ingress TE policy parameters, as described earlier in this chapter. These commands are critical to the function of the LISP mapping system because they trigger the ETR to tell the map server which EID prefixes are reachable with the RLOC address through the map register messages.

One useful optional command is **ipv4 map-request-source** *source-address*. By default, the ITR uses the RLOC address configured in the **database-mapping** command as the source address when sending map request messages to the MR. This command allows you to specify an IP address other than the RLOC address configured by the **database-mapping** command. Specifying the map request source may be useful when the ITR is positioned behind a network address translation (NAT) device, and the source IP address of any packet traversing the NAT device must match the NAT translation rules. You can configure the ITR to use the source IP address for the map request messages in accordance with translation rules defined in the NAT device.

Example 3-1 shows the configuration of the XTR1 device shown in the topology in Figure 3-2.

Example 3-1   *XTR1 IOS-XE LISP Router Configuration*

```
!Configuration on XTR1
!
hostname XTR1
!
interface Loopback0
 ip address 192.168.1.1 255.255.255.255
!
interface GigabitEthernet2
 ip address 172.16.1.1 255.255.255.0
 ip ospf network point-to-point
 ip ospf 1 area 0
!
interface GigabitEthernet3
 description link-to-ISP1
 ip address 10.1.10.1 255.255.255.0


!
interface GigabitEthernet4
 description link-to-ISP2
 ip address 10.1.20.1 255.255.255.0
!
router lisp
 eid-table default instance-id 0
  database-mapping 172.16.0.1/32 192.168.1.1 priority 1 weight 100
  database-mapping 172.16.1.0/24 192.168.1.1 priority 1 weight 100
  ipv4 map-request-source 192.168.1.1
  exit
 !
```

```
 ipv4 itr map-resolver 192.168.100.100
 ipv4 itr map-resolver 192.168.200.200
 ipv4 itr
 ipv4 etr map-server 192.168.100.100 key cisco
 ipv4 etr map-server 192.168.200.200 key cisco
 ipv4 etr
 exit
!
router ospf 1
 router-id 192.168.1.1
 default-information originate always
!
router bgp 64001
 bgp router-id 192.168.1.1
 bgp log-neighbor-changes
 no bgp default ipv4-unicast
 neighbor 10.1.10.10 remote-as 64100
 neighbor 10.1.20.20 remote-as 64200
 !
 address-family ipv4
  network 192.168.1.1 mask 255.255.255.255
  neighbor 10.1.10.10 activate
  neighbor 10.1.10.10 send-community
  neighbor 10.1.20.20 activate
  neighbor 10.1.20.20 send-community
```

The CE1 node attached to XTR1 does not run any LISP service or perform any LISP function, but it does act as a node inside a LISP site, advertising its loopback 0 IP address 172.16.1.1/32 as a LISP EID. The loopback 0 IP address is a /32 prefix similar to any host IP address that could exist in a LISP site. The link between CE1 and XTR1 is an attached EID prefix inside LISP site 1. Notice in the configuration that XTR1 adds to its LISP mapping database entries mapped to its RLOC address (192.168.1.1) for the loopback IP address of CE1 (172.16.1.1) and the directly attached network 172.16.11.0/24. XTR1 is telling the map server, "If anybody wants to get to IP address 172.16.1.1/32 or reach network 172.16.11.0/24, tell them to encapsulate LISP and send it to its RLOC IP address, which is 192.168.1.1."

Example 3-2 shows the configuration for the CE1 node in LISP site 1. Although it does not have any LISP-related configuration, the CE1 does have some basic routing configurations that need to be in place, as shown in this example.

Example 3-2 *CE1 Configuration: IOS/IOS-XE*

```
!Configuration of CE1 in LISP Site 1
!
hostname CE1
interface Loopback0
 ip address 172.16.0.1 255.255.255.255
 ip ospf 1 area 0
!
interface GigabitEthernet0/1
 ip address 172.16.1.2 255.255.255.0
 ip ospf network point-to-point
 ip ospf 1 area 0
!
router ospf 1
 router-id 172.16.0.1
```

MS-MR1 is a MS and MR LISP node configured on an IOS-XE router. The MS-MR1 configuration is presented next to complete the IOS-XE configuration examples.

To configure the MS/MR device on the IOS/IOS-XE OS, the following configurations steps are required:

Step 1. **Enable the LISP process.** The command **router lisp** takes you to the router configuration mode (config-router) to configure the LISP process. All LISP-related configuration commands are executed under the router configuration mode in both the IOS and IOS-XE platforms.

Step 2. **Configure the LISP site.** The command **site** *site name* creates a LISP site that represents a LISP network attached to a XTR.

Step 3. **Configure the authentication password.** The command **authentication-key** *key* creates a password for the site under the config-router-lisp-site mode. The password must match the password configured on the XTR for the respective site. If the keys do not match, the XTR cannot register the EID prefix for its attached site.

Step 4. **Configure the EID prefix.** The command **eid-prefix** *EID prefix* configures the subnet that is part of the LISP site. This command is also executed under the config-router-lisp-site mode.

Step 5. **Enable map server and map resolver functionality.** The commands **ipv4 map-server** and **ipv4 map-resolver** in the global configuration mode configure the local node as a LISP map server and map resolver, respectively.

To add another layer of security, the ETR RLOC address from which the map server will accept registration is specified with the command **allowed-located** *rloc-address* or **list** *prefix-list*. The purpose of the prefix list is to match the RLOC IP addresses permitted for the LISP site. This command is also executed under the config-router-lisp-site mode.

Example 3-3 shows the configuration of the MS-MR1 device shown in the topology in Figure 3-2.

Example 3-3 *MS-MR1 IOS-XE LISP Router Configuration*

```
hostname MS-MR1

interface Loopback0
 ip address 192.168.100.100 255.255.255.255

interface GigabitEthernet2
 ip address 10.10.100.100 255.255.255.0


router lisp
 site Site-1-AS-64001
  authentication-key cisco
  eid-prefix 172.16.0.1/32
  eid-prefix 172.16.1.0/24
  exit
 !
 site Site-2-AS-64002
  authentication-key cisco
  eid-prefix 172.16.0.2/32
  eid-prefix 172.16.2.0/24
  exit
 !
 site Site-3-AS-64003
  authentication-key cisco
  eid-prefix 172.16.0.3/32
  eid-prefix 172.16.3.0/24
  exit
 !
 ipv4 map-server
 ipv4 map-resolver
 exit

ip route 0.0.0.0 0.0.0.0 10.10.100.10
```

The XTR2 node is running the IOS-XR software. The LISP XTR deployment on the IOS-XR platform is similar in concept but slightly different in syntax. The key difference in IOS-XR is that you have to define any LISP configuration under an address family of choice and define the instance or virtual routing and forwarding (VRF) in which the EID and RLOC namespace exists.

To configure the XTR device on the IOS-XR platform, the following configuration steps are required:

Step 1. Enable the **LISP process.** The command **router lisp** *ID* starts the LISP process. The command is executed in global configuration mode (config). If you do not specify the process ID, the operating system uses the ID zero. Executing the command moves the prompt to LISP configuration mode (config-lisp).

Step 2. Enable the **address family.** If the LISP network is forwarding IPv4 packets, you need to enable the address family IPv4 by using the command **address-family ipv4 unicast**, which changes the command line to config-lisp-afi mode.

Step 3. Enable **ITR and ETR functionality.** Under the LISP address family mode, you use **etr** and **itr** commands to configure the XTR device as an egress tunnel router and ingress tunnel router, respectively.

Step 4. Configure the **map server and the map resolver.** The command **etr map-server** *map-server-address* { **key** [**clear** | **encrypted**] **LINE** | **proxy-reply** } configures the map server for the XTR. The **proxy-reply** option allows the map server to be an authoritative source for the EID prefixes registered by the XTR. This is communicated by the XTR to the map server by the turning on the proxy map reply flag (P bit) in the map register messages sent by the ETR to the map server. The key is a required configuration and must match between the ETR and the map server. To configure the map resolver, simply use the command **itr map-resolver** *map-resolver-address*.

Step 5. Configure the **EID-to-RLOC mapping database.** The EID-to-RLOC mapping database is called an EID table in IOS-XR. You must specify the routing context in which the EID prefix will exist. An EID table is mapped to a virtual routing forwarding (VRF) and LISP instance ID with the command **eid-table** { **default** | [**vrf** vrf_name] } **instance-id** *instance_id* in the config-lisp mode. Under the config-lisp-eid-table mode, you must specify the address family of the EID prefix with the command **address-family ipv4 unicast**, which moves your CLI to config-lisp-eid-table-afi, where you list your EID-to-RLOC mapping entries using the command **database-mapping** *EID prefix/prefix-length locator* **priority** *priority* **weight** *weight*. As part of the ITR function configuration, the map request message source IP is defined by the command **map-request-source** *ip_address*.

Step 6. Specify the **RLOC VRF.** Because you specified the VRF in which the EID prefix is reachable, the VRF of the RLOC also must be specified as part of the basic configuration. The command **locator-table** [**default** | **vrf** *vrf_name*] associates the VRF in which the RLOC is reachable with a LISP instance.

Note   Chapter 8, "LISP Network Virtualization/Multi-Tenancy," explains in more detail the use cases for instance ID and VRF in LISP networks. This chapter touches on the basic commands as they are part of the required configuration parameters for unicast routing. The examples shown in this chapter assume that all forwarding is in the default routing table.

Example 3-4 shows the configuration of the XTR2 device in the topology in Figure 3-2.

Example 3-4   *XTR2 IOS-XR LISP Configuration*

```
hostname XTR2

interface Loopback0
 ipv4 address 192.168.2.2 255.255.255.255


interface GigabitEthernet0/0/0/0
 ipv4 address 172.16.2.1 255.255.255.0
!
interface GigabitEthernet0/0/0/1
 description link-to-ISP1
 ipv4 address 10.2.10.2 255.255.255.0
!
interface GigabitEthernet0/0/0/2
description link-to-ISP2
 ipv4 address 10.2.20.2 255.255.255.0

router lisp
 address-family ipv4 unicast
  etr map-server 192.168.100.100 key cisco
  etr map-server 192.168.200.200 key cisco
  etr
  itr map-resolver 192.168.100.100
  itr map-resolver 192.168.200.200
  itr
 !
 eid-table default instance-id 0
  address-family ipv4 unicast
   database-mapping 172.16.0.2/32 192.168.2.2 priority 1 weight 100
   database-mapping 172.16.2.0/24 192.168.2.2 priority 1 weight 100
   map-request-source 192.168.2.2
  !
 !
 locator-table default

router ospf 2
 router-id 192.168.2.2
 default-information originate
 area 0
  interface GigabitEthernet0/0/0/0
  !
```

```
!
router bgp 64002
 bgp router-id 192.168.2.2
 address-family ipv4 unicast
  network 192.168.2.2/32
 !
 neighbor 10.2.10.10
  remote-as 64100
  address-family ipv4 unicast
  !
 !
 neighbor 10.2.20.10
  remote-as 64200
  address-family ipv4 unicast
  !
 !
!
```

MS-MR2 also provides MS and MR service to the LISP network. For completeness, Example 3-5 shows the configuration of MS-MR2 device in the topology in Figure 3-2.

Example 3-5   *MS-MR2 Configuration*

```
hostname MS-MR2

interface Loopback0
 ip address 192.168.200.200 255.255.255.255

interface GigabitEthernet0/0/0/0
 ip address 10.20.200.200 255.255.255.0


router lisp
 address-family ipv4 unicast
  map-resolver
  map-server
 !
 site Site-1-AS-64001
  eid-prefix 172.16.1.1/32
  eid-prefix 172.16.1.0/24
  authentication-key encrypted cisco
 !
 site Site-2-AS-64002
  eid-prefix 172.16.2.2/32
  eid-prefix 172.16.2.0/24
  authentication-key encrypted cisco
 !
```

```
 site Site-3-AS-64003
  eid-prefix 172.16.3.3/32
  eid-prefix 172.16.3.0/24
  authentication-key encrypted cisco
 !
locator-table vrf default
!

router static
 address-family ipv4 unicast
  0.0.0.0/0 10.20.200.20
```

The configuration for the MS or MR is similar on all the Cisco platforms. In IOS-XR, for any routing-related process configuration, you have to enable the address family for which you are enabling the routing service, as just shown with the **address-family ipv4** unicast command under **router lisp**. The **map-server** and **map-resolver** commands under the address family enable the map server and map resolver functionality. As a map server, the LISP site's EID prefix is defined, along with the authentication key expected from the ETR of each site, in the map register message.

The last XTR node, XTR3, is running the NX-OS image. These are the steps to configure LISP XTR on the NX-OS platform:

Step 1.   **Enable the LISP process.** The **feature lisp** command in the global configuration mode enables LISP. The LISP feature requires the Transport Services license. At the time of writing this book, LISP is not supported for F2 series modules. Remember that F2 is purely a Layer 2 module. The F3 and M3 series modules are supported as of NX-OS version 7.2(0)D1(1). The legacy M1 32-port, 10 Gigabit Ethernet (M1) module (N7K-M132XP-12 or N7K-M132XP-12L), with Electronic Programmable Logic Device (EPLD) version 186.008 or later also supports LISP.

Note   All the commands in this example are in the global configuration mode because both the RLOC and EID space are in the default routing table or VRF.

Step 2.   **Enable LISP ITR/ETR functionality.** A single command, **ip lisp itr-etr**, configures the device as both an ITR and XTR node. If there is a design requirement to enable only ITR or ETR functionality on a device, you can do so with the commands **ip lisp itr** and **ip lisp etr**, respectively.

Step 3.   **Configure the map server and the map resolver.** The **ip lisp itr map-resolver** *map-resolver-address* command configures the IPv4 locator address of the map resolver. Similarly, **ip lisp etr map-server** *map-server-address* **key** *key-type authentication-key* configures the IPv4 locator address of the map server with the required authentication key.

Step 4.   Configure an **EID-to-RLOC mapping database.** The command
ip database-mapping *EID-prefix/prefixlength locator* **priority** *priority*
weight *weight* creates an entry in the EID-to-RLOC mapping database on
the local ETR node for the EID prefixes attached to it with the ingress traffic
policy metric values for priority and weight.

One optional command, **ip lisp map-request-source** *source-address*, allows you to use
a certain IP address as the source of the ITR map request message. By default, the RLOC
address configured earlier with the **ip database-mapping** command is chosen as the
source address of any map request message.

Example 3-6 shows the configuration of the XTR3 device in the topology in Figure 3-2.

Example 3-6   *XTR3 Configuration*

```
hostname xTR3

interface loopback0
  ip address 192.168.3.3/32

interface Ethernet2/1
  no switchport
  ip address 172.16.3.1/24
  ip router ospf 3 area 0.0.0.0
  no shutdown

interface Ethernet2/2
  no switchport
  description link-to-ISP1
  ip address 10.3.10.3/24
  no shutdown

interface Ethernet2/3
  no switchport
  description link-to-ISP2
  ip address 10.3.20.3/24
  no shutdown

feature ospf
feature bgp
feature lisp

ip lisp itr-etr
ip lisp database-mapping 172.16.0.3/32 192.168.3.3 priority 1 weight 100
ip lisp database-mapping 172.16.3.0/24 192.168.3.3 priority 1 weight 100
ip lisp locator-vrf default
```

```
ip lisp itr map-resolver 192.168.100.100
ip lisp itr map-resolver 192.168.200.200
ip lisp etr map-server 192.168.100.100 key cisco
ip lisp etr map-server 192.168.200.200 key cisco
ip lisp map-request-source 192.168.3.3

router ospf 3
  router-id 192.168.3.3
  default-information originate always


router bgp 64003
  router-id 192.168.3.3
  address-family ipv4 unicast
    network 192.168.3.3/32
  neighbor 10.3.10.10 remote-as 64100
    address-family ipv4 unicast
  neighbor 10.3.20.20 remote-as 64200
    address-family ipv4 unicast
```

The ISP nodes function as core devices that provide the following:

- Connectivity between the MS/MR and XTR devices

- Connectivity between the XTR devices for LISP site-to-site communication

- Routing between the LISP and non-LISP sites to route through the core network infrastructure

The ISP nodes essentially provide the underlay transport service for the LISP sites. The configuration on the ISP devices only involves setting the basic routing protocol. Example 3-7 shows the configuration of ISP devices shown in the topology in Figure 3-2.

Example 3-7 *ISP Core Router Configurations*

```
!IOS-XE ISP1 configuration
hostname ISP1

interface Loopback0
 ip address 192.168.10.10 255.255.255.255
 !

interface GigabitEthernet0/1
 description link-to-XTR1
 ip address 10.1.10.10 255.255.255.0
```

```
interface GigabitEthernet0/2
  description link-to-XTR2
 ip address 10.2.10.10 255.255.255.0

interface GigabitEthernet0/3
  description link-to-XTR3
 ip address 10.3.10.10 255.255.255.0

!
interface GigabitEthernet0/4
  description link-to-MS/MR1
 ip address 10.10.100.10 255.255.255.0

!
router bgp 64100
 bgp router-id 192.168.10.10
 bgp log-neighbor-changes
 no bgp default ipv4-unicast
 neighbor 10.1.10.1 remote-as 64001
 neighbor 10.2.10.2 remote-as 64002
 neighbor 10.3.10.3 remote-as 64003
 !
 address-family ipv4
  network 192.168.10.10 mask 255.255.255.255
  redistribute connected
  redistribute static
  neighbor 10.1.10.1 activate
  neighbor 10.1.10.1 send-community
  neighbor 10.2.10.2 activate
  neighbor 10.2.10.2 send-community
  neighbor 10.3.10.3 activate
  neighbor 10.3.10.3 send-community
 exit-address-family
!

ip route 192.168.100.100 255.255.255.255 10.10.100.100

!IOS-XE ISP2 configuration

hostname ISP2

interface Loopback0
 ip address 192.168.20.20 255.255.255.255
!
```

```
interface GigabitEthernet0/1
 description link-to-XTR1
 ip address 10.1.20.20 255.255.255.0

interface GigabitEthernet0/2
  description link-to-XTR2
 ip address 10.2.20.20 255.255.255.0

interface GigabitEthernet0/3
  description link-to-XTR3
 ip address 10.3.20.20 255.255.255.0

!
interface GigabitEthernet0/4
  description link-to-MS/MR2
 ip address 10.20.200.20 255.255.255.0

!
router bgp 64200
 bgp router-id 192.168.20.20
 bgp log-neighbor-changes
 no bgp default ipv4-unicast
 neighbor 10.1.20.1 remote-as 64001
 neighbor 10.2.20.2 remote-as 64002
 neighbor 10.3.20.3 remote-as 64003
 !
 address-family ipv4
  network 192.168.20.20 mask 255.255.255.255
  redistribute connected
  redistribute static
  neighbor 10.1.20.1 activate
  neighbor 10.1.20.1 send-community
  neighbor 10.2.20.2 activate
  neighbor 10.2.20.2 send-community
  neighbor 10.3.20.3 activate
  neighbor 10.3.20.3 send-community
 exit-address-family
!

ip route 192.168.200.200 255.255.255.255 10.20.200.200
```

The basic configuration for this example is now complete. The following sections looks at how to verify the control plane.

LISP IPv4 Unicast Routing Control Plane Verification

A LISP network is broken into two routing domains: the RLOC and EID domains. Each of these routing domains, of course, has its own address space; in addition, each runs a unique instance of a routing protocol. In the example in Figure 3-2, the EID domain is running OSPF, while the RLOC domain is running BGP. The XTR nodes sit at the border of the two routing domains, running OSPF southbound toward its attached CE node and peering BGP northbound toward the ISP core routers. For LISP to work, the underlay routing in both the routing domains must be working. The underlay routing in the EID domain ensures that the endpoints in the LISP site can reach its local xTRs. In this example, the CE must be able to reach the local XTR, where the XTR can LISP encapsulate the packet to forward the traffic to the remote LISP site. The XTR nodes depend on the MS/MR nodes to resolve the EID-to-RLOC mapping to determine the RLOC to which the destination EID is attached. It is also important to verify that the XTR can reach its MS/MR nodes. Example 3-8 shows a quick check of the underlay routing in LISP site 1.

Example 3-8 *LISP Site 1 Underlay Routing Verification for the Figure 3-2 Topology*

```
!verifying OSPF peering


CE1# show ip ospf neighbor


Neighbor ID     Pri   State         Dead Time   Address         Interface
192.168.1.1       0   FULL/  -      00:00:31    172.16.11.1     GigabitEthernet0/1


!192.168.1.1 is the XTR1 loopback 0 IP. Ping the XTR loopback 0 interface.


CE1# ping 192.168.1.1 source loopback 0
Type escape sequence to abort.
Sending 5, 100-byte ICMP Echos to 192.168.1.1, timeout is 2 seconds:
Packet sent with a source address of 172.16.0.1
!!!!!
Success rate is 100 percent (5/5), round-trip min/avg/max = 3/4/6 ms


!On the XTR1 node verify the BGP peering is up with core ISP routers.


xTR1# show ip bgp summary
BGP router identifier 192.168.1.1, local AS number 64001
BGP table version is 16, main routing table version 16
15 network entries using 3720 bytes of memory
29 path entries using 3944 bytes of memory
13/7 BGP path/bestpath attribute entries using 3640 bytes of memory
8 BGP AS-PATH entries using 288 bytes of memory
0 BGP route-map cache entries using 0 bytes of memory
0 BGP filter-list cache entries using 0 bytes of memory
```

```
BGP using 11592 total bytes of memory
BGP activity 45/30 prefixes, 78/49 paths, scan interval 60 secs


Neighbor        V       AS MsgRcvd MsgSent   TblVer  InQ OutQ Up/Down  State/PfxRcd
10.1.10.10      4       64100      12      10      15   0    0 00:00:39       14
10.1.20.20      4       64200      13      10      15   0    0 00:00:42       14
```

!Through the ISP routers the XTR1 learns the transit network prefix and loopback IP
  !addresses of all XTR, ISP and MS/MR nodes as show in the routing table below.

xTR1# show ip route
```
Codes: L - local, C - connected, S - static, R - RIP, M - mobile, B - BGP
       D - EIGRP, EX - EIGRP external, O - OSPF, IA - OSPF inter area
       N1 - OSPF NSSA external type 1, N2 - OSPF NSSA external type 2
       E1 - OSPF external type 1, E2 - OSPF external type 2
       i - IS-IS, su - IS-IS summary, L1 - IS-IS level-1, L2 - IS-IS level-2
       ia - IS-IS inter area, * - candidate default, U - per-user static route
       o - ODR, P - periodic downloaded static route, H - NHRP, l - LISP
       a - application route
       + - replicated route, % - next hop override, p - overrides from PfR


Gateway of last resort is 10.255.0.1 to network 0.0.0.0

S*    0.0.0.0/0 [254/0] via 10.255.0.1
      10.0.0.0/8 is variably subnetted, 13 subnets, 3 masks
C        10.1.10.0/24 is directly connected, GigabitEthernet3
L        10.1.10.1/32 is directly connected, GigabitEthernet3
C        10.1.20.0/24 is directly connected, GigabitEthernet4
L        10.1.20.1/32 is directly connected, GigabitEthernet4
B        10.2.10.0/24 [20/0] via 10.1.10.10, 00:09:43
B        10.2.20.0/24 [20/0] via 10.1.20.20, 00:09:43
B        10.3.10.0/24 [20/0] via 10.1.10.10, 00:09:43
B        10.3.20.0/24 [20/0] via 10.1.20.20, 00:09:43
B        10.10.100.0/24 [20/0] via 10.1.10.10, 00:09:43
B        10.20.200.0/24 [20/0] via 10.1.20.20, 00:09:43
C        10.255.0.0/16 is directly connected, GigabitEthernet1
S        10.255.0.2/32 [254/0] via 10.255.0.1, GigabitEthernet1
L        10.255.1.182/32 is directly connected, GigabitEthernet1
      172.16.0.0/16 is variably subnetted, 3 subnets, 2 masks
O        172.16.0.1/32 [110/2] via 172.16.1.2, 04:09:15, GigabitEthernet2
C        172.16.1.0/24 is directly connected, GigabitEthernet2
L        172.16.1.1/32 is directly connected, GigabitEthernet2
      192.168.1.0/32 is subnetted, 1 subnets
C        192.168.1.1 is directly connected, Loopback0
```

```
        192.168.2.0/32 is subnetted, 1 subnets
B          192.168.2.2 [20/0] via 10.1.10.10, 00:09:43
        192.168.3.0/32 is subnetted, 1 subnets
B          192.168.3.3 [20/0] via 10.1.10.10, 00:09:43
        192.168.10.0/32 is subnetted, 1 subnets
B          192.168.10.10 [20/0] via 10.1.10.10, 00:09:43
        192.168.20.0/32 is subnetted, 1 subnets
B          192.168.20.20 [20/0] via 10.1.20.20, 00:09:43
        192.168.100.0/32 is subnetted, 1 subnets
B          192.168.100.100 [20/0] via 10.1.10.10, 00:09:43
        192.168.200.0/32 is subnetted, 1 subnets
B          192.168.200.200 [20/0] via 10.1.20.20, 00:09:43
```

In Example 3-8, note that XTR1 has only its own connected LISP site prefix, 172.16.11.0/24, in its routing table. XTR1 does not have the prefix information for the other LISP sites. XTR2 and XTR3 also only have their own connected LISP site network in their routing tables. The verification of the underlay routing for other sites would be similar but with variations in the **show** commands, depending on the platform.

The last basic underlay routing verification step is to make sure the xTR can ping its MS/MR devices, as shown in Example 3-9.

Example 3-9 *Verifying Connectivity Between XTR1, MS-MR1, and MS-MR2*

```
!pinging MS-MR1
xTR1# ping 192.168.100.100 source loopback0
Type escape sequence to abort.
Sending 5, 100-byte ICMP Echos to 192.168.100.100, timeout is 2 seconds:
Packet sent with a source address of 192.168.1.1
!!!!!
Success rate is 100 percent (5/5), round-trip min/avg/max = 5/5/6 ms


!pinging MS-MR2
xTR1# ping 192.168.200.200 source loopback0
Type escape sequence to abort.
Sending 5, 100-byte ICMP Echos to 192.168.200.200, timeout is 2 seconds:
Packet sent with a source address of 192.168.1.1
!!!!!
Success rate is 100 percent (5/5), round-trip min/avg/max = 3/4/5 ms
```

Note The focus of this book is LISP, and it is assumed that you are able to troubleshoot basic IGP and BGP protocols. Therefore, no further details about **show** commands are provided for verifying the underlay routing. A single example is shown to explain the interaction of the various underlay routing protocols configured.

Now that you have verified that the basic underlay connectivity is in place, you can proceed to understanding how the LISP control plane is operating in the network. Start first verifying whether the LISP process is enabled on each of the LISP devices, as shown in Example 3-10.

Example 3-10   *Verifying Whether LISP Functionality Is Enabled on XTR Devices*

```
!IOS-XE XTR1 LISP process verification
xTR1# show ip lisp
Instance ID:                            0
Router-lisp ID:                         0
Locator table:                          default
EID table:                              default
Ingress Tunnel Router (ITR):            enabled
Egress Tunnel Router (ETR):             enabled
Proxy-ITR Router (PITR):                disabled
Proxy-ETR Router (PETR):                disabled
NAT-traversal Router (NAT-RTR):         disabled
Mobility First-Hop Router:              disabled
Map Server (MS):                        disabled
Map Resolver (MR):                      disabled
Delegated Database Tree (DDT):          disabled
Site Registration Limit:                0
Map-Request source:                     192.168.1.1
ITR Map-Resolver(s):                    192.168.100.100, 192.168.200.200
ETR Map-Server(s):                      192.168.100.100 (02:10:39), 192.168.200.200
  (00:00:33)
xTR-ID:                                 0x550A5FD6-0xB04B031C-0x171BFDFA-0x51A155DE
site-ID:                                unspecified
ITR local RLOC (last resort):           192.168.1.1
ITR Solicit Map Request (SMR):          accept and process
  Max SMRs per map-cache entry:         8 more specifics
  Multiple SMR suppression time:        20 secs
ETR accept mapping data:                disabled, verify disabled
ETR map-cache TTL:                      1d00h
Locator Status Algorithms:
  RLOC-probe algorithm:                 disabled
  RLOC-probe on route change:           N/A (periodic probing disabled)
  RLOC-probe on member change:          disabled
  LSB reports:                          process
  IPv4 RLOC minimum mask length:        /0
  IPv6 RLOC minimum mask length:        /0
Map-cache:
  Static mappings configured:           0
  Map-cache size/limit:                 1/1000
  Imported route count/limit:           0/1000
```

```
   Map-cache activity check period:   60 secs
   Map-cache FIB updates:             established
   Persistent map-cache:              disabled
 Database:
   Total database mapping size:       2
   static database size/limit:        2/5000
   dynamic database size/limit:       0/1000
   route-import database size/limit:  0/1000
   Inactive (deconfig/away) size:     0
 Encapsulation type:                  lisp
```

```
! IOS-XR XTR2 LISP process verification
RP/0/0/CPU0:xTR2# show lisp ipv4 0
```

```
 Instance ID:                         0
 Router-lisp ID:                      0
 Locator table:                       default
   Cached IPv4 RLOC topology:         IPv4 default
   Cached IPv6 RLOC topology:         IPv6 default
 EID table:                           default
 Ingress Tunnel Router (ITR):         enabled
 Egress Tunnel Router (ETR):          enabled
 Proxy-ITR Router (PITR):             disabled
 Proxy-ETR Router (PETR):             disabled
 NAT-traversal Router (NAT-RTR):      disabled
 Mobility First-Hop Router:           disabled
 Map Server (MS):                     disabled
 Map Resolver (MR):                   disabled
 Delegated Database Tree (DDT):       disabled
 Map-Request source:                  192.168.2.2
 ITR Map-Resolver(s):                 192.168.100.100, 192.168.200.200
 ETR Map-Server(s):                   192.168.100.100 (00:00:47), 192.168.200.200
   (00:00:52)
 xTR-ID:                              unspecified
 site-ID:                             unspecified
 ITR local RLOC (last resort):        192.168.2.2
 ITR Solicit Map Request (SMR):       accept and process
   Max SMRs per map-cache entry:      8 more specifics
   Multiple SMR suppression time:     20 secs
 ETR accept mapping data:             disabled, verify disabled
 ETR map-cache TTL:                   1d00h
```

```
  Locator Status Algorithms:
    RLOC-probe algorithm:             disabled
    RLOC-probe on route change:       N/A (periodic probing disabled)
    RLOC-probe on member change:      disabled
    LSB reports:                      process
    IPv4 RLOC minimum mask length:    /0
    IPv6 RLOC minimum mask length:    /0
  Static mappings configured:         0
  Map-cache size/limit:               1/50000
  Imported route count/limit:         0/1000
  Map-cache activity check period:    60 secs
  Map-cache FIB updates:              established
  Total database mapping size:        0
    static database size/limit:       2/5000
    dynamic database size/limit:      0/1000
    route-import database size:       0


!NX-OS XTR3 LISP verification
xTR3# show ip lisp
LISP IP Configuration Information for VRF "default" (iid 0)
  Ingress Tunnel Router (ITR):        enabled
  Egress Tunnel Router (ETR):         enabled
  Proxy-ITR Router (PTR):             disabled
  Proxy-ETR Router (PETR):            disabled
  Map Resolver (MR):                  disabled
  Map Server (MS):                    disabled
  LISP Multicast:                     disabled
    GLT interface:                    glt1
  LISP control-plane security:        disabled
  Locator VRF:                        default
  Encap-Map-Request source:           192.168.3.3
  LISP-NAT Interworking:              disabled
  Use locators from BGP RIB:          disabled
  ITR send Map-Request:               enabled
  ITR send Data-Probe:                disabled
  LISP ALT-VRF:                       not configured
  LISP-DDT:                           disabled
  ITR Map-Resolver:                   192.168.100.100, last used: 00:53:57
  ITR Map-Resolver:                   192.168.200.200, last used: 00:53:57
  ETR Map-Server(s):                  192.168.100.100, 192.168.200.200
  Last Map-Register sent to MS:       00:00:26
  ETR merge-registrations:            disabled
  ETR glean mapping:                  disabled, verify disabled
  ETR accept mapping data:            disabled, verify disabled
  ETR map-cache TTL:                  24 hours
  ETR map-register TTL:               3 minutes
```

```
 Shortest EID-prefix allowed:    /16
 Locator Reachability Algorithms:
   Echo-nonce algorithm:          disabled
   TCP-counts algorithm:          disabled
   RLOC-probe algorithm:          disabled
 Static mappings configured:     0
 Map-cache limit:                18000
 Reserve-list:                   not configured
 Map-cache size:                 0
 ETR Database, global LSBs: 0x00000001:
   EID-prefix: 172.16.0.3/32, instance-id: 0, LSBs: 0x00000001
     Locator: 192.168.3.3, priority: 1, weight: 100
           Uptime: 03:55:26, state: up, local
   EID-prefix: 172.16.3.0/24, instance-id: 0, LSBs: 0x00000001
     Locator: 192.168.3.3, priority: 1, weight: 100
           Uptime: 03:55:26, state: up, local
```

The MS/MR nodes receive registration from the XTR nodes. An XTR node registers
with the map server that is reachable and configured. Verify whether this functionality is
enabled as shown in Example 3-11.

Example 3-11 *Verifying Whether LISP Functionality Is Enabled on MS/MR Devices*

```
!IOS-XE MS-MR1 LISP verification
MS-MR1# show lisp site detail
LISP Site Registration Information

Site name: Site-1-AS-64001
Allowed configured locators: any
Allowed EID-prefixes:

  EID-prefix: 172.16.0.1/32
    First registered:     04:16:46
    Last registered:      04:15:57
    Routing table tag:    0
    Origin:               Configuration
    Merge active:         No
    Proxy reply:          No
    TTL:                  1d00h
    State:                complete
    Registration errors:
      Authentication failures:  0
      Allowed locators mismatch: 0
```

```
    ETR 192.168.1.1:31542, last registered 04:15:57, no proxy-reply, map-notify
                        TTL 1d00h, no merge, hash-function sha1, nonce
                           0x5598D698-0x0272FC79
                        state complete, no security-capability
                        xTR-ID 0x550A5FD6-0xB04B031C-0x171BFDFA-0x51A155DE
                        site-ID unspecified
                        sourced by reliable transport
        Locator       Local  State      Pri/Wgt  Scope
        192.168.1.1   yes    up          1/100   IPv4 none


  EID-prefix: 172.16.1.0/24
     First registered:     04:16:46
     Last registered:      04:15:57
     Routing table tag:    0
     Origin:               Configuration
     Merge active:         No
     Proxy reply:          No
     TTL:                  1d00h
     State:                complete
     Registration errors:
        Authentication failures:  0
        Allowed locators mismatch: 0
     ETR 192.168.1.1:31542, last registered 04:15:57, no proxy-reply, map-notify
                        TTL 1d00h, no merge, hash-function sha1, nonce
                           0x5598D698-0x0272FC79
                        state complete, no security-capability
                        xTR-ID 0x550A5FD6-0xB04B031C-0x171BFDFA-0x51A155DE
                        site-ID unspecified
                        sourced by reliable transport
        Locator       Local  State      Pri/Wgt  Scope
        192.168.1.1   yes    up          1/100   IPv4 none
Site name: Site-2-AS-64002
Allowed configured locators: any
Allowed EID-prefixes:

  EID-prefix: 172.16.0.2/32
     First registered:     04:17:55
     Last registered:      00:00:14
     Routing table tag:    0
     Origin:               Configuration
     Merge active:         No
     Proxy reply:          No
     TTL:                  1d00h
     State:                complete
```

```
     Registration errors:
       Authentication failures:   0
       Allowed locators mismatch: 0
     ETR 192.168.2.2, last registered 00:00:14, no proxy-reply, map-notify
                     TTL 1d00h, no merge, hash-function sha1, nonce 0xFB547FF6-
                       0x4DC956A7
                     state complete, no security-capability
                     xTR-ID 0xBEF84B65-0xFCD931D3-0xFB40AC7D-0x7DBA373A
                     site-ID unspecified
       Locator       Local State      Pri/Wgt  Scope
       192.168.2.2   yes    up             1/100  IPv4 none


   EID-prefix: 172.16.2.0/24
     First registered:     04:17:55
     Last registered:      00:00:14
     Routing table tag:    0
     Origin:               Configuration
     Merge active:         No
     Proxy reply:          No
     TTL:                  1d00h
     State:                complete
     Registration errors:
       Authentication failures:   0
       Allowed locators mismatch: 0
     ETR 192.168.2.2, last registered 00:00:14, no proxy-reply, map-notify
                     TTL 1d00h, no merge, hash-function sha1, nonce 0xFB547FF6-
                       0x4DC956A7
                     state complete, no security-capability
                     xTR-ID 0xBEF84B65-0xFCD931D3-0xFB40AC7D-0x7DBA373A
                     site-ID unspecified
       Locator       Local State      Pri/Wgt  Scope
       192.168.2.2   yes    up             1/100  IPv4 none
Site name: Site-3-AS-64003
Allowed configured locators: any
Allowed EID-prefixes:


   EID-prefix: 172.16.0.3/32
     First registered:     04:17:38
     Last registered:      00:00:26
     Routing table tag:    0
     Origin:               Configuration
     Merge active:         No
     Proxy reply:          No
```

```
     TTL:                 00:03:00
     State:               complete
     Registration errors:
       Authentication failures:   0
       Allowed locators mismatch: 0
     ETR 192.168.3.3, last registered 00:00:26, no proxy-reply, no map-notify
                      TTL 00:03:00, no merge, hash-function sha1, nonce
                        0x00000000-0x00000000
                      state complete, no security-capability
                      xTR-ID N/A
                      site-ID N/A
       Locator       Local  State       Pri/Wgt  Scope
       192.168.3.3   yes    up              1/100  IPv4 none


   EID-prefix: 172.16.3.0/24
     First registered:    04:17:38
     Last registered:     00:00:26
     Routing table tag:   0
     Origin:              Configuration
     Merge active:        No
     Proxy reply:         No
     TTL:                 00:03:00
     State:               complete
     Registration errors:
       Authentication failures:   0
       Allowed locators mismatch: 0
     ETR 192.168.3.3, last registered 00:00:26, no proxy-reply, no map-notify
                      TTL 00:03:00, no merge, hash-function sha1, nonce
                        0x00000000-0x00000000
                      state complete, no security-capability
                      xTR-ID N/A
                      site-ID N/A
       Locator       Local  State       Pri/Wgt  Scope
       192.168.3.3   yes    up              1/100  IPv4 none

!IOS-XR MS-MR2 LISP verification.

RP/0/0/CPU0:MS-MR2# show lisp site rloc members registration
RP/0/0/CPU0:MS-MR2# show lisp site rloc members

LISP RLOC Membership for router lisp 0 IID 0
Entries: 3 valid / 3 total, Distribution disabled
```

```
RLOC                            Origin                  Valid
192.168.1.1                     Registration            Yes
192.168.2.2                     Registration            Yes
192.168.3.3                     Registration            Yes


RP/0/0/CPU0:MS-MR2# show lisp site


LISP Site Registration Information
* = Some locators are down or unreachable


Site Name       Last      Up   Who Last          Inst    EID Prefix
                Register       Registered        ID
Site-1-AS-64001 00:00:31  yes  10.1.20.1                 172.16.0.1/32
                00:00:31  yes  10.1.20.1                 172.16.1.0/24
Site-2-AS-64002 00:01:03  yes  192.168.2.2               172.16.0.2/32
                00:01:03  yes  192.168.2.2               172.16.2.0/24
Site-3-AS-64003 00:00:43  yes  192.168.3.3               172.16.0.3/32
                00:00:43  yes  192.168.3.3               172.16.3.0/24
```

The output in Example 3-11 confirms that all the xTRs can connect with both of the MS/MR nodes. To verify even further, the next step is to understand which MS/MR node processes the map register messages. You can see control plane message by using **debug** commands. On MS/MR routers, use the command **debug lisp control-plane map-server-registration**, as shown in Example 3-12.

Example 3-12 *Control Plane Registration Message on MS/MR Nodes*

```
!MS-MR2 control plane debug messages.


RP/0/0/CPU0:MS-MR2# debug lisp control-plane map-server-registration
!MS-MR site registration database was cleared to trigger re-registration from the
  ETRs
RP/0/0/CPU0:MS-MR2# clear lisp site *
!<SNIP>
RP/0/0/CPU0:MS-MR2#RP/0/0/CPU0:Mar 18 05:48:10.672 : lisp[1043]:  LISP:
  Processing received Map-Register(3) message on if:0x0 from 192.168.3.3:65491 to
  192.168.200.200:4342
!<SNIP>
RP/0/0/CPU0:Mar 18 05:48:10.672 : lisp[1043]:  LISP: Processing Map-Register mapping
  record for IID 0 172.16.0.3/32, ttl 3, action none, authoritative, 1 locator
  192.168.3.3 pri/wei=1/100 LpR
RP/0/0/CPU0:Mar 18 05:48:10.672 : lisp[1043]:  LISP-0: MS registration IID 0 prefix
  172.16.0.3/32 192.168.3.3 site Site-3-AS-64003, Created.
RP/0/0/CPU0:Mar 18 05:48:10.672 : lisp[1043]:  LISP: Processing Map-Register mapping
  record for IID 0 172.16.3.0/24, ttl 3, action none, authoritative, 1 locator
  192.168.3.3 pri/wei=1/100 LpR
RP/0/0/CPU0:Mar 18 05:48:10.672 : lisp[1043]:  LISP-0: MS registration IID 0 prefix
  172.16.3.0/24 192.168.3.3 site Site-3-AS-64003, Created.
```

```
RP/0/0/CPU0:Mar 18 05:48:27.931 : lisp[1043]:  LISP: Processing received
  Map-Register(3) message on if:0x0 from 10.1.20.1:4342 to 192.168.200.200:4342
!<SNIP>
RP/0/0/CPU0:Mar 18 05:48:27.931 : lisp[1043]:  LISP: Processing Map-Register mapping
  record for IID 0 172.16.0.1/32, ttl 1440, action none, authoritative, 1 locator
  192.168.1.1 pri/wei=1/100 LpR
RP/0/0/CPU0:Mar 18 05:48:27.931 : lisp[1043]:  LISP-0: MS registration IID 0 prefix
  172.16.0.1/32 10.1.20.1 site Site-1-AS-64001, Created.
RP/0/0/CPU0:Mar 18 05:48:27.931 : lisp[1043]:  LISP: Processing Map-Register mapping
  record for IID 0 172.16.1.0/24, ttl 1440, action none, authoritative, 1 locator
  192.168.1.1 pri/wei=1/100 LpR
RP/0/0/CPU0:Mar 18 05:48:27.931 : lisp[1043]:  LISP-0: MS registration IID 0 prefix
  172.16.1.0/24 10.1.20.1 site Site-1-AS-64001, Created.
RP/0/0/CPU0:Mar 18 05:48:35.760 : lisp[1043]:  LISP: Processing received
  Map-Register(3) message on if:0x0 from 192.168.2.2:4342 to 192.168.200.200:4342
!<SNIP>
RP/0/0/CPU0:Mar 18 05:48:35.760 : lisp[1043]:  LISP: Processing Map-Register mapping
  record for IID 0 172.16.0.2/32, ttl 1440, action none, authoritative, 1 locator .
  192.168.2.2 pri/wei=1/100 LpR
RP/0/0/CPU0:Mar 18 05:48:35.760 : lisp[1043]:  LISP-0: MS registration IID 0 prefix
  172.16.0.2/32 192.168.2.2 site Site-2-AS-64002, Created.
RP/0/0/CPU0:Mar 18 05:48:35.760 : lisp[1043]:  LISP: Processing Map-Register mapping
  record for IID 0 172.16.2.0/24, ttl 1440, action none, authoritative, 1 locator .
  192.168.2.2 pri/wei=1/100 LpR
RP/0/0/CPU0:Mar 18 05:48:35.760 : lisp[1043]:  LISP-0: MS registration IID 0 prefix
  172.16.2.0/24 192.168.2.2 site Site-2-AS-64002, Created.


!MS-MR1 control plane debug messages. I have filtered some of the output for brevity


MS-MR1# debug lisp control-plane map-server-registration
LISP control plane map-server registration debugging is on


*Mar 18 04:22:21.152: LISP: Processing received Map-Register(3) message on
  GigabitEthernet2 from 10.1.10.1:4342 to 192.168.100.100:4342
!<snip>
*Mar 18 04:22:21.152: LISP: Processing Map-Register mapping record for IID 0
  172.16.1.0/24 LCAF 255, ttl 1440, action none, authoritative, 1 locator .
    192.168.1.1 pri/wei=1/100 LpR
*Mar 18 04:22:21.152: LISP-0: MS registration IID 0 prefix 172.16.1.0/24 10.1.10.1
  SVC_IP_IAF_IPv4 site Site-1-AS-64001, Created new registration.
*Mar 18 04:22:21.154: LISP-0: MS registration IID 0 prefix 172.16.0.1/32 10.1.10.1
  SVC_IP_IAF_IPv4 site Site-1-AS-64001, Created new registration.
!<snip>
*Mar 18 04:22:38.584: LISP: Processing received Map-Register(3) message on
  GigabitEthernet2 from 192.168.3.3:65491 to 192.168.100.100:4342
!<SNIP>
*Mar 18 04:22:38.584: LISP: Processing Map-Register mapping record for IID 0
  172.16.0.3/32 LCAF 255, ttl 3, action none, authoritative, 1 locator .
    192.168.3.3 pri/wei=1/100 LpR
```

```
*Mar 18 04:22:38.586: LISP-0: MS registration IID 0 prefix 172.16.0.3/32 192.168.3.3
  SVC_IP_IAF_IPv4 site Site-3-AS-64003, Created new registration.
*Mar 18 04:22:38.587: LISP-0: MS registration IID 0 prefix 172.16.3.0/24 192.168.3.3
  SVC_IP_IAF_IPv4 site Site-3-AS-64003, Created new registration.
!<SNIP>
*Mar 18 04:22:57.697: LISP: Processing received Map-Register(3) message on
  GigabitEthernet2 from 192.168.2.2:4342 to 192.168.100.100:4342
!<SNIP>
*Mar 18 04:22:57.697: LISP: Processing Map-Register mapping record for IID 0
  172.16.0.2/32 LCAF 255, ttl 1440, action none, authoritative, 1 locator .
    192.168.2.2 pri/wei=1/100 LpR
*Mar 18 04:22:57.699: LISP-0: MS registration IID 0 prefix 172.16.0.2/32 192.168.2.2
  SVC_IP_IAF_IPv4 site Site-2-AS-64002, Created new registration.
*Mar 18 04:22:57.700: LISP-0: MS registration IID 0 prefix 172.16.2.0/24 192.168.2.2
  SVC_IP_IAF_IPv4 site Site-2-AS-64002, Created new registration.
```

The output in Example 3-12 shows that both MS/MRs are receiving registration from all the xTRs. If the xTRs can no longer reach MS-MR1, MS-MR2 continues to receives the registration from the xTRs, as shown in Example 3-13.

Example 3-13 *MS/MR Failure Behavior*

```
!Remove the static route from ISP1 to MS-MR1 to break network connectivity.

ISP1(config)# no ip route 192.168.100.100 255.255.255.255 10.10.100.100

!XTR1 cannot ping MS-MR1 now because ISP1 stop advertising the loopback IP of MS-MR1
  to !XTR routers.

xTR1# ping 192.168.100.100 source loopback 0
Type escape sequence to abort.
Sending 5, 100-byte ICMP Echos to 192.168.100.100, timeout is 2 seconds:
Packet sent with a source address of 192.168.1.1
.....
Success rate is 0 percent (0/5)

!XTR1 can still ping MS/MR-2. Static route to MS-MR2 was not removed on ISP2.

xTR1# ping 192.168.200.200 source loopback 0
Type escape sequence to abort.
Sending 5, 100-byte ICMP Echos to 192.168.200.200, timeout is 2 seconds:
Packet sent with a source address of 192.168.1.1
!!!!!
Success rate is 100 percent (5/5), round-trip min/avg/max = 4/5/8 ms

!Notice now on MS-MR1 the LISP site registration entries clearing
```

```
MS-MR1# show lisp site
LISP Site Registration Information
* = Some locators are down or unreachable
# = Some registrations are sourced by reliable transport

Site Name       Last       Up    Who Last            Inst    EID Prefix
                Register         Registered          ID
Site-1-AS-6400 04:38:41   yes   192.168.1.1:31542           172.16.0.1/32
               04:38:41   yes   192.168.1.1:31542           172.16.1.0/24
Site-2-AS-6400 never      no    --                          172.16.0.2/32
               never      no    --                          172.16.2.0/24
Site-3-AS-6400 never      no    --                          172.16.0.3/32
               never      no    --                          172.16.3.0/24

!manually clear the site registration entries on MS-MR1


MS-MR1# clear lisp site *




!No re-registration of from any XTR on MS-MR1


MS-MR1# show lisp site
LISP Site Registration Information
* = Some locators are down or unreachable
# = Some registrations are sourced by reliable transport

Site Name       Last       Up    Who Last            Inst    EID Prefix
                Register         Registered          ID
Site-1-AS-6400 never      no    --                          172.16.0.1/32
               never      no    --                          172.16.1.0/24
Site-2-AS-6400 never      no    --                          172.16.0.2/32
               never      no    --                          172.16.2.0/24
Site-3-AS-6400 never      no    --                          172.16.0.3/32
               never      no    --                          172.16.3.0/24

!MS-MR2 continues to receives registrations now and notice the entry is Updating.
  Showing !single XTR2 registration for brevity.


RP/0/0/CPU0:MS-MR2# debug lisp control-plane map-server-registration
RP/0/0/CPU0:Mar 18 05:56:09.879 : lisp[1043]:  LISP: Processing Map-Register mapping
  record for IID 0 172.16.0.2/32, ttl 1440, action none, authoritative, 1 locator .
  192.168.2.2 pri/wei=1/100 LpR
RP/0/0/CPU0:Mar 18 05:56:09.879 : lisp[1043]:  LISP-0: MS registration IID 0 prefix
  172.16.0.2/32 192.168.2.2 site Site-2-AS-64002, Updating.
```

```
!<SNIP>
RP/0/0/CPU0:Mar 18 05:56:09.879 : lisp[1043]:  LISP: Processing Map-Register mapping
   record for IID 0 172.16.2.0/24, ttl 1440, action none, authoritative, 1 locator .
   192.168.2.2 pri/wei=1/100 LpR
RP/0/0/CPU0:Mar 18 05:56:09.879 : lisp[1043]:  LISP-0: MS registration IID 0 prefix
   172.16.2.0/24 192.168.2.2 site Site-2-AS-64002. Updating.
RP/0/0/CPU0:Mar 18 05:56:19.389 : lisp[1043]:  LISP: Processing received
   Map-Register(3) message on if:0x0 from 192.168.3.3:65491 to 192.168.200.200:4342
<SNIP>
```

As shown in Example 3-13, when an MS/MR fails, the redundant MS/MR in the network
starts receiving all registration from the ETRs. The MS-MR1 router was no longer
reachable by the xTRs in each site, so all the xTRs started registering with MS-MR2. This
was confirmed by clearing the LISP site table on MS-MR1 after breaking the network
connectivity to MS-MR1 and enabling the **debug** command to confirm whether any
registration was being received on MS-MR1. The MS-MR1 LISP site table had no entries,
and the MS-MR2 LISP site table was fully populated with registration from all the LISP
sites, confirming the failover to MS-MR2.

The control plane verification example demonstrates the following steps in
troubleshooting LISP control plane registration failures between XTR nodes and
MS/MR:

Step 1. Using **show** commands to verify the LISP process state on each of the LISP
nodes to confirm proper LISP function assignment, such as ITR, ETR, and
MS/MR.

Step 2. Using **show** commands to verify the LISP map cache state in each of the ITR
nodes to confirm resolution of destination EID.

Step 3. Using **show** commands to verify the ETRs and EID prefixes registered on the
MS/MR nodes.

Step 4. Using **debug** commands to further verify receivers of registration messages
from ETRs on MS/MR nodes to confirm a proper process for registration
messages.

LISP IPv4 Unicast Routing Data Plane Verification

Forwarding of any packet involves the data plane in any networking device. LISP
packet forwarding between LISP sites is covered earlier in this chapter, in the section
"LISP IPv4 Unicast Routing Concepts." Earlier sections of this chapter also explain
how the control plane interactions are verified through the various **show** and **debug**
commands. This section continues using the scenario shown in Figure 3-2 to explain
some of the basic troubleshooting steps involved in verifying the forwarding of
LISP packets in the network. The scenario is simple: CE1 loopback0 in LISP site 1 is

communicating with CE2 loopback0 in LISP site 2 for the first time. The CE routers are the EID communicated between sites over the LISP overlay. The detailed packet walk is explained in this section, with packet captures to help you understand the data plane communication from one LISP site to another. The **show** commands are also shown used on the XTR to confirm that the LISP map cache has resolved and cached the destination EID prefixes.

Analyzing first-time communication is always interesting because it helps you see how cache entries are populated on the XTR routers, as shown in Example 3-14.

Note   The L in the first column of the **show ip route** output indicates a locally connected source, not LISP.

Example 3-14   *CE1 and CE2 Routing Table*

```
CE1# show ip route
<SNIP>
Gateway of last resort is 172.16.1.1 to network 0.0.0.0

O*E2  0.0.0.0/0 [110/1] via 172.16.1.1, 1w2d, GigabitEthernet0/1
       172.16.0.0/16 is variably subnetted, 3 subnets, 2 masks
C        172.16.0.1/32 is directly connected, Loopback0
C        172.16.1.0/24 is directly connected, GigabitEthernet0/1
L        172.16.1.2/32 is directly connected, GigabitEthernet0/1


!
CE2# show ip route
<SNIP>


Gateway of last resort is 172.16.2.1 to network 0.0.0.0

O*E2  0.0.0.0/0 [110/1] via 172.16.2.1, 1w2d, GigabitEthernet0/1
       172.16.0.0/16 is variably subnetted, 3 subnets, 2 masks
C        172.16.0.2/32 is directly connected, Loopback0
C        172.16.2.0/24 is directly connected, GigabitEthernet0/1
L        172.16.2.2/32 is directly connected, GigabitEthernet0/1
```

The routing table on the CE nodes only have a default route learned via OSPF from the local XTR routers, which act as gateways for the CE nodes. You need to verify whether the endpoints can ping their own local gateway IP address, as shown in Example 3-15.

Example 3-15 *CE-to-Gateway Reachability Verification*

```
CE1# ping 172.16.1.1 source loopback 0
Type escape sequence to abort.
Sending 5, 100-byte ICMP Echos to 172.16.1.1, timeout is 2 seconds:
Packet sent with a source address of 172.16.0.1
!!!!!
Success rate is 100 percent (5/5), round-trip min/avg/max = 2/4/7 ms

CE2# ping 172.16.2.2 source loopback 0
Type escape sequence to abort.
Sending 5, 100-byte ICMP Echos to 172.16.2.2, timeout is 2 seconds:
Packet sent with a source address of 172.16.0.2
!!!!!
Success rate is 100 percent (5/5), round-trip min/avg/max = 1/1/3 ms
```

Moving to the XTR device, notice in Example 3-16 that the LISP map cache is currently empty (that is, it has no RLOC-to-EID mapping entries), as no packets have been sent between LISP sites yet.

Example 3-16 *XTR1 and XTR2 Empty LISP Map Cache*

```
XTR1# show ip lisp  map-cache
LISP IPv4 Mapping Cache for EID-table default (IID 0), 1 entries

0.0.0.0/0, uptime: 1w0d, expires: never, via static-send-map-request
  Negative cache entry, action: send-map-request

RP/0/0/CPU0:XTR2# show lisp ipv4 map-cache
Mon Jul 16 05:39:56.868 UTC

LISP IPv4 Mapping Cache for EID-table default (IID 0), 1 entries

0.0.0.0/0, uptime: 1w0d, expires: never, via static send map-request
  Negative cache entry, action: send-map-request
```

The one 0.0.0.0/0 summarized default entry matches all destination EID prefix addresses with the action **send-map-request**. The purpose of this entry in the LISP map cache of the XTR is for any destination EID without a matching entry in the map cache of the XTR to trigger the resolution of the RLOC-to-EID mapping with the mapping system. When the resolution is complete, the XTR stores the learned RLOC-to-EID mapping entry in the map cache.

The NX-OS implementation is an exception with regard to the need for the 0.0.0.0/0 default entry in the LISP map cache. In the NX-OS platform device XTR3, a 0.0.0.0/0 default entry does not exist in the map cache by default because the platform is able to provide the same forwarding behavior without a need for a 0.0.0.0/0 default entry in the map cache. In the NX-OS platform, by default, when you enable LISP on the system, if no route is found in the routing table, the line card is programmed to send all packets for LISP resolution through lookups in the map cache, as shown in Example 3-17.

Example 3-17   *XTR3 Empty LISP Map Cache*

```
XTR3# show ip lisp map-cache
LISP IP Mapping Cache for VRF "default" (iid 0), 0 entries
XTR3#
```

As a basic check, verify that the mapping system has registration for local EID prefixes from all the xTRs, as shown in Example 3-18. The XTR must be able to reach the MS/MR to resolve the RLOC to which the destination EID attaches.

Example 3-18   *MS/MR XTR Registration Verification*

```
MS-MR1# show lisp site
LISP Site Registration Information
* = Some locators are down or unreachable
# = Some registrations are sourced by reliable transport


Site Name      Last      Up    Who Last            Inst    EID Prefix
               Register        Registered          ID
Site-1-AS-6400 00:21:15  yes#  192.168.1.1:28021           172.16.0.1/32
               00:21:15  yes#  192.168.1.1:28021           172.16.1.0/24
Site-2-AS-6400 00:00:26  yes   192.168.2.2:4342            172.16.0.2/32
               00:00:26  yes   192.168.2.2:4342            172.16.2.0/24
Site-3-AS-6400 00:00:10  yes   192.168.3.3:65491           172.16.0.3/32
               00:00:10  yes   192.168.3.3:65491           172.16.3.0/24


RP/0/0/CPU0:MS-MR2# show lisp site

LISP Site Registration Information
* = Some locators are down or unreachable

Site Name       Last      Up    Who Last            Inst    EID Prefix
                Register        Registered          ID
Site-1-AS-64001 00:00:53  yes   10.1.20.1                   172.16.0.1/32
                00:00:53  yes   10.1.20.1                   172.16.1.0/24
Site-2-AS-64002 00:00:26  yes   192.168.2.2                 172.16.0.2/32
                00:00:26  yes   192.168.2.2                 172.16.2.0/24
Site-3-AS-64003 00:00:40  yes   192.168.3.3                 172.16.0.3/32
                00:00:40  yes   192.168.3.3                 172.16.3.0/24
```

To test the connectivity between CE1 in LISP site 1 and CE2 in LISP site 2, initiate a **ping** sourced from CE1 loopback0 IP address 172.16.0.1 to CE2 loopback0 IP address 172.16.0.2, as shown in Example 3-19.

Example 3-19   *CE1 Sends a Ping Packet to CE2*

```
CE1# ping 172.16.0.2 source loopback 0
Type escape sequence to abort.
Sending 5, 100-byte ICMP Echos to 172.16.0.2, timeout is 2 seconds:
Packet sent with a source address of 172.16.0.1
..!!!
Success rate is 60 percent (3/5), round-trip min/avg/max = 9/9/11 ms
```

The **ping** does succeed, but the success rate is 60%. This is expected behavior for first-time communication. To establish this first-time communication, the CE1 node had to resolve the MAC address of its gateway IP address on the XTR1 device by using Address Resolution Protocol (ARP). The XTR1 device also had to resolve the RLOC address for the destination EID address 172.16.0.2. The capture in Figure 3-3 displays the LISP-encapsulated map request packet from XTR1 to the map server.

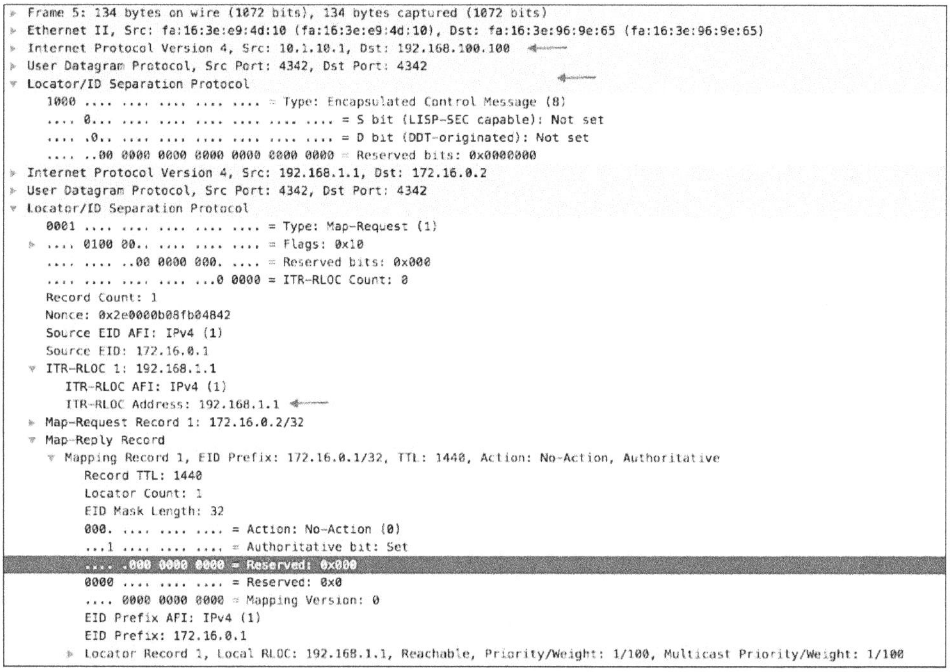

```
▶ Frame 5: 134 bytes on wire (1072 bits), 134 bytes captured (1072 bits)
▶ Ethernet II, Src: fa:16:3e:e9:4d:10 (fa:16:3e:e9:4d:10), Dst: fa:16:3e:96:9e:65 (fa:16:3e:96:9e:65)
▶ Internet Protocol Version 4, Src: 10.1.10.1, Dst: 192.168.100.100  ◀━━━
▶ User Datagram Protocol, Src Port: 4342, Dst Port: 4342               ◀━━━
▼ Locator/ID Separation Protocol
      1000 .... .... .... .... .... = Type: Encapsulated Control Message (8)
      .... 0... .... .... .... .... .... .... = S bit (LISP-SEC capable): Not set
      .... .0.. .... .... .... .... .... .... = D bit (DDT-originated): Not set
      .... ..00 0000 0000 0000 0000 0000 0000 = Reserved bits: 0x0000000
▶ Internet Protocol Version 4, Src: 192.168.1.1, Dst: 172.16.0.2
▶ User Datagram Protocol, Src Port: 4342, Dst Port: 4342
▼ Locator/ID Separation Protocol
      0001 .... .... .... .... .... = Type: Map-Request (1)
   ▶  .... 0100 00.. .... .... .... = Flags: 0x10
      .... .... ..00 0000 000. .... = Reserved bits: 0x000
      .... .... .... .... ...0 0000 = ITR-RLOC Count: 0
      Record Count: 1
      Nonce: 0x2e0000b08fb04842
      Source EID AFI: IPv4 (1)
      Source EID: 172.16.0.1
   ▼ ITR-RLOC 1: 192.168.1.1
         ITR-RLOC AFI: IPv4 (1)
         ITR-RLOC Address: 192.168.1.1  ◀━━━
   ▶ Map-Request Record 1: 172.16.0.2/32
   ▼ Map-Reply Record
      ▼ Mapping Record 1, EID Prefix: 172.16.0.1/32, TTL: 1440, Action: No-Action, Authoritative
            Record TTL: 1440
            Locator Count: 1
            EID Mask Length: 32
            000. .... .... .... = Action: No-Action (0)
            ...1 .... .... .... = Authoritative bit: Set
            .... .000 0000 0000 = Reserved: 0x000
            0000 .... .... .... = Reserved: 0x0
            .... 0000 0000 0000 = Mapping Version: 0
            EID Prefix AFI: IPv4 (1)
            EID Prefix: 172.16.0.1
         ▶ Locator Record 1, Local RLOC: 192.168.1.1, Reachable, Priority/Weight: 1/100, Multicast Priority/Weight: 1/100
```

Figure 3-3   *LISP Map Request Packet*

The map request packet outer IP header tells you that the map request packet is sent from XTR1 (10.1.10.1) toward MS-MR1 (192.168.100.100). MS-MR1 analyzes the map request packet and sees that the EID address being resolved is CE2's IP address, 172.16.0.2, and forward it to XTR2. The encapsulated map request packet also has the details of the ITR that initiated the map request so the ETR can reply directly to the ITR without having to go through the MS/MR.

In response to the map request notice in Figure 3-4, the LISP map reply control plane packet is sent directly from XTR2 (192.168.2.2) to XTR1 (192.168.1.1). In this case, XTR2 is the ETR responding directly to a map request sent by the ITR (XTR1 in this case).

```
▶ Frame 11: 82 bytes on wire (656 bits), 82 bytes captured (656 bits)
▶ Ethernet II, Src: fa:16:3e:5c:96:f5 (fa:16:3e:5c:96:f5), Dst: fa:16:3e:9f:55:c1 (fa:16:3e:9f:55:c1)
▼ Internet Protocol Version 4, Src: 192.168.2.2, Dst: 192.168.1.1  ◀——
    0100 .... = Version: 4
    .... 0101 = Header Length: 20 bytes (5)
  ▶ Differentiated Services Field: 0xc0 (DSCP: CS6, ECN: Not-ECT)
    Total Length: 68
    Identification: 0xd508 (54536)
  ▶ Flags: 0x4000, Don't fragment
    Time to live: 254
    Protocol: UDP (17)
    Header checksum: 0x228c [validation disabled]
    [Header checksum status: Unverified]
    Source: 192.168.2.2
    Destination: 192.168.1.1
▶ User Datagram Protocol, Src Port: 4342, Dst Port: 4342  ◀——
▼ Locator/ID Separation Protocol
    0010 .... .... .... .... .... = Type: Map-Reply (2)  ◀——
    .... 0... .... .... .... .... = P bit (Probe): Not set
    .... .0.. .... .... .... .... = E bit (Echo-Nonce locator reachability algorithm enabled): Not set
    .... ..0. .... .... .... .... = S bit (LISP-SEC capable): Not set
    .... ...0 0000 0000 0000 0000 = Reserved bits: 0x000000
    Record Count: 1
    Nonce: 0x882c64b8a741c30f
  ▼ Mapping Record 1, EID Prefix: 172.16.0.2/32, TTL: 1440, Action: No-Action, Authoritative  ◀——
      Record TTL: 1440
      Locator Count: 1
      EID Mask Length: 32
      000. .... .... .... = Action: No-Action (0)
      ...1 .... .... .... = Authoritative bit: Set
      .... .000 0000 0000 = Reserved: 0x000
      0000 .... .... .... = Reserved: 0x0
      .... 0000 0000 0000 = Mapping Version: 0
      EID Prefix AFI: IPv4 (1)
      EID Prefix: 172.16.0.2
    ▶ Locator Record 1, Local RLOC: 192.168.2.2, Reachable, Priority/Weight: 1/100, Multicast Priority/Weight: 0/0
```

Figure 3-4   *LISP Map Reply Packet*

In the packet capture of the LISP map reply packet, notice that the packet is sent as a UDP packet with destination port 4342, which is the reserved port for LISP control plane packets, as explained in Chapter 2. The LISP map reply control plane packet mapping record field in the LISP header section indicates the EID prefix (172.16.0.2/32), and the locator record RLOC field indicates the RLOC (192.168.2.2) mapped to the same EID prefix. The LISP control plane packet consists of IP, UDP, and LISP headers. The control plane communication all occurs in the underlay network part of the RLOC address space.

Note   Figure 3-4 describes only the resolution process for the CE2 IP address 172.16.0.2/32 from XTR1. However, XTR2 also has to resolve CE1 IP address 172.16.0.1/32 by sending an encapsulated map request to MS/MR and receiving a map reply from XTR1. Packet captures are shown only for one of the transaction for brevity.

The previously shown interaction to resolve LISP EID addresses by an ITR node from its mapping system can also be observed via **debug** commands on the MS/MR and XTR nodes, as demonstrated in the earlier section "LISP IPv4 Unicast Routing Control Plane Verification." The following is a list of handy **debug** commands you can use to analyze LISP control plane message exchanges on the IOS/IOS-XE platform to troubleshoot LISP:

> debug lisp control-plane map-server-map-request
>
> debug lisp control-plane map-server-registration
>
> debug lisp control-plane map-server-registration-errors
>
> debug lisp control-plane remote-eid-cache
>
> debug lisp forwarding remote-eid-prefix

The NX-OS platform **debug** commands are as follows:

> debug lisp control-plane etr-map-server
>
> debug lisp control-plane etr-map notify
>
> debug lisp control-plane solicit-map-request
>
> debug lisp control-plane map-server-registration
>
> debug lisp control-plane map-server-map-notify
>
> debug lisp control-plane messages

The **debug** commands must be enabled on the node where the particular LISP control plane message processing is occurring. For example, the PITR or ITR node would normally send out map request messages; therefore, the **debug** commands to view map request messages should be enabled on the ITR nodes.

Note   See the "LISP Command Reference Guide" for a platform on the Cisco.com website for **debug** command usage guidelines and examples. Separate command reference guides are provided for each platform.

The ping packet sourced from CE1 in the EID address space must traverse the RLOC address space via an overlay to reach its destination CE2 in another EID address space. Therefore, you see two IP headers, one for each address space the packet is forwarded through. Figure 3-5 shows the ICMP echo request packet sent from CE1 to CE2.

```
▶ Frame 14: 150 bytes on wire (1200 bits), 150 bytes captured (1200 bits)
▶ Ethernet II, Src: fa:16:3e:9f:55:c1 (fa:16:3e:9f:55:c1), Dst: fa:16:3e:5c:96:f5 (fa:16:3e:5c:96:f5)
▼ Internet Protocol Version 4, Src: 10.1.20.1, Dst: 192.168.2.2   ◀━━━━
      0100 .... = Version: 4
      .... 0101 = Header Length: 20 bytes (5)
    ▶ Differentiated Services Field: 0x00 (DSCP: CS0, ECN: Not-ECT)
      Total Length: 136
      Identification: 0x0048 (72)
    ▶ Flags: 0x4000, Don't fragment
      Time to live: 254
      Protocol: UDP (17)   ◀━━━━
      Header checksum: 0x9b70 [validation disabled]
      [Header checksum status: Unverified]
      Source: 10.1.20.1
      Destination: 192.168.2.2
▶ User Datagram Protocol, Src Port: 1283, Dst Port: 4341   ◀━━━━
▶ Locator/ID Separation Protocol (Data)   ◀━━━━
▼ Internet Protocol Version 4, Src: 172.16.0.1, Dst: 172.16.0.2   ◀━━━━
      0100 .... = Version: 4
      .... 0101 = Header Length: 20 bytes (5)
    ▶ Differentiated Services Field: 0x00 (DSCP: CS0, ECN: Not-ECT)
      Total Length: 100
      Identification: 0x006b (107)
    ▶ Flags: 0x0000
      Time to live: 254
      Protocol: ICMP (1)
      Header checksum: 0x640a [validation disabled]
      [Header checksum status: Unverified]
      Source: 172.16.0.1
      Destination: 172.16.0.2
▶ Internet Control Message Protocol
```

Figure 3-5   *LISP ICMP Echo Request Packet*

Notice the packet format with the outer IP, UDP, LISP, and inner IP headers. The UDP port of the packet is 4341, which is the reserved port allocated for LISP data packets.

All following pings succeed with a 100% success rate because the ARP and LISP map cache information has the forward information cached, avoiding the resolution process, as shown in Example 3-20.

Example 3-20   *CE1 Sending Ping Packet to CE2*

```
CE1# ping 172.16.0.2 source loopback 0
Type escape sequence to abort.
Sending 5, 100-byte ICMP Echos to 172.16.0.2, timeout is 2 seconds:
Packet sent with a source address of 172.16.0.1
!!!!!
Success rate is 100 percent (5/5), round-trip min/avg/max = 8/10/12 ms
```

Of course, each of these cached entries will have an age time in its respective database. Once the age time is reached, similar resolution processes have to occur again, as shown in Example 3-20. LISP by default has an age time of 24 hours for map cache entries.

To make sure there is connectivity between LISP sites 1 and 2 and LISP site 3, send a ping packet from CE1 to CE3 and CE2 to CE3, as shown in Example 3-21.

Example 3-21   *Verifying Connectivity to LISP Site 3*

```
CE1# ping 172.16.0.3 source loopback 0
Type escape sequence to abort.
Sending 5, 100-byte ICMP Echos to 172.16.0.3, timeout is 2 seconds:
Packet sent with a source address of 172.16.0.1
!!!!!
Success rate is 100 percent (5/5), round-trip min/avg/max = 8/9/11 ms

CE2# ping 172.16.0.3 source loopback0
Type escape sequence to abort.
Sending 5, 100-byte ICMP Echos to 172.16.0.3, timeout is 2 seconds:
Packet sent with a source address of 172.16.0.2
!!!!!
Success rate is 100 percent (5/5), round-trip min/avg/max = 8/10/11 ms
```

The LISP map cache databases on the XTR1, XTR2, and XTR3 are shown in
Example 3-22.

Example 3-22   *LISP Map Cache Databases on XTR Devices*

```
!XTR1 IOS-XE LISP map-cache

XTR1# show ip lisp map-cache detail
LISP IPv4 Mapping Cache for EID-table default (IID 0), 3 entries

0.0.0.0/0, uptime: 1w5d, expires: never, via static-send-map-request
  Sources: static-send-map-request
  State: send-map-request, last modified: 1w5d, map-source: local
  Exempt, Packets out: 6(684 bytes) (~ 00:22:40 ago)
  Configured as EID address space
  Negative cache entry, action: send-map-request
172.16.0.2/32, uptime: 01:30:05, expires: 22:29:54, via map-reply, complete
  Sources: map-reply
  State: complete, last modified: 01:30:05, map-source: 192.168.2.2
  Idle, Packets out: 9(1026 bytes) (~ 01:12:46 ago)
  Locator      Uptime     State      Pri/Wgt     Encap-IID
  192.168.2.2  01:30:05   up            1/100        -
    Last up-down state change:         01:30:05, state change count: 1
    Last route reachability change:    01:30:05, state change count: 1
    Last priority / weight change:     never/never
    RLOC-probing loc-status algorithm:
      Last RLOC-probe sent:            never
```

```
172.16.0.3/32, uptime: 00:22:44, expires: 23:37:15, via map-reply, complete
  Sources: map-reply
  State: complete, last modified: 00:22:44, map-source: 10.3.20.3
  Idle, Packets out: 9(1026 bytes) (~ 00:21:39 ago)
  Locator      Uptime    State     Pri/Wgt      Encap-IID
  192.168.3.3  00:22:44  up          1/100         -
    Last up-down state change:         00:22:44, state change count: 1
    Last route reachability change:    00:22:44, state change count: 1
    Last priority / weight change:     never/never
    RLOC-probing loc-status algorithm:
      Last RLOC-probe sent:            never


!XTR2 IOS-XR LISP map-cache

RP/0/0/CPU0:XTR2# show lisp ipv4 map-cache detail

LISP IPv4 Mapping Cache for EID-table default (IID 0), 3 entries

0.0.0.0/0, uptime: 1w5d, expires: never, via static send map-request
  Sources: static send map-request
  State: send-map-request, last modified: 1w5d, map-source: local
  Idle, Packets out: 0
  Configured as EID address space
  Negative cache entry, action: send-map-request
172.16.0.1/32, uptime: 01:38:28, expires: 22:29:57, via map-reply, complete
  Sources: map-reply
  State: complete, last modified: 01:38:28, map-source: 10.1.20.1
  Active, Packets out: 0
  Locator      Uptime    State     Pri/Wgt
  192.168.1.1  01:38:28  up          1/100
    Last up-down state change:         01:38:28, state change count: 1
    Last route reachability change:    01:38:28, state change count: 1
    Last priority / weight change:     never/never
    RLOC-probing loc-status algorithm:
      Last RLOC-probe sent:            never
172.16.0.3/32, uptime: 00:26:12, expires: 23:36:01, via map-reply, complete
  Sources: map-reply
  State: complete, last modified: 00:26:12, map-source: 10.3.20.3
  Active, Packets out: 0
  Locator      Uptime    State     Pri/Wgt
  192.168.3.3  00:26:12  up          1/100
    Last up-down state change:         00:26:12, state change count: 1
    Last route reachability change:    00:26:12, state change count: 1
```

```
       Last priority / weight change:      never/never
       RLOC-probing loc-status algorithm:
          Last RLOC-probe sent:            never


!XTR3 NX-OS LISP map-cache

XTR3# show ip lisp map-cache detail
LISP IP Mapping Cache for VRF "default" (iid 0), 4 entries

0.0.0.0/1, uptime: 00:14:03, expires: 00:00:56, via map-reply
  Negative cache entry, action: forward-native
  Last activity: 00:13:54
  Last modified: 00:14:03, map-source: 10.10.100.100

128.0.0.0/3, uptime: 00:14:03, expires: 00:00:56, via map-reply
  Negative cache entry, action: forward-native
  Last activity: 00:13:54
  Last modified: 00:14:03, map-source: 10.10.100.100

172.16.0.1/32, uptime: 00:33:08, expires: 23:26:51, via map-reply, auth
  Last activity: 00:32:50
  State: complete, last modified: 00:33:08, map-source: 10.1.20.1
  Pending hw update: FALSE
  Locator       Uptime    State      Priority/  Data      Control     MTU
                                     Weight     in/out    in/out
  192.168.1.1  00:33:08   up         1/100      0/8       1/1        1500
    Last up/down state change:          00:33:08, state change count: 0
    Last data packet in/out:            never/00:33:03
    Last control packet in/out:         00:33:10/00:33:10
    Last priority/weight change:        never/never

172.16.0.2/32, uptime: 00:28:09, expires: 23:31:50, via map-reply, auth
  Last activity: 00:27:59
  State: complete, last modified: 00:28:09, map-source: 192.168.2.2
  Pending hw update: FALSE
  Locator       Uptime    State      Priority/  Data      Control     MTU
                                     Weight     in/out    in/out
  192.168.2.2  00:28:09   up         1/100      0/8       2/1        1500
    Last up/down state change:          00:28:09, state change count: 0
    Last data packet in/out:            never/00:28:05
    Last control packet in/out:         00:28:09/00:28:11
    Last priority/weight change:        never/never
```

The map cache databases across all the platforms store very similar information, such as the EID prefix entry, the RLOCs mapped to the EID, the age time for the EID-to-RLOC entry, the RLOC priority/weight, and the RLOC state (up or down). Notice the default entries 0.0.0.0/1 and 128.0.0.0/3 in the NX-OS platform node, which XTR3 learned via map reply. As mentioned earlier in this chapter, on NX-OS devices, the moment LISP is enabled and a destination address does not match an entry in the routing table, the packet is punted to the LISP process for further lookup in the LISP map cache. If the EID-to-RLOC lookup process results in no entries in the map cache, the ITR tries to resolve the EID-to-RLOC mapping by forwarding the map request to the MS/MR. If the mapping system does not have in its database the information RLOC uses to map to the destination EID address, a negative map rely is returned. As a result of receiving a negative map reply, the ITR natively forwards the packet. The map-server is essentially telling the ITR that it does not have information about the prefixes in the range 0.0.0.0/1 and 128.0.0.0/3. The reason is because the map-server has the 172.x.x.x prefix configured for LISP site 3, and this prefix falls within the range 160.0.0.0–255.0.0.0. This entry optimizes EID-to-RLOC lookups by avoiding unnecessary lookups with a mapping system.

Internetworking LISP and Non-LISP Sites

As the incremental adoption of LISP occurs over time, there will be requirements for communication between LISP and non-LISP sites. No service, even within an enterprise data center, is turned on overnight. New services, hardware, and protocols are introduced in phases over different parts of a network. Because LISP is a completely new routing system, it will take time to adopt it across an enterprise and the Internet. LISP designers understood the challenges and addressed them by introducing devices with roles specifically designed to interconnect LISP site to non-LISP sites. Chapter 2 introduces PITR and PETR devices. Before delving into these devices further, let's review the fundamental challenge of interconnecting LISP and non-LISP sites and then look at how to address those challenges.

Given that the EID address space is non-routable and not advertised outside the LISP site, and given that the non-LISP site prefixes are not registered in the LISP mapping system, how do you establish communication between LISP and non-LISP sites? The challenge is to establish communication between two routing domains, LISP and non-LISP sites, that have two separate databases of connectivity information that are built using different control plane protocols. Maybe you could do some redistribution, but redistribution simply reintroduces the problem of scalability. Imagine redistributing BGP learned routes from a border router into LISP. Remember that the BGP synchronization command used to synchronize the BGP routes redistributed into an IGP like OSPF. As the Internet grew, OSPF could not handle the BGP routes. The same could happen with a LISP domain. To have two-way communication, you also have to redistribute LISP into BGP, which essentially makes LISP no different in operation from any IGP and, to complicate matters further, introduces another routing protocol into the plethora of routing protocols already existing in your networks. Network engineers know very well the challenges of two-way redistribution of routing protocols on various points in the networks and the challenges they bring in filtering routes to ensure optimal routing and avoid loops.

Another obvious approach might be to advertise the EID prefix into the global routing table or RLOC namespace to enable global reachability to the EID. This negates the entire purpose of LISP, which is locator and identifier separation. Plus, it contradicts the goal of LISP, which is to build a scalable address directory system. If you continue to advertise provider-independent EID prefixes on the Internet, the status quo is maintained: a non-scalable Internet routing system.

The first mechanism to establish communication between LISP and non-LISP sites is to introduce a new network element, a proxy ingress tunnel router (PITR). A PITR, as implied by the word *ingress*, allows non-LISP sites to send packets inbound to the LISP network toward LISP-enabled sites. The PITR attracts traffic from the non-LISP sites to the PITR by advertising coarse-aggregate prefixes for the LISP EID namespace into the non-LISP network. Upon receiving packets from a non-LISP site, the PITR encapsulates and forwards this traffic to LISP sites toward the destination RLOC ETR node. The LISP ingress Traffic Engineering policy applies to any traffic encapsulated by the PITR as it sends it to the destination ETR.

A recommended best practice is to advertise aggregated EID prefixes from the PITR to the global routing system to control the growth of the global routing table. If multiple PITRs exist, each PITR may advertise different aggregate prefixes to attract traffic for certain blocks of LISP EID prefixes, in effect distributing the traffic inbound from the non-LISP site to LISP sites.

PITR placement is an important design decision. The placement depends on several factors, such as which entity manages the PITR (service provider or customer), the geographic location of the PITR, whether the PITR is shared between customers, and traffic distribution requirements. Considering that the PITR is the entry point for packets from the non-LISP routing domain to the LISP routing domain, the PITR should ideally be placed near the non-LISP site to allow better load distribution across various PITRs. Multiple PITRs may advertise common EID prefix ranges out to the non-LISP site, using the same BGP next-hop IP address. The routers in the non-LISP site route to the nearest next-hop IP address for the EID prefix, based on the best routing metric. Routers in the non-LISP site then route to their nearest PITR, distributing traffic across the multiple PITRs for the same EID prefix advertised from the PITR to the non-LISP sites.

The entire packet communication process can be explained through an example of a packet walk between a non-LISP site and a LISP site, as depicted in Figure 3-6. This topology diagram shows a LISP site with a host with IP address 10.0.2.1/24 within the EID prefix 10.0.2.0/24. The LISP site has two xTR routers, XTR1 and XTR2, which act as both the ITR and ETR for the LISP site. Between the xTRs and PITR, the RLOC routing namespace allows LISP encapsulation between the PITR and XTR network devices. The PITR has connectivity to the non-LISP network, where no LISP encapsulation takes place. In the non-LISP routing domain are a PE router with a CE router hanging off it. The CE router has a client with IP address 10.20.2.1 sending packet to the client in the LISP site with IP address 10.0.2.1. The non-LISP site networking elements do not need any special configuration to communicate with the client in the LISP site. The PITR device acts as the gateway device between the non-LISP sites and traffic entering the LISP sites.

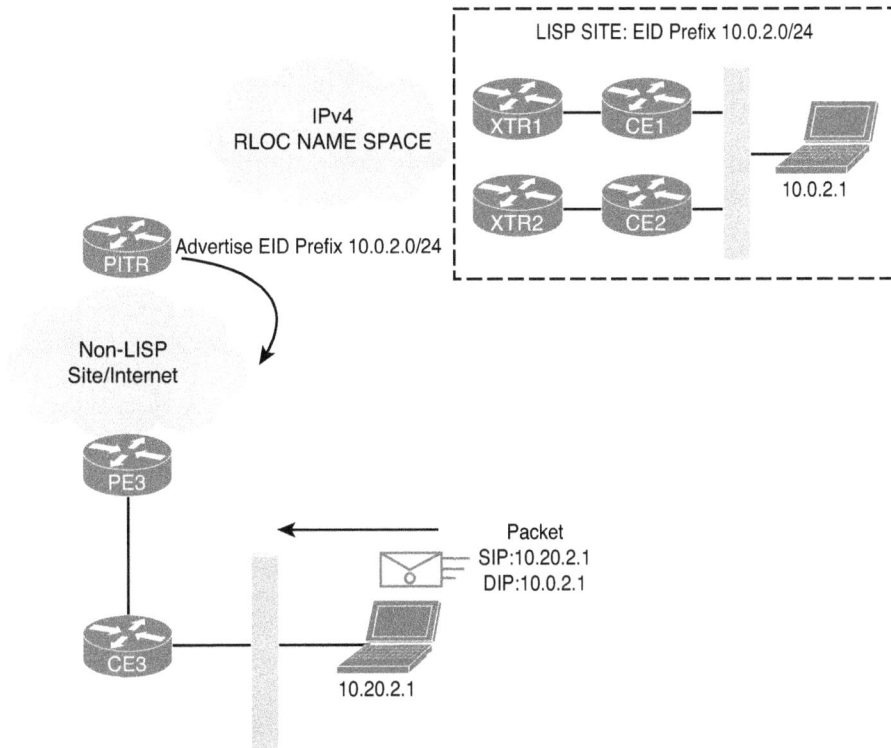

Figure 3-6   *PITR Packet Walk*

Here is a step-by-step look at how the packet exchange occurs:

Step 1.   The non-LISP site client resolves the IP address of the destination client EID address 10.0.2.1 via DNS. The client sends the packet with source IP address 10.20.2.1 and destination IP address 10.0.2.1 to its default gateway device, which is the CE3 router.

Step 2.   The CE3 router looks up the next-hop information for the destination address 10.0.2.1 and sends it to the PE3 router. The PE3 router may advertise a default route to CE3 or the exact EID prefix 10.0.2.0/24 to CE3. Advertising a default route is the most common and scalable method.

Step 3.   On receiving the packet, PE3 determines from its routing table that the PITR is the next hop for EID prefix 10.0.2.0/24 and continues to forward the packet toward the PITR.

Step 4.   On receiving the packet, the PITR refers to its local cache to resolve the RLOC address of the ETR that maps to EID prefix 10.0.2.0/24. The PITR follows a resolution process similar in operation to an ITR if the map cache is not prepopulated with the RLOC-to-EID mapping entry for the destination

EID prefix. The PITR then LISP encapsulates the packet with its own source RLOC, the destination RLOC of the preferred ETR or ETRs depending on priority/weight, the source EID 10.20.2.1, and the destination EID 10.0.2.1.

Step 5.   The ETRs of the LISP site receive the LISP-encapsulated packet, notice that it is destined for itself, de-encapsulates the LISP packet, verifies in its local routing table the next-hop CE to reach EID destination address 10.0.2.1, and sends the packet out to the locally attached CE router toward the destination client in the LISP site.

Step 6.   The response packet from the client in the LISP site to the client in the non-LISP site arrives at an ITR (XTR1 or XTR2), which on a Cisco platform triggers a lookup in the routing table first and then the LISP map cache for an entry for the 10.20.2.1 IP address, a non-EID address. (Other vendor implementations might do the opposite lookup process.) For a non-EID destination address, map cache look up and returns a negative map cache entry, telling the ITR that the destination site is not LISP enabled. The ITR then forwards the packet natively without LISP encapsulation. The packet may route out natively through the PITR if it is the only edge router between the LISP and non-LISP sites, or the packet might exit out another edge router that may have connectivity to the non-LISP sites; IGP determines the other edge router as the preferred next hop to reach the non-LISP destination address. In the case that the PITR is not used for return traffic from the LISP site to the non-LISP site, you see asymmetric routing behavior because the node to enter the LISP site is different from the node used to exit the LISP site.

The second mechanism to establish communication between the LISP and non-LISP sites is to introduce another network element called a proxy egress tunnel router (PETR). As the name implies, the PETR allows the communication from the LISP site out to the non-LISP site. The PETR acts like an ETR for traffic destined to non-LISP sites. The PETR receives LISP-encapsulated traffic from the ITR. Any packet destined outside the LISP site must be encapsulated at the ITR prior to being sent to the PETR. Any packets destined to a LISP site are directly sent to a resolved ETR RLOC address. This simplifies ITR forwarding logic; regardless of whether the packet is destined to a LISP site or not, the packet is LISP encapsulated. PETRs are used for the following reasons:

■ PETRs may be used to allow IPv6 LISP sites without native IPv6 RLOC connectivity (because the intermediate network is IPv4 only) to reach LISP sites that only have IPv6 RLOC connectivity.

■ The PETR can also be used to allow LISP sites with unicast reverse path forwarding (uRPF) restrictions to reach non-LISP sites. Return traffic from LISP sites to non-LISP sites in native forwarding format exposes the source EID address to the provider edge router bordering the non-LISP and LISP networks. The provider edge router does not have in its routing table the EID prefix; it contains only the

RLOC prefix for encapsulating traffic between RLOCs. If the provider edge router has strict uRPF enabled, the packet gets dropped. Remember that the EID prefix is a non-routable network on the Internet and completely separate from the RLOC namespace. One of the solutions is to encapsulate all packets sent to the PETR with the outer source IP address of ITR RLOC to ensure that the uRPF check on the provider edge routers does not drop the packet.

■ PETRs may be used to provide traffic symmetry when stateful inspection devices such as firewalls are deployed between LISP and non-LISP sites.

Using the topology in Figure 3-7, the packet walk is explained for a packet egressing a LISP site and forwarded toward a non-LISP site through the PETR. This diagram is similar to Figure 3-6, but now a PETR node is added, and traffic flow is from the LISP site to the non-LISP site. The packet is sourced from the client in the LISP site with source EID 10.0.2.1 and destination EID 10.20.2.1.

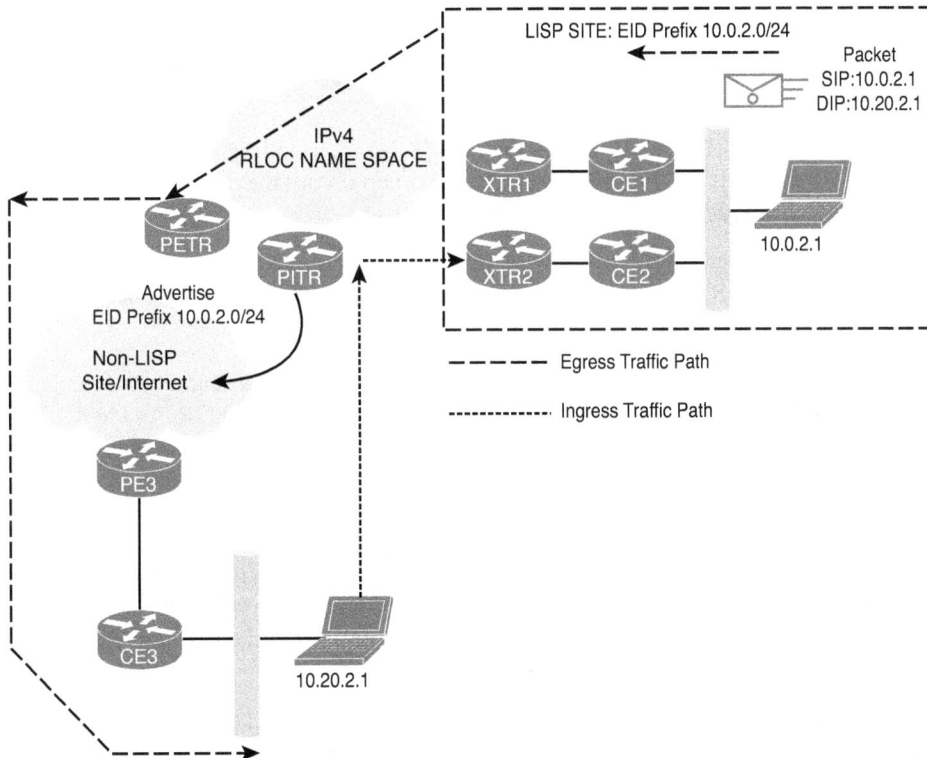

Figure 3-7 *PETR Packet Walk*

The packet exchange proceeds as follows:

Step 1.   The source host resolves the IP address through DNS resolution and gets the destination IP address 10.20.2.1 of the client in the non-LISP site.

Step 2.   The source host forwards the native IP packet toward its gateway router CE1 or CE2, depending on the first hop redundancy protocol used or the statically configured default gateway. The CE1 or CE2 router forwards the packet on to its downstream PE router XTR1 or XTR2. XTR1 and XTR2 are ITR routers configured to encapsulate packets destined to LISP and non-LISP sites. The ITR refers to its routing table first and then the LISP map cache. If the non-LISP destination prefix is not found in the routing table or in the LISP map cache, the ITR proceeds with the resolution process to learn the RLOC-to-EID mapping from the mapping system and receives a negative map reply containing the shortest prefix that contains the destination and does not cover any of the registered EID space. The ITR caches the prefix received in the negative map reply and binds it to the PETR address as the RLOC since the ITR is configured with the RLOC address of the PETR. The packet is then LISP encapsulated and sent to the PETR as a gateway LISP node to reach the non-LISP site.

Step 3.   The PETR de-encapsulates the LISP packet received from the ITR and natively forwards the original packet to its next hop toward the destination prefix 10.20.2.0/24 in the non-LISP site.

Step 4.   The return traffic from the non-LISP site back to the LISP site goes through the PITR, as described earlier in this chapter, in the section "Internetworking LISP and Non-LISP Sites."

You need to understand a few key deployment considerations regarding the PITR and PETR. The PETR is not meant to be deployed by itself, without the PITR. As a best practice, PITRs and PETRs should be provisioned on separate routers because PITRs are best deployed closest to non-LISP sites, and PETRs are best located close to the LISP sites for which they are de-encapsulating. But as an industry practice, the colocation of PITRs and PETRs is now a prevalent deployment practice. If a PETR and a PITR are implemented in the same router, such a node is referred to as a proxy XTR (PxTR). Implementing a PxTR node causes the packet forwarding path between LISP and non-LISP sites to always go through the PxTR device in both ingress and egress directions; this introduces symmetry in the traffic path.

Figure 3-8 shows the network used in this example to explain the configuration steps in deploying proxy XTR devices to establish communication between the three LISP sites and an Internet gateway (IGW) router that connects the LISP network to the Internet.

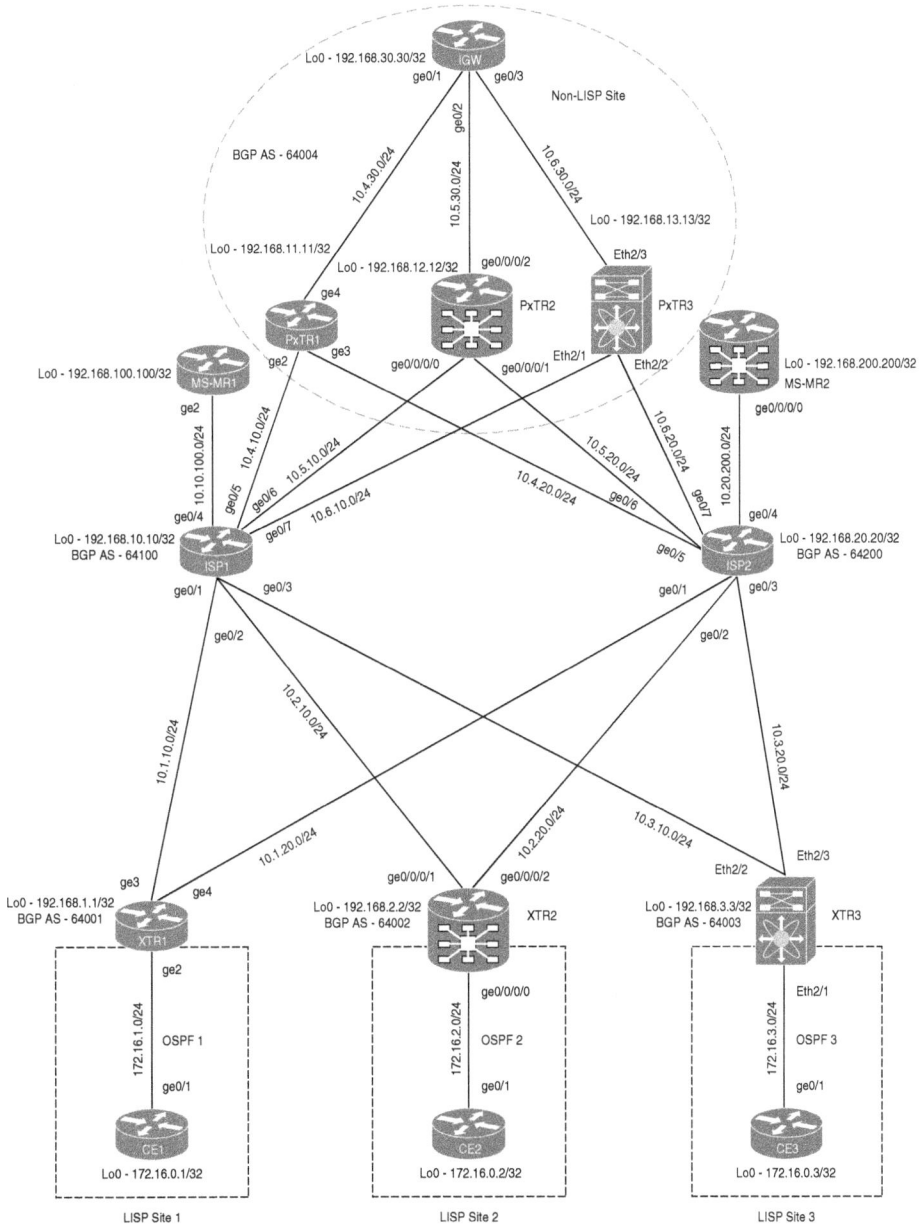

Figure 3-8 *LISP-to-Non-LISP Site Topology*

The PxTR devices are all part of a single BGP autonomous system (AS), number 64004. The PxTR nodes form an iBGP session with the IGW router while having an eBGP session with the ISP routers. The three LISP sites connect to the ISP that provide LISP infrastructure services such as MS/MR, proxy ITR, and proxy ETR to clients. This lowers a client's capital and operational expenditure as the client does not have to invest in equipment and humanpower for LISP infrastructure except for the customer edge router, which acts as the XTR. The customer edge router may also be part of the managed services provided by the service provider.

The client has three LISP sites that need Internet connectivity. The Internet reaches the LISP sites through the IGW router. Each PxTR advertises the aggregate of all the LISP site EID prefixes to the IGW router to attract traffic from the Internet to the PxTRs. The XTR devices at each LISP site are configured to use all the PxTRs to send packets to the IGW router.

PxTR1 is an IOS-XE platform router, PxTR2 is an IOS-XR platform router, and PxTR3 is an NX-OS platform multilayer switch. The implementation of routing between the LISP and non-LISP sites involves configuring the XTR and PxTR devices. The XTR devices are only configured to use the proxy ETR as an exit point out of the LISP network. The majority of the configuration steps are on the PxTR devices.

The general steps to configure internetworking between LISP and non-LISP sites are as follows:

Step 1.   Configure the proxy ETR node address on the XTR device.

Step 2.   Enable the LISP proxy ITR and proxy ETR functionality on the PxTR device.

Step 3.   Configure the map resolver on the PxTR device.

Step 4.   Configure the EID prefix map cache entry on the PxTR device.

Step 5.   Configure the IP source address used for the map request message by the PxTR device.

Step 6.   Configure the locator reachability algorithm.

The syntax across the various Cisco platforms is similar, but there are a few subtle differences, so this chapter provides examples for the various platforms.

The steps to configure a LISP xTR to use a proxy ETR on the IOS and IOS-XE platforms follow:

Step 1.   **Configure the proxy ETR IP address.** The command to specify the proxy ETR is **ipv4 use-petr** *locator-address* [**priority** *priority* **weight** *weight*] under the LISP router configuration mode (config-router). You can configure up to eight proxy ETRs per address family, IPv4 or IPv6, on the ITR or proxy ITR. Priority and weight are optional parameters. If they are not specified, the packets are load balanced to each proxy ETR based on a hashing algorithm. If the weight and priority are specified, then packets are load balanced according to the LISP priority and weight algorithm explained earlier in this chapter, in the section "LISP Ingress Traffic Engineering." Example 3-23 shows the complete LISP XTR configuration for XTR1.

Example 3-23 *Configuring PETR on XTR1*

```
!XTR1 IOS-XE LISP configuration
router lisp
 eid-table default instance-id 0
  database-mapping 172.16.0.1/32 192.168.1.1 priority 1 weight 100
  database-mapping 172.16.1.0/24 192.168.1.1 priority 1 weight 100
  ipv4 map-request-source 192.168.1.1
  exit
 !
 ipv4 itr map-resolver 192.168.100.100
 ipv4 itr map-resolver 192.168.200.200
 ipv4 itr
 ipv4 etr map-server 192.168.100.100 key cisco
 ipv4 etr map-server 192.168.200.200 key cisco
 ipv4 etr
 ipv4 use-petr 192.168.11.11
 ipv4 use-petr 192.168.12.12
 ipv4 use-petr 192.168.13.13
 exit
```

The remaining steps in the process of configuring the PxTR device on IOS-XE are configured on the PxTR1 node. Notice the similarities of these steps to the steps for configuring an ITR.

Step 2.   Enable the LISP proxy ITR and proxy ETR function. The command to configure a device as a LISP proxy ETR is **ipv4 proxy-etr** in the LISP router configuration (config-router) mode. In the same LISP router configuration mode, the command to enable the same device as a proxy ITR is **ipv4 proxy-itr** *ipv4-local-locator*. The locator address is the RLOC address for the proxy ITR and is used as the source address for LISP-encapsulated data packets.

Step 3.   Configure the map resolver IP address. As with the ITR device, the command to configure the IPv4 map resolver locator address is **ipv4 itr map-resolver** *map-resolver-address*. The ITR or proxy ITR device sends the map request to the specified map resolver locator address for EID-to-RLOC resolution.

Step 4.   Configure the EID prefix map cache entry. The proxy ITR must know for which EID prefix it should send a map request. The map cache is defined as a static list under the EID table, which is the EID namespace table. To configure an EID table, enter the command **eid-table** { **default** | **vrf** *vrf-name* } **instance-id** *iid* under the LISP router configuration (config-router) mode. The main purpose of the **eid-table** command is to map the EID namespace table within a VRF with a LISP instance ID. Instance ID 0 is the default

LISP process instance, and the VRF default is the global routing table. The prompt changes to the LISP EID table configuration mode (config-router-lisp-eid-table). Under the LISP EID table configure mode, insert the map cache entry by using the command **map-cache** *destination-EID-prefix / prefix-length* { **drop** | **map-request** | **native-forward** }. In this command, **drop**, **map-request**, and **native-forward** are packet-handling options for destinations that match the cached EID prefix entry. Proxy ITR must send a map request for the EID prefixes for which it is acting as a proxy.

Step 5. **Configure the map request source address.** The command to configure the map request message source address is **ipv4 map-request-source** *source-address*.

Step 6. **Configure the locator reachability algorithm.** To keep track of the locator status cached in the map cache of the PxTR, enable the locator reachability algorithm with the command **loc-reach-algorithm rloc-probing**. The only available locator reachability algorithm on the IOS or IOS-XE platform is rloc-probing. As explained earlier in this chapter, RLOC probing involves the exchange of map request and map reply messages in periodic intervals between the ITR and ETR devices to track locator reachability.

The complete configuration for the PxTR1 router is shown in Example 3-24.

Example 3-24 *PxTR1 LISP Routing Configuration*

```
!prefix list to match the EID prefix aggregate route and IGW network address.

ip prefix-list block_summary seq 5 permit 172.16.0.0/16
ip prefix-list block_summary seq 10 permit 192.168.30.30/32
!
!1st route-map statement denys the routes in prefix-list block_summary

route-map block_summary deny 10
 match ip address prefix-list block_summary
!2nd route-map statement is a permit all allowing all other routes.
route-map block_summary permit 20

router bgp 64004
 bgp router-id 192.168.11.11
 bgp log-neighbor-changes
 no bgp default ipv4-unicast
 neighbor 10.4.10.10 remote-as 64100
 neighbor 10.4.20.20 remote-as 64200
 neighbor 10.4.30.30 remote-as 64004
 !
```

```
address-family ipv4
  network 172.16.0.0
  network 192.168.11.11 mask 255.255.255.255
  redistribute connected
  neighbor 10.4.10.10 activate
  neighbor 10.4.10.10 send-community
  neighbor 10.4.10.10 route-map block_summary out
  neighbor 10.4.20.20 activate
  neighbor 10.4.20.20 send-community
  neighbor 10.4.20.20 route-map block_summary out
  neighbor 10.4.30.30 activate
  neighbor 10.4.30.30 send-community
 exit-address-family

router lisp
 locator-table default
 eid-table default instance-id 0
  map-cache 172.16.0.0/16 map-request
  exit
 !
 loc-reach-algorithm rloc-probing
 ipv4 itr map-resolver 192.168.100.100
 ipv4 itr map-resolver 192.168.200.200
 ipv4 map-request-source 192.168.11.11
 ipv4 proxy-etr
 ipv4 proxy-itr 192.168.11.11
 exit
```

Example 3-24 shows PxTR1 configured to have an iBGP session with the IGW router and eBGP sessions with the ISP routers. The PxTR acts as a handoff point in the network between LISP encapsulation and native IPv4 forwarding. As the traffic ingresses to the LISP site, the PxTR LISP encapsulates the traffic, and as the traffic leaves the XTR to route to a non-LISP site, the packets must also be LISP encapsulated. To ensure this forwarding behavior, two conditions must be met in the example network:

■ The IGW router must have a EID prefix pointing to the PxTR devices as the next hop. This is achieved by the PxTR devices advertising a summary route of 172.16.0.0/16 toward the IGW router. Under the BGP global address family, IPv4 network 172.16.0.0 advertises this summary route to the IGW router but filters it from being sent to the ISP routers because no EID prefix should exist in the global routing table, or the packets destined to the LISP site will not be LISP encapsulated.

Note   Notice the static route pointing to the null 0 interface for the summary route 172.16.0.0/16. This static route injects the summary route into the routing table of the PxTR device. Null 0 is a logical interface that never goes down, and therefore the static route remains permanently in the routing table. Under the BGP process, a network statement 172.16.0.0 is then used to advertise the summary route unconditionally to the IGW router. The aggregate address command is usually the command used to advertise summary routes in BGP. The BGP process only advertises summary routes using the aggregate address command when subnets falling under the summary route exist in the routing table. The PxTR is not directly attached to the LISP sites and therefore does not have any routes in the routing table in the EID address space. This behavior is by design, as you want all traffic to be LISP encapsulated between the PxTRs and xTRs.

■ The routers in the LISP RLOC space, such as ISP1, ISP2, and xTRs, cannot have the IGW router networks from the non-LISP site in their routing tables. In this example, the specific prefix of interest is 192.168.30.30/32, which is a loopback 0 IP address on the IGW router. In all the PxTRs BGP is configured to filter the 192.168.30.30/32 prefix from being advertised outbound toward the ISP routers. This again ensures that the non-LISP site network does not exist in the routing tables of the core devices in the RLOC namespace, which triggers the xTRs to punt all traffic destined to 192.168.30.30/32 to the LISP process for forwarding.

The prefix list and route maps are used to match and filter the IGW and EID prefix summary routes on the PxTR nodes. Example 3-25 shows how to verify the route map, prefix list, and BGP policy configurations on IOS and IOS-XE network operating systems.

Example 3-25   *Verifying BGP Routing Policy and LISP on PxTR1*

```
PxTR1# show ip prefix-list
ip prefix-list block_summary: 2 entries
   seq 5 permit 172.16.0.0/16
   seq 10 permit 192.168.30.30/32


PxTR1# show route-map
route-map block_summary, deny, sequence 10
  Match clauses:
    ip address prefix-lists: block_summary
  Set clauses:
  Policy routing matches: 0 packets, 0 bytes
route-map block_summary, permit, sequence 20
  Match clauses:
  Set clauses:
  Policy routing matches: 0 packets, 0 bytes
```

```
PxTR1# show ip bgp ipv4 unicast neighbors 10.4.10.10 policy
 Neighbor: 10.4.10.10, Address-Family: IPv4 Unicast
 Locally configured policies:
  route-map block_summary out
  send-community


!Verifying which routes were actually advertised to a particular neighbor
!Notice 172.16.0.0/16 and 192.168.30.30/32 is not advertised to ISP1

PxTR1# show ip bgp ipv4 unicast neighbors 10.4.10.10 advertised-routes
BGP table version is 29, local router ID is 192.168.11.11
Status codes: s suppressed, d damped, h history, * valid, > best, i - internal,
              r RIB-failure, S Stale, m multipath, b backup-path, f RT-Filter,
              x best-external, a additional-path, c RIB-compressed,
              t secondary path, L long-lived-stale,
Origin codes: i - IGP, e - EGP, ? - incomplete
RPKI validation codes: V valid, I invalid, N Not found

     Network          Next Hop          Metric LocPrf Weight Path
 *>  10.1.10.0/24     10.4.10.10             0             0 64100 ?
 *>  10.1.20.0/24     10.4.20.20             0             0 64200 ?
 *>  10.2.10.0/24     10.4.10.10             0             0 64100 ?
 *>  10.2.20.0/24     10.4.20.20             0             0 64200 ?
 *>  10.3.10.0/24     10.4.10.10             0             0 64100 ?
 *>  10.3.20.0/24     10.4.20.20             0             0 64200 ?
 *>  10.4.10.0/24     0.0.0.0                0         32768 ?
 *>  10.4.20.0/24     0.0.0.0                0         32768 ?
 *>  10.4.30.0/24     0.0.0.0                0         32768 ?
 *>  10.5.10.0/24     10.4.10.10             0             0 64100 ?
 *>  10.5.20.0/24     10.4.20.20             0             0 64200 ?
 *>  10.6.10.0/24     10.4.10.10             0             0 64100 ?
 *>  10.6.20.0/24     10.4.20.20             0             0 64200 ?
     Network          Next Hop          Metric LocPrf Weight Path
 *>  10.10.100.0/24   10.4.10.10             0             0 64100 ?
 *>  10.20.200.0/24   10.4.20.20             0             0 64200 ?
 *>  10.255.0.0/16    0.0.0.0                0         32768 ?
 *>  192.168.1.1/32   10.4.10.10                           0 64100 64001 i
 *>  192.168.2.2/32   10.4.10.10                           0 64100 64002 i
 *>  192.168.3.3/32   10.4.10.10                           0 64100 64003 i
 *>  192.168.10.10/32 10.4.10.10             0             0 64100 i
 *>  192.168.11.11/32 0.0.0.0                0         32768 i
 *>  192.168.20.20/32 10.4.20.20             0             0 64200 i
 *>  192.168.100.100/32
```

```
                        10.4.10.10              0           0 64100 ?
 *>    192.168.200.200/32
                        10.4.20.20              0           0 64200 ?


Total number of prefixes 24


PxTR1# show lisp service ipv4
  Instance ID:                      0
  Router-lisp ID:                   0
  Locator table:                    default
  EID table:                        default
  Ingress Tunnel Router (ITR):      disabled
  Egress Tunnel Router (ETR):       disabled
  Proxy-ITR Router (PITR):          enabled RLOCs: 192.168.11.11
  Proxy-ETR Router (PETR):          enabled
  NAT-traversal Router (NAT-RTR):   disabled
  Mobility First-Hop Router:        disabled
  Map Server (MS):                  disabled
  Map Resolver (MR):                disabled
  Delegated Database Tree (DDT):    disabled
  Site Registration Limit:          0
  Map-Request source:               192.168.11.11
  ITR Map-Resolver(s):              192.168.100.100, 192.168.200.200
  xTR-ID:                           0xF84C8169-0x7D66F253-0x0E57AF9A-0xE02744B9
  site-ID:                          unspecified
  ITR local RLOC (last resort):     192.168.11.11
  ITR Solicit Map Request (SMR):    accept and process
    Max SMRs per map-cache entry:   8 more specifics
    Multiple SMR suppression time:  20 secs
  ETR accept mapping data:          disabled, verify disabled
  ETR map-cache TTL:                1d00h
  Locator Status Algorithms:
    RLOC-probe algorithm:           enabled
    RLOC-probe on route change:     enabled
    RLOC-probe on member change:    disabled
    LSB reports:                    process
    IPv4 RLOC minimum mask length:  /0
    IPv6 RLOC minimum mask length:  /0
  Map-cache:
    Static mappings configured:     1
    Map-cache size/limit:           1/1000
    Imported route count/limit:     0/1000
```

```
  Map-cache activity check period:   60 secs
  Map-cache FIB updates:             established
  Persistent map-cache:              disabled
 Database:
  Total database mapping size:       0
  static database size/limit:        0/5000
  dynamic database size/limit:       0/1000
  route-import database size/limit:  0/1000
  Inactive (deconfig/away) size:     0
 Encapsulation type:                 lisp
```

The final step is to verify whether LISP site 1 node CE1 attached to XTR1 can communicate with the non-LISP site IGW using the PxTRs routers, as shown in Example 3-26.

Example 3-26 *Verifying Router Connectivity Between XTR1 and the Non-LISP Site IGW*

```
!Ping successful between CE1 loopback0 and IGW Loopback0 IP.


CE1# ping 192.168.30.30 source loopback0
Type escape sequence to abort.
Sending 5, 100-byte ICMP Echos to 192.168.30.30, timeout is 2 seconds:
Packet sent with a source address of 172.16.0.1
!!!!!
Success rate is 100 percent (5/5), round-trip min/avg/max = 9/9/10 ms


!XTR1 LISP forwarding verification to remote address in LISP and Non-LISP sites.


XTR1# show ip lisp map-cache
LISP IPv4 Mapping Cache for EID-table default (IID 0), 6 entries

0.0.0.0/0, uptime: 5d16h, expires: never, via static-send-map-request
  Negative cache entry, action: send-map-request
172.16.0.2/32, uptime: 00:13:49, expires: 23:46:10, via map-reply, complete
  Locator      Uptime     State      Pri/Wgt     Encap-IID
  192.168.2.2  00:13:49   up          1/100       -
172.16.0.3/32, uptime: 00:13:42, expires: 23:46:17, via map-reply, complete
  Locator      Uptime     State      Pri/Wgt     Encap-IID
  192.168.3.3  00:13:42   up          1/100       -
172.16.2.0/24, uptime: 00:14:43, expires: 23:45:16, via map-reply, complete
  Locator      Uptime     State      Pri/Wgt     Encap-IID
  192.168.2.2  00:14:43   up          1/100       -
```

```
172.16.3.0/24, uptime: 00:14:33, expires: 23:45:27, via map-reply, complete
  Locator       Uptime    State    Pri/Wgt     Encap-IID
  192.168.3.3  00:14:33  up            1/100        -
192.0.0.0/2, uptime: 00:15:07, expires: 00:14:45, via map-reply, forward-native
  Encapsulating to proxy ETR


XTR1# show ip lisp forwarding eid remote detail
Prefix               Fwd action  Locator status bits   encap_iid
0.0.0.0/0            signal      0x00000000            N/A
  packets/bytes      8/912
  path list 7EFBBFA09040, 3 locks, per-destination, flags 0x49 [shble, rif, hwcn]
    ifnums:
      LISP0(14)
    1 path
      path 7EFBBF9E6570, share 1/1, type attached prefix, for IPv4
        attached to LISP0, glean for LISP0
    1 output chain
      chain[0]: glean for LISP0
172.16.0.2/32        encap       0x00000001            N/A
  packets/bytes      4/456
  path list 7EFBBFA09180, 4 locks, per-destination, flags 0x49 [shble, rif, hwcn]
    ifnums:
      LISP0(14): 192.168.2.2
    1 path
      path 7EFBBF9E68E0, share 100/100, type attached nexthop, for IPv4
        nexthop 192.168.2.2 LISP0, IP midchain out of LISP0, addr 192.168.2.2
          7EFBEC452420
Prefix               Fwd action  Locator status bits   encap_iid
    1 output chain
      chain[0]: IP midchain out of LISP0, addr 192.168.2.2 7EFBEC452420
                IP adj out of GigabitEthernet4, addr 10.1.20.20 7EFBEC452DD0
172.16.0.3/32        encap       0x00000001            N/A
  packets/bytes      9/1026
  path list 7EFBBFA08DC0, 4 locks, per-destination, flags 0x49 [shble, rif, hwcn]
    ifnums:
      LISP0(14): 192.168.3.3
    1 path
      path 7EFBBF9E6780, share 100/100, type attached nexthop, for IPv4
        nexthop 192.168.3.3 LISP0, IP midchain out of LISP0, addr 192.168.3.3
          7EFBEC452610
    1 output chain
      chain[0]: IP midchain out of LISP0, addr 192.168.3.3 7EFBEC452610
                IP adj out of GigabitEthernet3, addr 10.1.10.10 7EFBB9253AF8
172.16.2.0/24        encap       0x00000001            N/A
  packets/bytes      4/456
```

```
   path list 7EFBBFA09180, 4 locks, per-destination, flags 0x49 [shble, rif, hwcn]
     ifnums:
       LISP0(14): 192.168.2.2
Prefix                    Fwd action  Locator status bits   encap_iid
     1 path
       path 7EFBBF9E68E0, share 100/100, type attached nexthop, for IPv4
         nexthop 192.168.2.2 LISP0, IP midchain out of LISP0, addr 192.168.2.2
           7EFBEC452420
     1 output chain
       chain[0]: IP midchain out of LISP0, addr 192.168.2.2 7EFBEC452420
                 IP adj out of GigabitEthernet4, addr 10.1.20.20 7EFBEC452DD0
172.16.3.0/24            encap       0x00000001            N/A
  packets/bytes        4/456
   path list 7EFBBFA08DC0, 4 locks, per-destination, flags 0x49 [shble, rif, hwcn]
     ifnums:
       LISP0(14): 192.168.3.3
     1 path
       path 7EFBBF9E6780, share 100/100, type attached nexthop, for IPv4
         nexthop 192.168.3.3 LISP0, IP midchain out of LISP0, addr 192.168.3.3
           7EFBEC452610
     1 output chain
       chain[0]: IP midchain out of LISP0, addr 192.168.3.3 7EFBEC452610
                 IP adj out of GigabitEthernet3, addr 10.1.10.10 7EFBB9253AF8
192.0.0.0/2             fwd native  0x00000000            N/A
  packets/bytes        9/1026
Prefix                    Fwd action  Locator status bits   encap_iid
   path list 7EFBBFA08FA0, 3 locks, per-destination, flags 0x49 [shble, rif, hwcn]
     ifnums:
       LISP0(14): 192.168.11.11, 192.168.12.12, 192.168.13.13
     3 paths
       path 7EFBBF9E6AF0, share 1/1, type attached nexthop, for IPv4
         nexthop 192.168.11.11 LISP0, IP midchain out of LISP0, addr 192.168.11.11
7EFBEC452800
       path 7EFBBF9E6BA0, share 1/1, type attached nexthop, for IPv4
         nexthop 192.168.12.12 LISP0, IP midchain out of LISP0, addr 192.168.12.12
7EFBEC452230
       path 7EFBBF9E6990, share 1/1, type attached nexthop, for IPv4
         nexthop 192.168.13.13 LISP0, IP midchain out of LISP0, addr 192.168.13.13
           7EFBEC4529F0
     1 output chain
       chain[0]: loadinfo 80007EFBEB7635A0, per-session, 3 choices, flags 0003,
         5 locks
                    flags [Per-session, for-rx-IPv4]
                    15 hash buckets
                      < 0 > IP midchain out of LISP0, addr 192.168.11.11 7EFBEC452800
                          IP adj out of GigabitEthernet3, addr 10.1.10.10
                            7EFBB9253AF8
```

```
Prefix                 Fwd action  Locator status bits   encap_iid
                    < 1 > IP midchain out of LISP0, addr 192.168.12.12 7EFBEC452230
                          IP adj out of GigabitEthernet3, addr 10.1.10.10
                             7EFBB9253AF8
                    < 2 > IP midchain out of LISP0, addr 192.168.13.13 7EFBEC4529F0
                          IP adj out of GigabitEthernet3, addr 10.1.10.10
                             7EFBB9253AF8
                    < 3 > IP midchain out of LISP0, addr 192.168.11.11 7EFBEC452800
                          IP adj out of GigabitEthernet3, addr 10.1.10.10
                             7EFBB9253AF8
                    < 4 > IP midchain out of LISP0, addr 192.168.12.12 7EFBEC452230
                          IP adj out of GigabitEthernet3, addr 10.1.10.10
                             7EFBB9253AF8
                    < 5 > IP midchain out of LISP0, addr 192.168.13.13 7EFBEC4529F0
                          IP adj out of GigabitEthernet3, addr 10.1.10.10
                             7EFBB9253AF8
                    < 6 > IP midchain out of LISP0, addr 192.168.11.11 7EFBEC452800
Prefix                 Fwd action  Locator status bits   encap_iid
                          IP adj out of GigabitEthernet3, addr 10.1.10.10
                             7EFBB9253AF8
                    < 7 > IP midchain out of LISP0, addr 192.168.12.12 7EFBEC452230
                          IP adj out of GigabitEthernet3, addr 10.1.10.10
                             7EFBB9253AF8
                    < 8 > IP midchain out of LISP0, addr 192.168.13.13 7EFBEC4529F0
                          IP adj out of GigabitEthernet3, addr 10.1.10.10
                             7EFBB9253AF8
                    < 9 > IP midchain out of LISP0, addr 192.168.11.11 7EFBEC452800
                          IP adj out of GigabitEthernet3, addr 10.1.10.10
                             7EFBB9253AF8
                    <10 > IP midchain out of LISP0, addr 192.168.12.12 7EFBEC452230
                          IP adj out of GigabitEthernet3, addr 10.1.10.10
                             7EFBB9253AF8
                    <11 > IP midchain out of LISP0, addr 192.168.13.13 7EFBEC4529F0
                          IP adj out of GigabitEthernet3, addr 10.1.10.10
                             7EFBB9253AF8
Prefix                 Fwd action  Locator status bits   encap_iid
                    <12 > IP midchain out of LISP0, addr 192.168.11.11 7EFBEC452800
                          IP adj out of GigabitEthernet3, addr 10.1.10.10
                             7EFBB9253AF8
                    <13 > IP midchain out of LISP0, addr 192.168.12.12 7EFBEC452230
                          IP adj out of GigabitEthernet3, addr 10.1.10.10
                             7EFBB9253AF8
                    <14 > IP midchain out of LISP0, addr 192.168.13.13 7EFBEC4529F0
                          IP adj out of GigabitEthernet3, addr 10.1.10.10
                             7EFBB9253AF8
               Subblocks:
               None
```

From the **show ip lisp map-cache** output in Example 3-26, you can confirm that the XTR1 is sending any packet destined to the 192.0.0.0/2 network to the PETR. This example confirms exactly which PETRs the xTR is forwarding to by using the command **show ip lisp forwarding eid remote detail**. The output clearly shows the three PxTR nodes at IP locator addresses 192.168.11.11, 192.168.12.12, and 192.168.13.13 as the next hops to reach 192.0.0.0/32 using the LISP0 interface. The outbound physical interface is GigabitEthernet3, which is the connection to ISP1 on XTR1.

As a final verification, it is always nice to see the packet capture to confirm the data plane forwarding. Two packet captures are necessary. First, you need to verify the packet egressing the LISP network toward the non-LISP site. This packet flow from the perspective of PxTR1 would be ingressing from the direction of ISP routers, and it would be expected to be LISP encapsulated. The second packet is the flow egressing the PxTR1 router toward the IGW router, which should have been de-encapsulated and forwarded natively because the IGW router is part of the non-LISP network.

The packet capture in Figure 3-9 shows the packet sent from CE1 LISP encapsulated at XTR1 toward its proxy ETR router destined to the IGW router.

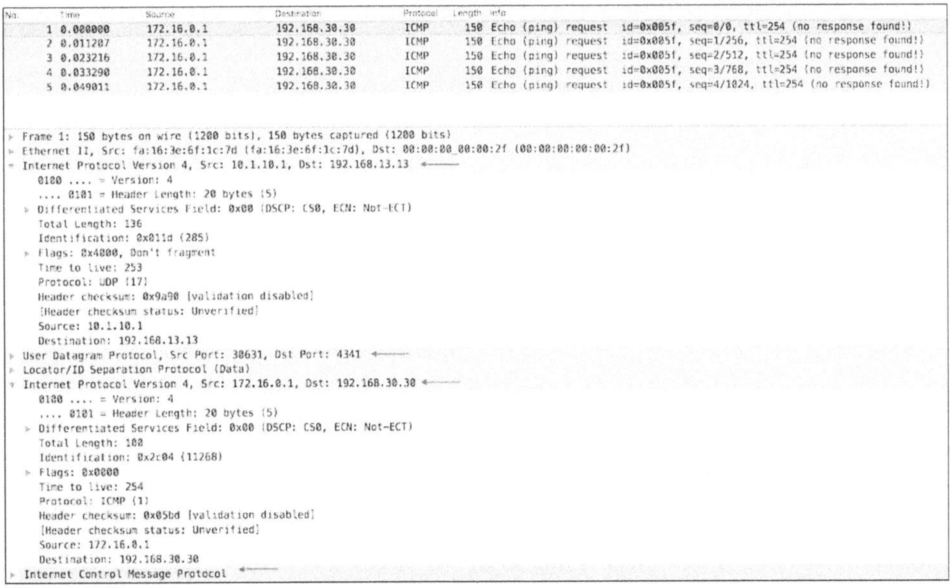

Figure 3-9 *Packet Capture from XTR1 to Proxy ETRs*

The packet capture in Figure 3-9 shows an ICMP echo request sent from 172.16.0.1 to 192.168.30.30 encapsulated in a LISP packet with UDP, LISP, and outer IP headers. The outer IP header has source IP address 10.10.10.1 (interface Ge3 on XTR1) and destination IP address 192.168.13.13 (PxTR3 locator address). Based on hash output, XTR1 chose to send the ICMP echo request packet to the proxy ETR node PxTR3. From PxTR3, the echo request packet was de-encapsulated and forwarded natively as an IPv4 packet out interface Eth2/3 toward the IGW, as shown in the packet capture in Figure 3-10.

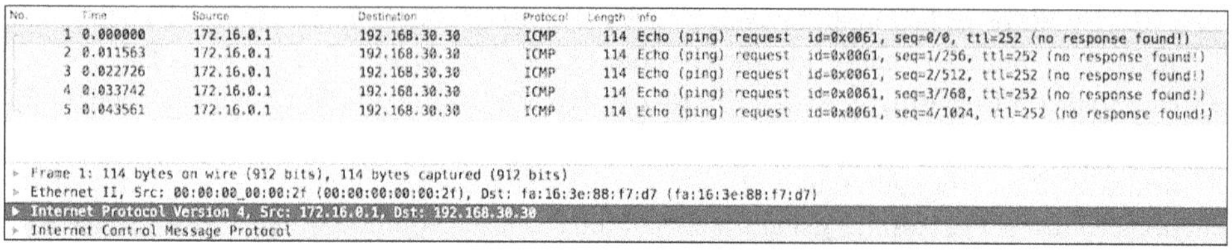

No.	Time	Source	Destination	Protocol	Length	Info
1	0.000000	172.16.0.1	192.168.30.30	ICMP	114	Echo (ping) request id=0x0061, seq=0/0, ttl=252 (no response found!)
2	0.011563	172.16.0.1	192.168.30.30	ICMP	114	Echo (ping) request id=0x0061, seq=1/256, ttl=252 (no response found!)
3	0.022726	172.16.0.1	192.168.30.30	ICMP	114	Echo (ping) request id=0x0061, seq=2/512, ttl=252 (no response found!)
4	0.033742	172.16.0.1	192.168.30.30	ICMP	114	Echo (ping) request id=0x0061, seq=3/768, ttl=252 (no response found!)
5	0.043561	172.16.0.1	192.168.30.30	ICMP	114	Echo (ping) request id=0x0061, seq=4/1024, ttl=252 (no response found!)

```
▶ Frame 1: 114 bytes on wire (912 bits), 114 bytes captured (912 bits)
▶ Ethernet II, Src: 00:00:00_00:00:2f (00:00:00:00:00:2f), Dst: fa:16:3e:88:f7:d7 (fa:16:3e:88:f7:d7)
▶ Internet Protocol Version 4, Src: 172.16.0.1, Dst: 192.168.30.30
▶ Internet Control Message Protocol
```

Figure 3-10 *Packet Capture from Proxy-ETR to IGW*

The IGW router then responds with an ICMP echo reply, as shown in Example 3-27.

Example 3-27 *IGW Echo Reply*

```
IGW# debug ip icmp
ICMP packet debugging is on
IGW#
*Jul 29 18:56:16.800: ICMP: echo reply sent, src 192.168.30.30, dst 172.16.0.1,
  topology BASE, dscp 0 topoid 0
*Jul 29 18:56:16.812: ICMP: echo reply sent, src 192.168.30.30, dst 172.16.0.1,
  topology BASE, dscp 0 topoid 0
*Jul 29 18:56:16.822: ICMP: echo reply sent, src 192.168.30.30, dst 172.16.0.1,
  topology BASE, dscp 0 topoid 0
*Jul 29 18:56:16.832: ICMP: echo reply sent, src 192.168.30.30, dst 172.16.0.1,
  topology BASE, dscp 0 topoid 0
*Jul 29 18:56:16.843: ICMP: echo reply sent, src 192.168.30.30, dst 172.16.0.1,
  topology BASE, dscp 0 topoid 0
```

Notice the info column of the Wireshark packet capture indicating "no response found."
This indicates that the echo reply packet did not return to PxTR3. So which path did
the echo reply packet take? It took the path the IGW router considered the best path to
reach the 172.16.0.0/16 network, which it learned from all the three PxTRs. The best path
depends on how the routing protocols are configured on the IGW. Example 3-28 shows
the BGP routing configuration and verification for the IGW router.

Example 3-28 *IGW Router BGP Configuration and Forwarding Verification*

```
!IGW IOS router BGP configuration

IGW# show run | section router bgp
router bgp 64004
 bgp router-id 192.168.30.30
 bgp log-neighbor-changes
 no bgp default ipv4-unicast
 neighbor 10.4.30.4 remote-as 64004
 neighbor 10.5.30.5 remote-as 64004
 neighbor 10.6.30.6 remote-as 64004
 !
```

```
 address-family ipv4
 network 192.168.30.30 mask 255.255.255.255
  aggregate-address 172.16.0.0 255.255.0.0 summary-only
  neighbor 10.4.30.4 activate
  neighbor 10.4.30.4 send-community
  neighbor 10.5.30.5 activate
  neighbor 10.5.30.5 send-community
  neighbor 10.6.30.6 activate
  neighbor 10.6.30.6 send-community
  maximum-paths ibgp 3
 exit-address-family


!IGW router iBGP neighbors including PxTR1, PxTR2 and PxTR3.


IGW# show ip bgp summary
BGP router identifier 192.168.30.30, local AS number 64004
BGP table version is 166, main routing table version 166
29 network entries using 4176 bytes of memory
73 path entries using 5840 bytes of memory
16 multipath network entries and 48 multipath paths
14/11 BGP path/bestpath attribute entries using 2128 bytes of memory
5 BGP AS-PATH entries using 120 bytes of memory
0 BGP route-map cache entries using 0 bytes of memory
0 BGP filter-list cache entries using 0 bytes of memory
BGP using 12264 total bytes of memory
BGP activity 93/64 prefixes, 512/439 paths, scan interval 60 secs


Neighbor        V         AS MsgRcvd MsgSent   TblVer  InQ OutQ Up/Down  State/PfxRcd
10.4.30.4       4      64004    9325    9294      166    0    0 5d20h          25
10.5.30.5       4      64004    8416    9233      166    0    0 5d19h          24
10.6.30.6       4      64004    8343    9150      166    0    0 5d18h          23


!BGP table entry for EID prefix summary route learned from PxTRs.


IGW# show ip bgp 172.16.0.0/16
BGP routing table entry for 172.16.0.0/16, version 148
Paths: (3 available, best #3, table default)
Multipath: iBGP
  Not advertised to any peer
  Refresh Epoch 1
  Local
    10.6.30.6 from 10.6.30.6 (192.168.13.13)
      Origin IGP, localpref 100, valid, internal, multipath
      rx pathid: 0, tx pathid: 0
  Refresh Epoch 1
  Local
```

```
      10.5.30.5 from 10.5.30.5 (192.168.12.12)
        Origin IGP, metric 0, localpref 100, valid, internal, multipath(oldest)
        rx pathid: 0, tx pathid: 0
    Refresh Epoch 1
    Local
      10.4.30.4 from 10.4.30.4 (192.168.11.11)
        Origin IGP, metric 0, localpref 100, valid, internal, multipath, best
        rx pathid: 0, tx pathid: 0x0

!IPv4 routing table entry.


IGW# show ip route 172.16.0.0 255.255.0.0
Routing entry for 172.16.0.0/16
  Known via "bgp 64004", distance 200, metric 0, type internal
  Last update from 10.4.30.4 5d18h ago
  Routing Descriptor Blocks:
  * 10.6.30.6, from 10.6.30.6, 5d18h ago
      Route metric is 0, traffic share count is 1
      AS Hops 0
      MPLS label: none
    10.5.30.5, from 10.5.30.5, 5d18h ago
      Route metric is 0, traffic share count is 1
      AS Hops 0
      MPLS label: none
    10.4.30.4, from 10.4.30.4, 5d18h ago
      Route metric is 0, traffic share count is 1
      AS Hops 0
      MPLS label: none

!IPv4 CEF forwarding entry.


IGW# show ip cef 172.16.0.0 255.255.0.0 detail
172.16.0.0/16, epoch 0, flags [rib only nolabel, rib defined all labels],
  per-destination sharing
  recursive via 10.4.30.4
    attached to GigabitEthernet0/1
  recursive via 10.5.30.5
    attached to GigabitEthernet0/2
  recursive via 10.6.30.6
    attached to GigabitEthernet0/3
```

The output in Example 3-28 tells you the following:

■ The IGW node has three iBGP neighbors (all PxTRs), from which it learns the 172.16.0.0/16 prefix.

■ The IGW router BGP process has **maximum-paths ibgp 3** configured, indicating that it will load balance across all three paths. But the BGP best path algorithm selects the path to the next-hop IP address 10.4.30.4 on the PxTR1 Ge4 interface as the best path.

■ The IGW router installs the three next hops to 172.16.0.0/16 in its routing and CEF tables.

In Figure 3-11 the packet capture on the PxTR1 Ge4 interface confirms that the echo reply packet is received on that interface from the IGW router IP address 192.168.30.30 to the CE1 IP address 172.16.0.1.

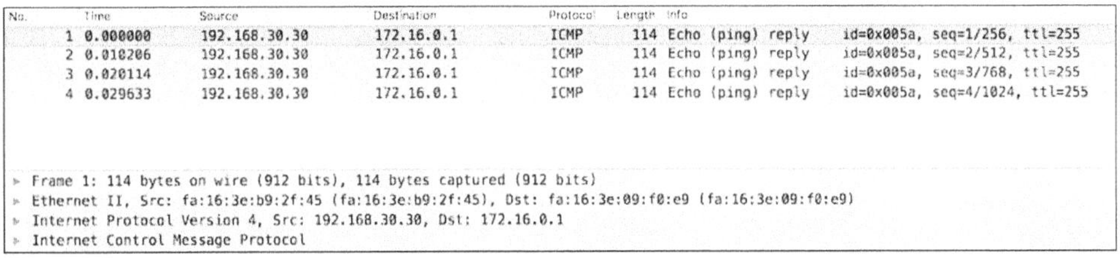

No.	Time	Source	Destination	Protocol	Length	Info
1	0.000000	192.168.30.30	172.16.0.1	ICMP	114	Echo (ping) reply id=0x005a, seq=1/256, ttl=255
2	0.018206	192.168.30.30	172.16.0.1	ICMP	114	Echo (ping) reply id=0x005a, seq=2/512, ttl=255
3	0.020114	192.168.30.30	172.16.0.1	ICMP	114	Echo (ping) reply id=0x005a, seq=3/768, ttl=255
4	0.029633	192.168.30.30	172.16.0.1	ICMP	114	Echo (ping) reply id=0x005a, seq=4/1024, ttl=255

```
▷ Frame 1: 114 bytes on wire (912 bits), 114 bytes captured (912 bits)
▷ Ethernet II, Src: fa:16:3e:b9:2f:45 (fa:16:3e:b9:2f:45), Dst: fa:16:3e:09:f0:e9 (fa:16:3e:09:f0:e9)
▷ Internet Protocol Version 4, Src: 192.168.30.30, Dst: 172.16.0.1
▷ Internet Control Message Protocol
```

Figure 3-11 *Packet Capture from IGW to PxTR1*

The PxTR1 router is also acting as a proxy ITR LISP node, so it has to resolve the destination IP address 172.16.0.1 and forward it to XTR1 encapsulated as a LISP packet. The packet in Figure 3-12 confirms the forwarding of the same ICMP echo reply packet received from the IGW router on PxTR1 toward XTR1 as a LISP-encapsulated packet.

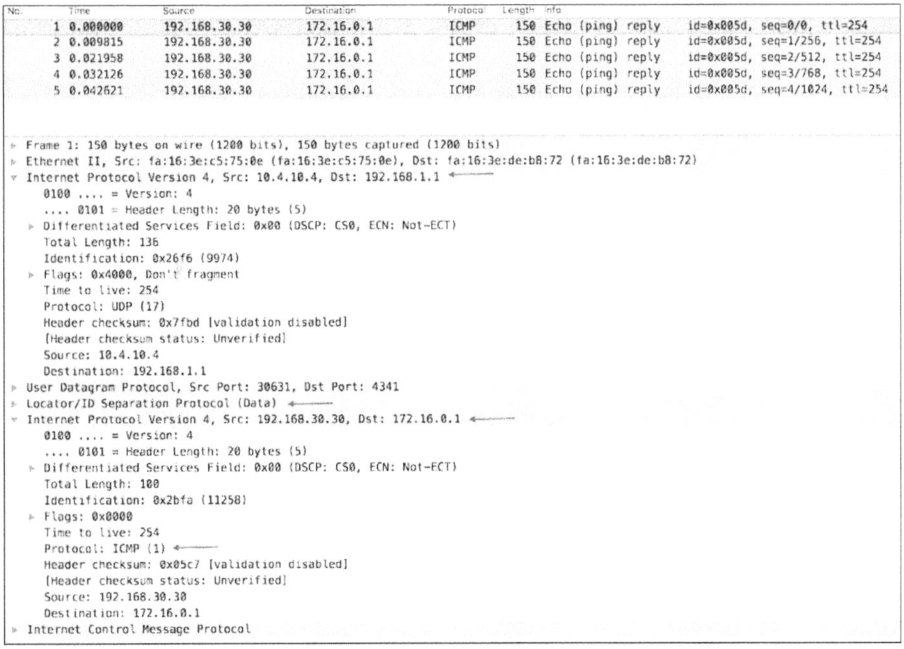

No.	Time	Source	Destination	Protocol	Length	Info
1	0.000000	192.168.30.30	172.16.0.1	ICMP	150	Echo (ping) reply id=0x005d, seq=0/0, ttl=254
2	0.009815	192.168.30.30	172.16.0.1	ICMP	150	Echo (ping) reply id=0x005d, seq=1/256, ttl=254
3	0.021958	192.168.30.30	172.16.0.1	ICMP	150	Echo (ping) reply id=0x005d, seq=2/512, ttl=254
4	0.032126	192.168.30.30	172.16.0.1	ICMP	150	Echo (ping) reply id=0x005d, seq=3/768, ttl=254
5	0.042621	192.168.30.30	172.16.0.1	ICMP	150	Echo (ping) reply id=0x005d, seq=4/1024, ttl=254

```
▷ Frame 1: 150 bytes on wire (1200 bits), 150 bytes captured (1200 bits)
▷ Ethernet II, Src: fa:16:3e:c5:75:0e (fa:16:3e:c5:75:0e), Dst: fa:16:3e:de:b8:72 (fa:16:3e:de:b8:72)
▽ Internet Protocol Version 4, Src: 10.4.10.4, Dst: 192.168.1.1  ◀━━━
    0100 .... = Version: 4
    .... 0101 = Header Length: 20 bytes (5)
  ▷ Differentiated Services Field: 0x00 (DSCP: CS0, ECN: Not-ECT)
    Total Length: 136
    Identification: 0x26f6 (9974)
  ▷ Flags: 0x4000, Don't fragment
    Time to live: 254
    Protocol: UDP (17)
    Header checksum: 0x7fbd [validation disabled]
    [Header checksum status: Unverified]
    Source: 10.4.10.4
    Destination: 192.168.1.1
▷ User Datagram Protocol, Src Port: 30631, Dst Port: 4341
▷ Locator/ID Separation Protocol (Data)  ◀━━━
▽ Internet Protocol Version 4, Src: 192.168.30.30, Dst: 172.16.0.1  ◀━━━
    0100 .... = Version: 4
    .... 0101 = Header Length: 20 bytes (5)
  ▷ Differentiated Services Field: 0x00 (DSCP: CS0, ECN: Not-ECT)
    Total Length: 100
    Identification: 0x2bfa (11258)
  ▷ Flags: 0x0000
    Time to live: 254
    Protocol: ICMP (1)  ◀━━━
    Header checksum: 0x05c7 [validation disabled]
    [Header checksum status: Unverified]
    Source: 192.168.30.30
    Destination: 172.16.0.1
▷ Internet Control Message Protocol
```

Figure 3-12 *Packet Capture from PxTR1 to XTR1*

Now, configuring communication between LISP and non-LISP sites on IOS-XR platform brings you to XTR2 and PxTR2. XTR2 needs a single command to tell it to which proxy ETR locator address to send packets destined to the IGW in the non-LISP network. The command used to specify the proxy ETR on XTR2 is **use-petr** *ip_address* [**priority** *priority* **weight** *weight*].

As you can see in Example 3-29, the configuration is very similar to the XTR1 configuration.

Example 3-29   *Configuring PETR on XTR2*

```
RP/0/0/CPU0:XTR2# show run router lisp

router lisp
 address-family ipv4 unicast
  etr map-server 192.168.100.100 key encrypted 060506324F41
  etr map-server 192.168.200.200 key encrypted 02050D480809
  etr
  itr map-resolver 192.168.100.100
  itr map-resolver 192.168.200.200
  itr
  use-petr 192.168.11.11
  use-petr 192.168.12.12
  use-petr 192.168.13.13
 !
 eid-table default instance-id 0
  address-family ipv4 unicast
   database-mapping 172.16.0.2/32 192.168.2.2 priority 1 weight 100
   database-mapping 172.16.2.0/24 192.168.2.2 priority 1 weight 100
   map-request-source 192.168.2.2
  !
 !
 locator-table default
!
```

The PxTR2 LISP configuration has similar implementation steps but with a few syntax differences, as shown in Example 3-29 for PxTR1. Example 3-30 shows the LISP and BGP routing configuration for PxTR2.

Example 3-30 *PxTR2 LISP and BGP Routing Configuration*

```
|filters to match EID Prefix summary and IGW Non-LISP site IP.

prefix-set block_summary
  172.16.0.0/16,
  192.168.30.30/32
end-set
!
!route-policy to match prefixes specified in the prefix set block_summary and drop
  while
!allowing all other prefixes.

route-policy block_summary
  if destination in block_summary then
    drop
  else
    pass
  endif
end-policy
!
!static route entry for unconditionally EID prefix summary route advertisement
router static
 address-family ipv4 unicast
  172.16.0.0/16 Null0
 !
!
router bgp 64004
 bgp router-id 192.168.12.12
 address-family ipv4 unicast
  network 172.16.0.0/16
  network 192.168.12.12/32
  redistribute connected
 !
 neighbor 10.5.10.10
  remote-as 64100
  address-family ipv4 unicast
   route-policy block_summary in
   route-policy block_summary out
  !
 !
```

```
neighbor 10.5.20.20
  remote-as 64200
  address-family ipv4 unicast
   route-policy block_summary in
   route-policy block_summary out
  !
 !
 neighbor 10.5.30.30
  remote-as 64004
  address-family ipv4 unicast
  !

!PxTR LISP configuration

router lisp
 address-family ipv4 unicast
  itr map-resolver 192.168.100.100
  itr map-resolver 192.168.200.200
  proxy-etr
  proxy-itr 192.168.12.12
  map-request-source 192.168.12.12
 !
 eid-table default instance-id 0
  address-family ipv4 unicast
   map-cache 172.16.0.0/16 map-request
  !
 !
 locator-table default
 loc-reach-algorithm rloc-probing
 !
```

Prefix set has the same function as an IP prefix list in IOS. Route policy has similar function to route maps in IOS but with much more powerful features and logic design that allow it to be applied almost like a programming language. Route policy is part of the route policy language feature in the IOS-XR platform. Again, you apply the route policy to a BGP peer in the inbound or outbound direction, depending on whether you want to filter routes going outbound from the local node or inbound from the peer node.

Example 3-31 demonstrates the verification of the internetworking between LISP site 2 and the non-LISP site IGW router on IOS-XR devices XTR2 and PxTR2.

Example 3-31   *XTR2 and PxTR2 LISP-to-Non-LISP Forwarding Verification*

```
!Ping test from LISP site 2 node CE2 towards Non-LISP site IGW router


CE2# ping 192.168.30.30 source loopback 0
Type escape sequence to abort.
Sending 5, 100-byte ICMP Echos to 192.168.30.30, timeout is 2 seconds:
Packet sent with a source address of 172.16.0.2
!!!!!
Success rate is 100 percent (5/5), round-trip min/avg/max = 11/11/13 ms


!XTR2 IOS-XR node LISP map cache.


RP/0/0/CPU0:XTR2# show lisp ipv4 map-cache


LISP IPv4 Mapping Cache for EID-table default (IID 0), 4 entries


0.0.0.0/0, uptime: 5d19h, expires: never, via static send map-request
  Negative cache entry, action: send-map-request
172.16.0.1/32, uptime: 03:29:23, expires: 20:48:32, via map-reply, complete
  Locator      Uptime      State      Pri/Wgt
  192.168.1.1  03:29:23  up            1/100
172.16.0.3/32, uptime: 00:00:21, expires: 23:59:40, via map-reply, complete
  Locator      Uptime      State      Pri/Wgt
  192.168.3.3  00:00:21  up            1/100
192.0.0.0/2, uptime: 00:04:03, expires: 00:11:17, via map-reply, forward-native
  Encapsulating to proxy ETR
!PxTR2 IOS-XR node LISP Proxy-ITR and Proxy-ETR function verification


RP/0/0/CPU0:PxTR2# show lisp ipv4


  Instance ID:                        0
  Router-lisp ID:                     0
  Locator table:                      default
    Cached IPv4 RLOC topology:        IPv4 default
    Cached IPv6 RLOC topology:        IPv6 default
  EID table:                          default
  Ingress Tunnel Router (ITR):        disabled
  Egress Tunnel Router (ETR):         disabled
  Proxy-ITR Router (PITR):            enabled RLOCs: 192.168.12.12
  Proxy-ETR Router (PETR):            enabled
  NAT-traversal Router (NAT-RTR):     disabled
  Mobility First-Hop Router:          disabled
```

```
    Map Server (MS):               disabled
    Map Resolver (MR):             disabled
    Delegated Database Tree (DDT): disabled
    Map-Request source:            192.168.12.12
    ITR Map-Resolver(s):           192.168.100.100, 192.168.200.200
    xTR-ID:                        unspecified
    site-ID:                       unspecified
    ITR local RLOC (last resort):  192.168.12.12
    ITR Solicit Map Request (SMR): accept and process
      Max SMRs per map-cache entry: 8 more specifics
      Multiple SMR suppression time: 20 secs
    ETR accept mapping data:       disabled, verify disabled
    ETR map-cache TTL:             1d00h
    Locator Status Algorithms:
      RLOC-probe algorithm:        enabled
      RLOC-probe on route change:  enabled
      RLOC-probe on member change: disabled
      LSB reports:                 process
      IPv4 RLOC minimum mask length: /0
      IPv6 RLOC minimum mask length: /0
    Static mappings configured:    1
    Map-cache size/limit:          2/50000
    Imported route count/limit:    0/1000
    Map-cache activity check period: 60 secs
    Map-cache FIB updates:         established
    Total database mapping size:   0
      static database size/limit:  0/5000
      dynamic database size/limit: 0/1000
      route-import database size:  0

!PxTR2 IOS-XR node lisp map cache

RP/0/0/CPU0:PxTR2# show lisp ipv4 map-cache

LISP IPv4 Mapping Cache for EID-table default (IID 0), 2 entries

172.16.0.0/16, uptime: 5d21h, expires: never, via static send map-request
  Negative cache entry, action: send-map-request
172.16.0.2/32, uptime: 5d20h, expires: 23:59:46, via map-reply, complete
  Locator     Uptime    State    Pri/Wgt
  192.168.2.2 5d20h     up       1/100
```

Consider two key observations from the **show lisp** command outputs. First, the XTR2 EID-to-RLOC map cache has an entry for the 192.0.0.0/2 EID prefix that is programmed to send to the proxy ETR node. Second, the PxTR2 map cache has an entry for EID prefix 172.16.0.2/32 mapped to RLOC 192.168.2.2 or XTR2, which it learned via a map reply which indicates that it resolved it from the MR.

Finally, you are ready for configuration examples between LISP and non-LISP sites on the NX-OS platforms. Example 3-32 shows the LISP configuration on XTR3.

Example 3-32   *XTR3 LISP Configuration*

```
!XTR3 NX-OS node LISP configuration

XTR3# show run lisp

feature lisp

ip lisp itr-etr
ip lisp use-petr 192.168.11.11 priority 50 weight 50
ip lisp use-petr 192.168.12.12 priority 50 weight 50
ip lisp use-petr 192.168.13.13 priority 50 weight 50
ip lisp database-mapping 172.16.0.3/32 192.168.3.3 priority 1 weight 100
ip lisp database-mapping 172.16.3.0/24 192.168.3.3 priority 1 weight 100
ip lisp locator-vrf default
ip lisp itr map-resolver 192.168.100.100
ip lisp itr map-resolver 192.168.200.200
ip lisp etr map-server 192.168.100.100 key 3 9125d59c18a9b015
ip lisp etr map-server 192.168.200.200 key 3 9125d59c18a9b015
ip lisp map-request-source 192.168.3.3
```

A key difference you can see on the NX-OS platform is that all the LISP configurations are configured in the global configuration mode (config). All the IPv4-related configuration commands start with **ip lisp**. The command to configure the proxy ETR locator address on the xTR is **ip lisp use-petr** *locator-address*.

Example 3-33 shows the BGP and LISP configuration for the PxTR3 NX-OS switch.

Example 3-33   *PxTR3 LISP and BGP Routing Configuration*

```
!static route for EID prefix summary route unconditional route advertisement.

ip route 172.16.0.0/16 Null0

!LISP configuration.

ip lisp proxy-itr 192.168.13.13
ip lisp proxy-etr
lisp loc-reach-algorithm rloc-probing
```

```
ip lisp locator-vrf default
ip lisp map-cache 172.16.0.0/16 map-request
ip lisp itr map-resolver 192.168.100.100
ip lisp itr map-resolver 192.168.200.200
ip lisp map-request-source 192.168.13.13


!prefix list filters to match EID Prefix summary and IGW Non-LISP site IP.


ip prefix-list block_summary seq 5 permit 172.16.0.0/16
ip prefix-list block_summary seq 10 permit 192.168.30.30/32


!route-map denying networks matched in prefix list block_summary and permitting all.

route-map block_summary deny 10
match ip address prefix-list block_summary
route-map block_summary permit 20


!route-map for matching connected interfaces for redistribution into BGP for next
  hop !reachability.


route-map connected permit 10
match interface Ethernet2/1 Ethernet2/2



router bgp 64004
  router-id 192.168.13.13
  address-family ipv4 unicast
    network 172.16.0.0/16
    network 192.168.13.13/32
    redistribute direct route-map connected
  neighbor 10.6.10.10 remote-as 64100
    address-family ipv4 unicast
      route-map block_summary out
  neighbor 10.6.20.20 remote-as 64200
    address-family ipv4 unicast
      route-map block_summary out
  neighbor 10.6.30.30 remote-as 64004
    address-family ipv4 unicast
```

Example 3-34 demonstrates the verification of the internetworking between LISP site 2 and the non-LISP site IGW router on NX-OS devices XTR3 and PxTR3.

Example 3-34 *XTR3 and PxTR3 LISP-to-Non-LISP Forwarding Verification*

```
!Ping test from LISP site 3 node CE3 towards Non-LISP site IGW router

CE3# ping 192.168.30.30 source loopback 0
Type escape sequence to abort.
Sending 5, 100-byte ICMP Echos to 192.168.30.30, timeout is 2 seconds:
Packet sent with a source address of 172.16.0.3
!!!!!
Success rate is 100 percent (5/5), round-trip min/avg/max = 13/13/13 ms


!XTR3 LISP map-cache

XTR3# show ip lisp map-cache
LISP IP Mapping Cache for VRF "default" (iid 0), 3 entries

172.16.0.1/32, uptime: 04:42:22, expires: 19:17:37, via map-reply, auth
  Locator      Uptime    State      Priority/  Data      Control      MTU
                                    Weight     in/out    in/out
  192.168.1.1  04:42:22  up         1/100      0/13      1/1          1500


172.16.0.2/32, uptime: 01:14:12, expires: 22:45:47, via map-reply, auth
  Locator      Uptime    State      Priority/  Data      Control      MTU
                                    Weight     in/out    in/out
  192.168.2.2  01:14:12  up         1/100      0/13      1/0          1500

192.0.0.0/2, uptime: 00:01:28, expires: 00:13:31, via petr, auth
  Locator        Uptime     State      Priority/  Data     Control       MTU
                                       Weight     in/out   in/out
  192.168.13.13  00:01:28   up         50/50      0/0      0/0           1500
  192.168.12.12  00:01:28   up         50/50      0/14     0/0           1500
  192.168.11.11  00:01:28   up         50/50      0/0      0/0           1500


!PxTR3 NX-OS LISP function verification

PxTR3# show ip lisp
LISP IP Configuration Information for VRF "default" (iid 0)
  Ingress Tunnel Router (ITR):      disabled
  Egress Tunnel Router (ETR):       disabled
  Proxy-ITR Router (PTR):           enabled
  PTR local locator:                192.168.13.13
  Proxy-ETR Router (PETR):          enabled
  Map Resolver (MR):                disabled
```

```
   Map Server (MS):              disabled
   LISP Multicast:               disabled
     GLT interface:              glt1
   LISP control-plane security:  disabled
   Locator VRF:                  default
   LISP-NAT Interworking:        disabled
   Use locators from BGP RIB:    disabled
   ITR send Map-Request:         enabled
   ITR send Data-Probe:          disabled
   LISP ALT-VRF:                 not configured
   LISP-DDT:                     disabled
   ITR Map-Resolver:             192.168.100.100, last used: 04:46:45
   ITR Map-Resolver:             192.168.200.200, last used: 04:46:39
   ETR merge-registrations:      disabled
   ETR glean mapping:            disabled, verify disabled
   ETR accept mapping data:      disabled, verify disabled
   ETR map-cache TTL:            24 hours
   ETR map-register TTL:         3 minutes
   Shortest EID-prefix allowed:  /16
   Locator Reachability Algorithms:
     Echo-nonce algorithm:       disabled
     TCP-counts algorithm:       disabled
     RLOC-probe algorithm:       enabled
   Static mappings configured:   1
   Map-cache limit:              18000
   Reserve-list:                 not configured
   Map-cache size:               3

!PxTR3 NX-OS node LISP map cache

PxTR3# show ip lisp map-cache detail
LISP IP Mapping Cache for VRF "default" (iid 0), 3 entries

172.16.0.0/16, uptime: 5d21h, expires: 0.000000, via static
  Negative cache entry, action: send-map-request
  Last activity: 01:27:55
  Last modified: 5d21h, map-source: *

172.16.0.3/32, uptime: 04:51:46, expires: 23:50:45, via map-reply, auth
  Last activity: 00:08:59
  State: complete, last modified: 04:51:46, map-source: 192.168.3.3
  Pending hw update: FALSE
```

```
Locator       Uptime    State       Priority/  Data     Control       MTU
                                     Weight     in/out   in/out
192.168.3.3  04:51:46  up           1/100      0/22     0/6          1500
  Last up/down state change:           04:51:46, state change count: 0
  Last data packet in/out:            never/00:11:08
  Last control packet in/out:         never/00:09:14
  Last priority/weight change:        never/never
  RLOC-probing loc-reach algorithm:
    Last RLOC-probe sent:             00:09:14
    Last RLOC-probe reply received: 00:09:14, rtt 0.004631

172.16.3.0/24, uptime: 04:51:52, expires: 19:10:01, via map-reply, auth
  Last activity: 04:49:52
  State: complete, last modified: 04:51:52, map-source: 192.168.3.3
  Pending hw update: FALSE
  Locator       Uptime    State       Priority/  Data     Control       MTU
                                      Weight     in/out   in/out
  192.168.3.3  04:51:52  up           1/100      0/3      0/2          1500
    Last up/down state change:           04:51:52, state change count: 0
    Last data packet in/out:            never/04:51:50
    Last control packet in/out:         never/04:49:58
    Last priority/weight change:        never/never
    RLOC-probing loc-reach algorithm:
      Last RLOC-probe sent:             04:49:58
      Last RLOC-probe reply received: 04:49:58, rtt 0.005495
```

The **show ip lisp map-cache** output confirms that the XTR3 node is configured with three PETR nodes, which it uses to reach any EID prefix that falls under the 192.0.0.0/2 range. From the LISP map cache of the PxTR3 node, you can see that PxTR3 will resolve any EID prefix in the 172.16.0.0/16 range by sending a map request to its configured map resolvers. PxTR3 has learned about the LISP site 3 EID prefixes from XTR3 RLOC through the LISP map reply message.

Summary

LISP is an overlay protocol that supports IPv4 unicast forwarding between LISP sites and non-LISP sites communicating with LISP sites. The communication between LISP sites requires two LISP nodes: the xTRs and the MS/MRs. The xTRs function as both ITR and ETRs. The ITRs encapsulate native IPv4 packets into LISP packets and route them over to the ETR by using the outer IP header (RLOC address). The ETRs de-encapsulate the LISP packet and forward the native IPv4 packet based on the inner IP header (EID address). ETR is the trusted source for EID prefixes that are stored in the MS. The MS has the mapping of the ETR locator address (RLOC) to the EID prefix registered by the ETR. The ETR registers its attached EID prefix with a shared password key with the mapping system. Only ETRs with shared secret key with MS can register its prefix. MS also compares its LISP site configuration to verify whether the authenticated ETR EID prefix entry is valid. The MS administrator must define in each MS the LISP site and the EID prefix for which the MS is acting as the mapping server. The XTRs have the data plane function of encapsulating and de-encapsulating LISP packets. The MR acts as the relay agent that redirects resolution requests to the single source of truth for EID-to-RLOC mapping: the MS. The MS is the control plane for the LISP network, providing the forwarding information to reach from one LISP to another.

Communication between LISP and non-LISP sites requires a proxy ITR device and a proxy ETR device. A proxy ETR is functionally an ETR that takes LISP packet sources from a LISP site, de-encapsulates them, and forwards them natively as IPv4 packets out to a non-LISP site. The proxy ITR does the reverse: It takes native IPv4 packets from non-LISP sites, encapsulates them into LISP packets, and routes the packets to the ETR locator address mapped to the destination address. A device playing both roles is called a proxy xTR, or PxTR. A PxTR acts as a handoff point or gateway between LISP and non-LISP networks. A PxTR device has two main configuration requirements. First, it must advertise the EID prefix summary route toward the non-LISP network devices to attract traffic toward the LISP network. Second, the PxTR must have entries in its cache for the EID-to-RLOC mapping for LISP sites for which it is acting as a proxy.

This chapter explains the control plane and data plane interaction for LISP IPv4 unicast routing for various use cases involving LISP sites and non-LISP sites across three Cisco platforms: IOS/IOS-XE, IOS-XR, and NX-OS. This chapter thoroughly explains configuration verification and troubleshooting methods and provides examples.

References

The following references provide more details on the topics discussed in this chapter:

RFC 6832, "Interworking Between Locator/ID Separation Protocol (LISP) and Non-LISP Sites"

Internet Draft, "The Locator/ID Separation Protocol (LISP)," draft-ietf-lisp-rfc6830bis-27

Internet Draft, "Locator/ID Separation Protocol (LISP) Control-Plane," draft-ietf-lisp-rfc6833bis-25

Cisco, "IOS IP Routing: LISP Command Reference," http://www.cisco.com

Cisco, "IOS-XE IP Routing: LISP Command Reference," http://www.cisco.com

Cisco, "Nexus 7000 LISP Configuration Guide," http://www.cisco.com

## Chapter 4

LISP IPv6 Unicast Routing

Because LISP is designed to address the scalability challenges of the Internet, it must support IPv6 as IPv6 adoption is increasing rapidly on the Internet and in enterprise networks. The focus of this chapter is on building a strong fundamental understanding of LISP unicast forwarding in IPv6 networks.

This chapter covers the following topics:

- LISP address family versatility, the basic attribute of LISP that allows easy coexistence of IPv4 and IPv6 and transition to IPv6 networks

- A brief review of existing IPv6 transition methods as they relate to LISP

- LISP IPv6 unicast forwarding packet walk

- Configuring and verifying the operation of a LISP IPv6 network

Address Family Versatility

The address family of an IP packet determines how the packet should be encoded. Currently IPv4 and IPv6 are the prevalent address families on the Internet and supported across the networking industry. The IANA assigned AF = 1 for IPv4 and AF = 2 for IPv6. Although today most networks are running on IPv4, the Internet is facing complete exhaustion of IPv4 addresses due to the exponential growth in demand for IP addresses for smartphones, tablets, laptops, sensors, and various wireless devices. The Internet is a critical tool that businesses use to operate and to interface with partners, customers, and other external institutions. The cloud enables users to access any resource anytime and anywhere as they move across buildings and geographies. The Internet of Things (IoT) connects our home appliances, cars, manufacturing tools, and many other items to the Internet to increase productivity, intelligence, and efficiency, improving the way we live and work. Many trends, including the ones just mentioned, are challenging the scalability of the Internet and leading to IPv4 address exhaustion. IPv6 is the answer to address exhaustion. LISP was designed to support easy migration to IPv6 by ensuring that LISP is incrementally deployable, affects a limited number of boxes, and will not disrupt the namespaces that are currently supported. The designers ensured that LISP can run in a IPv4-only and IPv6-only networks and also between IPv4 and IPv6 networks, making LISP a versatile protocol for interconnecting networks of various address families. As IPv6 becomes more prevalent than IPv6, endpoint identifiers (EIDs) will be necessary to scale the IPv6 Internet. The LISP EID, or routing locator (RLOC), can either be an IPv4 address or an IPv6 address. The LISP architecture supports the following encapsulation combinations:

■ IPv4 RLOC and IPv4 EID encapsulation, as shown in Figure 4-1

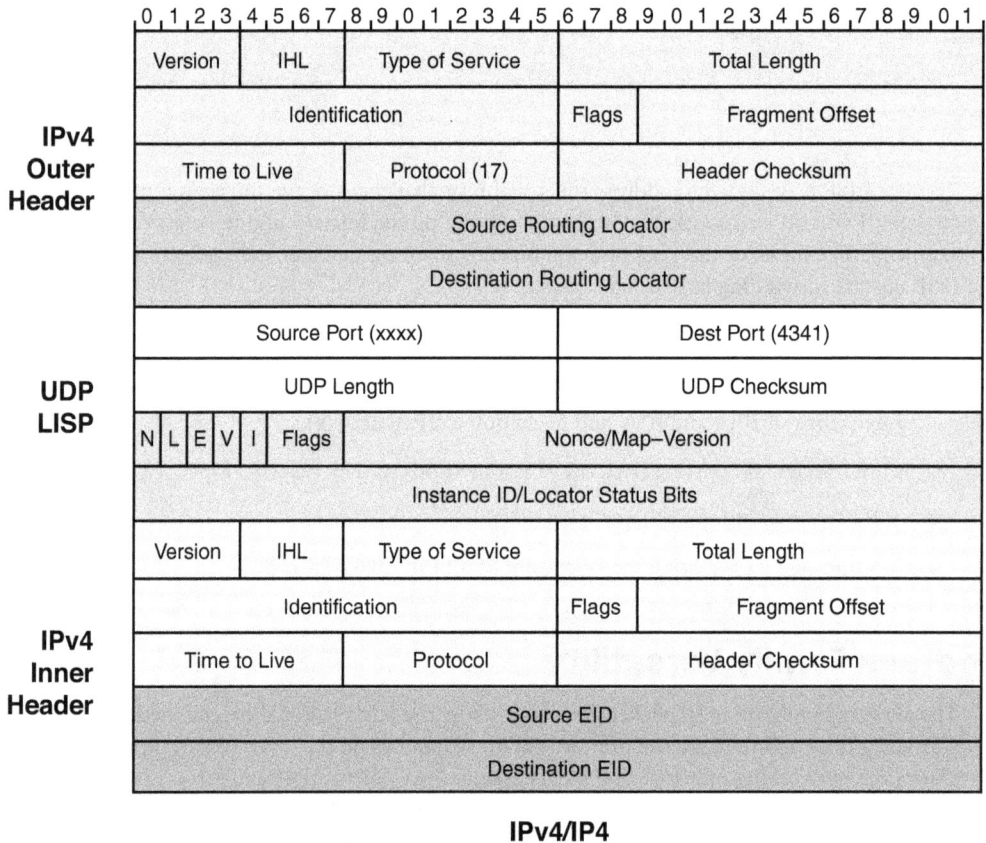

IPv4/IP4

Figure 4-1   *IPv4 RLOC and IPv4 EID LISP Packet Encapsulation*

■ IPv4 RLOC and IPv6 EID encapsulation, as shown in Figure 4-2

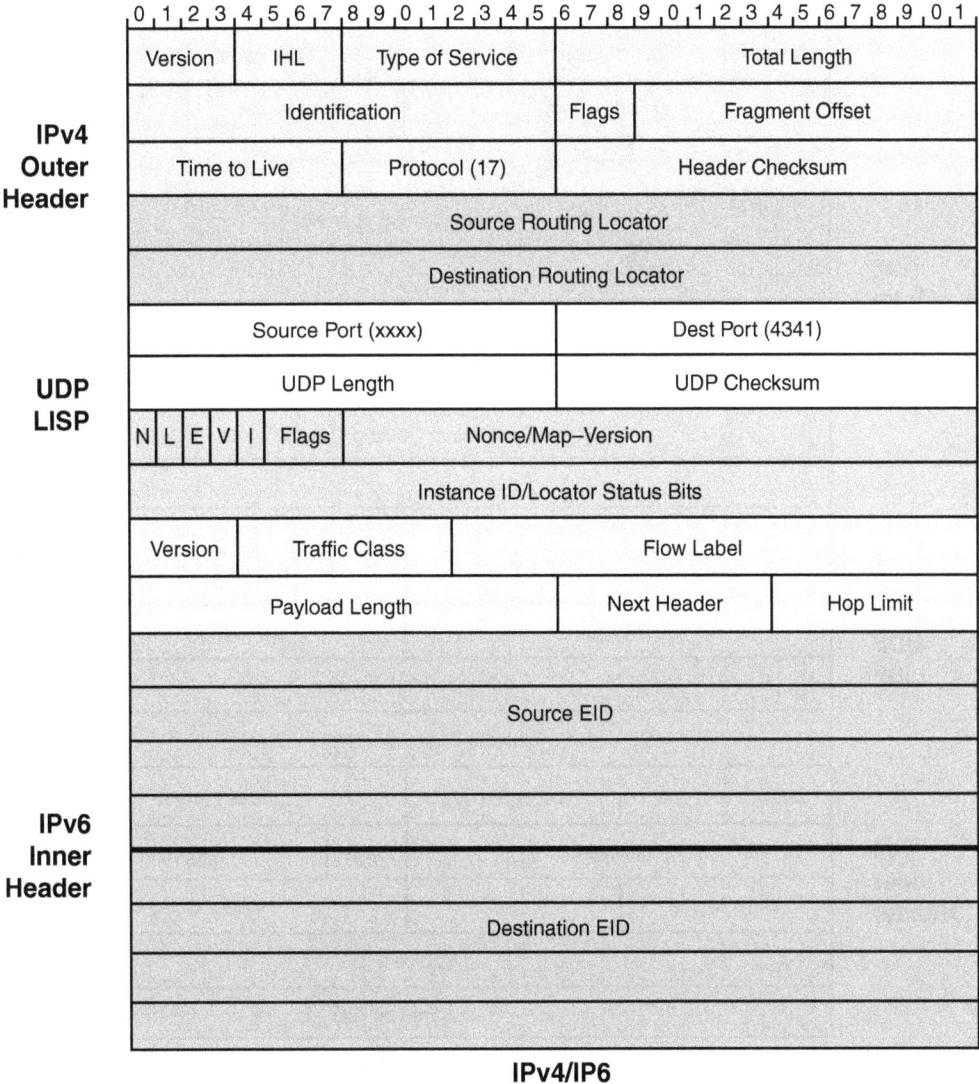

| 0 1 2 3 4 5 6 7 | 8 9 0 1 2 3 4 5 | 6 7 8 9 0 1 2 3 4 5 6 7 8 9 0 1 |

Figure 4-2 structure:

IPv4 Outer Header

Version	IHL	Type of Service	Total Length
Identification		Flags	Fragment Offset
Time to Live	Protocol (17)	Header Checksum
Source Routing Locator
Destination Routing Locator

UDP LISP

Source Port (xxxx)	Dest Port (4341)
UDP Length	UDP Checksum
N L E V I	Flags	Nonce/Map–Version
Instance ID/Locator Status Bits

| Version | Traffic Class | Flow Label |
| Payload Length | Next Header | Hop Limit |

IPv6 Inner Header

| Source EID |

| Destination EID |

IPv4/IP6

Figure 4-2 *IPv4 RLOC and IPv6 EID LISP Packet Encapsulation*

■ IPv6 RLOC and IPv4 EID encapsulation, as shown in Figure 4-3

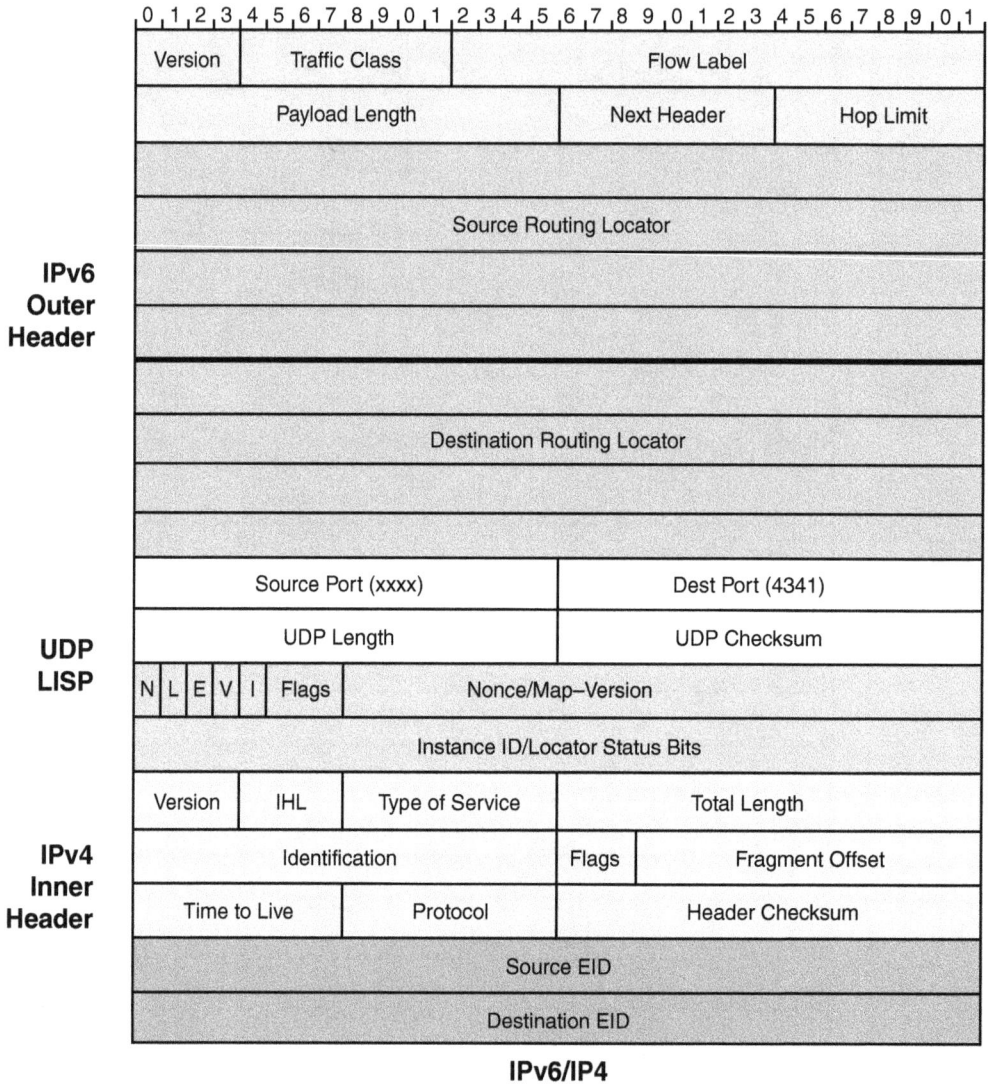

0 1 2 3 4 5 6 7 8 9 0 1	2 3 4 5 6 7 8 9 0 1	2 3 4 5 6 7 8 9 0 1

IPv6 Outer Header

Version	Traffic Class	Flow Label
Payload Length		Next Header	Hop Limit

Source Routing Locator

Destination Routing Locator

UDP LISP

Source Port (xxxx)	Dest Port (4341)
UDP Length	UDP Checksum

| N | L | E | V | I | Flags | Nonce/Map–Version |

Instance ID/Locator Status Bits

IPv4 Inner Header

Version	IHL	Type of Service	Total Length
Identification		Flags	Fragment Offset
Time to Live	Protocol	Header Checksum

Source EID

Destination EID

IPv6/IP4

Figure 4-3 *IPv6 RLOC and IPv4 EID LISP Packet Encapsulation*

■ IPv6 RLOC and IPv6 EID encapsulation, as shown in Figure 4-4

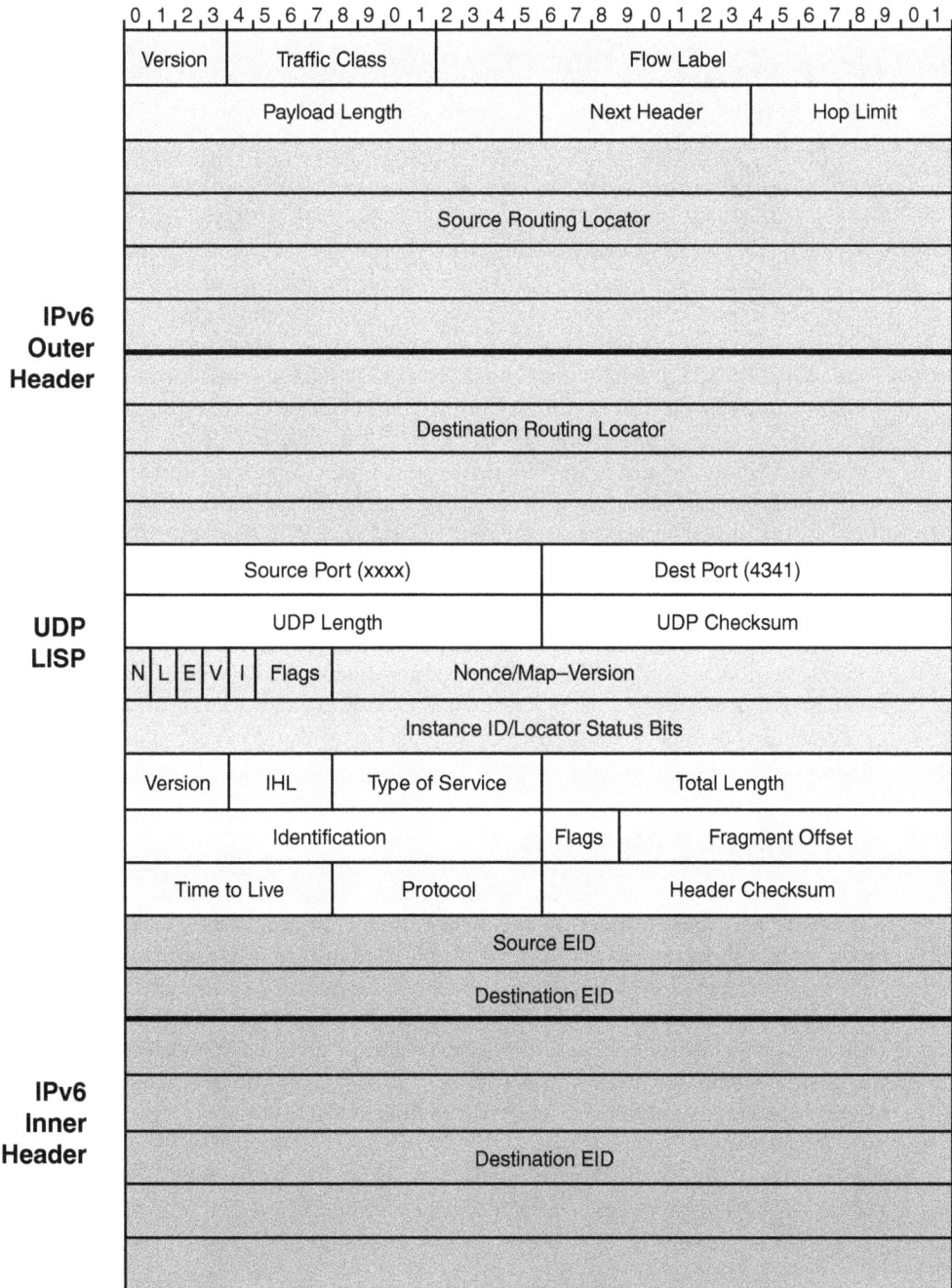

| 0 1 2 3 4 5 6 7 8 9 0 1 2 3 4 5 6 7 8 9 0 1 2 3 4 5 6 7 8 9 0 1 |

IPv6 Outer Header

| Version | Traffic Class | Flow Label |
| Payload Length | Next Header | Hop Limit |

Source Routing Locator

Destination Routing Locator

UDP LISP

Source Port (xxxx)	Dest Port (4341)
UDP Length	UDP Checksum
N L E V I Flags	Nonce/Map–Version
Instance ID/Locator Status Bits
Version	IHL	Type of Service	Total Length
Identification	Flags	Fragment Offset
Time to Live	Protocol	Header Checksum

Source EID

Destination EID

IPv6 Inner Header

Destination EID

IPv6/IP6

Figure 4-4 *IPv6 RLOC and IPv6 EID LISP Packet Encapsulation*

Within an address family, LISP can be extended further, to encapsulate IPv4 multicast EID with IPv4 unicast RLOC, IPv4 unicast EID with IPv4 multicast RLOC, and so on. An IPv4 multicast site traffic engineers its packets through an IPv4 unicast core service provider network. LISP multicast applications are discussed in Chapter 5, "LISP Multicast Routing Fundamentals."

LISP xTR routers can encapsulate IP packets inside other IP packets. When the LISP control plane protocol is integrated with Virtual Extensible LAN (VXLAN) as the data plane, Ethernet frames can also be encapsulated VXLAN packets. The entire Ethernet frame without the frame check sequence (FCS) and preamble is encapsulated inside a VXLAN packet. The destination User Datagram Protocol (UDP) port in the VXLAN packet is set to 4789. The source and destination media access control (MAC) addresses are used as source and destination EIDs. The LISP I bit is used to encode VXLAN virtual network identifier (VNID) or dot1q virtual LAN (VLAN) information through local configuration, mapped from a virtual routing and forwarding (VRF) VNI (that is, a Layer 3 VNI) or mapped from VLAN ID VNI (that is, a Layer 2 VNI). LISP is used on the control plane to learn endpoint and network IP prefix information. When configuring LISP in software-defined access (SDA) fabrics, an administrator must configure LISP to use VXLAN, rather than LISP, as the encapsulation protocol. By default, LISP encapsulation is used on Cisco platforms. Refer to Cisco's "Software-Defined Access Deployment Guide" to learn more about how to implement LISP in SDA fabrics. The focus of this book is LISP IP encapsulation.

You can see from the various encapsulation combinations with different address families that LISP is a strong tool for migration and interconnecting networks of various transport types. For example, with LISP, a service provider with an IPv4 Multiprotocol Label Switching (MPLS) core can easily connect IPv6 islands of customers.

IPv6 Transition Methods

For any organization, the decision to migrate to IPv6 is based on technical and business goals. Some decisions are based on long-term goals, and some are based on short-term goals. An organization may need to migrate to IPv6 because it is out of IPv4 addresses but is continuing to grow; information technology (IT) infrastructure has become a tool to help improve business processes and enable growth. Purchasing IPv4 address pools from providers is difficult because they have been depleted in many Internet registries; however, IPv6 pools are still plentiful. IPv6 is an attractive option for helping grow the IT infrastructure. An enterprise or a service provider might also want to deploy IPv6 to provide innovative new applications, such as IPv6 4G/LTE connectivity, IoT, and seamless mobile connectivity for collaborative applications across the cloud. A lot of government organizations mandate that any business doing business with a government entity be IPv6 enabled as a standard requirement.

There are several methods of migrating a network from IPv4 to IPv6. This section provides a brief overview of a variety of IPv6 transition methods that fall into several categories:

- Dual stack
- Translation

- Tunneling

- MPLS

- LISP

These transition types are compared and contrasted with LISP in mind.

A dual stack network has both IPv4 and IPv6 fully deployed across the infrastructure. Dual stack may involve running multiple routing protocols to support the two separate address families, such as Open Shortest Path First version 2 (OSPFv2) for IPv4 and OSPFv3 for IPv6 routing. Intermediate System to Intermediate System (IS-IS) can run a single instance of the routing protocol but in multi-topology mode, which involves having a separate Shortest Path First (SPF) instance and database for each address family. Dual stack takes extra control plane Routing Information Base (RIB) and data plane Forwarding Information Base (FIB) resources. Every node in the path must support IPv6. If the long-term goal is to move to IPv6 permanently, when the network reaches the target state of migration to IPv6, the IPv4 services and protocols are decommissioned.

Two methods are used for translation: IP address translation and address family translation (AFT). AFT refers to the translation of one address family into another. For example, translation of IPv6 to IPv4 is called NAT64, and translation of IPv4 to IPv6 is called NAT46. Network address translation (NAT) refers to the translation of one IP address to another IP address within the same address family (for example, translating a single IPv4 source IP address to another IPv4 source IP address). There are three types of NAT: static, dynamic, and port address translation (PAT). The following general challenges and caveats apply to deploying NAT in any form:

- NAT breaks the end-to-end model of IP.

- Not all applications work with NAT.

- Scaling NAT in a very large network requires special hardware, such as carrier-grade NAT modules in service provider environments.

- NAT breaks end-to-end network security.

- NAT translation mechanisms require reengineering of the Domain Name System (DNS) infrastructure to support IPv6.

Tunneling mechanisms come in various forms, such as IP-in-IP and IP-in-L2 tunnel. IP-in-IP involves encapsulating an IPv6 packet inside another address family IP packet. This includes technologies such as IPv6 over generic routing encapsulation (GRE) or IPv6 over IPv4 (6to4). IP-in-L2 refers to encapsulating IPv6 traffic inside a Layer 2 virtual private network (VPN) tunnel over an IPv4 transport network. IP-in-L2 includes IPv6 over Layer 2 Tunneling Protocol (L2TP) or IPv6 over L2TPv3. A lot of these tunneling mechanisms require manual provisioning, which prevents these solutions from scaling. In addition, increased control plane complexity increases the encapsulation overhead. The routers sourcing and terminating the tunnels must be dual stacked. Some tunneling mechanisms, such as 6to4 and 6rd, require the cooperation of the service provider.

MPLS enables IPv6 through two solutions: 6PE and 6VPE. 6PE uses IPv6 over an MPLS Multiprotocol BGP (MP-BGP) IPv4 transport network between IPv6 islands in the global routing table. 6VPE facilitates IPv6 over an MPLS MP-BGP IPv4 transport network between IPv6 islands existing in unique VPNs assigned to their own VRFs. In either case, an MPLS transport network is required to tunnel IPv6 traffic across the IPv4 core. 6VPE requires the use of MP-BGP and a strong understanding of MPLS L3 VPN technologies.

Finally, let's examine LISP as the IPv6 transition method. LISP encapsulates IPv4 into IPv6 and IPv6 into IPv4 packets. This is similar to other IP-in-IP solutions except that LISP is more versatile when it comes to options of underlays to forward IPv6 packets. LISP works in an IPv4-only or IPv6-only underlay, whereas other transition strategies, such as 6to4 and IPv6 over GRE, assume an IPv4-only underlay. LISP has no dependency on any specific routing protocol or label signaling protocol, such as MP-BGP or Label Distribution Protocol (LDP), when deploying 6PE or 6VPE. LISP simply is implemented at the edge of the network, with no requirement to be dual stacked, eliminating the need to run multiple instances of routing protocols such as OSPFv2 and OSPFv3. The address family–agnostic nature of LISP reduces the need to make any major changes to the network infrastructure. In addition, the various rich features of LISP, such as inherent multihoming, ingress traffic engineering, and mobility, are added benefits for long-term deployments.

The LISP map-n-encap forwarding mechanism eliminates all dependency on manual configuration of tunnels, adding scale and simplifying network management. Any ingress tunnel router (ITR) node simply has to resolve the RLOC address of any address family to forward to a EID of any address family. Any modification to the EID space is dynamically updated by the egress tunnel router (ETR) to the mapping system. Figure 4-5 illustrates how IPv4 and IPv6 LISP sites communicate through cores with the same or a different address family.

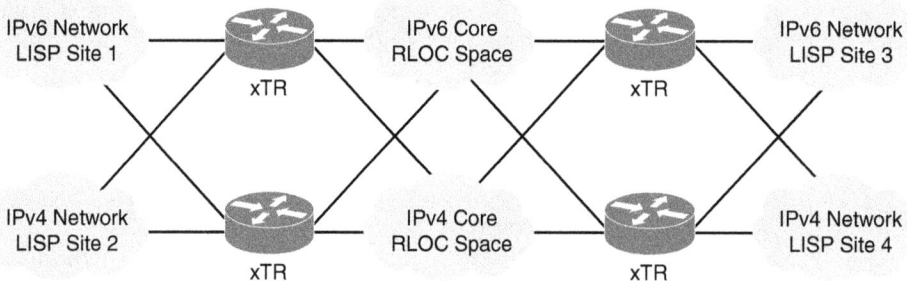

Figure 4-5   *LISP Internetworking Between IPv4 and IPv6 Sites*

Figure 4-5 shows islands of IPv4 and IPv6 networks separated by IPv6 and IPv4 networks. LISP-enabled routers are designed to interconnect IPv6 islands through IPv4 core and IPv4 islands through IPv6 core. A feature that is very unique to LISP is allowing incremental deployment of technologies and features from various address families. Let's look at how this works with some examples.

Connecting IPv6 Islands Using LISP

An organization in the initial phases of IPv6 adoption has IPv4 networks for most of its core infrastructure. Some sites and departments may have migrated to IPv6 networks. Say that an organization is currently migrating only small to medium branches to IPv6, starting at the edges of the network and moving toward the core. The network has islands of IPv6 networks separated by an IPv4 network, as depicted in Figure 4-6.

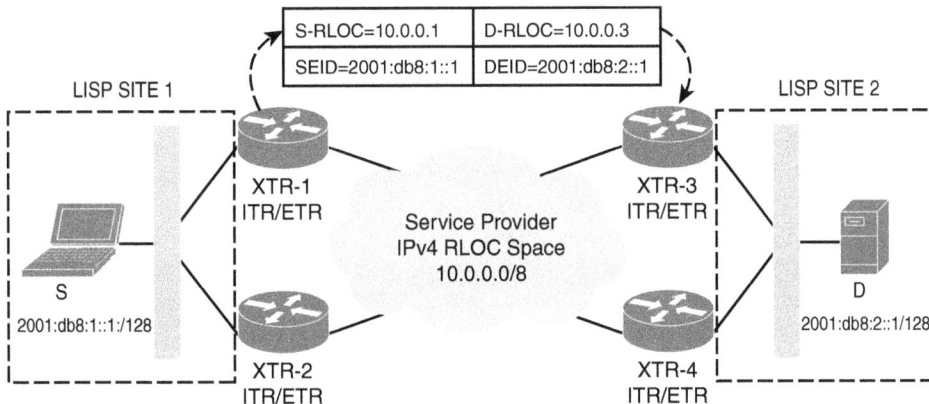

Figure 4-6   *Connecting IPv6 Islands Using LISP*

The client S represents the source EID with IPv6 address 2001:db8:1::1 that is sending packets to the destination EID server D with IPv6 address 2001:db8:2::1 on the right. The client and server each exist in a LISP site, separated by service provider networks in between. Each LISP site is multihomed to its service provider with IPv4 core networks. The LISP site sits behind the ITRs and ETRs, which are the customer edge routers encapsulating LISP packets when sending traffic out of the LISP site toward the provider and de-encapsulating LISP packets when receiving traffic from the provider destined to the EID attached to it.

The packet processing from client S connecting to a web application hosted on server D with hostname D.abc.com is similar to the packet walk described in the previous example on communication between two IPv4 LISP sites but with one critical difference: The LISP packets leave the ITR with IPv6 EID addresses from client S as the source and to server D as the destination. The outer IP header has IPv4 RLOC addresses with the source RLOC address of the ITR and the RLOC address of the ETR as the destination. (The packet exchange process is explained in Chapter 3, "LISP IPv4 Unicast Routing," and is therefore not repeated in this section.)

Connecting to the IPv6 Internet Using LISP

Say that Corporation ABC just migrated its entire data center, it campus, and it WAN sites to IPv6. To complete migration to IPv6 end to end, ABC corporation must ensure that all sites have connectivity to the IPv6 Internet. ABC's local service provider currently does not have IPv6 enabled at locations peering with ABC corporation edge routers. ABC Corporation's service provider has suggested LISP as a solution to interconnect the various IPv6 sites to the IPv6 Internet through the service provider IPv4 backbone. ABC Corporation is delighted to know the migration can be completed on time. ABC Corporation is proceeding with LISP to connect its new IPv6 sites to the IPv6 Internet.

A LISP site requiring connectivity to the IPv6 Internet requires proxy ingress tunnel routers (PITRs) and proxy egress tunnel routers (PETRs). (The role of PITRs and PETRs in internetworking between LISP and non-LISP sites is explained in detail in Chapter.) A PITR is a LISP infrastructure device that provides connectivity between non-LISP sites and LISP sites by attracting non-LISP traffic destined to LISP sites and encapsulating that traffic to LISP sites. The PITR attracts traffic to the LISP site by advertising a summary address of the EID prefix address space on behalf of the LISP site to the non-LISP site. For example, in Figure 4-7, the PITR advertises a summary prefix for the LISP sites with addresses 2001:db8:2::/48 and 2001:db8:1::/48 out to the IPv6 Internet. It is important to note that prefixes are provider independent. The routers existing in the IPv6 Internet learn the LISP EID prefix routes from the PITR, making the PITR the next hop to reach the LISP EID site networks. In Figure 4-7, notice the IPv4 service provider network; in this case, the PITR attracts IPv6 non-LISP traffic and forwards it to a LISP site, using the IPv4 transport network.

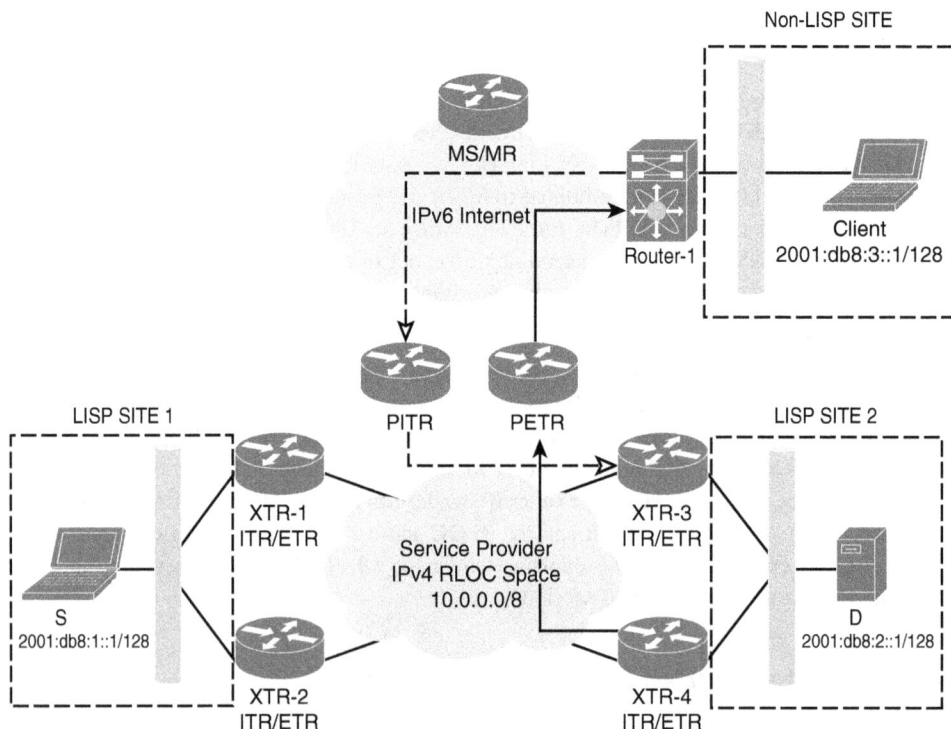

Figure 4-7   *Connecting to IPv6 Internet Using LISP*

The PETR acts as the gateway device for traffic egressing a LISP site destined to a non-LISP site. In the IPv6 transition case shown in Figure 4-7, the PETR allows the IPv6 LISP sites that have only IPv4 RLOC connectivity to reach LISP and non-LISP sites that have only IPv6 RLOC connectivity.

Note The selection of the ITR and ETR depends purely on the Interior Gateway Protocol (IGP) preferred path, according to the direction of traffic leaving or entering the LISP site.

Let's end this section by looking at a packet walk for packets sent from a client existing in the IPv6 Internet to destination server D inside the IPv6 LISP site:

Step 1. IPv6 packets sourced from the client with IPv6 address 2001:db8:3::1 are routed to the PITR, which is dual stacked (connected to the IPv4 Internet and the IPv6 Internet), connected to the LISP mapping system, and advertising an aggregate prefix covering the LISP Site 2 EID prefix into the IPv6 Internet to attract non-LISP traffic that is destined to LISP Site 2.

Step 2. The PITR encapsulates these packets to LISP Site 2 XTR3 using an IPv4 locator, as specified by the LISP Site 2 xTR LISP traffic engineering policy.

Step 3. The LISP Site 2 ETR router, XTR3, de-encapsulates the IPv4 LISP header and forwards the IPv6 packet to the web server.

Step 4. Return traffic from the web server flows back to the LISP Site 2 XTR4 based on IGP lowest cost for an EID route.

Step 5. The ETR node XTR4 refers to its local map cache and LISP encapsulates these IPv6 packets to the PETR using its IPv4 locator based on the EID-RLOC mapping in its local cache. As the packets leaves ETR node XTR4, the inner IP header has the IPv6 source EID address 2001:db8:2::1, the destination EID address 2001:db8:3::1, source RLOC address of XTR4, and destination RLOC address of PETR.

Step 6. The PETR de-encapsulates the LISP-encapsulated packets and forwards them natively within the IPv6 Internet to the IPv6 user, using the inner header IPv6 EID address fields.

Configuring LISP IPv6 Unicast Routing

Figure 3-8 shows the topology used to explain how to configure LISP IPv6 unicast routing in this section; it is the same topology used to show LISP IPv4 unicast routing in Chapter 3. This topology is used to explain both LISP-to-LISP site and LISP-to-non-LISP site IPv6 unicasting. This example builds on the information in Chapter 3 but now with a focus on IPv6 unicast routing. All the IPv6 configurations—both for the underlay and the LISP overlay—have been added to the nodes.

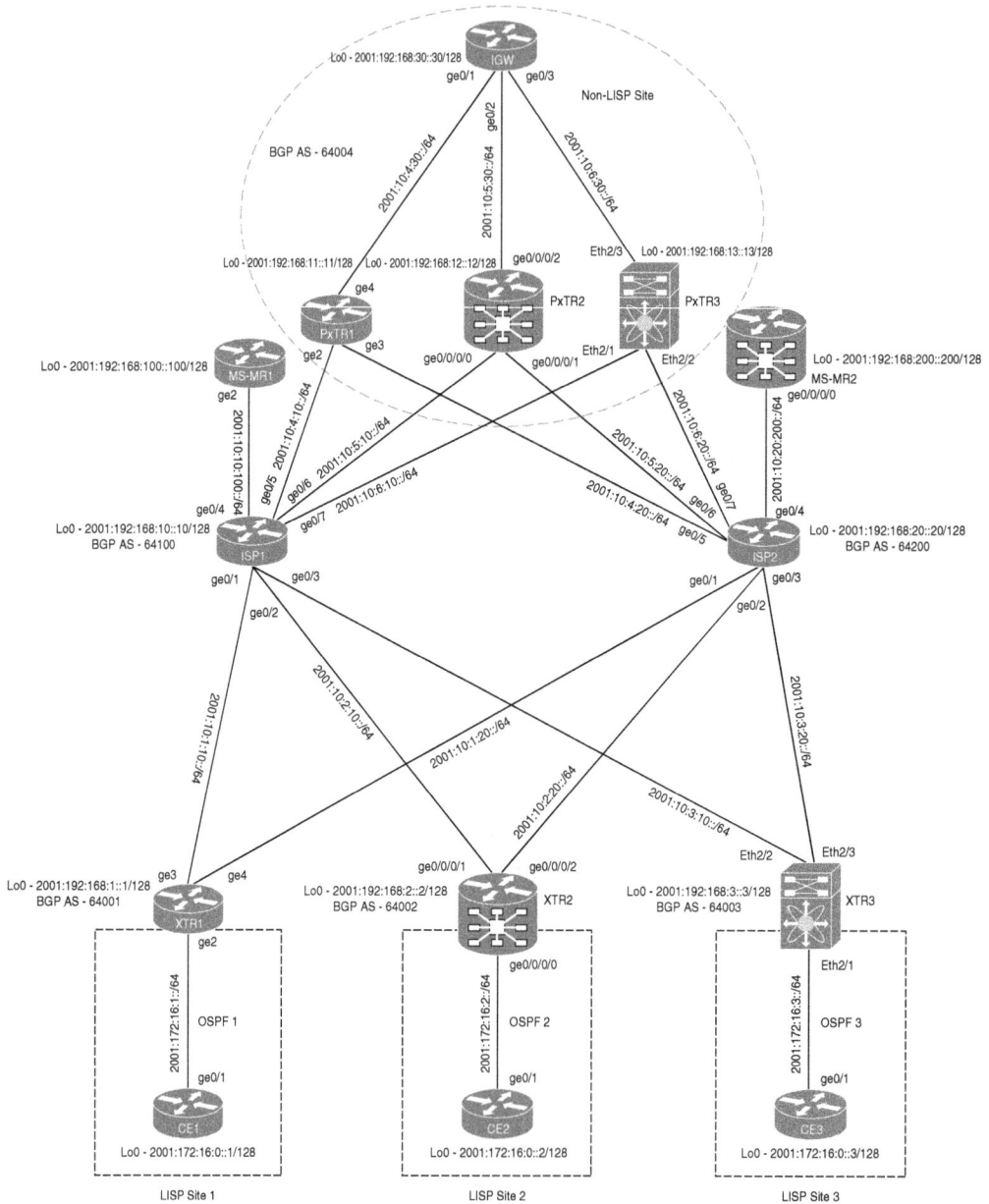

Figure 4-8 *LISP IPv6 Unicast Routing Topology*

The IPv6 addresses assigned to the nodes are similar to the IPv4 addresses originally used. Each IPv4 address was encoded inside the IPv6 address of each of a node interface and prepended with 2001. For example, the loopback 0 IPv4 address 172.16.0.1/32 now has IPv6 address 2001:172:16:0::1/128. In this example, IPv6 is configured end to end in the core, from LISP site and non-LISP site. As explained in earlier sections, communication between two IPv6 LISP sites does not require that the core be IPv6 enabled. Because this chapter is focused on IPv6 unicast forwarding, the underlay and overlay end to end are configured for IPv6 forwarding.

Note   This chapter assumes that you are comfortable configuring IPv6 routing protocols such as OSPFv3, MP-BGP, and static routing. The focus of the explanations in this chapter is on LISP. The examples that follow show only the IPv6-related configurations.

The syntax and steps to configure LISP IPv6 unicast routing are the same as for IPv4 unicast routing except that a few commands are specifically needed to configure IPv6-related parameters. Because the syntax for LISP IPv6 unicast routing configurations matches closely that of the LISP IPv4 unicast routing configurations, this chapter does not provide an exhaustive step-by-step explanation of all the commands. Refer to Chapter 3 for a detailed explanation of the LISP IPv4 command-line syntax that correlates with the IPv6-related configurations covered in this section. The patterns will become clear as you go through the examples.

Configuring xTR nodes involves the following steps:

Step 1.   Enable the LISP process.

Step 2.   Enable the LISP ITR/ETR functionality.

Step 3.   Configure the map server and map resolver.

Step 4.   Configure an EID-to-RLOC mapping database.

Configuring internetworking between LISP and non-LISP sites involves the following steps:

Step 1.   Configure the PETR node address on the xTR device.

Step 2.   Enable the LISP PITR and PETR functionality on the PxTR device.

Step 3.   Configure the map resolver on the PxTR device.

Step 4.   Configure the EID prefix map cache entry on the PxTR device.

Step 5.   Configure the IP source address used for the map request message by the PxTR device.

Step 6.   Configure the locator reachability algorithm.

Note   In IOS-XE version 16.6.1, the new CLI model for LISP configuration was redesigned with improvements to the structure and flow of the commands as part of the development effort around the campus fabric solution, which later evolved into SDA. Most LISP-specific configuration guides still adhere to old LISP CLI structure. The old and common CLI structure is followed in this book. Refer to Cisco's configuration guides for IOS-XE campus fabric or SDA for more details on the new LISP CLI structure on. Current versions of IOS-XE support both CLI structures.

In the topology shown in Figure 4-8, XTR1 is acting as the ITR and ETR LISP node forwarding IPv6 unicast packets for LISP Site 1. XTR1 also has three PxTRs configured for routing to non-LISP sites. Example 4-1 shows the complete XTR1 node LISP IPv6 unicast routing configuration.

Example 4-1   *XTR1 LISP IPv6 Unicast Routing Configuration*

```
!XTR1 IOS-XE LISP IPv6 configuration
hostname XTR1

ipv6 unicast-routing

interface Loopback0
 ipv6 address 2001:192:168:1::1/128
!
interface GigabitEthernet2
 ipv6 address 2001:172:16:1::1/64
 ipv6 ospf network point-to-point
 ipv6 ospf 1 area 0

interface GigabitEthernet3
 description link-to-ISP1
 ipv6 address 2001:10:1:10::1/64

interface GigabitEthernet4
 description link-to-ISP2
 ipv6 address 2001:10:1:20::1/64
!
router lisp
 eid-table default instance-id 0
  database-mapping 2001:172:16:0::1/128 2001:192:168:1::1 priority 1 weight 100
  database-mapping 2001:172:16:1::/64 2001:192:168:1::1 priority 1 weight 100
  ipv6 map-request-source 2001:192:168:1::1
  exit
 !
 ipv6 itr map-resolver 2001:192:168:100::100
 ipv6 itr map-resolver 2001:192:168:200::200
 ipv6 itr
 ipv6 etr map-server 2001:192:168:100::100 key cisco
 ipv6 etr map-server 2001:192:168:200::200 key cisco
 ipv6 etr
 ipv6 use-petr 2001:192:168:11::11
```

```
 ipv6 use-petr 2001:192:168:12::12
 ipv6 use-petr 2001:192:168:13::13
 exit
!
router ospfv3 1
 router-id 192.168.1.1
 !
 address-family ipv6 unicast
  default-information originate always
 exit-address-family
!
router bgp 64001
 bgp router-id 192.168.1.1
 bgp log-neighbor-changes
 no bgp default ipv4-unicast
 neighbor 2001:10:1:10::10 remote-as 64100
 neighbor 2001:10:1:20::20 remote-as 64200
 !
 address-family ipv6
  network 2001:192:168:1::1/128
  neighbor 2001:10:1:10::10 activate
  neighbor 2001:10:1:10::10 send-community
  neighbor 2001:10:1:20::20 activate
  neighbor 2001:10:1:20::20 send-community
 exit-address-family
!
```

As mentioned earlier, the commands to configure LISP IPv6 unicast routing are like the commands to configure LISP IPv4 unicast routing; however, note that the IPv6-related commands start with **ipv6** instead of **ip**. Across all protocols and services supported on the IOS and IOS-XE platforms, any command that starts with **ip** is generally intended for IPv4-related configuration, and any command that starts with **ipv6** is for IPv6-related configuration. The **ipv6 unicast-routing** command in the global configuration mode enables IPv6 protocol services on the router.

The same patterns of commands used in Chapter 3 for IPv4 are used here, but the address-related configuration parameters are populated with the IPv6 address. Consider these examples:

■ The **database-mapping** *EID-prefix/prefix length locator* **priority** *priority* **weight** *weight* command allows the ETR to populates its local LISP mapping database with the local EID-to-RLOC entries.

■ The **ipv6 itr** command is used to configure a device as an ITR node, and **ipv6 etr** is used to configure a device as an ETR node.

- The command to specify which map server an ETR should register to is
  ipv6 etr map-server *map-server-address* **key** *key-type authentication-key*. The
  command to specify which map resolver the ITR sends map request messages to for
  resolving IPv4 EID to RLOC is **ipv6 itr map-resolver** *map-resolver-address*.

- The command to specify the PETR is **ipv6 use-petr** *locator-address* [**priority**
  priority **weight** *weight*].

The PxTR1 router acts as both a PITR and as a PETR. The command to enable the PITR
function for IPv6 routing is **ipv6 proxy-itr** *ipv6-local-locator* [*ipv4-local-locator*], and
the command to enable the PETR function is **ipv6 proxy-etr**. The local locator address
for the PITR can be an IPv6 address or an IPv4 address. The use case for an IPv4 local
locator address is when the RLOC space in the core of the network is an IPv4 network,
while the EID prefix exists in an IPv6 network destined to an IPv6 non-LISP site. Of
course, the xTR attached to an IPv6 network would have to configure its PETR with an
IPv4 locator address by using the **ipv6 use-petr** command. In this case, the XTR1 encapsulates the packet with an inner IPv6 header (EID space) and an outer IPv4 header (RLOC
space) to the PETR. When the PETR receives the LISP packets, it strips the outer IPv4
header and natively forwards the IPv6 packet toward the non-LISP site.

Example 4-2 shows the PxTR1 node configuration running an IOS-XE image.

Example 4-2 *PxTR1 LISP IPv6 Unicast Routing Configuration*

```
!PxTR1 IOS-XE LISP IPv6 unicast routing complete configuration.

hostname PxTR1

ipv6 unicast-routing

interface Loopback0
 ipv6 address 2001:192:168:11::11/128

interface GigabitEthernet2
 descriptio1n link-to-ISP1
 ipv6 address 2001:10:4:10::4/64

!
interface GigabitEthernet3
 description link-to-ISP2
 ipv6 address 2001:10:4:20::4/64

!
interface GigabitEthernet4
 description link-to-IGW
 ipv6 address 2001:10:4:30::4/64

ipv6 route 2001:172:16::/64 Null0
```

```
ipv6 prefix-list block_summary_v6 seq 5 permit 2001:172:16::/64
ipv6 prefix-list block_summary_v6 seq 10 permit 2001:192:168:30::30/128
!
!
route-map block_summary_v6 deny 10
 match ipv6 address prefix-list block_summary_v6
!
route-map block_summary_v6 permit 20

router bgp 64004
 bgp router-id 192.168.11.11
 bgp log-neighbor-changes
 no bgp default ipv4-unicast
 neighbor 2001:10:4:10::10 remote-as 64100
 neighbor 2001:10:4:20::20 remote-as 64200
 neighbor 2001:10:4:30::30 remote-as 64004
 !
 address-family ipv6
  network 2001:172:16::/64
  network 2001:192:168:11::11/128
  redistribute connected
  neighbor 2001:10:4:10::10 activate
  neighbor 2001:10:4:10::10 send-community
  neighbor 2001:10:4:10::10 route-map block_summary_v6 out
  neighbor 2001:10:4:20::20 activate
  neighbor 2001:10:4:20::20 send-community
  neighbor 2001:10:4:20::20 route-map block_summary_v6 out
  neighbor 2001:10:4:30::30 activate
  neighbor 2001:10:4:30::30 send-community
 exit-address-family

router lisp
 eid-table default instance-id 0
  map-cache 2001:172:16::/64 map-request
  exit
 !
 loc-reach-algorithm rloc-probing
 locator-table default
 ipv6 itr map-resolver 2001:192:168:100::100
 ipv6 itr map-resolver 2001:192:168:200::200
 ipv6 map-request-source 2001:192:168:11::11
 ipv6 proxy-etr
 ipv6 proxy-itr 2001:192:168:11::11
 exit
 exit
```

A routing policy is required on the PxTR nodes to match and filter the non-LISP IPv6 route from the IGW node 2001:192:168:30::30/128 and the EID IPv6 summary prefix 2001:172:16::/64 from being advertised to the ISP devices in the RLOC address space. The following is a summary of the commands used to configure the routing policy:

- **ipv6 route:** This command configures a static route to the summarized EID prefix with a next hop of Null 0. Then, under the BGP routing process, the **network** command is used to unconditionally advertise the summary of the EID prefixes to the non-LISP site. The advertisement is unconditional because the static route points to a logical interface null0, which never goes down.

- **ipv6 prefix-list:** This command configures a prefix list to match the non-LISP site routes and the EID prefix summary route. The name of the IPv6 prefix list is **block_summary_v6**.

- **route-map:** This command, which is the first statement in sequence 10, denies any route that matches the prefix list **block_summary_v6**. The sequence 20 statement is an implicit **permit all** statement as the action is **permit**, and there is no **match** statement. The name of the route map is **block_summary_v6**.

- **route-map block_summary_v6:** This command is used in the BGP peering between the PxTR1 toward the ISP routers as an outbound filter to block the 2001:172:16::/64 and 2001:192:168:30::30/128 from being advertised to the ISP routers while permitting all other routes.

The routing policy is required to make sure the ISP routers that live in the RLOC address space have no knowledge of the EID address space or the non-LISP site networks. This ensures that all the traffic in any of the LISP sites toward the non-LISP site and traffic from the non-LISP site toward the LISP site is LISP encapsulated.

Example 4-3 shows the MS/MR LISP IPv6 configuration for the IOS-XE platform on the MS/MR1 node.

Example 4-3 *MS/MR1 LISP IPv6 Site Configuration*

```
!MS/MR1 IOS-XE IPv6 site configuration

hostname MS-MR1

ipv6 unicast-routing

interface Loopback0
 ipv6 address 2001:192:168:100::100/128

interface GigabitEthernet2
 description link-to-ISP1
 ipv6 address 2001:10:10:100::100/64
```

```
router lisp
 site Site-1-AS-64001
  authentication-key cisco
  eid-prefix 2001:172:16:0::1/128
  eid-prefix 2001:172:16:1::/64
  exit
 !
 site Site-2-AS-64002
  authentication-key cisco
  eid-prefix 2001:172:16:0::2/128
  eid-prefix 2001:172:16:2::/64
  exit
 !
 site Site-3-AS-64003
  authentication-key cisco
  eid-prefix 2001:172:16:0::3/128
  eid-prefix 2001:172:16:3::/64
  exit
 !
 ipv6 map-server
 ipv6 map-resolver
 exit

ipv6 route ::/0 2001:10:10:100::10
```

The MS/MR configuration is very simple and occurs on the same sites that were config-ured for LISP for IPv4 EID prefix configured earlier—but with the IPv6 EID prefix added for the same LISP sites. The same MS/MR nodes are used here for both IPv6 and IPv4 LISP unicast routing.

The second MS/MR2 node running the IOS-XR image is also configured as an MS/MR node, as shown in Example 4-4.

Example 4-4   *MS/MR2 LISP IPv6 Site Configuration*

```
!MS/MR2 IOS-XR LISP IPv6 site configuration

hostname MS-MR2

interface Loopback0
 ipv6 address 2001:192:168:200::200/128

interface GigabitEthernet0/0/0/0
 description link-to-ISP2
 ipv6 address 2001:10:20:200::200/64
```

```
router lisp
 address-family ipv6 unicast
  map-resolver
  map-server
 !
 site Site-1-AS-64001
  eid-prefix 2001:172:16:0::1/128
  eid-prefix 2001:172:16:1::/64
  authentication-key encrypted cisco
 !
 site Site-2-AS-64002
  eid-prefix 2001:172:16:0::2/128
  eid-prefix 2001:172:16:2::/64
  authentication-key encrypted cisco
 !
 site Site-3-AS-64003
  eid-prefix 2001:172:16:0::3/128
  eid-prefix 2001:172:16:3::/64
  authentication-key encrypted cisco
 !

 locator-table vrf default
!

router static
 address-family ipv6 unicast
   ::/0 2001:10:20:200::20
```

The MS/MR2 IOS-XR configuration syntax is very similar in structure to that of the MS/MR1 IOS-XE node. Keep in mind the following factors that are specific to IOS-XR:

■ The **address-family ipv6 unicast** command is required to enable the LISP protocol for IPv6 unicast forwarding.

■ The **map-resolver** and **map-server** commands must be enabled under the IPv6 address family so the authoritative ETRs register their IPv6 EID prefixes with the MS/MR and the ITRs resolve IPv6 EID prefixes.

Under the same sites that were previously configured as part of the LISP IPv4 unicast routing example, the IPv6 EID prefixes entries are added to the same site.

The LISP Site 2 XTR2 node is also configured as an ITR and an ETR for a LISP IPv6 site. Example 4-5 shows the XTR2 node LISP IPv6 unicast routing configuration.

Example 4-5 *XTR2 LISP IPv6 Unicast Routing Configuration*

```
!XTR2 IOS-XR LISP IPv6 unicast routing configuration

hostname XTR2

interface Loopback0
 ipv6 address 2001:192:168:2::2/128

interface GigabitEthernet0/0/0/0
 ipv6 address 2001:172:16:2::1/64

!
interface GigabitEthernet0/0/0/1
 description link-to-ISP1
 ipv6 address 2001:10:2:10::2/64

!
interface GigabitEthernet0/0/0/2
description link-to-ISP2
 ipv6 address 2001:10:2:20::2/64

router lisp
 address-family ipv6 unicast
  etr map-server 2001:192:168:100::100 key cisco
  etr map-server 2001:192:168:200::200 key cisco
  etr
  itr map-resolver 2001:192:168:100::100
  itr map-resolver 2001:192:168:200::200
  itr
  use-petr 2001:192:168:11::11
  use-petr 2001:192:168:12::12
  use-petr 2001:192:168:13::13
 !
 eid-table default instance-id 0
  address-family ipv6 unicast
   database-mapping 2001:172:16:0::2/128 2001:192:168:2::2 priority 1 weight 100
   database-mapping 2001:172:16:2::/64 2001:192:168:2::2 priority 1 weight 100
   map-request-source 2001:192:168:2::2
  !
 !
```

```
  locator-table default

router ospfv3 2
 router-id 192.168.2.2
 default-information originate always
 area 0
  interface GigabitEthernet0/0/0/0
  network point-to-point
  !

!
route-policy passall
pass

router bgp 64002
 bgp router-id 192.168.2.2
 address-family ipv6 unicast
  network 2001:192:168:2::2/128
 !
 neighbor 2001:10:2:10::10
  remote-as 64100
  address-family ipv6 unicast
   route-policy passall in
   route-policy passall out
  !
 !
 neighbor 2001:10:2:20::20
  remote-as 64200
  address-family ipv6 unicast
   route-policy passall in
   route-policy passall out
  !
```

Observe the following in the configuration shown in Example 4-5:

■ All the LISP IPv6 configurations, such as the locator IPv6 addresses of the map server, map resolver, and ETR plus the enablement of the ITR/ETR function for the local device are applied in the **address-family ipv6 unicast** mode under the LISP router process (config-lisp-afi)#.

■ The local IPv6 EID-to-RLOC table entries for the ETR are configured in the EID table mapped to LISP instance 0; in this example, instance ID 0 is mapped to **vrf default** because we are not doing any virtualization. This occurs in the **address-family ipv6 unicast** mode under the LISP router process (config-lisp-eid-table-afi)#.

Example 4-6 shows an example for the IOS-XR platform configuration of the PxTR2 node.

Example 4-6   *PxTR2 LISP IPv6 Unicast Routing Configuration*

```
!PxTR2 IOS-XR LISP IPv6 unicast routing configuration.

hostname PxTR2

interface Loopback0
 ipv6 address 2001:192:168:12::12/128
!

interface GigabitEthernet0/0/0/0
 description link-to-ISP1
 ipv6 address 2001:10:5:10::5/64
!
interface GigabitEthernet0/0/0/1
 description link-to-ISP2
 ipv6 address 2001:10:5:20::5/64
!
interface GigabitEthernet0/0/0/2
 description link-to-IGW
 ipv6 address 2001:10:5:30::5/64
!
end

prefix-set block_summary_v6
  2001:172:16::/64,
  2001:192:168:30::30/128
end-set

route-policy block_summary_v6
  if destination in block_summary_v6 then
    drop
  else
    pass
  endif
end-policy

router static
 address-family ipv6 unicast
  2001:172:16::/64 Null0
```

```
router bgp 64004
 bgp router-id 192.168.12.12
 address-family ipv6 unicast
  network 2001:172:16::/64
  network 2001:192:168:12::12/128
  redistribute connected
 !
 neighbor 2001:10:5:10::10
  remote-as 64100
  address-family ipv6 unicast
   route-policy block_summary_v6 in
   route-policy block_summary_v6 out
  !
 !
 neighbor 2001:10:5:20::20
  remote-as 64200
  address-family ipv6 unicast
   route-policy block_summary_v6 in
   route-policy block_summary_v6 out
  !
 !
 neighbor 2001:10:5:30::30
  remote-as 64004
  address-family ipv6 unicast

!
router lisp
 address-family ipv6 unicast
  itr map-resolver 2001:192:168:100::100
  itr map-resolver 2001:192:168:200::200
  proxy-etr
  proxy-itr 2001:192:168:12::12
  map-request-source 2001:192:168:12::12
 !
 eid-table default instance-id 0
  address-family ipv6 unicast
   map-cache 2001:172:16::/64 map-request
  !
 !
 locator-table default
 loc-reach-algorithm rloc-probing
!
end
```

The routing policy configured on the PxTR2 node is like that of the PxTR1 router. The prefix set is equivalent to a prefix list in the IOS/IOS-XE platform, and the route policy has a similar function to the route map in the IOS-XE platform. The purpose of the routing policy is the same as on the PxTR1: to prevent the non-LISP site and the LISP site routes from being advertised into the RLOC address space.

As in the previous two examples, the PxTR2 node is an IOS-XR device; to enable the PITR and PETR function for IPv6 LISP sites, the **proxy-itr** and **proxy-etr** commands are configured in the **address-family ipv6 unicast** mode under the LISP router process. To configure which IPv6 EID prefixes the PxTR2 should send, the map request for the **map-cache** command is configured in the **address-family ipv6 unicast** mode inside the EID table under the LISP router process.

The last set of configurations required in this example is for the NX-OS devices. The XTR3 node is also configured as a LISP site with the OSPFv3 routing protocol to provide IPv6 unicast forwarding. Example 4-7 shows the complete LISP IPv6 unicast routing configuration for XTR3.

Example 4-7 *XTR3 LISP IPv6 Unicast Routing Configuration*

```
!XTR3 NX-OS LISP IPv6 unicast routing configuration

hostname XTR3

interface loopback0
  ipv6 address 2001:192:168:3::3/128

interface Ethernet2/1
  no switchport
  ipv6 address 2001:172:16:3::1/64
  ospfv3 network point-to-point
  ipv6 router ospfv3 3 area 0.0.0.0

interface Ethernet2/2
  no switchport
  description link-to-ISP1
  ipv6 address 2001:10:3:10::3/64

interface Ethernet2/3
  no switchport
  description link-to-ISP2
  ipv6 address 2001:10:3:20::3/64

feature ospfv3
feature bgp
feature lisp
```

```
ipv6 lisp itr-etr
ipv6 lisp use-petr 2001:192:168:11::11 priority 50 weight 50
ipv6 lisp use-petr 2001:192:168:12::12 priority 50 weight 50
ipv6 lisp use-petr 2001:192:168:13::13 priority 50 weight 50
ipv6 lisp database-mapping 2001:172:16:0::3/128 2001:192:168:3::3 priority 1
  weight 100
ipv6 lisp database-mapping 2001:172:16:3::/64 2001:192:168:3::3 priority 1
  weight 100
ipv6 lisp locator-vrf default
ipv6 lisp itr map-resolver 2001:192:168:100::100
ipv6 lisp itr map-resolver 2001:192:168:200::200
ipv6 lisp etr map-server 2001:192:168:100::100 key cisco
ipv6 lisp etr map-server 2001:192:168:200::200 key cisco
ipv6 lisp map-request-source 2001:192:168:3::3

router ospfv3 3
  router-id 192.168.3.3
  address-family ipv6 unicast
    default-information originate always

router bgp 64003
  router-id 192.168.3.3
  address-family ipv6 unicast
    network 2001:192:168:3::3/128
  neighbor 2001:10:3:10::10 remote-as 64100
    address-family ipv6 unicast
  neighbor 2001:10:3:20::20 remote-as 64200
    address-family ipv6 unicast
```

The syntax here looks very similar to the syntax used for configuring LISP IPv4 unicast routing in Chapter 3. All the IPv6 LISP configurations are applied globally rather than under a router process (in contrast to the configuration on IOS-XE and IOS-XR software). All the LISP IPv6-related configurations start with the command **ipv6 lisp**, and the remaining command options are similar, but instead of specifying IPv4 addresses for the EID prefixes or RLOC addresses, you enter IPv6 addresses for those same parameters.

Example 4-8 shows the final configuration for the PxTR3 node.

Example 4-8 *PxTR3 LISP IPv6 Unicast Routing Configuration*

```
!PxTR3 NX-OS LISP IPv6 unicast routing configuration

hostname PxTR3

interface loopback0
  ipv6 address 2001:192:168:13::13/128

interface Ethernet2/1
  description link-to-ISP1
  ipv6 address 2001:10:6:10::6/64
  no shutdown

interface Ethernet2/2
  description link-to-ISP2
  ipv6 address 2001:10:6:20::6/64
  no shutdown

interface Ethernet2/3
  description link-to-IGW
  ipv6 address 2001:10:6:30::6/64
  no shutdown

ipv6 route 2001:172:16::/64 Null0

ipv6 prefix-list block_summary_v6 seq 5 permit 2001:172:16::/64
ipv6 prefix-list block_summary_v6 seq 10 permit 2001:192:168:30::30/128

route-map block_summary_v6 deny 10
  match ipv6 address prefix-list block_summary_v6
route-map block_summary_v6 permit 20

route-map connected permit 10
  match interface Ethernet2/1 Ethernet2/2

router bgp 64004
  router-id 192.168.13.13
  address-family ipv6 unicast
    network 2001:172:16::/64
    network 2001:192:168:13::13/128
    redistribute direct route-map connected
  neighbor 2001:10:6:10::10 remote-as 64100
```

```
    address-family ipv6 unicast
      route-map block_summary_v6 out
  neighbor 2001:10:6:20::20 remote-as 64200
    address-family ipv6 unicast
      route-map block_summary_v6 out
  neighbor 2001:10:6:30::30 remote-as 64004
    address-family ipv6 unicast

ipv6 lisp proxy-itr 2001:192:168:13::13
ipv6 lisp proxy-etr
lisp loc-reach-algorithm rloc-probing
ipv6 lisp locator-vrf default
ipv6 lisp map-cache 2001:172:16::/64 map-request
ipv6 lisp itr map-resolver 2001:192:168:100::100
ipv6 lisp itr map-resolver 2001:192:168:200::200
ipv6 lisp map-request-source 2001:192:168:13::13
```

Because PxTR3 is a PITR and PETR device, just like PxTR1 and PxTR2, you need to configure the same parameters: Enable the ITR and PETR functions and specify the map resolver and EID map cache entries to send map request messages for. To configure all these parameters, start with **ipv6 lisp**, as described earlier.

Note   To better understand the steps and syntax needed to configure either of the address family protocols, study the LISP IPv4 unicast routing configuration examples in Chapter 3 and compare them with the LISP IPv6 unicast routing examples covered in this chapter. The same topology and IP addressing pattern are purposely used in this chapter and Chapter 3 for easier understanding of the examples.

LISP IPv6 Unicast Routing Control Plane Verification

The routing in LISP networks consists of two layers: the underlay and the overlay network. In terms of the LISP packet headers, the outer IP header is the underlay, and the inner IP header represents the overlay network. The traffic from the LISP sites sourced and destined to the EID addresses are overlaid on top of the core network. The underlay forwards based on the next-hop or RLOC address to reach the specific EID. The underlay has no knowledge of the EID prefixes, and it is this lack of knowledge that triggers the LISP resolution process on the xTR node, which is the edge device attached to a LISP site that borders the core transport network. The xTR nodes in the topology shown in Figure 4-8 have no entries in their routing table of any of the LISP sites except the one that is directly attached. It is important to understand the various routing layers and their attributes as you troubleshoot a LISP network.

In the topology in Figure 4-8, the CE1, CE2, and CE3 routers each exist in a LISP site. The Internet gateway (IGW) router exists in the non-LISP site. There are two MS/MR devices attached to the core network. The xTR devices in each LISP site are configured to be both ITRs and ETRs. xTRs tunnel traffic to each other for communication between the LISP sites. When the traffic needs to go from a LISP site to a non-LISP site, the packet is forwarded to one of the three PxTRs, which all act as both PITRs and PETRs.

With the LISP protocol, the control plane is decoupled from the data plane. The MS/MR stores the forwarding information for LISP sites to communicate with each other and for the non-LISP site to communicate with the LISP site. The specific forwarding information is a mapping of the RLOC to the EID prefix for each LISP site. If MS/MR does not know about the existence of an EID prefix in a site or the PxTR does not have the locator address of the map resolver, the forwarding information is not available for the PxTR or xTR to encapsulate the LISP packet to the destination EID.

To verify that MS/MR1 and MS/MR2 are functioning as map server and resolver nodes, you must use the **show ipv6 lisp** command, as shown in Example 4-9.

Example 4-9 *MS/MR LISP Function Verification*

```
!MS/MR1 IOS-XE MS/MR function verification

MS-MR1# show ipv6 lisp
  Instance ID:                          0
  Router-lisp ID:                       0
  Locator table:                        default
  EID table:                            default
  Ingress Tunnel Router (ITR):          disabled
  Egress Tunnel Router (ETR):           disabled
  Proxy-ITR Router (PITR):              disabled
  Proxy-ETR Router (PETR):              disabled
  NAT-traversal Router (NAT-RTR):       disabled
  Mobility First-Hop Router:            disabled
  Map Server (MS):                      enabled
  Map Resolver (MR):                    enabled
  Delegated Database Tree (DDT):        disabled
  Site Registration Limit:              0
  Map-Request source:                   derived from EID destination
  ITR local RLOC (last resort):         *** NOT FOUND***
  ITR Solicit Map Request (SMR):        accept and process
    Max SMRs per map-cache entry:       8 more specifics
    Multiple SMR suppression time:      20 secs
  ETR accept mapping data:              disabled, verify disabled
  ETR map-cache TTL:                    1d00h
```

```
  Locator Status Algorithms:
    RLOC-probe algorithm:              disabled
    RLOC-probe on route change:        N/A (periodic probing disabled)
    RLOC-probe on member change:       disabled
    LSB reports:                       process
    IPv4 RLOC minimum mask length:     /0
    IPv6 RLOC minimum mask length:     /0
  Map-cache:
    Static mappings configured:        0
    Map-cache size/limit:              0/1000
    Imported route count/limit:        0/1000
    Map-cache activity check period:   60 secs
    Map-cache FIB updates:             established
    Persistent map-cache:              disabled
  Database:
    Total database mapping size:       0
    static database size/limit:        0/5000
    dynamic database size/limit:       0/1000
    route-import database size/limit:  0/1000
    Inactive (deconfig/away) size:     0
  Encapsulation type:                  lisp


!MS/MR2 IOS-XR MS/MR function verification


RP/0/0/CPU0:MS-MR2# show lisp ipv6

  Instance ID:                       0
  Router-lisp ID:                    0
  Locator table:                     default
    Cached IPv4 RLOC topology:       IPv4 default
    Cached IPv6 RLOC topology:       IPv6 default
  EID table:                         N/A
  Ingress Tunnel Router (ITR):       disabled
  Egress Tunnel Router (ETR):        disabled
  Proxy-ITR Router (PITR):           disabled
  Proxy-ETR Router (PETR):           disabled
  NAT-traversal Router (NAT-RTR):    disabled
  Mobility First-Hop Router:         disabled
  Map Server (MS):                   enabled
  Map Resolver (MR):                 enabled
  Delegated Database Tree (DDT):     disabled
  Map-Request source:                derived from EID destination
  ITR local RLOC (last resort):      *** NOT FOUND***
```

```
ITR Solicit Map Request (SMR):      accept and process
  Max SMRs per map-cache entry:     8 more specifics
  Multiple SMR suppression time:    20 secs
ETR accept mapping data:            disabled, verify disabled
ETR map-cache TTL:                  1d00h
Locator Status Algorithms:
  RLOC-probe algorithm:             disabled
  RLOC-probe on route change:       N/A (periodic probing disabled)
  RLOC-probe on member change:      disabled
  LSB reports:                      process
  IPv4 RLOC minimum mask length:    /0
  IPv6 RLOC minimum mask length:    /0
Static mappings configured:         0
Map-cache size/limit:               0/50000
Imported route count/limit:         0/1000
Map-cache activity check period:    60 secs
Map-cache FIB updates:              pre-init
Total database mapping size:        0
  static database size/limit:       0/5000
  dynamic database size/limit:      0/0
  route-import database size:       0
```

Note The LISP protocol was initially an IP overlay solution, but it has evolved to support other encapsulation types, such as Ethernet for VXLAN packet forwarding. There is an IETF draft for LISP extensions titled "LISP Generic Protocol Extension draft-lewis-lisp-gpe." The Cisco SDA/campus fabric solution uses LISP as the control plane protocol and VXLAN as the data plane protocol in the IOS-XE platform. Notice that the MS/MR2 IOS-XR node does not have the LISP encapsulation type specified because it supports only IPv4 and IPv6 overlays with LISP encapsulation.

Example 4-10 shows the authoritative ETRs and the EIDs registered to the MS/MR nodes for each site.

Example 4-10 *MS/MR Site Registration Details*

```
!MS/MR1 IOS-XE site registration details

MS-MR1# show lisp site detail
LISP Site Registration Information

Site name: Site-1-AS-64001
Allowed configured locators: any
```

```
Allowed EID-prefixes:
  EID-prefix: 172.16.0.1/32
    First registered:     6d14h
    Last registered:      6d14h
    Routing table tag:    0
    Origin:               Configuration
    Merge active:         No
    Proxy reply:          No
    TTL:                  1d00h
    State:                complete
    Registration errors:
      Authentication failures:   0
      Allowed locators mismatch: 0
    ETR 192.168.1.1:49845, last registered 6d14h, no proxy-reply, map-notify
                          TTL 1d00h, no merge, hash-function sha1, nonce
                            0xCAF78EA6-0x1C61B042
                          state complete, no security-capability
                          xTR-ID 0x394428FD-0x6D1BE5DC-0x6CE78839-0x356F9618
                          site-ID unspecified
                          sourced by reliable transport
      Locator      Local State      Pri/Wgt  Scope
      192.168.1.1  yes   up            1/100  IPv4 none

  EID-prefix: 172.16.1.0/24
    First registered:     6d14h
    Last registered:      6d14h
    Routing table tag:    0
    Origin:               Configuration
    Merge active:         No
    Proxy reply:          No
    TTL:                  1d00h
    State:                complete
    Registration errors:
      Authentication failures:   0
      Allowed locators mismatch: 0
    ETR 192.168.1.1:49845, last registered 6d14h, no proxy-reply, map-notify
                          TTL 1d00h, no merge, hash-function sha1, nonce
                            0xCAF78EA6-0x1C61B042
                          state complete, no security-capability
                          xTR-ID 0x394428FD-0x6D1BE5DC-0x6CE78839-0x356F9618
                          site-ID unspecified
                          sourced by reliable transport
      Locator      Local State      Pri/Wgt  Scope
      192.168.1.1  yes   up            1/100  IPv4 none
```

```
EID-prefix: 2001:172:16::1/128
  First registered:      6d14h
  Last registered:       6d14h
  Routing table tag:     0
  Origin:                Configuration
  Merge active:          No
  Proxy reply:           No
  TTL:                   1d00h
  State:                 complete
  Registration errors:
    Authentication failures:    0
    Allowed locators mismatch:  0
  ETR 2001:192:168:1::1.23456, last registered 6d14h, no proxy-reply, map-notify
                               TTL 1d00h, no merge, hash-function sha1, nonce
                                 0x1A72AAC8-0xA0334153
                               state complete, no security-capability
                               xTR-ID 0x394428FD-0x6D1BE5DC-0x6CE78839-0x356F9618
                               site-ID unspecified
                               sourced by reliable transport
    Locator            Local  State     Pri/Wgt  Scope
    2001:192:168:1::1  yes    up          1/100  IPv6 none

EID-prefix: 2001:172:16:1::/64
  First registered:      6d14h
  Last registered:       6d14h
  Routing table tag:     0
  Origin:                Configuration
  Merge active:          No
  Proxy reply:           No
  TTL:                   1d00h
  State:                 complete
  Registration errors:
    Authentication failures:    0
    Allowed locators mismatch:  0
  ETR 2001:192:168:1::1.23456, last registered 6d14h, no proxy-reply, map-notify
                               TTL 1d00h, no merge, hash-function sha1, nonce
                                 0x1A72AAC8-0xA0334153
                               state complete, no security-capability
                               xTR-ID 0x394428FD-0x6D1BE5DC-0x6CE78839-0x356F9618
                               site-ID unspecified
                               sourced by reliable transport
    Locator            Local  State     Pri/Wgt  Scope
    2001:192:168:1::1  yes    up          1/100  IPv6 none
```

```
Site name: Site-2-AS-64002
Allowed configured locators: any
Allowed EID-prefixes:

  EID-prefix: 172.16.0.2/32
    First registered:    6d14h
    Last registered:     00:01:01
    Routing table tag:   0
    Origin:              Configuration
    Merge active:        No
    Proxy reply:         No
    TTL:                 1d00h
    State:               complete
    Registration errors:
      Authentication failures:   0
      Allowed locators mismatch: 0
    ETR 192.168.2.2, last registered 00:01:01, no proxy-reply, map-notify
                  TTL 1d00h, no merge, hash-function sha1, nonce
                    0x86E09BAC-0xF66E6AC5
                  state complete, no security-capability
                  xTR-ID 0x0158C515-0x20C1C5C9-0x4CB68CB6-0x7C853161
                  site-ID unspecified
      Locator      Local  State    Pri/Wgt  Scope
      192.168.2.2  yes    up          1/100  IPv4 none

  EID-prefix: 172.16.2.0/24
    First registered:    6d14h
    Last registered:     00:01:01
    Routing table tag:   0
    Origin:              Configuration
    Merge active:        No
    Proxy reply:         No
    TTL:                 1d00h
    State:               complete
    Registration errors:
      Authentication failures:   0
      Allowed locators mismatch: 0
    ETR 192.168.2.2, last registered 00:01:01, no proxy-reply, map-notify
                  TTL 1d00h, no merge, hash-function sha1, nonce
                    0x86E09BAC-0xF66E6AC5
                  state complete, no security-capability
                  xTR-ID 0x0158C515-0x20C1C5C9-0x4CB68CB6-0x7C853161
                  site-ID unspecified
      Locator      Local  State    Pri/Wgt  Scope
      192.168.2.2  yes    up          1/100  IPv4 none
```

```
EID-prefix: 2001:172:16::2/128
  First registered:      6d14h
  Last registered:       00:00:01
  Routing table tag:     0
  Origin:                Configuration
  Merge active:          No
  Proxy reply:           No
  TTL:                   1d00h
  State:                 complete
  Registration errors:
    Authentication failures:   0
    Allowed locators mismatch: 0
  ETR 2001:192:168:2::2, last registered 00:00:01, no proxy-reply, map-notify
                         TTL 1d00h, no merge, hash-function sha1, nonce
                           0x0A3DD0E6-0x8E05F323
                         state complete, no security-capability
                         xTR-ID 0x0158C515-0x20C1C5C9-0x4CB68CB6-0x7C853161
                         site-ID unspecified
    Locator           Local  State    Pri/Wgt  Scope
    2001:192:168:2::2 yes    up        1/100   IPv6 none

EID-prefix: 2001:172:16:2::/64
  First registered:      6d14h
  Last registered:       00:00:01
  Routing table tag:     0
  Origin:                Configuration
  Merge active:          No
  Proxy reply:           No
  TTL:                   1d00h
  State:                 complete
  Registration errors:
    Authentication failures:   0
    Allowed locators mismatch: 0
  ETR 2001:192:168:2::2, last registered 00:00:01, no proxy-reply, map-notify
                         TTL 1d00h, no merge, hash-function sha1, nonce
                           0x0A3DD0E6-0x8E05F323
                         state complete, no security-capability
                         xTR-ID 0x0158C515-0x20C1C5C9-0x4CB68CB6-0x7C853161
                         site-ID unspecified
    Locator           Local  State    Pri/Wgt  Scope
    2001:192:168:2::2 yes    up        1/100   IPv6 none
Site name: Site-3-AS-64003
Allowed configured locators: any
Allowed EID-prefixes:
```

```
EID-prefix: 172.16.0.3/32
  First registered:     6d14h
  Last registered:      00:00:27
  Routing table tag:    0
  Origin:               Configuration
  Merge active:         No
  Proxy reply:          No
  TTL:                  00:03:00
  State:                complete
  Registration errors:
    Authentication failures:   0
    Allowed locators mismatch: 0
  ETR 192.168.3.3, last registered 00:00:27, no proxy-reply, no map-notify
                TTL 00:03:00, no merge, hash-function sha1, nonce
                  0x00000000-0x00000000
                state complete, no security-capability
                xTR-ID N/A
                site-ID N/A
  Locator       Local State      Pri/Wgt  Scope
  192.168.3.3   yes   up         1/100    IPv4 none

EID-prefix: 172.16.3.0/24
  First registered:     6d14h
  Last registered:      00:00:27
  Routing table tag:    0
  Origin:               Configuration
  Merge active:         No
  Proxy reply:          No
  TTL:                  00:03:00
  State:                complete
  Registration errors:
    Authentication failures:   0
    Allowed locators mismatch: 0
  ETR 192.168.3.3, last registered 00:00:27, no proxy-reply, no map-notify
                TTL 00:03:00, no merge, hash-function sha1, nonce
                  0x00000000-0x00000000
                state complete, no security-capability
                xTR-ID N/A
                site-ID N/A
  Locator       Local State      Pri/Wgt  Scope
  192.168.3.3   yes   up         1/100    IPv4 none

EID-prefix: 2001:172:16::3/128
  First registered:     6d14h
  Last registered:      00:00:27
```

```
        Routing table tag:    0
        Origin:               Configuration
        Merge active:         No
        Proxy reply:          No
        TTL:                  00:03:00
        State:                complete
        Registration errors:
          Authentication failures:   0
          Allowed locators mismatch: 0
        ETR 2001:10:3:10::3, last registered 00:00:27, no proxy-reply, no map-notify
                        TTL 00:03:00, no merge, hash-function sha1, nonce
                          0x00000000-0x00000000
                        state complete, no security-capability
                        xTR-ID N/A
                        site-ID N/A
          Locator            Local  State       Pri/Wgt  Scope
          2001:192:168:3::3  yes    up            1/100  IPv6 none

    EID-prefix: 2001:172:16:3::/64
      First registered:     6d14h
      Last registered:      00:00:27
      Routing table tag:    0
      Origin:               Configuration
      Merge active:         No
      Proxy reply:          No
      TTL:                  00:03:00
      State:                complete
      Registration errors:
        Authentication failures:   0
        Allowed locators mismatch: 0
      ETR 2001:10:3:10::3, last registered 00:00:38, no proxy-reply, no map-notify
                      TTL 00:03:00, no merge, hash-function sha1, nonce
                        0x00000000-0x00000000
                      state complete, no security-capability
                      xTR-ID N/A
                      site-ID N/A
        Locator            Local  State       Pri/Wgt  Scope
        2001:192:168:3::3  yes    up            1/100  IPv6 none

MS-MR1# show lisp site summary
                    ----------- IPv4 ----------- ----------- IPv6 -----------
Site name           Configured Registered Incons Configured Registered Incons
Site-1-AS-64001              2          2      0          2          2      0
Site-2-AS-64002              2          2      0          2          2      0
Site-3-AS-64003              2          2      0          2          2      0
```

```
Number of configured sites:                    3
Number of registered sites:                    3
Sites with inconsistent registrations:         0
IPv4
  Number of configured EID prefixes:           6
  Number of registered EID prefixes:           6
IPv6
  Number of configured EID prefixes:           6
  Number of registered EID prefixes:           6


!MS/MR2 IOS-XR site registration details

RP/0/0/CPU0:MS-MR2# show lisp site

LISP Site Registration Information
* = Some locators are down or unreachable

Site Name       Last     Up   Who Last          Inst    EID Prefix
                Register      Registered        ID
Site-1-AS-64001 00:00:59 yes  10.1.20.1                 172.16.0.1/32
                00:00:59 yes  10.1.20.1                 172.16.1.0/24
                00:00:01 yes  2001:10:1:20::1           2001:172:16::1/128
                00:00:01 yes  2001:10:1:20::1           2001:172:16:1::/64
Site-2-AS-64002 00:00:41 yes  192.168.2.2               172.16.0.2/32
                00:00:41 yes  192.168.2.2               172.16.2.0/24
                00:00:07 yes  2001:192:168:2::2         2001:172:16::2/128
                00:00:07 yes  2001:192:168:2::2         2001:172:16:2::/64
Site-3-AS-64003 00:00:13 yes  192.168.3.3               172.16.0.3/32
                00:00:13 yes  192.168.3.3               172.16.3.0/24
                00:00:13 yes  2001:10:3:20::3           2001:172:16::3/128
                00:00:13 yes  2001:10:3:20::3           2001:172:16:3::/64


RP/0/0/CPU0:MS-MR2# show lisp site summary

                ----------- IPv4 ----------- ----------- IPv6 -----------
Site name       Configured Registered Incons Configured Registered Incons
Site-1-AS-64001          2          2      0          2          2      0
Site-2-AS-64002          2          2      0          2          2      0
Site-3-AS-64003          2          2      0          2          2      0


Number of configured sites:                    3
Number of registered sites:                    3
```

```
Sites with inconsistent registrations:        0
IPv4
  Number of configured EID prefixes:          6
  Number of registered EID prefixes:          6
IPv6
  Number of configured EID prefixes:          6
  Number of registered EID prefixes:          6
```

In the output in Example 4-10, you can see that the MS/MR1 and MS/MR2 nodes are map servers for both the IPv4 and IPv6 address families. The LISP sites are dual stacked with both IPv4 and IPv6 EID prefixes. The **detail** option provides a lot of details on the registration state in the MS/MR nodes for each site, including whether there were any registration failures due to password mismatch or ETR trying to register and not being listed as one of the allowed locators for the LISP site. In the detailed output of the MS/MR1 node, **allowed configured locators: any** indicates that currently the MS/MR1 is accepting EID prefix registration from any ETR locator address for the site. It is possible to filter which ETR locator address for a specific site can register its attached EID prefix with the MS/MR nodes, adding a second layer of security on top of the required shared key between the ETR and the map server. The configuration command to specify which ETR locator address can register for a particular site on the map server is **allowed-locator** *rloc* under the (config-router-lisp-site)# mode. After specifying the allowed locators, the map server not only checks the shared key in the map register message from the ETR but also makes sure the locator address in the map register message matches the locator list specified for the site.

The MS/MR2 router examples provide a summarized view of map server registration–related state information, such as which ETRs registered which prefixes in each site and some total count statistics for each address family.

In some circumstances, LISP site connectivity might fail. A common reason is control plane packet exchange failures. Statistics on the LISP control plane packet exchange help narrow down the root cause of why the map server, map resolver, or xTR node may not be processing a control plane message or why the LISP control plane packet is having any sort of packet errors. Example 4-11 shows the commands to verify LISP control plane packet exchange statistics.

Example 4-11 *LISP IPv6 Control Plane Packet Statistics*

```
!MS/MR1 IOS-XE node LISP IPv6 control plane packet statistics

MS-MR1# show ipv6 lisp statistics
LISP EID Statistics for instance ID 0 - last cleared: never
Control Packets:
  Map-Requests in/out:                     0/13
    Encapsulated Map-Requests in/out:      0/13
    RLOC-probe Map-Requests in/out:        0/0
    SMR-based Map-Requests in/out:         0/0
    Map-Requests expired on-queue/no-reply 0/0
```

```
        Map-Resolver Map-Requests forwarded:      31
        Map-Server Map-Requests forwarded:        13
      Map-Reply records in/out:                   0/651
        Authoritative records in/out:             0/651
        Non-authoritative records in/out:         0/0
        Negative records in/out:                  0/651
        RLOC-probe records in/out:                0/0
        Map-Server Proxy-Reply records out:       0
      WLC Map-Subscribe records in/out:           2/0
        Map-Subscribe failures in/out:            0/0
      WLC Map-Unsubscribe records in/out:         0/0
        Map-Unsubscribe failures in/out:          0/0
      Map-Register records in/out:                36693/0
        Map-Server AF disabled:                   2
        Authentication failures:                  0
      WLC Map-Register records in/out:            0/0
        WLC AP Map-Register in/out:               0/0
        WLC Client Map-Register in/out:           0/0
        WLC Map-Register failures in/out:         0/0
      Map-Notify records in/out:                  0/17892
        Authentication failures:                  0
      WLC Map-Notify records in/out:              0/0
        WLC AP Map-Notify in/out:                 0/0
        WLC Client Map-Notify in/out:             0/0
        WLC Map-Notify failures in/out:           0/0
      Dropped control packets in input queue:     0
      Deferred packet transmission:               0/0
        DDT referral deferred/dropped:            0/0
        DDT request deferred/dropped:             0/0
        Map-Reply deferred/dropped:               0/0
        MR negative Map-Reply deferred/dropped:   0/0
        MR Map-Request fwd deferred/dropped:      0/0
        MS Map-Request fwd deferred/dropped:      0/0
        MS proxy Map-Reply deferred/dropped:      0/0
        xTR mcast Map-Notify deferred/dropped:    0/0
        MS Info-Reply deferred/dropped:           0/0
        RTR Map-Register fwd deferred/dropped:    0/0
        RTR Map-Notify fwd deferred/dropped:      0/0
        ETR Info-Request deferred/dropped:        0/0
Errors:
      Map-Request invalid source rloc drops:      0
      Map-Register invalid source rloc drops:     0
      DDT ITR Map-Requests dropped:               0 (nonce-collision: 0, bad-xTR-nonce: 0)
```

```
Cache Related:
  Cache entries created/deleted:           0/0
  NSF CEF replay entry count               0
  Number of EID-prefixes in map-cache:     0
  Number of negative entries in map-cache: 0
  Total number of RLOCs in map-cache:      0
  Average RLOCs per EID-prefix:            0
Forwarding:
  Number of data signals processed:        0 (+ dropped 0)
  Number of reachability reports:          0 (+ dropped 0)
LISP RLOC Statistics - last cleared: never
Control Packets:
    RTR Map-Requests forwarded:            0
    RTR Map-Notifies forwarded:            0
  DDT-Map-Requests in/out:                 0/0
  DDT-Map-Referrals in/out:                0/0
Errors:
  Map-Request format errors:               0
  Map-Reply format errors:                 0
  Map-Referral format errors:              0
  Mapping record TTL alerts:               0
  DDT Requests failed:                     0
LISP Miscellaneous Statistics - last cleared: never
Errors:
  Invalid IP version drops:                0
  Invalid IP header drops:                 0
  Invalid IP proto field drops:            0
  Invalid packet size dropss:              0
  Invalid LISP control port drops:         0
  Invalid LISP checksum drops:             0
  Unsupported LISP packet type drops:      0
  Unknown packet drops:                    0


!MS/MR2 IOS-XR LISP IPv6 control plane packets statistics

RP/0/0/CPU0:MS-MR2# show lisp ipv6 statistics

LISP EID Statistics for instance ID 0 - last cleared: never
Control Packets:
  Map-Requests in/out:                     2/0
    Encapsulated Map-Requests in/out:      2/0
    RLOC-probe Map-Requests in/out:        0/0
    SMR-based Map-Requests in/out:         0/0
```

```
      Map-Requests expired on-queue/no-reply  0/0
      Map-Resolver Map-Requests forwarded:    0
      Map-Server Map-Requests forwarded:      0
    Map-Reply records in/out:                 0/2
      Authoritative records in/out:           0/2
      Non-authoritative records in/out:       0/0
      Negative records in/out:                0/2
      RLOC-probe records in/out:              0/0
      Map-Server Proxy-Reply records out:     0
    Map-Register records in/out:              254/0
      Map-Server AF disabled:                 0
      Authentication failures:                0
    Map-Notify records in/out:                0/168
      Authentication failures:                0
    Deferred packet transmission:             0/0
      DDT referral deferred/dropped:          0/0
      DDT request deferred/dropped:           0/0
      Map-Reply deferred/dropped:             0/0
      MR negative Map-Reply deferred/dropped: 0/0
      MR Map-Request fwd deferred/dropped:    0/0
      MS Map-Request fwd deferred/dropped:    0/0
      MS proxy Map-Reply deferred/dropped:    0/0
      xTR mcast Map-Notify deferred/dropped:  0/0
      MS Info-Reply deferred/dropped:         0/0
      RTR Map-Register fwd deferred/dropped:  0/0
      RTR Map-Notify fwd deferred/dropped:    0/0
      ETR Info-Request deferred/dropped:      0/0
Errors:
  Map-Request invalid source rloc drops:      0
  Map-Register invalid source rloc drops:     0
  DDT ITR Map-Requests dropped:               0 (nonce-collision: 0, bad-xTR-nonce: 0)
Cache Related:
  Cache entries created/deleted:              0/0
  NSF CEF replay entry count                  0
  Number of EID-prefixes in map-cache:        0
  Number of negative entries in map-cache:    0
  Total number of RLOCs in map-cache:         0
  Average RLOCs per EID-prefix:               0
Forwarding:
  Number of data signals processed:           0 (+ dropped 0)
  Number of reachability reports:             0 (+ dropped 0)
```

```
LISP RLOC Statistics - last cleared: never
Control Packets:
    RTR Map-Requests forwarded:          0
    RTR Map-Notifies forwarded:          0
  DDT-Map-Requests in/out:               0/0
  DDT-Map-Referrals in/out:              0/0
Errors:
  Map-Request format errors:             0
  Map-Reply format errors:               0
  Map-Referral format errors:            0
  Mapping record TTL alerts:             0
  DDT Requests failed:                   0
LISP Miscellaneous Statistics - last cleared: never
Errors:
  Invalid IP version drops:              0
  Invalid IP header drops:               0
  Invalid IP proto field drops:          0
  Invalid packet size dropss:            0
  Invalid LISP control port drops:       0
  Invalid LISP checksum drops:           0
  Unsupported LISP packet type drops:    0
  Unknown packet drops:                  0
```

A similar set of commands can be applied both to the xTR and PxTR nodes to confirm the LISP control plane operation. For example, Example 4-12 shows XTR3 and PxTR3 output to give you an idea of what types of information can be extracted. For brevity, this example does not show output from every xTR and PxTR; however, the commands across the platforms are similar, and Chapter 3 shows examples across all platforms for similar verification steps.

Example 4-12 *XTR3 LISP Control Plane Verification*

```
!XTR3 NX-OS LISP control plane verification.

XTR3# show ipv6 lisp
LISP IPv6 Configuration Information for VRF "default" (iid 0)
  Ingress Tunnel Router (ITR):     enabled
  Egress Tunnel Router (ETR):      enabled
  Proxy-ITR Router (PTR):          disabled
  Proxy-ETR Router (PETR):         disabled
  Map Resolver (MR):               disabled
  Map Server (MS):                 disabled
  LISP Multicast:                  disabled
    GLT interface:                 glt1
```

```
    LISP control-plane security:    disabled
    Locator VRF:                    default
    Encap-Map-Request source:       2001:192:168:3::3
    LISP-NAT Interworking:          disabled
    Use locators from BGP RIB:      disabled
    ITR send Map-Request:           enabled
    ITR send Data-Probe:            disabled
    LISP ALT-VRF:                   not configured
    LISP-DDT:                       disabled
    ITR Map-Resolver:               2001:192:168:100::100, last used: 00:13:59
    ITR Map-Resolver:               2001:192:168:200::200, last used: 00:13:59
    ETR Map-Server(s):              2001:192:168:100::100, 2001:192:168:200::200
    Last Map-Register sent to MS:   00:00:41
    ETR merge-registrations:        disabled
    ETR glean mapping:              disabled, verify disabled
    ETR accept mapping data:        disabled, verify disabled
    ETR map-cache TTL:              24 hours
    ETR map-register TTL:           3 minutes
    Shortest EID-prefix allowed:    /48
    Use Proxy-ETRs:
       2001:192:168:13::13, priority: 50, weight: 50
       2001:192:168:12::12, priority: 50, weight: 50
       2001:192:168:11::11, priority: 50, weight: 50
    Locator Reachability Algorithms:
       Echo-nonce algorithm:        disabled
       TCP-counts algorithm:        disabled
       RLOC-probe algorithm:        disabled
    Static mappings configured:     0
    Map-cache limit:                18000
    Reserve-list:                   not configured
    Map-cache size:                 6
    ETR Database, global LSBs: 0x00000001:
       EID-prefix: 2001:172:16::3/128, instance-id: 0, LSBs: 0x00000001
          Locator: 2001:192:168:3::3, priority: 1, weight: 100
                Uptime: 6d17h, state: up, local
       EID-prefix: 2001:172:16:3::/64, instance-id: 0, LSBs: 0x00000001
          Locator: 2001:192:168:3::3, priority: 1, weight: 100
                Uptime: 6d19h, state: up, local

XTR3# show lisp proxy-itr
Discovered Proxy-ITRs (PITRs) in VRF "default"
  2001:192:168:12::12  2001:192:168:13::13  2001:192:168:11::11  2001:10:4:10::4

XTR3# show ipv6 lisp statistics
LISP Statistics for VRF "default" - last cleared: never
```

```
Data Forwarding:
  IPv6-in-IPv4 encap/decap packets:      0/0
  IPv6-in-IPv6 encap/decap packets:      57/0
  Translated packets in/out:             0/0
  Map-cache lookup succeeded/failed:     57/11
  LISP-ALT lookup succeeded/failed:      0/0
  Loc-reach-bit changes local/remote:    0/0
Control Packets:
  Data-Probes in/out:                    0/0
  Map-Requests in/out:                   9122/1148
    Encapsulated Map-Requests in/out:    9/1148
    RLOC-probe Map-Requests in/out:      9113/0
    SMR-based Map-Requests in/out:       0/0
  Map-Replies in/out:                    1131/9122
    Security header included in/out:     0/0
    Authoritative in/out:                1131/9122
    Non-authoritative in/out:            0/0
    Negative Map-Replies in/out:         1127/0
    RLOC-probe Map-Replies in/out:       0/9113
  Map-Registers in/out:                  0/19148
    Authentication failures:             0
  Map-Notifies in/out:                   0/0
    Authentication failures:             0
  Map-Notify-Acks in/out:                0/0
  Map-Referrals in/out:                  0/0
  EID Map-Registers in/out:              0/0
  EID Map-Notifies in/out:               0/0
  EID Map-Notify-Acks in/out:            0/0
Errors:
  Encapsulations failed:                 11
  Map-Request format errors:             0
  Map-Reply format errors:               0
  Map-Reply spoof alerts:                0
  Map-Reply signature failed:            0
  Map-cache recursive-loop occurrences:  0
  Map-Register UDP length too small:     0
Cache Related:
  Cache entries created/timed-out:       976/968
  Number of EID-prefixes in map-cache:   3
  Number of negative map-cache entries:  0
  Number of translation cache entries:   0
  Total number of RLOCs in map-cache:    5
  Number of best-priority RLOCs:         5
  Average RLOCs per EID-prefix:          1
```

> **Note**   The command **show ipv6 lisp statistics** is also very useful for viewing counters
> related to failure in the data plane seen from cache- and forwarding-related counter values.

The output from XTR3 in Example 4-12 shows the following.

- Whether the node was configured as an ITR or ETR

- Which map servers, map resolvers, and PETRs are configured, whether they are
  reachable, and when the last communication occurred

- The locally attached EID prefix entries for the ETR

- Time-to-live (TTL) values for cached entries and entry limits

- The ETR map register time, which in this case is 3 minutes, which means the ETR
  will register its EID prefixes every 3 minutes

- The PITRs that the node discovered

- LISP control plane and data plane packet statistics

Example 4-13 shows the PxTR3 control plane verification commands. This example
shows information about PxTR3 as a PxTR device.

Example 4-13   *PxTR3 Control Plane Verification*

```
!PxTR3 NX-OS control plane verification

PxTR3# show ipv6 lisp
LISP IPv6 Configuration Information for VRF "default" (iid 0)
  Ingress Tunnel Router (ITR):    disabled
  Egress Tunnel Router (ETR):     disabled
  Proxy-ITR Router (PTR):         enabled
  PTR local locator:              2001:192:168:13::13
  Proxy-ETR Router (PETR):        enabled
  Map Resolver (MR):              disabled
  Map Server (MS):                disabled
  LISP Multicast:                 disabled
    GLT interface:                glt1
  LISP control-plane security:    disabled
  Locator VRF:                    default
  LISP-NAT Interworking:          disabled
  Use locators from BGP RIB:      disabled
  ITR send Map-Request:           enabled
  ITR send Data-Probe:            disabled
  LISP ALT-VRF:                   not configured
  LISP-DDT:                       disabled
  ITR Map-Resolver:               2001:192:168:100::100, last used: 08:21:00
```

```
ITR Map-Resolver:              2001:192:168:200::200, last used: 08:21:18
ETR merge-registrations:       disabled
ETR glean mapping:             disabled, verify disabled
ETR accept mapping data:       disabled, verify disabled
ETR map-cache TTL:             24 hours
ETR map-register TTL:          3 minutes
Shortest EID-prefix allowed:   /48
Locator Reachability Algorithms:
  Echo-nonce algorithm:        disabled
  TCP-counts algorithm:        disabled
  RLOC-probe algorithm:        enabled
Static mappings configured:    1
Map-cache limit:               18000
Reserve-list:                  not configured
Map-cache size:                4


PxTR3# show ipv6 lisp statistics
LISP Statistics for VRF "default" - last cleared: never
Data Forwarding:
  IPv6-in-IPv4 encap/decap packets:   0/0
  IPv6-in-IPv6 encap/decap packets:   18/0
  Translated packets in/out:          0/0
  Map-cache lookup succeeded/failed:  24/0
  LISP-ALT lookup succeeded/failed:   0/0
  Loc-reach-bit changes local/remote: 0/0
Control Packets:
  Data-Probes in/out:                 0/0
  Map-Requests in/out:                0/17
    Encapsulated Map-Requests in/out: 0/6
    RLOC-probe Map-Requests in/out:   0/11
    SMR-based Map-Requests in/out:    0/0
  Map-Replies in/out:                 17/0
    Security header included in/out:  0/0
    Authoritative in/out:             17/0
    Non-authoritative in/out:         0/0
    Negative Map-Replies in/out:      0/0
    RLOC-probe Map-Replies in/out:    11/0
  Map-Registers in/out:               0/0
    Authentication failures:          0
  Map-Notifies in/out:                0/0
    Authentication failures:          0
  Map-Notify-Acks in/out:             0/0
  Map-Referrals in/out:               0/0
  EID Map-Registers in/out:           0/0
```

```
  EID Map-Notifies in/out:           0/0
  EID Map-Notify-Acks in/out:        0/0
Errors:
  Encapsulations failed:             6
  Map-Request format errors:         0
  Map-Reply format errors:           0
  Map-Reply spoof alerts:            0
  Map-Reply signature failed:        0
  Map-cache recursive-loop occurrences: 0
  Map-Register UDP length too small:  0
Cache Related:
  Cache entries created/timed-out:    7/3
  Number of EID-prefixes in map-cache:  4
  Number of negative map-cache entries: 1
  Number of translation cache entries:  0
  Total number of RLOCs in map-cache:   4
  Number of best-priority RLOCs:        4
  Average RLOCs per EID-prefix:         1
```

Finally, a variety of debugging commands can be used to do more active troubleshooting and view real-time LISP packet transactions. Of course, you must always use **debug** commands with caution in a production environment. A few best practices can help you avoid a lot of unnecessary problems and provide the required logs to get to root cause for any issue—for example, disabling logging on the console for the **debug** commands and allocating buffer space in memory to store the debug outputs to view with the **show logging** command.

Example 4-14 shows the registration process using **debug** commands between XTR3 and one of the map servers, MS/MR2.

Example 4-14 *XTR3 Map-Register Messages to Map Server MS/MR2*

```
!XTR3 NX-OS map-register messages to map servers.
!Only showing IPv6 register messages


XTR3# debug lisp mapping register
<SNIP>
2018 Sep  4 20:28:49.475775 lisp: <default> Build IPv6 Map-Register
2018 Sep  4 20:28:49.475827 lisp: <default> Mapping record for EID
  2001:172:16::3/128 (iid 0), ttl: 3, locator count: 1, a-bit: 1, send_withdraw:
  FALSE
2018 Sep  4 20:28:49.475869 lisp: <default>   Locator: 2001:192:168:3::3, geo: none,
  upriority/uweight: 1/100, mpriority/mweight: 255/0, loc-bits: LpR
2018 Sep  4 20:28:49.475909 lisp: <default> Mapping record for EID
  2001:172:16:3::/64 (iid 0), ttl: 3, locator count: 1, a-bit: 1, send_withdraw:
  FALSE
```

```
2018 Sep  4 20:28:49.475955 lisp: <default>   Locator: 2001:192:168:3::3, geo: none,
  upriority/uweight: 1/100, mpriority/mweight: 255/0, loc-bits: LpR
2018 Sep  4 20:28:49.476757 lisp: <default> Send IPv6 Map-Register to Map-Server
  2001:192:168:100::100 using sha1
2018 Sep  4 20:28:49.476821 lisp: <default> Build IPv6 Map-Register
2018 Sep  4 20:28:49.477200 lisp: <default> Mapping record for EID
  2001:172:16::3/128 (iid 0), ttl: 3, locator count: 1, a-bit: 1, send_withdraw:
  FALSE
2018 Sep  4 20:28:49.477247 lisp: <default>   Locator: 2001:192:168:3::3, geo: none,
  upriority/uweight: 1/100, mpriority/mweight: 255/0, loc-bits: LpR
2018 Sep  4 20:28:49.477287 lisp: <default> Mapping record for EID
  2001:172:16:3::/64 (iid 0), ttl: 3, locator count: 1, a-bit: 1, send_withdraw:
  FALSE
2018 Sep  4 20:28:49.477326 lisp: <default>   Locator: 2001:192:168:3::3, geo: none,
  upriority/uweight: 1/100, mpriority/mweight: 255/0, loc-bits: LpR
2018 Sep  4 20:28:49.478133 lisp: <default> Send IPv6 Map-Register to Map-Server
  2001:192:168:200::200 using sha1


!MS/MR2 IOS-XR map-register messages
!Only showing outputs for LISP Site 3 IPv6 EID prefix registration from XTR3.


RP/0/0/CPU0:MS-MR2# debug lisp control-plane map-server-registration
<SNIP>
RP/0/0/CPU0:Sep  4 20:23:31.732 : lisp[1043]:  LISP: Processing received
  Map-Register(3) message on if:0x0 from 2001:10:3:20::3.65520 to
  2001:192:168:200::200.4342
RP/0/0/CPU0:Sep  4 20:23:31.732 : lisp[1043]:  LISP: Processing Map-Register no
  proxy, no map-notify, no merge, no security, no mobile-node, not to-RTR, fast-
  map-register, no EID-notify, no ID-included, 2 records, nonce
  0x00000000-0x00000000, key-id 1, auth-data-len 20, hash-function sha1
RP/0/0/CPU0:Sep  4 20:23:31.732 : lisp[1043]:  LISP: Processing Map-Register mapping
  record for IID 0 2001:172:16::3/128, ttl 3, action none, authoritative,
  1 locator .  2001:192:168:3::3 pri/wei=1/100 LpR
RP/0/0/CPU0:Sep  4 20:23:31.732 : lisp[1043]:  LISP-0: MS registration IID 0 prefix
  2001:172:16::3/128 2001:10:3:20::3 site Site-3-AS-64003, Updating.
RP/0/0/CPU0:Sep  4 20:23:31.732 : lisp[1043]:  LISP: Processing Map-Register mapping
  record for IID 0 2001:172:16:3::/64, ttl 3, action none, authoritative,
  1 locator .  2001:192:168:3::3 pri/wei=1/100 LpR
RP/0/0/CPU0:Sep  4 20:23:31.732 : lisp[1043]:  LISP-0: MS registration IID 0 prefix
  2001:172:16:3::/64 2001:10:3:20::3 site Site-3-AS-64003, Updating.
```

Debug output may seem a bit cryptic, but if you follow the highlighted text in Example 4-14, you will understand that the XTR3 with RLOC address 2001:192:168:3::3 registered two IPv6 prefixes with the map server MS/MR2, which has the locator address 2001:192:168:200::200. The two prefixes registered with the map server are 2001:172:16::3/128 and 2001:172:16:3::/64, and they are part of a LISP site named Site-3-AS-64003. The default frequency of registration is every 3 minutes, as explained earlier, with the ETR map register TTL value in the **show ipv6 lisp** output in Example 4-12.

Note   As of IOS-XE release 16.10.1, a user can enter the **debug lisp filter** command up to four times. The **debug lisp filter** command provides a mechanism to reduce the debugging output displayed on the terminal by matching only the parameters of interest, such as the specific EID, RLOC, or LISP instance identifier (IID). Refer to the IOS-XE LISP command reference guide, available on cisco.com, for further details.

LISP IPv6 Unicast Routing Data Plane Verification

LISP packet encapsulation from any LISP site starts at the xTR device. Traffic must be sourced from a node present inside the EID prefix of an xTR device. In Example 4-15, CE1 present in LISP Site 1 pings three destinations: The first one is the CE2 router in LISP Site 2, the second is CE3 in LISP Site 3, and the last is the IGW router that is part of the non-LISP site network.

Example 4-15   *LISP Site 1 Communication to LISP Site 2, LISP Site 3, and the Non-LISP Site*

```
!pinging CE2 in LISP site 2
CE1# ping ipv6 2001:172:16::2 source loopback 0
Type escape sequence to abort.
Sending 5, 100-byte ICMP Echos to 2001:172:16::2, timeout is 2 seconds:
Packet sent with a source address of 2001:172:16::1
!!!!!
Success rate is 100 percent (5/5), round-trip min/avg/max = 9/13/27 ms


!pinging CE3 in LISP site 3
CE1# ping ipv6 2001:172:16::3 source loopback 0
Type escape sequence to abort.
Sending 5, 100-byte ICMP Echos to 2001:172:16::3, timeout is 2 seconds:
Packet sent with a source address of 2001:172:16::1
!!!!!
Success rate is 100 percent (5/5), round-trip min/avg/max = 5/7/10 ms


!pinging IGW router in Non-LISP site
CE1# ping ipv6 2001:192:168:30::30 source loopback 0
Type escape sequence to abort.
Sending 5, 100-byte ICMP Echos to 2001:192:168:30::30, timeout is 2 seconds:
Packet sent with a source address of 2001:172:16::1
!!!!!
Success rate is 100 percent (5/5), round-trip min/avg/max = 8/8/11 ms
```

The xTR node caches the remote LISP site destination EID entries resolved through the mapping system, and entries for any other destination without a match in the map cache are sent to the configured PETRs, as shown in Example 4-16. Certain platforms display the map cache slightly differently, particularly for entries such as the default entry or the ones created to convey the ranges of EID prefixes that are sent to the PETR node.

Example 4-16 *xTR Node LISP IPv6 Map Caches*

```
!XTR1 IOS-XE node IPv6 LISP map cache


XTR1# show ipv6 lisp map-cache
LISP IPv6 Mapping Cache for EID-table default (IID 0), 4 entries

::/0, uptime: 1w0d, expires: never, via static-send-map-request
  Negative cache entry, action: send-map-request
2001:172:16::2/128, uptime: 09:30:13, expires: 14:29:46, via map-reply, complete
  Locator           Uptime    State     Pri/Wgt    Encap-IID
  2001:192:168:2::2  09:30:13  up           1/100        -
2001:172:16::3/128, uptime: 09:30:03, expires: 14:29:56, via map-reply, complete
  Locator           Uptime    State     Pri/Wgt    Encap-IID
  2001:192:168:3::3  09:30:03  up           1/100        -
2001:180::/25, uptime: 00:16:38, expires: 00:13:13, via map-reply, forward-native
  Encapsulating to proxy ETR


!XTR2 IOS-XR node LISP IPv6 map cache


RP/0/0/CPU0:XTR2# show lisp ipv6 map-cache


LISP IPv6 Mapping Cache for EID-table default (IID 0), 4 entries

::/0, uptime: 1w0d, expires: never, via static send map-request
  Negative cache entry, action: send-map-request
2001:172:16::1/128, uptime: 09:22:34, expires: 15:25:36, via map-reply, complete
  Locator           Uptime    State     Pri/Wgt
  2001:192:168:1::1  09:22:34  up           1/100
2001:172:16::3/128, uptime: 09:18:25, expires: 15:29:24, via map-reply, complete
  Locator           Uptime    State     Pri/Wgt
  2001:192:168:3::3  09:18:25  up           1/100
2001:180::/25, uptime: 00:00:17, expires: 00:14:44, via map-reply, forward-native
  Encapsulating to proxy ETR


!XTR3 NX-OS node LISP IPv6 map cache


XTR3# show ipv6 lisp map-cache
LISP IPv6 Mapping Cache for VRF "default" (iid 0), 7 entries
```

```
0::/3, uptime: 6d23h, expires: 00:08:07, via petr, auth
  Locator            Uptime    State    Priority/  Data      Control     MTU
                                        Weight     in/out    in/out
  2001:192:168:13::13  6d23h    up        50/50     0/0       4/4        1500
  2001:192:168:12::12  6d23h    up        50/50     0/0       0/9412
  1500
  2001:192:168:11::11  6d23h    up        50/50     0/0       0/0        1500


2001:172:16::1/128, uptime: 09:23:01, expires: 14:36:58, via map-reply, auth
  Locator            Uptime    State    Priority/  Data      Control     MTU
                                        Weight     in/out    in/out
  2001:192:168:1::1  09:23:01  up        1/100     0/18      1/1        1500


2001:172:16::2/128, uptime: 09:19:00, expires: 14:40:59, via map-reply, auth
  Locator            Uptime    State    Priority/  Data      Control     MTU
                                        Weight     in/out    in/out
  2001:192:168:2::2  09:19:00  up        1/100     0/23      1/0        1500


2001:180::/25, uptime: 00:08:18, expires: 00:06:41, via petr, auth
  Locator            Uptime    State    Priority/  Data      Control     MTU
                                        Weight     in/out    in/out
  2001:192:168:13::13  00:08:18  up        50/50     0/9       0/0        1500
  2001:192:168:12::12  00:08:18  up        50/50     0/0       0/0        1500
  2001:192:168:11::11  00:08:18  up        50/50     0/0       0/0        1500


2002::/15, uptime: 00:06:52, expires: 00:08:07, via petr, auth
  Locator            Uptime    State    Priority/  Data      Control     MTU
                                        Weight     in/out    in/out
  2001:192:168:13::13  00:06:52  up        50/50     0/0       0/0        1500
  2001:192:168:12::12  00:06:52  up        50/50     0/0       0/0        1500
  2001:192:168:11::11  00:06:52  up        50/50     0/0       0/0        1500


2400::/6, uptime: 00:06:52, expires: 00:08:07, via petr, auth
  Locator            Uptime    State    Priority/  Data      Control     MTU
                                        Weight     in/out    in/out
  2001:192:168:13::13  00:06:52  up        50/50     0/0       0/0        1500
  2001:192:168:12::12  00:06:52  up        50/50     0/0       0/0        1500
  2001:192:168:11::11  00:06:52  up        50/50     0/0       0/0        1500


8000::/1, uptime: 00:06:52, expires: 00:08:07, via petr, auth
  Locator            Uptime    State    Priority/  Data      Control     MTU
                                        Weight     in/out    in/out
  2001:192:168:13::13  00:06:52  up        50/50     0/0       0/0        1500
  2001:192:168:12::12  00:06:52  up        50/50     0/0       0/0        1500
  2001:192:168:11::11  00:06:52  up        50/50     0/0       0/0        1500
```

Let's look at bit more closely at LISP packet forwarding. In topologies where there are multiple equal-cost multipath (ECMP) paths between XTR devices in the underlay, it may be useful to confirm the outbound interface in certain failure scenarios. Most Cisco platforms perform a hash operation of some sort with various IP packet header fields to select outbound interfaces. Example 4-17 shows output for XTR1, with the outbound interface chosen for LISP packet forwarding for entries in the map cache.

Example 4-17 *XTR1 Node LISP IPv6 Unicast Forwarding*

```
!XTR1 IOS-XE node IPv6 unicast forwarding

XTR1# show ipv6 lisp forwarding eid remote detail
Prefix               Fwd action  Locator status bits   encap_iid
::/0                 signal      0x00000000            N/A
  packets/bytes      9/1026
  path list 7F3272EE6460, 3 locks, per-destination, flags 0x49 [shble, rif, hwcn]
    ifnums:
      LISP0(13)
    1 path
      path 7F3295772D10, share 1/1, type attached prefix, for IPv6
        attached to LISP0, glean for LISP0
    1 output chain
      chain[0]: glean for LISP0
2001:172:16::2/128     encap      0x00000001            N/A
  packets/bytes      14/1596
  path list 7F3272EE5EC0, 3 locks, per-destination, flags 0x49 [shble, rif, hwcn]
    ifnums:
      LISP0(13): 2001:192:168:2::2
    1 path
      path 7F3295772580, share 100/100, type attached nexthop, for IPv6
        nexthop 2001:192:168:2::2 LISP0, IPV6 midchain out of LISP0, addr
          2001:192:168:2::2 7F3291170078
Prefix               Fwd action  Locator status bits   encap_iid
    1 output chain
      chain[0]: IPV6 midchain out of LISP0, addr 2001:192:168:2::2 7F3291170078
                IPV6 adj out of GigabitEthernet3, addr FE80::F816:3EFF:FE55:E584
                  7F3291170648
2001:172:16::3/128     encap      0x00000001            N/A
  packets/bytes      24/2736
  path list 7F3272EE6320, 3 locks, per-destination, flags 0x49 [shble, rif, hwcn]
    ifnums:
      LISP0(13): 2001:192:168:3::3
    1 path
      path 7F3295772BB0, share 100/100, type attached nexthop, for IPv6
        nexthop 2001:192:168:3::3 LISP0, IPV6 midchain out of LISP0, addr
          2001:192:168:3::3 7F329116FE88
```

```
    1 output chain
      chain[0]: IPV6 midchain out of LISP0, addr 2001:192:168:3::3 7F329116FE88
               IPV6 adj out of GigabitEthernet3, addr FE80::F816:3EFF:FE55:E584
               7F3291170648
2001:180::/25            fwd native  0x00000000           N/A
  packets/bytes          9/1026
  path list 7F3272EE61E0, 3 locks, per-destination, flags 0x49 [shble, rif, hwcn]
Prefix                Fwd action  Locator status bits   encap_iid
    ifnums:
      LISP0(13): 2001:192:168:11::11, 2001:192:168:12::12, 2001:192:168:13::13
    3 paths
      path 7F3295772A50, share 1/1, type attached nexthop, for IPv6
        nexthop 2001:192:168:11::11 LISP0, IPV6 midchain out of LISP0, addr
          2001:192:168:11::11 7F329E1CB778
      path 7F3295772840, share 1/1, type attached nexthop, for IPv6
        nexthop 2001:192:168:12::12 LISP0, IPV6 midchain out of LISP0, addr
          2001:192:168:12::12 7F329E1CB588
      path 7F32957728F0, share 1/1, type attached nexthop, for IPv6
        nexthop 2001:192:168:13::13 LISP0, IPV6 midchain out of LISP0, addr
          2001:192:168:13::13 7F329E1CB398
    1 output chain
      chain[0]: loadinfo 80007F329D346AA0, per-session, 3 choices, flags 0005,
        5 locks
                 flags [Per-session, for-rx-IPv6]
                 15 hash buckets
          < 0 > IPV6 midchain out of LISP0, addr 2001:192:168:11::11
                  7F329E1CB778
                IPV6 adj out of GigabitEthernet3, addr FE80::F816:
                  3EFF:FE55:E584 7F3291170648
          < 1 > IPV6 midchain out of LISP0, addr 2001:192:168:12::12
                  7F329E1CB588
Prefix                Fwd action  Locator status bits   encap_iid
                IPV6 adj out of GigabitEthernet3, addr
                  FE80::F816:3EFF:FE55:E584 7F3291170648
          < 2 > IPV6 midchain out of LISP0, addr 2001:192:168:13::13
                  7F329E1CB398
                IPV6 adj out of GigabitEthernet3, addr FE80::F816:
                  3EFF:FE55:E584 7F3291170648
          < 3 > IPV6 midchain out of LISP0, addr 2001:192:168:11::11
                  7F329E1CB778
                IPV6 adj out of GigabitEthernet3, addr
<SNIP>
```

The packet capture in Figure 4-9 shows the echo request packet sent from CE1 in LISP
Site 1 to CE2 in LISP Site 2.

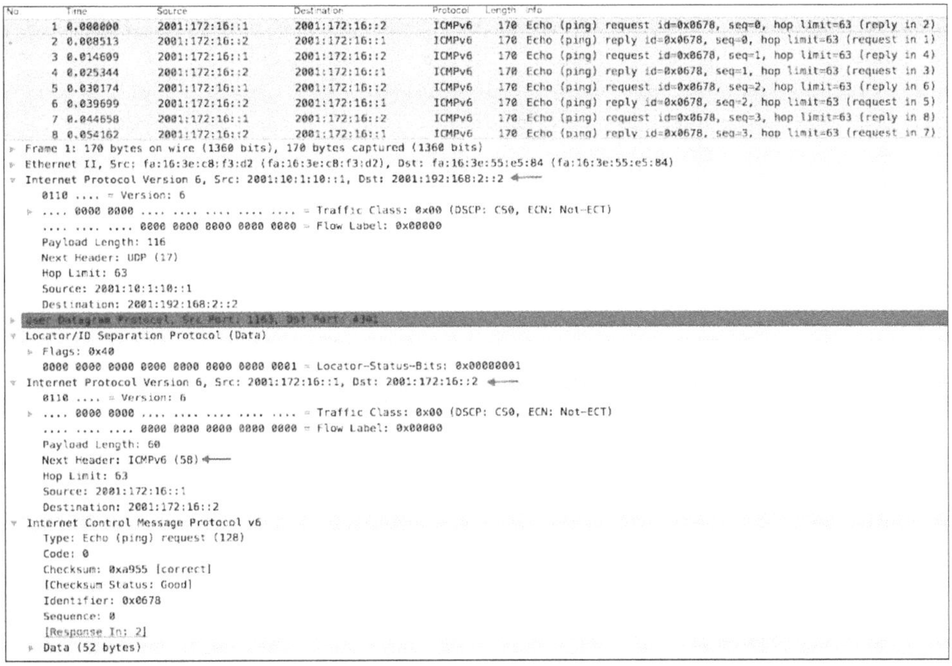

Figure 4-9 *CE1 to CE2 IPv6 LISP Data Packet Capture*

The packet capture in Figure 4-9 clearly shows two IPv6 headers; the outer header (RLOC address space) has as a destination the XTR2 RLOC address of 2001:192:168:2::2, to which CE2 is attached. The inner IPv6 header (EID address space) has the EID source and destination addresses 2001:172:16::1 and 2001:172:16::2, respectively. The inner IPv6 header also has the Next Header field encoded as ICMPv6. UDP destination port 4341 is the reserved port for LISP data plane traffic.

Let's move on to verifying the LISP IPv6 unicast forwarding data plane state on the PxTR nodes. Example 4-18 shows the map cache entries on all the PxTR nodes, one by one.

Example 4-18 *PxTR Node LISP IPv6 Unicast Map Cache Entries*

```
!PxTR1 IOS-XE LISP IPv6 unicast map cache entries

PxTR1# show ipv6 lisp map-cache
LISP IPv6 Mapping Cache for EID-table default (IID 0), 4 entries

2001:172:16::/64, uptime: 1w0d, expires: never, via static-send-map-request
  Negative cache entry, action: send-map-request
2001:172:16::1/128, uptime: 10:32:40, expires: 23:45:02, via map-reply, complete
  Locator          Uptime     State     Pri/Wgt     Encap-IID
  2001:192:168:1::1  10:32:40  up         1/100        -
```

```
2001:172:16::2/128, uptime: 10:32:13, expires: 23:46:38, via map-reply, complete
  Locator          Uptime    State     Pri/Wgt      Encap-IID
  2001:192:168:2::2  10:32:13  up          1/100      -
2001:172:16::3/128, uptime: 10:31:50, expires: 23:40:53, via map-reply, complete
  Locator          Uptime    State     Pri/Wgt      Encap-IID
  2001:192:168:3::3  10:31:50  up          1/100      -


!PxTR2 IOS-XR LISP IPv6 unicast map cache entries
RP/0/0/CPU0:PxTR2# show lisp ipv6 map-cache


LISP IPv6 Mapping Cache for EID-table default (IID 0), 4 entries

2001:172:16::/64, uptime: 1w0d, expires: never, via static send map-request
  Negative cache entry, action: send-map-request
2001:172:16::1/128, uptime: 1w0d, expires: 23:59:41, via map-reply, complete
  Locator          Uptime    State     Pri/Wgt
  2001:192:168:1::1  1w0d       up          1/100
2001:172:16::2/128, uptime: 1w0d, expires: 23:59:12, via map-reply, complete
  Locator          Uptime    State     Pri/Wgt
  2001:192:168:2::2  1w0d       up          1/100
2001:172:16::3/128, uptime: 1w0d, expires: 23:59:17, via map-reply, complete
  Locator          Uptime    State     Pri/Wgt
  2001:192:168:3::3  1w0d       up          1/100


!PxTR3 NX-OS LISP IPv6 unicast map cache entries

PxTR3# show ipv6 lisp map-cache
LISP IPv6 Mapping Cache for VRF "default" (iid 0), 4 entries

2001:172:16::/64, uptime: 1w0d, expires: 0.000000, via static
  Negative cache entry, action: send-map-request

2001:172:16::1/128, uptime: 10:34:07, expires: 23:16:04, via map-reply, auth
  Locator          Uptime    State     Priority/  Data     Control    MTU
                                       Weight     in/out   in/out
  2001:192:168:1::1  10:34:07  up          1/100    0/10     0/6       1500

2001:172:16::2/128, uptime: 10:33:36, expires: 22:48:24, via map-reply, auth
  Locator          Uptime    State     Priority/  Data     Control    MTU
                                       Weight     in/out   in/out
  2001:192:168:2::2  10:33:36  up          1/100    0/6      4/3       1500

2001:172:16::3/128, uptime: 10:33:18, expires: 22:41:17, via map-reply, auth
  Locator          Uptime    State     Priority/  Data     Control    MTU
                                       Weight     in/out   in/out
  2001:192:168:3::3  10:33:18  up          1/100    0/5      0/4       1500
```

The static entries shown in Example 4-18 define the LISP EID space for which local PITR is proxying. Notice that the action is send-map-request. This entry defines the EID prefix range for which the PITR will map request messages to populate its local map cache when receiving traffic from a non-LISP site to the LISP site it is proxying for.

As CE1 sends the packet to a non-LISP site, it must go through one of the PxTRs. On XTR1, LISP encapsulates the Internet Control Message Protocol (ICMP) packet received from CE1 destined to the non-LISP site IGW router to PxTR1, as shown in the packet capture in Figure 4-10.

```
Frame 2: 170 bytes on wire (1360 bits), 170 bytes captured (1360 bits)
Ethernet II, Src: fa:16:3e:61:8e:05 (fa:16:3e:61:8e:05), Dst: fa:16:3e:39:1d:5f (fa:16:3e:39:1d:5f)
Internet Protocol Version 6, Src: 2001:10:1:10::1, Dst: 2001:192:168:11::11
    0110 .... = Version: 6
    .... 0000 0000 .... .... .... .... .... = Traffic Class: 0x00 (DSCP: CS0, ECN: Not-ECT)
    .... .... .... 0000 0000 0000 0000 0000 = Flow Label: 0x00000
    Payload Length: 116
    Next Header: UDP (17)
    Hop Limit: 62
    Source: 2001:10:1:10::1
    Destination: 2001:192:168:11::11
User Datagram Protocol, Src Port: 1312, Dst Port: 4341
Locator/ID Separation Protocol (Data)
Internet Protocol Version 6, Src: 2001:172:16::1, Dst: 2001:192:168:30::30
    0110 .... = Version: 6
    .... 0000 0000 .... .... .... .... .... = Traffic Class: 0x00 (DSCP: CS0, ECN: Not-ECT)
    .... .... .... 0000 0000 0000 0000 0000 = Flow Label: 0x00000
    Payload Length: 60
    Next Header: ICMPv6 (58)
    Hop Limit: 63
    Source: 2001:172:16::1
    Destination: 2001:192:168:30::30
Internet Control Message Protocol v6
```

Figure 4-10 *CE1 to IGW IPv6 LISP Data Packet Capture*

Summary

From its inception, LISP has been designed as a protocol that can be introduced in a network in phases to minimize downtime. LISP can natively interoperate with IPv4 networks and smoothly transition to IPv6 because it can support multiple address families, both in the underlay and in the overlay.

The fundamental concepts, operation, and configuration of LISP IPv6 unicast routing are like those of LISP IPv4 unicast routing, explored in Chapter 3. The verification steps and commands use similar approaches and commands on the various platforms.

References

Cisco, "Software Defined Access 1.0" white paper, http://www.cisco.com

Cisco, "Cisco Nexus 7000 LISP Configuration Guide," http://www.cisco.com

Cisco, "Cisco IOS-XR LISP Configuration Guide," http://www.cisco.com

Cisco, "Cisco IOS LISP Configuration Guide," http://www.cisco.com

Cisco, "Cisco IOS-XE LISP Configuration Guide," http://www.cisco.com

Cisco, "Enterprise IPv6 Transition Strategy Using the Locator/ID Separation Protocol" white paper, http://www.cisco.com

## Chapter 5

LISP Multicast Routing Fundamentals

In an enterprise or data center network environment, it is very common to have applications with multidestination traffic—that is, traffic destined to multiple end users/receivers, which might be geographically dispersed. Most of these multi-destination applications use multicast, and thus it is vital that the infrastructure be capable of carrying multicast. LISP infrastructure also provides support for multicast traffic, but there is a difference between how LISP handles unicast packets and how it handles multicast packets.

This chapter covers the following topics:

- LISP multicast routing concepts

- LISP multicast routing configuration and verification

- Troubleshooting LISP multicast

LISP Multicast Routing Concepts

Unicast and multicast routing work on different LISP semantics. For unicast packets, LISP semantics require mapping of both source and destination addresses, whereas for multicast, LISP semantics only require the mapping of the source addresses. This means that the source addresses are more topologically significant than the group addresses. RFC 6831 describes the LISP support for multicast environments and explains the different replication methods available for multicast.

LISP multicast supports various replication methods. But before we discuss replication, it's important to go over some basic terminology:

- **Source endpoint identifier (S-EID):** The S-EID is the source host.

- **Receiver endpoint identifier (R-EID):** The R-EID is the receiver host.

- **Rendezvous point endpoint identifier (RP-EID):** The RP-EID is the host/node where the RP resides.

- **Source routing locator (S-RLOC):** The S-RLOC is the ingress tunnel router (ITR) on a multicast tree.

- **Receiver routing locator (R-RLOC):** The R-RLOC is the RLOC for the receiver host.

- **Rendezvous point routing locator (RP-RLOC):** The RP-RLOC is the RLOC for the RP.

For LISP multicast, the group addresses have neither ID nor location semantics. Thus, the group for example named G is topologically opaque and can be used everywhere.

A LISP-enabled network uses two replication methods for delivering multicast packets across the network:

- Unicast head-end replication

- Native multicast replication

Unicast head-end replication is also known as the unicast tunneling method. In this method, the replication of multicast traffic happens at the root site, which makes it possible to carry multicast traffic over a network that does not support native multicast. The multicast packets are forwarded as LISP unicast packets to the remote sites. Unicast replication for an (S-EID, G) flow requires the downstream LISP tunnel router (xTR) to tunnel join/prune messages to the upstream xTR via a LISP tunnel interface. The upstream xTR encapsulates data packets to each and every downstream xTR for which it has received a join message.

For native multicast replication, the downstream xTR must also join the same group in the core by sending a native (S-RLOC, G). The upstream site encapsulates (S-EID,G) packets inside an (S-RLOC, G) packet.

LISP IPv4 Multicast

Figure 5-1 provides an example to help you understand how LISP IPv4 multicast works and how LISP unicast head-end replication is used to construct a multicast tree to transmit multicast data under LISP architecture. In this topology, the source is connected to an ITR on Site A, and the receiver is connected to the egress tunnel router (ETR) on Site B. In this scenario, receivers and the source are not directly connected to the xTR routers.

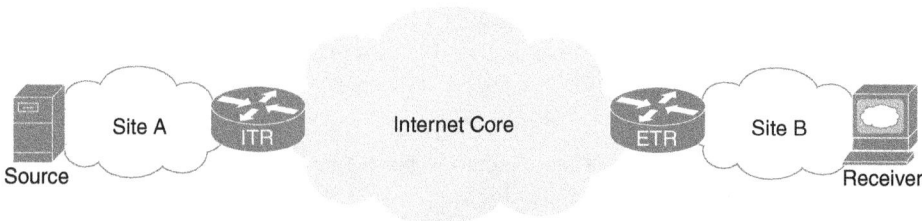

Figure 5-1 *A Typical LISP Multicast Topology*

LISP supports only source-specific multicast (SSM) and any-source multicast (ASM).

Note   SSM uses Internet Group Management Protocol version 3 (IGMPv3) with the default SSM group 232.0.0.0/8 and specifies a single particular source for the group. It eliminates the need for a rendezvous point (RP). On the other hand, ASM forms a shared tree (*, G) and requires an RP. It is a form of multicast that can have multiple senders for the same group.

These following steps explain the typical control plane flow for LISP SSM, using the topology in Figure 5-1:

Step 1.   If receiver R wants to join SSM multicast group G with source S, it sends an IGMPv3 join for SSM group G with source S toward the last-hop router (LHR), which is a router that is directly connected to the receiver. Note that for an xTR, R can be represented as the R-EID, which is in Site B, and S can be represented as the S-EID, which resides in Site A.

Step 2.   Because the sender and the receiver are not in the same site, PIM join packets are created by the LHR and intermediate routers in Site B and sent toward the core. Note that in the case of SSM, this is an (S, G) join.

Step 3.   On receiving the PIM join packet, the ETR connected to Site B performs a LISP map cache lookup for the S-EID.

Step 4.   When the ETR's map cache is updated with the information for the S-EID, the ETR encapsulates the packet inside a LISP header and forwards the Protocol Independent Multicast (PIM) join packet to the ITR connected through the core.

Step 5.   At the ITR, the packet from the ETR is de-encapsulated, and the PIM join packet is processed and sent to the first-hop router (FHR) that is directly connected to the S-EID. This completes the building of the multicast tree for (S-EID, G).

The data plane for the multicast traffic is done in the reverse manner, from the ITR site to the ETR site. When the multicast packets are being sent from the source (S-EID) to a particular group G, the data packets eventually reach the ITR, following the (S, G) state at each hop that was built using the PIM join messages. The ITR is aware of all the destination sites that have joined the group G. The ITR then encapsulates the data packets and forwards them through the core. On receiving the multicast data packets, the ETR router de-encapsulates the outer LISP header and replicates the multicast data stream to the receiver that has joined the group G within the ETR's site. It is important to note that the multicast LISP overlay packets and messages will be carried over either the unicast headend router (HER) or multicast through the core.

In ASM, there is an extra component that comes into play: the rendezvous point (RP). In a LISP architecture, the RP can be deployed at a site that is different from the sites with the S-EID and R-EID. If the RP resides in the same site as the S-EID, the PIM join packet is sent toward the RP-EID instead of the S-EID. But if the RP resides in a different site than the R-EID or the S-EID, the control flow differs a bit, and two trees are built:

- (*, G) RP tree rooted at the RP

- (S, G) tree rooted at the source

To further understand the control plane flow of ASM multicast, examine the topology shown in Figure 15-2. In this topology, the S-EID is present in Site A and can be reached through xTR1. In addition, xTR2 is acting as both the xTR and the RP, and the receiver (R-EID) is present in Site C and can be reached through xTR3.

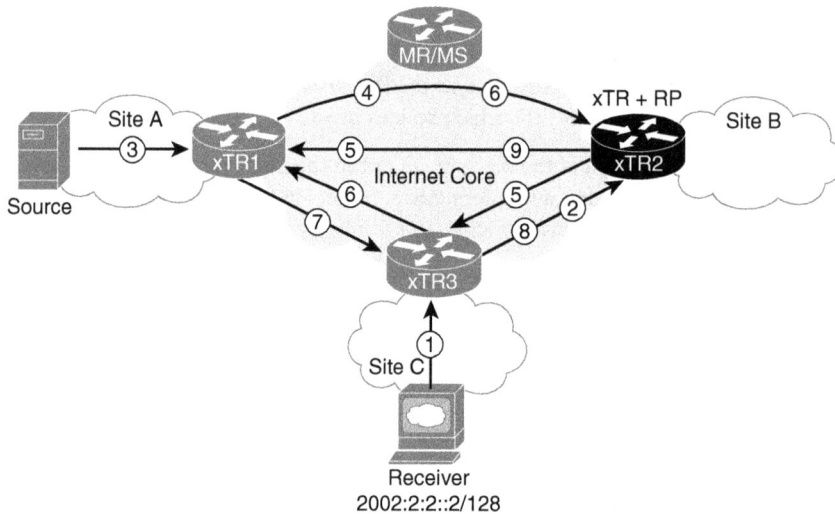

Figure 5-2 *LISP ASM Multicast Topology*

Figure 5-2 shows the control plane flow in a step-by-step process:

Step 1.   The receiver sends an IGMP join for the group G. PIM join packets are created by the LHR and intermediate routers in Site C. On receiving the PIM join, xTR3 forms the (*, G) entry.

Step 2.   Because the RP does not reside locally in Site C, xTR3 performs a LISP map cache lookup for the RP-EID. When the map cache is updated, xTR3 encapsulates the PIM join for the group G inside a LISP header and forwards it to xTR2, where the RP actually resides. At this point, the (*, G) entry is built on xTR2, with the incoming interface as the RP de-encapsulation tunnel and the outgoing interface list (OIL) populated with the LISP interface with the xTR3 RLOC as the next hop.

Step 3.   The source S sends multicast traffic for group G to the FHR. On receiving the multicast packet, the FHR sends a PIM register message toward the RP. At this point, the FHR creates an (S, G) entry in the mroute table, and the OIL is populated with the RP encapsulation tunnel.

Step 4. Because the S-EID is present on xTR1, it performs a LISP map cache lookup for the RP-EID. When the map cache is updated, xTR1 encapsulates the PIM register message and forwards it toward the RP on xTR2. xTR2 de-encapsulates the PIM register message and is consumed by the RP to program the (S, G) entry.

Step 5. xTR2 forwards the multicast traffic to xTR3, which is connected to the receiver on the shared tree. xTR2 also sends a PIM join to the FHR, which is connected on xTR1. On receiving the PIM join, xTR1 updates the (S, G) OIL entry with the LISP tunnel interface that has the xTR2 RLOC as the next hop.

Step 6. xTR1 sends multicast traffic that is encapsulated with the LISP header to xTR2. On xTR3, because the multicast traffic was received from the source S, the (S, G) entry is installed in the mroute table with the xTR1 RLOC as the reverse path forwarding (RPF) neighbor. Also, the LHR sends a PIM join toward the source S-EID, which resides on xTR1. On receiving the PIM join from xTR3, xTR1 updates the (S, G) entry and adds another OIL interface with a LISP overlay interface with a next hop of xTR3 RLOC.

Step 7. When the OIL is updated on xTR1, xTR1 forwards the multicast traffic to xTR3.

Step 8. xTR3 sends a PIM prune message with the RP-bit set for (*, G) to the RP (that is, xTR2).

Step 9. xTR2 sends a PIM prune message for (S-EID, G) to xTR1. This removes the OIL on xTR1 for the xTR2 RLOC.

These steps demonstrate the forwarding of multicast traffic on LISP infrastructure over the shortest path tree (that is, directly between xTR1 and xTR3). LISP multicast functionality is not just supported between LISP sites but also between LISP and non-LISP sites.

Configuring LISP IPv4 Multicast

LISP multicast is currently supported only on IOS/IOS-XE and NX-OS platforms. Implementation of LISP multicast currently has a few limitations:

- XE platforms support both unicast head-end replication and multicast replication, whereas NX-OS (Nexus 7000) supports only the unicast head-end replication method.

- LISP multicast supports only any-source multicast (ASM) and source-specific multicast (SSM) service models.

- LISP multicast supports only static RP configurations.

■ LISP multicast can be used across different virtual routing and forwarding (VRF) and instance IDs.

■ NX-OS platforms support only LISP IPv4 multicast. XE platforms support both LISP IPv4 and IPv6 multicast.

Note   Refer to the Cisco Feature Navigator and the CCO documentation for more specifics about the LISP multicast features on different XE and NX-OS platforms.

LISP multicast on IOS/IOS-XE platforms is enabled in two simple steps:

Step 1.   Enable multicast globally by using the command **ip multicast-routing** [**vrf** *vrf-name*] **distributed**.

Step 2.   Enable PIM sparse mode under the LISP interface and the customer-facing interfaces by using **ip pim sparse-mode** command.

On NX-OS, LISP multicast is enabled using the command **ip lisp multicast**. To enable the customer edge (CE)–facing interfaces with PIM sparse mode, PIM needs to be enabled using the command **feature pim**, and then the interfaces can be configured using the command **ip pim sparse-mode**. There is no additional configuration required when deploying IPv4 LISP multicast with unicast head-end replication. To deploy IPv4 LISP multicast with multicast replication, you need to use the additional command **ip pim lisp transport multicast** under the LISP interface. To better understand how LISP multicast is deployed and how to verify and troubleshoot LISP multicast issues, examine the topology shown in Figure 5-3. In this figure, the source is connected to xTR1, and the receiver is connected to xTR3. xTR1 also has the RP-EID, which is configured locally. Thus, xTR1 is acting as both the xTR and the RP.

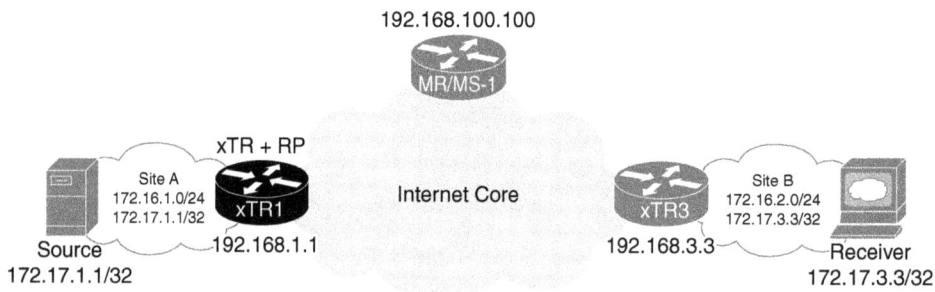

Figure 5-3   *LISP Multicast Topology*

Example 5-1 shows the configuration for enabling LISP multicast on both XE and NX-OS platforms.

Example 5-1 *Configuring LISP Multicast*

```
xTR1 - IOS-XE
! xTR1 Base Configuration

router lisp
 locator-table default
 service ipv4
  itr map-resolver 192.168.100.100
  itr
  etr map-server 192.168.100.100 key cisco
  etr
  map-request-source 192.168.1.1
  exit-service-ipv4
 !
 instance-id 1
  decapsulation filter rloc source member
  service ipv4
   eid-table default
   database-mapping 172.16.1.0/24 192.168.1.1 priority 1 weight 100
   database-mapping 172.17.1.1/32 192.168.1.1 priority 1 weight 100
   map-request-source 192.168.1.1
   exit-service-ipv4
  !
  service ipv6
   eid-table default
   exit-service-ipv6
  !
  exit-instance-id
 !
 instance-id 101
  service ipv4
   eid-table vrf FOO
   database-mapping 172.16.101.0/24 192.168.1.1 priority 1 weight 100
   database-mapping 172.17.101.1/32 192.168.1.1 priority 1 weight 100
   map-request-source 192.168.1.1
   exit-service-ipv4
  !
  service ipv6
   eid-table vrf FOO
   exit-service-ipv6
  !
  exit-instance-id
 !
```

```
 decapsulation filter rloc source member
 exit-router-lisp

! xTR1 LISP Multicast Configuration

xTR1(config)# ip multicast-routing distributed
xTR1(config)# interface lisp0.1
xTR1(config-if)# ip pim sparse-mode
xTR1(config)# interface lisp0.101
xTR1(config-if)# ip pim sparse-mode
xTR1(config-if)# interface GigabitEthernet4
xTR1(config-if)# ip pim sparse-mode
xTR1(config-if)# interface GigabitEthernet5
xTR1(config-if)# ip pim sparse-mode
```

```
xTR3 - NX-OS
! xTR3 Base Configuration

ip lisp itr-etr
ip lisp database-mapping 172.16.3.0/24 192.168.3.3 priority 1 weight 100
ip lisp database-mapping 172.17.3.3/32 192.168.3.3 priority 1 weight 100
lisp instance-id 1
ip lisp locator-vrf default
ip lisp itr map-resolver 192.168.100.100
ip lisp etr map-server 192.168.100.100 key 3 9125d59c18a9b015
ip lisp map-request-source 192.168.3.3

vrf context FOO
  ip lisp itr-etr
  ip lisp database-mapping 172.16.103.0/24 192.168.3.3 priority 1 weight 100
  lisp instance-id 101
  ip lisp locator-vrf default
  ip lisp itr map-resolver 192.168.100.100
  ip lisp etr map-server 192.168.100.100 key 3 9125d59c18a9b015

! xTR3 LISP Multicast Configuration

xTR3(config)# feature pim
xTR3(config)# ip lisp multicast
xTR3(config)# vrf context FOO
xTR3(config-vrf)# ip lisp multicast
xTR3(config)# interface Ethernet2/3-4
xTR3(config-if)# ip pim sparse-mode
```

Note   The LISP configuration for IPv4/IPv6 EID tables remains the same with multicast as for without it. No other changes are required specifically for LISP multicast.

The next step is to configure the rendezvous point (RP) for the customer edge (CE) network. Because the CE network can be part of the global routing table or a VRF routing table, you need to specify the RP for the source and receivers in the appropriate routing table. The RP configuration is required only when implementing ASM. For SSM, there is no RP required. Example 5-2 shows the configuration of RP on xTR1 and xTR2 for sources and receivers that are part of the global routing table as well as the VRF routing table.

Example 5-2   *Enabling RP for CE Networks*

```
xTR1 - IOS-XE
xTR1(config)# ip pim rp-add 172.16.1.1
xTR1(config)# ip pim vrf FOO rp-address 172.16.103.1


xTR3 - NX-OS
xTR3(config)# ip pim rp-address 172.16.1.1
xTR3(config)# vrf context FOO
xTR3(config-vrf)# ip pim rp-address 172.16.103.1
```

Because the destination group addresses are not topology dependent, mapping is only required for multicast source addresses as LISP endpoint identifiers (EIDs). Thus, no extra configuration changes are required on the map resolver (MR)/map server (MS) or the xTR devices. The same configuration is required on the proxy tunnel routers (PxTRs) that connect the source or the receivers.

Verifying LISP Multicast

Once LISP multicast is enabled on the xTR devices connected to both the receivers and the source, you need to verify a few things to ensure successful flow of the multicast stream, as shown in the following steps:

Step 1.   Ensure that LISP multicast is enabled on the ITR and the ETR (xTRs). On NX-OS, verify this by using the command **show ip lisp** [**vrf** *vrf-name*]. (There is no similar command for IOS/IOS-XE devices.) For IOS/IOS-XE, use the command **show ip multicast** [**vrf** *vrf-name*] **interface** [*interface-id*] and verify whether multicast routing is enabled for the LISP interface. Example 5-3 shows verification that multicast routing is enabled for LISP on both xTR1 and xTR3.

Example 5-3   *Verifying LISP Multicast State*

```
xTR1 - IOS-XE
xTR1# show ip multicast interface
LISP0.1 is up, line protocol is up
  Interface is unnumbered. Using address of GigabitEthernet4 (172.16.1.1)
  Multicast routing: enabled
  Multicast switching: fast
  Multicast packets in/out: 0/2
  Multicast TTL threshold: 0
  Multicast Tagswitching: disabled
GigabitEthernet4 is up, line protocol is up
  Internet address is 172.16.1.1/24
  Multicast routing: enabled
  Multicast switching: fast
  Multicast packets in/out: 74/0
  Multicast TTL threshold: 0
  Multicast Tagswitching: disabled


xTR1# show ip multicast vrf FOO interface
LISP0.101 is up, line protocol is up
  Interface is unnumbered. Using address of GigabitEthernet5 (172.16.101.1)
  Multicast routing: enabled
  Multicast switching: fast
  Multicast packets in/out: 0/0
  Multicast TTL threshold: 0
  Multicast Tagswitching: disabled
GigabitEthernet5 is up, line protocol is up
  Internet address is 172.16.101.1/24
  Multicast routing: enabled
  Multicast switching: fast
  Multicast packets in/out: 29/0
  Multicast TTL threshold: 0
  Multicast Tagswitching: disabled
```

```
xTR3 - NX-OS
xTR3# show ip lisp
LISP IP Configuration Information for VRF "default" (iid 1)
  Ingress Tunnel Router (ITR):    enabled
  Egress Tunnel Router (ETR):     enabled
  Proxy-ITR Router (PTR):         disabled
  Proxy-ETR Router (PETR):        disabled
```

```
   Map Resolver (MR):              disabled
   Map Server (MS):                disabled
   LISP Multicast:                 enabled
     GLT interface:                glt1
   LISP control-plane security:    disabled
   Locator VRF:                    default
   Encap-Map-Request source:       192.168.3.3
   LISP-NAT Interworking:          disabled
   Use locators from BGP RIB:      disabled
   ITR send Map-Request:           enabled
   ITR send Data-Probe:            disabled
   LISP ALT-VRF:                   not configured
! Output omitted for brevity


xTR3# show ip lisp vrf FOO
LISP IP Configuration Information for VRF "FOO" (iid 101)
   Ingress Tunnel Router (ITR):    enabled
   Egress Tunnel Router (ETR):     enabled
   Proxy-ITR Router (PTR):         disabled
   Proxy-ETR Router (PETR):        disabled
   Map Resolver (MR):              disabled
   Map Server (MS):                disabled
   LISP Multicast:                 enabled
     GLT interface:                glt1
   LISP control-plane security:    disabled
   Locator VRF:                    default    *** VRF cross-over ***
   Encap-Map-Request source:       192.168.3.3
   LISP-NAT Interworking:          disabled
   Use locators from BGP RIB:      disabled
   ITR send Map-Request:           enabled
   ITR send Data-Probe:            disabled
   LISP ALT-VRF:                   not configured
! Output omitted for brevity
```

Step 2.   Verify whether PIM is enabled on both the overlay LISP interface and the
CE-facing interfaces. Example 5-4 shows verification that PIM is enabled on
the relevant interfaces on both the xTRs. Note that on xTR1 running XE, the
neighbor count on the LISP0.101 interface is 1. The XE platforms establish a
unidirectional PIM neighbor toward the upstream xTR as they will be sending
the PIM join/prune messages toward the RP. It is important to note that the
PIM control traffic across the LISP tunnel interface is strictly restricted to
join/prune messages.

Example 5-4 *Verifying PIM Interfaces on xTRs*

```
xTR1
xTR1# show ip pim interface

Address            Interface              Ver/   Nbr    Query  DR      DR
                                          Mode   Count  Intvl  Prior
172.16.1.1         LISP0.1                v2/S   0      30     1       172.16.1.1
172.16.1.1         GigabitEthernet4       v2/S   1      30     1       172.16.1.2

xTR1# show ip pim vrf FOO interface

Address            Interface              Ver/   Nbr    Query  DR      DR
                                          Mode   Count  Intvl  Prior
172.16.101.1       LISP0.101              v2/S   1      30     1       172.16.101.1
172.16.101.1       GigabitEthernet5       v2/S   1      30     1       172.16.101.2


xTR3
xTR3# show ip pim interface brief
PIM Interface Status for VRF "default"
Interface          IP Address      PIM DR Address   Neighbor  Border
                                                    Count     Interface
g1t4               192.168.3.3     192.168.3.3      0         no
g1t5               192.168.3.3     192.168.3.3      0         no
g1t6               192.168.3.3     192.168.3.3      0         no
g1t1               192.168.3.3     192.168.3.3      0         no
g1t2               192.168.3.3     192.168.3.3      0         no
g1t3               192.168.3.3     192.168.3.3      0         no
Ethernet2/3        172.16.3.1      172.16.3.2       1         no


xTR3# show ip pim interface brief vrf FOO
PIM Interface Status for VRF "FOO"
Interface          IP Address      PIM DR Address   Neighbor  Border
                                                    Count     Interface
Ethernet2/4        172.16.103.1    172.16.103.2     1         no
```

Step 3.   When the xTR or the LHR receives an IGMP join request for the group G, the (*, G) entry is built on the LHR. If the LHR is not the xTR, a PIM join message is sent toward the RP, traversing via the xTR. In this case, xTR3 RLOC holds the receiver EID (R-EID) for group 239.1.1.1 in the global routing table, and xTR1 RLOC holds the R-EID for 239.1.1.3 in the vrf FOO mroute table. Example 5-5 shows validation of the (*, G) entry for both the global routing table and the vrf FOO mroute table. In the highlighted output in Example 5-5, xTR3 is having the incoming interface as glt1, which is the generic LISP tunnel (GLT), interface with the RPF neighbor for xTR1 (192.168.1.1), which has the RP-RLOC. Similarly, the highlighted output for the vrf FOO mroute table on xTR1 displays the LISP0.101 interface with RPF neighbor 192.168.3.3, which has the RP-RLOC for the multicast group 239.1.1.3.

Example 5-5 *Mroute Table for the (*, G) Entry*

```
xTR3
xTR3# show ip mroute 239.1.1.1
IP Multicast Routing Table for VRF "default"

(*, 239.1.1.1/32), uptime: 03:24:12, pim ip
  Incoming interface: glt1, RPF nbr: 192.168.1.1
  Outgoing interface list: (count: 1)
    Ethernet2/3, uptime: 03:24:12, pim

xTR3# show ip mroute 239.1.1.3 vrf FOO
IP Multicast Routing Table for VRF "FOO"

(*, 239.1.1.3/32), uptime: 11:01:41, pim ip
  Incoming interface: Ethernet2/4, RPF nbr: 172.16.103.1
  Outgoing interface list: (count: 1)
    glt1, uptime: 11:01:41, pim
```

```
xTR1
xTR1# show ip mroute 239.1.1.1
IP Multicast Routing Table
| Output omitted for brevity
Outgoing interface flags: H - Hardware switched, A - Assert winner, p - PIM Join
 Timers: Uptime/Expires
 Interface state: Interface, Next-Hop or VCD, State/Mode

(*, 239.1.1.1), 03:22:49/00:03:05, RP 172.16.1.1, flags: S
  Incoming interface: Null, RPF nbr 0.0.0.0
  Outgoing interface list:
    LISP0.1, 192.168.3.3, Forward/Sparse, 03:22:49/00:03:05

xTR1# show ip mroute vrf FOO 239.1.1.3
IP Multicast Routing Table
Outgoing interface flags: H - Hardware switched, A - Assert winner, p - PIM Join
 Timers: Uptime/Expires
 Interface state: Interface, Next-Hop or VCD, State/Mode
```

```
(*, 239.1.1.3), 11:03:31/00:02:48, RP 172.16.103.1, flags: S
  Incoming interface: LISP0.101, RPF nbr 192.168.3.3
  Outgoing interface list:
    GigabitEthernet5, Forward/Sparse, 11:03:31/00:02:48
```

Step 4.   When the source starts sending the traffic, the (S, G) entry is built following the steps explained earlier for LISP ASM. Example 5-6 displays the mroute table with the (S, G) entry when the source starts sending the traffic. In the highlighted output in Example 5-6, the OIL for group 239.1.1.1 is now populated on xTR1 with the LISP0.1 interface, which indicates that the traffic will be LISP encapsulated when sent to the receiver site. Similarly, the OIL for group 239.1.1.3 in the vrf FOO mroute table is now populated with GLT interface on xTR3.

Example 5-6   *Mroute Table with the (S, G) Entry*

```
xTR1
xTR1# show ip mroute 239.1.1.1
IP Multicast Routing Table
! Output omitted for brevity
Outgoing interface flags: H - Hardware switched, A - Assert winner, p - PIM Join
 Timers: Uptime/Expires
 Interface state: Interface, Next-Hop or VCD, State/Mode

(*, 239.1.1.1), 04:07:51/stopped, RP 172.16.1.1, flags: S
  Incoming interface: Null, RPF nbr 0.0.0.0
  Outgoing interface list:
    LISP0.1, 192.168.3.3, Forward/Sparse, 04:07:51/00:03:12

(172.16.1.2, 239.1.1.1), 00:00:06/00:03:28, flags: T
  Incoming interface: GigabitEthernet4, RPF nbr 172.16.1.2
  Outgoing interface list:
    LISP0.1, 192.168.3.3, Forward/Sparse, 00:00:06/00:03:23

xTR1# show ip mroute vrf FOO 239.1.1.3
IP Multicast Routing Table
Outgoing interface flags: H - Hardware switched, A - Assert winner, p - PIM Join
 Timers: Uptime/Expires
 Interface state: Interface, Next-Hop or VCD, State/Mode

(*, 239.1.1.3), 11:05:27/stopped, RP 172.16.103.1, flags: S
  Incoming interface: LISP0.101, RPF nbr 192.168.3.3
  Outgoing interface list:
   GigabitEthernet5, Forward/Sparse, 11:05:27/00:02:50
```

```
(172.16.103.2, 239.1.1.3), 00:00:30/00:02:29, flags: T
  Incoming interface: LISP0.101, RPF nbr 192.168.3.3
  Outgoing interface list:
    GigabitEthernet5, Forward/Sparse, 00:00:30/00:02:59
```

```
xTR3
xTR3# show ip mroute 239.1.1.1
IP Multicast Routing Table for VRF "default"

(*, 239.1.1.1/32), uptime: 04:10:34, pim ip
  Incoming interface: glt1, RPF nbr: 192.168.1.1
  Outgoing interface list: (count: 1)
    Ethernet2/3, uptime: 04:10:34, pim

(172.16.1.2/32, 239.1.1.1/32), uptime: 00:00:40, pim mrib ip
  Incoming interface: glt1, RPF nbr: 192.168.1.1
  Outgoing interface list: (count: 1)
    Ethernet2/3, uptime: 00:00:40, pim

xTR3# show ip mroute 239.1.1.3 vrf FOO
IP Multicast Routing Table for VRF "FOO"

(*, 239.1.1.3/32), uptime: 11:02:39, pim ip
  Incoming interface: Ethernet2/4, RPF nbr: 172.16.103.1
  Outgoing interface list: (count: 1)
    glt1, uptime: 11:02:39, pim

(172.16.103.2/32, 239.1.1.3/32), uptime: 00:00:08, ip mrib pim
  Incoming interface: Ethernet2/4, RPF nbr: 172.16.103.2
  Outgoing interface list: (count: 1)
    glt1, uptime: 00:00:08, pim
```

Step 5. Note that PIM join/prune, PIM register, and the multicast traffic between
the sites are LISP encapsulated when sent between the xTR nodes via the ISP
core network. Figure 5-4 shows the Wireshark packet analyzer displaying the
LISP-encapsulated traffic.

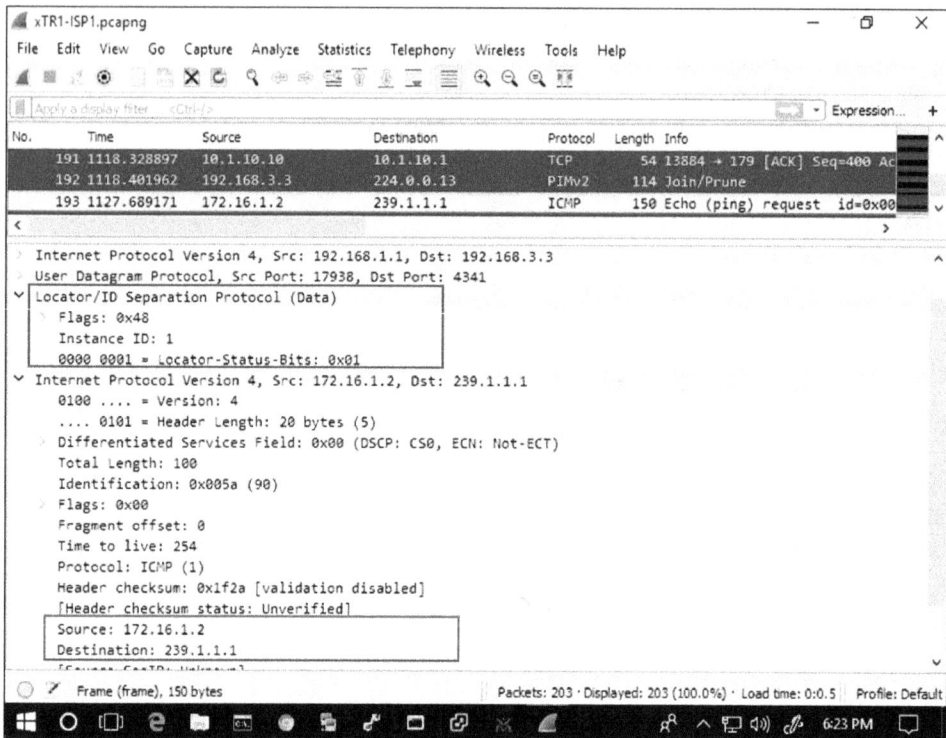

Figure 5-4 *LISP-Encapsulated Multicast Traffic in Wireshark*

Troubleshooting LISP Multicast on IOS-XE and NX-OS

Multiple components on both IOS-XE and NX-OS come into play when building a successful multicast flow. But before troubleshooting the issue from a multicast perspective, it is important to validate that the unicast flows are working fine and that the LISP map cache has relevant entries. For instance, in the case of LISP ASM, the LHR or xTR for the receiver site should have the LISP map cache updated with both the source and the RP. Example 5-7 shows the verification of RP and its corresponding LISP map cache entry.

Example 5-7 *Verifying RP Mapping and the LISP Map Cache*

```
xTR3 - NX-OS
xTR3# show ip pim rp
PIM RP Status Information for VRF "default"
BSR disabled
Auto-RP disabled
BSR RP Candidate policy: None
BSR RP policy: None
Auto-RP Announce policy: None
Auto-RP Discovery policy: None
```

```
RP: 172.16.1.1, (0),
 uptime: 22:34:50   priority: 0,
 RP-source: (local),
 group ranges:
 224.0.0.0/4


xTR3# show ip lisp map-cache
LISP IP Mapping Cache for VRF "default" (iid 1), 1 entries


172.16.1.0/24, uptime: 22:32:25, expires: 01:27:34, via map-reply, auth
  Locator       Uptime     State         Priority/  Data     Control      MTU
                                         Weight     in/out   in/out
   192.168.1.1  22:32:25   up            1/100      0/0      1/0         1500
```

```
xTR1
xTR1# show ip pim vrf FOO rp mapping
PIM Group-to-RP Mappings


Group(s): 224.0.0.0/4, Static
    RP: 172.16.103.1 (?)


xTR1# show ip lisp instance-id 101 map-cache
LISP IPv4 Mapping Cache for EID-table vrf FOO (IID 101), 2 entries


0.0.0.0/0, uptime: 22:36:10, expires: never, via static-send-map-request
  Negative cache entry, action: send-map-request
172.16.103.0/24, uptime: 22:33:09, expires: 01:26:50, via map-reply, complete
  Locator       Uptime     State      Pri/Wgt      Encap-IID
   192.168.3.3  22:33:09   up         1/100        -
```

After you verify the RP mappings and unicast forwarding across LISP and non-LISP sites, IGMP comes into play. The source and the receivers are usually not directly connected to the xTRs, and thus IGMP may not come into play when troubleshooting from the perspective of the xTR. From the perspective of the LHR, you need to verify IGMP to make sure the LHR is receiving the IGMP request for the relevant groups. This is verified using the command **show ip igmp** [**vrf** *vrf-name*] **groups** on IOS-XE platforms and **show ip igmp groups** [**vrf** *vrf-name*] on NX-OS.

The xTRs usually receives PIM join messages from the LHR. NX-OS provides both the **show** command for PIM route and the **event-history** command, which captures all the events related to the control plane messages. Use the command **show ip pim route** *mcast-address* [**vrf** *vrf-name*] to validate the PIM route and the command **show ip pim**

event-history join-prune to verify the event history logs for the PIM join/prune messages. On IOS-XE, there is no event trace for PIM feature. Thus, debugging is required to troubleshoot PIM-related issues. Use the command **debug ip pim** [**vrf** *vrf-name*] *mcast-address* to validate the message exchange from a PIM perspective.

Example 5-8 shows the PIM route and event history for group 239.1.1.1 on NX-OS and PIM debugs on IOS-XE when a PIM join is received. In the output on XTR3, notice that the PIM route points the incoming interface glt1 with RPF neighbor to 192.168.1.1, which has the RP-RLOC. The information populated in the **show ip pim route** command can be validated in the event history logs. PIM receives a join message for (*, 239.1.1.1/32) with wildcard bit set and RP bit set. It then adds the interface Eth2/3 on the OIL and then sends the join/prune message to LISP xTR 192.168.1.1 over the glt1 interface. On XTR1, the **debug ip pim** logs show that the PIM join was received for (*, 239.1.1.1). IOS/IOS-XE platforms creates PIM de-encapsulation tunnels on the RP and PIM encapsulation tunnels on all routers, including the FHR and LHR. The PIM tunnels are verified using the command **show ip pim** [**vrf** *vrf-name*] **tunnel**. After receiving the PIM join from xTR3, xTR1 adds a PIM register de-encapsulation tunnel as the accepting interface and adds a LISP overlay interface to the OIL.

Example 5-8   *Verifying PIM Logs for Join/Prune Messages*

```
xTR3
xTR3# show ip pim route 239.1.1.1
PIM Routing Table for VRF "default" - 2 entries


(*, 239.1.1.1/32), RP 172.16.1.1, expires 00:03:00, RP-bit
  Incoming interface: glt1, RPF nbr **192.168.1.1**
  Oif-list: (1) 00000000, Timeout-list: (0) 00000000
  Timeout-interval: 4, JP-holdtime round-up: 4


xTR3# show ip pim event-history join-prune
 join-prune events for PIM process


19:35:24.066734 pim [5913]: : Send Join-Prune on glt1 using LISP encapsulation,
  length: 44 in context 1
19:35:24.066731 pim [5913]: : pim_send_jp: Successfully encapsulated Mcast LISP
  packet
19:35:24.066718 pim [5913]: : pim_send_jp: IP header: ip.tl = 64, source addr
  192.168.3.3 -> dest addr 224.0.0.13, protocol 103
19:35:24.066715 pim [5913]: : pim_send_jp: Sending the Join/Prune msg to LISP xTR
  192.168.1.1 on context 1 for interface glt1 using source rloc 192.168.3.3
19:35:24.066190 pim [5913]: : Put (*, 239.1.1.1/32), WRS in join-list for nbr
  192.168.1.1
19:35:24.066187 pim [5913]: : wc_bit = TRUE, rp_bit = TRUE
19:35:24.064052 pim [5913]: : -----
19:35:24.064043 pim [5913]: : Add Ethernet2/3 to all (S,G)s for group 239.1.1.1
```

```
19:35:24.063834 pim [5913]: : No (*, 239.1.1.1/32) route exists, to us

19:35:24.063828 pim [5913]: : pim_receive_join: We are target comparing with iod

19:35:24.063795 pim [5913]: : pim_receive_join: route: (*, 239.1.1.1/32), wc_bit:
  TRUE, rp_bit: TRUE

19:35:24.063786 pim [5913]: : Received Join-Prune from 172.16.3.2 on Ethernet2/3,
  length: 34, MTU: 1500, ht: 210
xTR1
xTR1# debug ip pim 239.1.1.1
PIM debugging is on

19:35:16.307: PIM(0): J/P Transport Attribute, Transport Type: Unicast

19:35:16.307: PIM(0): Join-list: (*, 239.1.1.1), RPT-bit set, WC-bit set, S-bit set

19:35:16.308: PIM(0): Check RP 172.16.1.1 into the (*, 239.1.1.1) entry

19:35:16.308: PIM(0): Adding register decap tunnel (Tunnel2) as accepting interface
  of (*, 239.1.1.1).

19:35:16.308: PIM(0): Add LISP0.1/192.168.3.3 to (*, 239.1.1.1), Forward state, by
  PIM *G Join

19:35:26.551: PIM(0): J/P Transport Attribute, Transport Type: Unicast

19:35:26.551: PIM(0): Join-list: (*, 239.1.1.1), RPT-bit set, WC-bit set, S-bit set

19:35:26.552: PIM(0): Update LISP0.1/192.168.3.3 to (*, 239.1.1.1), Forward state,
  by PIM *G Join

19:36:14.632: PIM(0): Building Periodic (*,G) Join / (S,G,RP-bit) Prune message for
  239.1.1.1


xTR1# show ip pim tunnel
Tunnel0
  Type       : PIM Encap
  RP         : 172.16.1.1*
  Source     : 172.16.1.1
  State      : UP
  Last event : Created (23:30:37)
Tunnel2*
  Type       : PIM Decap
  RP         : 172.16.1.1*
  Source     : -
  State      : UP
  Last event : Created (23:30:33)
```

Note A PIM encapsulation tunnel is dynamically created whenever a group-to-RP mapping is learned. The PIM encapsulation tunnel is used to encapsulate multicast packets sent by first-hop designated routers that have directly connected sources.

A PIM de-encapsulation tunnel is dynamically created on RP whenever a group-to-RP mapping is learned. The RP uses the PIM de-encapsulation tunnel to de-encapsulate PIM register messages. PIM encapsulation and de-encapsulation tunnels are specific to IOS-XE platforms.

Once the source starts sending the traffic, the FHR sends a PIM register message to the RP. Because the RP resides on xTR1, it receives the PIM register message. The first time it receives the PIM register message, the PIM de-encapsulation tunnel is added as the accepting interface for the (S, G) entry. Then a PIM join/prune message is built and sent to the source from the RP. On receiving another register message from the source, the LISP overlay interface is added to the OIL of the (S, G) entry where the source is 172.16.1.2 and the group is 239.1.1.1.

When the multicast packet is received from the source over the shared tree, the LHR sends another PIM join message for the group, but this time it includes the source address. On NX-OS, the PIM event history for join/prune messages shows that another PIM join message is received from the LHR. This (S, G) join message is LISP encapsulated and sent to xTR1, where the RP resides. Example 5-9 shows the PIM debug logs and PIM event history logs for this event.

Example 5-9 *PIM Events on the Source Register*

```
xTR1
xTR1# debug ip pim 239.1.1.1
PIM debugging is on
19:39:50.823: PIM(0): Received v2 Register on GigabitEthernet4 from 172.16.1.2
19:39:50.823:        for 172.16.1.2, group 239.1.1.1
19:39:50.824: PIM(0): Adding register decap tunnel (Tunnel2) as accepting interface
  of (172.16.1.2, 239.1.1.1).
19:39:50.824: PIM(0): Insert (172.16.1.2,239.1.1.1) join in nbr 172.16.1.2's queue
19:39:50.825: PIM(0): Building Join/Prune packet for nbr 172.16.1.2
19:39:50.825: PIM(0):  Adding v2 (172.16.1.2/32, 239.1.1.1), S-bit Join
19:39:50.825: PIM(0): Send v2 join/prune to 172.16.1.2 (GigabitEthernet4)
19:39:50.835: PIM(0): Removing register decap tunnel (Tunnel2) as accepting inter-
  face of (172.16.1.2, 239.1.1.1).
19:39:50.835: PIM(0): Installing GigabitEthernet4 as accepting interface for
  (172.16.1.2, 239.1.1.1).
19:39:50.872: PIM(0): J/P Transport Attribute, Transport Type: Unicast
19:39:50.872: PIM(0): Join-list: (172.16.1.2/32, 239.1.1.1), S-bit set
19:39:50.872: PIM(0): Update LISP0.1/192.168.3.3 to (172.16.1.2, 239.1.1.1), Forward
  state, by PIM SG Join
19:39:55.832: PIM(0): Received v2 Register on GigabitEthernet4 from 172.16.1.2
19:39:55.832:        for 172.16.1.2, group 239.1.1.1
19:39:55.832: PIM(0): Send v2 Register-Stop to 172.16.1.2 for 172.16.1.2, group
  239.1.1.1
xTR1#
19:40:11.131: PIM(0): Building Periodic (*,G) Join / (S,G,RP-bit) Prune message for
  239.1.1.1
19:40:42.515: PIM(0): J/P Transport Attribute, Transport Type: Unicast
19:40:42.515: PIM(0): Join-list: (*, 239.1.1.1), RPT-bit set, WC-bit set, S-bit set
19:40:42.515: PIM(0): Update LISP0.1/192.168.3.3 to (*, 239.1.1.1), Forward state,
  by PIM *G Join
```

```
19:40:42.515: PIM(0): Update LISP0.1/192.168.3.3 to (172.16.1.2, 239.1.1.1), Forward
  state, by PIM *G Join
19:40:42.515: PIM(0): Join-list: (172.16.1.2/32, 239.1.1.1), S-bit set
19:40:42.515: PIM(0): Update LISP0.1/192.168.3.3 to (172.16.1.2, 239.1.1.1), Forward
  state, by PIM SG Join
xTR3
xTR3# show ip pim route 239.1.1.1 172.16.1.2
PIM Routing Table for VRF "default" - 3 entries


(172.16.1.2/32, 239.1.1.1/32), expires 00:02:55
  Incoming interface: glt1, RPF nbr **192.168.1.1**
  Oif-list:      (1) 00000000, Timeout-list: (0) 00000000
  Immediate-list: (1) 00000000, Immediate-timeout-list: (0) 00000000
  Sgr-prune-list: (0) 00000000  Timeout-interval: 3, JP-holdtime round-up: 4


xTR3# show ip pim event-history join-prune
 join-prune events for PIM process


19:39:58.783595 pim [5913]: : Send Join-Prune on glt1 using LISP encapsulation,
  length: 44 in context 1
19:39:58.783591 pim [5913]: : pim_send_jp: Successfully encapsulated Mcast LISP
  packet
19:39:58.783569 pim [5913]: : pim_send_jp: IP header: ip.tl = 64, source addr
  192.168.3.3 -> dest addr 224.0.0.13, protocol 103
19:39:58.783563 pim [5913]: : pim_send_jp: Sending the Join/Prune msg to LISP xTR
  192.168.1.1 on context 1 for interface glt1 using source rloc 192.168.3.3
19:39:58.782775 pim [5913]: : Put (172.16.1.2/32, 239.1.1.1/32), S in join-list for
  nbr 192.168.1.1
19:39:58.782767 pim [5913]: : wc_bit = FALSE, rp_bit = FALSE
19:39:58.780922 pim [5913]: : -----
19:39:58.780625 pim [5913]: : No (172.16.1.2/32, 239.1.1.1/32) route exists, to us
19:39:58.780618 pim [5913]: : pim_receive_join: We are target comparing with iod
19:39:58.780578 pim [5913]: : pim_receive_join: route: (172.16.1.2/32,
  239.1.1.1/32), wc_bit: FALSE, rp_bit: FALSE
19:39:58.780564 pim [5913]: : Received Join-Prune from 172.16.3.2 on Ethernet2/3,
  length: 34, MTU: 1500, ht: 210
```

Note In the previous two examples, the PIM events and debugs are shown only for multicast in the default table. The PIM debug and event history logs are similar for the vrf FOO table.

On IOS-XE, the information from PIM gets populated into the Multicast Routing Information Base (MRIB), which then gets pushed down to the Multicast Forwarding Information Base (MFIB). The MRIB entry is verified using the command **show ip mrib** [**vrf** *vrf-name*] **route** *mcast-address*. Example 5-10 shows the MRIB table output for both (*, G) and (S, G). In the output, notice that for group 239.1.1.1, the default table has the forward flag (F) set on the LISP tunnel interface and the accept flag (A) set on the Tunnel2 interface, which is the PIM de-encapsulation tunnel.

Example 5-10   *MRIB Table Output*

```
xTR1
xTR1# show ip mrib route 239.1.1.1
IP Multicast Routing Information Base
Entry flags: L - Domain-Local Source, E - External Source to the Domain,
    C - Directly-Connected Check, S - Signal, IA - Inherit Accept, D - Drop
    ET - Data Rate Exceeds Threshold,K - Keepalive,DDE - Data Driven Event
    ME - MoFRR ECMP Flow based, MNE - MoFRR Non-ECMP Flow based,
    MP - Primary MoFRR Non-ECMP Flow based entry
Interface flags: F - Forward, A - Accept, IC - Internal Copy,
    NS - Negate Signal, DP - Don't Preserve, SP - Signal Present,
    II - Internal Interest, ID - Internal Disinterest, LI - Local Interest,
    LD - Local Disinterest, MD - mCAC Denied, MI - mLDP Interest
    A2 - MoFRR ECMP Backup Accept


(*,239.1.1.1) RPF nbr: 0.0.0.0 Flags: C
  LISP0.1 Flags: F NS   Next-hop: 192.168.3.3
  Tunnel2 Flags: A


(172.16.1.2,239.1.1.1) RPF nbr: 172.16.1.2 Flags:
  GigabitEthernet4 Flags: A
  LISP0.1 Flags: F NS   Next-hop: 192.168.3.3

xTR1# show ip mrib vrf FOO route 239.1.1.3
IP Multicast Routing Information Base
! Output omitted for brevity


(*,239.1.1.3) RPF nbr: 192.168.3.3 Flags: C
  LISP0.101 Flags: A
  GigabitEthernet5 Flags: F NS


(172.16.103.2,239.1.1.3) RPF nbr: 192.168.3.3 Flags:
  LISP0.101 Flags: A
  GigabitEthernet5 Flags: F NS
```

The MRIB component is a platform-independent (PI) component; in other words, it is information in software. The information is pushed down to the MFIB table, which is validated using the command **show ip mfib** [**vrf** *vrf-name*] **route** *mcast-address* [**detail**]. As shown in Example 5-11, both the incoming and outgoing interfaces have their adjacency programmed in Cisco Express Forwarding (CEF), along with the flags that confirm the entry was accepted in MRIB (RA) and also in MFIB (MA). Along with the flags, the MFIB component is used to verify the hardware and software switched counters for the multicast traffic, using the command **show ip mfib [vrf** *vrf-name*] *mcast-address* **count**. Note that if the SW forwarding counters are incrementing for the source tree, this might indicate that the information is not properly programmed in the hardware or the adjacency is not complete and is causing the packets to get software switched.

Example 5-11 *Verifying Information in MFIB and Hardware Counters*

```
xTR1
xTR1# show ip mfib route 239.1.1.1 detail
Entry Flags:     C - Directly Connected, S - Signal, IA - Inherit A flag,
                 ET - Data Rate Exceeds Threshold, K - Keepalive
                 DDE - Data Driven Event, HW - Hardware Installed
                 ME - MoFRR ECMP entry, MNE - MoFRR Non-ECMP entry, MP - MFIB
                 MoFRR Primary, RP - MRIB MoFRR Primary, P - MoFRR Primary
                 MS  - MoFRR  Entry in Sync, MC - MoFRR entry in MoFRR Client.
I/O Item Flags: IC - Internal Copy, NP - Not platform switched,
                 NS - Negate Signalling, SP - Signal Present,
                 A - Accept, F - Forward, RA - MRIB Accept, RF - MRIB Forward,
                 MA - MFIB Accept, A2 - Accept backup,
                 RA2 - MRIB Accept backup, MA2 - MFIB Accept backup


Forwarding Counts: Pkt Count/Pkts per second/Avg Pkt Size/Kbits per second
Other counts:       Total/RPF failed/Other drops
I/O Item Counts:   FS Pkt Count/PS Pkt Count
Default
 (*,239.1.1.1) C K; epoch 0
   LISP0.1, 192.168.3.3 RF F NS; epoch 0
     CEF: Adjacency
   Tunnel2 RA A MA; epoch 0
 (172.16.1.2,239.1.1.1) K DDE; epoch 0
   LISP0.1, 192.168.3.3 RF F NS; epoch 0
     CEF: Adjacency
   GigabitEthernet4 RA A MA; epoch 0
     CEF: Adjacency

xTR1# show ip mfib 239.1.1.1 count
Forwarding Counts: Pkt Count/Pkts per second/Avg Pkt Size/Kilobits per second
Other counts:       Total/RPF failed/Other drops(OIF-null, rate-limit etc)
Default
 11 routes, 7 (*,G)s, 2 (*,G/m)s
Group: 239.1.1.1
  RP-tree,
   SW Forwarding: 5/0/100/0, Other: 0/0/0
```

```
  HW Forwarding:    0/0/0/0, Other: 3/3/0
 Source: 172.16.1.2,
  SW Forwarding: 0/0/0/0, Other: 0/0/0
 HW Forwarding:    78/0/114/0, Other: 0/0/0
xTR1# show ip mfib vrf FOO route 239.1.1.3 detail


Forwarding Counts: Pkt Count/Pkts per second/Avg Pkt Size/Kbits per second
Other counts:      Total/RPF failed/Other drops
I/O Item Counts:   FS Pkt Count/PS Pkt Count
VRF FOO
 (*,239.1.1.3) C K; epoch 0
   GigabitEthernet5 RF F NS; epoch 0
     CEF: Adjacency
   LISP0.101 RA A MA; epoch 0
     CEF: Adjacency
 (172.16.103.2,239.1.1.3) K DDE; epoch 0
   GigabitEthernet5 RF F NS; epoch 0
     CEF: Adjacency
   LISP0.101 RA A MA; epoch 0
     CEF: Adjacency


xTR1# show ip mfib vrf FOO 239.1.1.3 count
Forwarding Counts: Pkt Count/Pkts per second/Avg Pkt Size/Kilobits per second
Other counts:      Total/RPF failed/Other drops(OIF-null, rate-limit etc)
VRF FOO
 10 routes, 7 (*,G)s, 2 (*,G/m)s
Group: 239.1.1.3
  RP-tree,
   SW Forwarding: 0/0/0/0, Other: 0/0/0
   HW Forwarding:   3/0/150/0, Other: 0/0/0
  Source: 172.16.103.2,
   SW Forwarding: 0/0/0/0, Other: 0/0/0
   HW Forwarding:   103/0/150/0, Other: 0/0/0
  Totals - Source count: 1, Packet count: 106
```

Both the (*, G) and (S, G) entries in MFIB are bound to an object interface list, which includes both the incoming and outgoing interfaces. This information can be validated on both the RP and the FP. To verify whether the (*, G) and (S, G) entries are present in the QuantumFlow Processor (QFP) software programming of MFIB, use the command **show platform software ip fp active mfib**. This command displays the entries along with the mapping object IDs. These object IDs are queried in the multicast list (MList) entries using the command **show platform software mlist fp active index** *index*. The output provides a list of output chain element (OCE) that points to the interfaces bound to that adjacency. This is validated both on the route processor (RP) and the forwarding processor (FP), also known as the forwarding engine (FE), using the command **show platform software adjacency [rp | fp] active index** *index*. Example 5-12 demonstrates the validation of the MFIB programming on the ASR1000 platform.

Example 5-12 *Verifying QFP Programming on the ASR1000 Platform*

```
xTR1
xTR1# show platform software ip fp active mfib
Route flags:
S - Signal;          C - Directly connected;
IA - Inherit A Flag;   L - Local;
BR - Bidir route
*, 224.0.0.0/4 --> OBJ_INTF_LIST (0x44)
             Obj id: 0x44, Flags: C
             aom id: 189, HW handle: 0x55c7439b7c98 (created)
*, 224.0.1.40/32 --> OBJ_INTF_LIST (0x4c)
             Obj id: 0x4c, Flags: C, AUTORP Internel Copy
             aom id: 205, HW handle: 0x55c743a01a08 (created)
*, 239.1.1.1/32 --> OBJ_INTF_LIST (0x6e)
             Obj id: 0x6e, Flags: C
             aom id: 285, HW handle: 0x55c743a22808 (created)
239.1.1.1, 172.16.1.2/64 --> OBJ_INTF_LIST (0xa)
             Obj id: 0xa, Flags: unknown
             aom id: 304, HW handle: 0x55c743a483a8 (created)

xTR1# show platform software mlist fp active index 0x6e
Multicast List entries

OCE Flags:
NS - Negate Signalling; IC - Internal copy;
A - Accept;            F - Forward;

OCE            Type           OCE Flags      Interface
-----------------------------------------------------------------------------
  ---
0x6d           OBJ_ADJACENCY  NS, F          LISP0.1
0xf8000166     OBJ_ADJACENCY  A              Tunnel2

xTR1# show platform software mlist fp active index 0xa
Multicast List entries

OCE Flags:
NS - Negate Signalling; IC - Internal copy;
A - Accept;            F - Forward;
```

```
OCE              Type          OCE Flags      Interface
--------------------------------------------------------------------------------
0x6d             OBJ_ADJACENCY  NS, F          LISP0.1
0xf80000a1       OBJ_ADJACENCY  A              GigabitEthernet4


xTR1# show platform software adjacency fp active index 0x6d
Number of adjacency objects: 22

Adjacency id: 0x6d (109)
  Interface: LISP0.1, IF index: 18, Link Type: MCP_LINK_IP
  Encap: 45:0:0:0:0:0:40:0:0:11:f5:98:c0:a8:1:1:c0:a8:3:3:0:0:10:f5:0:0:0:0:48:0:0:
  0:0:0:1:1
  Encap Length: 36, Encap Type: MCP_ET_LISP, MTU: 1464
  Flags: midchain
  Incomplete behavior type: None
  Fixup: unknown
  Fixup_Flags_2: unknown
  Nexthop addr: 192.168.3.3
  IP FRR MCP_ADJ_IPFRR_NONE 0
  aom id: 281, HW handle: 0x55c743a21998 (created)


xTR1# show platform software adjacency fp active index 0xf80000a1
Number of adjacency objects: 22

Adjacency id: 0xf80000a1 (4160749729)
  Interface: GigabitEthernet4, IF index: 10, Link Type: MCP_LINK_IP
  Encap: 1:0:5e:0:0:0:c:70:eb:13:3b:3:8:0
  Encap Length: 14, Encap Type: MCP_ET_ARPA, MTU: 1500
  Flags: no-l3-inject, p2mp-type
  Incomplete behavior type: None
  Fixup: unknown
  Fixup_Flags_2: unknown
  Nexthop addr: 225.0.0.0
  IP FRR MCP_ADJ_IPFRR_NONE 0
  aom id: 197, HW handle: 0x55c7439c9978 (created)
```

Note   The commands may vary between different IOS-XE software versions and platforms. The output in Example 5-12 is taken from an ASR1000 platform running the 16.8.1 release.

If for any reason the multicast routing table is not being built or the (S, G) entry is not being formed, you should use the command **debug ip mrouting** [**vrf** *vrf-name*] *mcast-address*. This **debug** command displays the multicast routing events along with the relevant flags and OIL information. Example 5-13 displays the debug output for the group 239.1.1.1. It is important to remember that multicast routing comes into play only after you validate the information from a PIM perspective.

Example 5-13 *debug ip mrouting Command Output*

```
xTR1
xTR1# debug ip mrouting 239.1.1.1
IP multicast routing debugging is on
xTR1#
16:19:08.651: MRT(0): Create (*,239.1.1.1), RPF (unknown, 0.0.0.0, 0/0)
16:19:08.651: MRT(0): WAVL Insert LISP interface: LISP0.1 in (* ,239.1.1.1) Next-
  hop: 192.168.3.3 Outer-source: 0.0.0.0 Successful
16:19:08.651: MRT(0): set min mtu for (172.16.1.1, 239.1.1.1) 0->17892
16:19:08.651: MRT(0): Add LISP0.1/192.168.3.3 to the olist of (*, 239.1.1.1), For-
  ward state - MAC not built
16:19:08.651: MRT(0): Set the PIM interest flag for (*, 239.1.1.1)
16:19:13.547: MRT(0): Reset the z-flag for (172.16.1.2, 239.1.1.1)
16:19:13.547: MRT(0): (172.16.1.2,239.1.1.1), RPF install from /0.0.0.0 to Giga-
  bitEthernet4/172.16.1.2
16:19:13.547: MRT(0): Create (172.16.1.2,239.1.1.1), RPF (GigabitEthernet4,
  172.16.1.2, 0/0)
16:19:13.547: MRT(0): WAVL Insert LISP interface: LISP0.1 in (172.16.1.2,239.1.1.1)
  Next-hop: 192.168.3.3 Outer-source: 0.0.0.0 Successful
16:19:13.547: MRT(0): set min mtu for (172.16.1.2, 239.1.1.1) 18010->17892
16:19:13.547: MRT(0): Add LISP0.1/192.168.3.3 to the olist of (172.16.1.2,
  239.1.1.1), Forward state - MAC not built
16:19:13.557: MRT(0): Set the T-flag for (172.16.1.2, 239.1.1.1)
16:19:13.574: MRT(0): Update LISP0.1/192.168.3.3 in the olist of (172.16.1.2,
  239.1.1.1), Forward state - MAC not built
```

As stated earlier, IOS-XE does not have an event history as NX-OS does, but it does have event traces, which are similar to event history. IOS-XE provides event trace logs for the MFIB database. These logs are useful in case relevant messages are received by the PIM and processed by multicast routing and inserted into the MRIB but not added to the MFIB. The MFIB database event trace is viewed using the command **show monitor event-trace mfib db all** [**detail**]. Example 5-14 shows the MFIB event trace for the group 239.1.1.1. The output shown in this example highlights the sequence of events for both the (*, G) and (S, G) entries, along with the incoming and OIL interfaces and their respective flags (from the MRIB and MFIB command output shown in previous examples).

Example 5-14   *MFIB Database Event Trace on IOS-XE*

```
xTR1
xTR1# show monitor event-trace mfib db all detail
07:38:55.469: (0x0/Default) 0x7FC02C55C958 (*,239.1.1.1) Attached
07:38:55.469: (0x0/Default) 0x7FC02C55C958 (*,239.1.1.1) add Creator, now Temp
07:38:55.469: (0x0/Default) 0x7FC02C55C958 (*,239.1.1.1) del Creator, now <deleted>
07:38:55.469: (0x0/Default) 0x7FC02C55C958 (*,239.1.1.1) add Creator, now MRIB
07:38:55.469: (0x0/Default) 0x7FC02C55C958 (*,239.1.1.1) Activated with None
07:38:55.469: (0x0/Default) 0x7FC02C55C958 (*,239.1.1.1) Set Attr to C/K
07:38:55.474: (0x0/Default) 0x7FC02C55C958 (*,239.1.1.1) LISP0.1, 192.168.3.3
  Attached
07:38:55.474: (0x0/Default) 0x7FC02C55C958 (*,239.1.1.1) LISP0.1, 192.168.3.3 add
  Creator, now Temp
07:38:55.474: (0x0/Default) 0x7FC02C55C958 (*,239.1.1.1) LISP0.1, 192.168.3.3 del
  Creator, now <deleted>
07:38:55.474: (0x0/Default) 0x7FC02C55C958 (*,239.1.1.1) LISP0.1, 192.168.3.3 add
  Creator, now MRIB
07:38:55.474: (0x0/Default) 0x7FC02C55C958 (*,239.1.1.1) add Creator, now MRIB/
  IOitem
07:38:55.474: (0x0/Default) 0x7FC02C55C958 (*,239.1.1.1) LISP0.1, 192.168.3.3
  Activated with None
07:38:55.474: (0x0/Default) 0x7FC02C55C958 (*,239.1.1.1) LISP0.1, 192.168.3.3 Set
  Attr to F/NS/RF
07:38:55.474: (0x0/Default) 0x7FC02C55C958 (*,239.1.1.1) Tunnel2 Attached
07:38:55.474: (0x0/Default) 0x7FC02C55C958 (*,239.1.1.1) Tunnel2 add Creator, now
  Temp
07:38:55.474: (0x0/Default) 0x7FC02C55C958 (*,239.1.1.1) Tunnel2 del Creator, now
  <deleted>
07:38:55.474: (0x0/Default) 0x7FC02C55C958 (*,239.1.1.1) Tunnel2 add Creator, now
  MRIB
07:38:55.474: (0x0/Default) 0x7FC02C55C958 (*,239.1.1.1) Tunnel2 Activated with None
07:38:55.474: (0x0/Default) 0x7FC02C55C958 (*,239.1.1.1) Tunnel2 Set Attr to A/RA/MA
! Output omitted for brevity
07:39:13.741: (0x0/Default) 0x7FC26BA80958 (172.16.1.2,239.1.1.1) Attached
07:39:13.741: (0x0/Default) 0x7FC26BA80958 (172.16.1.2,239.1.1.1) add Creator, now
  DDC
07:39:13.741: (0x0/Default) 0x7FC26BA80958 (172.16.1.2,239.1.1.1) GigabitEthernet4
  Attached
07:39:13.741: (0x0/Default) 0x7FC26BA80958 (172.16.1.2,239.1.1.1) GigabitEthernet4
  add Creator, now DDC
07:39:13.741: (0x0/Default) 0x7FC26BA80958 (172.16.1.2,239.1.1.1) del Creator, now
  <deleted>
07:39:13.743: (0x0/Default) 0x7FC26BA80958 (172.16.1.2,239.1.1.1) GigabitEthernet4
  add Creator, now DDC/Signal
07:39:13.743: (0x0/Default) 0x7FC26BA80958 (172.16.1.2,239.1.1.1) add Creator, now
  IOitem
07:39:13.743: (0x0/Default) 0x7FC26BA80958 (172.16.1.2,239.1.1.1) Activated with
  None
```

```
07:39:13.745: (0x0/Default) 0x7FC26BA80958 (172.16.1.2,239.1.1.1) GigabitEthernet4
  Activated with SP

07:39:13.746: (0x0/Default) 0x7FC26BA80958 (172.16.1.2,239.1.1.1) GigabitEthernet4
  del Creator, now Signal

07:39:13.745: (0x0/Default) 0x7FC26BA80958 (172.16.1.2,239.1.1.1) GigabitEthernet4
  Set Attr to SP

07:39:13.746: (0x0/Default) 0x7FC26BA80958 (172.16.1.2,239.1.1.1) add Creator, now
  MRIB/IOitem

07:39:13.746: (0x0/Default) 0x7FC26BA80958 (172.16.1.2,239.1.1.1) Set Attr to K/DDE

07:39:13.747: (0x0/Default) 0x7FC26BA80958 (172.16.1.2,239.1.1.1) GigabitEthernet4
  add Creator, now MRIB/Signal

07:39:13.747: (0x0/Default) 0x7FC26BA80958 (172.16.1.2,239.1.1.1) GigabitEthernet4
  Set Attr to A/SP/RA

07:39:13.747: (0x0/Default) 0x7FC26BA80958 (172.16.1.2,239.1.1.1) GigabitEthernet4
  del Creator, now MRIB

07:39:13.746: (0x0/Default) 0x7FC26BA80958 (172.16.1.2,239.1.1.1) Tunnel2 Attached

07:39:13.746: (0x0/Default) 0x7FC26BA80958 (172.16.1.2,239.1.1.1) Tunnel2 add
  Creator, now Temp

07:39:13.746: (0x0/Default) 0x7FC26BA80958 (172.16.1.2,239.1.1.1) Tunnel2 del
  Creator, now <deleted>

07:39:13.746: (0x0/Default) 0x7FC26BA80958 (172.16.1.2,239.1.1.1) Tunnel2 Set Attr
  to None

07:39:13.746: (0x0/Default) 0x7FC26BA80958 (172.16.1.2,239.1.1.1) Sweeping

07:39:13.746: (0x0/Default) 0x7FC26BA80958 (172.16.1.2,239.1.1.1) Tunnel2 Discarded

07:39:13.746: (0x0/Default) 0x7FC26BA80958 (172.16.1.2,239.1.1.1) LISP0.1,
  192.168.3.3 Attached

07:39:13.746: (0x0/Default) 0x7FC26BA80958 (172.16.1.2,239.1.1.1) LISP0.1,
  192.168.3.3 add Creator, now Temp

07:39:13.746: (0x0/Default) 0x7FC26BA80958 (172.16.1.2,239.1.1.1) LISP0.1,
  192.168.3.3 del Creator, now <deleted>

07:39:13.746: (0x0/Default) 0x7FC26BA80958 (172.16.1.2,239.1.1.1) LISP0.1,
  192.168.3.3 add Creator, now MRIB

07:39:13.746: (0x0/Default) 0x7FC26BA80958 (172.16.1.2,239.1.1.1) LISP0.1,
  192.168.3.3 Activated with None

07:39:13.746: (0x0/Default) 0x7FC26BA80958 (172.16.1.2,239.1.1.1) LISP0.1,
  192.168.3.3 Set Attr to F/NS/RF
```

On the NX-OS software, different components interact with each other to program both the software and hardware for LISP multicast. Figure 5-5 highlights some of the high-level component interactions between components to program the multicast entries in both software and hardware. The primary concern in LISP multicast is the scenario when the RPF source of a route (the S-EID in the case of SSM or the RP-EID in the case of ASM) and the R-EID are located at two different customer sites, separated by the provider core network. To understand the component interaction, assume that PIM receives a PIM join packet for the first time. PIM performs both route lookup in both the Unicast Routing Information Base (URIB) and LISP to the RPF source of the route. PIM chooses the best prefix returned by LISP and the URIB and then installs the route to the MRIB. PIM also waits for a notification from the MRIB, which also listens to notifications from the

URIB and the LISP component. When RPF information is available, PIM sends the join packet to the upstream neighbor (toward the RPF source). The other events take place in a regular way: After the multicast tree is built, the data packets are sent downstream to the receiver site, which is across the LISP tunnel in the forwarding plane. In this case, the multicast forwarding distribution manager (MFDM) instructs the FIB to perform LISP encapsulation. Note that the encapsulation information is preprogrammed by the MRIB. The multicast forwarding (MCASTFWD) component is used for processing data packets in software.

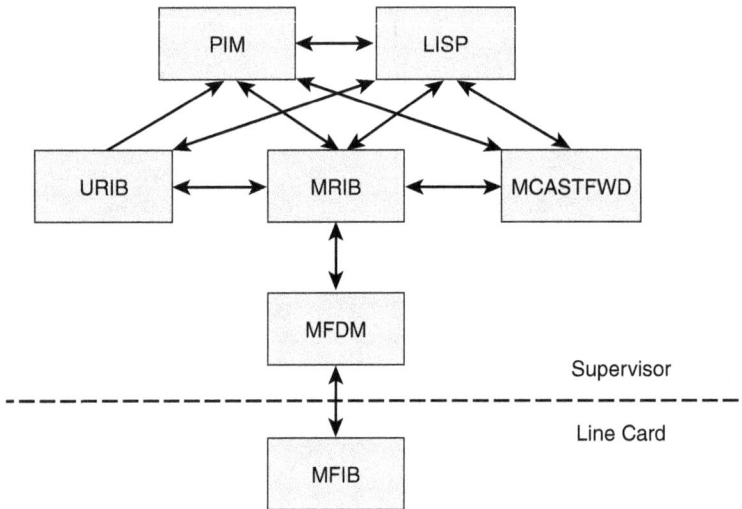

Figure 5-5   *NX-OS Component Interaction for LISP Multicast*

Examples 5-8 and 5-9, earlier in this chapter, show the information present in the PIM component. Because the PIM exchanges the information with the MRIB, the multicast route is verified in the MRIB by using the command **show routing ip multicast** *mcast-address* [**detail**] [**vrf** *vrf-name*]. The information present in the MRIB output can be cross-validated using the MRIB event history, which is verified using the command **show routing ip multicast internal event-history rib**. Example 5-15 shows the MRIB information for the multicast route 239.1.1.1. Notice that from the event history, it is clear that when the information is received from PIM for both the (*, G) and (S, G) routes, the MRIB performs an RPF lookup, and it looks into both the URIB and LISP components. When the information is available from both components, it then compares the information and choses the best route to the RPF neighbor. Because the RPF neighbor in this case is on a remote LISP site, the route from the LISP component is used, and the RPF neighbor is chosen to be the xTR1 RLOC address.

Example 5-15 *MRIB Route and Event History*

```
xTR3
xTR3# show routing ip multicast 239.1.1.1 detail
IP Multicast Routing Table for VRF "default"


Total number of routes: 3
Total number of (*,G) routes: 1
Total number of (S,G) routes: 1
Total number of (*,G-prefix) routes: 1


(*, 239.1.1.1/32) Route ptr: 0x62202648 , uptime: 00:02:26, pim(1) ip(0)
  RPF-Source: 172.16.1.1 [0/0]
  Data Created: No
  Stats: 0/0 [Packets/Bytes], 0.000   bps
  LISP Source RLOC address : 192.168.3.3
  Incoming interface: glt1, RPF nbr: 192.168.1.1
  Outgoing interface list: (count: 1)
    Ethernet2/3, uptime: 00:02:26, pim


(172.16.1.2/32, 239.1.1.1/32) Route ptr: 0x62202840 , uptime: 00:02:26, pim(1)
  mrib(0) ip(0)
  RPF-Source: 172.16.1.2 [0/0]
  Data Created: No
  Stats: 22/2200 [Packets/Bytes], 186.667 bps
  LISP Source RLOC address : 192.168.3.3
  Incoming interface: glt1, RPF nbr: 192.168.1.1
  Outgoing interface list: (count: 1)
    Ethernet2/3, uptime: 00:02:26, pim


xTR3# show routing ip multicast internal event-history rib


 rib events for MRIB process
09:07:00.381929 mrib [5898]: : "pim" add route (172.16.1.2/32, 239.1.1.1/32)
  (Ethernet2/3), rpf glt1 192.168.1.1(172.16.1.2), iod 40, mdt_encap_index 0, src_
  rloc 0.0.0.0, dst_rloc 0.0.0.0, bidir: 0, multi-route, use_rpf_source
09:07:00.381920 mrib [5898]: : RPF change for (172.16.1.2/32, 239.1.1.1/32)
  (172.16.1.2), iif: glt1 (iod 40), RPF nbr: 192.168.1.1
09:07:00.381916 mrib [5898]: : RPF lookup for route (172.16.1.2/32, 239.1.1.1/32)
  RPF Source 172.16.1.2 is iif: glt1 (iod 40), RPF nbr: 192.168.1.1,  path_type 0
09:07:00.381909 mrib [5898]: : mrib_rpf_lookup: Comparing LISP and URIB route.
  Lookup for EID 172.16.1.2 returns dest-rloc 192.168.1.1 and source-rloc
  192.168.3.3. urib_prefix_masklen: 0 lisp_mask_len: 24
09:07:00.381906 mrib [5898]: : mrib_rpf_lookup: LISP lookup returns if-index
  0x22280001, source-rloc 192.168.3.3, dest-rloc 192.168.1.1, forward-native FALSE,
  static-drop FALSE
```

```
09:07:00.381873 mrib [5898]: : mrib_rpf_lookup: This is xTR, looking up rpf route
   for 172.16.1.2
09:07:00.381866 mrib [5898]: : URIB RPF lookup failed: urib_get_route_for_multicast_
   source: src = 172.16.1.2, grp = 239.1.1.1, tableId = 1: No route found
09:07:00.381857 mrib [5898]: : Route: (172.16.1.2/32, 239.1.1.1/32), tableid: 1
09:07:00.381842 mrib [5898]: [5927]: mrib_add_oifs: add oifs mpib:pim
09:07:00.381834 mrib [5898]: : "pim" add route (*, 239.1.1.1/32) (Ethernet2/3), rpf
   glt1 192.168.1.1(172.16.1.1), iod 40, mdt_encap_index 0, src_rloc 0.0.0.0, dst_
   rloc 0.0.0.0, bidir: 0, use_rpf_source
09:07:00.381817 mrib [5898]: : RPF change for (*, 239.1.1.1/32) (172.16.1.1), iif:
   glt1 (iod 40), RPF nbr: 192.168.1.1
09:07:00.381814 mrib [5898]: : RPF lookup for route (*, 239.1.1.1/32) RPF Source
   172.16.1.1 is iif: glt1 (iod 40), RPF nbr: 192.168.1.1,  path_type 0
09:07:00.381803 mrib [5898]: : mrib_rpf_lookup: Comparing LISP and URIB route.
   Lookup for EID 172.16.1.1 returns dest-rloc 192.168.1.1 and source-rloc
   192.168.3.3. urib_prefix_masklen: 0 lisp_mask_len: 24
09:07:00.381800 mrib [5898]: : mrib_rpf_lookup: LISP lookup returns if-index
   0x22280001, source-rloc 192.168.3.3, dest-rloc 192.168.1.1, forward-native FALSE,
   static-drop FALSE
09:07:00.381754 mrib [5898]: : mrib_rpf_lookup: This is xTR, looking up rpf route
   for 172.16.1.1
09:07:00.381712 mrib [5898]: : URIB RPF lookup failed: urib_get_route_for_multicast_
   source: src = 172.16.1.1, grp = 239.1.1.1, tableId = 1: No route found
09:07:00.381699 mrib [5898]: : Route: (*, 239.1.1.1/32), tableid: 1
```

Because the LISP component interacts with the MRIB component, LISP stores the information for multicast routes that use the LISP map cache for their RPF neighbor. This is
verified using the command **show lisp internal ip multicast routes**. The LISP component
provides event history for its interaction with the MRIB. This is verified using the command **show lisp internal event-history multicast**. Example 5-16 shows the multicast
routes using the LISP map cache. In the output in Example 5-16, notice that the entry
(172.16.1.1, 239.1.1.1), which is for the RPF lookup for the RP of group 239.1.1.1, is using
the same map cache entry for (S, G), where S is the actual source 172.16.1.2.

Example 5-16 *LISP Event History for Multicast*

```
xTR3
xTR3# show lisp internal ip multicast routes

Multicast routes using LISP map-cache :
        (172.16.1.1, 239.1.1.1) Cache 172.16.1.0/24
        (172.16.1.2, 239.1.1.1) Cache 172.16.1.0/24

xTR3# show lisp internal event-history multicast
printing event history for instance 14
19:39:58.782012 lisp [5180]: (default): Sending ack: xid: eeee0075
```

```
19:39:58.781978 lisp [5180]: (default): RPF_SOURCE_ADD_FLAG_IS_SET for 172.16.1.2.
  Adding route: src 172.16.1.2, grp: 239.1.1.1, iod: 40
19:39:58.781971 lisp [5180]: (default): Received Join notify for (172.16.1.2/32,
  239.1.1.1/32), rpf_source 172.16.1.2,RPF iod is 40
19:39:58.781960 lisp [5180]: (default): Received a Join notify message from MRIB
  xid: 4008575093 count 0
19:35:24.064807 lisp [5180]: (default): Sending ack: xid: eeee0071
19:35:24.064784 lisp [5180]: (default): RPF_SOURCE_ADD_FLAG_IS_SET for 172.16.1.1.
  Adding route: src 0.0.0.0, grp: 239.1.1.1, iod: 40
19:35:24.064780 lisp [5180]: (default): Received Join notify for (*, 239.1.1.1/32),
  rpf_source 172.16.1.1,RPF iod is 40
19:35:24.064773 lisp [5180]: (default): Received a Join notify message from MRIB
  xid: 4008575089 count 0
```

The MRIB component shares the information further down to the MFDM. The MFDM
component receives routes programmed by the MRIB and pushes this information down to
the MFIB component. The multicast route information in the MFDM is verified using the
command **show forwarding distribution multicast route [group** *mcast-address*] **[source**
ip-address]. The interaction between the MFDM and the MRIB is verified using the command **show routing ip multicast internal event-history mfdm-debugs**. Example 5-17 shows
the route information present in MFDM along with the MRIB event history for MFDM
debugs. Note that the RPF is pointing to GLT, which in this case is referenced by RPF-IOD 40.

Example 5-17   *MFDM Route and Event History*

```
xTR3
xTR3# show forwarding distribution multicast route group 239.1.1.1


  (*, 239.1.1.1/32), RPF Interface: glt1, flags:
    Received Packets: 0 Bytes: 0
    Number of Outgoing Interfaces: 1
    Outgoing Interface List Index: 3
      Ethernet2/3


  (172.16.1.2/32, 239.1.1.1/32), RPF Interface: glt1, flags:
    Received Packets: 0 Bytes: 0
    Number of Outgoing Interfaces: 1
    Outgoing Interface List Index: 3
      Ethernet2/3


xTR3# show routing ip multicast internal event-history mfdm-debugs

 mfdm-debugs events for MRIB process
09:07:00.383255 mrib [5898]: : default: Received update-ack from MFDM, route-buffer
  0x0826ed5c, route-count 2, xid 0x0, Used buffer queue count:0, Free buffer queue
  count:10
```

```
09:07:00.383234 mrib [5898]: [5922]: Received update-ack from MFDM route-count: 2,
  xid: 0xaa0c
09:07:00.382071 mrib [5898]: : default: Sending update-route buffer 0x0x826ed5c, xid
  0xaa0c, count 2 of size 136 to MFDM
09:07:00.382069 mrib [5898]: [5917]: default: Moving MFDM txlist member marker to
  version 37, routes skipped 0
09:07:00.382064 mrib [5898]: : Inserting add-op-update for (172.16.1.2/32,
  239.1.1.1/32) (context 1) from txlist into MFDM route buffer
09:07:00.382062 mrib [5898]: :        OIF interface: Ethernet2/3
09:07:00.382060 mrib [5898]: : RPF-iod: 40,iif:40(v) rpf_s:ac100102(a) oif-list:
  00000000 (1), number of GLT intf 0,  Bidir-RP Ordinal: 0, mfdm-flags: dpgbrufo-
  vnl3r3
09:07:00.382057 mrib [5898]: : MRIB-MFDM-IF:Non-vpc mode. Invoked mfdm_mrib_add_reg_
  oif for non-oiflist oif Ethernet2/3
09:07:00.382055 mrib [5898]: : default: Insert add-op (172.16.1.2/32, 239.1.1.1/32)
  into MFDM buffer
09:07:00.382053 mrib [5898]: :        OIF interface: Ethernet2/3
09:07:00.382049 mrib [5898]: : Inserting add-op-update for (*, 239.1.1.1/32) (con-
  text 1) from txlist into MFDM route buffer
09:07:00.382046 mrib [5898]: :        OIF interface: Ethernet2/3
09:07:00.382044 mrib [5898]: : RPF-iod: 40,iif:40(v) rpf_s:ac100101(a) oif-list:
  00000000 (1), number of GLT intf 0,  Bidir-RP Ordinal: 0, mfdm-flags: dpgbrufovnl3r3
09:07:00.382037 mrib [5898]: : MRIB-MFDM-IF:Non-vpc mode. Invoked mfdm_mrib_add_reg_
  oif for non-oiflist oif Ethernet2/3
09:07:00.382033 mrib [5898]: : default: Insert add-op (*, 239.1.1.1/32) into MFDM
  buffer
09:07:00.382028 mrib [5898]: :        OIF interface: Ethernet2/3
```

The multicast route from MFDM is then pushed to the MFIB, which is validated using
the command **show forwarding ip multicast route** [group *mcast-address*] [**source**
ip-address]. The same route is validated on the forwarding engine on the line card, using
the command **show system internal forwarding multicast route** [group *mcast-address*]
[**source** *ip-address*] [**detail**] [**module** *slot-number*]

Note   In the event of any issues with LISP multicast on NX-OS, collect output for the
following **show tech** commands and share it with Cisco TAC for further investigation:

- **show tech ip multicast**

- **show tech forwarding l3 multicast detail**

- **show tech lisp**

In case of any issues with LISP multicast on IOS-XE, collect the following logs:

- **show tech lisp**

- **show tech ipmulticast**

- **show tech mfib** [**ipv4** | **ipv6**] [**vrf** *vrf-name*]

LISP IPv6 Multicast

In the past, enterprises used IPv4 addressing. However, due to the scale of IPv6 addressing and other benefits that IPv6 addressing provides, such as security, a shift occurred in network addressing requirements. Most enterprises and data centers are now interested in deploying just IPv6-enabled hosts or dual-stack hosts with both IPv4 and IPv6 addressing. Moreover, applications today are designed to support both IPv4 and IPv6 infrastructure. These changing requirements created a need to support IPv6 multicast over the LISP infrastructure so that multicast applications using IPv6 addressing can communicate across multiple LISP sites.

LISP IPv6 multicast support was added on the IOS-XE platform starting in the 16.2 release. Prior to this release, IOS-XE platforms supported only LISP IPv4 multicast. LISP IPv6 multicast functions the same way as LISP IPv4 multicast. The IPv6 PIM messages are sent to remote LISP or non-LISP sites using IPv4 transport. To understand the working behavior of LISP IPv6 multicast across LISP and non-LISP sites, examine the topology shown in Figure 5-6. In this topology, the source is connected to a non-LISP site (PxTR1), the receiver resides on xTR2, and the IPv6 RP resides on xTR1.

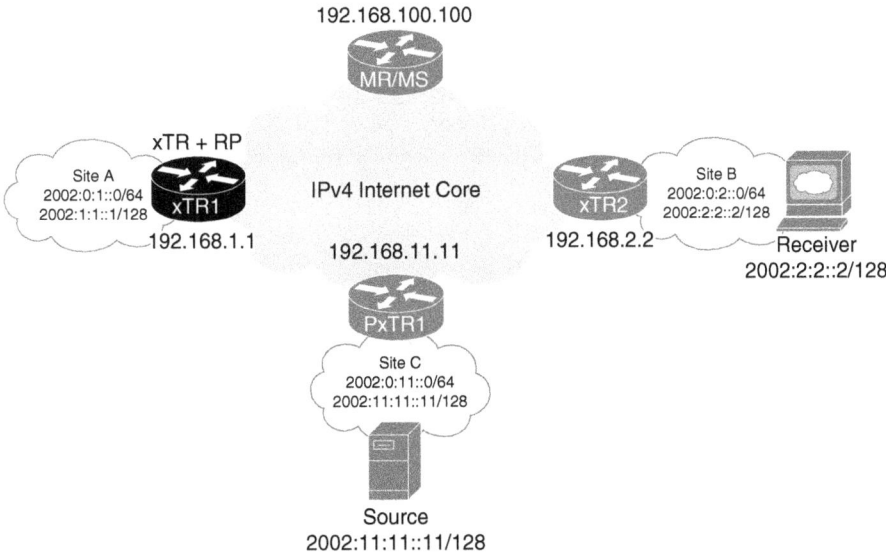

Figure 5-6 *LISP IPv6 Multicast Topology with LISP and Non-LISP Sites*

The following control plane exchanges happen between the three sites:

1. Because the hosts are IPv6 enabled, their membership is managed via the IPv6 Multicast Listener Discovery (MLD) protocol. The receiver sends a join for group G, which is discovered by MLD. Then IPv6 PIM join packets are created by the LHR and intermediate routers in LISP Site B. When xTR2 receives the PIM join, it forms the (*, G) entry.

2. Because the RP does not reside locally in Site B, xTR2 performs a LISP map cache lookup for the RP-EID. When the map cache is updated, xTR2 encapsulates the PIM join for group G inside a LISP header and forwards it to xTR1, where the RP actually resides. At this point, the (*, G) entry is built on the xTR1, with the incoming interface as the RP de-encapsulation tunnel and the OIL populated with the LISP interface with the xTR2 RLOC as the next hop.

3. The source S sends multicast traffic for group G to the FHR. On receiving the multicast packet, the FHR sends a PIM register message toward the RP. At this point, the FHR creates an (S, G) entry in the mroute table with the OIL populated with the RP encapsulation tunnel.

4. Because the S-EID is present on PxTR1, it performs a LISP map cache lookup for the RP-EID. When the map cache is updated, xTR1 encapsulates the PIM register message with the LISP header and forwards it toward the RP on xTR1. xTR1 de-encapsulates the PIM register message, and the RP consumes it and programs the (S, G) entry.

5. xTR1 forwards the multicast traffic to xTR2, which is connected to the receiver on the shared tree. Because the LHR receives the traffic from source S, it sends an IPv6 PIM join for group G with source S. The xTR2 then initiates a LISP query for the prefix S. Because the source S couldn't be resolved by MR/MS, the query is defaulted to PxTR1. PxTR1 sends a map reply for the source S to xTR2. xTR2 then sends a PIM join to the FHR, which is connected on PxTR1. On receiving the PIM join, PxTR1 updates the (S, G) OIL entry with LISP tunnel interface with the xTR2 RLOC as the next hop.

6. PxTR1 sends multicast traffic that is encapsulated with the LISP header to xTR2. On xTR2, because the multicast traffic was received from the source S, the (S, G) entry is installed in the mroute table with the RPF neighbor of PxTR1. Also, the LHR sends a PIM join toward the source S-EID that resides on xTR1. On receiving the PIM join from xTR3, xTR1 updates the (S, G) entry and adds another OIL interface with LISP overlay interface with the xTR3 RLOC as the next hop.

7. When the OIL is updated on xTR1, PxTR1 forwards the multicast traffic to xTR2.

8. xTR2 sends a PIM prune message with the RP bit set for (*, G) to the RP (that is, xTR1).

9. xTR1 sends PIM prune message for (S-EID, G) to PxTR1. This removes the OIL on PxTR1 for the xTR1 RLOC.

The current implementation supports only IPv6 SSM and IPv6 ASM over LISP infrastructure on IOS-XE platforms with statically defined RP. Note that the RLOC space being used for LISP IPv6 multicast is IPv4.

Configuring and Verifying LISP IPv6 Multicast

To set up LISP IPv6 multicast, we can use the same topology shown in Figure 5-6. To enable LISP IPv6 multicast, first you need to run **ipv6 multicast-routing** [**vrf** *vrf-name*] on the xTRs and PxTRs. Enabling IPv6 multicast automatically enables IPv6 PIM on the interfaces. Configure the static IPv6 RP by using the command **ipv6 pim** [**vrf** *vrf-name*] **rp-address** *v6-address*. Finally, under the LISP overlay interface, run the command **ipv6 pim lisp transport unicast ipv4**. This command allows the IPv6 PIM to use IPv4 transport over LISP. This configuration is required for the unicast head-end replication method. To deploy LISP IPv6 multicast with multicast replication, use the command **ipv6 pim lisp transport multicast**. Example 5-18 displays the configuration of xTR1 and PxTR1. Notice that this example also demonstrates a new way of configuring IPv4 and IPv6 database mappings as part of the IPv4 and IPv6 services.

Example 5-18   *LISP IPv6 Multicast Configuration*

```
xTR1
ipv6 unicast-routing
ipv6 multicast-routing
!
ipv6 pim rp-address 2002:0:1::1
!
router lisp
 locator-table default
!
 service ipv6
  itr map-resolver 192.168.100.100
  itr
  etr map-server 192.168.100.100 key cisco
  etr
  use-petr 192.168.11.11
  exit-service-ipv6
 !
 instance-id 1
  service ipv6
   eid-table default
   database-mapping 2002:0:1::/64 192.168.1.1 priority 100 weight 100
   database-mapping 2002:1:1::1/128 192.168.1.1 priority 100 weight 100
   exit-service-ipv6
  !
  exit-instance-id
 !
 exit-router-lisp
!
interface LISP0.1
 ipv6 pim lisp transport unicast ipv4
PxTR1
ipv6 unicast-routing
ipv6 multicast-routing
!
```

```
ipv6 pim rp-address 2002:0:1::1
!
router lisp
 locator-table default
!
 service ipv6
  itr map-resolver 192.168.100.100
  proxy-etr
  proxy-itr 192.168.11.11
  exit-service-ipv6
 !
 instance-id 1
  service ipv6
   eid-table default
   map-cache ::/0 map-request
   no map-cache-persistent
   exit-service-ipv6
  !
  exit-instance-id
 !
 exit-router-lisp
!
interface LISP0.1
 ipv6 pim lisp transport unicast ipv4
```

Note   Before implementing LISP IPv6 multicast with multicast replication, check the Cisco documentation for feature support on specific hardware platforms and software.

When the configuration is complete for all sites and IPv6 multicast is enabled, you need to verify the PIM neighbor on each xTR and PxTR node. Example 5-19 examines the PIM neighbors on all the xTR and PxTR routers. Notice that on xTR2, the PIM neighbor is seen for three interfaces. The IPv6 PIM neighbor over LISP interfaces is seen only when there is a join sent via the xTR over the LISP tunnel interface. Notice that the local PIM neighbor is formed over the link-local address, whereas the PIM neighbor across the LISP overlay is formed over IPv6 mapped IPv4 address.

Example 5-19 *Verifying IPv6 PIM Neighbors*

```
xTR1
xTR1# show ipv6 pim neighbor
PIM Neighbor Table
Mode: B - Bidir Capable, G - GenID Capable
Neighbor Address          Interface         Uptime    Expires  Mode DR pri


FE80::A8BB:CCFF:FE00:700  GigabitEthernet3  1d22h     00:01:26 B G  DR 1
xTR2
xTR2# show ipv6 pim neighbor
PIM Neighbor Table
Mode: B - Bidir Capable, G - GenID Capable
Neighbor Address          Interface         Uptime    Expires  Mode DR pri


FE80::A8BB:CCFF:FE00:900  GigabitEthernet3  1d22h     00:01:22 B G  DR 1
::FFFF:192.168.1.1        LISP0.1           1d22h     00:01:33       N/A
::FFFF:192.168.11.11      LISP0.1           02:27:43  00:01:23       N/A
PxTR1
PxTR1# show ipv6 pim neighbor
PIM Neighbor Table
Mode: B - Bidir Capable, G - GenID Capable
Neighbor Address          Interface         Uptime    Expires  Mode DR pri


FE80::A8BB:CCFF:FE00:800  GigabitEthernet3  22:06:12  00:01:17 B G  DR 1
```

When LISP and IPv6 multicast are enabled on all the xTR, PxTR, and CE routers and when PIM neighborship is set up, the receiver can initiate an MLD join for the group FF5A:11:11::11 from the CE2 router connecting to xTR2. Because the LHR is the CE2 router, it sends an IPv6 PIM join/prune message to xTR2, which is destined to the RP. On receiving the IPv6 PIM join, xTR2 builds a (*, G) entry for the group FF5A:11:11::11. Because the RP resides on xTR1, a map request is sent to MR/MS for the RP-EID. When the map cache is updated with the RP-RLOC, the incoming interface is set to the LISP overlay interface. This information is also verified using the command **debug ipv6 pim group** *mcast-group*. Example 5-20 shows the IPv6 multicast route on both xTR1, which is the RP-RLOC, and xTR2, where R-EID resides. The output also displays the PIM de-encapsulation tunnel using the command **show ipv6 pim tunnel**.

Example 5-20 *Mroute Table After an MLD Join*

```
xTR2
xTR2# show ipv6 mroute
Multicast Routing Table
! Output omitted for brevity
Timers: Uptime/Expires
Interface state: Interface, State

(*, FF5A:11:11::11), 06:35:40/00:02:46, RP 2002:0:1::1, flags: S
  Incoming interface: LISP0.1
  RPF nbr: ::FFFF:192.168.1.1
  Immediate Outgoing interface list:
    GigabitEthernet3, Forward, 06:35:40/00:02:46


xTR2# debug ipv6 pim group FF5A:11:11::11
IPv6 PIM group debugging is on for group FF5A:11:11::11


07:13:05.033: IPv6 PIM: J/P entry: Join root: 2002:0:1::1 group: FF5A:11:11::11
  Sender: FE80::A8BB:CCFF:FE00:900 flags:  RPT WC S
07:13:05.033: IPv6 PIM: (*,FF5A:11:11::11) Create entry
07:13:05.033: IPv6 PIM: (*,FF5A:11:11::11) Extranet RPF update, RPF interface
  LISP0.1 VRF [0xFFFF]->[0x0]
07:13:05.033: IPv6 PIM: (*,FF5A:11:11::11/128) MRIB modify DC
07:13:05.033: IPv6 PIM: (*,FF5A:11:11::11/128) LISP0.1 MRIB modify A
07:13:05.033: IPv6 PIM: (::,FF5A:11:11::11) ole GigabitEthernet3 created as Generic
  type
07:13:05.033: IPv6 PIM: (*,FF5A:11:11::11/128) GigabitEthernet3 MRIB modify !MD
07:13:05.033: IPv6 PIM: (*,FF5A:11:11::11) GigabitEthernet3 J/P state changed from
  Null to Join
07:13:05.034: IPv6 PIM: (*,FF5A:11:11::11) GigabitEthernet3 Raise J/P expiration
  timer to 210 seconds
07:13:05.034: IPv6 PIM: (*,FF5A:11:11::11) GigabitEthernet3 FWD state change from
  Prune to Forward
07:13:05.034: IPv6 PIM: (*,FF5A:11:11::11/128) GigabitEthernet3 MRIB modify F NS
07:13:05.034: IPv6 PIM: (*,FF5A:11:11::11) Updating J/P status from Null to Join
07:13:05.034: IPv6 PIM: (*,FF5A:11:11::11) J/P scheduled in 0.0 secs
07:13:05.035: IPv6 PIM: (*,FF5A:11:11::11) Processing timers
07:13:05.035: IPv6 PIM: (*,FF5A:11:11::11) J/P processing
07:13:05.035: IPv6 PIM: (*,FF5A:11:11::11) Upstream Mode changed from None to PIM
07:13:05.035: IPv6 PIM: (*,FF5A:11:11::11) Periodic J/P scheduled in 60 secs. Exact
  schedule time including jitter is: 59042 msec
07:13:05.035: IPv6 PIM: (*,FF5A:11:11::11) J/P adding Join on LISP0.1
xTR1 (RP)
xTR1# show ipv6 mroute FF5A:11:11::11
Multicast Routing Table
! Output omitted for brevity
```

```
Timers: Uptime/Expires
Interface state: Interface, State

(*, FF5A:11:11::11), 06:50:21/00:03:16, RP 2002:0:1::1, flags: S
  Incoming interface: Tunnel2
  RPF nbr: 2002:0:1::1
  Immediate Outgoing interface list:
    LISP0.1, NH 10.2.20.2, Forward, 06:50:21/00:03:16

xTR1# show ipv6 pim tunnel
Tunnel0*
  Type : PIM Encap
  RP   : Embedded RP Tunnel
  Source: 2002:0:1::1
Tunnel1*
  Type : PIM Encap
  RP   : 2002:0:1::1*
  Source: 2002:0:1::1
Tunnel2*
  Type : PIM Decap
  RP   : 2002:0:1::1*
  Source: -

xTR1# debug ipv6 pim group FF5A:11:11::11
IPv6 PIM group debugging is on for group FF5A:11:11::11

07:13:05.008: IPv6 PIM: J/P entry: Join root: 2002:0:1::1 group: FF5A:11:11::11
  Sender: FE80::21E:49FF:FE84:BC00 flags: RPT WC S
07:13:05.009: IPv6 PIM: (*,FF5A:11:11::11) Create entry
07:13:05.009: IPv6 PIM: (*,FF5A:11:11::11) Extranet RPF update, RPF interface
  Tunnel2 VRF [0xFFFF]->[0x0]
07:13:05.009: IPv6 PIM: (*,FF5A:11:11::11/128) MRIB modify DC
07:13:05.009: IPv6 PIM: (*,FF5A:11:11::11/128) Tunnel2 MRIB modify A
07:13:05.009: IPv6 PIM: (::,FF5A:11:11::11) ole LISP0.1 NH:10.2.10.2 created as
  NBMA type
07:13:05.009: IPv6 PIM: (*,FF5A:11:11::11/128) LISP0.1 NH:10.2.10.2 MRIB modify !MD
07:13:05.009: IPv6 PIM: (*,FF5A:11:11::11) LISP0.1 NH:10.2.10.2 J/P state changed
  from Null to Join
07:13:05.010: IPv6 PIM: (*,FF5A:11:11::11) LISP0.1 NH:10.2.10.2 Raise J/P expiration
  timer to 210 seconds
07:13:05.010: IPv6 PIM: (*,FF5A:11:11::11) LISP0.1 FWD state change from Prune to
  Forward
07:13:05.010: IPv6 PIM: (*,FF5A:11:11::11/128) LISP0.1 NH:10.2.10.2 MRIB modify F
07:13:05.010: IPv6 PIM: (*,FF5A:11:11::11) Updating J/P status from Null to Join
07:13:05.010: IPv6 PIM: (*,FF5A:11:11::11) J/P scheduled in 0.0 secs
```

```
07:13:05.010: IPv6 PIM: (*,FF5A:11:11::11) Processing timers
07:13:05.011: IPv6 PIM: (*,FF5A:11:11::11) J/P processing
07:13:05.011: IPv6 PIM: (*,FF5A:11:11::11) Upstream Mode changed from None to PIM
07:13:05.011: IPv6 PIM: (*,FF5A:11:11::11) Periodic J/P scheduled in 60 secs. Exact
  schedule time including jitter is: 59583 msec
```

When the source starts sending the traffic, the FHR sends a PIM register message toward the RP for the group FF5A:11:11::11 with source 2002:11:11::11. On receiving the PIM register, the RP builds the (S, G) entry. Example 5-21 shows the mroute table with the (S, G) entry. Notice that on the RP (xTR1), there are two (S, G) entries. The first entry is with the incoming interface of the de-encapsulation tunnel and the outgoing interface of the LISP overlay tunnel with the xTR2 RLOC as the next hop . This entry is formed when the source registers for the group G. The second entry is with the incoming interface of the LISP overlay with the RPF neighbor PxTR1 and the outgoing interface as the LISP overlay with the xTR2 RLOC as the next hop . This entry is built when traffic is received from the source. The OIL for this second entry is inherited from the OIL of the first (S, G) entry. PxTR1, on the other hand, initially builds the (S, G) entry with the OIL pointing toward the RP-RLOC. Because the source, receiver, and RP all reside on different sites, xTR2 sends another join after receiving traffic on the shared tree toward PxTR1 with the SPT bit set, and PxTR1 adds the LISP overlay interface with the xTR2 RLOC as the next hop. At the same time, it receives a prune message from the RP and thus removes the xTR1 RLOC from the OIL and directly forwards the multicast traffic to xTR2.

Example 5-21   *Mroute Table with an (S, G) Entry*

```
PxTR1
PxTR1# show ipv6 mroute FF5A:11:11::11
Multicast Routing Table
Flags: D - Dense, S - Sparse, B - Bidir Group, s - SSM Group,
       C - Connected, L - Local, I - Received Source Specific Host Report,
       P - Pruned, R - RP-bit set, F - Register flag, T - SPT-bit set,
       J - Join SPT, Y - Joined MDT-data group,
       y - Sending to MDT-data group
       g - BGP signal originated, G - BGP Signal received,
       N - BGP Shared-Tree Prune received, n - BGP C-Mroute suppressed,
       q - BGP Src-Active originated, Q - BGP Src-Active received
       E - Extranet
Timers: Uptime/Expires
Interface state: Interface, State

(2002:11:11::11, FF5A:11:11::11), 00:04:26/00:03:12, flags: ST
  Incoming interface: GigabitEthernet3
  RPF nbr: FE80::A8BB:CCFF:FE00:800
  Immediate Outgoing interface list:
LISP0.1, NH 10.2.10.2, Forward, 00:04:26/00:03:12
```

```
PxTR1# debug ipv6 pim group FF5A:11:11::11
IPv6 PIM group debugging is on for group FF5A:11:11::11


20:08:57.988: IPv6 PIM: J/P entry: Join root: 2002:11:11::11 group: FF5A:11:11::11
  Sender: FE80::21E:7AFF:FEB3:E900 flags:  S
20:08:57.988: IPv6 PIM: (2002:11:11::11,FF5A:11:11::11) Create entry
20:08:57.989: IPv6 PIM: (2002:11:11::11,FF5A:11:11::11) RPF changed from ::/- to
  FE80::A8BB:CCFF:FE00:800/GigabitEthernet3
20:08:57.989: IPv6 PIM: (2002:11:11::11,FF5A:11:11::11) Source metric changed from
  [0/0] to [1/110]
20:08:57.989: IPv6 PIM: (2002:11:11::11,FF5A:11:11::11/128) MRIB modify DC
20:08:57.989: IPv6 PIM: (2002:11:11::11,FF5A:11:11::11/128) NULLIF-skip MRIB
  modify A
20:08:57.989: IPv6 PIM: (2002:11:11::11,FF5A:11:11::11) ole LISP0.1 NH:10.1.10.1
  created as NBMA type
20:08:57.989: IPv6 PIM: (2002:11:11::11,FF5A:11:11::11/128) LISP0.1 NH:10.1.10.1
  MRIB modify !MD
20:08:57.990: IPv6 PIM: (2002:11:11::11,FF5A:11:11::11) LISP0.1 NH:10.1.10.1 J/P
  state changed from Null to Join
20:08:57.990: IPv6 PIM: (2002:11:11::11,FF5A:11:11::11) LISP0.1 NH:10.1.10.1 FWD
  state change from Prune to Forward
20:08:57.990: IPv6 PIM: (2002:11:11::11,FF5A:11:11::11) Updating J/P status from
  Null to Join
20:08:57.990: IPv6 PIM: (2002:11:11::11,FF5A:11:11::11) J/P scheduled in 0.0 secs
20:08:57.990: IPv6 PIM: (2002:11:11::11,FF5A:11:11::11/128) GigabitEthernet3 MRIB
  modify NS
20:08:57.991: IPv6 PIM: (2002:11:11::11,FF5A:11:11::11) Set SPT bit
20:08:57.991: IPv6 PIM: (2002:11:11::11,FF5A:11:11::11/128) MRIB modify !DC
20:08:57.991: IPv6 PIM: (2002:11:11::11,FF5A:11:11::11/128) NULLIF-skip MRIB
  modify !A
20:08:57.991: IPv6 PIM: (2002:11:11::11,FF5A:11:11::11/128) GigabitEthernet3 MRIB
  modify A !NS
20:08:57.991: IPv6 PIM: (2002:11:11::11,FF5A:11:11::11/128) LISP0.1 NH:10.1.10.1
  MRIB modify F
20:08:57.992: IPv6 PIM: (2002:11:11::11,FF5A:11:11::11) LISP0.1 NH:10.1.10.1 Raise
  J/P expiration timer to 210 seconds
20:08:57.992: IPv6 PIM: (2002:11:11::11,FF5A:11:11::11) Processing timers
20:08:57.992: IPv6 PIM: (2002:11:11::11,FF5A:11:11::11) J/P processing
20:08:57.992: IPv6 PIM: (2002:11:11::11,FF5A:11:11::11) Upstream Mode changed from
  None to PIM
20:08:57.992: IPv6 PIM: (2002:11:11::11,FF5A:11:11::11) Periodic J/P scheduled in
  60 secs. Exact schedule time including jitter is: 59362 msec
20:08:57.992: IPv6 PIM: (2002:11:11::11,FF5A:11:11::11) J/P adding Join on
  GigabitEthernet3
20:08:58.008: IPv6 PIM: J/P entry: Join root: 2002:11:11::11 group: FF5A:11:11::11
  Sender: FE80::21E:49FF:FE84:BC00 flags:  S
```

```
20:08:58.009: IPv6 PIM: (2002:11:11::11,FF5A:11:11::11) ole LISP0.1 NH:10.2.10.2
   created as NBMA type

20:08:58.009: IPv6 PIM: (2002:11:11::11,FF5A:11:11::11/128) LISP0.1 NH:10.2.10.2
   MRIB modify !MD

20:08:58.009: IPv6 PIM: (2002:11:11::11,FF5A:11:11::11) LISP0.1 NH:10.2.10.2 J/P
   state changed from Null to Join

20:08:58.009: IPv6 PIM: (2002:11:11::11,FF5A:11:11::11) LISP0.1 NH:10.2.10.2 FWD
   state change from Prune to Forward

20:08:58.010: IPv6 PIM: (2002:11:11::11,FF5A:11:11::11/128) LISP0.1 NH:10.2.10.2
   MRIB modify F

20:08:58.010: IPv6 PIM: (2002:11:11::11,FF5A:11:11::11) LISP0.1 NH:10.2.10.2 Raise
   J/P expiration timer to 210 seconds

20:08:58.015: IPv6 PIM: J/P entry: Prune root: 2002:11:11::11 group: FF5A:11:11::11
   Sender: FE80::21E:7AFF:FEB3:E900 flags:  S

20:08:58.015: IPv6 PIM: (2002:11:11::11,FF5A:11:11::11) LISP0.1 NH:10.1.10.1 J/P
   state changed from Join to Null

20:08:58.016: IPv6 PIM: (2002:11:11::11,FF5A:11:11::11) LISP0.1 NH:10.1.10.1 FWD
   state change from Forward to Prune

20:08:58.016: IPv6 PIM: (2002:11:11::11,FF5A:11:11::11/128) LISP0.1 NH:10.1.10.1
   MRIB modify !F

20:08:58.016: IPv6 PIM: (2002:11:11::11,FF5A:11:11::11) LISP0.1 NH:10.1.10.1
   Processing timers

20:08:58.016: IPv6 PIM: (2002:11:11::11,FF5A:11:11::11) Processing timers
xTR1

xTR1# show ipv6 mroute FF5A:11:11::11
Multicast Routing Table
Flags: D - Dense, S - Sparse, B - Bidir Group, s - SSM Group,
       C - Connected, L - Local, I - Received Source Specific Host Report,
       P - Pruned, R - RP-bit set, F - Register flag, T - SPT-bit set,
       J - Join SPT, Y - Joined MDT-data group,
       y - Sending to MDT-data group
       g - BGP signal originated, G - BGP Signal received,
       N - BGP Shared-Tree Prune received, n - BGP C-Mroute suppressed,
       q - BGP Src-Active originated, Q - BGP Src-Active received
       E - Extranet
Timers: Uptime/Expires
Interface state: Interface, State


(2002:11:11::11, FF5A:11:11::11), 00:00:04/00:03:26, RP 2002:0:1::1, flags: SPR
  Incoming interface: Tunnel2
  RPF nbr: 2002:0:1::1
  Immediate Outgoing interface list:
    LISP0.1, NH 10.2.20.2, Null, 00:00:04/00:03:24


(2002:11:11::11, FF5A:11:11::11), 00:00:04/00:03:26, flags: S
  Incoming interface: LISP0.1
```

```
   RPF nbr: ::FFFF:192.168.11.11
   Inherited Outgoing interface list:
      LISP0.1, NH 10.2.20.2, Forward, 06:54:33/00:03:04


xTR1# debug ipv6 pim group FF5A:11:11::11
IPv6 PIM group debugging is on for group FF5A:11:11::11


*Jul 28 20:08:57.952: IPv6 PIM: (2002:11:11::11,FF5A:11:11::11) Received Register
  from 2002:0:11::2
*Jul 28 20:08:57.952: IPv6 PIM: (2002:11:11::11,FF5A:11:11::11) Create entry
*Jul 28 20:08:57.952: IPv6 PIM: (2002:11:11::11,FF5A:11:11::11) RPF changed from
  ::/- to ::/-
*Jul 28 20:08:57.952: IPv6 PIM: (2002:11:11::11,FF5A:11:11::11) Source metric
  changed from [0/0] to [4294967295/2147483647]
*Jul 28 20:08:57.952: IPv6 PIM: (2002:11:11::11,FF5A:11:11::11) Extranet RPF update,
  RPF interface - VRF [0x0]->[0xFFFF]
*Jul 28 20:08:57.953: IPv6 PIM: (2002:11:11::11,FF5A:11:11::11/128) MRIB modify DC
*Jul 28 20:08:57.953: IPv6 PIM: (2002:11:11::11,FF5A:11:11::11/128) Tunnel2 MRIB
  modify A
*Jul 28 20:08:57.953: IPv6 PIM: (2002:11:11::11,FF5A:11:11::11/128) LISP0.1
  NH:10.2.10.2 MRIB modify F
*Jul 28 20:08:57.954: IPv6 PIM: (2002:11:11::11,FF5A:11:11::11) Set alive timer to
  210 sec
*Jul 28 20:08:57.954: IPv6 PIM: (2002:11:11::11,FF5A:11:11::11) Updating J/P status
  from Null to Join
*Jul 28 20:08:57.954: IPv6 PIM: (2002:11:11::11,FF5A:11:11::11) J/P scheduled in
  0.0 secs
*Jul 28 20:08:57.954: IPv6 PIM: (2002:11:11::11,FF5A:11:11::11/128) NULLIF-skip MRIB
  modify NS
*Jul 28 20:08:57.954: IPv6 PIM: (2002:11:11::11,FF5A:11:11::11/128) MRIB modify L
*Jul 28 20:08:57.955: IPv6 PIM: (2002:11:11::11,FF5A:11:11::11) Processing timers
*Jul 28 20:08:57.955: IPv6 PIM: (2002:11:11::11,FF5A:11:11::11) J/P processing
*Jul 28 20:08:57.956: IPv6 PIM: (2002:11:11::11,FF5A:11:11::11) Upstream Mode
  changed from None to PIM
*Jul 28 20:08:57.956: IPv6 PIM: (2002:11:11::11,FF5A:11:11::11) Periodic J/P
  scheduled in 60 secs. Exact schedule time including jitter is: 59793 msec
*Jul 28 20:08:57.956: IPv6 PIM: (2002:11:11::11,FF5A:11:11::11) No RPF neighbor to
  send J/P
*Jul 28 20:08:57.964: IPv6 PIM: (2002:11:11::11,FF5A:11:11::11) RPF changed from
  ::/- to ::FFFF:192.168.11.11/LISP0.1
*Jul 28 20:08:57.964: IPv6 PIM: (2002:11:11::11,FF5A:11:11::11/128) NULLIF-skip MRIB
  modify !NS
*Jul 28 20:08:57.964: IPv6 PIM: (2002:11:11::11,FF5A:11:11::11/128) LISP0.1 MRIB
  modify NS
*Jul 28 20:08:57.964: IPv6 PIM: (2002:11:11::11,FF5A:11:11::11) Source metric
  changed from [4294967295/2147483647] to [1/1]
*Jul 28 20:08:57.965: IPv6 PIM: (2002:11:11::11,FF5A:11:11::11) J/P scheduled in
  0.0 secs
```

```
*Jul 28 20:08:57.965: IPv6 PIM: (2002:11:11::11,FF5A:11:11::11) Extranet RPF update,
RPF interface LISP0.1 VRF [0xFFFF]->[0x0]

*Jul 28 20:08:57.966: IPv6 PIM: (2002:11:11::11,FF5A:11:11::11) Processing timers

*Jul 28 20:08:57.966: IPv6 PIM: (2002:11:11::11,FF5A:11:11::11) J/P processing

*Jul 28 20:08:57.966: IPv6 PIM: (2002:11:11::11,FF5A:11:11::11) Periodic J/P
scheduled in 60 secs. Exact schedule time including jitter is: 58932 msec

*Jul 28 20:08:57.967: IPv6 PIM: (2002:11:11::11,FF5A:11:11::11) J/P adding Join on
LISP0.1

*Jul 28 20:08:57.988: IPv6 PIM: J/P entry: Prune root: 2002:11:11::11 group:
FF5A:11:11::11 Sender: FE80::21E:49FF:FE84:BC00 flags:  RPT S

*Jul 28 20:08:57.988: IPv6 PIM: (2002:11:11::11,FF5A:11:11::11)RPT Create entry

*Jul 28 20:08:57.989: IPv6 PIM: (2002:11:11::11,FF5A:11:11::11) ole LISP0.1
NH:10.2.10.2 created as NBMA type

*Jul 28 20:08:57.989: IPv6 PIM: (2002:11:11::11,FF5A:11:11::11/128) LISP0.1
NH:10.2.10.2 MRIB modify !MD

*Jul 28 20:08:57.989: IPv6 PIM: (2002:11:11::11,FF5A:11:11::11)RPT LISP0.1
NH:10.2.10.2 J/P state changed from Null to Prune

*Jul 28 20:08:57.989: IPv6 PIM: (2002:11:11::11,FF5A:11:11::11)RPT LISP0.1
NH:10.2.10.2 FWD state change from Forward to Prune

*Jul 28 20:08:57.989: IPv6 PIM: (2002:11:11::11,FF5A:11:11::11/128) LISP0.1
NH:10.2.10.2 MRIB modify !F

*Jul 28 20:08:57.990: IPv6 PIM: (2002:11:11::11,FF5A:11:11::11) Updating J/P status
from Join to Null

*Jul 28 20:08:57.990: IPv6 PIM: (2002:11:11::11,FF5A:11:11::11) J/P scheduled in
0.0 secs

*Jul 28 20:08:57.990: IPv6 PIM: (2002:11:11::11,FF5A:11:11::11/128) LISP0.1 MRIB
modify !NS

*Jul 28 20:08:57.990: IPv6 PIM: (2002:11:11::11,FF5A:11:11::11)RPT Updating J/P
status from Null to Prune

*Jul 28 20:08:57.990: IPv6 PIM: (2002:11:11::11,FF5A:11:11::11)RPT J/P scheduled in
0.0 secs

*Jul 28 20:08:57.990: IPv6 PIM: (2002:11:11::11,FF5A:11:11::11)RPT LISP0.1
NH:10.2.10.2 Raise J/P expiration timer to 210 seconds

*Jul 28 20:08:57.991: IPv6 PIM: (2002:11:11::11,FF5A:11:11::11) Processing timers

*Jul 28 20:08:57.991: IPv6 PIM: (2002:11:11::11,FF5A:11:11::11) J/P processing

*Jul 28 20:08:57.991: IPv6 PIM: (2002:11:11::11,FF5A:11:11::11) Periodic J/P stopped

*Jul 28 20:08:57.991: IPv6 PIM: (2002:11:11::11,FF5A:11:11::11) J/P adding Prune on
LISP0.1

*Jul 28 20:08:57.991: IPv6 PIM: (2002:11:11::11,FF5A:11:11::11)RPT Processing timers

*Jul 28 20:08:57.992: IPv6 PIM: (2002:11:11::11,FF5A:11:11::11)RPT J/P processing

*Jul 28 20:08:57.992: IPv6 PIM: (2002:11:11::11,FF5A:11:11::11) Suppress J/P to
ourselves

*Jul 28 20:08:57.992: IPv6 PIM: (2002:11:11::11,FF5A:11:11::11)RPT Upstream Mode
changed from None to PIM

*Jul 28 20:08:57.992: IPv6 PIM: (2002:11:11::11,FF5A:11:11::11) Suppress J/P to
ourselves

*Jul 28 20:08:57.992: IPv6 PIM: (2002:11:11::11,FF5A:11:11::11) Suppress J/P to
ourselves
```

```
*Jul 28 20:08:59.950: IPv6 PIM: (2002:11:11::11,FF5A:11:11::11) Received Register
  from 2002:0:11::2
*Jul 28 20:08:59.950: IPv6 PIM: (2002:11:11::11,FF5A:11:11::11) Set alive timer to
  210 sec
*Jul 28 20:08:59.950: IPv6 PIM: (2002:11:11::11,FF5A:11:11::11) Send Register-Stop
  to 2002:0:11::2
xTR2
xTR2# show ipv6 mroute FF5A:11:11::11
Multicast Routing Table
! Output omitted for brevity
Timers: Uptime/Expires
Interface state: Interface, State


(2002:11:11::11, FF5A:11:11::11), 00:02:54/00:02:44, flags: ST
  Incoming interface: LISP0.1
  RPF nbr: ::FFFF:192.168.11.11
  Immediate Outgoing interface list:
    GigabitEthernet3, Forward, 00:02:54/00:02:44


xTR2# debug ipv6 pim group FF5A:11:11::11
IPv6 PIM group debugging is on for group FF5A:11:11::11


20:08:58.001: IPv6 PIM: J/P entry: Join root: 2002:11:11::11 group: FF5A:11:11::11
  Sender: FE80::A8BB:CCFF:FE00:900 flags:  S
20:08:58.001: IPv6 PIM: (2002:11:11::11,FF5A:11:11::11) Create entry
20:08:58.001: IPv6 PIM: (2002:11:11::11,FF5A:11:11::11) RPF changed from ::/- to
  ::/-
20:08:58.001: IPv6 PIM: (2002:11:11::11,FF5A:11:11::11) Source metric changed from
  [0/0] to [4294967295/2147483647]
20:08:58.001: IPv6 PIM: (2002:11:11::11,FF5A:11:11::11) Extranet RPF update, RPF
  interface - VRF [0x0]->[0xFFFF]
20:08:58.002: IPv6 PIM: (2002:11:11::11,FF5A:11:11::11/128) MRIB modify DC
20:08:58.002: IPv6 PIM: (2002:11:11::11,FF5A:11:11::11/128) LISP0.1 MRIB modify A
20:08:58.003: IPv6 PIM: (2002:11:11::11,FF5A:11:11::11/128) GigabitEthernet3 MRIB
  modify F NS
20:08:58.003: IPv6 PIM: (2002:11:11::11,FF5A:11:11::11) ole GigabitEthernet3 created
  as Generic type
20:08:58.003: IPv6 PIM: (2002:11:11::11,FF5A:11:11::11/128) GigabitEthernet3 MRIB
  modify !MD
20:08:58.003: IPv6 PIM: (2002:11:11::11,FF5A:11:11::11) GigabitEthernet3 J/P state
  changed from Null to Join
20:08:58.003: IPv6 PIM: (2002:11:11::11,FF5A:11:11::11) GigabitEthernet3 Imm FWD
  state change from Prune to Forward
20:08:58.004: IPv6 PIM: (2002:11:11::11,FF5A:11:11::11) Updating J/P status from
  Null to Join
20:08:58.004: IPv6 PIM: (2002:11:11::11,FF5A:11:11::11) J/P scheduled in 0.0 secs
```

```
20:08:58.004: IPv6 PIM: (2002:11:11::11,FF5A:11:11::11/128) NULLIF-skip MRIB
modify NS

20:08:58.004: IPv6 PIM: (2002:11:11::11,FF5A:11:11::11) GigabitEthernet3 Raise J/P
expiration timer to 210 seconds

20:08:58.004: IPv6 PIM: (2002:11:11::11,FF5A:11:11::11) Processing timers

20:08:58.004: IPv6 PIM: (2002:11:11::11,FF5A:11:11::11) J/P processing

20:08:58.005: IPv6 PIM: (2002:11:11::11,FF5A:11:11::11) Upstream Mode changed from
None to PIM

20:08:58.005: IPv6 PIM: (2002:11:11::11,FF5A:11:11::11) Periodic J/P scheduled in
60 secs. Exact schedule time including jitter is: 59850 msec

20:08:58.005: IPv6 PIM: (2002:11:11::11,FF5A:11:11::11) No RPF neighbor to send J/P

20:08:58.009: IPv6 PIM: (2002:11:11::11,FF5A:11:11::11) RPF changed from ::/- to
::FFFF:192.168.11.11/LISP0.1

20:08:58.010: IPv6 PIM: (2002:11:11::11,FF5A:11:11::11/128) NULLIF-skip MRIB
modify !NS

20:08:58.010: IPv6 PIM: (2002:11:11::11,FF5A:11:11::11) Source metric changed from
[4294967295/2147483647] to [1/1]

20:08:58.010: IPv6 PIM: (2002:11:11::11,FF5A:11:11::11) Set SPT bit

20:08:58.010: IPv6 PIM: (2002:11:11::11,FF5A:11:11::11/128) MRIB modify !DC

20:08:58.010: IPv6 PIM: (2002:11:11::11,FF5A:11:11::11/128) LISP0.1 MRIB modify !A

20:08:58.011: IPv6 PIM: (2002:11:11::11,FF5A:11:11::11/128) LISP0.1 MRIB modify A
!NS

20:08:58.011: IPv6 PIM: (2002:11:11::11,FF5A:11:11::11/128) GigabitEthernet3 MRIB
modify F NS

20:08:58.011: IPv6 PIM: (2002:11:11::11,FF5A:11:11::11)RPT Updating J/P status from
Null to Prune

20:08:58.011: IPv6 PIM: (2002:11:11::11,FF5A:11:11::11)RPT Create entry

20:08:58.011: IPv6 PIM: (2002:11:11::11,FF5A:11:11::11)RPT J/P scheduled in 0.0 secs

20:08:58.011: IPv6 PIM: (2002:11:11::11,FF5A:11:11::11) J/P scheduled in 0.0 secs

20:08:58.012: IPv6 PIM: (2002:11:11::11,FF5A:11:11::11) Extranet RPF update, RPF
interface LISP0.1 VRF [0xFFFF]->[0x0]

20:08:58.013: IPv6 PIM: (2002:11:11::11,FF5A:11:11::11)RPT Processing timers

20:08:58.013: IPv6 PIM: (2002:11:11::11,FF5A:11:11::11)RPT J/P processing

20:08:58.013: IPv6 PIM: (2002:11:11::11,FF5A:11:11::11)RPT Upstream Mode changed
from None to PIM

20:08:58.014: IPv6 PIM: (2002:11:11::11,FF5A:11:11::11)RPT J/P adding Prune on
LISP0.1

20:08:58.014: IPv6 PIM: (2002:11:11::11,FF5A:11:11::11)RPT Delete entry

20:08:58.014: IPv6 PIM: (2002:11:11::11,FF5A:11:11::11) Processing timers

20:08:58.014: IPv6 PIM: (2002:11:11::11,FF5A:11:11::11) J/P processing

20:08:58.014: IPv6 PIM: (2002:11:11::11,FF5A:11:11::11) Periodic J/P scheduled in
60 secs. Exact schedule time including jitter is: 59671 msec

20:08:58.014: IPv6 PIM: (2002:11:11::11,FF5A:11:11::11) J/P adding Join on LISP0.1
```

The information from PIM is pushed down to the MRIB and from the MRIB to the MFIB table. This is verified using the commands **show ipv6 mrib route** *mcast-address* and **show ipv6 mfib** *mcast-address* [**verbose**], as shown in Example 5-22. Note that the MFIB table displays the software and hardware forwarding counters. These counters are useful in troubleshooting multicast forwarding issues and help validate whether the packets are getting hardware switched or software switched or whether they are not being forwarded at all.

Example 5-22   *IPv6 MRIB and MFIB Table*

```
PxTR1
PxTR1# show ipv6 mrib route FF5A:11:11::11
IP Multicast Routing Information Base
Entry flags: L - Domain-Local Source, E - External Source to the Domain,
    C - Directly-Connected Check, S - Signal, IA - Inherit Accept, D - Drop
    ET - Data Rate Exceeds Threshold,K - Keepalive,DDE - Data Driven Event
    ME - MoFRR ECMP Flow based, MNE - MoFRR Non-ECMP Flow based,
    MP - Primary MoFRR Non-ECMP Flow based entry
Interface flags: F - Forward, A - Accept, IC - Internal Copy,
    NS - Negate Signal, DP - Don't Preserve, SP - Signal Present,
    II - Internal Interest, ID - Internal Disinterest, LI - Local Interest,
    LD - Local Disinterest, MD - mCAC Denied, MI - mLDP Interest
    A2 - MoFRR ECMP Backup Accept

(2002:11:11::11,FF5A:11:11::11) RPF nbr: FE80::A8BB:CCFF:FE00:800 Flags:
  LISP0.1 Flags: F      Next-hop: 10.2.10.2
  GigabitEthernet3 Flags: A


PxTR1# show ipv6 mfib FF5A:11:11::11 verbose
Entry Flags:     C - Directly Connected, S - Signal, IA - Inherit A flag,
                 ET - Data Rate Exceeds Threshold, K - Keepalive
                 DDE - Data Driven Event, HW - Hardware Installed
                 ME - MoFRR ECMP entry, MNE - MoFRR Non-ECMP entry, MP - MFIB
                 MoFRR Primary, RP - MRIB MoFRR Primary, P - MoFRR Primary
                 MS  - MoFRR  Entry in Sync, MC - MoFRR entry in MoFRR Client.
I/O Item Flags: IC - Internal Copy, NP - Not platform switched,
                 NS - Negate Signalling, SP - Signal Present,
                 A - Accept, F - Forward, RA - MRIB Accept, RF - MRIB Forward,
                 MA - MFIB Accept, A2 - Accept backup,
                 RA2 - MRIB Accept backup, MA2 - MFIB Accept backup


Forwarding Counts: Pkt Count/Pkts per second/Avg Pkt Size/Kbits per second
Other counts:       Total/RPF failed/Other drops
I/O Item Counts:    FS Pkt Count/PS Pkt Count
Default
(2002:11:11::11,FF5A:11:11::11) Flags: K HW
   0x45  OIF-IC count: 0, OIF-A count: 1
   SW Forwarding: 0/0/0/0, Other: 0/0/0
   HW Forwarding:   1/0/114/0, Other: 0/0/0
```

```
      GigabitEthernet3 Flags: RA A MA
    LISP0.1, 10.2.10.2 Flags: RF F
      CEF: Adjacency with MAC:
            4500000000004000FF1153D30A0B0A0B0A020A02000010F50000000008000000000000100
      Pkts: 0/0
xTR1
xTR1# show ipv6 mrib route FF5A:11:11::11
IP Multicast Routing Information Base
Entry flags: L - Domain-Local Source, E - External Source to the Domain,
   C - Directly-Connected Check, S - Signal, IA - Inherit Accept, D - Drop
   ET - Data Rate Exceeds Threshold,K - Keepalive,DDE - Data Driven Event
   ME - MoFRR ECMP Flow based, MNE - MoFRR Non-ECMP Flow based,
   MP - Primary MoFRR Non-ECMP Flow based entry
Interface flags: F - Forward, A - Accept, IC - Internal Copy,
   NS - Negate Signal, DP - Don't Preserve, SP - Signal Present,
   II - Internal Interest, ID - Internal Disinterest, LI - Local Interest,
   LD - Local Disinterest, MD - mCAC Denied, MI - mLDP Interest
   A2 - MoFRR ECMP Backup Accept


(*,FF5A:11:11::11) RPF nbr: 2002:0:1::1 Flags: C
  LISP0.1 Flags: F      Next-hop: 10.2.20.2
  Tunnel2 Flags: A


(2002:11:11::11,FF5A:11:11::11) RPF nbr: 2002:0:1::1 Flags: L C
  Tunnel2 Flags: A


xTR1# show ipv6 mfib FF5A:11:11::11 verbose
Entry Flags:    C - Directly Connected, S - Signal, IA - Inherit A flag,
                ET - Data Rate Exceeds Threshold, K - Keepalive
                DDE - Data Driven Event, HW - Hardware Installed
                ME - MoFRR ECMP entry, MNE - MoFRR Non-ECMP entry, MP - MFIB
                MoFRR Primary, RP - MRIB MoFRR Primary, P - MoFRR Primary
                MS  - MoFRR  Entry in Sync, MC - MoFRR entry in MoFRR Client.
I/O Item Flags: IC - Internal Copy, NP - Not platform switched,
                NS - Negate Signalling, SP - Signal Present,
                A - Accept, F - Forward, RA - MRIB Accept, RF - MRIB Forward,
                MA - MFIB Accept, A2 - Accept backup,
                RA2 - MRIB Accept backup, MA2 - MFIB Accept backup


Forwarding Counts: Pkt Count/Pkts per second/Avg Pkt Size/Kbits per second
Other counts:      Total/RPF failed/Other drops
I/O Item Counts:   FS Pkt Count/PS Pkt Count
Default
  (*,FF5A:11:11::11) Flags: C K HW
```

```
  0x65  OIF-IC count: 0, OIF-A count: 1
  SW Forwarding: 6/0/100/0, Other: 0/0/0
  HW Forwarding:   NA/NA/NA/NA, Other: NA/NA/NA
  Tunnel2 Flags: RA A MA
  LISP0.1, 10.2.10.2 Flags: RF F
    CEF: Adjacency with MAC:
         4500000000004000FF1153E70A010A010A020A02000010F500000000048000000000000101
    Pkts: 0/6
 (2002:11:11::11,FF5A:11:11::11) Flags: C K HW
   0x67  OIF-IC count: 0, OIF-A count: 1
   SW Forwarding: 0/0/0/0, Other: 0/0/0
   HW Forwarding:   NA/NA/NA/NA, Other: NA/NA/NA
   Tunnel2 Flags: RA A MA
xTR2
xTR2# show ipv6 mrib route FF5A:11:11::11
IP Multicast Routing Information Base
Entry flags: L - Domain-Local Source, E - External Source to the Domain,
    C - Directly-Connected Check, S - Signal, IA - Inherit Accept, D - Drop
    ET - Data Rate Exceeds Threshold,K - Keepalive,DDE - Data Driven Event
    ME - MoFRR ECMP Flow based, MNE - MoFRR Non-ECMP Flow based,
    MP - Primary MoFRR Non-ECMP Flow based entry
Interface flags: F - Forward, A - Accept, IC - Internal Copy,
    NS - Negate Signal, DP - Don't Preserve, SP - Signal Present,
    II - Internal Interest, ID - Internal Disinterest, LI - Local Interest,
    LD - Local Disinterest, MD - mCAC Denied, MI - mLDP Interest
    A2 - MoFRR ECMP Backup Accept


(*,FF5A:11:11::11) RPF nbr: ::FFFF:192.168.1.1 Flags: C
  GigabitEthernet3 Flags: F NS
  LISP0.1 Flags: A


(2002:11:11::11,FF5A:11:11::11) RPF nbr: ::FFFF:192.168.11.11 Flags:
  LISP0.1 Flags: A
  GigabitEthernet3 Flags: F NS


xTR2# show ipv6 mfib FF5A:11:11::11 verbose
! Output omitted for brevity

Forwarding Counts: Pkt Count/Pkts per second/Avg Pkt Size/Kbits per second
Other counts:      Total/RPF failed/Other drops
I/O Item Counts:   FS Pkt Count/PS Pkt Count
Default
 (*,FF5A:11:11::11) Flags: C K HW
   0x95  OIF-IC count: 0, OIF-A count: 1
```

```
  SW Forwarding: 0/0/0/0, Other: 0/0/0
  HW Forwarding:   4/0/150/0, Other: 0/0/0
  LISP0.1 Flags: RA A MA
  GigabitEthernet3 Flags: RF F NS
    CEF: Adjacency with MAC: 3333000000110CD89D7A840286DD
    Pkts: 0/0
(2002:11:11::11,FF5A:11:11::11) Flags: K HW
  0xC4  OIF-IC count: 0, OIF-A count: 1
  SW Forwarding: 0/0/0/0, Other: 0/0/0
  HW Forwarding:   157/0/150/0, Other: 0/0/0
  LISP0.1 Flags: RA A MA
  GigabitEthernet3 Flags: RF F NS
    CEF: Adjacency with MAC: 3333000000110CD89D7A840286DD
    Pkts: 0/0
```

On IOS-XE platforms, you can also validate the platform software counters for both IPv4 and IPv6 multicast by using the command **show platform software multicast stats**. This command not only displays the message counters but also maintains the counters for any failures. Example 5-23 shows the counters for messages added, modified, and deleted for the IPv6 MFIB and other IPv6 MFIB counters.

Example 5-23   *show platform software multicast stats Command Output*

```
xTR1
xTR1# show platform software multicast stats
Statistics for platform multicast operations:
 0 Number of bad fman stats
 0 Number of access to entries without platform markings
 0 Number of punts without subblocks
 0 v5-mfib-entry add messages
 0 v5-mfib-entry modify messages
 0 v5-mfib-entry delete messages
 0 Number of duplicate v4 entry deletes
 0 v5-mfib-outgoing-interface add messages
 0 v5-mfib-outgoing-interface modify messages
 0 v5-mfib-outgoing-interface delete messages
 2 v5-interface enable messages
 0 v5-interface disable messages
 0 Oif v4 adds, missing adjacency
 0 Oif v4 missing adj's added
 0 Oif v4 adj creation skipped
 0 Oif v4 adj creation failure
 0 Oif v4 ID creation failure
```

```
0 Oif v4 deletes, missing adj using cached ID
0 Oif v4 deletes, missing ID cache
0 Oif v4 add/modify, IC flag update failure
0 Oif v4 deletes, IC flag update failure
17662 mGRE, non-AutoRP Packets for AutoRP groups
0 mGRE, AutoRP Packets injected to p2MP interface
46 v6-mfib-entry add messages
46 v6-mfib-entry modify messages
13 v6-mfib-entry delete messages
0 Number of duplicate v6 entry deletes
45 v6-mfib-outgoing-interface add messages
20 v6-mfib-outgoing-interface modify messages
39 v6-mfib-outgoing-interface delete messages
20 v6-interface enable messages
4 v6-interface disable messages
15 Oif v6 adds, missing adjacency
15 Oif v6 missing adj's added
0 Oif v6 adj creation skipped
0 Oif v6 adj creation failure
0 Oif v6 ID creation failure
11 Oif v6 deletes, missing adj using cached ID
0 Oif v6 deletes, missing ID cache
0 Oif v6 add/modify, IC flag update failure
0 Oif v6 delete, IC flag update failure
0 Number of downloads with unknown AF
0 Oif IC count add/modify failure
0 Oif IC count deletes failure
0 Oif A count add/modify failure
0 Oif A count deletes failure
```

Finally, when the information is programmed in the MFIB, the MFIB programming on the forwarding engine on an ASR1000 series router is verified using the command **show platform software ipv6 fp active mfib group** *mcast-address/len* [**brief**]. This command returns the multicast list that holds the output chain elements (OCEs) mapping to incoming and outgoing interfaces. You can view the multicast list by using the command **show platform software mlist fp active** [**index** *index*]. Using the OCE indexes, you can validate the adjacency information on both the RP and the FP by using the command **show platform software adjacency** [**rp** | **fp**] **active index** *index*. Example 5-24 shows the verification of hardware programming for the IPv6 multicast group FF5a:11:11::11 on the PxTR1 router.

Example 5-24   *Verifying Platform Programming on an ASR1000 for IPv6 Multicast*

```
PxTR1
PxTR1# show platform software ipv6 fp active mfib group ff5a:11:11::11/128 brief
ff5a:11:11::11, 2002:11:11::11/256 --> List: 0xc (2 OCEs)
                HW list: 0x55d302b70b98 (created)


PxTR1# show plat software mlist fp active
Index           OCEs     Info
---------------------------------------------------------
0xc             2        HW list: 0x55d302b70b98 (creat
0x20            0        HW list: 0x55ae15cadf18 (creat
! Output omitted for brevity
0x3d            0        HW list: 0x55ae15cb89f8 (creat
0x45            0        HW list: 0x55ae15d217d8 (creat


PxTR1# show plat software mlist fp active index 0xc
Multicast List entries


OCE Flags:
NS - Negate Signalling; IC - Internal copy;
A - Accept;             F - Forward;


OCE             Type            OCE Flags       Interface
--------------------------------------------------------------------------------
0x16            OBJ_ADJACENCY   F               LISP0.1
0xf8000092      OBJ_ADJACENCY   A               GigabitEthernet3

PxTR1# show plat software adjacency rp active index 0x16
Number of adjacency objects: 14


Adjacency id: 0x16 (22)
  Interface: LISP0.1, IF index: 18, Link Type: MCP_LINK_IPV6
  Next Object Type: OBJ_ADJACENCY, Handle: 67
  Flags: midchain
  IP FRR MCP_ADJ_IPFRR_NONE 0
  OM handle: 0x34804f2060



PxTR1# show plat software adjacency fp active index 0x16
Number of adjacency objects: 14
```

```
Adjacency id: 0x16 (22)
  Interface: LISP0.1, IF index: 18, Link Type: MCP_LINK_IPV6
  Encap: 45:0:0:0:0:0:40:0:ff:11:53:d3:a:b:a:b:a:2:a:2:0:0:10:f5:0:0:0:0:8:0:0:0:0:
  0:1:0
  Encap Length: 36, Encap Type: MCP_ET_LISP, MTU: 1464
  Flags: midchain
  Incomplete behavior type: None
  Fixup: unknown
  Fixup_Flags_2: unknown
  Nexthop addr: 10.2.10.2
  IP FRR MCP_ADJ_IPFRR_NONE 0
  aom id: 309, HW handle: 0x55d302b72a58 (created)

PxTR1# show plat software adjacency rp active index 0xf8000092
Number of adjacency objects: 16

Adjacency id: 0xf8000092 (4160749714)
  Interface: GigabitEthernet3, IF index: 9, Link Type: MCP_LINK_IPV6
  Encap: 33:33:0:0:0:0:c:d8:9d:37:eb:2:86:dd
  Encap Length: 14, Encap Type: MCP_ET_ARPA, MTU: 1500
  Flags: no-l3-inject, p2mp-type
  Incomplete behavior type: None
  Fixup: unknown
  Fixup_Flags_2: unknown
  Nexthop addr: ff0e::
  IP FRR MCP_ADJ_IPFRR_NONE 0
  OM handle: 0x34804ed4e8

PxTR1# show plat software adjacency fp active index 0xf8000092
Number of adjacency objects: 14

Adjacency id: 0xf8000092 (4160749714)
  Interface: GigabitEthernet3, IF index: 9, Link Type: MCP_LINK_IPV6
  Encap: 33:33:0:0:0:0:c:d8:9d:37:eb:2:86:dd
  Encap Length: 14, Encap Type: MCP_ET_ARPA, MTU: 1500
  Flags: no-l3-inject, p2mp-type
  Incomplete behavior type: None
  Fixup: unknown
  Fixup_Flags_2: unknown
  Nexthop addr: ff0e::
  IP FRR MCP_ADJ_IPFRR_NONE 0
  aom id: 196, HW handle: 0x55d302b52508 (created)
```

Note In the event of any problems, collect the following logs from IOS-XE:

- **show tech ipmulticast** [vrf *vrf-name*]
- **show tech mfib** [ipv4 | ipv6]

LISP Multicast with the VXLAN Data Plane

LISP multicast is not supported only over the LISP data plane but also over the VXLAN data plane. The control plane behavior of both LISP IPv4 and IPv6 multicast does not change, except that all the control plane messages in the core are VXLAN encapsulated. Both the ITR and the ETR encapsulate the packet into a VXLAN header before sending it toward the remote xTR. The LISP instance ID is copied as the VXLAN virtual network identifier (VNID) in the VXLAN header, and the packet is then sent out. The VXLAN control plane packet being received by the remote xTR is de-encapsulated and then processed. To enable VXLAN encapsulation for IPv4 and IPv6, use the command **encapsulation vxlan** under the **service ipv4** and **service ipv6** configuration sections on IOS-XE. Figure 5-7 shows the VXLAN encapsulation LISP IPv6 multicast packet.

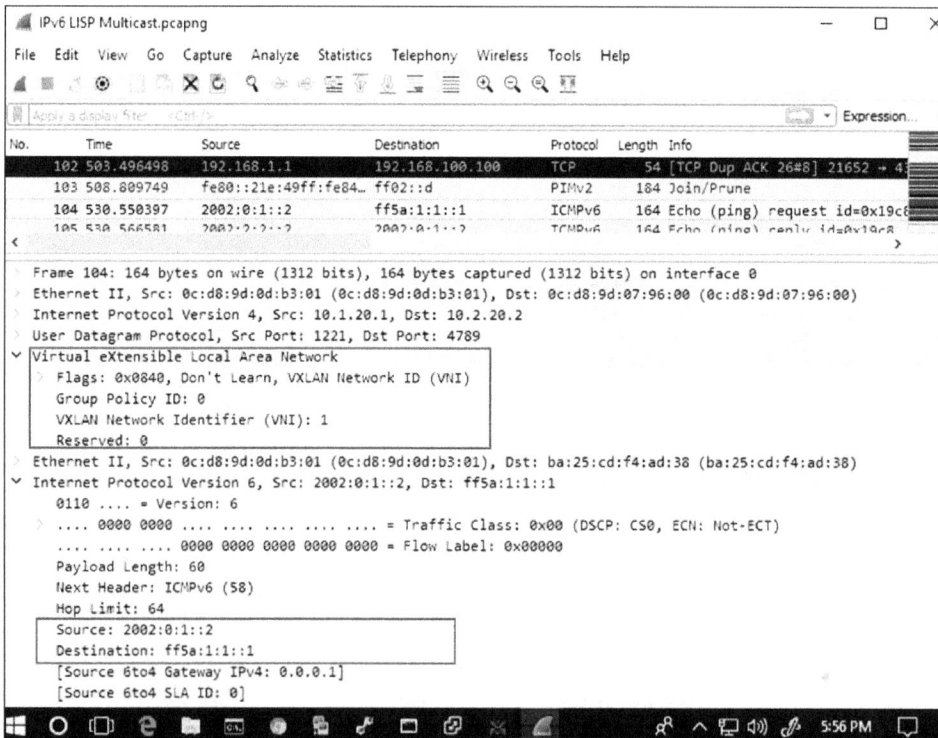

Figure 5-7 *LISP IPv6 Multicast Packet with VXLAN Data Plane*

Summary

LISP multicast, as defined in RFC 6831, leverages the LISP architecture to carry multicast between the source and the receiver, which are geographically dispersed. LISP multicast is enabled using two methods:

- Unicast head-end replication

- Native multicast replication

In the unicast head-end replication method, the Internet service provider (ISP) core network is not enabled with native multicast, and the packets are replicated at the source site itself. Unicast replication for an (S-EID, G) flow requires the downstream xTR to tunnel join/prune messages to the upstream xTR via a LISP tunnel interface. The upstream xTR encapsulates data packets to each and every downstream xTR for which it has received a join message. On the other hand, where the core is enabled with native multicast, the downstream xTR must additionally join the same group in the core by sending a native (S-RLOC, G). The upstream site encapsulates (S-EID, G) packets inside an (S-RLOC, G) packet and sends it toward the receiver site.

LISP multicast has the following restrictions:

- LISP multicast supports only SSM and ASM modes.

- LISP multicast supports only static RP configurations.

- LISP IPv6 multicast is supported only on IOS-XE platforms.

- Nexus does not support native multicast replication.

This chapter covers control plane and data plane interaction for both IPv4 and IPv6 LISP multicast between LISP and non-LISP sites. This chapter explains various configuration options on both IOS-XE and Nexus platforms, along with the components involved in verification and in performing troubleshooting of LISP multicast issues on each platform.

References

The following references provide more details on the topics discussed in this chapter:

RFC 6831, "The Locator/ID Separation Protocol (LISP) for Multicast Environments"

RFC 8378, "Signal-Free Locator/ID Separation Protocol (LISP) Multicast"

Cisco, "Cisco IOS Software Configuration Guides," http://www.cisco.com

Chapter 6

LISP IP Mobility in Traditional Data Center Network

Operational continuity with disaster avoidance (DA), business resilience, and disaster recovery (DR) are core capabilities of the data center IT infrastructure. The emergence of cloud computing have further highlighted the need for extremely robust network resilience strategies that address security, availability, and virtual machine (VM) mobility while maintaining the flexibility and agility of a cloud model. As the operational continuity model evolves, the time to recover in the event of a roaming application—either due to an outage or due to a migration toward a cloud infrastructure—must be reduced to its shortest value; at the same time, when it is required, dynamic localization of applications should be leveraged to automatically reroute traffic directly to the site where it is active.

The challenges of supporting operational continuity are not limited to a single data center. The elasticity and flexibility of the network architecture must be addressed as well. Therefore, the compute and network components may not necessarily reside in the same physical location. These resources could be placed at different locations and interconnected using routed Layer 3 transport or transparent Layer 2 transport. In addition, with the modern data center fabric networks, it is critical to maintain the end-to-end network segmentation, regardless of where the software framework and hardware platforms reside, because it is essential that IP localization techniques are multi-tenant capable.

This chapter covers the following topics:

- The principal traditional and modern solutions to extend bridge domains across different locations

- The solutions available to optimize the inbound workflow and localize roamers to redirect the IP data packets directly toward the site to which they belong

■ The LISP IP mobility models deployed with traditional data center networks, conventionally named LISP IP Mobility with Extended Subnet Mode (ESM) and LISP IP Mobility Across Subnets Mode (ASM)

■ A subfunction of LISP called Interior Gateway Protocol (IGP) Assist, which dynamically advertises host routes toward the Layer 3 core layer

Design Considerations Related to Interconnecting Data Centers

One of the key concepts of cloud computing is automatically and dynamically providing resources for a given service in a virtual environment. The virtual environment can be spread over multiple racks within a data center or across multiple data centers where hardware and software resources are available. To offer availability of those components seamlessly to distant locations, the network architecture must be built with efficient tools to support operational continuity throughout the live mobility of the applications and the network services, regardless of the physical location, as long as some crucial rules are addressed; for example, the movement of applications (software components or virtual machines) between two geographically dispersed locations should happen seamlessly from an operations point of view. During and after the migration of an application, its availability should not be impacted by long interruption, the same level of security must be maintained, and application performance should not be impacted by the distance from the new location. The operational continuity model is conventionally made of two key building blocks. First, a pair of tightly coupled data center leads, separated by metro distances for low latency, to avoid any interruption and allow synchronous data replication. Therefore, from a computer and application perspective, as well as from a storage point of view, the two twin data centers are seen as a single data center at all the stacks: network, compute, services, and storage. And from an operational point of view, they are seen as a logical entity. Second, a third data center located at a regional or international distance is deployed to recover the business in case of a major disaster in the twin data centers. Asynchronous data replication is therefore the only option to store user data at long distances. This third data center is often known as the disaster recovery data center or backup site. The backup site is typically used to run local applications independently from the other locations while all three sites are working properly. This solution architecture offers the ability to absorb the impact of a disaster and continue to provide an acceptable level of service according to the criticality levels of the enterprise's applications.

Figure 6-1 shows a classical deployment for operational continuance where applications and services are distributed across metro and geo distances. The left side shows typical twin data centers interconnected by short distances for low latency offering seamless migration and synchronous data replication for an active/active operational service. A third data center that is shown in the right side acts as a backup site so that the software infrastructure from the main location can be switched over to recover critical applications and services in case a global outage occurs and prevents the primary location from being operational. In addition to the disaster recovery function, the backup site can also be leveraged to support additional applications and services.

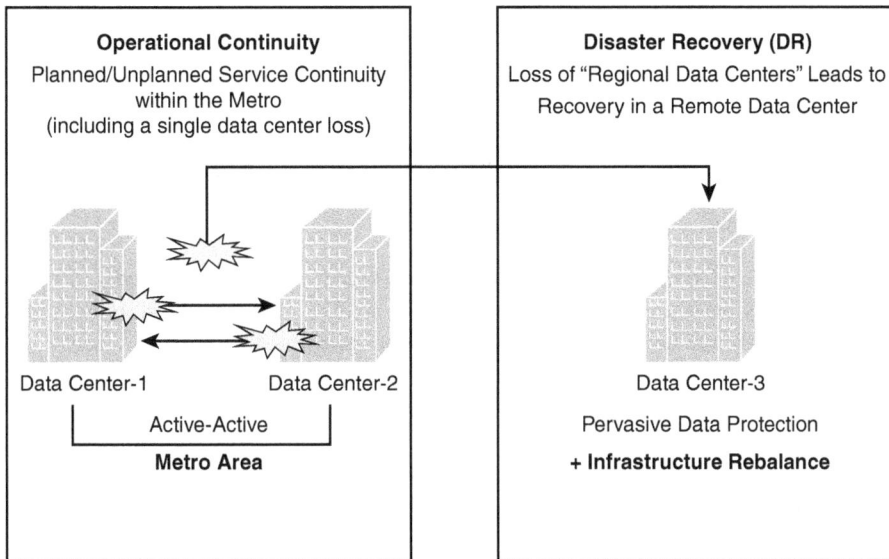

Figure 6-1   *Main Logical Data Center for Operational Continuity with a Third Data Center for a Disaster Recovery Plan*

As a consequence, from an applications and services point of view, both tightly coupled sites appear as a single logical data center, which improves scalability and resiliency. Having a physical separation of the two data centers offers the required level of redundancy for resource availability in case one office experiences any access issues for any applications. Thus, it is crucial for the network interconnection to offer the same level of independence. The following section elaborates on data center interconnection design considerations.

Operational continuity refers to the ability to always be able to get access to the information, regardless of any critical event. The applications and software framework must be able to migrate dynamically where the hardware resources are available, and it must be able to migrate seamlessly or to recover from an unplanned (or even planned) interruption in a remote data center located within the metro area to offer a level of disaster avoidance (DA). In the event of an unplanned major disaster or planned interruption at the main sites, a disaster recovery plan (DRP) is manually or automatically triggered to recover from the loss of these two primary data centers in a distant backup site. Processes to fail over applications to new locations have evolved in the past two decades, from manual legacy operations that took up to several days to dynamic migration of applications where resources are available; these improvements are thanks to the concept of a virtualized computer stack for seamless migration. The network access to reach the concerned application has also reduced the latency between the end user and the application, either from a manual action to activate the network redirection after a disaster recovery (DNS, routing metrics) or to automatically reroute the network traffic to the site of interest according to the location of the virtual machine handling the targeted application. The latter can be assisted with solutions such as LISP host mobility, discussed in this chapter and in Chapter 7, "LISP IP Mobility in Modern Data Center Fabrics." Application and data recovery today can take between a few seconds and several minutes, depending of the software frameworks and whether the network construct is deployed in the most optimal way for a DA or DRP requirement.

Three key technical network services are fundamental for supporting the high level of flexibility, resiliency, resource availability, and transparent resource connectivity required for cloud computing:

- The Layer 3 network must offer traditional as well as multi-tenancy routed connectivity between remote sites and provide end-user access to cloud services. Consequently, the Layer 3 segmentation must be maintained between all tenants or security zones residing on any locations. For the reference disaster recovery architecture previously discussed, the Layer 2 network is not necessarily required between the twin data centers and the backup site. As discussed further in the section "IP Mobility Using LISP Across Subnets Mode," later in this chapter, cold migration can be achieved across a pure Layer 3 network.

- The extended Layer 2 network (VLANs) between the two tightly coupled data centers must offer transparent transport and support application and operating system stateful mobility.

- IP localization is required to dynamically optimize northbound workflow, or north–south traffic, as well as server-to-server communication, also known as east–west traffic.

Data Center Interconnect (DCI) solutions are aiming to address the operational continuity needs of enterprise and service provider cloud implementations without interruption. DCI reference transports support the extension of Layer 2 and Layer 3 networks as well as network services across multiple data centers that are geographically distributed.

DA capabilities provide operational continuity without service interruption and without performance impact while manually or automatically moving VMs between different physical hosts. As mentioned earlier, the destination hosts can be located in the same data center as the source host, or they can be in a different physical data center. However, to offer a seamless live mobility with efficiency, without interruption, the same bridge domain must be extended from end to end and from site to site. Latency is a key element to take into consideration because it can have a serious impact on application performance. To reduce the latency to its lowest number, the external traffic must be steered automatically to the data center where the application of interest resides. This is usually referred as *endpoint IP localization*. It involves several techniques, such as probing the endpoints or listening for Address Resolution Protocol (ARP) messages either to trigger a host route or to update a centralized endpoint mapping database. If advertising a host route can be an efficient mechanism using a more specific route to steer the traffic directly where the destination is physically located, in some context, this mechanism cannot be used. Host route injection to the upstream router is often used by large enterprises that own and manage their routed core network. If injecting /32 prefixes into the Layer 3 wide area network (WAN)/metropolitan area network (MAN) is not disruptive in a private network, however, when the Layer 3 network is managed by one or multiple operators, host routing is ordinarily not permitted. The key reason is because the providers can't support all host routes for all enterprises for scalability and network address translation purposes. In such a case, one solution for routing traffic based on endpoint identifiers while maintaining the privacy of the network is to run an overlay on the top of the managed Layer 3 network. A mapping database is updated dynamically with the locations of roaming endpoints, and a tunnel is established between the source location and a destination data center. This situation, known as *LISP IP mobility*, is a key technique discussed later in this chapter.

Network Extension Solutions for Interconnecting Data Centers

As mentioned earlier, extending a LAN (also known as a bridge domain) between two sites is one of the fundamental requirements for supporting hot live migration and high-availability clustering frameworks. To allow the same bridge domain to exist on all far-end sites, different techniques are used to extend the concerned Layer 2 segments— from longstanding models limited to extending the Layer 2 network to modern solutions offering support for multi-tenancy while reducing the failure domain to its smallest diameter. This section discusses a variety of network designs, transports, and solutions that are used to extend broadcast domains. It provides a little reminder about legacy DCI solutions and elaborates on the latest recommended designs and deployment options.

Evolving Requirements for Extending Layer 2

For more than a decade, it has been a common practice to extend Layer 2 networks across multiple locations. Although the network team understands the risks of extending the traditional broadcast domain beyond the data center due to the well-known weaknesses of Layer 2 and the risks of disrupting the whole extended network across all locations, it is agreed that there are some decisive situations where this requirement is essential. Requirements for extending Layer 2 are evolving with the experiences and the evolution of network technologies. The following are the key use cases:

- For many years, the traditional high-availability cluster deployment was evolving from covering a single campus to being geographically dispersed, with cluster members spread across distant locations to improve the DRP for highly critical applications.

- With the evolution of virtual machines and virtualized services, it has been a common tradition to leverage simplicity and efficiency of migration in real-time software frameworks. When possible and according to the criticality level of the concerned applications, this should be achieved with a minimum period of interruption to avoid affecting the business. The migration of virtual machines can be achieved manually or dynamically toward physical host resources available at different data centers. This method addresses the elasticity required to offer efficient operational continuity with zero interruption at lower cost.

- For cost containment, it might be simpler and faster (and hence cost-effective) to migrate bare-metal servers, mainframes, or virtual machines without changing their host TCP/IP reachability information when moving from one location to another.

- With the growing adoption of multi-cloud solutions, to reduce cost and mitigate the risks, a network manager may now automate deployment and manage workloads between private or public clouds and on-premises data centers. Maintaining the same host identifiers across multi-cloud scenarios is crucial for operational continuity and cost control.

Layer 2 transport carried throughout the metro network using direct fibers or over the WAN with very long distances (whether it is a native Ethernet frame format or a Layer 2 over TCP/IP over any type of transport) should not have any performance impact except for the latency imposed by the physical distance between distant sites. Switching technologies are used to extend the Layer 2 network over Layer 3 (overlay network), and obviously the native Layer 2 protocol must be supported by the hardware (ASIC) to establish network overlay tunnels and transport data packets at line rate. The choice for the distances between two sites is imposed by the maximum latency supported by the applications and software framework. For example, vSphere 6.0 offers a long-distance vMotion feature that supports a maximum round-trip latency for the vMotion networks of up to 150 milliseconds. The maximum latency supported with vSphere 5.0 for vMotion network is 10 milliseconds.

The Layer 2 network transport is not sensitive to latency per se, but its sturdiness relies on propagation of uncontrolled flooding. The geographic zone where the flooding occurs is usually called the *failure domain* because most Layer 2 failures are due to propagation of flooding everywhere across the broadcast domain. As a result, using modern transport flood-and-learn techniques in conjunction with extended bridge domains can finally be avoided outside a single data center, and when possible, flooding can be reduced to the smallest diameter (the switch itself). With an efficient control plane, flood-and-learn techniques are not required to extend the Layer 2 domain across data center sites.

For many years, to qualify the model of transport used to extend VLANs, one of the foremost questions was the number of sites to interconnect: two (point-to-point) or more (point-to-multipoint)? Some legacy solutions that were used to interconnect two data centers in a back-to-back or point-to-point fashion were simpler to deploy and to maintain using direct fibers or xWDM managed services. However, the drawbacks to rudimentary point-to-point technology are limited scalability and flexibility concerns. These solutions can be a serious disadvantage as the need to add a third data center might be a barrier; however, increasing the number of resources geographically distributed across multiple remote sites is becoming more critical than ever. For multipoint infrastructure requirements, overlay solutions such as VPLS or OTV have been leveraged, reducing the triangulation of traffic flow due to Spanning Tree Protocol imposed with classical Ethernet transport. More importantly, as mentioned previously with an extended native Layer 2 transport or with legacy Layer 2 pseudowires using VPLS, the network weaknesses are spread across the two data centers due to flood-and-learn techniques, and there are risks of disrupting all data center locations in the event of a major network disaster in one site.

With modern fabrics such as Virtual Extensible Local Area Network (VXLAN) with a Multiprotocol Border Gateway Protocol (MP-BGP) and the Address Family Ethernet virtual private network (AF-EVPN) or the Application Centric Infrastructure (ACI), the solution to extend Layer 2 and/or Layer 3 connectivity between two or more sites is integrated into the whole network architecture, forming a more solid and efficient hierarchical solution at a lower cost. With modern network fabrics offering integrated and hierarchical solutions to extend Layer 2 and Layer 3 segmentation, the failure domain is reduced to its smallest diameter. As a consequence, enterprises and service providers should study any possible future expansion of their cloud networking and the need to operate without disruption when considering Layer 2 extension technologies. Solutions for interconnecting multiple sites should offer the same simplicity as solutions for interconnecting two sites, with transparent impact for the entire data center. Dynamically adding or removing one or several resource sites in an autonomous fashion is often referred to as *point-to-cloud site integration*. With such a solution, the network team should be able to seamlessly insert or remove a new data center on demand to extend the Layer 2 and Layer 3 segment across the concerned sites without modifying the existing interconnections and regardless of the status of the other remote sites.

Modern fabrics usually require multi-tenant support throughout the same extended infrastructure. Therefore, the elasticity of the service offered by the cloud must be very granular and enabled per tenant.

Whatever DCI technology solution is chosen to extend the Layer 2 VLANs between remote sites, the network transport over the WAN must also provide secure ingress and egress access into those data centers.

When extending Layer 2, a number of rules must be applied to improve the reliability and effectiveness of distributed cloud networking:

- Do not extend the spanning tree domain beyond a local data center, even though all the links and switches that provide Layer 2 extension must be fully redundant and all active.

- The broadcast traffic must be controlled and reduced when possible by the DCI edge devices to mitigate the risk of polluting remote sites. A high level of broadcast traffic may have a negative impact on network resources and compute performances.

- All existing paths between the data centers must be forwarding, and communication between application tiers should be comprised inside the same data center when possible in order to use the available bandwidth between data centers more efficiently and to better control the latency across sites.

- Within the same broadcast domain, the Layer 3 services from the WAN/MAN may not be able to natively locate where the destination endpoint is attached or to identify the position of a VM that migrated from one host to another. If this is the expected behavior of any routed traffic, it may not be efficient enough when the Layer 2 network (aka broadcast or bridge domain) is extended over long distances and hosts are spread over different locations. Therefore, it might be essential to redirect the incoming traffic dynamically on the physical site where virtualized applications were activated (north–south traffic flows). Similarly, the traffic to and from the default gateway can be controlled and restricted onto each local data center when appropriate (east–west traffic flows).

■ For inter-site communication, mechanisms to protect the links must be enabled and rapid convergence algorithms must be provided to keep any failures of the transport as transparent as possible.

■ The VLANs to be extended must have been previously identified by the server and network team. Extending all existing VLANs, regardless of the need to do so, may consume excessive hardware resources and increase the risk of failures and impact the time to converge. Nevertheless, the DCI solution for LAN extension must provide the flexibility to dynamically remove or add any elected VLAN on demand without disrupting production traffic.

■ Optimize multicast traffic, especially in a cloud architecture made up of multiple geographically dispersed resources (more than two sites).

In a summary, the diversity of services required in a data center infrastructure and in a cloud computing environment and the constraints related to the type of applications moving over the extended network require a set of expanded DCI components. Two distinct technical solutions that meet these criteria are Layer 2 extension and path optimization.

Today, it is interesting to dissociate traditional data center networking that relies on classical Ethernet IEEE-802.1Q standard-based transport from modern data center fabric built with VXLAN transport.

Interconnecting Traditional Data Center Networks

The network design interconnecting traditional data centers at Layer 2 is constantly evolving. With the development of new network transport and protocols, some legacy solutions may be considered less efficient than modern solutions. The following sections cover different designs and transport, from the native Ethernet back-to-back connectivity between two sites to modern overlay network transport interconnecting multiple distant data centers and clarifies which solution is recommended.

Layer 2 Back-to-Back vPC for Interconnecting Traditional Data Center

For many years, for back-to-back interconnections between two classical Ethernet-based data centers, either using a dedicated fiber or a managed fiber with a protected dense wavelength-division multiplexing (DWDM) mode, Multi-Chassis EtherChannel (MEC) solutions were leveraged to allow multiple physical links to form a virtual port channel distributed over two different chassis. This method is also known as Multi-chassis Link Aggregation Layer (MLAG or MC-LAG). MEC is also available throughout all Nexus switch series, and it is formally called virtual port channel (vPC). The interconnection between the two data centers consists of configuring a vPC domain on each site in a back-to-back fashion. This design is also known as double-sided vPC.

Figure 6-2 shows a physical view of a pair of fully redundant switches connected in the back-to-back fashion using two distinct links, resulting in transparent transport simulating a resilient logical switch on each side for optimal data packet flow.

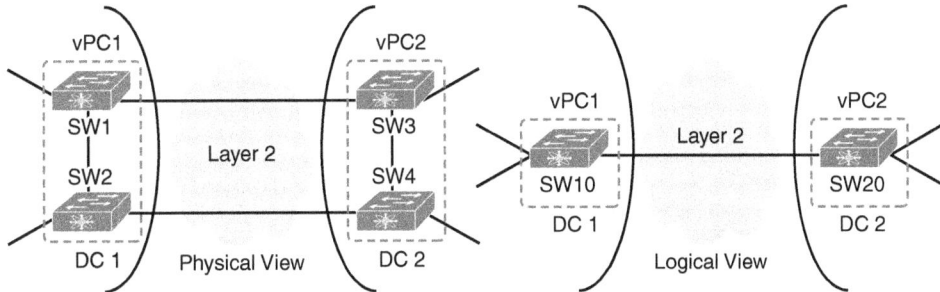

Figure 6-2   *Double-Sided vPC*

This solution has the advantage of being simple while allowing all vPC peer devices and inter-site links to be active without extending the spanning tree to control the loops. However, if most of native back-to-back solutions technically can offer Layer 2 extension between two data centers, it is not the best-in-class DCI architecture per se. It is quite important to be conscious about the weaknesses of extending native Ethernet frames without a solid DCI solution. This is mainly due to the quality of and service-level agreements (SLAs) related to any xWDM links, as well as the risks of disrupting both data center networks in the event of a major Layer 2 outage at one site. Nevertheless, from the point of view of xWDM efficiency, remote shutdown is strongly recommended in case of fiber link bouncing.

Although it may be technically possible to adopt this double-sided solution when the enterprise owns the fiber that interconnects different buildings (for example, within a campus) to form tightly coupled data centers, it is not a good idea to consider this option to connect a remote data center for a disaster avoidance and recovery plan. As mentioned previously, it is important to understand the risks due to the failure domain being extended across both locations.

MPLS Layer 2 Virtual Private Networks (VPNs)

Ethernet over Multiprotocol Label Switching (EoMPLS) pseudowire was set up for many years by service providers and large enterprises for interconnecting two data center networks across long distances. EoMPLS service is still supported natively on most network platforms, but it is less commonly used because more sophisticated modern transport protocols are more efficient.

Note   Ethernet over MPLS is also known as Virtual Private Wire Service (VPWS). Both EoMPLS and VPWS are MPLS Layer 2 VPN service and terms used to define point-to-point Layer 2 circuits.

It is imperative to understand that EoMPLS, like any other encapsulated method, is just a tunnel-based transport. Hence, EoMPLS must be diverted from its initial function and adapted accordingly to address some of the DCI requirements that are not natively embedded. Undeniably, for resiliency purposes, an EoMPLS pseudowire alone is not a desired option for interconnecting a distant data center; rather, such interconnection requires a two-box deployment, making the solution quite a bit more complex to implement. However, as discussed previously, a double-sided vPC solution can be leveraged as a redundant solution without involving the spanning tree protocol between remote sites.

Note   A vPC back-to-back design and, more generally speaking, any MC-LAG back-to-back solution using direct fibers or "Xconnect pseudowires" based on EoMPLS should no longer be considered as an efficient and reliable DCI solution since new integrated solutions based on modern transport exist (as discussed next). The older design relies on a flood-and-learn data plane mechanism. It is missing the efficient control plane that locally learns the endpoint reachability information and distributes that information across all network devices, reducing the risk of widespread failure on both sites at the same time. Interface Xconnect transparently transports any packet getting into the physical port as is, toward the egress associated port. This simulates a cross-connect cable with an infinite length, as it is transported through the MPLS network.

In parallel to EoMPLS, historically, Virtual Private LAN Service (VPLS) has been deployed for interconnecting multiple traditional data centers. Like EoMPLS, VPLS is not natively built to interconnect multiple data center networks. Indeed, it also requires configuration of a multi-chassis design such as MC-LAG or vPC techniques to aggregate the pseudowires across two physical platforms in each site to improve high availability as the redundant physical devices and links act as a single logical device. However, a circuit must be set up and maintained with all VPLS peer devices, which makes deployment and operation quite complex for the network teams.

Another drawback to EoMPLS and VPLS is that they are typically managed services from a provider. A service provider needs to be involved to implement changes to the Layer 2 extension, which may take some time. Solutions such as LISP IP Mobility give control to the network operator since the service provider only provides basic IP connectivity between sites.

For service providers, the alternatives to VPLS are Multi-protocol Label Switching - Ethernet VPN (MPLS-EVPN), Provider Backbone Bridging EVPN (PBB-EVPN), and even VXLAN EVPN as double encapsulation is also supported for multi-tenancy purposes. EVPN is different from existing VPLS offerings. Whereas VPLS relies on flooding to learn MAC addresses, EVPN relies on its control plane for MAC-based learning over the core.

EVPN is the next-generation solution that provides Ethernet multipoint services using an IP network, including over the top of an IP or an MPLS transport. EVPN was designed from the ground up to handle sophisticated access redundancy scenarios and per-flow load balancing and to provide operational simplicity.

PBB-EVPN inherits all of the benefits of EVPN while combining PBB (IEEE 802.1ah) and EVPN functions in a single node. Compared to EVPN, this combination allows PBB-EVPN to simplify control-plane operations in the core, provide faster convergence, and enhance scalability. PBB-EVPN differs from MPLS-EVPN as it transports the C-VLAN for each upstream client network independently, using MAC-in-MAC encapsulation. As a result, the network devices that sit in the provider backbone (service provider network) only learn the MAC addresses of the provider edge (PE) devices, offering the gateway between the customer edge (CE) and the provider backbone, ignoring the MAC addresses from the client's data center networks. This hierarchical solution addresses the need for a highly scalable architecture, aside from offering Layer 2 managed services.

Note   It may be worth noting that for point-to-point, RFC 8214 describes how EVPN is used to support VPWS in MPLS/IP networks. At the time of writing this book, there is not yet a deployment of it, so we do not cover it.

Overlay Transport Virtualization (OTV)

Overlay Transport Virtualization (OTV) was introduced in 2010 as the reference DCI solution for extending Layer 2 traffic between multiple sites over a Layer 3 network.

Figure 6-3 shows a data packet walk from the OTV internal interface facing the endpoints with the MAC lookup that triggers the IP encapsulation toward the remote OTV devices.

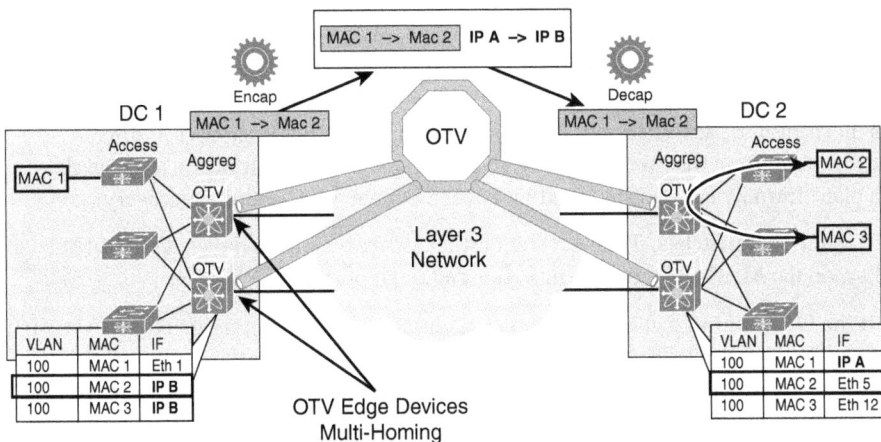

Figure 6-3   *OTV Packet Walk*

OTV dynamically encapsulates Layer 2 packets into an IP header for the traffic sent to the remote data centers. It uses either Ethernet over generic routing encapsulation (GRE) or the User Datagram Protocol (UDP) header encapsulation introduced with the latest hardware line cards. With the latter, the header format is similar to the header format used for the VXLAN header defined in the RFC 7348 and discussed further below. Forwarding Layer 2 traffic on top of a Layer 3 network is known as *MAC routing transport*. MAC routing leverages the use of a control protocol to propagate MAC address reachability information (push model); this is in contrast with the traditional data plane learning used in legacy technologies like EoMPLS or VPLS, as mentioned previously.

Figure 6-3 shows a high-level packet walk across two data centers interconnected using OTV:

■ Host 1 with MAC 1 is sending a data packet to Host 2, identified with MAC 2. On the MAC table of the OTV edge device in DC 1, the Layer 2 lookup shows that MAC 1 is a local address (Eth1), while the destination MAC 2 belongs to a remote location that is reachable via the IP B, which is the remote OTV edge device located in DC 2. What differs from other traditional Layer 2 switches is that when the destination belongs to a remote site, a traditional Layer 2 lookup is performed, but in this case, the destination MAC address information in the MAC table does not point to a local Ethernet interface but to the IP address of the remote OTV edge device that advertised the MAC reachability information.

■ Given the IP address as an egress interface to reach the destination MAC of interest, the local OTV-ED in DC 1 encapsulates the Layer 2 frame using an IP header with the IP destination IP B. When the remote IP B of the OTV-ED (OED) receives the data packet from the OTV edge device in DC 1, it removes the IP header, does a Layer 2 lookup, and, as a result, forwards the frames to its internal interface (Eth 5, in this example). Consequently, the local Layer 2 traffic is treated like any classical Ethernet switch (that is, between MAC 2 and MAC 3 on DC 2).

The key advantage provided by OTV is the control plane protocol used to exchange MAC reachability information between remote OTV edge devices, while the learning process inside the data center is performed as in any traditional Layer 2 switch. This mechanism of advertisement destined to the remote OTV edge device differs fundamentally from that in classical Layer 2 switches, which traditionally leverage the data plane learning mechanism based on Layer 2 source MAC address discovery.

With traditional switches, if the Layer 2 destination address is unknown after a MAC lookup on the MAC table, the traffic is flooded to all ports in the VLAN.

With the OTV control plane, the process for learning MAC addresses involves advertising the local MAC tables to all remote OTV edge devices. Consequently, if a destination MAC address is not known, the packet destined to the remote data center is dropped. This technical innovation has the advantage of removing the risk of broadcasting data packets with unknown unicast destination addresses from one site to another. This technique is based on a routing protocol and provides a very stable and efficient mechanism of MAC address learning and Layer 2 extension while maintaining the failure domain inside each data center.

In addition to dropping broadcast traffic of unknown unicast, OTV implements a mechanism called ARP optimization to reduce the number of ARP requests to be sent across the OTV overlay infrastructure. The local OTV edge device is capable of snooping the ARP replies to cache the contained reachability information (for example, MAC, IP) of remote endpoints in a local data structure. All subsequent ARP requests destined for the same IP address are intercepted by the local OTV edge device, which locally answers to the ARP request, removing the need to send the ARP request across the DCI infrastructure toward the distant destination machine.

While OTV natively maintains the Spanning Tree Protocol and the failure domain within each local data center, it provides the ability to deploy multiple OTV edge devices in the same data center, all in active mode. This function is known as *multihoming*.

OTV works across any type of transport extended between the remote sites (for example, fiber, TCP/IP, MPLS) with the reliability and effectiveness of a Layer 3 protocol.

If OTV natively suppresses broadcast flows of unknown unicast and embeds a caching mechanism to reduce the ARP messages sent across all remote sites, it still needs to reduce or completely suppress the amount of Layer 2 broadcast traffic sent across the overlay, such as ARP requests, by using broadcast rate limiters. The reason is always to protect remote sites against Layer 2 outages such as broadcast storms.

Deployment Considerations for Legacy Layer 2 DCI Solutions

The know-hows in regard to OTV and reflections around the evolution of multi-tenancy abetted and accelerated the innovation, few years ago with the development of VXLAN in conjunction with its control plane MP-BGP EVPN.

While most modern solutions leverage the features listed in the previous section, OTV was designed almost 10 years ago to interconnect traditional data centers and extend the Layer 2 network from site to site. If it relies on a flexible encapsulation format, either IP-GRE or IP-UDP (VXLAN type header) for its data plane, the control plane is not natively multi-tenant capable, and separate platforms are required to extend and maintain the Layer 2 and Layer 3 segmentations from site to site for each particular tenant. Consequently, with the fast evolution of multi-tenancy requirements, OTV is not necessarily the most appropriate solution for interconnecting modern multi-tenant-based fabrics. As a result, OTV is no longer considered the best platform of choice for interconnecting traditional data centers, which may have to evolve to modern fabric-based networking.

With the evolution of modern overlay networks elaborated in the following sections, it is important to note that native MC-LAG, vPC double-sided for classical Ethernet, EoMPLS, VPLS, and OTV must be considered legacy techniques to extend Layer 2 between two or multiple classical Ethernet-based data center networks. Although some of these solutions, such as VPLS or OTV, have demonstrated their efficiency and robustness in the past, they should no longer be chosen as the primary solution to interconnect a data center network due to the lack of possibility of evolving to support modern data center network fabrics.

For classical Ethernet-based data centers, generally speaking for an enterprise deployment, VXLAN EVPN Multi-Site, discussed next, is now the recommended solution for interconnecting two or more legacy data centers.

Interconnecting VXLAN MP-BGP EVPN-Based Fabrics

As discussed earlier in this chapter, a DCI solution represents a network architecture that extends Layer 2 and Layer 3 segmented networks across two or more data centers. A DCI architecture relies on a data plane for the transport forwarding user data and a control plane for an efficient and solid mechanism for endpoint discovery and distribution between sites, including propagation of host routes and prefixes to or from an external network.

VXLAN, described in RFC 7348, is an encapsulation-type model that dynamically establishes an overlay tunnel between two virtual tunnel endpoints (VTEPs); it's not a network architecture per se. Nonetheless, the VXLAN data plane encapsulation transport can be deployed in conjunction with a control plane such as MP-BGP AF EVPN or another control plane, such as LISP. For data center networks, including software-defined networking (SDN)–based fabrics such as ACI, VXLAN is becoming, de facto, the foremost data plane forwarding transport within and to the outside of the network fabric.

In the context of network overlay, the control plane objective is to leverage unicast transport while processing VTEP and host discovery and distribution processes. This method significantly reduces flooding for unknown unicast traffic within a fabric and across multiple sites. That being said, the fact that VXLAN with its control plane MP-BGP EVPN can be deployed on top of a Layer 3 network doesn't imply that it can be considered as a comprehensive DCI solution. Some network solutions relying on VXLAN are positioned as simple DCI solutions. This can be a bit of a concern when you realize that the second data center also offers the role of a backup site for operational continuity. If a major outage arises in one data center, it must not disrupt the other sites. VXLAN EVPN was designed to make the traffic inside a data center solid and efficient. There is nothing new in it to claim that it offers a DCI transport just by magic. The rule to keep in mind is that all remote data centers must still be protected from any form of severe disruption, such as a broadcast storm.

For a DCI solution to be considered an efficient and solid solution, VXLAN MP-BGP EVPN requires the following additional features:

- Distributed Layer 3 anycast gateways (east–west traffic localization using the anycast default gateway)

- Anycast border gateway functions offering multihoming site-to-site connectivity

- Data plane domain isolation

- Unknown unicast suppression

- Selective storm control for broadcast unknown unicast and multicast (BUM) traffic

- Native Layer 2 loop detection and protection

As mentioned earlier, for many years, DCI solutions were designed to essentially interconnect classical Ethernet-based data center network solutions. Data center networking is evolving very quickly from the traditional network architecture to the VXLAN-based fabric model and gaining strong momentum in enterprises, which are adopting it to optimize modern applications, computing resources, mobility, high scale-out, costs, and operational benefits. If independent DCI technologies has been widely exploited in the past for extending Layer 2 networks between traditional data center networks, VXLAN EVPN Multi-Site is now de facto the recommended solution to interconnect legacy data centers and, hence, ease the migration to modern fabrics, also protecting the investment as the Multi-Site function is integrated into the same device. The same border gateway node provides all-in-one functions such as Layer 2 and Layer 3 extension across the same VXLAN transport, VRF Lite, network service attachment, and computer node attachment or connectivity to a legacy network. As a consequence, a new innovative solution called VXLAN EVPN Multi-Site integrated within the same border device has been created to address the extension of Layer 2 and Layer 3 networks using a single transport, VXLAN EVPN, across multiple sites, forming a hierarchical end-to-end architecture.

Note   The concepts of VXLAN Multi-Pod, Multi-Fabric and Multi-Site discussed in this section concerns VXLAN MP-BGP EVPN-based fabrics, also known as stand-alone VXLAN fabrics, which are different from the Cisco enhanced SDN-based fabrics, also known as ACI fabrics. If both models rely on VXLAN as the network overlay transport within the fabric, they use different solutions for interconnecting multiple fabrics together. ACI Multi-Site and ACI Multi-Pod are discussed later in this chapter.

Cisco introduced the use of the MP-BGP EVPN–based control plane for VXLAN in 2015. Since then, a couple network architectures have been proposed to help enterprises divert VXLAN EVPN for improved DCI purposes, such as VXLAN EVPN Multi-Pod and VXLAN EVPN Multi-Fabric. Cisco has also developed an embedded DCI solution, called VXLAN EVPN Multi-Site, to interconnect VXLAN EVPN fabrics locally or over unlimited distances. Although VXLAN EVPN Multi-Pod and Multi-Fabric solutions are not recommended anymore, the following sections cover them to answer questions a network manager might have about all the existing options and clarify the functional differences that make VXLAN Multi-Site the modern DCI solution of choice.

VXLAN EVPN Multi-Pod

Cisco created VXLAN EVPN Multi-Pod in 2015 to build a single logical VXLAN EVPN fabric in which multiple pods were dispersed to different locations using a Layer 3 underlay to interconnect the pods. Also known as *stretched fabric*, this option was more commonly called *VXLAN EVPN Multi-Pod fabric*. This model has been promoted by Cisco network architects to mitigate risks by stretching the same VXLAN EVPN domain across long distances. However, it was not aiming to be referenced as a DCI solution per se; indeed, from a VXLAN overlay point of view, there is no demarcation between one pod and another. A unique data plane and a single control plane are stretched across all pods.

VXLAN overlay networks are established from end to end across all pods. This architecture model was used to interconnect multiple pods within a building or campus area as well as across metropolitan areas.

Figure 6-4 shows the legacy VXLAN EVPN Multi-Pod architecture, highlighting the establishment of the VXLAN tunnel from pod to pod. Each pod is constructed with its own IGP area for underlay network connectivity, in conjunction with its own iBGP autonomous system number for the overlay network. An MP-eBGP EVPN address family session is established to transit routing between the pods with the IPv4 address family. The MP-eBGP sessions can be established between the pairs of transit leaf nodes deployed within each pod (as shown in Figure 6-4), or they can be established between the route reflectors on the spine nodes.

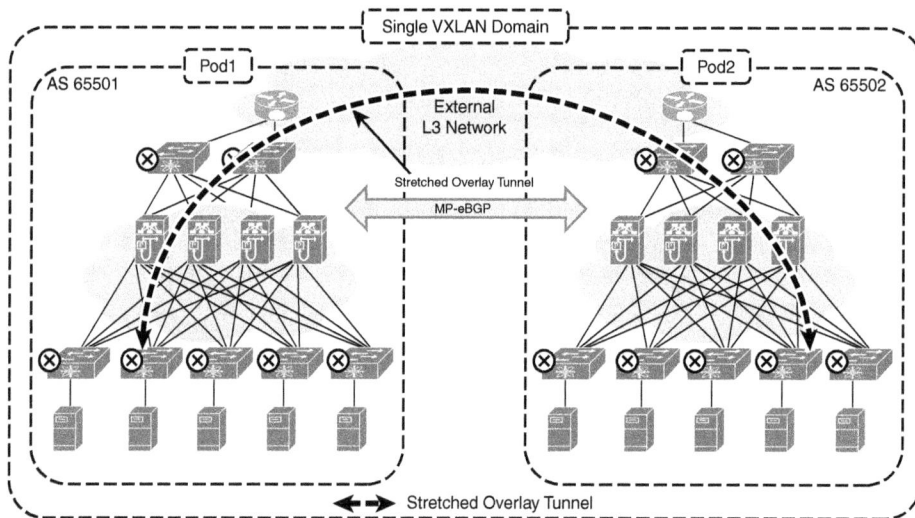

Figure 6-4   *VXLAN EVPN Multi-Pod Architecture*

Although with the VXLAN Multi-Pod methodology, the underlay and overlay control planes were optimized to offer a more robust end-to-end architecture than is available with a basic stretched fabric, the same VXLAN EVPN fabric is overextended across different locations. Subsequently, the reachability information for all VTEPs, as well as that of endpoints, is extended across the whole VXLAN domain, extending the failure domain across all the pods, while the scalability remains the same as it is in a single VXLAN fabric. Consequently, although this solution was simple and easy to deploy, it lacks sturdiness with the same data plane and control plane shared across all geographically dispersed pods. With the evolution of the hardware and software, this model is not considered a DCI solution.

VXLAN EVPN Multi-Fabric

An evolution of the network architecture, VXLAN EVPN Multi-Fabric, came out in 2016 to interconnect multiple VXLAN EVPN fabrics in a more solid fashion by inserting an independent DCI solution, extending Layer 2 and Layer 3 connectivity services between independent VXLAN fabrics, and maintaining segmentation for multi-tenancy purposes. Compared to the VXLAN EVPN Multi-Pod fabric design, the VXLAN EVPN Multi-Fabric architecture offered a higher level of separation for each of the data center network fabrics from a data plane and control plane point of view. The reachability information for all VTEPs is contained within each single VXLAN EVPN fabric. As a result, VXLAN tunnels are initiated and terminated inside each data center fabric (in the same location).

The VXLAN EVPN Multi-Fabric model also offered higher scalability than the VXLAN Multi-Pod approach, supporting a larger total number of leaf nodes and endpoints across all fabrics.

Figure 6-5 describes two autonomous VXLAN EVPN domains where the data planes and control planes from the fabrics are running independently from each other. A dedicated DCI solution is inserted between VXLAN fabrics to extend the Layer 2 VLANs. In addition, the establishment of a separated Layer 3 network transport between the VXLAN EVPN fabrics is also required to maintain the Layer 3 segmentations using VRF Lite hand-off.

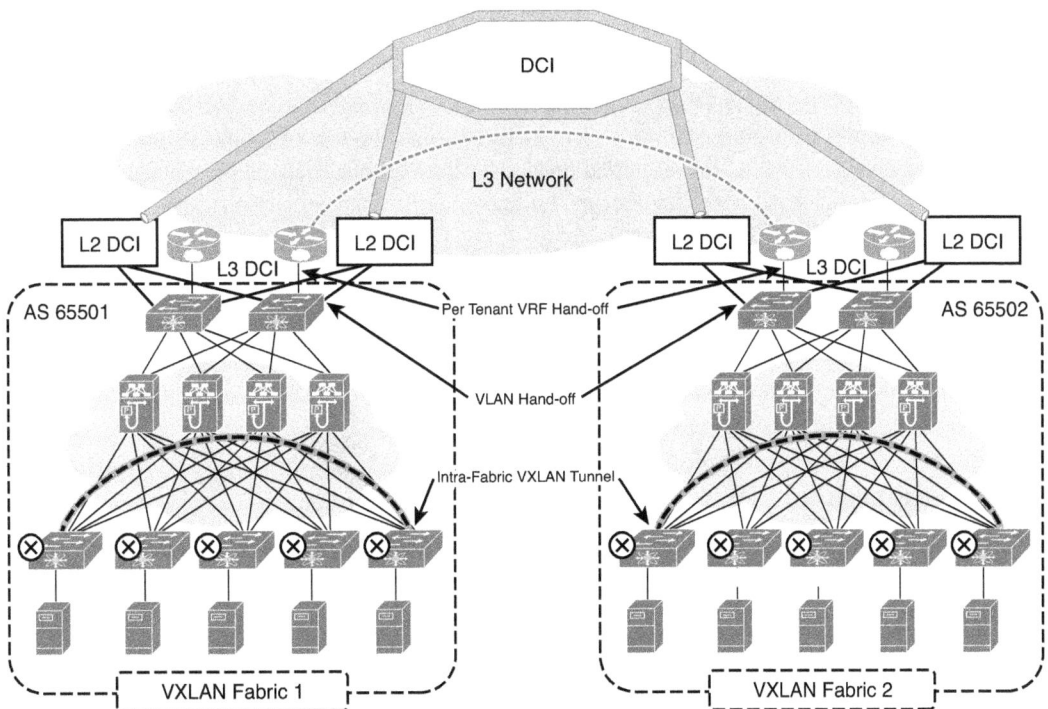

Figure 6-5   *VXLAN EVPN Multi-Fabric Architecture*

However, the big disadvantage of this solution is that, due to the native multi-tenancy nature of VXLAN EVPN, it requires complex and manual configurations for dedicated Layer 2 and Layer 3 extensions between the VXLAN EVPN fabrics. In addition, the original protocol responsible for Layer 2 and Layer 3 segmentation must hand off at the egress side of the border leaf nodes (respectively, Dot1Q hand-off and VRF Lite hand-off). Finally, in addition to the dual-box design for dedicated Layer 2 and Layer 3 DCI services, endpoints cannot be locally attached to DCI devices themselves.

Although the VXLAN EVPN Multi-Fabric solution improved the strength of the end-to-end solution, there is no integration per se between the VXLAN fabrics and the different DCI transports for Layer 2 and Layer 3 extension, making the deployment complex to operate and to manage. With the evolution of the hardware and software, this model is no longer considered a DCI solution.

Interconnecting Multiple VXLAN EVPN Fabrics: A Chronological Evolution

Now that we have discussed temporary solutions for extending Layer 2 and Layer 3 networks across VXLAN EVPN fabrics, it is crucial to note that they are now considered obsolete since a new solution architecture, VXLAN EVPN Multi-Site, became available in 2017, with the NX-OS software release 7.0(3)I7(1).

The timeline in Figure 6-6 shows the fast evolution of the solutions for interconnecting VXLAN EVPN domains. The VXLAN EVPN Multi-Pod and VXLAN EVPN Multi-Fabric solutions discussed previously are solutions encompassing multiple independent network components, brought together manually to mitigate risks due to the weaknesses of the stretched fabric or to gather the network transport to be extended with an independent DCI solution. The VXLAN EVPN Multi-Site solution discussed in the following section offers a more efficient integrated and hierarchical solution and is easy to deploy.

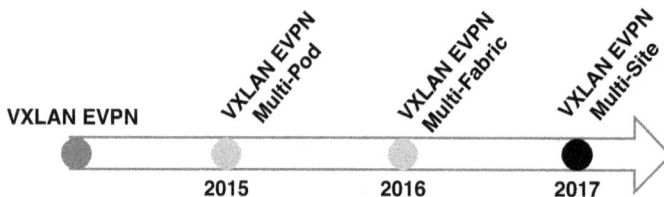

Figure 6-6   *Evolution of Interconnecting Multiple VXLAN EVPN Fabrics*

Note   A related IETF draft is available for further details; see https://tools.ietf.org/html/draft-sharma-Multi-Site-evpn.

VXLAN EVPN Multi-Site

The focus of the VXLAN EVPN Multi-Site solution is on interconnecting Greenfield VXLAN EVPN fabrics or Brownfield legacy data center network or interconnecting VXLAN EVPN–based fabric with a classical Ethernet-based data center network—either in the same building, in the same campus, or geographically dispersed at different sites across unlimited distances—to reduce the failure domain by organizing a hierarchical architecture.

VXLAN EVPN Multi-Site integrates Layer 2 and Layer 3 services. The need for separate physical devices for Layer 2 and Layer 3 VXLAN tunnels is eliminated thanks to the new border gateways concept. This model relies on Layer 2 VNI stitching, meaning that a VXLAN tunnel terminates and is initiated from the same VTEP without using either old-fashioned Dot1Q hand-off or VRF Lite hand-off. A new function, known as a border gateway, is responsible for that integrated extension. As a result, a site-internal VXLAN tunnel that requires extension toward remote sites terminates at a border gateway, which, from the same VTEP interface, re-initiates a new VXLAN tunnel toward the remote sites (the sites-external DCI). The Layer 2 and Layer 3 services are extended using the same protocol. This new innovation combines the simplicity and flexibility of VXLAN Multi-Pod with the sturdiness of VXLAN Multi-Fabric.

The stitching together of the Layer 2 and Layer 3 VXLAN network segment IDs (VNIs)—site-internal fabric overlay networks and site-external DCI overlay networks— happens in the same physical border nodes (leaf or spine). The border node running the EVPN Multi-Site function is known as a border gateway (BGW). The border gateway offers a unique function, gathering internal VXLAN tunnels with the external VXLAN tunnels, using the same hardware at line rate.

Note   A border gateway function requires a Cisco Cloud Scale ASIC (the second generation of the Nexus 9000-EX and -FX series).

The other non-border gateway network devices within the VXLAN EVPN fabric, such as spine and leaf nodes, are not required to support the function of VXLAN EVPN Multi-Site—either in hardware or in software. As a result, for any VXLAN EVPN fabric based on the first generation of the Nexus 9000 series or based on any merchant-silicon switches, compliant with the VXLAN EVPN standard, it is possible to deploy VXLAN EVPN Multi-Site by simply adding the pair of required devices that support the border gateway function. It is worth mentioning that even any legacy data centers running classical Ethernet can be interconnected using this solution. The BGW multi-site integrates and extends Layer 2 and Layer 3 networks from the site-internal fabric toward the site-external DCI network, and it also offers Layer 3 VPN network external connectivity (per tenant) from the fabric to the core Layer 3 network.

VXLAN EVPN Multi-Site offers an all-in-one-box solution with, if desired, the possibility to locally attach endpoints for other purposes (computers, firewalls, load balancers, WAN edge routers, and so on).

Figure 6-7 shows a VXLAN EVPN Multi-Site architecture highlighting border gateway functions initiated to stitch VXLAN site-internal tunnels with site-external tunnel in a single-box paradigm. The data plane and the control plane are extended using the same encapsulated transport.

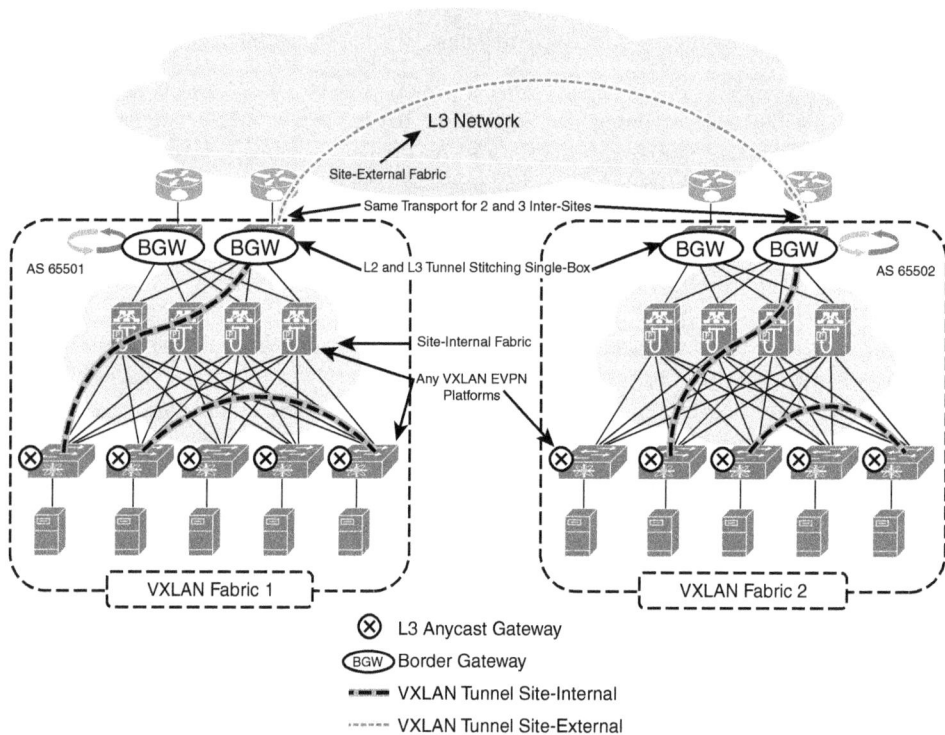

Figure 6-7   *VXLAN EVPN Multi-Site: A Hierarchical Integrated DCI Solution*

VXLAN EVPN Multi-Site offers a level of simplicity and flexibility that has never before been reached. Indeed, the border gateway function can be initiated from dedicated devices known as Anycast border gateways (BGP-based BGWs), as depicted in Figure 6-7, or from existing vPC-based border leaf nodes, offering seamless migration from traditional to multi-site architectures, as shown in Figure 6-8 in Site 2. This vPC-based option allows for locally attached dual-homed endpoints at Layer 2.

Nevertheless, at the time of writing this book, in anycast mode it is possible to deploy up to six independent border leaf nodes per site when configured in anycast BGW mode, relying on BGP delivering the function of border gateway in a cluster fashion, all active with the same virtual IP (VIP) address. With Anycast mode, Layer 3 services (for example, firewalls, routers, server load balancers) can be attached on the same BGW nodes.

Finally, it is also possible to initiate the Multi-Site function with its border gateway role directly from the spine layer. Either BGP anycast BGW mode or vPC BGW mode can fully interoperate with each other's modes, from the Border Spine nodes or from the Border Leaf nodes, as depicted in Figure 6-8.

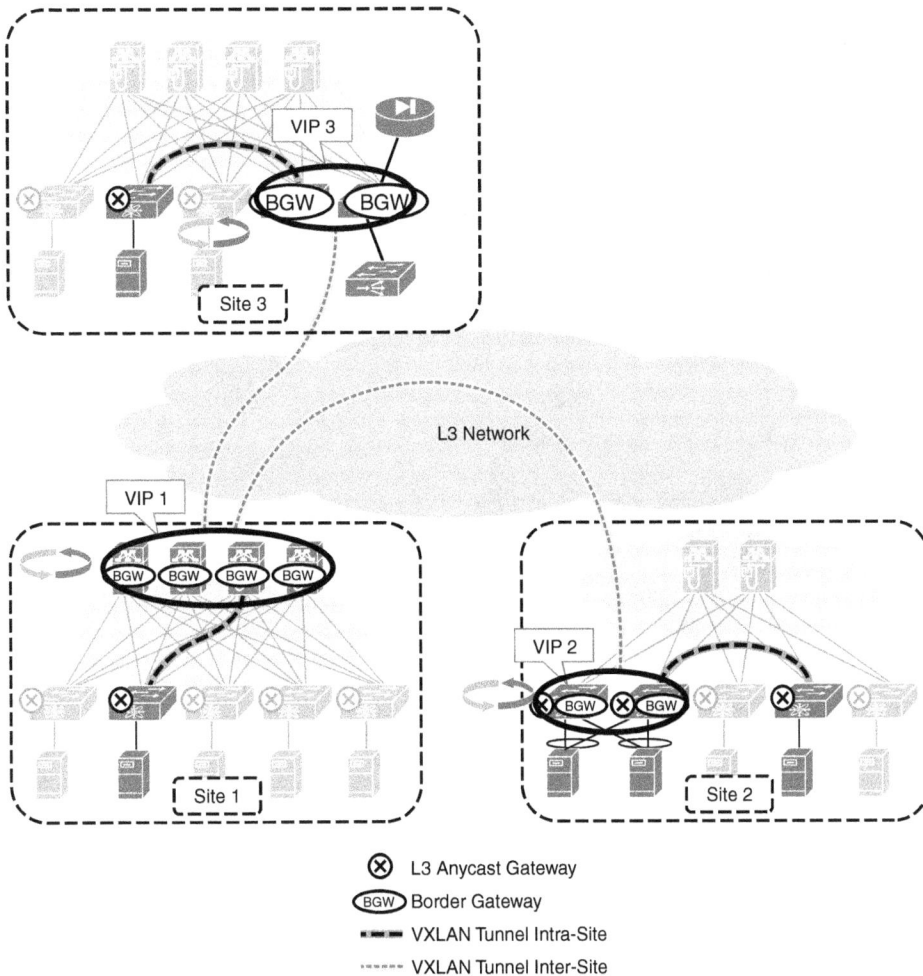

VIP 3

BGW   BGW

Site 3

L3 Network

VIP 1

BGW   BGW   BGW   BGW

Site 1

VIP 2

BGW   BGW

Site 2

⊗ L3 Anycast Gateway

BGW Border Gateway

▬▬▬ VXLAN Tunnel Intra-Site

------ VXLAN Tunnel Inter-Site

Figure 6-8   *VXLAN EVPN Multi-Site: BGW Placement*

When the border gateways are deployed in Anycast mode, the cluster is built with up to six nodes sharing the same VIP address across the associated members. The same border gateway VIP address is used for the virtual networks initiated inside the VXLAN fabric as well as for the VXLAN tunnels established with the remote sites.

The architecture of VXLAN EVPN Multi-Site is transport agnostic. It can be established between two sites connected with direct fiber links in a back-to-back fashion or across an external native Layer 3 WAN/MAN or Layer 3 VPN core (MPLS VPN) to interconnect multiple data centers across any distances. This integrated DCI solution offers higher reliability and resiliency for the end-to-end design, with all redundant devices delivering fast convergence in case of link or device failure.

VXLAN EVPN Multi-Site and Rate Limiters

The de-encapsulation and encapsulation of tunnels happens inside the same VTEP interface. This method makes it possible to enable traffic policers per tenant to control the rate of storms independently for broadcast, unknown unicast, or multicast traffic. Therefore, failure containment is controlled through the granular mechanism of BUM rate limiters, protecting remote sites from any broadcast storms.

Figure 6-9 emphasizes one of the most critical DCI features, with storm control for BUM traffic required to preserve the failure domain from being extended using granular rate limiters. The rate-limiting function is applied between the internal VXLAN segment and the external VXLAN extended outside the fabric for DCI purposes, rate limiting BUM traffic from 0% to 100%.

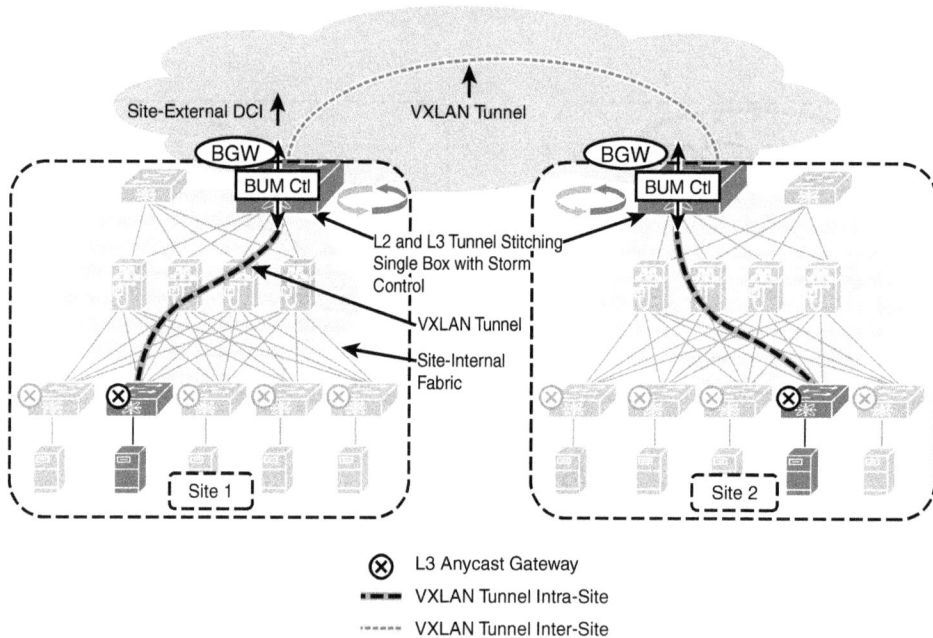

Figure 6-9 *VXLAN EVPN Multi-Site: Storm Control Rate Limiter*

VXLAN EVPN Multi-Site with Legacy Data Centers

The VXLAN EVPN Multi-Site solution is not limited to interconnecting modern Greenfield data centers. It offers two additional flavors for network connectivity with Brownfield data centers.

The first use case is with a legacy data center alone, devoid of any DCI service. For this option, if the enterprise wants to build two new Greenfield data centers and keep the original one, with all sites interconnected, it is possible to deploy a pair of border gateways, dual-homed toward the aggregation layer, as shown with DC 1 in Figure 6-10. This function of border gateway mapping Dot1Q to VXLAN is known as *vPC BGW*. The VLANs of interest are extended using VXLAN EVPN toward the Greenfield VXLAN EVPN Multi-Site, as shown in Figure 6-10.

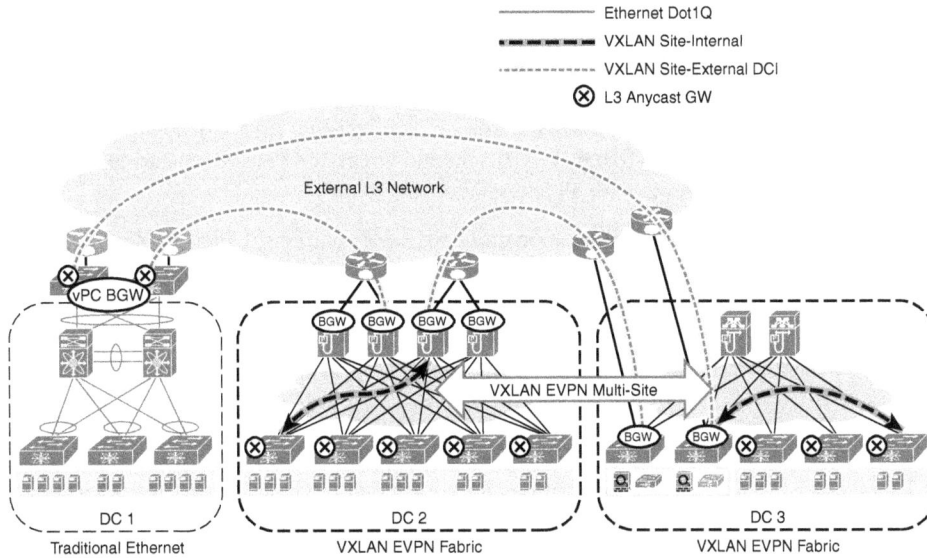

Figure 6-10 *Traditional DC Integration with VXLAN EVPN Multi-Site*

The second use case concerns traditional data center networks interconnected for Layer 2 extension. With that migration in mind, it is possible to leverage the vPC BGW mode by using VXLAN EVPN Multi-Site as shown in Figure 6-11.

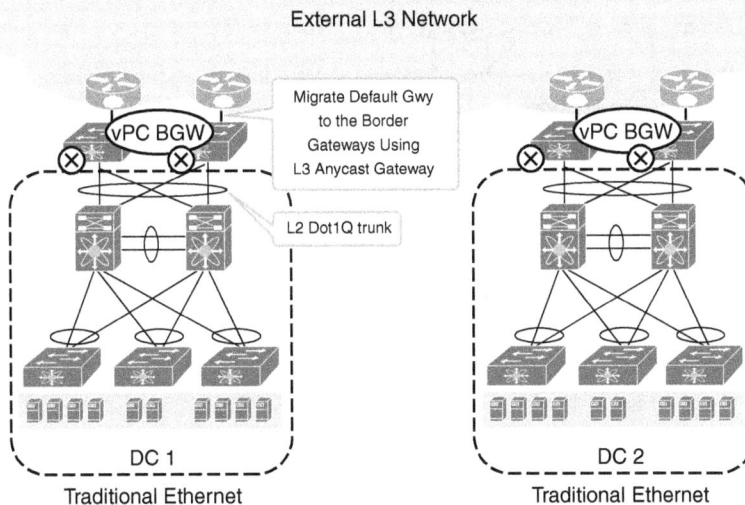

Figure 6-11 *VXLAN EVPN Multi-Site Interconnecting Traditional Data Centers*

Figure 6-11 illustrates two legacy data center infrastructures interconnected using the vPC BGW mode. This solution offers a smooth migration process from the classical Ethernet-based data center to VXLAN EVPN-based fabric. This option leverages a pair of vPC BGWs inserted in each legacy site to extend Layer 2 and Layer 3 connectivity between sites. These BGWs may be reused seamlessly afterward for full Multi-Site functions. This solution offers a slow phase-out of the legacy networks, replacing them with VXLAN EVPN fabrics. It allows migration from existing legacy default gateways (for example, HSRP, VRRP) to a more efficient and integrated Layer 3 anycast gateway, offering the default gateways for all endpoints.

vPC BGW multi-site offers a more solid and integrated solutions than a simple VXLAN EVPN-based solution, with natively embedded features from the border gateway nodes to improve the sturdiness from end to end (for example, split horizon, designated forwarding for BUM traffic, traffic control of BUM [disable or rate based], control plane with selective advertisement for Layer 2 and Layer 3 segments).

VXLAN EVPN Multi-Site and External Layer 3 Connectivity

This section discusses the design options for connecting the fabric part of a VXLAN Multi-Site architecture to the external network domain. Every data center fabric needs external connectivity to the campus or core network (WAN/MAN). The VXLAN EVPN fabric can be connected across Layer 3 boundaries using MPLS Layer 3 VPN (L3VPN) or virtual routing and forwarding (VRF) IP routing (VRF Lite). The integration can occur for the Layer 3 segmentation toward a WAN/MAN, built with a native or segmented Layer 3 network. When required, each tenant defined inside the VXLAN EVPN fabric can connect to a specific Layer 3 VPN network. In this case, VRF Lite is handed off at the border leaf nodes to be bound with the respective external segmentations using subinterfaces for north–south (N–S) traffic flow (1), as illustrated in Figure 6-12 with Site 1. Using a separate set of interfaces (2), the routed network maintains the Layer 3 connectivity between the remote sites in order to establish the VXLAN EVPN Multi-Site site-external overlay network for east–west (E–W) traffic flow (5).

In deployments with a very large number of extended VRF instances, the number of eBGP sessions or IGP neighbors can lead to scalability issues and configuration complexity. Traditionally with such deployments it is necessary to maintain the segmentation between the border leaf node using VRF Lite hand-off and the provider equipment (PE), which imposes a two-box solution. However, it is now possible to merge the Layer 3 segmentation with the external Layer 3 connectivity (provider edge router) for a single-device solution.

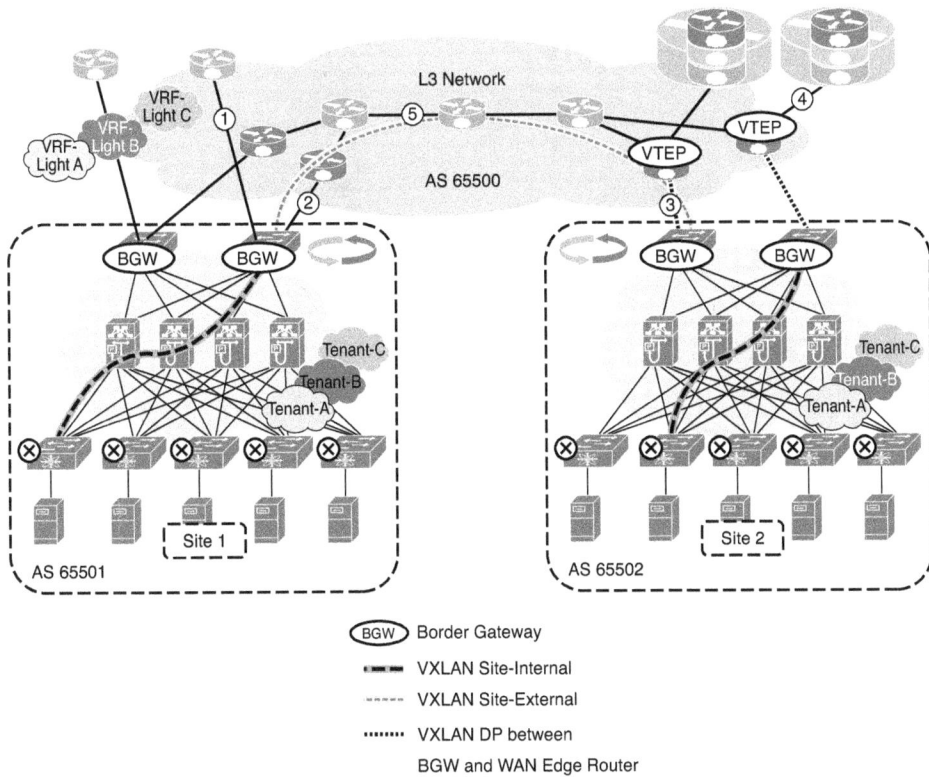

Figure 6-12 *VXLAN EVPN Multi-Site: Layer 3 Segmentation Connectivity to the External Layer 3 Domain*

In Figure 6-12 Site 2 depicts a full integration of the Layer 3 segmentation initiated inside the VXLAN EVPN fabric (tenants), extended for external connectivity from the BGW devices to an MPLS L3VPN network. This option allows extension of the VXLAN tunnel toward the external core router (VTEP) that terminates the tunnel (3). In this scenario, it is possible to use a single set of interfaces for E–W and N–S traffic flow destined to the PE. This integration makes it possible to stitch the Layer 3 VNI from the VXLAN fabric to an MPLS Layer 3 VPN network (4). The routed network maintains the Layer 3 connectivity between sites to establish the VXLAN EVPN Multi-Site site-external overlay network (5). This model requires that the core router be border provider edge (border PE) capable. This feature is supported with the Nexus 7000/M3, ASR 1000, and ASR 9000.

With VXLAN BGP EVPN, the advertisement of host routes (/32) is performed by default. This is crucial to help ensure that external traffic from end users is steered directly to the data center where the endpoints are active, reducing the hairpinning through a distant site, as highlighted in Figure 6-13.

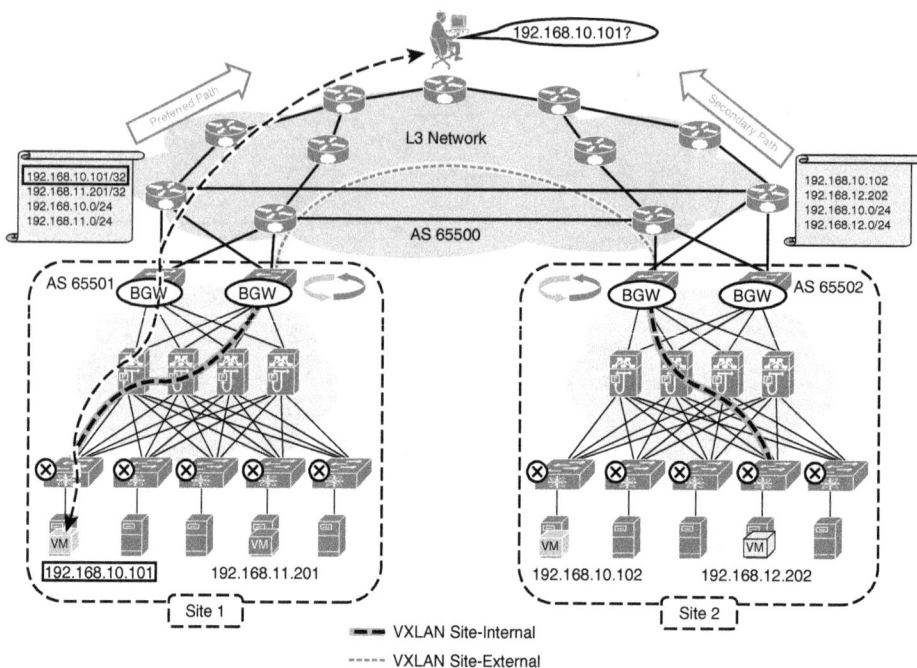

Figure 6-13   *VXLAN EVPN Multi-Site: Host Route Advertisement to the External Layer 3 Domain*

Interconnecting ACI Fabrics

This following section covers the various past and present solutions for interconnecting two or more ACI points of delivery (PoD) or ACI fabrics. It provides an overview of the different solutions, ranging from DCI-independent services inherited from traditional networks to hierarchical and integrated solutions into the ACI domain.

Interconnecting Multiple ACI Fabrics: A Chronological Evolution

As with stand-alone VXLAN EVPN, when the ACI platform became available through its first release, the need to extend networks and policies outside the local data center became a crucial constraint. Network and policy extension requirements were first deployed with traditional methods, either by stretching the same ACI fabric beyond a single location or by interconnecting multiple independent ACI fabrics using traditional DCI solutions.

The need to offer solid and efficient architectures interconnecting multiple ACI domains has evolved quickly, as shown in Figure 6-14. Currently, the two architectures qualified to interconnect multiple pods or fabrics are ACI Multi-Pod and ACI Multi-Site:

■ **ACI Multi-Pod:** This architecture allows you to connect various ACI pods via an external IP-routed network called the inter-pod network (IPN). You can deploy applications across these pods, stretching VRF instances, BD, EPGs, and policies across a VXLAN between pods. All of this operational activity is managed under a single Application Policy Infrastructure Controller (APIC) cluster. You therefore get single policy plane, fault isolation at the pod level, and the ability to move applications around without having to re-address the endpoints' identities.

■ **ACI Multi-Site:** This architecture allows you to manage and automate the connectivity between multiple ACI fabrics spread across long distances, each with its own local APIC, through a single management pane known as the ACI Multi-Site Orchestrator (MSO), which offers a global view of network policy automatically federated between APIC clusters. This greatly simplifies the handling of both disaster recovery and scale-out, allowing you to deploy applications across multiple data centers through common policy, enable application mobility, isolate failure domains, and greatly improve availability and scalability.

Note Unlike VXLAN EVPN Multi-Pod, ACI Multi-Pod is a fully validated solution deployed to interconnect multiple ACI pods, as discussed in the next section.

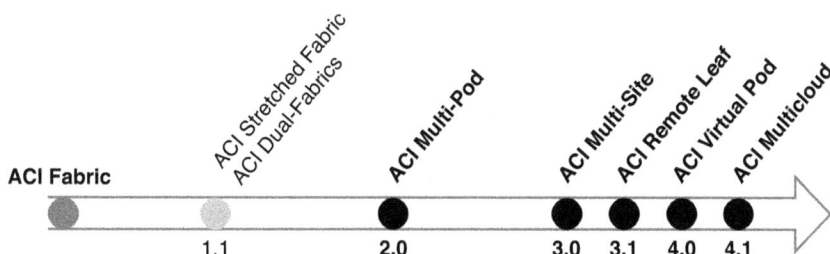

Figure 6-14 *Evolution with ACI Anywhere*

ACI Remote Leaf Node

You can extend ACI to remote data center or IaaS environments. Since APIC release 3.1(1) this can be accomplished through a remote physical switch connected on an on-premises data center by a standard IP network.

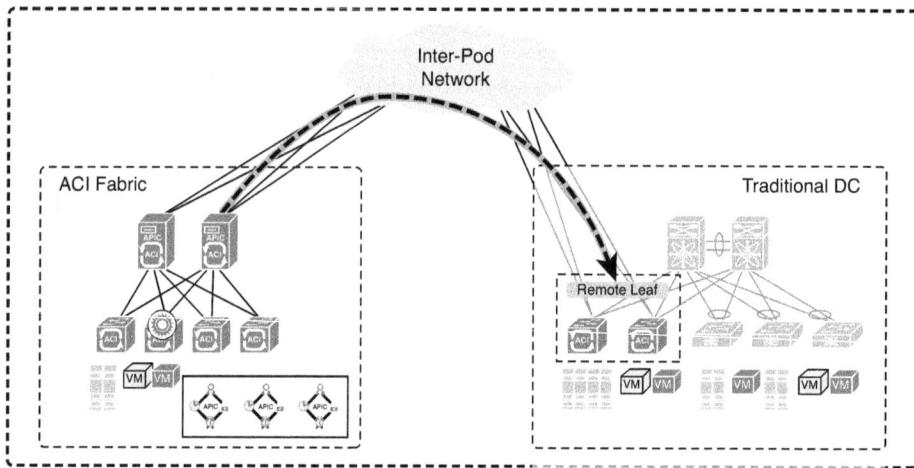

Figure 6-15 *ACI Fabric Extension to a Remote Data Center, Using Remote Physical Leaf Nodes*

ACI Multi-Pod

ACI Multi-Pod relies on a single APIC cluster that is dispersed across multiple locations to build an ACI domain. It is usually deployed within a metropolitan area or geographically distributed across longer distances, with up to 50 ms of maximum latency between pods. As a result, a single ACI domain exists from end to end, managed by the same APIC SDN controller.

The deployment of a unique APIC cluster simplifies the management and operational features of the solution, as every pod appears like a single ACI fabric: Each configured tenant component (for example, VRF instances, bridge domains, endpoint group) and policy is made available across all the pods, simplifying the connections and mobility of endpoints across the whole ACI domain from any pod to any pod.

From a network point of view, the key difference between VXLAN EVPN Multi-Pod and an ACI stretched fabric is that ACI Multi-Pod reduces the failure domain to a single pod. Indeed, ACI Multi-Pod offers a boundary that separates the different control plane protocols from each pod. As shown with Figure 6-16, the instances of IS-IS, COOP, and MP-BGP protocols that exist inside each pod run independently. As a result, any issues due to any of those protocols is contained within a pod, without affecting the rest of the ACI domain. This is a key DCI requirement for extending Layer 2 segments beyond a single location that clearly makes ACI Multi-Pod the recommended design option for spreading the same ACI domain across different locations.

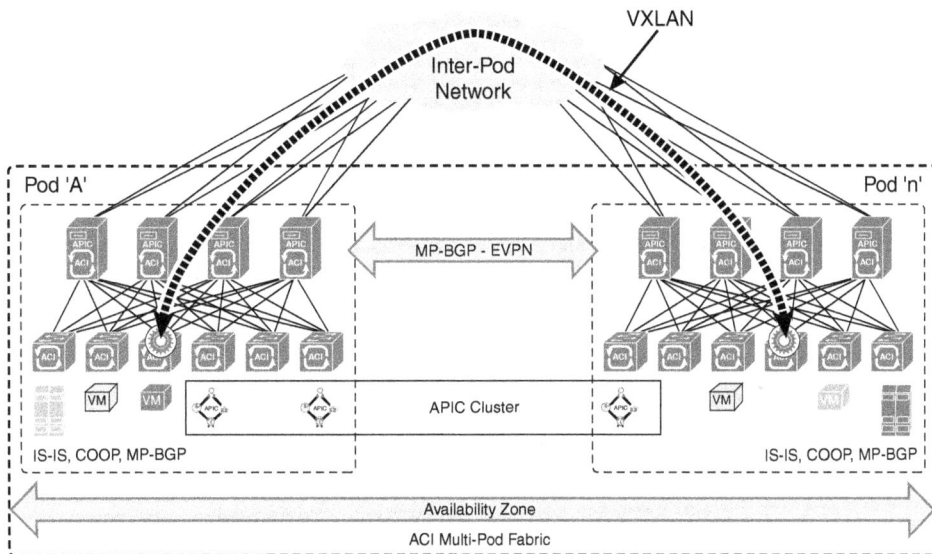

Figure 6-16 *ACI 2.0: Multiple Networks (Pods) in a Single Availability Zone (ACI Fabric)*

From a physical connectivity point of view, each pod bonds from the spine layer to the IPN. The IPN is a pure Layer 3 network, typically dedicated to inter-pod communication. It is crucial that the IPN network support Multicast Bidirectional Protocol Independent Multicast (BIDIR-PIM) as well as the Dynamic Host Configuration Protocol (DHCP) relay and Open Shortest Path First (OSPF) between the spine layer and the Layer 3 first-hop IPN device. The maximum transmit unit (MTU) size must be large enough to accommodate VXLAN encapsulation (which requires at least an additional 50 bytes). At the time of writing this book, back-to-back connectivity using direct fiber is not yet supported.

ACI Multi-Pod is the solution of choice for active/active data center fabric deployment. The advantage of ACI Multi-Pod design is support for active/active firewall deployment. All geographically dispersed pods are managed as if they were logically a single entity. As mentioned earlier, ACI Multi-Pod architecture is managed as a single fabric (APIC domain). As a result, any change configuration within a tenant applies across all the pods. ACI Multi-Pod introduces specific enhancements to isolate as much as possible the failure domains between pods, contributing to increasing the overall design resiliency. Although this behavior contributes to operational simplicity, it may raise concerns about the propagation of configuration errors across any remote pods.

ACI Multi-Site

To address the latter concerns just mentioned with ACI Multi-pod, ACI version 3.0 came with a new approach called ACI Multi-Site that offers a solution architecture for interconnecting independent ACI fabrics at Layer 2 and/or Layer 3. Each ACI domain is therefore identified as a separate availability zone. An availability zone is delimited by the centralized SDN management using the APIC cluster. With ACI Multi-Site, not only are the data plane and control plane isolated between sites, but the SDN controller, commonly called the *APIC cluster*, runs independently within each availability zone. However, to facilitate the day 1 and day 2 operations across multiple ACI domains, ACI Multi-Site introduces the concept of the Multi-Site Orchestrator, which is responsible for deploying any configuration changes across all sites of interest to which an ACI fabric belongs, using a single pane of management. Consequently, policy definitions and enforcement can be provisioned from end to end with a centralized management engine. This solution provides a granular level of control to push the concerned policies to a selected set of ACI fabric representing a single source of truth for these policies. In addition, the Multi-Site Orchestrator offers support for the network manager to monitor the health score states for each ACI fabric domain independently.

Much as with ACI Multi-Pod, the inter-site control plane exchanges the endpoint reachability information using a VXLAN MP-BGP EVPN control plane transport. Layer 2 and Layer 3 communication between endpoints connected to different sites is accomplished through a VXLAN overlay from ACI spine to ACI spine layer, across a generic IP network called the ISN that interconnects the various sites. The IP network has no specific functional requirements other than the capability to support routing and increased MTU size according to the extra header for VXLAN encapsulation (an extra 50 bytes minimum).

Figure 6-17 shows an ACI multi-site architecture with two ACI domain fabrics.

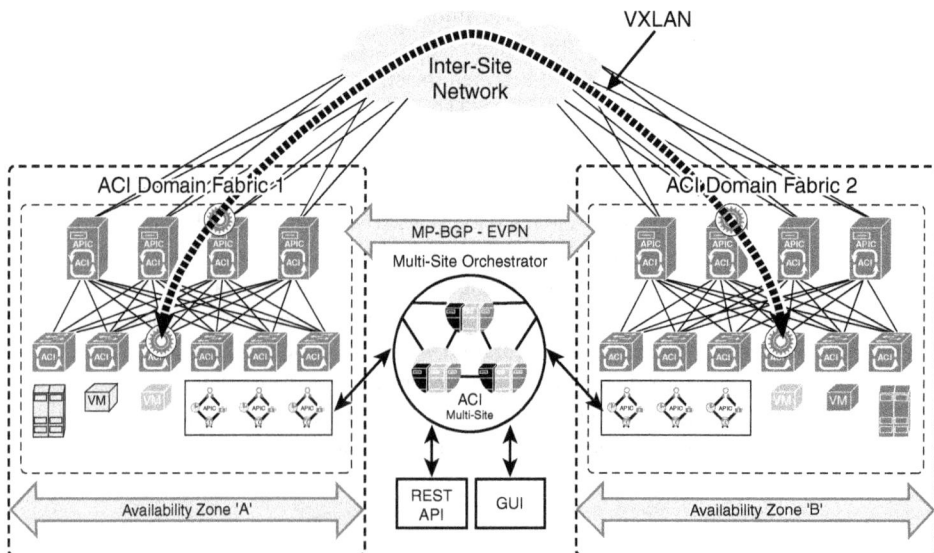

Figure 6-17   *Using ACI Multi-Site to Interconnect Independent ACI Domains*

ACI Multi-Site offers different flexible use cases based on business requirement. Notice that for all use cases, the communication locally or between distant endpoint groups (EPGs) is achieved only if the appropriate policy is applied between them.

ACI Multi-Site brings the capability of supporting IP mobility for endpoints roaming across ACI fabrics. This is achieved by allowing the endpoints to preserve their IP addresses, both for live migration (as, for example, in the case of vSphere vMotion) and cold migration scenarios (as, for example, for a DR use case). One of the distinctive capability offered by ACI Multi-Site consists in allowing those IP mobility use cases without flooding broadcast traffic across sites, which is a critical functionality to ensure that disruptive events are not propagated between them.

In addition, ACI Multi-Site can be leveraged to offer business continuity with zero interruption selectively for critical applications that rely on high-availability clusters. This model requires Layer 2 adjacency between application nodes deployed across the ACI fabrics, so it is possible to selectively enable inter-site BUM flooding only for the BDs requiring this functionality.

The third traditional use case is when only Layer 3 connectivity is required between sites. In this case, only routed communication is established across different ACI fabrics. In this specific scenario, neither Layer 2 extension nor flooding is permitted between the sites of interest. Only bridge domains configured with different IP subnets are active in different ACI domain sites.

The ACI Multi-Pod and ACI Multi-Site solutions sounds fairly similar, however they differ in a few crucial aspects. Only one single APIC cluster is required for managing all of ACI Multi-Pods, which results in a single availability zone, while ACI Multi-Site deploys an independent APIC cluster for each ACI domain, offering multiple availability zones. The Multi-Site Orchestrator is leveraged to keep consistency between policies across concerned sites. As a result, ACI Multi-Site is more adapted for solid DRP. ACI Multi-Pod is certainly more adapted for active/active data centers, even though ACI Multi-Site offers both. As previously stated, ACI Multi-Site offers the choice to extend between sites, Layer 2, with or without flooding, or only Layer 3.

ACI and External Layer 3 Connectivity

Traditionally with an ACI single site, ACI Multi-Pod, or ACI Multi-Site, the Layer 3 connections to outside the fabric (L3Out) are established from the ACI border leaf nodes. Figure 6-18 illustrates the L3Out connection from the ACI border leaf nodes.

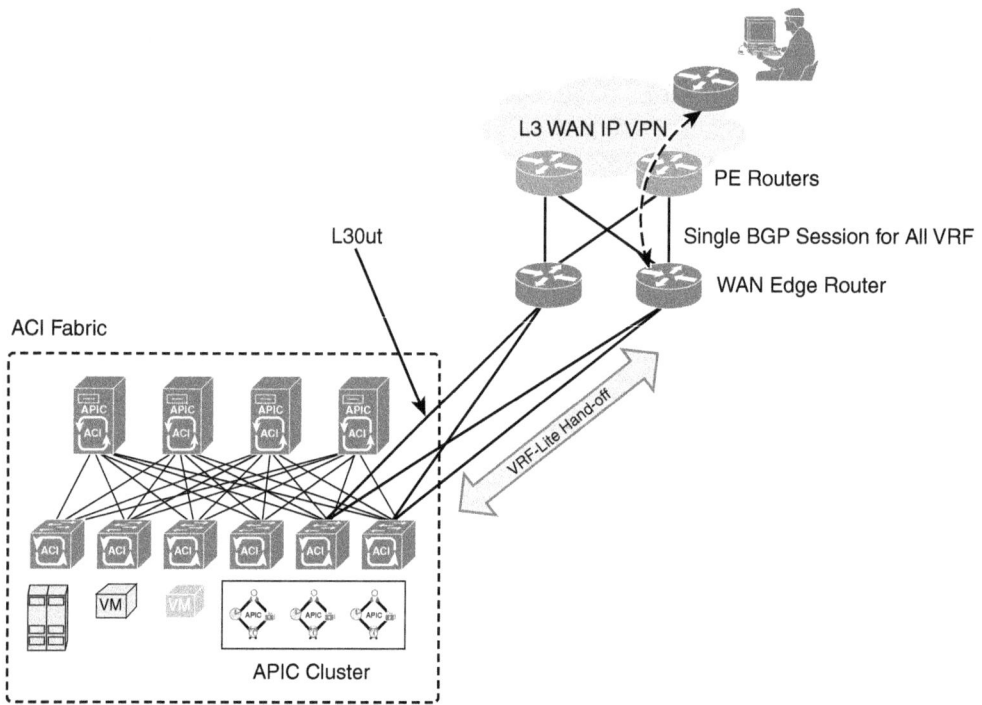

Figure 6-18   *L3Out Connection from the ACI Border Leaf*

However, an alternative approach when deploying ACI across multiple locations is Giant Overlay Fabric (GOLF). GOLF (also known as Layer 3 EVPN Services for Fabric WAN) offers a more efficient and scalable ACI fabric to extend a tenant network connectivity toward an external Layer 3 VPN. As shown in Figure 6-19, GOLF allows the creation of L3Out connections from the ACI spine layer to establish a VXLAN MP-BGP EVPN session with the external Layer 3 devices that connect to the WAN/MAN network.

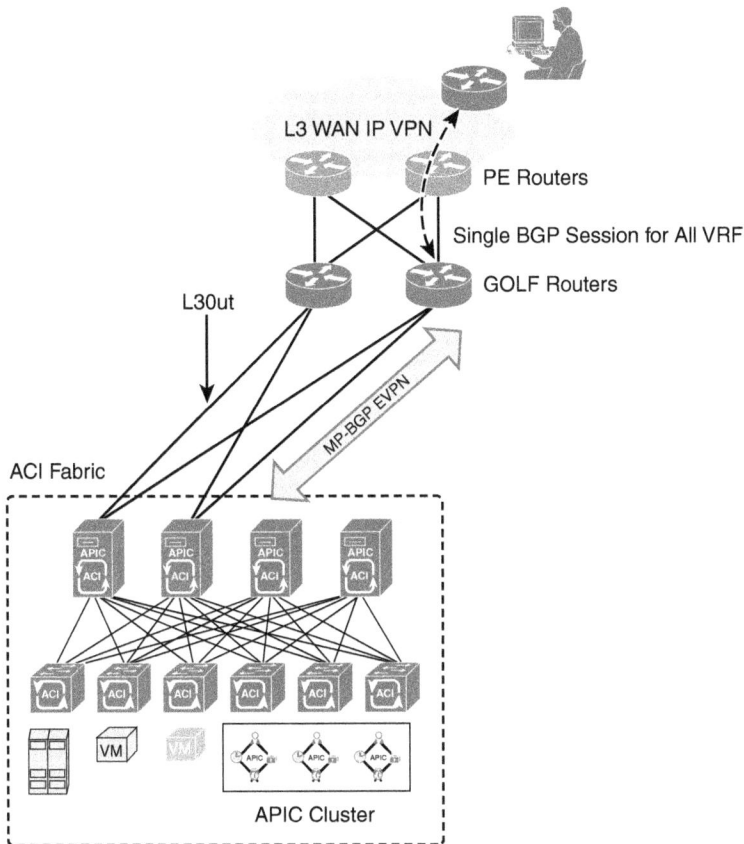

Figure 6-19 *L3Out Connection from the ACI Spine Nodes*

Each of the external tenant connections uses a single session from the spine devices where the GOLF routers are connected.

GOLF offers more efficiency and higher scalability because it establishes a single BGP session for all tenants/VRF instances, therefore reducing the number of tenant sessions and the amount of configuration required for all of them and simplifying the tenant L3Out configuration. Another specific feature that concerns this book is that this model supports host route advertisement using EVPN type 2 from the ACI fabric spine nodes toward the WAN. Host routes for endpoints that belong to a public subnet in the concerned ACI pod or fabric are injected by the WAN edge router into the WAN if the enterprise owns the WAN/MAN or the endpoint identifier is registered into a LISP mapping database (see Chapter 7).

Note   Host route advertisement using GOLF requires, at a minimum, APIC release software 2.1.x.

Figure 6-20 shows an ACI Multi-Pod architecture with the GOLF function used to steer the traffic from the WAN toward the ACI pod where the destination endpoint is currently active.

Either when multiple ACI pods or ACI fabrics are dispersed geographically across different locations, it might be useful to optimize the ingress traffic to directly hit the place where the application is active to reduce the latency due to hairpinning workflow.

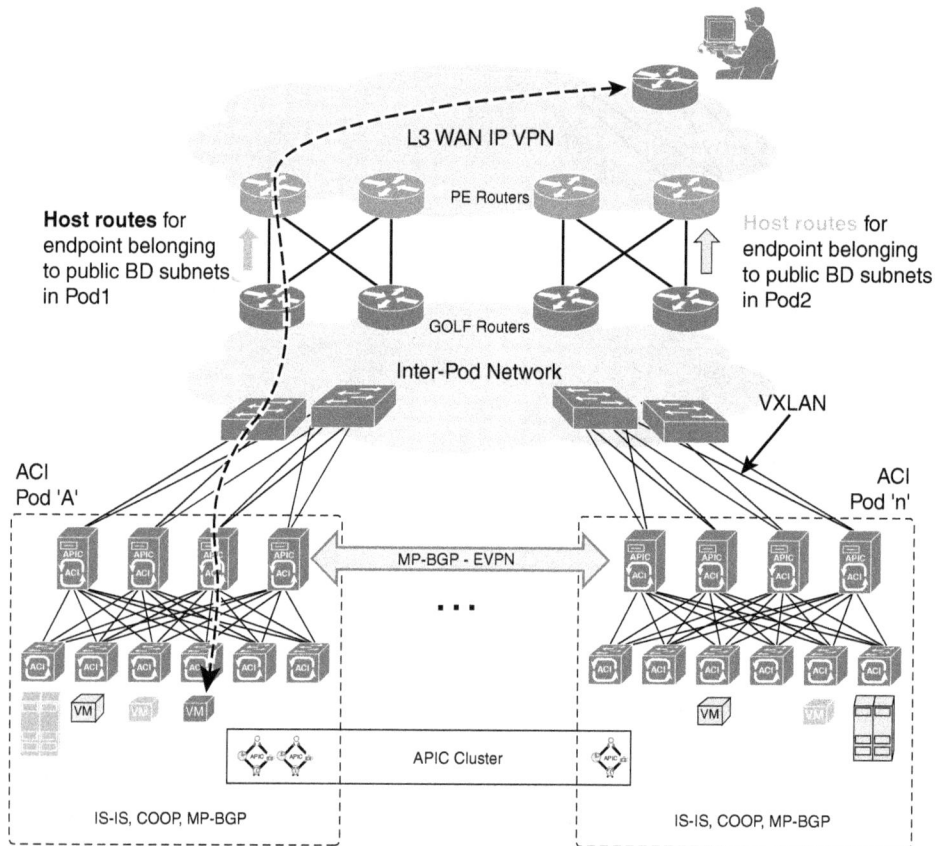

Figure 6-20 *ACI Multi-Pod with GOLF for Host Route Injection*

In summary, to optimize the ingress traffic, it is possible to leverage the host route to steer the traffic to the fabric where the destination endpoint is attached. There are two solutions:

■ **GOLF L3Out:** As previously discussed, an external WAN edge device tightly coupled with the ACI fabric, called the GOLF device, is responsible for sending the IP prefixes and pushing the specific host routes toward the Layer 3 VPN network. As a result, the ingress traffic is always steered to the site where the destination endpoint is located.

■ **ACI border leaf host route:** Since ACI 4.0, host routes can be advertised directly from the ACI fabric border leaf nodes. More precisely, the public IP addresses of endpoints that must be accessible from outside are injected toward the next Layer 3 core router out of the local pod in which they are connected and active. These host route advertisements are performed from the local border leaf devices along with the subnet. The local endpoint host routes are never advertised through remote border leaf nodes that belong in different locations. On the other hand, when an endpoint is moved away from its local pod—either because it was stopped or became silent after a timeout of inactivity or because it moved to another location—its host route information is immediately withdrawn from the local pod. In case of live migration of a virtual machine from one data center to a different site, its prefix is firstly revoked from the initial pod and announced afterward from the new location. This approach natively brings optimal performance for ingress communication to be directed to the right location dynamically.

Figure 6-21 shows the new feature advertising host route available with ACI 4.0.

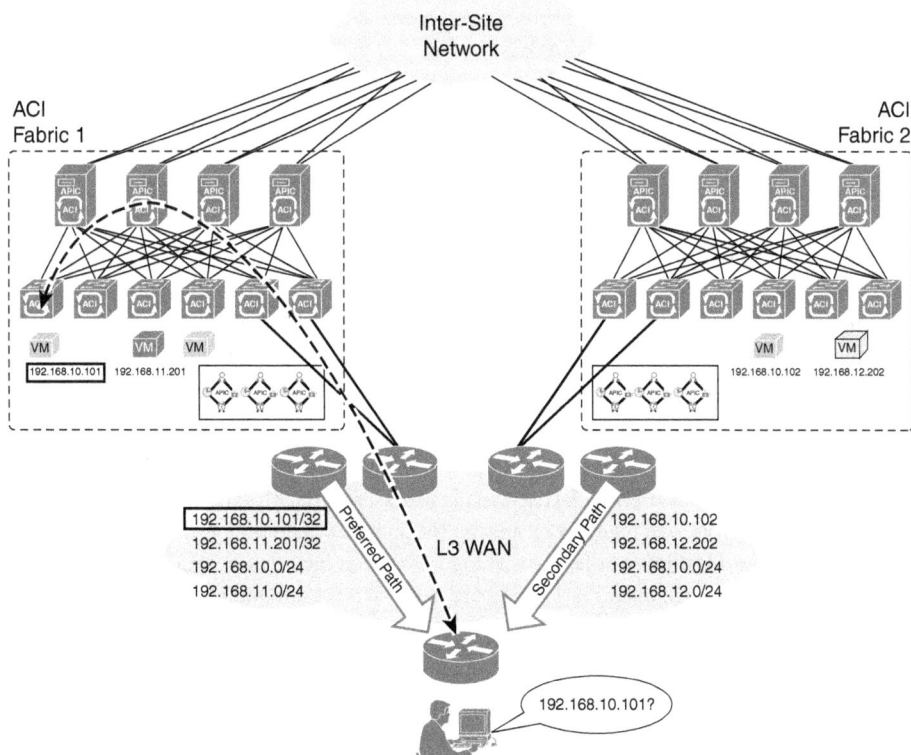

Figure 6-21 *Host-Route Injection from the ACI Border Leaf Nodes in the Context of ACI Multi-Site*

The previous sections introduce and compare the various ways of providing DCI connectivity using architectures that range from traditional to integrated hierarchical

DCI. The latter has been elaborated for interconnecting VXLAN MP-BGP EVPN fabrics as well as ACI fabrics. The purpose of these DCI solutions is to provide a seamless way of offering workload or application mobility that can meet the needs of automatic resource allocation or business continuity and disaster recovery planning or that can allow the network to scale to the requirements of the business. The different types of workload mobility are covered in the following section.

Workload Mobility Types

The compute stack and application layer are currently agnostic about the extension of the network. However, unlike in the overlay network, the software components in the compute stack and application layer can be very sensitive to latency. When deploying a high-availability cluster frameworks or hypervisor with live mobility, it is important to understand the maximum latency supported between two cluster members or two hosts. Each software framework has its own numbers. Also, multitier applications work similarly, regardless of whether the peer tier is local or distant. Thus, it is critical when deploying a multi-site architecture with an extended VLAN to understand the traffic flow that exists between each next hop; thus, deployment of stateful devices such as firewalls or application delivery controllers (ADCs) is vital.

From a network point of view, *workload mobility* means that an endpoint is moving from one physical location to another while maintaining its initial reachability information (MAC and IP addresses). The network should be able to identify in real time the new location of the endpoint, and the traffic intended to it must be carried accordingly to the expected destination. In this case, the location is the interface, and the switch (usually, but not always, the top of the rack) is changing. The network immediately updates (within a subsecond) its host tables accordingly, even if the migration is stateful, which means no interruption of the active sessions. The hypervisor sends an ARP message (GARP or RARP) after the move to inform the network about its new location. When it's a cold move, typically the host also sends an ARP message (an ARP request) during the boot sequence.

Different use cases imply workload scenarios such as hot live migration with virtual machines or cold or warm migration for high-availability cluster members, based on physical or virtual nodes. For the latter, usually an assisted health-check probing triggers a failover process from one member to another node while maintaining the same IP characteristics. And last but not least, workload scenarios include operational cost containment as well, such as migration of bare metal servers and mainframes.

These are the most popular workload types inside a data center, but other scenarios may exist. Nevertheless, all of these use cases require either the extension of the concerned VLANs or the existence of the same subnet on multiple locations without LAN extension. The difference is subtle but crucial:

- For extension of VLANs to be possible, Layer 2 adjacency must exist between the source and the target location, with broadcast traffic flooding allowed across the extension. This requires a DCI solution to extend the Layer 2 broadcast domain between the two sites.

▪ Extension of a subnet means that the same subnet exists on different locations without a bridge domain in between to allow flooding. A routed network offers the Layer 3 connectivity between the two sites.

Bare-Metal Servers

In the context of a data center, a computer running an operating system directly on hardware offering applications and services for a single-user environment is commonly called a *bare-metal server*. The user environment is also known as a *tenant*. In comparison, a computer host runs a hypervisor server that hosts multiple virtual machines, each independently running operating system software serving multiple user environments or multiple tenants. High-availability clustering is one of the most important resilient software frameworks requiring Layer 2 extension between physical nodes. For business continuity requirements, it is often desired to spread the members of a high-availability cluster across different locations.

High-Availability Clusters

Certainly, the early requirement for Layer 2 extensions between different data centers comes from the high-availability cluster. The primary purpose of high-availability clusters is to provide uninterrupted access to the data and applications a cluster is supporting. There are several high-availability cluster platforms from different vendors, but most of them were designed to offer high availability inside the campus. In the most basic implementation, a high-availability cluster consists of at least two server machines (referred to as *nodes*, or *members*) that "share" common data storage for the applications supported. The data is saved to this storage, and if one node cannot provide access to it, another member of the cluster takes over the client requests. During normal operation, only one member is processing client requests and has access to the storage; however, this may vary among different vendors, depending on the implementation of clustering. A high-availability cluster usually accepts several hundred milliseconds of latency, so it can also be deployed in different facilities at various distances, including intercontinental distances. A first Layer 2 communication must exist between members of a high-availability cluster in order to check the health of the active node. The member probes its peers by sending *heartbeats*. Heartbeats are hello packets that are exchanged across a private network at regular intervals via the heartbeat interfaces of the cluster nodes. In case of failure on the primary active member, the standby node immediately processes the following end-user requests while it has full write access to the shared database. This network is known as a private Layer 2 network as it is limited for communication between the high-availability cluster. Because the new active node shares the same device reachability information, another Layer 2 network should also exist in the front-end network of the cluster reachability to share the same IP address. This network, known as public Layer 2 network, is traditionally advertised outside the data centers. As a result, regardless of whether the cluster is local or the cluster members are stretched across different locations, it is required to extend at least two distinct Layer 2 segments between locations of the cluster nodes.

Cost Containment

Bare-metal machines are not as flexible as virtual machines, but for cost containment, when moving a bare-metal system from one physical location to another, it is often desired to maintain the same IP parameters. This implies that the same subnet should exist on both sides but doesn't necessarily require a Layer 2 broadcast domain extension per se; however, for easy deployment, the extension of the VLANs to retrieve the same subnet on both sites may help avoid IP address renumbering. Not only does this ease the migration of the applications supported by mainframes, it reduces the risks and accelerates the deployment of those bare-metal services. Nonetheless, a Layer 2 network is often deployed between the data centers to maintain the same host reachability parameters.

This is where LISP IP Mobility Across Subnets Mode (ASM) can be very helpful. This mode can be deployed to address cold migration requirements in a fully routed environment, without extending the broadcast domain across multiple data centers, providing dynamic redirection to the active node. LISP ASM is discussed later in this chapter section.

Virtual Machines

A virtual machine (VM) is usually an operating system or an application installed on a software environment supported by a dedicated physical host. The VM simulates exactly the behavior of a physical host. Typically, a hypervisor framework is responsible for creating and controlling the virtual environment and its components (virtual machines, network, storage) deployed on top of multiple physical hosts. Different vendors provide distinct virtualization management tools, such as VMware vCenter, Microsoft Hyper-V, and Citrix XenServer.

An individual virtual machine is decoupled from the physical device that hosts it. This means is that, from a network point of view, the VM is not physically bound to a physical network interface. In addition, the virtual machine can move, manually or automatically, from one physical host to another device, with or without the active sessions being discontinued. This is typically possible if the targeted physical host shares the same storage with enough hardware resources to support the new machine. There are two distinct options that rely on the enterprise business requirements. The first option is for the critical applications to be always available, with zero interruption, which means the virtual machine must follow a seamless process for hot live migration. To achieve a hot live migration without interruption, a Layer 2 network must exist between the source and destination hosts. The other option is to interrupt an application for a few seconds in order for the application to restart on a different location; this move is known as a warm or cold migration. For this use case, it is not mandatory to extend the Layer 2 network, but for the sake of simplification, the same subnet can exist in both locations. This use case is usually performed for disaster recovery. Several software tools exist, such as VMware Site Recovery Manager (SRM) and Azure Site Recovery. The number of VMs that can be hosted in a physical device is variable and depends on the hardware resources available (for example, central processing unit [CPU], memory, storage) used to build the virtual machines with their expected performances.

Workload Mobility Flows Between Data Centers

Whatever the number of sites deployed and the distances between data centers, the need to extend Layer 2 segments results in workload behavior similar to that of a single data center—but with higher distances between two machines or to the next hops. That is to say, the data packet between an external user and the front-end tier of an application (also known as the north–south traffic flow) and between the multiple tiers of a concerned application (also known as an east–west traffic flow) might zigzag, and hence it may need to be optimized due to the distances, while the same level of security may need to be maintained.

Northbound Traffic

It is crucial to notice that a Layer 3 network is not natively capable of identifying the location of an endpoint within the same broadcast domain. In a disaster avoidance network architecture where the bridge domain supporting the concerned application is extended across multiple locations, it is usually required to dissociate the data centers where the machines are connected. The concept of the primary and secondary data centers relying on the best metric to steer the traffic for a specific subnet to the so-called primary data center was traditionally used for many years.

For example, say that Data Center 1 is the authoritative site to support the applications that belong to the subnet 192.168.10.0/24. Data Center 2 is the backup site in the event that Data Center 1 becomes unavailable. As an illustration, the network manager might set a better metric for the Subnet A 192.168.10.0 advertised from Data Center 1 using a netmask set to 255.255.255.128. The same subnet is also announced from Data Center 2, using a netmask set to 255.255.255.0. As a consequence, the external data packets from the WAN are always steered toward Data Center 1 for traffic destined to subnet 192.168.10.0, as long as subnet A/25 is announced from Data Center 1. Usually, the same model is duplicated for other subnets, and the higher metric is balanced between the two locations. Each data center is therefore active and provides backup for the other for a set of subnets. The data centers are both active but for different subnets.

With the live mobility function allowed for virtual machines, it is currently common to move an application from Data Center 1 to Data Center 2. As a result, after the migration of an application from the primary data center to the secondary one, the ingress traffic destined to the concerned application is still sent to Data Center 1. The extended Layer 2 network allows the traffic to reach the targeted endpoint that sits in the secondary data center. If the network transport is usually not sensitive to latency, application performance may be seriously impacted, depending on the latency introduced to hit the destination endpoint and return. It is important to note that the return traffic has to hit the original firewall, as shown in Figure 6-22. As mentioned previously, the same level of network and application security as well as optimization must be maintained as if the workload happened inside a single data center.

East–West Traffic

As with northbound traffic, for east–west traffic (that is, for the server-to-server communication inside the data center), the network and application security services as well as optimization process must be maintained as if they were inside a single data center.

Network services are usually performed using stateful devices such as firewalls and application delivery controllers (ADCs), which include load balancers and web application security or Secure Sockets Layer (SSL) offloaders. These stateful devices are typically initiated in line with the data packets of a particular session. One of the key statements to address when using a stateful device is that only one active engine owns the current active session, and the return traffic must always hit the owner of that session; otherwise, the traffic is dropped for security reasons. Indeed, generally speaking, asymmetric flow is not well supported.

After the move of the application, without any optimization techniques, the original data center continues to receive new requests from outside destined to the moved endpoint prior to sending them throughout the extended Layer 2 network in order to reach the final destination endpoint (which at this time is located in the remote location). This is the expected behavior, and it is possible because the same Layer 2 domain is extended across all sites of concern. The routing takes the best path at the lowest cost, following the most specific route. That behavior requires the requested workflow to follow a round-trip path from site to site, adding pointless latency that may have some performance impact on applications distributed across long distances. This round trip is commonly called *hairpinning* or *zigzagging* or a *Ping Pong effect*. Figure 6-22 shows the traffic hairpinning after the VM has migrated from DC 1 to DC 2. As expected in a traditional situation without any IP localization optimization techniques, the ingress traffic from the end user is still steered toward the primary data center after the migration of the virtual machine. The traffic is secured using the firewall and eventually optimized with a load balancer engine before hitting the target on the remote site. Because it is crucial that the same session continue to use the same stateful device, the return traffic must be steered toward the perpetual appliance that owns this session.

With the increasing demand for dynamic workload mobility across multiple data centers, it becomes important to localize the data center where the application resides in order to dynamically redirect the data workload to the right location—all in a transparent manner for the end users as well as the applications and without any interruption to workflow.

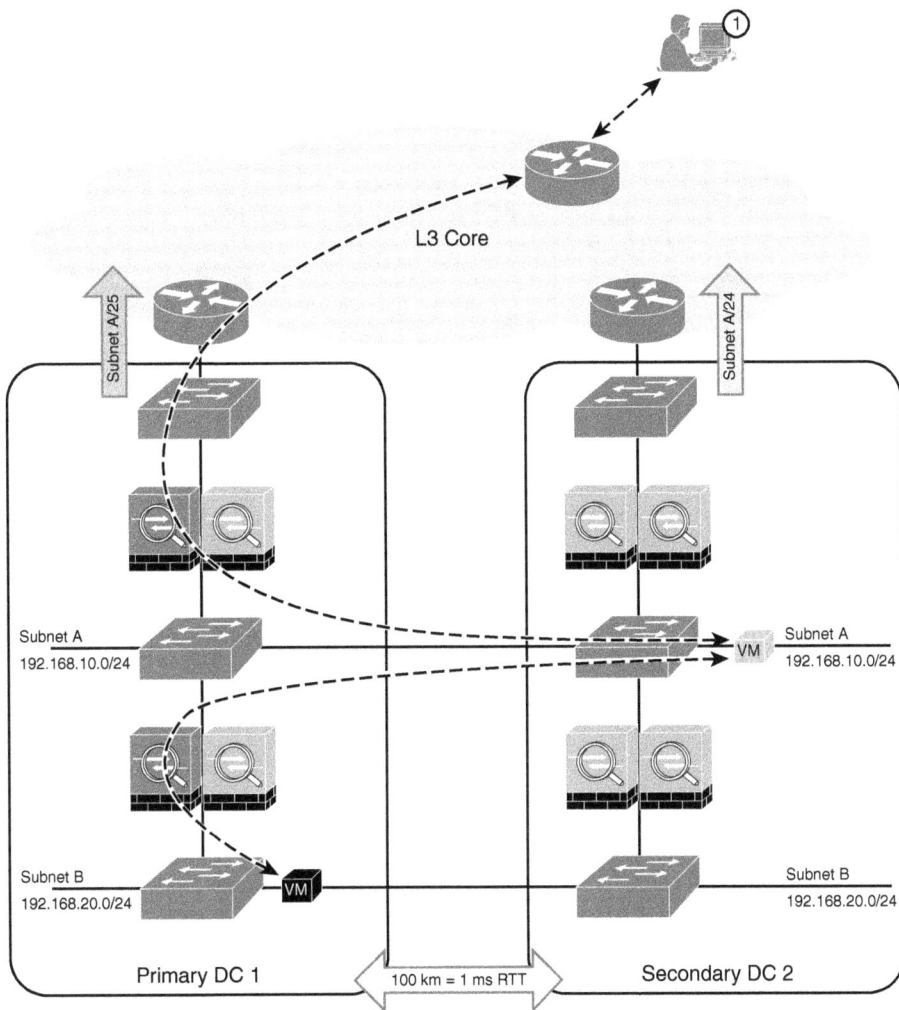

Figure 6-22 *Traffic Hairpinning Between Two Sites*

The goal is to dynamically inform the upward Layer 3 network of the physical location of the target (virtual machines, applications, high-availability clusters, and so on) while maintaining the statefulness of the active sessions and allowing new sessions to be established directly to the site where the application resides. Maintaining the statefulness of the sessions imposes one-way symmetry, meaning that the return traffic must hit the original firewall that owns the session. However, all new sessions must take advantage of the path optimization, using dynamic redirection through local firewalls. In that case, to be fully optimized, it is important to take into consideration the active functions of the closest stateful devices, the Layer 3 next-hop services where the endpoint resides. One additional action to reduce the hairpinning effect between the two distant locations is to specify a tight relationship between a group of virtual machines and a group of hosts that communicate together, such as a multi-tier application, using the host affinity rule for the migration stage. As a consequence, when migrating a multi-tier application from a local site to a remote one, all the related virtual machines belonging to the same multi-tier application are moved together accordingly. Figure 6-23 shows how the data flow should be carried to provide an efficient ingress path after a destined application moves from DC 1 to DC 2. In this example, a more specific route (/32) advertised to the Layer 3 core is used to steer the traffic directly to the location where the target endpoint resides. The active firewall in DC 2 is used to locally secure the traffic toward the front-end tier, and east–west traffic from the front-end layer to the back-end layer is kept local. The same occurs for the return traffic.

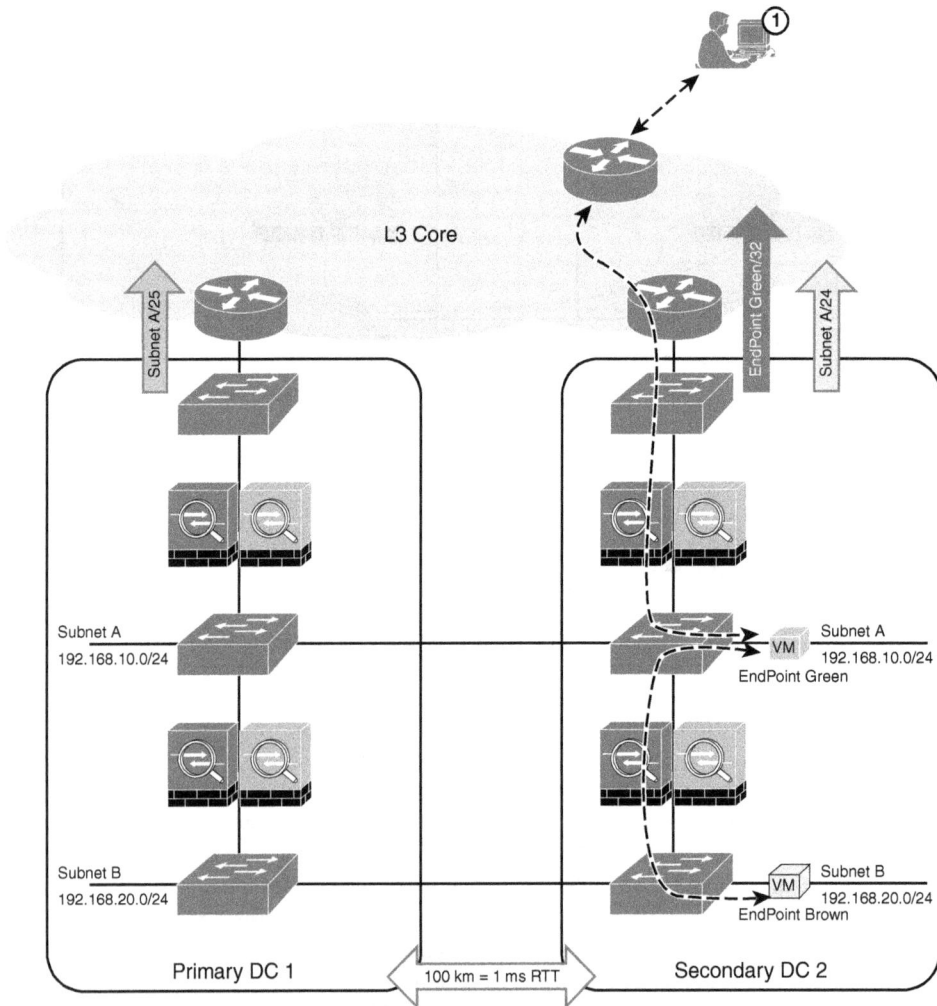

Figure 6-23   *Traffic Hairpinning Reduced Inside the Local Data Center*

Optimization for ingress traffic is traditionally not directly related to the egress traffic. These two mechanisms must be treated separately.

Traditional IP Mobility Solutions

For multiple data centers and business continuance, there have been several ways to control how to redirect the traffic in a different location. Historically, and for many years, these methods were described under Global Server Load Balancing. These technologies were leveraged with dedicated network service devices to accelerate disaster recovery service by dynamically redirecting the traffic toward the backup data center or by distributing the workload between the primary and secondary data centers. These traditional solutions to load balancing between different sites rely on three major technologies:

- An intelligent domain name system (DNS) known as the Global Site Selector (GSS) redirects the requests from end users to the physical location where the application is active. This model assumes that every time a machine moves, it is reassigned a new IP address from a subnet that belongs to the designed data center. In addition, the GSS can be used to distribute traffic across multiple active sites, either in collaboration with the local services such as a server load balancing (SLB) engine. Some vendors provide enhanced SLB devices, which, when deployed in different data centers, can inform a GSS appliance of the health of the application it serves locally. For example, if Application A is active on DC 1, the SLB device from DC 1 periodically notifies the intelligent DNS server about the status of Application A. When Application A stops in DC 1 and restarts in DC 2, the SLB device in DC 2 detects that Application A is active locally and accordingly informs its GSS device about it, while the original SLB device withdraws the application from its side. As a consequence, the GSS device can dynamically update its domain name space entry for Application A associated with the IP address used for DC 2. Other methods based on the load of the network or in collaboration with the existing WAN edge routers in the data center (for example, redirection based on the physical distance between the user and the destination application) can be leveraged. These solutions were commonly deployed for cold migration with proper IP address reassignment. Each data center uses its own network subnets. The user traffic is consequently distributed across the routed WAN.

  The weakness of the GSS is that the local DNS cache may impact the convergence time for the migration. Nonetheless, GSS works only for name-based connections, while other applications are using an IP-based connection model.

- The network service devices can go further in case of insufficient resources. For example, a local SLB device can return a Hypertext Transfer Protocol (HTTP) redirection message type (HTTP status code 3xx) to the end user so that the web browser of the client is automatically and transparently redirected to the elected backup data center where resources and information are available.

- Certainly the most popular mechanism to control the traffic to be redirected to the site of interest was route health injection (RHI), usually available from smart SLB devices. RHI provides real-time, granular distribution of user traffic across multiple sites, based on application availability. This method is initiated by an SLB engine that continuously probes a server (IP) or a server farm (VIP) and dynamically informs the upward router about the state of selected applications. This notification is achieved by injecting or removing a more specific route from the destination place where the endpoint moved into the routing protocol. More precisely, this means injection of the host route of the machine that has moved. The host route is then usually routed to the private core network. The host route injection is based on accurate information of the local application itself. This information is usually associated to the state of the application that it supports, such as the application being locally active (inject the /32 to the upstream router) or not responding anymore (withdraw the /32 entry). However, other criteria can be used, such as server resources, thresholds, specific period of time during the day, and so on. Thus, the redirection of the user request to a remote site can occur automatically in real time, based on different conditions.

The downsides of this latter approach using RHI are that it greatly consumes routing table resources, and it may require initiating a lot of probes from the SLB appliance. In the case of too many probes, it may cause a large amount of churn in the routing protocol and overwhelm the host, resulting false positives. This could lead to instabilities and overall loss of connectivity.

Note As discussed earlier in this chapter, a classical Ethernet-based data center requires additional techniques diverted from their original usage to inject a host route toward the Layer 3 WAN based on probing or signaling. These options are beyond the scope of this book.

The alternative based on host route advertisement from the endpoints' default gateway, usually referred as the first-hop router (FHR) toward the external Layer 3 devices, is to leverage native routing function from the Layer 3 switch to detect and inject the /32 route into the IGP routing table. The endpoint MAC and IP information are learned on the FHR based on control plane and data plane communication. More specifically, when a virtual machine completes its live migration process, the hypervisor hosting it generates a control plane frame on its behalf. The Microsoft Hyper-V hypervisor or the Xen hypervisor generates a Gratuitous ARP (GARP) frame, allowing the FHR to learn both the MAC and IP information for the virtual machine. The VMware ESXi hypervisor instead generates Reverse ARP (RARP) frames, allowing the FHR to only learn the MAC address information for the relocated workload. The IP address then needs to be learned from ARP control plane frames (ARP reply or GARP) generated directly by the VM.

In the context of a traditional data center network, because the FHR is a subfunction of LISP IP Mobility, this solution is called LISP IGP Assist and is covered in detail later in this chapter, in the section "IP Mobility Using LISP IGP Assist." LISP IGP Assist can be helpful only for legacy data center networks, whereas modern fabrics such as VXLAN MP-BGP EVPN and ACI provide natively similar functions with host route advertisements. Nonetheless, another similar solution was discussed previously with ACI fabrics with GOLF L3Out connections; this provides an option for exchanging specific host route information between an ACI fabric and the external Layer 3 intranet domain. Contrary to a classical Ethernet-based solution, the reachability information of all endpoints in learned by each leaf node where endpoints are connected and distributed across the fabric. ACI 4.0 and above support injection of host route notification directly toward the Layer 3 intranet network via the border leaf L3Out connections.

Similarly, host route advertisement to outside the data center fabric can also be enforced from the VXLAN MP-BGP EVPN control plane for the same reasons. Indeed, endpoint reachability information learned by the VXLAN EVPN leaf node where the IP address is connected is natively distributed across the VXLAN domain and to outside the fabric.

As mentioned earlier, it is worth noting that host routing is normally restricted to private intranet networks because, by definition, it is not allowed to inject host route prefixes toward the Internet network managed by an Internet service provider. Host routing requires that the WAN/MAN network accept route advertisement from the data center with a prefix subnet mask of 32 bits (/32). Technically, this is perfectly acceptable when the enterprise owns the end-to-end Layer 3 network. However, if the Layer 3 network is managed by one or multiple service providers, this is usually not allowed. As a result, to address host mobility across Layer 3 managed services, an overlay network can be initiated to encapsulate and transport the original traffic on top of the provider network using a public address name space across the core Layer 3 network. In addition, this necessitates a mechanism to discover and distribute the information about the locations of endpoints, and thus traffic intended to the roamer of interest can be routed directly to the right location without hairpinning workflow. This is possible because with the IP encapsulation transport, the original private subnet from the enterprise is kept transparent for the service provider.

LISP IP Mobility provides a solution for workload mobility with optimal effectiveness. The following section describes the LISP IP Mobility solution in contrast with host route advertisement options and provides specific guidance for deploying and configuring the LISP Host Mobility solution.

LISP IP Mobility

LISP IP Mobility, also commonly called LISP Host Mobility or LISP VM Mobility, allows any IP addressable device such as a host to move, or "roam," from its subnet to land to either an extension of its subnet in a different location or to a totally different subnet while, most importantly, maintaining its original IP address.

Traditional IPv4 and IPv6 Address Schemas

In a traditional scenario, an IP address (whether IPv4 or IPv6) combines two main functions. First, it provides the location of the host in a Layer 3 network to establish a path for the particular subnet to which the host belongs. Second, it identifies the host with a unique identity to establish a network communication directly with it. The location and identity forming the unique IP address of the host can't be dissociated. This is, for example, a classical behavior that happens multiple times per day with your laptop moving from home to the office or to a public hotspot, where it gets a new IP address at each location, as shown in Figure 6-24. On the other hand, when an endpoint migrates to a distant place while maintaining the same subnet—for example, with the Layer 2 domain extended between the initial location and the remote site—its IP address remains the same. As a consequence, it is usually difficult to determine the physical location of the roamer across the whole extended Layer 2 domain as the location remains the same.

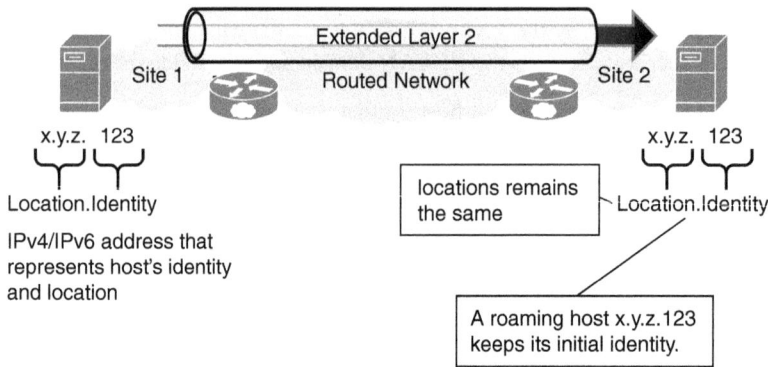

Figure 6-24   *Traditional Moving of Endpoints*

LISP IP Mobility Overview

In the context of LISP IP Mobility, the initial IPv4/IPv6 address of the endpoint represents the device's identity only, and the LISP site router identifies the location (routing locator [RLOC]) where the endpoint identifier landed. The original IP reachability is maintained during and after the migration; only the RLOC changed, as depicted in Figure 6-25. After the move of an endpoint, the initial flow is still sent to exactly the same IP destination; it is encapsulated toward the new location, also known as the RLOC, and de-encapsulated at the destination by the LISP router.

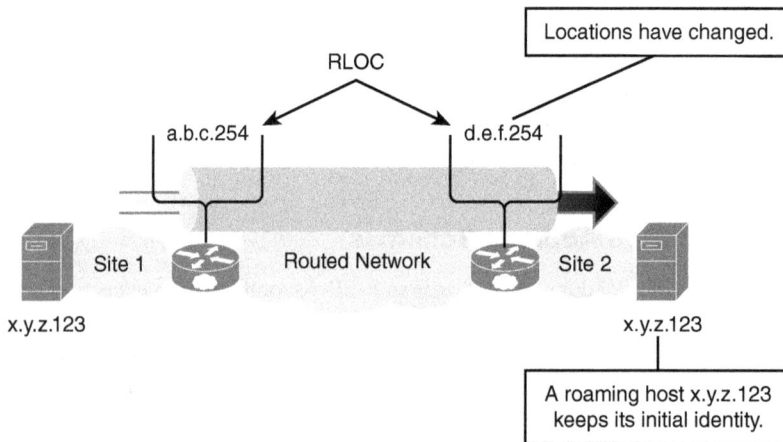

Figure 6-25   *Roaming Device with LISP IP Mobility*

LISP IP Mobility deployed in conjunction with Layer 2 VLAN/subnets extended across distant sites is called *LISP IP Mobility with Extended Subnet Mode (ESM)*. The key concern to address is that, in a traditional routing environment, when the Layer 2 network is geographically extended, a specific endpoint IP subnet/VLAN is no longer associated to a single location, as the Layer 2 domain itself is not localized either. As a result, the location of an endpoint is undetermined, and applications' performance may suffer due to higher latency with endpoints dispersed across distant sites. LISP IP Mobility ESM is used to provide seamless ingress path optimization by dynamically detecting the movement of the endpoints and directly rerouting the traffic according to the new place where the endpoint is active. Unlike other traditional routing protocols, LISP relies on a pull-based model, in which only LISP routers ask a mapping database for information about the location to take. This results in smaller endpoint tables, thus maintaining a low consumption of hardware resources for other purposes.

LISP IP Mobility in which subnets are different between distant sites and no LAN extensions are deployed across the data centers is called *LISP IP Mobility Across Subnets Mode (ASM)*. With LISP IP Mobility ASM, the IT manager still needs to migrate applications but does not need to reassign new IP parameters to the mobile machines. This is typically the scenario used for DRP or for extending resources to a cloud provider data center while managing cost containment. This model, in which an endpoint can move to a different IP subnet while retaining its original IP address, is commonly associated to cold migration scenarios. In these use cases, LISP provides both IP Mobility and dynamic inbound traffic path optimization functionalities without any manual human action.

It is essential to notice that there are some deployment scenarios in which the LISP IP Mobility functionality alone may be sufficient to address the workload mobility requirements, eliminating the need for Layer 2 extensions. For these particular use cases, such as disaster recovery and cold moves of hosts, LISP ASM can be very efficient, optimizing the ingress workflow to the data center where the destination endpoints reside without the need to extend the bridge domain between sites.

This transport method is also very useful for hybrid cloud services, in which a service provider can move and host the data center of the enterprise without necessarily changing the full address space of network devices and servers. This solution is elaborated later in this chapter, in the section "IP Mobility Using LISP Across Subnets Mode."

In LISP terminology, a device that moves is often called a *roaming device*, and its IP address is called its *dynamic endpoint identifier (EID)*. The LISP router is called the *LISP site gateway*. From a control plane point of view, one of the major responsibilities of the LISP site gateway to dynamically notify a LISP mapping database as soon as a new endpoint identifier is discovered. From a routing aspect point of view, it also updates its routing table with the host route accordingly. This LISP registration is done with the LISP map server of the LISP mapping database. The LISP site gateway's IP addresses are therefore used as the locators (RLOCs) by the LISP map server for each endpoint and IP subnet. The LISP site gateway is responsible for data plane IP tunneling transport:

- It provides a LISP ingress tunnel router (ITR) function or LISP ITR role, encapsulating the traffic coming from its internal site interface to be sent to the external Layer 3 domain destined to a remote LISP router.

■ It provides a LISP egress tunnel router (ETR) function or LISP ETR role for de-encapsulating the inbound traffic coming from the external Layer 3 domain, commonly from the LISP branch router, and original data packet are sent toward the destined host inside the data center network, typically the dynamic EID.

Note that because the same LISP site gateway can provide either the ingress or egress tunnel routing functions, it is commonly called a *LISP xTR*. The LISP site gateway xTR devices dynamically determine when a dynamic EID moves on or off one of its directly connected subnets.

■ It is possible to implement xTR functions on behalf of non-LISP sites with a proxy function called LISP proxy [ingress/egress] tunnel router (LISP PxTR). Typically, the LISP PxTR is used when a LISP site needs to send or receive LISP-encapsulated traffic to and from non-LISP sites. The PxTR function runs in a LISP-capable router normally deployed near an ISP's networks where a non-LISP site resides to allow remote customers from those networks to connect to LISP sites.

Before looking in more detail into the mechanisms that allow a roaming device to move between physical locations, it is important to introduce the concepts of the LISP site and the data center site and to clarify their relationship.

Figure 6-26 provides a general overview of LISP deployment, including the essential components in the LISP IP Mobility environment.

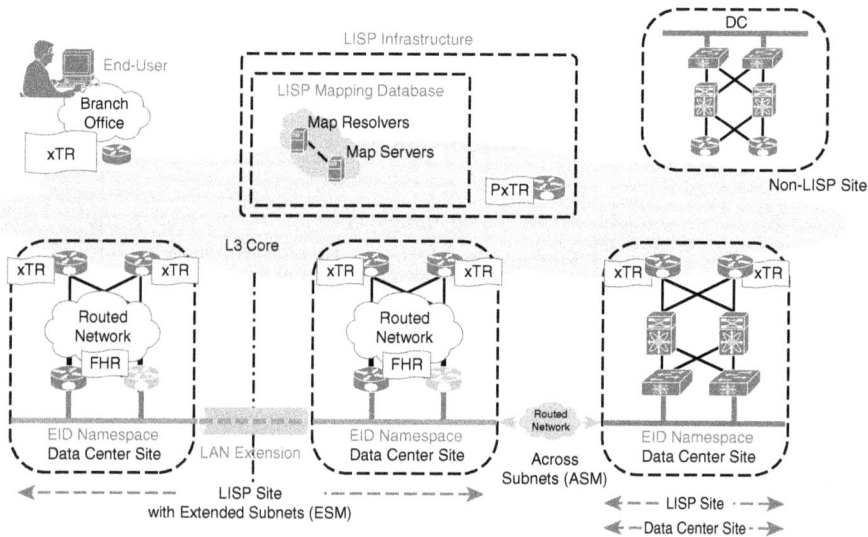

Figure 6-26   *LISP IP Mobility Environment*

The following bullets provides the list of LISP components with their depiction used in this chapter.

■ The data center site is a physical site comprising one or more LISP site gateway xTRs participating in a LISP site.

■ The LISP site is a logical view comprising one or more EID prefixes that have a unique locator set.

  ■ A LISP site can be made of two or more data center sites in which the EID prefix(es) and the locator set are distributed across multiple data center sites. This is possible when LISP is deployed in conjunction with an extended subnet (DCI/LAN extension). In this case, a single LISP site includes multiple data center sites. This is typically the case when LISP IP Mobility is deployed using Extended Subnet Mode (ESM)

    ■ A LISP site comprises a single data center site when the EID prefix(es) and the unique locator set are wholly contained within that single data center site. In this case, a single data center site constitutes and is equivalent to an entire LISP site. In this case, there is no LAN extended across multiple data centers. This is typically the case when LISP IP Mobility is deployed in Across Subnets Mode (ASM).

■ The LISP infrastructure includes a mapping database, which is composed of multiple map servers and map resolvers, as well as the xTR proxy.

■ The LISP EID namespace represents customer end sites in the same way that end sites are defined in non-LISP environments—but with one difference: The IP addresses used within these LISP sites are not advertised within the non-LISP Internet.

■ With a dynamic EID, a host (a physical or virtual machine) participating in VM mobility is capable of moving among multiple Layer 3 hops. When a dynamic EID moves, the roaming can be achieved via exactly the same network prefix (and can match that of the dynamic EID), or it can have different network prefixes.

■ When the roaming device matches the same network prefix as the dynamic EID, LISP IP Mobility is configured with "extended subnet" (ESM) command and functionality. When this is the case, a Layer 2 extension mechanism (DCI), as discussed previously, must also be deployed.

■ When the roaming device matches a different network prefix from that of the dynamic EID, LISP IP Mobility is configured with "across subnets" (ASM) command and functionality. When this is the case, the extension of the Layer 2 is not required.

Typically, an IP address uses a unique identifier assigned to a specific subnet prefix that represents the location determined by a mask to be naturally unique. The external Layer 3 network uses this endpoint IP address to also determine the network entity's location, based on the IP subnet. This is possible because conventionally a particular subnet exists only in a single physical place where the broadcast domain for that subnet is contained. When the Layer 2 domain is stretched beyond a single physical site, the location of an identifier might exist anywhere else the bridge domain exists, and thus the same subnet is extended across it. Therefore, the host's IP address no longer suffices to locate the endpoint to a physical place. Consequently, when a virtual machine migrates from one data center to another, the usual IP address schema retains its original unique identity and location even though the physical location actually changed. This is a result of extending the Layer 2 bridge domain used to transport a particular IP subnet between different physical locations. The TCP/IP identifiers of the machines that move remain the same from end to end, and the traffic follows the broadcast domain to communicate with all endpoints that belong to it, creating hairpinning workflows between the distant locations, as depicted in Figure 6-22, which is necessary to maintain active sessions for roaming applications.

To identify the location of a network entity, LISP separates the identifier of the network device and its location, known as the locator or RLOC. Once the separation is done, a LISP mapping system maintains an association between these two distinct EID and RLOC address spaces. From the data plane point of view, the IP address of the identifier is preserved by being encapsulated in a traditional IP frame for which the destination IP is the location (RLOC) of the site where the endpoint is currently active. When a data packet is destined to an identified network that exists in the LISP mapping database, it is intercepted by a LISP router, which processes a lookup into the LISP map cache to retrieve the location of the target data center where that particular prefix resides or, in the event of a lookup miss, asks the LISP mapping database about the dynamic EID reachability information. The LISP mapping database is also known as the RLOC mapping database. The LISP router sends a map request to the LISP mapping database when it doesn't know the location of the concerned endpoint or when it has been informed that the location previously recorded in its cache is not valid anymore. Therefore, when it knows the destined RLOC, the LISP router encapsulates the data packet with a LISP IP header encompassing the IP destination node of the selected RLOC and routes it toward the location where the endpoint belongs.

A traditional routed network underneath provides reachability to the locator, while the IP address of the endpoint can dynamically migrate to a new location without modification of the routing information relevant to the locator space. The original reachability information of the end-user data packet is transparent for the underlay Layer 3 core layer.

When a virtual machine migrates from one data center to another, the movement is detected in real time, and the association between the endpoint identifier and the locator is immediately updated into the LISP mapping database. Only the information in the mapping database is updated, and the endpoint identifier is mapped to its new locator. All the traffic destined for the endpoint is dynamically, automatically, and transparently redirected to the new location.

Figure 6-27 provides a high-level overview of the dynamic redirection process.

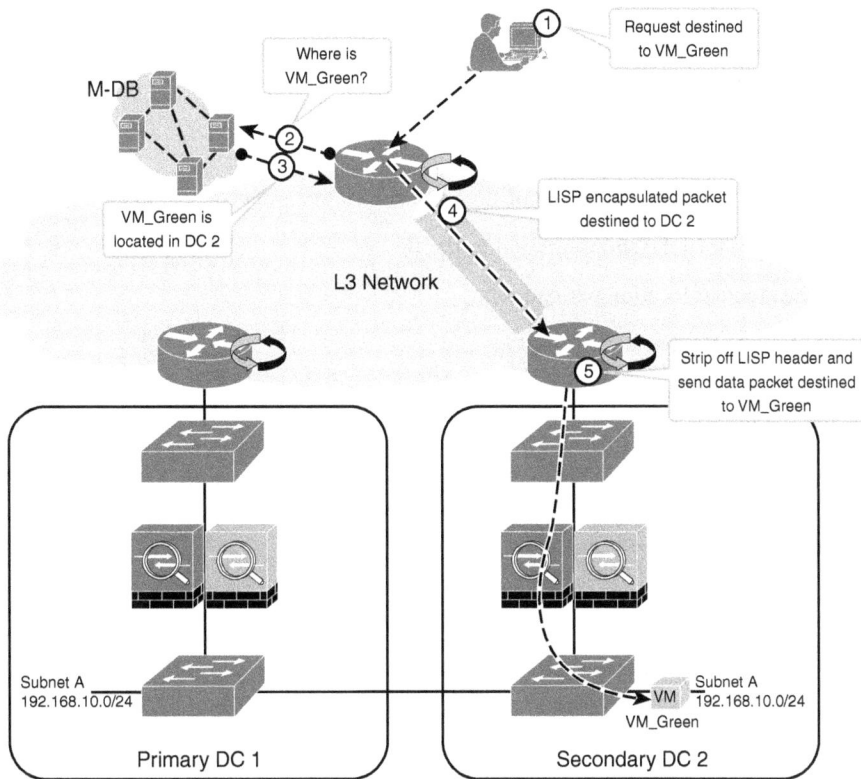

Figure 6-27   *LISP IP Mobility High-Level Overview*

The steps shown in Figure 6-27 are as follows:

Step 1.   The end user sends a data packet destined to VM_Green.

Step 2.   The traffic hits the local LISP router, which runs a LISP lookup in its map cache. In this example, it is assumed that this is the first data packet destined to this dynamic EID. Consequently, to this cache miss, the LISP router solicits the LISP mapping database for that particular location of VM_Green.

Step 3.   The LISP ITR gets in return the RLOC associated with VM_Green.

Step 4.   The LISP ITR uses the received RLOC information as the IP destination to encapsulate the data packet. The traffic is normally routed until it reaches the destination LISP site gateway.

Step 5.   The LISP ETR strips off the LISP IP header and forwards the initial data packet to the early destination endpoint.

As described earlier in this chapter, LISP is an IP-based solution that allows a subnet to be geographically dispersed across multiple locations, seamlessly offering ingress path optimization dynamically wherever the endpoint is physically located. LISP IP Mobility provides an automated solution to endpoint mobility with the following characteristics:

- Guaranteed optimal shortest-path routing

- Seamless hot live migration (ESM) or cold migration (ASM)

- Support for any combination of IPv4 and IPv6 addressing

- Transparent to the endpoints and to the IP core

- Fine granular location per endpoint

- Autonomous system agnosticity

- Multi-tenancy support

Note   Extending Layer 2 networks is a decision to be made with caution and with serious thought. It is imperative to consider the valid reasons for Layer 2 networks to be extended geographically across distant locations.

IP Mobility Using LISP Extended Subnet Mode

This section discusses workload mobility through the combination of LISP IP Mobility and LAN extensions to offer a transparent stateful live migration (with no interruption). As explained previously, this mode is known as LISP IP Mobility with Extended Subnet Mode (ESM). LISP ESM is agnostic of the DCI solution used to extend the Layer 2 networks. Any DCI solutions for classical Ethernet-based data centers (discussed earlier in "Interconnecting Traditional Data Center Networks") is supported. When deployed in conjunction with a DCI solution for extending VLAN across sites, LISP IP Mobility is responsible for offering ingress path optimization using the shortest path toward the data center where the endpoint is currently active.

The following section describes the mechanism for detection and notification of movement of endpoints across multiple sites and how the ingress traffic is redirected using the shortest path from the end user to the new location supporting the active application.

LISP detects the dynamic endpoint identifier (EID) and notifies all the LISP routers of the same LISP site about its new location. It therefore allows automatic and dynamic redirection of the initial request directly toward the site that hosts the destination application (endpoint), reducing the hairpinning workflows via the primary data center. As mentioned earlier, LISP relies on a system database that maps the endpoints with their current locations and provides this information when requested by the ITR. LISP signaling is triggered for each new discovered EID, and the localization of the endpoints is constantly updated in real time. That is, as soon as an IP address of the endpoint moves to a remote location, this information is signaled to the local LISP router, which updates the LISP mapping database accordingly.

To better understand the control plane and the data plane, it is crucial to outline the roles of the LISP infrastructure devices.

The LISP mapping database is the core repository for information on LISP IP Mobility. It is the source point for a successful LISP environment. This system database is responsible for dynamically maintaining the mapping between the subnet prefixes, the endpoint reachability information, and the location known as the RLOC. (The RLOC is the IP addresses identifying a LISP site gateway in a LISP site.)

A LISP EID namespace consists of the initial IP addresses and prefixes identifying the endpoints that are part of the LISP site (in enterprise data centers). Only EIDs from the LISP mobile subnets are involved in the LISP IP Mobility process. The EID reachability information with its location among multiple LISP sites is achieved by resolving EID-to-RLOC mappings from the LISP mapping database.

The LISP mapping database provides two specific roles:

- The LISP mapping database has a map server (MS) function, in which the LISP site gateways from each site register their local EID prefixes. The MS stores the registered EID prefixes in a mapping database, where they are associated to RLOCs.

- The LISP mapping database has a map resolver (MR) function, resolving EID-to-RLOC mappings as soon as it receives a LISP MR query from a LISP ITR.

LISP IP Mobility ESM Control Plane Operations

The LISP control plane is responsible for discovering the endpoints and informing the ingress and egress tunnel routers (xTRs). One of the key control plane functions of LISP IP Mobility is dynamically registering the discovered EIDs in a shared LISP mapping database.

LISP Site Gateways

A LISP site gateway is a network service that is typically enabled at the boundary of the data center; usually this function is initiated from the WAN edge router or a core router that connects the data center to the external Layer 3 network. This is the preferred place in the architecture as it is the gateway between the original data packet inside the data center and the encapsulated traffic between sites. Theoretically, when LISP IP Mobility is deployed in its simplest design, it is also responsible for detecting the movement of IP machines and notifying the LISP mapping database accordingly. To achieve this function in a legacy data center network, it must be the first-hop router for the endpoints that it needs to identify. This implies that there is a single Layer 3 hop between the endpoints and the LISP site gateway.

Note With modern fabrics such as VXLAN EVPN and ACI infrastructure, the function of endpoint discovery is embedded with the fabric directly managed by the control plane. This integrated function allows the VXLAN EVPN fabric to advertise the host route of the discovered endpoints from the fabric border leaf node toward the LISP site gateways (xTRs), which can be located at multiple Layer 3 hops from the endpoints.

LISP Multihop

An important component in LISP is the function of LISP multihop. Actually, in a production network, it is not usual to attach the servers that host the business applications directly to the WAN edge router—and hence to the LISP site gateway (xTR) router. For security and optimization reasons, stateful devices such as firewalls, IPSs, and load balancers, are commonly deployed between the applications and the WAN edge router—and, thus, for our concern, function as a LISP tunnel routers. Inside the data center, network services are not LISP encapsulation aware, so the LISP traffic cannot exist inside the data center network. Therefore, due to the fact that multiple routed hops may exist between the application supported by a machine (EID) and the LISP site gateway (xTR) initiated at the WAN edge layer, it is challenging for the LISP site gateway to be the default gateway of the endpoints, and thus detecting the endpoint reachability directly from the LISP xTR device is not possible. As a result, in a traditional data center network, a LISP agent located in the default gateway of the endpoints, known as the first-hop router, must be present to discover the endpoint or to detect the movement of the machines and to notify its local LISP site gateway over the routed network inside the data center. Consequently, the local LISP site gateway xTR in its turn notifies the LISP mapping database for an update of the EID with its new location. This service is called LISP multihop (LISP MH); however, the function itself initiated in the default gateway is called the LISP first-hop router (LISP FHR). In a modern fabric (for example, VXLAN EVPN, ACI), the default gateway is distributed and offered by the leaf nodes; as a result, there are multiple Layer 3 hops between the endpoint and the LISP site gateway.

Figure 6-28 compares LISP single-hop, where the two main functions of LISP site gateway and first-hop router are initiated from the same device, with LISP multihop, where the two functions are separated by a routed network.

For the purpose of LISP IP Mobility ESM, the scenarios are elaborated with the concept of multihop as, in a production network, the chance that the LISP site gateway is also the default gateway of the servers is limited. It is worth reiterating that the first-hop router function discussed in the next sections exists only in the context of traditional data center networks. As elaborated in Chapter 7 with modern fabrics (VXLAN EVPN and ACI), the function of the first-hop router is provided directly by the fabric, using the control plane.

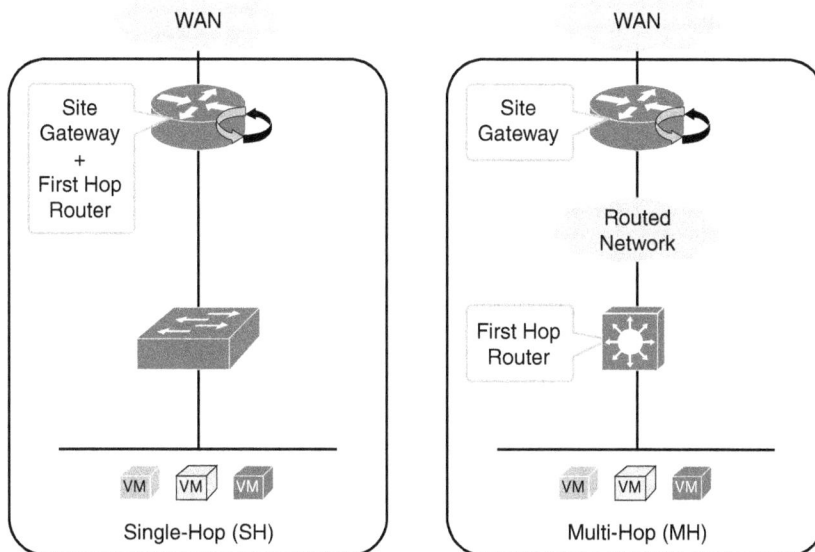

Figure 6-28   *LISP Single-Hop (Testbed Environment) and Multihop Designs (Production Environment)*

In addition to the multihop deployment, consider egress path optimization: You want the outbound traffic to take the same path as the inbound traffic. From a default gateway point of view, there are two options:

■ In the case of traditional data centers, the most useful option is to filter the hello messages for First-Hop Resiliency Protocol (FHRP) between the two data centers so that the default gateway is maintained active in each site with the same Layer 2 and Layer 3 reachability information.

■ In case of VXLAN EVPN or ACI, the embedded distributed Layer 3 anycast feature by default offers the same default gateway parameters from each first-hop router, including across multiple sites. Hence, by default, the egress data traffic is sent locally to the outside of the data center fabric.

Note   The deployment of LISP IP Mobility with VXLAN EVPN and ACI is elaborated in detail in Chapter 7.

LISP Mapping Database Updates in a Single-Hop Environment

Figure 6-29 depicts the high-level control plane signaling exchanged between LISP infrastructure components to localize subnet prefixes. Notice that the map resolver and map server are software processes that can run on the same device(s). They can also be combined with the LISP xTR role. This packet walk is similar in a multihop environment, as discussed shortly.

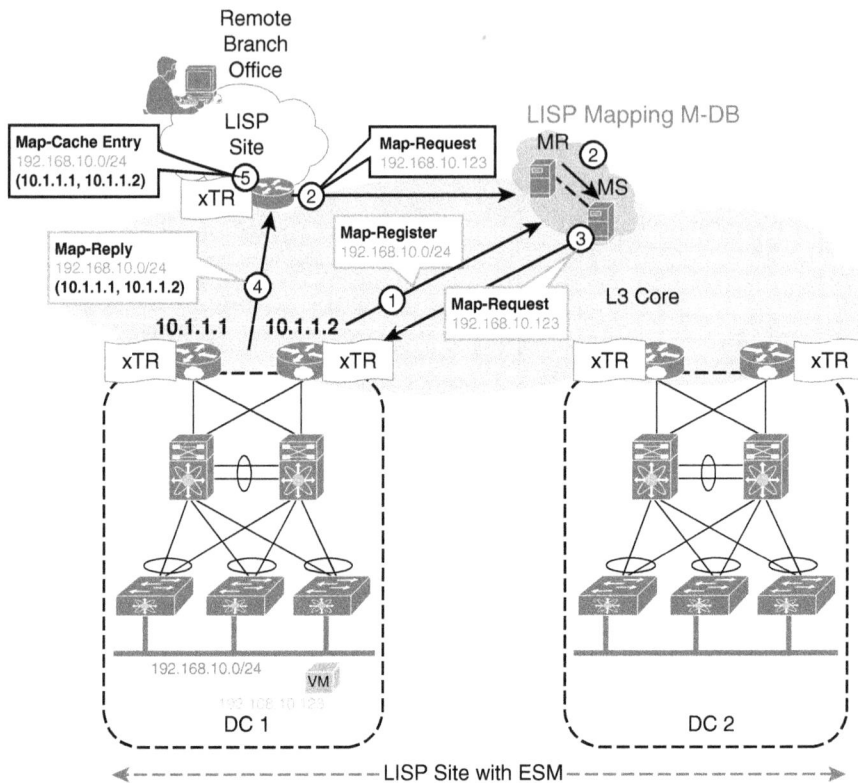

Figure 6-29 *LISP IP Mobility Control Plane Operation to Localize Subnet Prefixes*

The steps shown in Figure 6-29 are as follows:

Step 1.   Both LISP ETRs from DC 1 register to the map server (MS) the EID subnets that are locally defined from the LISP router configuration and from which network prefixes they are authoritative. In this example, the EID subnet configured for the LISP IP Mobility process is 192.168.10.0/24. For consistency, map registration messages are sent every 60 seconds by each ETR.

In this high-level scenario, an end user located in a remote branch office that is a LISP-enabled site initiates a request to the destination host 192.168.10.123. This IP address relates to a LISP EID prefix subnet deployed at one of the LISP-enabled data centers. The end-user workstation is agnostic of the LISP process. However, a LISP router in the branch office intercepts the data packet destined to the EID, which triggers a Layer 3 lookup. The prefix subnet, which could be a private network, is not part of the traditional routing table, but it is configured as a LISP prefix subnet. In this scenario, it is assumed that the LISP ITR at the remote branch office does not yet have any entry in its local map cache for the endpoint 192.168.10.123.

Step 2.   The LISP ITR at the remote branch office sends a map request to the LISP map resolver (MR) for 192.168.10.123.

Step 3.   Consequently, the MR forwards the map request to the map server, which forwards the original map request for 192.168.10.123 to one of the LISP ETRs that last registered the EID subnet.

Step 4.   As soon as it receives the map request, the LISP site gateway returns a map reply directly to the source ITR with the mapping for the subnet of interest, 192.168.10.0/24, and its locators, 10.1.1.1 and 10.1.1.2. The assumption in this scenario is that the two local ETRs in DC 1 are announced with the same weight. Such a configuration is usually recommended to load balance inbound traffic across both RLOCs. This direct notification is intended to ensure that there is accessibility communication between the destination ETR and the source LISP ITR.

After receiving the map reply, the LISP ITR in the branch office installs the mapping information for subnet 192.168.10.0/24 into its local LISP map cache. Data plane communication between the end user and the application in DC 1 starts.

Step 5.   As a consequence, from the forwarding data plane point of view, the LISP ITR in the branch office encapsulates the data packet from the user and sends it toward either the destination LISP ETR 10.1.1.1 or 10.1.1.2.

The LISP handshake learning process for a particular subnet belonging to one single data center DC 1 being described with the previous steps, it is crucial to include the second data center into the end-to-end network architecture.

First of all, it is important to understand the prerequisites that make LISP IP Mobility ESM efficient. In addition (and as mentioned previously), you need to understand how the LISP first-hop router exchanges the EID information with the LISP xTR and how the moves of an EID are detected by the FHR and how the other LISP nodes are notified about those moves. The cloud between the WAN edge layer (LISP router) and the server farm (endpoints) in Figure 6-30 represents the routed network required for network services traditionally deployed inside a data center infrastructure.

As mentioned earlier, due to the extended bridge domain across the two data centers where EIDs might reside, to prevent asymmetric traffic flow, the default gateway should be active in both sides. Thus, the egress traffic can exit toward the WAN from the local WAN edge routers where the endpoint is active. The concept is to deploy a pair of active/standby first-hop routers (FHRs) on each site. By filtering FHRP hello messages across the legacy data centers, the FHRs become active/active on both sites. The default gateway reachability information (vMAC and VIP) in both data centers remains consistent, allowing the end-to-end migration without interruption as the endpoint continues to send packets to its default GW IP address after the live move is done.

When a VM migrates from one data center to another, the movement of the machine is detected in real time by the LISP FHR. As a result, the association between the EID and the locator is immediately updated into the RLOC mapping database by the LISP xTR. All traffic destined to the VM is dynamically, automatically, and transparently redirected to the new location.

LISP Mapping Database Update in a Multihop Environment

In the scenario illustrated in Figure 6-30, it is assumed that the endpoint 192.168.10.123 is live migrating from DC 1 to DC 2 via an extended bridge domain. Prior to the move, in each data center, the local IGP routing table contains the subnet 192.168.10.0/24. Notice that two /25 Null0 routes (192.168.10.0/25 and 192.168.10.128/25) are automatically installed in the IGP routing table by the LISP process. This is achieved as soon as the **lisp extended-subnet-mode** command is configured for the subnet 192.168.10.0, as described later in this chapter. These routes are needed to allow the LISP xTR devices to punt to the CPU the first packet received from a mobile workload so that the LISP xTR can dynamically discover it and register the specific host route prefix (/32) with the LISP map server. The two 192.168.10.x/25 Null0 routes in this example are created to cover the entire 192.168.10.0/24 subnet. This is required to enable mobility for the hosts belonging to the full /24 mobile subnet. The existence of these /25 Null0 routes also has another motivating side effect: Because they are more specific than the local /24 subnet, traffic originating from the Layer 3 domain (for example, from a remote client) is never routed immediately to the mobile subnet but is first dropped because of the /25 Null0 routes until the destination endpoint is discovered. This allows the discovery process to learn the EID punting the endpoint IP address to the CPU. Indeed, for the punting to CPU to happen, an analogous unicast Reverse Path Forwarding logic (uRPF-like) against /25 is enabled automatically on an interface configured for LISP Host Mobility.

In the LISP IP Mobility with Extended Subnet Mode implementation, the communication with the roaming machine that belongs to a LISP mobile subnet is established only after that endpoint is dynamically discovered by the local LISP router, regardless of which data center the machine belongs to.

The LISP first-hop router discovers the EID either from the data plane or from the control plane. When the roaming device sends an IP data packet (Layer 3 packet), it triggers the discovery event as described here. This learning process is referred to as *data plane discovery*. When the roaming machine sends an ARP packet (which is a Layer 2 frame) containing the IP address of the endpoint in the payload, a discovery event triggered by ARP messages is referred to as *control plane discovery*. A typical scenario occurs during the boot sequence of a physical host or virtual machine since it would usually send out a Gratuitous ARP (GARP) frame to detect a duplicate IP address, including in the payload its own IP address.

To visualize the handshake mechanism, Figure 6-30 shows the sequence of events with a data plane discovery process using a LISP IP Mobility ESM deployment:

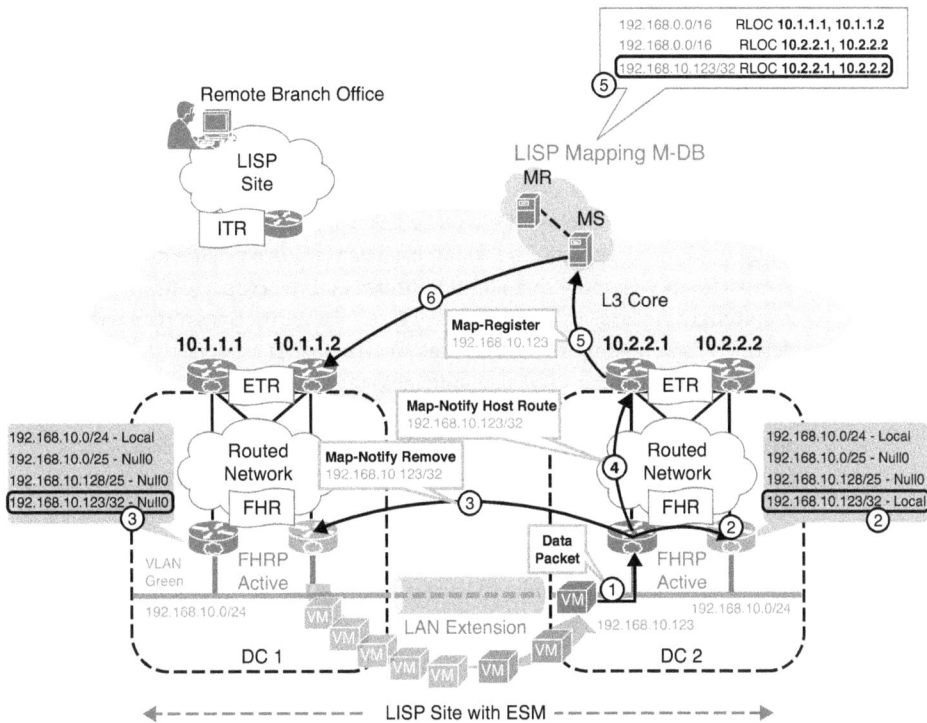

Figure 6-30   *LISP IP Mobility Control Plane Operation to Localize EIDs*

Step 1.   After its move to DC 2, the roaming EID generates an IP data packet that is received by the FHR on the interface enabled for LISP Host Mobility where the switch virtual interface (SVI) is configured with 192.168.10.254. The Layer 3 traffic from the roaming machine is routed through its local gateway.

The LISP logic inspects the IP address of the received packet. To get a successful handling, the packet must be received on the interface that the router uses to forward the return packet. However, as depicted in this scenario, the /25 Null0 routes are more specific than the /24 subnet directly connected via the SVI. Consequently, because the packet matches one of the 192.168.10.x/25 Null0 routes by LISP which is more specific than the /24 subnet directly connected via the SVI, the packet is punted to the CPU, triggering the EID dynamic discovery process.

Step 2.   The local active LISP FHR injects the host route of the roaming EID 192.168.10.123/32 into its local IGP routing table. Subsequently, the discovering LISP FHR sends out a map notify group multicast message that reaches the other FHRs and also travels through the LAN extension connection toward the two remote LISP FHRs. Receiving the map notify group multicast message, the second local FHRP router, identified as the its FHR peer, adds the local /32 route of the discovered EID to its routing table.

Step 3.   The remote FHR that is active on the source data center receives the map notify group multicast message. As a result, it installs a LISP Null0 entry for the roamer EID of interest (192.168.10.123/32) into its IGP routing table. This Null0 is required since the workload has been discovered in a different data center site to guarantee that all LISP infrastructure components are updated accordingly. As a result, if the LISP xTR of interest receives a data packet destined for a host route (/32) to that particular EID associated with a Null0 entry, it replies with a LISP signaling message (solicitation map request) to inform the source ITR that it exists in a new location for that destination IP address. Updating the IGP routing table is crucial because inbound traffic from a remote xTR may be delivered to either data center device, so it is important that both of them have local routing information to allow traffic to the destination EID.

Step 4.   After its IGP tables are updated with the host route information of the discovered EID (local or Null0), the discovering FHR sends a LISP notification toward its local LISP site gateways (ETRs). (As a reference, this is the LISP multihop design depicted on the right side of the Figure 6-28.)

Step 5.   Each local LISP site gateway in DC 2 registers the /32 prefix with the map server by sending a map registry control plane message to the LISP map server.

Step 6.   The map server, in its turn, updates the last LISP site gateways (xTRs) in the original DC 1 where the roaming EID initially belonged, to inform it about the new location (RLOC mapping) for that particular EID. This automatically results in the installation of a Null0 entry for that EID.

In addition to the LISP routers of each data center and the LISP mapping database being updated with the new location of the roaming device, the remaining LISP component to be updated is the ITR from the branch office.

Remote End-User Communication with a Roaming Application

If you took a snapshot of the content in the map cache belonging to the LISP ITR running in the remote branch office after the device 192.168.10.123 landed at the new data center DC 2 but before a data packet from the user was sent, the RLOC for the concerned EID would still refer to the DC 1, as shown in Figure 6-31.

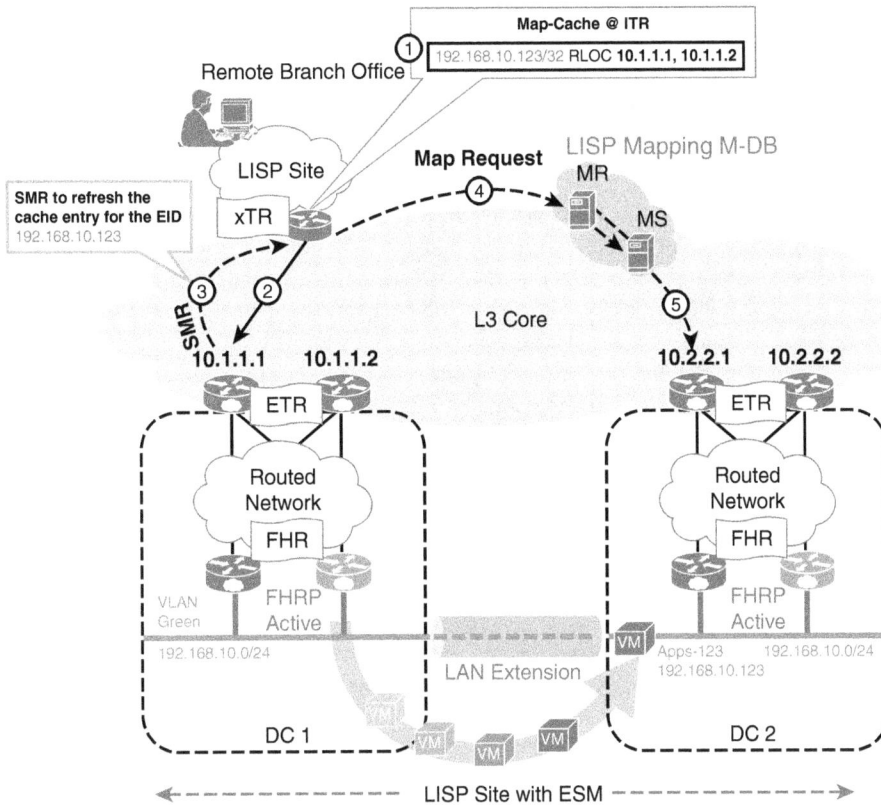

Figure 6-31 *Remote xTR Map Cache Entry Update (Part 1)*

The steps shown in Figure 6-31 and Figure 6-32 are as follows:

Step 1.   After the seamless migration of the machine, data packets from the end
user continue to be sent toward Apps-123, hosted by the dynamic EID
192.168.10.123, without any change in configuration. The LISP router ITR
from the branch office does a LISP lookup from its map cache and finds the
initial RLOCs 10.1.1.1 and 10.1.1.2 associated with this dynamic EID.

Step 2.   The LISP router ITR from the branch office encapsulates the user data packet
with either 10.1.1.1 or 10.1.1.2 as the destination LISP ETR. In this example,
assume that the hashing algorithm has elected 10.1.1.1 as the destination
LISP ETR.

The LISP ETR 10.1.1.1 receives the encapsulated data packet from the remote
ITR. The receiving LISP site gateway applies a Layer 3 lookup in its routing
table and notices a Null0 entry for the EID of interest. This allows the traffic
to be punted to the CPU and, hence, to be passed to the LISP process that
generates the solicit map request (SMR) destined to the remote xTR.

Step 3. The SMR is sent to the remote source LISP ITR that generated the user data packet. This handshake mechanism is fundamental for two reasons:

- First, it is important to inform the remote LISP ITR immediately that there is a need to refresh its map cache information because the destination workload was moved to a different location.

- Second, this process ends the LISP signaling loop and guarantees that all LISP infrastructure components were updated accordingly. It is important to note that the SMR message is created because there is a Null0 entry for a host route (/32) associated with that particular EID. Hence, for this handshake to be efficient, it is critical that the xTRs in the original site are map notified and correctly updated with the new entry when the roaming EID is discovered in DC 2. Therefore, it is crucial that the LISP site gateway be notified using two dynamic parallel processes. First, a routing update is initiated from the FHR routing table for the concerned endpoint being withdrawn. This routing update is performed through the interface facing the dynamic EID. Second, a LISP notification is sent from the LISP mapping database about the new location of the roaming endpoint.

Step 4. The ITR from the remote branch office receives the SMR and sends a new map request to the LISP map resolver for the roaming device's IP address 192.168.10.123, which afterward forwards the request to the map server.

Step 5. The map server forwards the map request to the LISP site gateway in DC 2 that last registered the 192.168.10.123/32 IP address for the roaming EID. It is assumed that the hashing algorithm sends the traffic to 10.2.2.1.

Step 6. As shown in Figure 6-32, the elected LISP site gateway 10.2.2.1 sends a map reply with the updated mapping information for 192.168.10.123 directly to the LISP ITR from the remote branch office that originated the LISP map request. The key reason for this direct return map reply is to guarantee that the Layer 3 reachability is validated between the ETRs in the new location (DC 2) and the initial ITR (remote branch office).

Step 7. The remote ITR from the branch office updates the new EID mapping information in its map cache, replacing the old RLOCs 10.1.1.1 and 10.1.1.2 with the RLOCs of the xTRs deployed in the DC 2 (that is, 10.2.2.1 and 10.2.2.2). Traffic can now be optimally steered toward the DC 2 site without any interruption.

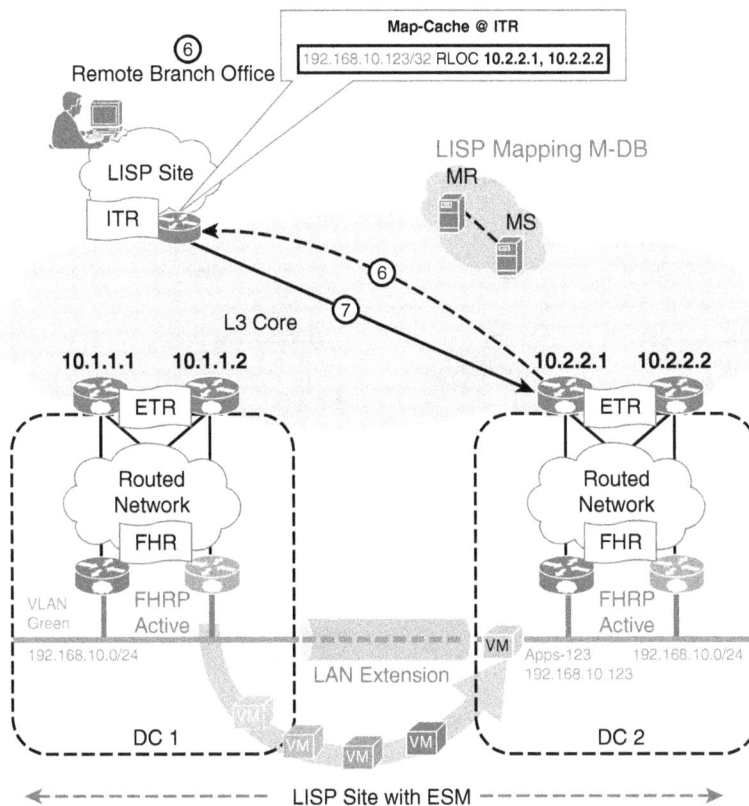

Figure 6-32 *Remote xTR Map Cache Entry Update (Part 2)*

LISP IP Mobility ESM Data Plane Operation

The device responsible for the data plane function of LISP IP Mobility is the LISP site gateway that initiates the overlay tunnel between the original source site and the destination data center. The encapsulation of the original user data packet with a LISP IP header is initiated by the LISP ITR function. This IP-in-IP encapsulation might also be performed from a proxy tunnel router (PxTR) that intercepts the concerned traffic destined to a LISP EID. This PxTR function must happen when no ITR exists locally when the source end user resides in the non-LISP site. A PxTR is a LISP device that provides connectivity between non-LISP sites and LISP sites by attracting non-LISP traffic destined to LISP sites and encapsulating this traffic toward the ETR devices deployed at LISP sites. When the PxTR receives the data packets from the requester's side, it behaves exactly like a LISP ITR. In either role, it encapsulates the data, solicits a map request if needed, and routes the packet toward the appropriate data center. The tunnel terminates at the target data center where the destination endpoint is discovered. When the data packet is received at the destination, the overlay tunnel network is de-encapsulated from the LISP ETR and forwarded to the endpoint of interest.

Figure 6-33 shows the placement of the LISP infrastructure components comprising the LISP site gateways (ETRs) located in the LISP data centers, the LISP router initiated in the branch office (ITR), and the proxy LISP router (PxTR) in the path, intercepting the traffic from a non-LISP site destined to a LISP mobile prefix subnet. On the other hand, the LISP mapping database represents the function that can be initiated either from dedicated devices or combined with the LISP routers.

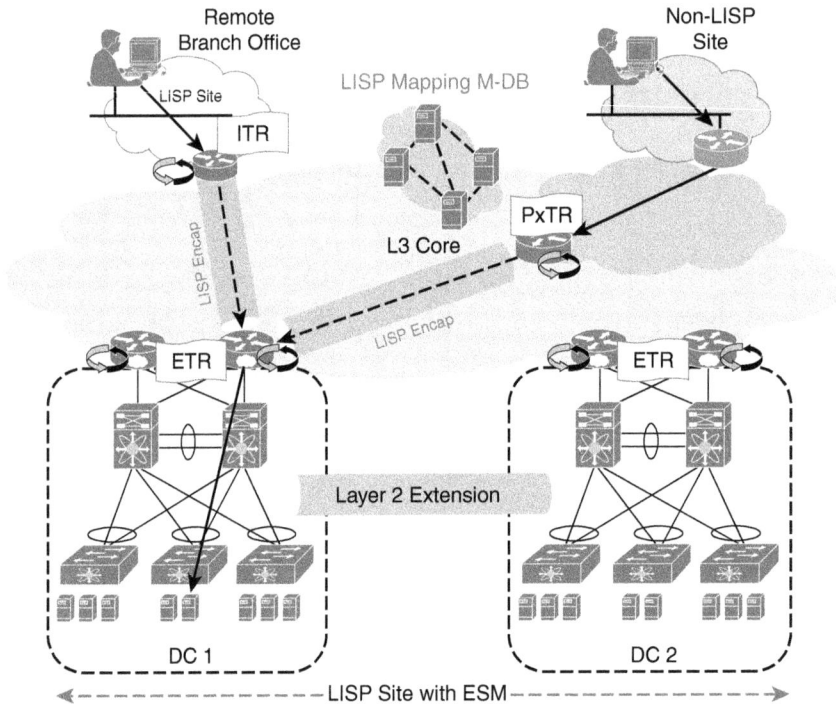

Figure 6-33   *LISP Site Gateway Placement*

The reachability within the ITR and the ETR is achieved by traditional routing methods in the Layer 3 WAN network infrastructure—either the enterprise core network or a Layer 3 network managed by a service provider.

The forwarding data plane is quite straightforward and seamless for the data workflow. As demonstrated in Figure 6-34 the end user from the branch office sends a request for the application Apps-123. As with any traditional network requests, this workstation first queries through a DNS request the IP address of the destination Apps-123, regardless of where the application is running. From a source-to-destination communication process point of view, the server that hosts the application App-123 can be located in a conventional data center, or it can be deployed at one of the LISP-enabled data center sites. The DNS server returns to the end user's station the unique IP address for that particular machine. This EID IP address is unique and will be kept the same, wherever the machine moved. Traffic originated from the client is steered toward the local LISP-enabled device.

Note Notice that if there is no LISP xTR locally deployed in the branch office, the traffic destined to a LISP EID is steered toward a LISP PxTR. Nevertheless, the following description remains exactly the same whether it is a local LISP ITR or a LISP PITR.

Figure 6-34 shows the north–south flow. As each LISP router offers the two roles, ETR and IRT, a similar mechanism is used for the return traffic originated by the EID located in DC 2 and destined to the remote end user, where the LISP devices exchange their respective roles of ITRs (DC 2) and ETRs (branch office).

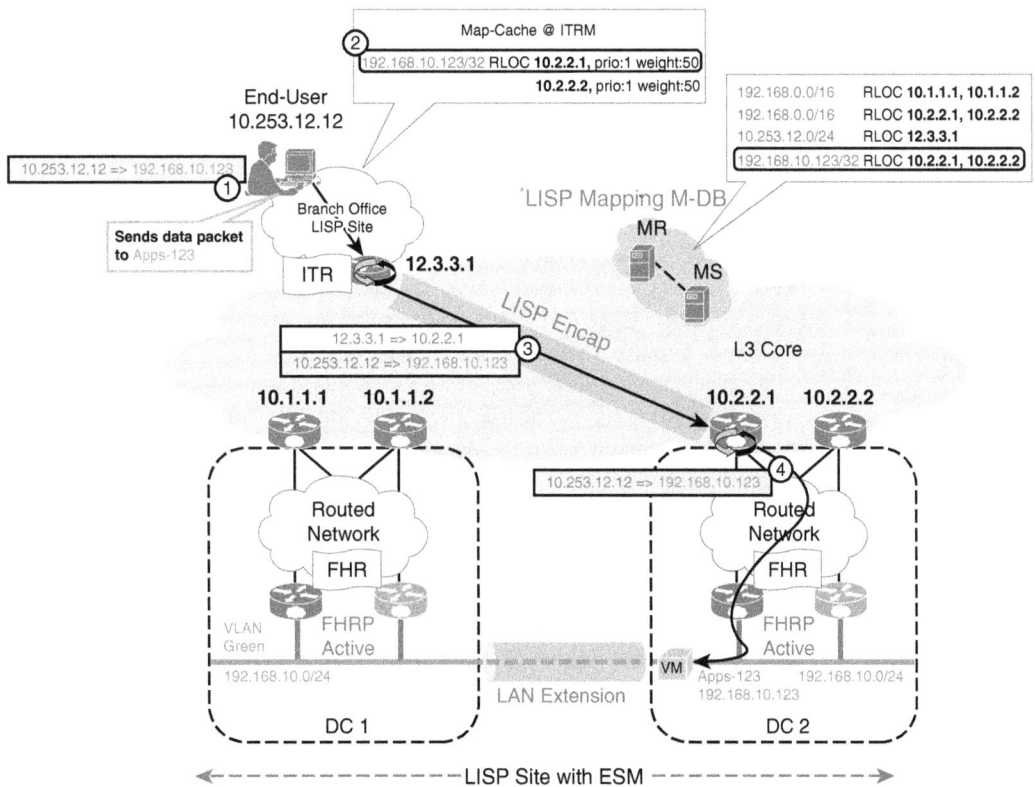

Figure 6-34 *LISP IP Mobility Data Plane Workflow*

The steps shown in Figure 6-34 are as follows:

Step 1. The end-user workstation sends the data packet destined for 192.168.10.123. The LISP ITR can be the client's default gateway or the WAN edge router of the branch office. This LISP router first performs a lookup for the destination (192.168.10.123) in its routing table.

Step 2.   As described with the previous control plane signaling mechanism, the RLOC for that particular endpoint was updated in its map cache with the LISP site gateway's DC 2 as the new locator. Notice that if it was the first data packet, the EID is not present in the RLOC mapping space, and hence the lookup fails, triggering the LISP map request control plane handshake.

In the LISP mapping database, the 192.168.0.0/16 network is configured as the global LISP EID space on all the xTR devices belonging to the same LISP sites (that is, part of both DC 1 and DC 2).

Note   The dynamic EID prefixes need to be more specific of the subnet mask configured on the Layer 3 interface where the dynamic EID map is applied (SVI Green in the scenario discussed in this example). In the example depicted in Figure 6-34, /16 is the mask associated with the prefix in the global mapping, and /24 is used as the mask for the IP subnet associated with the end-user network 10.253.12.0.

The destination EID (192.168.10.123) is associated to the RLOCs identifying both ETR devices located in DC 2. Each entry has associated priority and weight values that are controlled by the destination site to influence the way inbound traffic is received from the transport infrastructure. The priority is used to determine whether both LISP ETR devices can be used to receive LISP encapsulated traffic destined to a local EID subnet (load-balancing scenario). If desired, it is possible to provide different weight values to allow tuning of the amount of traffic received by each LISP ETR in a weighted load-balancing scenario. The weight values are therefore efficient only with the equal priority given for the xTR in the same data center.

Step 3.   After a lookup in its map cache, the ITR performs a LISP encapsulation of the original user's data packet and sends it into the transport infrastructure with an IP destination: one of the ETRs belonging to DC 2. With the same priority and weight values, the selection of the specific ETR RLOC is done on a per-flow basis, based on hashing performed on the 5-tuple Layer 3 and Layer 4 information of the original client's IP packet. In this example, the elected RLOC is 10.2.2.1.

Step 4.   The ETR 10.2.2.1 receives the IP data packet, de-encapsulates it, and sends the original data packet into the internal site destined to the EID.

LISP IP Mobility ESM Configuration

The previous section details the step-by-step operation involved in dynamically discovering the location of the mobile endpoints and how the ingress traffic is optimized using the direct data center site where the targeted active endpoint resides. The following section provides details on the configuration for each LISP device.

Configuring the LISP Mapping Database

Use Figure 6-35 as reference for the following configuration examples.

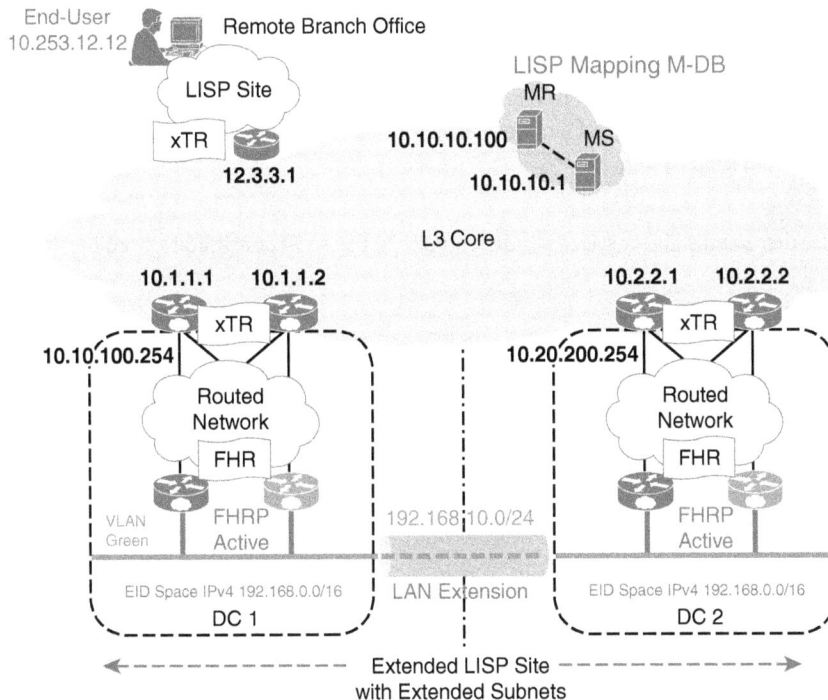

Figure 6-35 *LISP ESM Configuration Example*

As mentioned previously, the map server and the map resolver are the key components in a LISP deployment, dynamically providing the accurate locations of prefix subnets and endpoint identifiers. Hence, the distribution of the mapping database must be deployed in a resilient form, which can be achieved with a cluster of machines (active/active nodes).

These map server and map resolver tasks can be hosted by a shared mapping database cluster, such as pair of IOS routers. For assessment purposes, it is, however, possible to combine these two functions within the LISP site gateways, as is done with a Nexus 7000 in the following examples.

Note   The mapping database can also be fully distributed, and MS/MR functions can be enabled onto separate physical nodes. There are different ways to achieve a distribution of the mapping database for large scales. For a more exhaustive list of distributed mapping database deployments, refer to http://lisp.cisco.com.

The configuration snapshots given in the following command lines are particular for the NX-OS platforms that traditionally belong to data centers (LISP site gateways and LISP mapping database). For the branch office, IOS is used. Almost all IOS, IOS-XE, NX-OS, and IOS-XR routers offer the functions of the LISP site gateway and LISP mapping database. A summary is provided later in this chapter, in the section "LISP Feature Support by Operating System."

Note   For further details about specific routers, refer to the LISP configuration guides for the concerned platforms.

For this scenario, the LISP mapping database is enabled onto the LISP site gateways (or xTR). Two LISP site gateways per LISP data center are installed, as depicted in Figure 6-35.

Notice that the configuration samples provided in Example 6-1 are for one LISP xTR and one LISP MH on each site, as the configurations are very similar.

Example 6-1   *Enabling the LISP Feature, Defining LISP Roles, and Defining the Loopback Interfaces*

```
!
feature lisp
ip lisp map-resolver
ip lisp map-server
!
 interface loopback0
      description Map-Resolver
      IP Address ip address 10.10.10.100/32
! duplicate this above IP address between all Map-Resolvers
!
interface loopback1
      description Map-Server IP Address
      ip address 10.10.10.1/32
!this above IP address is unique per Map-Server
```

Subject to the type of network operating system and platform, the LISP feature must be enabled to get the LISP function, and the role must be explicitly defined, as shown in Example 6-1 with the function of map server and a map resolver. As previously mentioned, these two functions can run from independent appliances or can be combined within the same device, and they can also be combined with other functions, such as LISP xTRs.

For the cluster deployment with two nodes, an anycast IP address is used on both cluster nodes for the function of map resolver (10.10.10.100/32). Consequently, a map request that originated from a LISP ITR device is sent to the closest map resolver from a routing metric point of view. For the map server, however, a unique IP address is used for each physical node. As a result, each LISP ETR registers its EID subnets with both map servers, as shown with the LISP site gateway configuration in Example 6-1.

Note For a small deployment where a single device hosts the roles of MS and MR, it is possible to use a unique IP address for both functions; this is demonstrated in Chapter 7.

For this scenario, the remote site is deployed using a Cisco ISR router configured as a LISP ITR/ETR, hosting the 10.253.12.0/24 EID space, which is the end-user space. The configuration of the LISP site in the remote branch office for the subnet Green extended across the two data centers is required; see Example 6-2.

Example 6-2 *LISP ITR/ETR Configuration in a Remote Branch Office*

```
lisp site BRANCH
!notice number of site is not limited to one
      eid-prefix 10.253.12.0/24
      authentication-key 0 thisisthepassword
 !
 !
lisp site LISP_VLAN_Green
      eid-prefix 192.168.10.0/24 accept-more-specifics
! the previous CLI is important to accept /32 prefixes
      authentication-key 0 thisisthepassword
 !
exit
```

An authentication key must match the one that is configured on the LISP routers to receive the map register control packets from the LISP site gateway.

Configuring LISP Multihop with Extended Subnet Mode

As mentioned previously and depicted in Figure 6-28, in a production network architecture, the LISP site gateway is seldom the first-hop router for the endpoints. Network services, such as firewalls and load balancers, are usually inserted between the first-hop router, which offers the default gateway for the machines, and the LISP xTR. Consequently, you need to dissociate the function of the LISP xTR from the function of the LISP first-hop router onto two different devices.

Configuring the LISP First-Hop Router in DC 1

The configuration of the LISP FHR makes it possible to dynamically send notifications for presence of EID toward the local LISP router xTR with the specified IP address 192.168.100.254. This notification is maintained securely, along with the authentication key used with the LISP gateway xTR. Notice that this IP address 192.168.100.254 is the site-internal interface of the local LISP gateway xTRs configured using HSRP. This configuration of the local LISP router xTR is detailed in Example 6-7.

VLAN 10 is the extended VLAN Green that is used for this scenario. The VLAN Green is associated with the 192.168.10.0/24 network and is extended between these two data centers using a validated LAN extension technology. LISP IP Mobility is not directly related to the model of DCI solution that is deployed. However, with the DCI solution deployed for Layer 2 extension, the extended VLAN stretches the single LISP site across the two data center sites.

Migration of endpoints that belong to VLAN Green happens between the two data centers, DC 1 and DC 2. The network 192.168.10.0/24 is configured as the dynamic EID space with both RLOCs in DC 1.

LISP is multi-tenant capable. However, in this context of LISP IP Mobility in conjunction with legacy data centers, the VRF segmentation is not leveraged.

Note   LISP IP Mobility deployment with modern fabric with support for VRF segmentation is discussed in Chapter 7.

The LISP feature must be enabled on the LISP FHR. The role of LISP ETR must be enabled within the first-hop router, as shown in Example 6-3.

Example 6-3   *LISP First-Hop Router 1 in DC 1*

```
feature lisp
ip lisp etr
lisp dynamic-eid VLAN-Green
      database-mapping 192.168.10.0/24 10.1.1.1 priority 1 weight 50
      database-mapping 192.168.10.0/24 10.1.1.2 priority 1 weight 50
 eid-notify 192.168.100.254 key thisisthepassword
 map-notify-group 239.1.1.2
 !
```

The LISP FHR configuration can apply optionally to one or multiple specific VRF contexts. Hence, if needed, configuration of the FHR function can be initiated under the specified VRF routing context. Example 6-3 provides the FHR configuration for the default VRF.

The **eid-notify** command makes it possible to send notifications of the presence of dynamic EID to a LISP gateway xTR with the specified IP address, along with the authentication key used with the gateway xTR. This is usually the xTR interface facing the inside the data center, but it must be a loopback address configured in the LISP site gateway that is reachable by the LISP FHR in order to leverage all physical paths available to connect to it.

The **map-notify-group** command is used to send a map notify message to all other LISP FHRs within the same data center site and toward the remote site via the extended VLAN to which the LISP roamer belonged prior to its migration. Hence, each LISP FHR determines in real time the location of the discovered dynamic EID (either inject a /32 or add a Null0 for the endpoints of interest).

Example 6-4 shows the configuration of the extended VLAN across the two data centers in the access device acting as the default gateway for the roamers as well as the LISP FHR.

Example 6-4 *Extended VLAN Green Configuration in DC 1*

```
interface Vlan10
 description VLAN Green
 lisp mobility VLAN-Green
 lisp extended-subnet-mode
 ip address 192.68.10.251/24
 ip ospf passive-interface
 ip router ospf 100 area 0.0.0.1
 hsrp 1
    preempt delay reload 300
    priority 130
    ip 192.168.10.254
```

The "**lisp mobility**" command is used to attach the dynamic EID policy configuration **VLAN-Green** to this interface connecting to the LISP mobile subnet where endpoints can migrate. Because the access device is the first-hop router—and hence the default gateway of the roamer—the Layer 3 interface is typically a VLAN interface (SVI).

For interconnecting multiple traditional DC networks in conjunction with LISP IP Mobility ESM, the default gateway on each site must be active. There are various techniques to allow the default gateway to become active on both sites offering the same local SVI with the same VIP and vMAC on each site. As an example, with OTV it is typical to leverage a VLAN access list to filter the gateway reachability information as well as FHRP hello messages between sites. (Other methods exist that are beyond the scope of this book.)

Notice that when deploying LISP IP Mobility with VXLAN EVPN fabric and ACI fabric (as discussed in Chapter 7), the embedded Layer 3 anycast gateway function automatically ensures the availability of a consistent virtual IP (VIP) address and virtual MAC (vMAC) address for the default gateway on both sites without requiring the creation of a specific VACL or PACL.

Example 6-5 provides the configuration for the LISP first-hop router in the access device.

Example 6-5   *LISP First-Hop Router 2 in DC 1*

```
ip lisp etr
lisp dynamic-eid VLAN-Green
       database-mapping 192.168.10.0/24 10.1.1.1 priority 1 weight 50
       database-mapping 192.168.10.0/24 10.1.1.2 priority 1 weight 50
 eid-notify 192.168.100.254 key thisisthepassword
 map-notify-group 239.1.1.2
!
interface Vlan10
 description VLAN Green
 lisp mobility VLAN-Green
 lisp extended-subnet-mode
 ip address 192.68.10.252/24
 ip ospf passive-interface
 ip router ospf 100 area 0.0.0.1
 hsrp 1
    priority 120
    ip 192.168.10.254
```

Configuring the LISP First-Hop Router in DC 2

The configuration given in Example 6-6 is identical to the LISP FHR configuration in DC 1, but for DC 2, the locations (RLOCs) are the two LISP xTRs located in DC 2, and the target for the EID notification is local to DC 2 as well.

Example 6-6   *LISP First-Hop Router 1 in DC 2*

```
ip lisp etr
lisp dynamic-eid VLAN-Green
       database-mapping 192.168.10.0/24 10.2.2.1 priority 1 weight 50
       database-mapping 192.168.10.0/24 10.2.2.2 priority 1 weight 50
 eid-notify 192.168.200.254 key thisisthepassword
 map-notify-group 239.1.1.2
!
interface Vlan10
 description VLAN Green
 lisp mobility VLAN-Green
 lisp extended-subnet-mode
 ip address 192.68.10.253/24
 ip ospf passive-interface
 ip router ospf 100 area 0.0.0.1
 hsrp 1
    ip 192.168.10.254
```

As previously mentioned, the HSRP VIP address for VLAN Green is duplicated, and as a result of the HSRP filter (not shown here), both SVIs for VLAN Green are active on both data centers.

Note The configuration for the LISP first-hop router peer located in DC 2 is not provided in the configuration examples because the configuration is very similar to the DC 1 configuration. The slight difference remains with the primary IP address of the interface VLAN 10 that must be specific for each device.

Configuring LISP xTR Site Gateways with Extended Subnet Mode

DC 1 hosts servers and services belong to the network 192.168.0.0/16. The mobility events are received from the LISP first-hop router and registered to the LISP mapping system by the local LISP site gateway xTRs.

With the **ip lisp database-mapping** command, the 192.168.0.0/16 network is configured as the global LISP EID space on all the xTR devices belonging to the same LISP data center. As the LISP sites extend both LISP DC 1 and DC 2, each site will configure the same network respectively with its local xTRs.

As is conventionally done, both data centers here are multihomed to the Layer 3 core.

In Example 6-6, the LISP VLAN Green with dynamic EIDs is covering prefixes for host detection. With the **lisp dynamic-eid** command, the system can detect a host in the 192.168.10.0/24 range and register the host with the RLOC set (plus priorities and weights) specified for each database mapping entry.

The LISP feature must be enabled. The roles of LISP ETR (for de-encapsulating LISP traffic received from the Layer 3 domain of the network) and ITR (for encapsulating LISP traffic destined for remote locations) must be initiated in the LISP site gateway router.

Example 6-7 shows the configuration for the LISP site gateway in DC 1.

Example 6-7 *LISP Site Gateway xTR 1 in DC 1*

```
feature lisp
ip lisp itr-etr
!
ip lisp database-mapping 192.168.0.0/16 10.1.1.1 priority 1 weight 50
ip lisp database-mapping 192.168.0.0/16 10.1.1.2 priority 1 weight 50
ip lisp itr map-resolver 10.10.10.100
ip lisp etr map-server 10.10.10.1 key thisisthepassword
!
lisp dynamic-eid EXTENDED_VLAN_GREEN
      database-mapping 192.168.10.0/24 10.1.1.1 priority 1 weight 50
        eid-notify authentication-key thisisthepassword
      database-mapping 192.168.10.0/24 10.1.1.2 priority 1 weight 50
        eid-notify authentication-key thisisthepassword
      map-notify-group 239.1.1.2
```

It is critical to ensure that the prefixes specified under the dynamic EID are more specific than the ones listed for the global **ip lisp database-mapping** section in Example 6-7. Because the LISP database mapping command is configured in the dynamic EID map configuration mode, the LISP ETR registers a /32 host prefix with the mapping system after a dynamic EID is detected in the configured range. If the site is assigned multiple dynamic EID prefix blocks, the database mapping is configured for each dynamic EID prefix block assigned to the site and for each locator from which the EID prefix block can be reached. In addition, the subnet associated with the dynamic EID prefixes must be more specific than the one used in the global database mapping configuration and the one used for the SVIs on which the LISP map is applied. In Example 6-7, /16 is the mask associated with the prefix in the global mapping, and /24 is used as a mask for the IP subnet associated with the SVI.

Example 6-8 shows the configuration for internal interface VLAN 100, used for network connectivity with the LISP first-hop router, as configured for the LISP MH for its EID notification target. It is also possible to configure routed interfaces to connect a LISP site gateway to the internal network.

Example 6-8   *Internal VLAN Interface Configuration*

```
!
interface Vlan100
 description Inside DC 1
ip address 10.10.100.251/24
 ip ospf passive-interface
 ip router ospf 100 area 0.0.0.1
 hsrp 1
    preempt delay reload 300
    priority 130
    ip 10.10.100.254
!
```

Example 6-9 shows the configuration for the redundant LISP router.

Example 6-9   *Configuration of the LISP Site Gateway xTR 2 in DC 1*

```
feature lisp
ip lisp itr-etr
ip lisp database-mapping 192.168.0.0/16 10.1.1.1 priority 1 weight 50
ip lisp database-mapping 192.168.0.0/16 10.1.1.2 priority 1 weight 50
ip lisp itr map-resolver 10.10.10.100
ip lisp etr map-server 10.10.10.1 key thisisthepassword
!
lisp dynamic-eid EXTENDED_VLAN_GREEN
      database-mapping 192.168.10.0/24 10.1.1.1 priority 1 weight 50
      database-mapping 192.168.10.0/24 10.1.1.2 priority 1 weight 50
      map-notify-group 239.1.1.2
!
```

```
interface Vlan100
 description Inside DC 1
ip address 10.10.100.252/24
 ip ospf passive-interface
 ip router ospf 100 area 0.0.0.1
 hsrp 1
    ip 10.10.100.254
 !
```

Because in Extended Subnet Mode there is a single LISP site spanning separate DC locations, the LISP xTR devices are configured identically for the global **ip lisp database-mapping** configuration, and the RLOCs of all the xTRs belonging to the same LISP data center must be listed.

Regarding the dynamic EID configuration, however, notice that only RLOCs that exist on the physical data center must be registered. As a result, the incoming LISP traffic from other xTR traffic is load balanced equally. The weight can be used to change the load, if desired.

Example 6-10 shows the configuration for the second data center.

Example 6-10   *Configuration of the LISP Site Gateway xTR 1 in DC 2*

```
feature lisp
ip lisp itr-etr
ip lisp database-mapping 192.168.0.0/16 10.2.2.1 priority 1 weight 50
ip lisp database-mapping 192.168.0.0/16 10.2.2.2 priority 1 weight 50
ip lisp itr map-resolver 10.10.10.100
ip lisp etr map-server 10.10.10.1 key thisisthepassword
 !
lisp dynamic-eid EXTENDED_VLAN_GREEN
      database-mapping 192.168.10.0/24 10.2.2.1 priority 1 weight 50
      database-mapping 192.168.10.0/24 10.2.2.2 priority 1 weight 50
      map-notify-group 239.1.1.2
 !
interface Vlan200
 description VLAN Green
 ip address 10.10.200.251/24
 ip ospf passive-interface
 ip router ospf 100 area 0.0.0.1
 hsrp 1
    ip 10.10.200.254
 !
```

VLAN 200 is the internal interface VLAN used for network connectivity with the LISP first-hop router, as configured for the LISP MH for its EID notification target.

As the peer LISP xTR is similar to this sample configuration, except for the primary interface for VLAN 200, its configuration is not shown in this section.

There are several options for managing the load between different data centers, and hence there are different ways to configure the LISP site gateway. Some enterprises might want to extend the LISP subnets equally between distant data centers. In this case, the LISP endpoints are spread across the LISP data centers, and traffic is steered to the concerned site, based on the locations (RLOCs) of the dynamic EIDs.

As is done in Example 6-10, some enterprises want the registrations from one data center to have only RLOCs belonging to that location, say DC 1, and the registrations from the remote data center to only have RLOCs belonging to the remote site, say DC 2.

It is also possible to register all four RLOCs on the data centers and adapt the priority of the local RLOCs with better values than the priority of the remote RLOCs. This provides a fallback mechanism in case the local RLOCs become unavailable.

With the particular configuration shown in the last two examples, each LISP site gateway registers respectively the dynamic EID (/32s) located in the DC 1 (Example 6-9) with the RLOCs belonging to DC 1 and the dynamic EID (/32s) located in DC 2 (Example 6-10) with the RLOCs belonging to DC 2. This approach allows all the traffic destined for a particular endpoint (/32) to go directly to the site in which it is currently hosted, preventing traffic to be evenly load balanced across DC 1 and DC 2 for registered EIDs.

IP Mobility Using LISP Across Subnets Mode

As mentioned earlier, with the acceleration of operational continuity, one of the most recent use cases is deploying LISP IP Mobility Across Subnets Mode (ASM) to offer automatically transparent migration to a secondary independent site without IP address renumbering. This is achieved without extending the Layer 2 network between sites, although subnet networks are different on each location. LISP IP Mobility ASM can be very efficient, allowing the migration of endpoints from site to site across a routed network only. In addition, LISP IP Mobility ASM dynamically reroutes the ingress traffic directly toward the data center of interest where roaming endpoints were localized. This is possible as long as the sessions established prior to the move can be restarted in a host with the same reachability parameters in a new location. This movement of IP entities is traditionally called a *cold* or *warm migration*, and it typically (but not always) is used with a disaster recovery site. Other use cases, such as moving a software framework from an on-premises infrastructure to a cloud environment, may leverage this stateless migration scenario.

Avoiding IP address renumbering not only eases the migration of the applications from the enterprise premise equipment but also mitigates risks related to not having to extend broadcast domain between distant data centers while it continues to accelerate the deployment of roaming servers.

For many years, disaster recovery solutions were worked in cold standby mode, with appropriately configured backup resources located in a safe remote location. Hardware and software components, network access, and data restoration were implemented and started manually as needed. This legacy type of disaster recovery not only requires restarting applications on the backup site but also requires enabling network redirection to the secondary data center. Several options are available, either with a new IP address association from the DNS server triggered with special probes or from manual changes of routing metrics. Although the cold standby model is traditionally easy to maintain and still remains valid for some enterprises, it requires a substantial delay to evolve from a standby mode to full operational capability, and such a delay might have a negative impact for an enterprise's business. The recovery point objective (RPO), which is the maximum data loss during the recovery process, is habitually quite high and can't be improved very much because it relies on the data storage replication service tools and, above all, on the distances over which the data replication occurs. However, the time to recover, also known as the recovery time objective (RTO), which historically was up to several weeks for a full operational state after a cold restart situation, can be improved with virtualization and automation components. For example, in warm standby mode, the applications at the secondary data center can be ready to take over. Resources and services are started but are kept in a standby mode, ready to switch to active as soon as the primary data center goes out of service. In both modes, LISP IP Mobility ASM can help accelerate the migration without the need to re-address the endpoints; LISP IP Mobility ASM can also improve the network traffic redirection to the new location automatically and dynamically, based on the presence of the application (dynamic EID), and thus the RTO can be reduced to several minutes or seconds, depending the process restart mode available with the high-availability software framework.

During the process of migrating physical servers to a new data center, some applications, such as a mainframe, may be difficult to re-address at Layer 3. Avoiding IP address renumbering may ease physical migration projects and reduces their costs substantially.

With a hybrid cloud, enterprise private/internal cloud resources are moved to a public/external cloud location. In addition, LISP guarantees optimal routing to the active application, removing the hairpin effect and therefore improving the response time to access the service.

Finally, keep in mind that the move of an endpoint doesn't imply that the current sessions with this particular destination IP address must be stateful per se all the time. In some cases, depending on the criticality level of an application, such as "business operational" or "business administrative," a stateful live migration is not necessarily needed, and the current sessions can be interrupted and recovered just after the move. In a virtual environment, restarting an application in a remote location may take a few minutes or even less. Therefore, the concerned roaming machine can be suspended prior to running a cold move to the target location, and the software processes can be restarted immediately afterward. Several factors are crucial: The network reachability information on reaching the application must remain the same for the end user, and redirection must be achieved in real time seamlessly, without blackholes due to DNS caching. LISP IP Mobility Across Subnets Mode allows migration to occur without the need to renumber the endpoints;

this saves time by avoiding the change management procedure and by automatically rerouting the traffic destined to the concerned application toward the new location.

As highlighted in Figure 6-36, in a typical deployment, LISP IP Mobility ASM can be deployed for a backup data center (DR) in conjunction with a LISP IP Mobility ESM deployment between two primary coupled main data centers. In addition, the remote data center is evolving more frequently to a "host" or "public cloud" provider infrastructure for other use cases. The infrastructure remains the same, with the twin data centers, DC 1 and DC 2, representing the customer's traditional data center or on-premises cloud infrastructure and the remote site representing the cloud provider. In such a scenario, the Layer 2 extension exists between the tightly coupled primary data centers, and the same extended subnets are spread across the extended LISP site, as discussed previously with LISP IP Mobility ESM. Also, Layer 3-only connectivity exists between the two main data centers and the remote site.

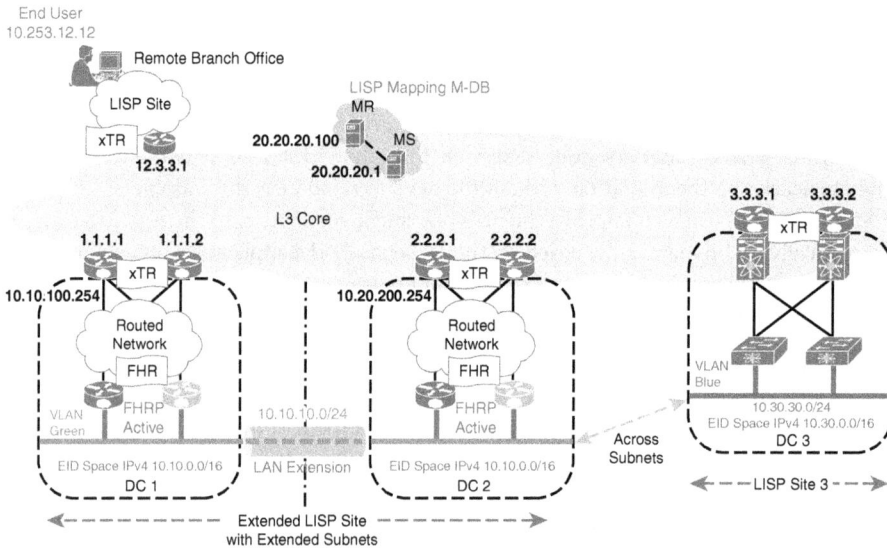

Figure 6-36   *LISP IP Mobility Across Subnets Mode as a DR Site*

The subnets that live on the two primary data centers and the remote site are totally different, and no LAN extension techniques are required toward the remote location DC 3. In some other cases, LISP IP Mobility ESM is not required at all because the distance between DC 1 and DC 2 is short enough to ignore the latency and the disruptive trombone effects. Hence, other scenarios exist with LISP IP Mobility Across Subnets Mode only deployed between two or more sites. Indeed, some enterprises and service providers don't consider the extension of the Layer 2 network as an option, although they still want to offer a certain level of mobility services between different locations.

As the technology and software frameworks evolve, more scenarios will be addressed. In the future, network architects will have more options between a Layer 2– and a Layer 3–based solution to satisfy the requirements for interconnecting multiple data centers that traditionally were focused exclusively on Layer 2 solutions.

In summary, the key functionality with LISP IP Mobility ASM is that it allows endpoints to migrate to a remote site and land in a different IP subnet while retaining its original IP address. In this particular scenario, LISP provides both IP mobility and inbound traffic path optimization functionalities.

LISP IP Mobility ASM Control Plane Operation

The control plane signaling with LISP IP Mobility Across Subnets Mode is pretty similar to the signaling discussed previously with LISP IP Mobility Extended Subnet Mode. However, one key difference is that the default gateway in the landing site needs to be emulated, as the roaming workload must be able to continue sending traffic to its default gateway after the move is completed even though the landing subnet is different. Although the roamer can migrate from one subnet to the remote site while retaining its original IP addresses, there is no need to define an SVI in the new landing data center for the original subnet of the mobile endpoint. This is a key advantage of the LISP IP Mobility functionality across Layer 3 network domains.

With LISP ASM, a proxy ARP function must be enabled from the default gateway of the roamer. The proxy ARP function allows the migrating machine to communicate after the move with the new gateway belonging to the remote data center site. In addition, it is crucial that the same vMAC exist between all SVIs concerned with the LISP mobile subnets (leaving and landing). Thus, when configuring the HSRP VIP address with different groups, exactly the same vMAC address must be specified between the original LISP mobile subnets and the landing subnet, as discussed in in the configuration samples that follow.

Another important difference with LISP ESM is that, as shown in Figure 6-37, prefix subnets are different on each site. In this scenario, DC 1 is the home site for the VLAN Green, associated to the subnet 10.10.10.0/24, which only exists in DC 1, which is different from the VLAN Blue, associated to the subnet 10.30.30.0/24, which is only hosted in DC 2.

The following section clarifies how the learning for EID is accomplished throughout the LISP infrastructure components, including with the LISP mapping database.

EID Migration and the LISP Mapping Database Update

Figure 6-38 shows a cold migration scenario in which the endpoint 10.10.10.123 is roaming from the subnet 10.10.10.0/24 and landing in the subnet 10.30.30.0/24, homed in DC 2.

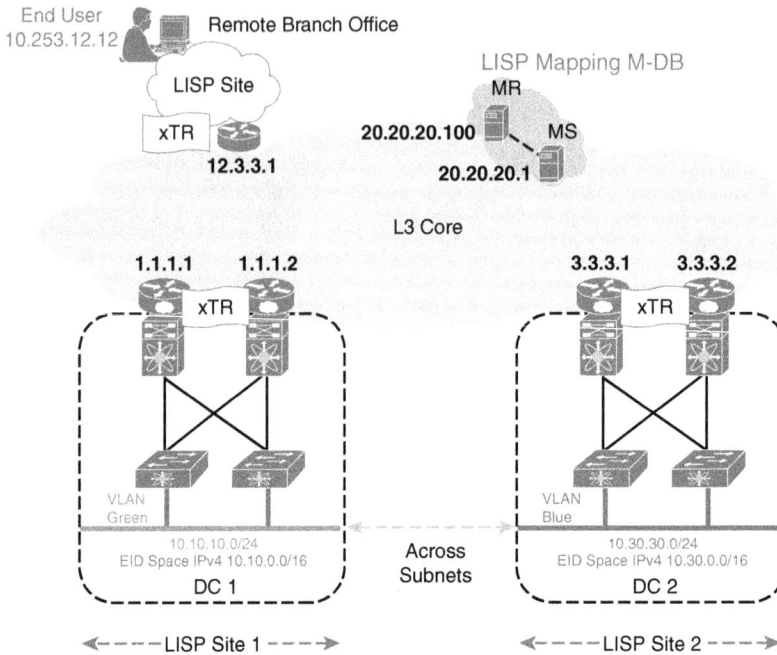

Figure 6-37   *LISP IP Mobility Across Subnets Mode with Two Sites*

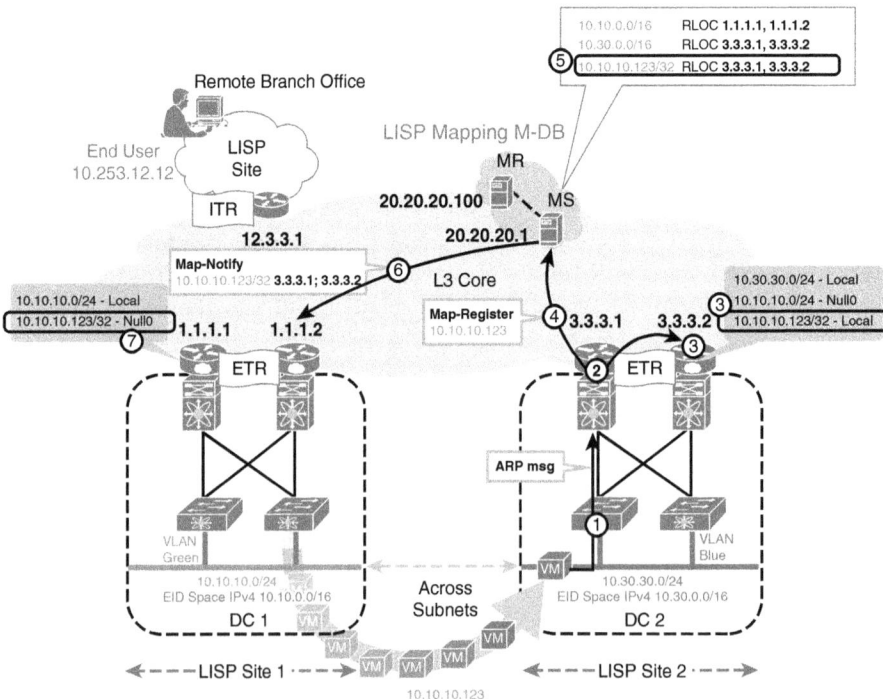

Figure 6-38   *LISP IP Mobility Across Subnets Mode Control Plane*

Note   IP packets sourced by the roaming machine are steered toward the local gateway because of the proxy ARP function. This is possible only because this is a cold restart, and hence the ARP table of the roamer is empty after the move. The effect is to send an ARP message prior to initiating communication with a data packet, which is treated seamlessly by the local gateway, even though the SVI of the landing subnet is different.

The steps shown in Figure 6-38 are as follows:

Step 1.   The roaming machine sends an ARP message when it lands in DC 2.

Step 2.   The LISP site gateway that receives the ARP message injects the host route of the roaming EID 10.10.10.123/32 into its local IGP routing table. ARP messages are key to allowing communication to be established with the roaming workflow since that traffic is methodically avoided by the /24 Null0 entry configured in the LISP site gateway (xTR).

Step 3.   The discovering LISP site gateway sends out a map notify group multicast message that reaches the other local LISP router. Receiving the map notify group multicast message, the second local LISP router peer adds a local /32 route of the discovered EID into its routing table (local). Notice that with LISP ASM, the map notify group multicast is not sent to the initial LISP site, as this multicast is not forwarded outside the local LISP data center.

Step 4.   The initial LISP router sends a map register message for the /32 EID address to the map server, which updates its mapping database with the entry for the specific EID 10.10.10.123, which is now associated with the RLOCs 3.3.3.1 and 3.3.3.2, which are the locations assigned for the two LISP xTRs in DC 2.

Step 5.   The map server updates the last LISP site gateways in the original data centers from which the roaming EID was coming to inform them about the new location (RLOC 3.3.3.1 or and 3.3.3.2) for each EID.

Step 6.   The two initial LISP routers in DC 1 sequentially receive the map notify message from the map server and add to their respective routing tables a /32 Null0 route associated to the EID 10.10.10.123. Meanwhile, each LISP xTR also notifies, as an alternative update, its peer by leveraging a site-local map notify message.

Step 7.   The initial LISP routers in the original data center (DC 1 in this example) receiving the map notification from the LISP map server sends a Gratuitous ARP locally toward the subnet of interest (Subnet Green in this example). Then, all local machines belonging to VLAN Green will withdraw from the ARP cache table the entry associated with 10.10.10.123.

The LISP routers in the data centers and the LISP mapping database are updated accordingly with the new location of the roaming device, and the remaining LISP component to be updated is the ITR from the branch office.

Remote End-User Communication with a Roaming Application

Unlike with LISP IP Mobility with Extended Subnet Mode, with LISP IP Mobility ASM, the LISP xTRs do not dynamically discover local steady endpoints that are part of the LISP mobile subnet. There is no entry in the local dynamic EID table or in the map server for the hosts that are still active in their original locations. The traffic sent from a remote end user destined for an endpoint residing in its home site is directed by the LISP branch office router toward the home site, where the subnet of the concerned EID is associated. The dynamic EID reachability information is not distributed until it moves to a remote LISP site. Nonetheless, the traffic is received in one of the LISP gateways in DC 1. It is de-encapsulated by the elected local LISP ETR and routed toward the locally attached EID subnet. In this scenario, prior to the endpoint 10.10.10.123 to migrate to a remote LISP site, any traffic from the Layer 3 core destined to this particular machine is routed to the prefix 10.10.10.0/24 hosted in DC 1. Traffic is de-encapsulated by either 1.1.1.1 or 1.1.1.2 and forwarded to VLAN Green with the initial retained IP destination address 10.10.10.123.

Let's look at what happens after a migration of the roamer. If you were to take a picture of the entries at the LISP map cache in the ITR running in the remote branch office just after the device 10.10.10.123 landed into the new data center DC 2 but before a new data packet from the user was sent, there would be no entry for the concerned dynamic EID. Instead, the LISP ITR would look at the mapping database for the aggregate prefix subnet and select one of the RLOCs referring to the locators in DC 1 (step 1), where the endpoint resides from a routing point of view.

In summary, prior to moving a mobile EID, with a LISP IP Mobility Across Subnets Mode implementation, the communication to the roamer belonging to a LISP mobile subnet and still active in its initial home site can be established without the need to dynamically discover that EID prefix. Nonetheless, when an original roamer is moved back from a remote data center to its home site (but only in this case), the roaming machine is dynamically discovered and registered in the local dynamic EID table and with the map server for a short period of time.

As depicted in Figure 6-39, in the map cache of the LISP router in the branch office, the 10.10.0.0/16 network is configured as the global LISP EID space on all the RLOC devices belonging to the LISP site in DC 1. The 10.30.0.0/16 network is configured as the global LISP EID space on all the RLOC devices belonging to the LISP site in DC 2.

Note   The LISP xTRs do not dynamically discover endpoints that are connected to the home site that sources IP traffic in the local LISP site gateway direction (as happens in Extended Subnet Mode). The only exception to this behavior is when a workload is initially moved back to the original site from a remote data center. In this case, the workload is to be dynamically discovered and temporarily registered in the local dynamic EID table and with the map server as a normal roamer.

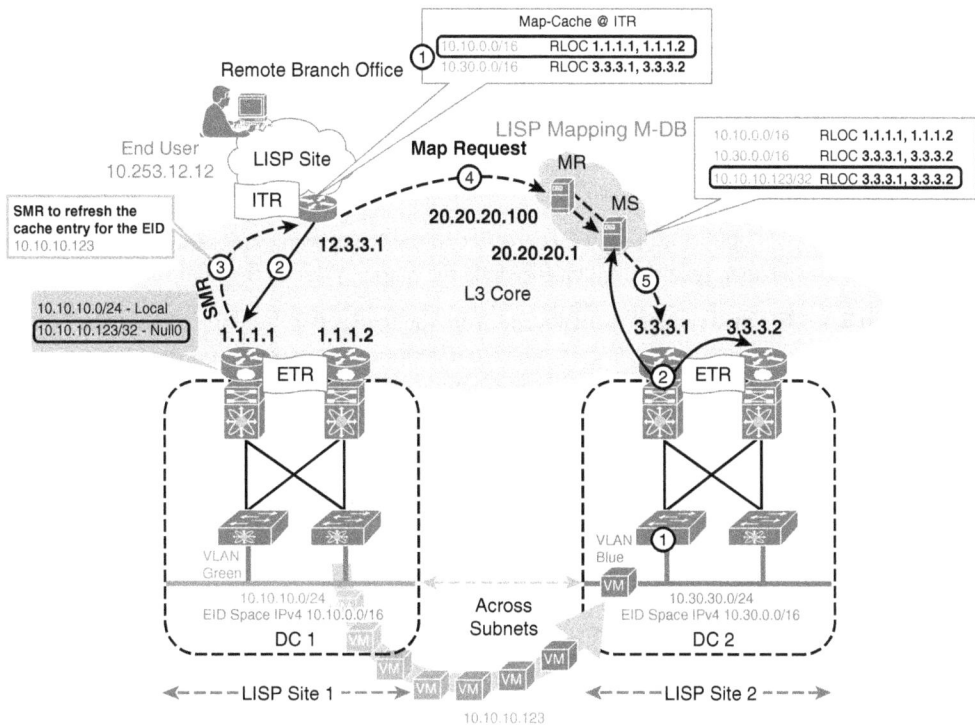

Figure 6-39 *Remote xTR Map Cache Entry Update (Part 1)*

Before we look at LISP IP Mobility signaling and the data plane workflow, it is worth noting that LISP doesn't replace the DNS server function. Both roles are complementary and are required to address their respective functions. As with the establishment of any traditional network communication, the end user sends a request to access the application of interest. The request is forwarded to the local DNS server to resolve the name of the application of interest. As a result, the DNS server returns to the requestor the unique IP address for the particular targeted application. This EID IP address is unique and will be kept the same wherever the machine moves. The same behavior happens with LISP IP Mobility ESM or ASM.

The process shown in Figure 6-39 and Figure 6-40 is as follows:

Step 1.   As soon as the end user sends a data packet to the mobile endpoint 10.10.10.123, the LISP ITR from the branch office identifies the location of the site where the subnet 10.10.0.0/16 is known from its LISP map cache with RLOCs 1.1.1.1 and 1.1.1.2.

Step 2.   In this example, the LISP ITR router in the branch office encapsulates the packet with RLOC 1.1.1.1 as the destination IP and routes the traffic to the initial DC 1 where the EID was initially active. The LISP ETR 1.1.1.1 in DC 1 that receives the data packet destined to the EID 10.10.10.123 removes the LISP header and performs a Layer 3 lookup in its routing table for the destination endpoint. It finds a Null0 for the destination 10.10.10.123 previously installed as a result of the notification received from the LISP map server.

Step 3. The original LISP ETR router triggers a solicit map request (SMR) message back to the LISP branch office ITR that sent the traffic to the concerned machine.

Step 4. The LISP ITR in the branch office initiates a new map request process with the map resolver, which forwards the map request to the map server engine.

Step 5. The map request is forwarded from the map server function toward the LISP site gateway in DC 2, to which the endpoint has moved, and then toward the last LISP site gateway that registered the roaming EID of interest.

Figure 6-40 shows the process of validating the RLOC in DC 2, which replies directly to the remote LISP ITR. The reception of the map reply confirms the connectivity between the remote LISP ITR and the LISP xTR in DC 2.

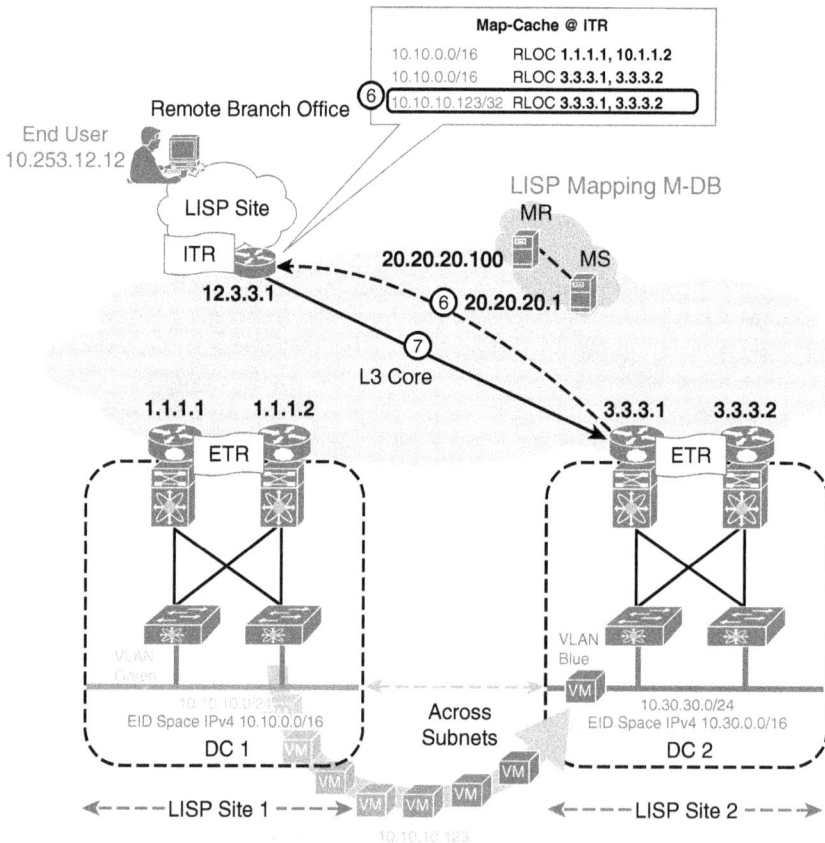

Figure 6-40 *Remote xTR Map Cache Entry Update (Part 2)*

Step 6.   The LISP router from the new DC 2 that receives the map request destined to 10.10.10.123 immediately sends a map reply directly to the LISP ITR that initiated the map request. The LISP ITR from the branch office immediately updates its LISP map cache.

Step 7.   The LISP ITR encapsulates the user data packet and sends the traffic destined to 10.10.10.123 directly toward DC 2, to either RLOC 3.3.3.1 or 3.3.3.2.

LISP IP Mobility ASM Data Plane Operation

From a branch office to a LISP site, the forwarding data plane with LISP IP Mobility ASM is quite straightforward and similar to that in LISP IP Mobility ESM. As shown in Figure 6-41, the end user from the branch office sends a request for the application Apps-123. As with any traditional network requests, the end-user workstation queries the IP address of the destination Apps-123 through a conventional DNS request, regardless of where the application is running. Up to this stage, from the perspective of establishing a source-to-destination communication, the server that hosts the application App-123 can be located in a conventional data center or deployed at one of the LISP-enabled data center sites.

Note   The name server translating the text-based identifier into a numeric identifier is still required and is complementary to LISP IP Mobility signaling.

Figure 6-41 shows the LISP-encapsulated traffic between the remote LISP ITR and the LISP ETR belonging to the data center where the destination is active:

Step 1.   The end-user workstation sends data packet destined to App-123 (10.10.10.123). The traffic that originated from the client is steered toward the local LISP-enabled router located in the remote branch office.

Step 2.   This LISP router in the branch office performs a lookup for the destination (10.10.10.123) in its routing table. As described with the previous control plane signaling mechanism, the RLOC for that particular endpoint was updated in its map cache with the LISP site gateway belonging to DC 2.

The destination EID (10.10.10.123) is associated with the RLOCs identifying both ETR devices located in DC 2—3.3.3.1 and 3.3.3.2. Each entry has associated priority and weight values that are controlled by the destination site to influence the way inbound traffic is received from the transport infrastructure. The priority is used to determine whether both LISP ETR devices can be used to receive LISP-encapsulated traffic destined to a local EID subnet (in a load-balancing scenario). If desired, it is possible to provide different weight values to tune the amount of traffic received by each LISP ETR in a weighted load-balancing scenario. The weight values are therefore efficient only when equal priority is given for the xTRs in the same data center.

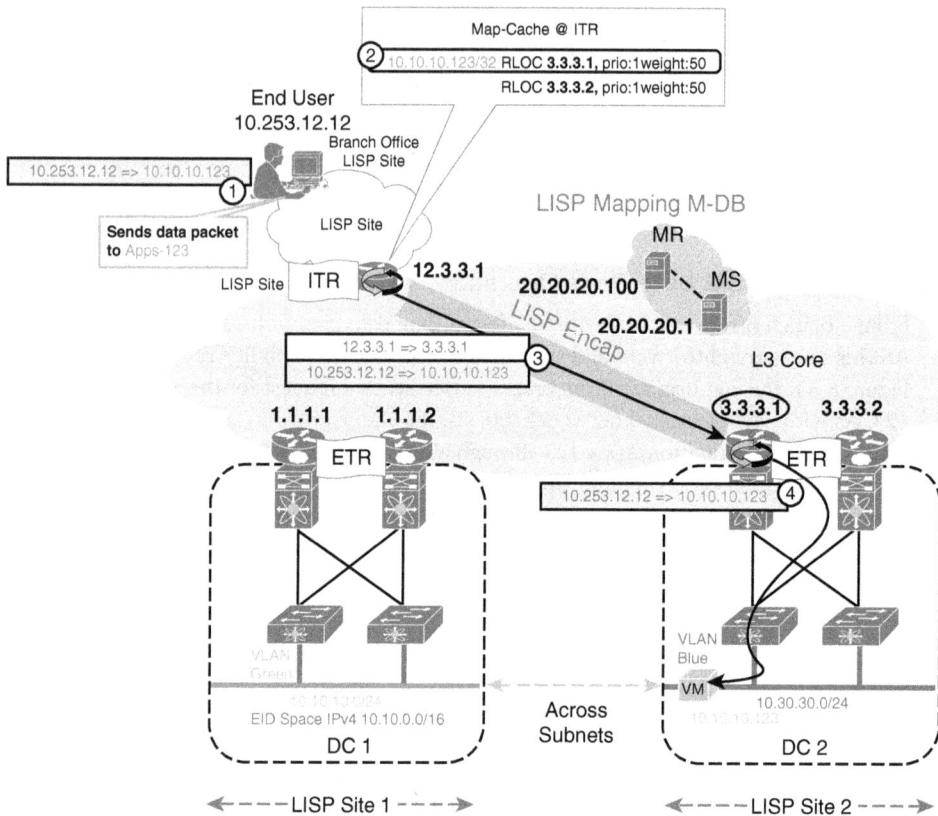

Figure 6-41   *Data Plane Forwarding with LISP ASM*

Step 3.   After a LISP lookup in its map cache, the ITR appliance located in the branch office performs a LISP encapsulation of the original user's data packet and routes it over the Layer 3 transport infrastructure with, as the IP destination, one of the LISP ETRs belonging to DC 2. With the same priority and weight values, the selection of the specific ETR RLOC is done on a per-flow basis, based on hashing performed on the 5-tuple Layer 3 and Layer 4 information of the original client's IP packet. In this example, the elected RLOC is 3.3.3.1.

Step 4.   The LISP ETR 3.3.3.1 receives the IP data packet, de-encapsulates it, applies the Layer 3 lookup in the original data packet, and routes it into the internal interface VLAN Blue, for which the particular IP address for the destined EID has been associated with subnet 10.10.10.0/24.

Figure 6-41 shows the north–south traffic flow. As each LISP router offers the two roles, ETR and ITR, a similar mechanism is used for the return traffic originated by the EID located in DC 2 and destined to the remote end user, where the LISP devices exchange their respective roles of ITRs (DC 2) and ETRs (branch office).

Another key difference with LISP IP Mobility ESM is that for intra-subnet communication across a LISP site, data packets between machines belonging to the same subnet are routed across the Layer 3 core, with LISP encapsulation as the transport.

Note   With LISP IP Mobility ESM, intra-subnet communication is directly established across the Layer 2 extension as a transport.

This section has discussed the communication established between an end user from a branch office and a roaming machine moved to a secondary site. Say that the roamer that landed in DC 2 needs to communicate with another machine sharing the same subnet that is still located in its original data center, DC 1. With LISP IP Mobility ASM, it is now understood that there is no Layer 2 adjacent communication extended between the two endpoints. Let's now look at the packet walk in this scenario to clarify how the intra-subnet communication is established.

As discussed previously, because LISP ASM offers migration without an extended VLAN, the only option for communicating between the two distant sites is over the routed Layer 3 transport.

With LISP ASM, only a move of a roamer to a remote LISP site dictates the remote site to be discovered, and thus the content of the mapping database is updated accordingly after the migration. Hence, we can take into consideration the two ways of communication separately.

Figure 6-42 shows the first workflow. The endpoint App-1 from its home site DC 1 initiates communication with the roamer App-123, which landed in the LISP site DC 2. It is assumed that this is the first establishment between those two machines and that their respective ARP tables are empty. Because they belong to the same broadcast domain, App-1 initiates an ARP request destined to App-123.

Keep in mind that as soon as the source LISP router (DC 1) receives a map notification from the LISP map server about the move and the new RLOC of the roaming dynamic EID, it sends a Gratuitous ARP toward the concerned subnet (VLAN Green in this example). This is crucial for the whole migration process as endpoints belonging to the same subnet are separated by a routed network. As a result, all local machines from VLAN Green withdraw the entry associated to 10.10.10.123 from their respective ARP cache tables, causing the local machines to send an ARP request prior to communicating with the roaming device.

As stated previously, the SVIs for the mobile subnets are configured with the proxy ARP function. As a result, the local LISP site gateway receives the broadcasted ARP request from App-1 destined to App-123 on its interface VLAN Green, which triggers two actions. The LISP site gateway ARP replies on behalf of target endpoint App-123 with the vMAC configured for the default gateway. This is possible because the LISP site gateways in DC 1 have a Null0 value associated to the host App-123 in its routing table. This also confirms that the LISP routers are aware that App-123 landed at the other site. Notice that no proxy ARP happens if the destination endpoint is in the home site.

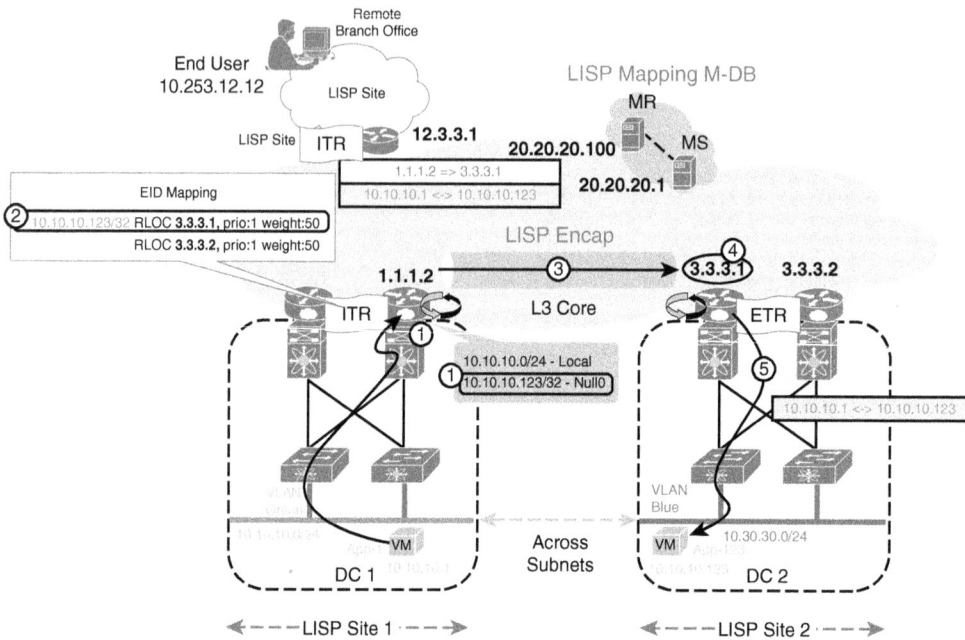

Figure 6-42 *LISP ASM Intra-Subnet Communication Across Remote Sites (Stage 1)*

Once the ARP table of App-1 has been populated, data plane connectivity with App-123 in the remote site can be established via the following process (refer to Figure 6-42):

Step 1. App-1 sends the data packet destined to App-123 with the vMAC associated to the VIP HSRP as the destination MAC address. The packet hits the LISP site gateway in DC 1, configured with the HSRP vMAC given with the proxy ARP for the SVI of interest. The Layer 3 lookup for destination 10.10.10.123 hits Null0 for that particular host route, and the data packet is punted to the CPU, which triggers the LISP lookup for the dynamic EID 10.10.10.123.

Step 2. The LISP map caches on LISP routers in DC 1 are updated with the LISP map notify sent by the LISP map server.

Step 3. The LISP router takes the role of ITR and encapsulates the data packet from App-1.

Step 4. The LISP router sends the data traffic to one of the remote RLOCs deployed in DC 2 (3.3.3.1 in this example).

Step 5. The receiving LISP ETR strips off the LISP encapsulation and routes the packet destined to the VLAN Green, with which the LISP IP Mobility was associated.

Note   The receiving LISP ETR router may need to use ARP for the destination. This ARP request must be sent on an SVI configured in a different IP subnet. This is possible because of the LISP IP Mobility configuration.

Another scenario is that App-123 might need to establish a Layer 2 communication to reply to the host App-1, as shown with Figure 6-43.

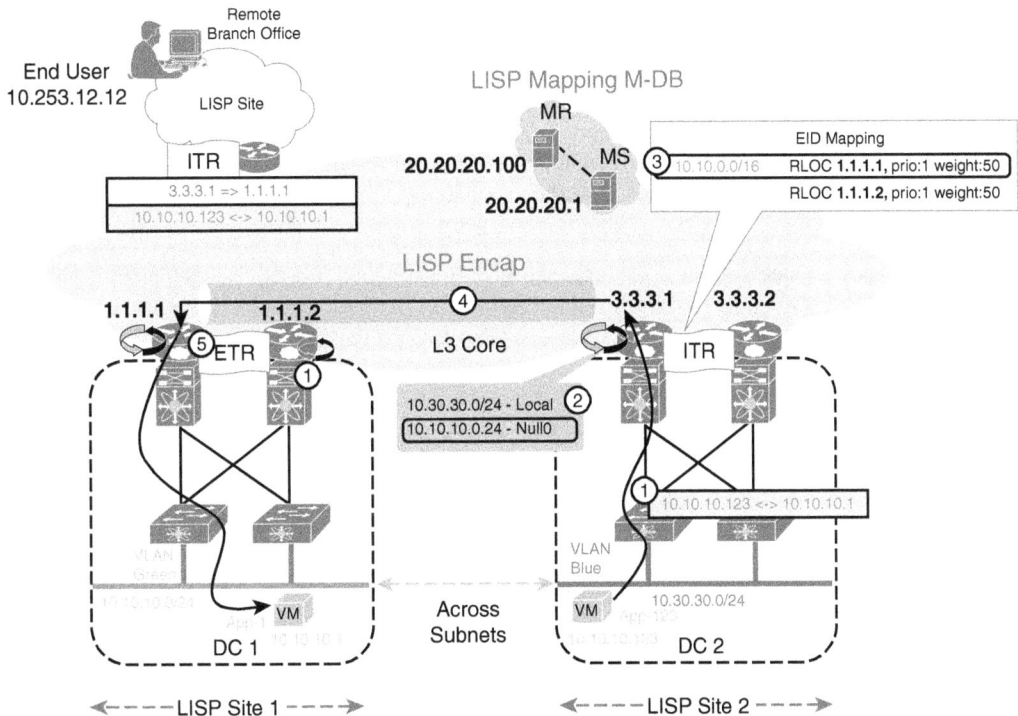

Figure 6-43   *LISP ASM Intra-Subnet Communication Across Remote Sites (Stage 2)*

The process shown in Figure 6-43 is as follows:

Step 1.   Due to the cold migration, the ARP table of App-123 is cleaned up. This triggers an ARP request from App-123 to discover the MAC address of App-1 as, theoretically, the data packet is destined to the same broadcast domain. Under the assumption that this is a cold migration (only for ARP requests), 10.10.10.123 would use an ARP message to discover the MAC address for 10.10.10.1. The proxy-ARP function enabled on the SVI for VLAN Blue provides the vMAC of the default gateway as a response. It is important to keep in mind that the LISP routers in DC 2 have a Null0 statement for the subnet 10.10.10.0/24. This Null0 was installed by LISP with the mapping configuration of the dynamic EID.

Step 2.   The packet hits the LISP site gateway in DC 2, configured with the HSRP vMAC given with the proxy ARP for the SVI of interest. The Layer 3 lookup for destination 10.10.10.1 hits the Null0 for the subnet 10.10.10.0/24. As a result, the first data packet sent from App-123 in DC 2 is punted to the CPU, which triggers a LISP mapping lookup for the dynamic EID 10.10.10.1.

Step 3.   Because App-1, belonging to the same LISP mobile subnet, is still active in its initial home site DC 1, the dynamic EID notification for App-1 is not triggered by the LISP router in DC 1. As a result, the LISP site gateway in DC 2 runs the lookup for 10.10.10.1. Nonetheless, the communication can be established without the need to dynamically discover and install the EID host route in its LISP map cache. Indeed, the global database mapping 10.10.0.0/16 encompasses the prefix subnet to which the destination EID belongs.

Step 4.   The elected LISP ITR in DC 2 (3.3.3.1 in this example) encapsulates the data packet and routes it to the destination 1.1.1.1, one of the RLOCs associated with the LISP xTRs located in DC 1.

Step 5.   Because the ARP exchange already happened to establish the communication in Figure 6-42, when the LISP ETR in DC 1 receives the LISP packet, it removes the LISP encapsulation, applies a Layer 3 lookup, and routes the original data packet to the subnet Green with App-1 as the IP destination.

In summary, the LISP Host Mobility ASM solution provides the key benefits of automatically detecting and updating the LISP mapping database as soon as an endpoint moves from one LISP site to another. As a result, the traffic is always steered to the location where the roamer is currently active. In addition, it preserves intra-subnet communication across Layer 3 by LISP encapsulating the data traffic over a Layer 3 network. This prevents the extension of the Layer 2 networks for cold or warm migration across long distances.

Configuring LISP IP Mobility Across Subnets Mode

This section details the minimum configuration required to deploy LISP IP Mobility ASM communication. Figure 6-44 shows the reachability information required for the configuration for the different LISP components.

This configuration example is constructed with two different LISP subnets, one on each LISP site. We can refer to them as "home subnets." VLAN Green with the home subnet 10.10.10.0/24 belongs to DC 1, and VLAN Blue with the home subnet 10.30.30.0/24 belongs to DC 2.

In the configuration examples that follow, it is assumed that LISP IP Mobility is allowed from DC 1 subnet Green to subnet Blue in DC 2, and subnet Green is the referencing LISP IP Mobility subnet configured in both interface VLANs, Green and Blue. Finally, the remote site is hosting the network 10.253.12.0/24.

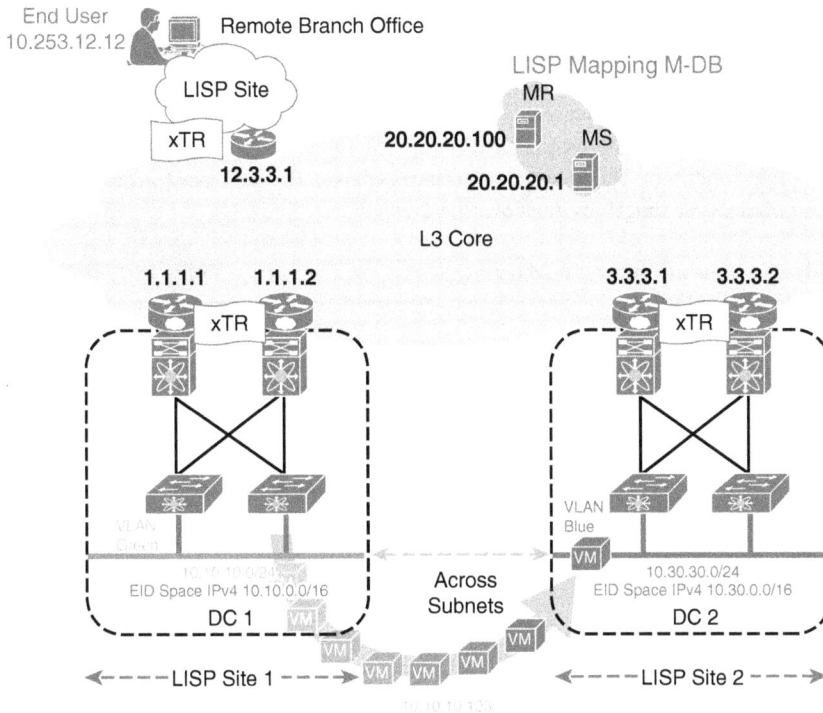

Figure 6-44 *LISP IP Mobility ASM Topology*

The configurations given shortly for the LISP mapping database and the site gateways in DC 1 and DC 2 rely on the command-line interface (CLI) for the Nexus 7000 series. The configuration for the branch office shows the CLI for an ASR 1000 series. For other LISP platforms, the configuration differs slightly, so check with the appropriate configuration guide for further details.

The configurations between the pairs of local LISP devices are quite similar; only the interface VLAN where roamers exist differs by having a unique primary IP address. As a result, the following examples include only one device per site.

In a production network, the recommendation is to either dedicate a cluster of servers to run the two functions of the LISP mapping database separately or to configure such a cluster on each site. The same recommendation in a typical enterprise deployment applies with LISP IP Mobility ASM, as distinct devices perform the roles of LISP map server and LISP map resolvers and LISP site gateways, and they work in a completely stateless fashion. Nonetheless, LISP IP Mobility offers the flexibility to enable different roles in a single appliance, if desired, as demonstrated with the following configuration examples. In this scenario, all three roles—MS, MR, and LISP xTR—are combined in the same LISP site gateway.

LISP Mapping Database Configuration

For all LISP devices, the LISP feature must be enabled to get the LISP functionality, and the LISP role must be explicitly defined, as shown in Example 6-11 for the map server and map resolver functions. As previously mentioned, these two functions can run from independent appliances or can be combined within the same device, such as a LISP xTR, along with other functions. The loopback interfaces used as IP addresses for the map resolver and map server functions must also be created.

Example 6-11 *Configuration for the Mapping Database Functions: Roles and Interfaces*

```
feature lisp
ip lisp map-resolver
ip lisp map-server
!
interface loopback0
description Map-Resolver IP Address
ip address 20.20.20.100/32
!
interface loopback1
description Map-Server IP Address
ip address 20.20.20.1/32
```

Example 6-12 shows the configuration for the remote branch office and the data centers.

Example 6-12 *Configuration for the Mapping Database Components: Remote Branch Site(s) and Data Center(s)*

```
 lisp site BRANCH
!notice number of site is not limited to one
  eid-prefix 10.253.12.0/24
  authentication-key 0 thisisthepassword
!
lisp site DC 1
 eid-prefix 10.10.0.0/16 accept-more-specifics
! the previous CLI is important to accept /32 prefixes
 authentication-key 0 thisisthepassword
 !
 lisp site DC 2
 eid-prefix 10.30.0.0/16 accept-more-specifics
 authentication-key 0 thisisthepassword
```

It is imperative to specify the **accept-more-specifics** keyword associated with the DC global EID prefix for which the LISP Host Mobility is enabled in the DC xTRs because specific /32 prefixes that are part of the larger aggregate prefix are registered after moves of dynamic EIDs.

LISP Site Gateway Configuration

If the LISP mapping database is enabled within dedicated platforms, it is necessary to enable the LISP feature for the LISP site gateway. It is also necessary to specify the roles the mapping database and LISP site gateway are going to perform, which are, respectively, the LISP ITR for encapsulating ingress traffic destined to remote LISP locations and the LISP egress tunnel router ETR for de-encapsulating the traffic received from the Layer 3 network.

It is essential to configure the global database mapping to identify all the IP subnets deployed in each data center's LISP site, as highlighted in Example 6-13. The aggregate prefixes encompass the IP subnets where the mobile endpoints belong. The aggregate prefixes can also include the subnets that are not used for LISP IP Mobility.

Example 6-13 *LISP Site Gateway (ETR 1) in DC 1: LISP Feature and Network Prefix Configuration*

```
feature lisp
ip lisp itr-etr
!
ip lisp database-mapping 10.10.0.0/16 1.1.1.1 priority 1 weight 50
ip lisp database-mapping 10.10.0.0/16 1.1.1.2 priority 1 weight 50
lisp dynamic-eid Subnet-Green
  database-mapping 10.10.10.0/24 1.1.1.1 priority 1 weight 25
  database-mapping 10.10.10.0/24 1.1.1.2 priority 1 weight 25
  map-notify-group 239.1.1.1
```

The global mappings shown in Example 6-13 associate the aggregate prefix 10.10.0.0/16 with the local LISP site gateway xTRs, known as RLOCs for DC 1. To keep the communication with each RLOC successful, as long as a valid Layer 3 path connects the LISP xTR with the Layer 3 core network, it is a best practice to leverage the loopback interface for that particular usage.

Priority and a weight can be associated to each mapping statement. These values can be tuned to balance the traffic through a specific LISP router. In this sample configuration, the values are identical to ensure fair distribution across both LISP xTRs in DC 1. In this example, the same load sharing behavior applies on both data centers.

A dynamic mapping is required to identify the IP subnets to which the mobile machines belong. In this example, the mobile subnet 10.10.10.0 is a /24 prefix, which is associated with the same two RLOCs in the data center that were previously used for the global mapping. Priorities and weights are kept the same in this case to achieve inbound load balancing for traffic destined to the mobile subnet. A multicast address (called map notify group) must also be associated to the dynamic EID mapping. Unlike with LISP IP Mobility with ESM, this multicast group will be unique per LISP site as, with LISP ASM, there is no LAN extension, and hence the map notification group will be only local.

The mask associated to the dynamic EID prefix should always be more specific that the one used in the global mapping statements.

Some additional factors around the length of the network prefix specified in the dynamic EID mapping must be taken into consideration. In a production environment, multiple mobile subnets are configured. Consequently, it is possible to either define different LISP dynamic EID components for each subnet or to use a broader prefix that includes all subnets.

The multicast address of the map notify group can be the same across multiple IP subnets in the same LISP site.

The next step involves defining the IP addresses of the LISP map servers and map resolvers. In a production deployment, it is a best practice to activate multiple map resolvers by using an anycast IP address. The same applies with deployment of multiple physical map servers, which should be configured with their respective unique IP addresses; in this example, however, only one map server is used.

As mentioned previously, in a typical enterprise deployment, two separate devices perform the roles of MS and MR and work in a completely stateless fashion. That recommendation is not applied in the sample given here.

Example 6-14 shows the configuration for the interface VLAN associated with the mobile subnet (that is, the VLANs to which roaming machines will belong).

Example 6-14   *LISP Site Gateway (ETR 1) in DC 1: MS/MR and Interface VLAN Configuration*

```
! Define MS and MR
 ip lisp itr map-resolver 20.20.20.100
!An anycast IP address shared among multiple MR
 ip lisp etr map-server 20.20.20.1 key thisisthepassword
! additional MS can be listed below
!
interface vlan 10
  ip address 10.10.10.3/24
  lisp mobility Subnet-Green
  ip proxy-arp
  hsrp 1
    mac-address CAFE.CAFE.CAFE
    preempt delay reload 300
    priority 130
    ip 10.10.10.254
```

In Example 6-14, the **lisp mobility** command is used to attach the dynamic EID policy configuration **Subnet-Green** to this interface. The VLAN 10 interface is related to the LISP mobile subnet to and from which endpoints can migrate. Because the LISP router is the first-hop router, and hence the default gateway of the roamer, its Layer 3 interface is typically that VLAN interface (SVI).

As discussed previously, the **ip proxy-arp** command is essential to allow the roamers to communicate successfully with the default gateway for two key reasons: Either a local endpoint in DC 1 initiates a data packet destined to a roamer that was moved to a remote LISP site or the roamer establishes a communication after its migration to the remote data center site DC 2. Notice the static configuration of the vMAC as part of the HSRP configuration. The same vMAC must be configured on the remote LISP site gateway interface VLAN Blue, where roamers from VLAN Green are allowed to land. The reason for specifying the vMAC under the HSRP configuration is to ensure that even if the HSRP group is different across the remote sites, the vMAC remains the same; this is crucial for a successful migration.

Because the interface setup is the only configuration that differs between the two local LISP xTRs belonging to the same LISP site, Example 6-15 shows only that SVI setup.

Example 6-15   *LISP Site Gateway (ETR 2) in DC 1: Interface VLAN Configuration*

```
interface vlan 10
  ip address 10.10.10.2/24
  lisp mobility Subnet-Green
  ip proxy-arp
  hsrp 1
    mac-address CAFE.CAFE.CAFE
    ip 10.10.10.254
```

As with the LISP xTR in DC 1, it is necessary to enable the LISP feature and specify that the roles the xTRs are going to perform, which are the LISP ITR for encapsulating ingress traffic destined to remote LISP locations and the LISP ETR for de-encapsulating the traffic received from the Layer 3 network.

The global database mapping is different from that of the DC 1, as it identifies the IP subnets deployed in DC 2, as shown in Example 6-16.

Example 6-16   *LISP Site Gateway (ETR 1) in DC 2: LISP Network Prefix Configuration*

```
 feature lisp
 ip lisp itr-etr
!
 ip lisp database-mapping 10.30.0.0/16 3.3.3.1 priority 1 weight 50
 ip lisp database-mapping 10.30.0.0/16 3.3.3.2 priority 1 weight 50
 lisp dynamic-eid Subnet-Green
   database-mapping 10.10.10.0/24 3.3.3.1 priority 1 weight 25
! mobile subnet in DC 1 RLOC1
   database-mapping 10.10.10.0/24 3.3.3.2 priority 1 weight 25
!mobile subnet in DC 1 RLOC 2
   map-notify-group 239.2.2.2 ↔ multicast group is different from the one used in
     DC 1
```

The mapping given in Example 6-16 associates the aggregate prefix 10.30.0.0/16 with the local LISP site gateway xTRs, known as RLOCs for DC 2.

Notice that the prefix in the dynamic EID mapping identifying the mobile subnet is identical to the one defined on the DC 1 xTRs since it identifies the IP subnet where the LISP mobile endpoints belong. However, the prefix 10.10.10.0/24 is specified with the RLOCs that belong to DC 2.

The multicast group is unique for each LISP site, as with LISP ASM, as there is no LAN extension and hence the map notification is local.

The next step involves defining the IP addresses of the LISP map servers and map resolvers. As mentioned earlier, additional LISP map servers, if there are multiple devices, can be added with their respective IP addresses (one unique IP address per map server). In this example, only one map server is used:

```
ip lisp itr map-resolver 20.20.20.100
 ip lisp etr map-server 20.20.20.1 key thisisthepassword
```

Same additional factors related to the length of the network prefix specified in the dynamic EID mapping must be taken into consideration with this use case. Regarding the configuration for the interface associated with the mobile subnets and the fact that roaming machines migrate from a subnet that doesn't exist in the DC 2 LISP site while they sustain their original IP addresses, there is no need to define an SVI belonging to subnets in DC 1. In Example 6-17, there is no need to configure the VLAN 10 for subnet 10.10.10.0/24 in DC 2. However, the local interface VLAN 30 is associated with the LISP IP Mobility subnet Green.

Example 6-17   *Interface VLAN Configuration for ETR 1 in DC 2*

```
interface vlan 30
  ip address 10.30.30.3/24
  lisp mobility Subnet-Green
  ip proxy-arp
  hsrp 2
    mac-address CAFE.CAFE.CAFE
    preempt delay reload 300
    priority 110
    ip 10.30.30.254
```

The **lisp mobility** command is used to attach the dynamic EID policy configuration **Subnet-Green** to this interface, which connects to the LISP mobile subnet from which endpoints migrate.

ip proxy-arp command is required to permit communication with the roamer after the migration to the remote data center site.

The HSRP group configured on the LISP xTRs in DC 2 can be different from the one used in DC 1. In this case, however, it is essential to configure exactly the same static HSRP vMAC (CAFE.CAFE.CAFE in Example 6-17) to ensure that a migrated workload can consistently send traffic to the default gateway, regardless of its location. The static configuration of the vMAC is part of the HSRP configuration.

LISP xTR in Branch Office Configuration

The configuration for the remote xTR is quite simple because there is no need to configure the requirement for mobile EIDs. Example 6-18 shows the configuration for an IOS router, which differs slightly from the previous NX-OS configuration. For example, the LISP configuration must be added under **Router lisp**. This model follows the regular approach used for configuring other routing protocols in IOS.

The first configuration enables the database mapping for the network where the clients communicate with data centers where roamers are deployed.

Example 6-18   *LISP Network Prefix Configuration for an ETR in the Branch Office*

```
Router lisp
   database-mapping 10.253.12.0/24 12.3.3.1 priority 1 weight 50
   ipv4 itr map-resolver 20.20.20.100
   ipv4 etr map-server 20.20.20.1 key thisisthepassword
```

The RLOC address associated with the EID prefix may be a loopback address (as recommended for the LISP routers in LISP sites). Notice in this example that only one RLOC is used for the branch office. Traditionally, in a production environment, redundant LISP routers are deployed, so, as shown for the data center LISP xTR configuration, two RLOCs can be associated to the database mapping.

The map server and the map resolver anycast addresses must be configured like the other LISP infrastructure components.

Finally, the configuration given for a single branch office can be duplicated as many times as needed for multiple remote sites. It is important to configure the LISP mapping database appropriately in the LISP mapping database.

LISP Feature Support by Operating System

Table 6-1 lists the LISP features by platform OS at the time of writing of this book. For an accurate and updated list, visit the LISP site http://lisp.cisco.com/lisp_hwsw.html#HW.

Table 6-1   LISP Features by Platform OS

Roles	IOS	IOS XE	NX-OS	IOS XR
ITR/ETR	Yes	Yes	Yes	Yes
PITR/PETR	Yes	Yes	Yes	Yes
MS/MR	Yes	Yes	Yes	Yes
EID IPv4/IPv6	Yes	Yes	Yes	Yes
RLOC IPv4/IPv6	Yes	Yes	IPv4 only	Yes
Functions				
ESM/ASM	Yes	Yes	Yes	N/A
ESM multihop	Yes	Yes	Yes	N/A
ESM/FHR	No	No	Yes	N/A

IP Mobility Using LISP IGP Assist

The section "Traditional IP Mobility Solutions," earlier in this chapter, examines network services capable of injecting a host route toward the Layer 3 domain to steer the traffic destined toward the mobile endpoints using the optimal path. The side effects of such a legacy solution are that dedicated network services such as server load balancers must be deployed, the configuration may quickly become complex as the number of roamers increase, and there are scalability limits involved with probing hundreds of endpoints.

Still, in the context of multiple traditional data centers, it is possible to leverage LISP IP Mobility to detect and signal the presence of an endpoint without the need to encapsulate the traffic. In particular, the LISP IP Mobility process detects the host routes of the endpoints roaming over a LISP subnet and then redistributes them into IGP or BGP. The host routes might be provided end to end across all data centers. In that case, there is no LISP encapsulation or de-encapsulation involved, and the configuration is reduced to the LISP multihop function. This might be useful when the enterprise owns the Layer 3 core. Although this solution is similar to a route health injection driven by a load balancer (discussed earlier in this chapter), it is embedded with the LISP first-hop router, and so it is much more scalable. There is no need to deploy dedicated SLB devices to inject the host routes. This solution is well adapted to a traditional hierarchical data center network infrastructure where the default gateways (SVI) are initiated from the aggregation layer.

However, such an old-school solution is useful only for classical Ethernet-based data centers. Indeed, host route advertisement to outside a data center fabric can also be dynamically advertised from the VXLAN EVPN fabric or ACI fabric control plane (as discussed in Chapter 7). With modern network fabrics, endpoint reachability and location (next-hop) information learned by the fabric control plane is natively distributed across the VXLAN domain, but more importantly for ingress path optimization, the host route is natively advertised to outside the fabric.

LISP IGP Assist with Extended Subnet Mode

LISP control plane operations are required to dynamically discover endpoints and their locations.

LISP IGP Assist Control Plane Operation

The same rules discussed for LISP IP Mobility ESM apply to IGP Assist. A hot live migration requires the concerned VLAN to be extended across the remote sites. Because the default gateway must be active on both sites, it is imperative to enable HSRP filtering for that purpose. In this section, we use the same scenario that was used earlier for LISP IP Mobility ESM.

As shown in Figure 6-45, say that you have DC 1 and DC 2 with a DCI solution to extend the concerned LAN between the two sites. A roaming machine, App-123, 192.168.10.123, migrates from DC 1 to DC 2. Because it's a live migration, the endpoint continues to communicate via its default gateway without any interruption. The mechanism to discover the host route is the same as for the LISP first-hop router in the context of LISP IP Mobility ESM.

Figure 6-45 shows the packet walk for LISP IGP Assist without any LISP infrastructure (that is, no LISP mapping database)

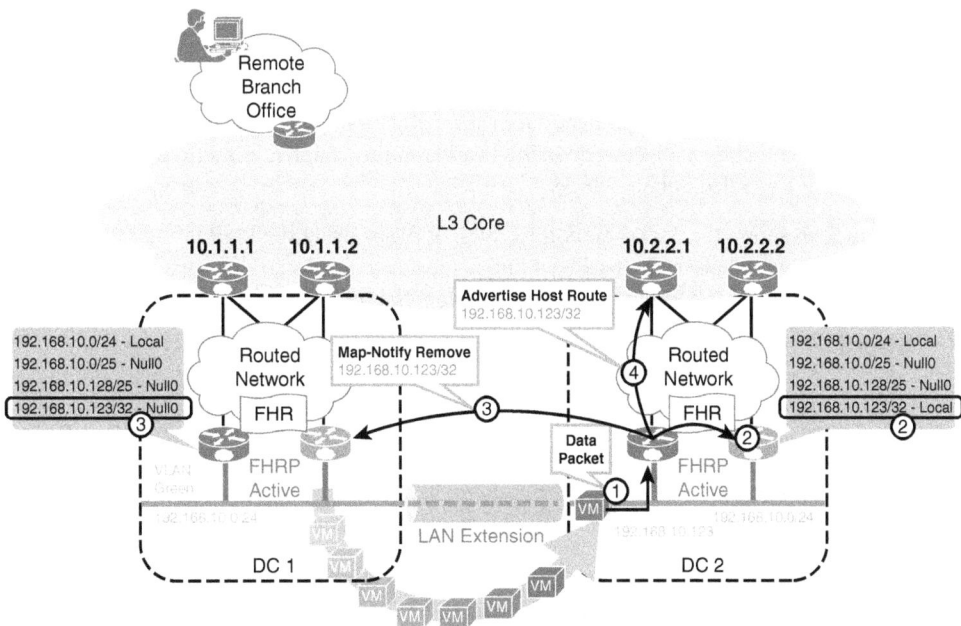

Figure 6-45 *LISP IGP Assist with Extended Subnet Mode: Classical Phase 1*

The process shown in Figure 6-45 is as follows:

Step 1.   After the migration of 192.168.10.123, the roamer sends out an IP data packet that is intercepted by one of the LISP local first-hop routers (FHRs). Because of the inconsistency with Null0 automatically installed for the prefix subnet 192.168.10.0/25, the data packet is punted to the CPU. This triggers a data plane–driven EID discovery event. (Note that for this to happen, the packet must be an IP packet containing the source IP address of the EID.) Once the EID is discovered, it is added to the dynamic EID table of the discovering LISP FHR.

Step 2.   The discovering first-hop router injects a /32 into the IGP routing table and map notifies its local peer with that host route /32, using the map notify group multicast. The map notify group (**Map-Notify**) multicast message (configured with the 239.1.1.1 multicast group) reaches the other local FHR and, via the LAN extension connection, the map notification hits the two remote xTRs in DC 1. On local peers, 192.168.10.123/32 is more specific than the initial /25.

Step 3.   On the remote FHR, a Null0 entry is added for that particular host route.

Step 4.   The routing table in the LISP FHR in DC 2 injects a host route toward the WAN edge routers, and traffic from the branch office is steered toward DC 2.

You could stop the configuration here, but to get a resilient notification process, you can leverage the existing LISP mapping database to maintain an up-to-date directory for the mobile prefix subnet and the related roaming EIDs.

If you want to improve the resiliency for the notification, you need to configure the LISP map server and map resolver as described earlier in this chapter, in section "IP Mobility Using LISP Extended Subnet Mode."

Figure 6-46 shows the packet walk for LISP IGP Assist using the LISP infrastructure (LISP mapping database). Steps 1 to 4 in this figure are similar to the steps in the previous scenario without LISP infrastructure. In addition, the following steps occur:

Step 5.   Following the local routing update with the host route /32 and the map notify group to update all LISP FHRs, the local FHR also triggers a LISP host registration to the LISP map server, which adds the new EID to the database.

Step 6.   The map server map notifies the last LISP first-hop router in the original data center DC 1, to which the roaming EIDs initially belonged, to inform them about the new location (RLOC mapping) for the particular EID.

For a production deployment, it is a best practice to use a LISP mapping database as a secondary mechanism to notify the remote LISP FHRs.

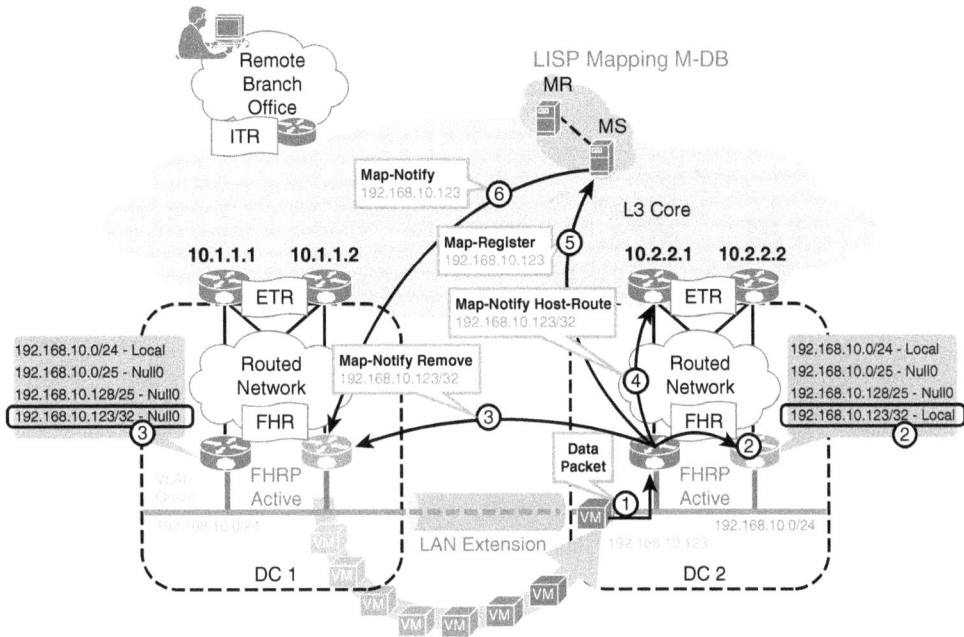

Figure 6-46 *LISP IGP Assist with Extended Subnet Mode: With LISP Mapping Database Stage 2*

LISP IGP Assist Data Plane Operation

Figure 6-47 shows the forwarding plane for a remote user to communicate with the application App-123. The steps shown in this figure are as follows:

Step 1.   As soon as the LISP first-hop router in DC 2 discovers the endpoints, it injects the host route (/32) information of App-123 (192.168.10.123) into its IGP routing table.

Step 2.   The host route is injected toward the WAN edge router, which in turn injects the host route across the routed Layer 3 domain. As a result, the data packet to App-123 initiated by end user 10.253.12.12 is sent to the user's local default gateway. The local traditional router in the branch office does a Layer 3 lookup and notices the route for 192.168.10.123/32. Traffic is natively routed in a traditional fashion toward DC 2, using the optimal routing path to reach the final destination.

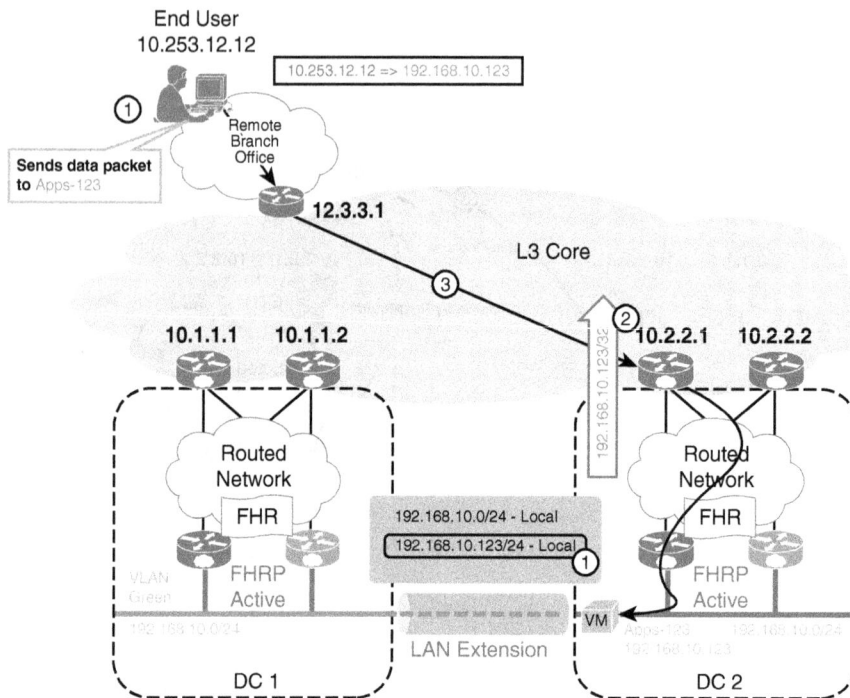

Figure 6-47 *LISP First-Hop Router Data Plane*

Now let's go a bit further with a particular use case to better understand the workflow and the configuration in a multi-tenant environment.

LISP IGP Assist with Network Services

LISP IGP Assist allows the use of local network services such as default gateways, load balancers, and security engines distributed across each location. It helps reduce the inter-subnet server-to-server communication latency (east–west workflows). This solution is useful only for traditional data center networks. Modern fabrics such as VXLAN EVPN and ACI can natively advertise the host route.

Endpoint Localization for East–West Traffic

For the scenario used throughout the following pages, subnets are stretched across multiple locations using a Layer 2 DCI solution. As discussed previously, several use cases require LAN extension between multiple sites, such as hot live migration and health-check probing for high-availability clusters (heartbeats). This scenario assumes that due to the long distances between sites, the network services are duplicated and deployed in active/standby mode on each of the sites to reduce the trombone effect.

Communication Within and Between Sites

Remember that traditionally, an IP address uses a unique identifier assigned to a specific network device, such as physical system, virtual machine or firewall, default gateway, and so on. An IP address has two fundamental functions: It identifies the host, and it provides the location of the host in the network. The routed WAN uses the identifier to also determine the network entity's location in the IP subnet. When a virtual machine migrates from one data center to another, the traditional IP address schema retains its original unique identifier and location, despite the fact that the physical location has actually changed. As a result, the extended VLAN must share the same subnet so that the TCP/IP parameters of the VM remain the same from site to site; this is necessary to maintain active sessions for migrated applications.

When deploying a logical data center architecture stretched across multiple locations, with duplicated active network services, a couple critical behaviors must be taken into consideration. First, it is extremely important to maintain transparently, with no interruption, the same level of security within and across sites before, during, and after live migration of any endpoints. Second, while machines follow a stateful migration process (hot live migration) from site to site, each security and network service that owns currently active sessions should not reject any sessions due to an asymmetric workflow. It is mandatory for the round-trip data packet flow to always reach the stateful device that owns the current session; otherwise, the session is broken by the stateful device. To achieve the required symmetric workflow, it is fundamental that each IP endpoint be localized dynamically, and any movement of virtual machines requires notification in real time to update all relevant routing tables.

Note   The scenario discussed in the following pages covers security appliances in routed mode. However, the same behavior applies with any stateful devices, such as SLB engines, physical appliances, and virtual services.

In the following use case, two physical data centers are interconnected using a Layer 2 DCI solution, which offers a single logical data center from a multitiered application framework point of view. This solution is agnostic to the DCI transport as long as a method to filter FHRP exists between data centers.

Figure 6-48 shows a generic deployment of multiple sites interconnected with a Layer 2 overlay network extended over the Layer 3 connection. The two data centers, which are tightly coupled by the Layer 2 extension, are organized to support multi-tenancy with tenant Red and tenant Green. The firewalls are both active and independent from each other. A standby firewall exists for each active firewall.

The goal is to utilize the required services from local stateful devices to reduce latency for server-to-server communication in a multi-tenant environment, while traffic flows are kept symmetric from end to end.

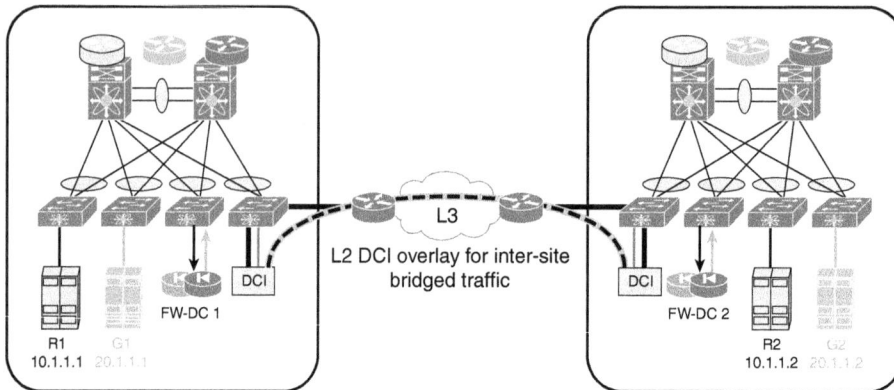

Figure 6-48   *Data Center with Multiple Sites: High-Level Physical Architecture*

In Figure 6-49, when host R1 (R for Red) from tenant Red communicates with host G1 (G for Green) from tenant Green, both located in DC 1, the traffic is inspected by the local firewall in DC 1. On the other site, when host R2 communicates with host G2, the traffic is inspected by the local firewall in DC 2. The default gateways are provided by the aggregation layer. The communication between VRF Red and VRF Green is achieved through the firewalls.

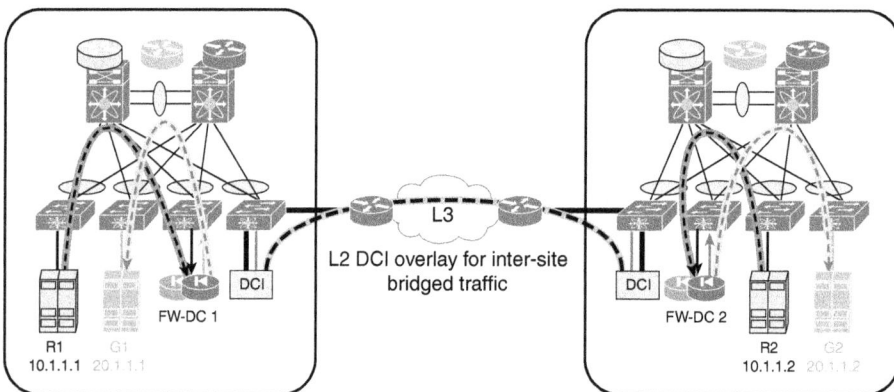

Figure 6-49   *Data Center with Multiple Sites: Localized East–West Traffic*

If this behavior sounds obvious for independent data centers with geographically dispersed data centers, it might become a concern when the broadcast domains are extended across multiple sites, with duplicate active stateful devices. The logical view in Figure 6-50 depicts the issue. The traffic from VLAN 10 (subnet Red) destined to VLAN 20 (subnet Green) is routed via each local active firewall. As a result, when host R1 (VLAN 10) in DC 1 needs to communicate with host G2 (VLAN 20) in DC 2, its data packet is routed toward its local firewall in DC 1, which in turn routes the traffic destined to G2 (subnet Green) extended to the remote site. It is therefore necessary to extend the Layer 2 network for those subnets to reach the endpoints wherever they are located. The routed traffic is therefore forwarded toward host G2 across the extended subnet Green (with Layer 2 overlay connectivity established across the DCI transport). G2 receives the data packets and replies as expected to R1, using its local default gateway, which in turn routes toward its local firewall (DC 2) the response destined to R1 (subnet Red). In this design, by default the local firewall on each site receives the preferred paths for subnet Red and subnet Green from its local fabric. Hence, routing between endpoints belonging to those two IP subnets is always kept local to a site. As a result, this behavior affects the workflow, which becomes asymmetrical, and consequently the firewall in DC 2 terminates that current session for security reasons.

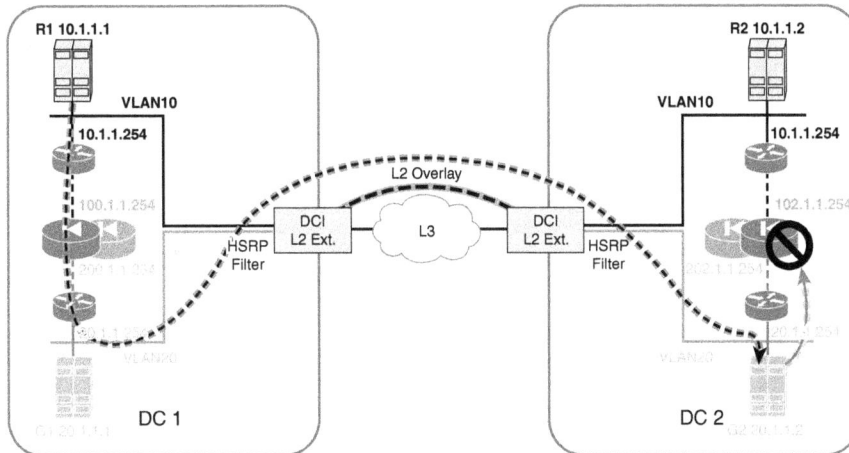

Figure 6-50 *Asymmetric Flow with Stateful Devices Not Allowed*

Two scenarios exist based on host routing to provide the physical location of the IP endpoint—with and without Layer 2 segments extended between multiple locations. The concept relies on more specific routes (/32) propagated to multiple host databases (DC 1 and DC 2). Having a dynamic database of endpoints associated with their physical locations makes it possible to redirect the traffic destined to IP machines of interest over a specific Layer 3 path.

LISP IGP Assist and Host Route Injection

The following section describes a subfunction of LISP that consists of injecting the host route toward the IGP protocol in conjunction with extended subnets across distant locations, as described earlier in this chapter for LISP IGP Assist ESM. LISP IGP Assist is agnostic to the DCI technology deployed, but because IGP Assist uses a multicast group to transport host route notifications from site to site, it is important that IP multicast traffic be routed across the DCI network.

Note   The fact that IP multicast traffic must be routed across the DCI network doesn't mean that the WAN must be IP multicast capable; it means that multicast data packets should be carried across all remote locations. Therefore, it is important to select the DCI solution that supports transporting multicast traffic using at least head-end replication.

LISP IGP Assist can be leveraged to dynamically trigger an update in its EID database for each detection of a new machine that belongs to a selected subnet. As soon as an endpoint is powered on or moved to a new physical host, it is automatically detected by its default gateway (the LISP first-hop router function). The LISP process running on the relevant switch (DG) registers the new host reachability information (host route) to its EID database with its location and notifies all remote first-hop routers accordingly, using a dedicated multicast group across the Layer 2 DCI. When the host routes are installed in the local routing table, the FHR can advertise the host routes to an upstream Layer 3 device using the routing protocol of choice (IGP or BGP).

The key concept is to propagate the host routes dynamically to the remote site by using a dedicated Layer 3 DCI network. As a result, a more specific route (/32) is announced to steer the traffic to the EID of interest using a specific path. This Layer 3 DCI connectivity is shown in Figure 6-51 as the secure Layer 3 DCI connection for inter-site, inter-VRF routed traffic. The firewalls must establish the Layer 3 peering with the local LISP FHR devices and between them via the Layer 3 DCI connection:

■ R1 and G1 host routes are propagated toward DC 2 over the Layer 3 DCI.

■ R2 and G2 host routes are propagated toward DC 1 over the Layer 3 DCI.

Figure 6-51 provides further details that are used for this scenario.

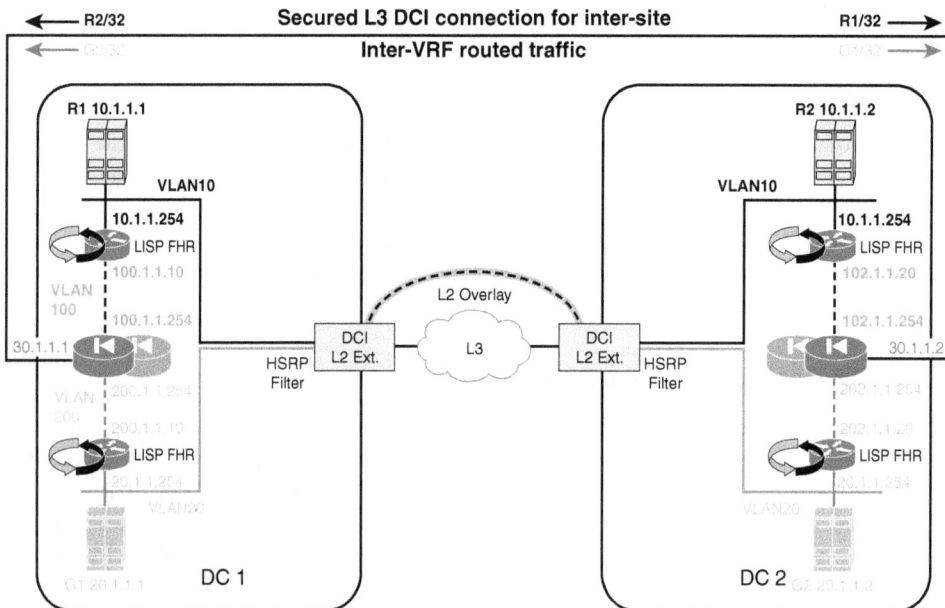

Figure 6-51   *IGP Assist for Host Route Injection over a Layer 3 DCI*

To summarize the logical view in Figure 6-51:

- Hosts R1 and R2 belong to the same VLAN 10 within tenant Red, while G1 and G2 share the same VLAN 20 that belongs to tenant Green.

- VLAN 10 and VLAN 20 are extended across the Layer 2 DCI connection established using a Layer 2 DCI solution.

- Hosts R1 and G1 are located in DC 1, and Hosts R2 and G2 are located in DC 2.

- Intra-subnet and inter-subnet communication belonging to a given demilitarized zone (DMZ) or tenant happens freely, while inter-tenant packet flows must be enforced through the firewall as the route to reach the remote endpoint from a different VRF is more specific using the dedicated Layer 3 DCI connection.

- A Layer 3 segmentation (VRF) is performed between tenants to force the routed traffic to use the firewall. VLAN 10 belongs to VRF Red and VLAN 20 to VRF Green.

- FHRP filtering is enabled in conjunction with the DCI Layer 2 transport so that the same SVI can be active on both sites.

- The LISP FHR must be configured as the default gateway for every host of interest because it needs to be the first-hop router to discover the endpoints either using the data plane or using the control plane, depending on whether the hypervisor deployed offers live mobility. When the endpoint sends an IP data packet (Layer 3 packet), this learning process is referred to as *data plane discovery*. When the roaming machine sends an ARP packet (which is a Layer 2 frame) containing the IP address of the endpoint in the payload, a discovery event triggered by ARP messages is referred to as *control plane discovery*.

- An active firewall on each site is used to secure the routed traffic between VRF Red and VRF Green.

Note   It is assumed but not discussed in this section that in a production environment, the network services—such as SVI, LISP, firewalls, server load balancers, and DCI edge devices—are fully redundant (active/standby mode per site).

Consider three types of data flows:

- **Intra-subnet communication via the Layer 2 DCI:** Bridged traffic destined for a remote host within the same broadcast domain uses the Layer 2 DCI connectivity. Note that additional security services in transparent mode and/or encryption can be leveraged, if needed, to secure the Layer 2 DCI connectivity without impacting this scenario, as shown in Figure 6-52.

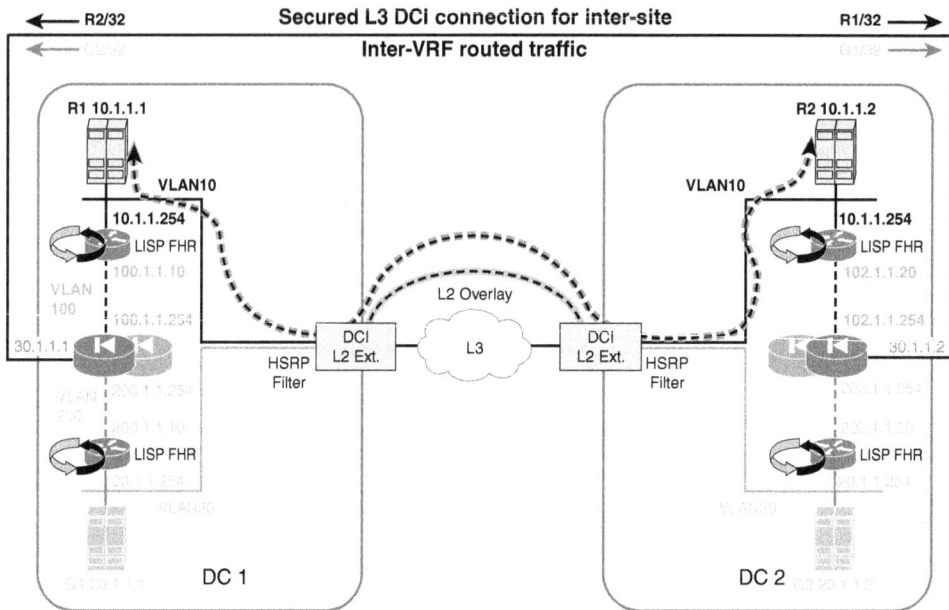

Figure 6-52   *Intra-Subnet Communication via the Layer 2 DCI*

■ **Local routed inter-tenant intra-DC traffic:** Routed traffic destined for a local machine that belongs to a different DMZ (VRF) uses the local firewalls. Each firewall within a data center is first of all used to secure the local traffic between the two VRFs. Firewalls are configured using dynamic routing, as shown in Figure 6-53.

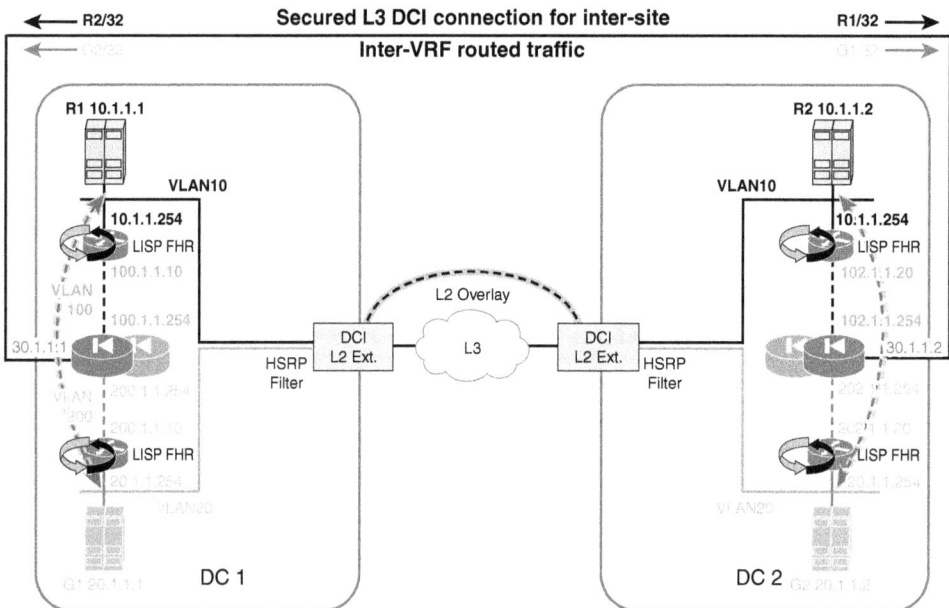

Figure 6-53   *Local Inter-VRF Secure Communication (Using the Local Firewall)*

■ **Routed inter-tenant inter-DC traffic:** Routed traffic destined for a remote machine that belongs to a different DMZ or VRF uses both firewalls from each site. The traffic is routed using a dedicated Layer 3 DCI connection (depicted in Figure 6-53 as Backbone Inter-DMZ link), preventing asymmetric traffic. To achieve this symmetric routing using the dedicated Layer 3 DCI network, as soon as the first-hop router first discovers an endpoint, it injects a /32 into its IGP routing table and notifies the remote FHR via the LAN extension for the host route of interest using the map notify group multicast. As a result, the distant FHR removes the concerned /32 host route from its routing table. Once the host routes are installed in the local routing table, the FHR can advertise the host routes to an upstream Layer 3 device, which is the firewall, using the routing protocol of choice (IGP or BGP). As a result, the route to reach the target host is now more specific using the remote firewall as the next hop. As a result, the relevant traffic inter-VRF is transported across the dedicated Layer 3 DCI path toward the remote firewall, as shown in Figure 6-54.

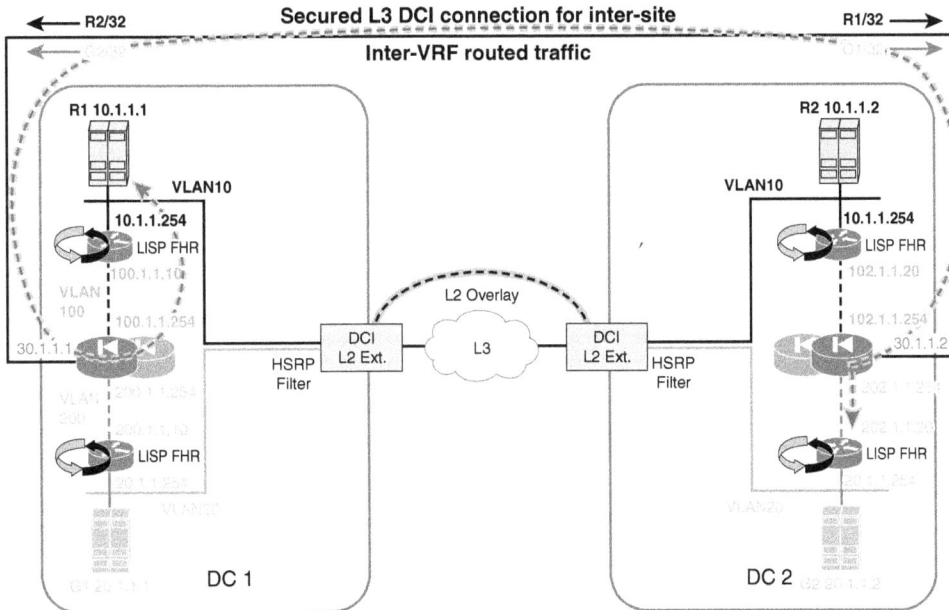

Figure 6-54 *Site-to-Site Inter-VRF Secure Communication (Both Firewalls)*

LISP IGP Assist Basic Configuration

The following sections provides the configuration for LISP IGP Assist for DC 1 and DC 2.

LISP IGP Assist in DC 1

The minimum configuration required for LISP IGP Assist is quite simple. The first step is to enable PIM to distribute the host route notification using a multicast group. All interfaces of interest must be configured with PIM sparse mode. In this setup, as shown in Example 6-19, a single RP is configured in DC 1 using the same loopback address used for the LISP locator.

Example 6-19 *DC 1 LISP Loopback Address Configuration*

```
interface loopback10
 description LISP Loopback
 ip address 10.10.10.10/32
 ip router ospf 1 area 0.0.0.0
 ip pim sparse-mode
!
ip pim rp-address 10.10.10.10 group-list 224.0.0.0/4
ip pim ssm range 232.0.0.0/8
```

Next, you need to configure the route map to advertise the host routes toward the local firewall. The command shown in Example 6-20 is global for any subnets, but more specific prefixes can be used. The route map is redistributed via the OSPF process for each VRF. In this case OSPF is used for establishing Layer 3 peering between the LISP FHR and the local firewall.

Example 6-20 *DC 1 Route Map Configuration for Host Route Advertisement*

```
ip prefix-list HOST-ROUTES seq 5 permit 0.0.0.0/0 eq 32
route-map ADV-HOST-ROUTES deny 5
 match interface Null0
route-map ADV-HOST-ROUTES permit 10
 match ip address prefix-list HOST-ROUTES
router ospf 100
 router-id 1.1.1.2
 vrf GREEN
 redistribute lisp route-map ADV-HOST-ROUTES
 vrf RED
 redistribute lisp route-map ADV-HOST-ROUTES
```

Because this is a multi-tenant environment, LISP IGP Assist is configured under each relevant VRF. The notification of host routes is achieved using a dedicated multicast group 239.1.1.n for each tenant. A dedicated LISP instance is also required for each tenant. The subnet 20.1.1.0/24 used for VRF Green is added into the local mapping database (actually the loopback address 10.10.10.10 in DC 1). Subnet 10.1.1.0/24, used for the VRF Red, is added to the same local mapping database. In this testbed, the notifications of EID (host route) are performed using the multicast group 239.1.1.2, as shown in Example 6-21.

Example 6-21 *DC 1 LISP Configuration Associated with Each VRF*

```
vrf context GREEN
 ip pim ssm range 232.0.0.0/8
 ip lisp itr-etr
 lisp instance-id 2
 ip lisp locator-vrf default
 lisp dynamic-eid LISP_EXTENDED_SUBNET
 database-mapping 20.1.1.0/24 10.10.10.10 priority 1 weight 50
 map-notify-group 239.1.1.2
 no route-export away-dyn-eid
!
vrf context RED
 ip pim ssm range 232.0.0.0/8
 ip lisp itr-etr
 lisp instance-id 1
 ip lisp locator-vrf default
 lisp dynamic-eid LISP_EXTENDED_SUBNET
 database-mapping 10.1.1.0/24 10.10.10.10 priority 1 weight 50
 map-notify-group 239.1.1.1
 no route-export away-dyn-eid
```

All concerned interface VLANs must be configured to use the LISP dynamic EID process, as shown in Example 6-22.

Example 6-22 *DC 1 LISP Mobile Subnets*

```
interface Vlan10
 no shutdown
 vrf member RED
 lisp mobility LISP_EXTENDED_SUBNET
 lisp extended-subnet-mode
 ip address 10.1.1.251/24
 ip ospf passive-interface
 ip pim sparse-mode
 hsrp 10
 preempt
 priority 110
 ip 10.1.1.254
!
```

```
interface Vlan20
 no shutdown
 vrf member GREEN
 lisp mobility LISP_EXTENDED_SUBNET
 lisp extended-subnet-mode
 ip address 20.1.1.251/24
 ip ospf passive-interface
 ip pim sparse-mode
 hsrp 20
 preempt
 priority 110
 ip 20.1.1.254
```

Example 6-22 shows the minimum required (highlighted in bold) with IGP Assist to detect and inject the host route dynamically toward the upward Layer 3 device—in this case, the firewall—offering more specific routes for remote endpoints.

LISP IGP Assist in DC 2

The same configuration just described for DC 1 is duplicated on each site with the changes shown in Example 6-23.

Example 6-23 *DC 1 LISP IGP Assist*

```
interface loopback20
  description LISP Loopback
  ip address 20.20.20.20/24
  ip router ospf 1 area 0.0.0.0
  ip pim sparse-mode
!
ip pim rp-address 10.10.10.10 group-list 224.0.0.0/4
ip pim ssm range 232.0.0.0/8
!
ip prefix-list HOST-ROUTES seq 5 permit 0.0.0.0/0 eq 32
  match interface Null0
route-map ADV-HOST-ROUTES deny 5
route-map ADV-HOST-ROUTES permit 10
  match ip address prefix-list HOST-ROUTES
!
vrf context GREEN
  ip pim ssm range 232.0.0.0/8
  ip lisp itr-etr
  lisp instance-id 2
  ip lisp locator-vrf default
  lisp dynamic-eid LISP_EXTENDED_SUBNET
```

```
      map-notify-group 239.1.1.2
      database-mapping 20.1.1.0/24 20.20.20.20 priority 1 weight 50
      no route-export away-dyn-eid
  !
vrf context RED
  ip pim ssm range 232.0.0.0/8
  ip lisp itr-etr
  lisp instance-id 1
  ip lisp locator-vrf default
  lisp dynamic-eid LISP_EXTENDED_SUBNET
      database-mapping 10.1.1.0/24 20.20.20.20 priority 1 weight 50
      map-notify-group 239.1.1.1
      no route-export away-dyn-eid
  !
interface Vlan10
  no shutdown
  vrf member RED
  lisp mobility LISP_EXTENDED_SUBNET
  lisp extended-subnet-mode
  ip address 10.1.1.252/24
  ip ospf passive-interface
  ip pim sparse-mode
  hsrp 10
    preempt
    priority 120
    ip 20.1.1.254
    ip 10.1.1.254
  !
interface Vlan20
  no shutdown
  vrf member GREEN
  lisp mobility LISP_EXTENDED_SUBNET
  lisp extended-subnet-mode
  ip address 20.1.1.252/24
  ip ospf passive-interface
  ip pim sparse-mode
  hsrp 20
    preempt
    priority 120
  router-id 1.1.1.2
  !
router ospf 100
  vrf GREEN
    redistribute lisp route-map ADV-HOST-ROUTES
  vrf RED
    redistribute lisp route-map ADV-HOST-ROUTES
no system default switchport shutdown
```

LISP IGP Assist Verification

It's important to check the dynamic EID database on each site to verify the LISP IGP Assist configuration. (In the following examples, the output has been reduced to make it readable.)

The EID reachability information is as follows for the VRFs:

- **R1:** 10.1.1.1

- **R2:** 10.1.1.2

- **G1:** 20.1.1.1

- **G2:** 20.1.1.2

Example 6-24 shows the dynamic EID summary for VRF Red in DC 1.

Example 6-24   *Data Center 1 (Left)*

```
LISP-IGP_DC 1# show lisp dynamic-eid summary vrf RED
LISP Dynamic EID Summary for VRF "RED"
LISP_EXTENDED_SUBNET      10.1.1.1    Vlan10
!
LISP-IGP_DC 1# show lisp dynamic-eid summary vrf GREEN
LISP Dynamic EID Summary for VRF ""GREEN"
LISP_EXTENDED_SUBNET      20.1.1.1    Vlan20
```

Example 6-25 shows out the dynamic EID summary for VRF Red in DC 2.

Example 6-25   *Data Center 2 (Right)*

```
LISP-IGP_DC 2# show lisp dynamic-eid summary vrf RED
LISP Dynamic EID Summary for VRF "RED"
LISP_EXTENDED_ SUBNET      10.1.1.2    Vlan10
!
LISP-IGP_DC 2# show lisp dynamic-eid summary vrf GREEN
LISP Dynamic EID Summary for VRF "GREEN"
LISP_EXTENDED_SUBNET      20.1.1.2    Vlan20
```

Next, it's important to check the routing table. (The following examples show just the relevant EIDs.) From VRF Red, R1 is 10.1.1.1/32, locally attached to VLAN 10. R2 (10.1.1.2), G1 (20.1.1.1), and G2 (20.1.1.2) are reachable via the next-hop router (100.1.1.254), as shown in Example 6-26. 100.1.1.254 is the local active firewall in from the topology shown in Figure 6-54.

Example 6-26 *Data Center 1 (Left)*

```
LISP-IGP_DC 1# show ip route vrf RED
IP Route Table for VRF "RED"
...
10.1.1.1/32, ubest/mbest: 1/0, attached
 *via 10.1.1.1, Vlan10, [240/0], 00:31:42, lisp, dyn-eid
10.1.1.2/32, ubest/mbest: 1/0
 *via 100.1.1.254, Vlan100, [110/1], 00:32:49, ospf-100, type-2
...
20.1.1.1/32, ubest/mbest: 1/0
 *via 100.1.1.254, Vlan100, [110/1], 00:31:40, ospf-100, type-2
20.1.1.2/32, ubest/mbest: 1/0
 *via 100.1.1.254, Vlan100, [110/1], 00:32:47, ospf-100, type-2
..//..
```

In Example 6-27, the firewall shows the two host routes from different paths. The local host 10.1.1.1 is reachable locally (100.1.1.10), and the remote host 10.1.1.2 from DC 2 is reachable through the Layer 3 DCI (30.1.1.2).

Example 6-27 *Firewall in DC 1*

```
FW-DC 1# show route
..//..
O E2 10.1.1.2 255.255.255.255 [110/1] via 30.1.1.2, 60:53:29, Inter-DMZ
<== via L3 DCI toward DC 2
O E2 10.1.1.1 255.255.255.255 [110/1] via 100.1.1.10, 60:52:56, RED
<== via local LISP FHR device
..//..
```

In the Example 6-28, the firewall shows the two host routes from different paths. The local host 10.1.1.2 is reachable locally (102.1.1.20), and the remote host 10.1.1.1 from DC 1 is reachable through the Layer 3 DCI (30.1.1.1).

Example 6-28 *Firewall in DC 2*

```
FW-DC 2# show route

..//..
O E2 10.1.1.1 255.255.255.255 [110/1] via 30.1.1.1, 2d12h, Inter-DMZ
<== via L3 DCI toward DC 1
O E2 10.1.1.2 255.255.255.255 [110/1] via 102.1.1.20, 2d12h, RED
<== via local LISP FHR device
..//..
```

From VRF Green, G1 (20.1.1.1) is locally attached to VLAN 20. R1 (10.1.1.1/32), R2 (10.1.1.2), and G2 (20.1.1.2) are reachable via the next-hop router (200.1.1.254), which is the local active firewall in the topology, as shown in Example 6-29.

Example 6-29   *Route Next Hop from VRF Green*

```
LISP-IGP_DC 1# show ip route vrf GREEN
IP Route Table for VRF "GREEN"
...
10.1.1.1/32, ubest/mbest: 1/0
    *via 200.1.1.254, Vlan200, [110/1], 01:04:23, ospf-100, type-2
10.1.1.2/32, ubest/mbest: 1/0
    *via 200.1.1.254, Vlan200, [110/1], 01:05:30, ospf-100, type-2
...
20.1.1.1/32, ubest/mbest: 1/0, attached
    *via 20.1.1.1, Vlan20, [240/0], 01:04:22, lisp, dyn-eid
20.1.1.2/32, ubest/mbest: 1/0
    *via 200.1.1.254, Vlan200, [110/1], 01:05:28, ospf-100, type-2
```

If you perform a live migration with R1 moving to DC 2 and R2 moving to DC 1, as soon as the migration is complete, the dynamic EID mapping database is updated accordingly in DC 1, as shown in Example 6-30.

Example 6-30   *Host Routes Learned from the Firewall in Data Center 1*

```
LISP-IGP_DC 1# show lisp dynamic-eid summary vrf red
LISP Dynamic EID Summary for VRF "RED"
LISP_EXTENDED_SUBNET       10.1.1.2     Vlan10

FW-DC 1# show route
../..
O E2 10.1.1.2 255.255.255.255 [110/1] via 100.1.1.10, 0:01:15, RED
<== Local routed traffic
O E2 10.1.1.1 255.255.255.255 [110/1] via 30.1.1.2, 0:01:19, Inter-DMZ
<== via L3 DCI toward DC 1
../..
```

After the migration, the dynamic EID mapping database is updated accordingly in DC 2, as shown in Example 6-31.

Example 6-31 *Host Routes Learned from the Firewall in Data Center 2*

```
LISP-IGP_DC 2# show lisp dynamic summary vrf red
LISP Dynamic EID Summary for VRF "RED"
LISP_EXTENDED_ SUBNET      10.1.1.1    Vlan10


FW-DC 2# sho route
../..//..
O E2     10.1.1.1 255.255.255.255 [110/1] via 30.1.1.1, 2d12h, Inter-DMZ
<== via L3 DCI toward DC 1
O E2     10.1.1.2 255.255.255.255 [110/1] via 102.1.1.20, 2d12h, RED
<== Local routed traffic
../..//..
```

Ping and Secure Shell (SSH) sessions inter-DC between the two VRFs continue to work, with a slight delay of few seconds during the migration.

LISP IGP Assist Full Configuration

As previously mentioned, the LISP IGP Assist setup just discussed is the minimum configuration required to notify the EID dynamically using the multicast protocol across the Layer 2 DCI links and redistribute the host route into the IGP routing table. As long as the multicast group can reach the remote LISP mapping database using the Layer 2 DCI extension, the solution works as expected.

It is optionally possible, and recommended, to add an alternative mechanism to notify the EID through a routing protocol established with a LISP map server in case the primary mechanism fails. If, for any reason, the multicast transport or Layer 2 extension stops working, the map server notifies the remote mapping database about the new EID using the routing protocol. Actually, this is the method used for IGP Assist in ASM (Across Subnets Mode without any Layer 2 extension) when no extended VLAN exists across data centers to carry the multicast for each VRF.

The LISP mapping database (M-DB) is responsible for maintaining the location of the EID in real time, and it comprises two subfunctions: map resolver (MR) and map server (MS).

The map resolver is responsible for receiving map requests from remote ITRs to retrieve the mapping between an EID and its current location. This specific scenario does not have any inbound path optimization or ITR, ETR, or LISP encapsulation. Hence, only the map server function is relevant for this solution as a backup mechanism to trigger the endpoint notifications. In the context of IGP Assist, the map server system is responsible for exchanging EID mapping between all other LISP devices. The M-DB can cohabit on the same device as the LISP FHR, and multiple mapping databases can be distributed over dedicated hosts. For this scenario, the function of the MS runs on the same switch device.

Example 6-32 shows the configuration for the LISP map server on each LISP IGP router.

Example 6-32 *LISP Map Server Configuration in DC 1*

```
ip lisp itr-etr
ip lisp map-server
lisp site DATA_CENTER
  eid-prefix 10.1.0.0/16 instance-id 1 accept-more-specifics
  eid-prefix 20.1.0.0/16 instance-id 2 accept-more-specifics
  authentication-key 3 9125d59c18a9b015
ip lisp etr map-server 10.10.10.10 key 3 9125d59c18a9b015
ip lisp etr map-server 20.20.20.20 key 3 9125d59c18a9b015
```

Example 6-33 shows the configuration for the LISP map server on each LISP IGP router.

Example 6-33 *LISP Map Server Configuration in DC 2*

```
ip lisp itr-etr
ip lisp map-server
lisp site DATA_CENTER
  eid-prefix 10.1.0.0/16 instance-id 1 accept-more-specifics
  eid-prefix 20.1.0.0/16 instance-id 2 accept-more-specifics
  authentication-key 3 9125d59c18a9b015
ip lisp etr map-server 10.10.10.10 key 3 9125d59c18a9b015
ip lisp etr map-server 20.20.20.20 key 3 9125d59c18a9b015
```

Summary

This chapter describes different use cases for extending Layer 2 and Layer 3 networks across multiple sites and using LISP IP Mobility to dynamically improve the ingress data workflow. Different solutions for extending Layer 2 are described in this chapter, from legacy DCI solutions to modern overlay networks. The data center network is evolving drastically into modern network fabrics, either using VXLAN transport with a BGP EVPN as a standalone control plane or using a sophisticated SDN controller such as Cisco ACI. LISP IP Mobility is detailed in this chapter in conjunction with traditional data center networks. Chapter 7 focuses on LISP IP Mobility deployment with modern data center network fabrics.

References

The following references provide more details on the topics discussed in this chapter:

RFC6830, "LISP," https://tools.ietf.org/html/rfc6830

RFC 8214, "Virtual Private Wire Service Support in Ethernet VPN" https://tools.ietf.org/html/rfc8214

Cisco, "LISP Deep Dive Resources…," http://lisp.cisco.com/lisp_tech.html#CG

Cisco, "LISP Hardware and Software Support," http://lisp.cisco.com/lisp_hwsw.html#HW

Cisco, "LISP IGP Assist," http://lisp.cisco.com/docs/LISP_IGP_ASSIST_WHITEPAPER.pdf

Cisco, "LISP Frequently Asked Questions," http://lisp.cisco.com/lisp_faq.html

Cisco, "LISP NX-OS Configuration Guide," https://www.cisco.com/c/en/us/td/docs/switches/datacenter/nexus7000/sw/lisp/config/cisco_nexus7000_lisp_config_guide_8x.html

Cisco, "LISP IOS XE Configuration Guide," https://www.cisco.com/c/en/us/td/docs/ios-xml/ios/iproute_lisp/configuration/xe-16/irl-xe-16-book/irl-lisp-esm-multihop-mobility.html

Chapter 7

LISP IP Mobility in Modern Data Center Fabrics

With modern fabrics such as integrated Virtual Extensible LAN (VXLAN), Ethernet Virtual Private Network (EVPN), or Application Centric Infrastructure (ACI), Locator/ID Separation Protocol (LISP) Internet Protocol (IP) Mobility is a solution that offers ingress path optimization in an easy way: LISP IP Mobility dynamically handles multi-tenant connectivity toward the physical site where an active destination endpoint is located. Modern fabrics natively offer the function of dynamically advertising the host route to the external Layer 3 network, eliminating the requirement to activate the role of the LISP first-hop router inside the data center network.

This chapter is organized into two main sections that describe how to integrate LISP IP Mobility with modern fabrics. This chapter demonstrates how LISP IP Mobility can help solve route optimization problems that result from workload mobility across data center fabrics. It covers the following topics:

- LISP IP Mobility integration with a VXLAN EVPN Multi-Site infrastructure
- LISP IP Mobility integration with ACI Multi-Pod infrastructure

LISP IP Mobility Deployment with Modern Fabrics

As mentioned in Chapter 6, "LISP IP Mobility in Traditional Data Center Network," traditionally LISP IP Mobility Multihop in a LISP data center combines two major LISP components:

- The LISP first-hop router (FHR), which is deployed on the default gateway used for mobile subnets, is responsible for detecting the presence of the LISP dynamic endpoint identifiers (EIDs):
  - From the control plane point of view, the LISP FHR signaling notifies the discovered existence of IP endpoints toward its local LISP site gateways.

- From a data plane point of view, as the default gateway, the LISP FHR routes the data packet to and from the upstream Layer 3 device.

- The LISP router or LISP site gateway deployed on the WAN edge router supports the functions of the LISP tunnel router (xTR) as well as the Layer 3 forwarding functions:

  - From a control plane point of view, the LISP site gateway registers the discovered roaming endpoint identifiers (EIDs) just previously advertised by the LISP FHR with the LISP mapping database.

  - From a data plane point of view, as an ingress tunnel router (ITR), the LISP router performs LISP encapsulation of the user data packet inside a LISP header with one of its routing locators (RLOCs) as the IP source address toward a remote RLOC as the IP destination inside the LISP header. As an egress tunnel router (ETR), it also performs LISP de-encapsulation of the traffic being received from the remote LISP router.

The LISP mapping database is the authoritative repository that comprises the mobile subnets concerned with the roaming EID and the dynamic EID with their respective locations, known as RLOCs, identifying the LISP site gateway where the concerned dynamic EID is currently active. The LISP mapping database is constantly updated by the LISP site gateways, from which it serves to reply to all the map requests from the remote LISP routers with the location of interest.

The following sections describe the integration of VXLAN EVPN and ACI fabrics with the function of LISP site gateway leveraged for ingress path optimization.

Unlike traditional data centers, based on classical Ethernet, VXLAN EVPN and ACI fabrics, natively offer three important network concepts:

- **Layer 3 anycast gateway:** The function of the default gateway, distributed across all leaf nodes, which stands as the first-hop router for the endpoints

- **Multi-tenancy:** The network separation of multiple tenants inside the fabric that remains separated from the data center throughout the external routed network

- **Endpoint identifier discovery:** The dynamic detection of endpoints and advertisement of their respective host routes into the external Layer 3 domain

Consequently, the role of the LISP first-hop router is simply replaced by the discovery and distribution signaling embedded within the fabric via the control plane.

VXLAN EVPN Multi-Site with LISP IP Mobility

As shown in Figure 7-1, VXLAN EVPN Multi-Site offers a large combination of roles from the border leaf devices. A first important function needed from any VXLAN EVPN domain consists of providing Layer 3 connectivity to the external network domain and advertising public prefix networks from the fabric to the outside Layer 3 domain.

This is represented at the bottom side of the fabric from the border leaf (BL) nodes. A second function specific to EVPN Multi-Site is the role of the border gateway (BGW) in establishing the inter-site overlay networks across the distant data centers, also known as the site-external network. These overlay networks rely on a single VXLAN EVPN domain interconnecting each location using the border gateway nodes from each local VXLAN EVPN fabric domain. The objective is to extend and maintain the segmentation of the Layer 2 and Layer 3 networks from site to site, using a hierarchical integrated infrastructure.

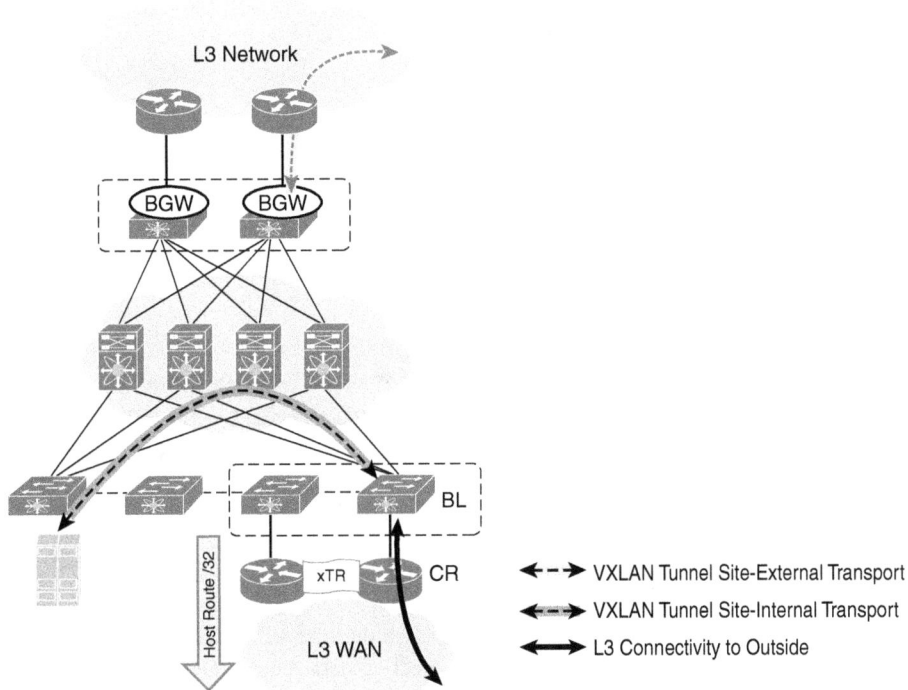

Figure 7-1 *Border Leaf and Border Gateway Roles from Separate Physical Nodes*

In Figure 7-1 the roles of border leaf nodes and border gateways are played by separate physical devices and separate network infrastructures. One Layer 3 infrastructure is dedicated for multi-site (east–west traffic), while the Layer 3 WAN network is used for outside connectivity only (northbound traffic). For LISP IP Mobility purposes, the LISP site gateway (xTR) is enabled on the core router (CR) facing the BL node.

VXLAN EVPN architecture with Multi-Site extension is very flexible as it doesn't impose a fixed configuration. As shown in Figure 7-2, the same network devices combine both functions: the role of BL nodes and the role of Multi-Site BGW.

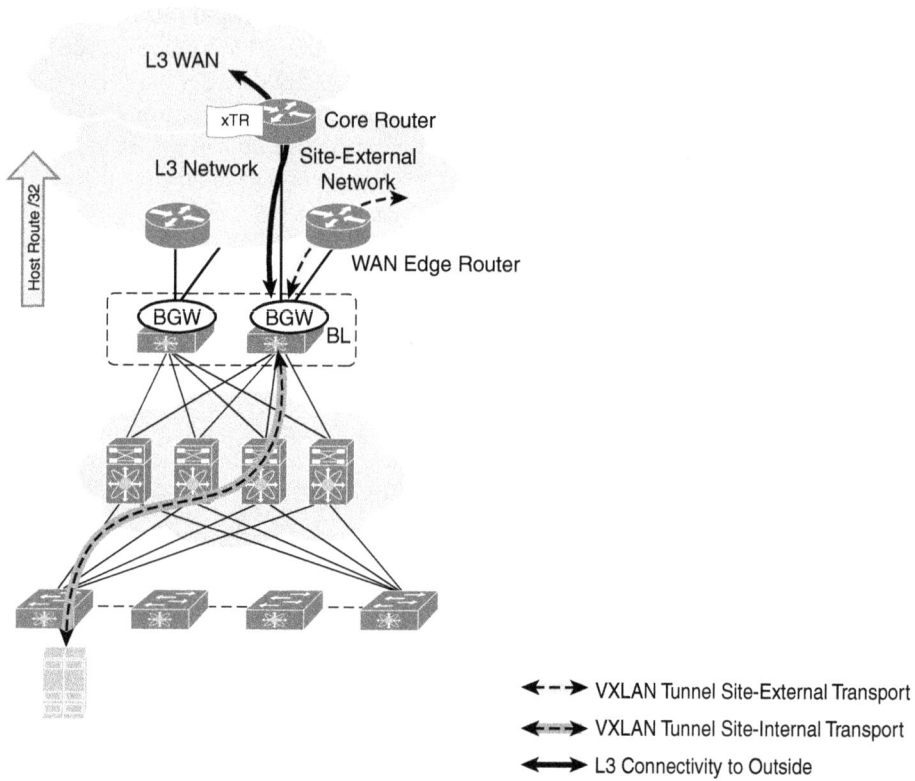

Figure 7-2　*Border Leaf and Border Gateways Roles from the Same Physical Nodes*

These two separate network infrastructures are available for connections with the external WAN network (for north–south traffic flow) and for site-external network connections (for east–west traffic flow). This is often the case when dedicated high-speed connections between sites are used for interconnecting data centers (DCI). In such cases, the BGW and BL roles are tightly coupled in the same border nodes to use a set of links to connect to the inter-site network routers (which could also be back-to-back fiber connections between the two sites) and to use another separate set of links to connect to the core routers for WAN access.

As shown in Figure 7-3, the same network infrastructure can be used for WAN access and for inter-site network connectivity. In this case, the BGW/BL nodes connect to the same pair of external routers for both types of communications.

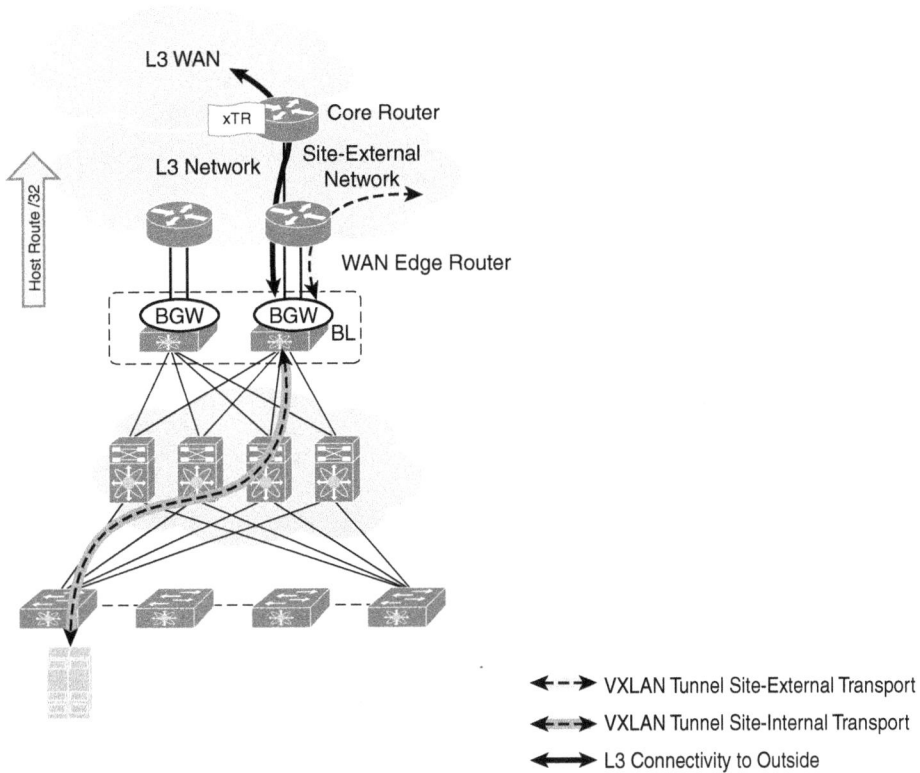

Figure 7-3 *Border Leaf and Border Gateways Roles from the Same Physical Nodes (Subcase 1)*

Two subcases can be leveraged. First of all, from the same BGW/BL nodes, you can use VRF Lite for segmented Layer 3 connectivity to the WAN edge routers, which implies the use of subinterfaces for all the connected VRF instance(s). In addition, from the same nodes connecting to the same WAN edge routers, it is possible to use separate links for site-external transport to create the VXLAN EVPN Multi-Site infrastructure. This is often done when the same WAN/MAN offering external network connections is leveraged to multiple interconnected data centers.

With the second subcase, illustrated in Figure 7-4, you can use VXLAN EVPN to connect to the WAN edge routers with "shared router" as a generic role; this is often referenced as a border provider edge (BorderPE) router for bounding the site-internal Layer 3 segments with the MPLS IP VPN network. In this case, the same set of physical links can be leveraged for both WAN connectivity (that is, for northbound communication) and for site-external network connection (that is, for east–west communication), because it is always VXLAN encapsulated traffic. The shared border nodes operate as in a traditional virtual tunnel endpoint (VTEP); however, the tunnel endpoint function is performed outside the VXLAN fabric, and thus it is conventionally called *site-external VTEP*. The site-internal VXLAN segment terminates at the BGW nodes from which a new VXLAN tunnel is either stitched to the upstream site-external VTEP (shared router) or the BGW initiates a new VXLAN tunnel toward the remote BGWs. The BGWs receive the external routes via EVPN from the site-external VTEP and injects them inside the local VXLAN EVPN fabric. All the site-internal VTEPs see the BGWs as the next hop toward the external destinations.

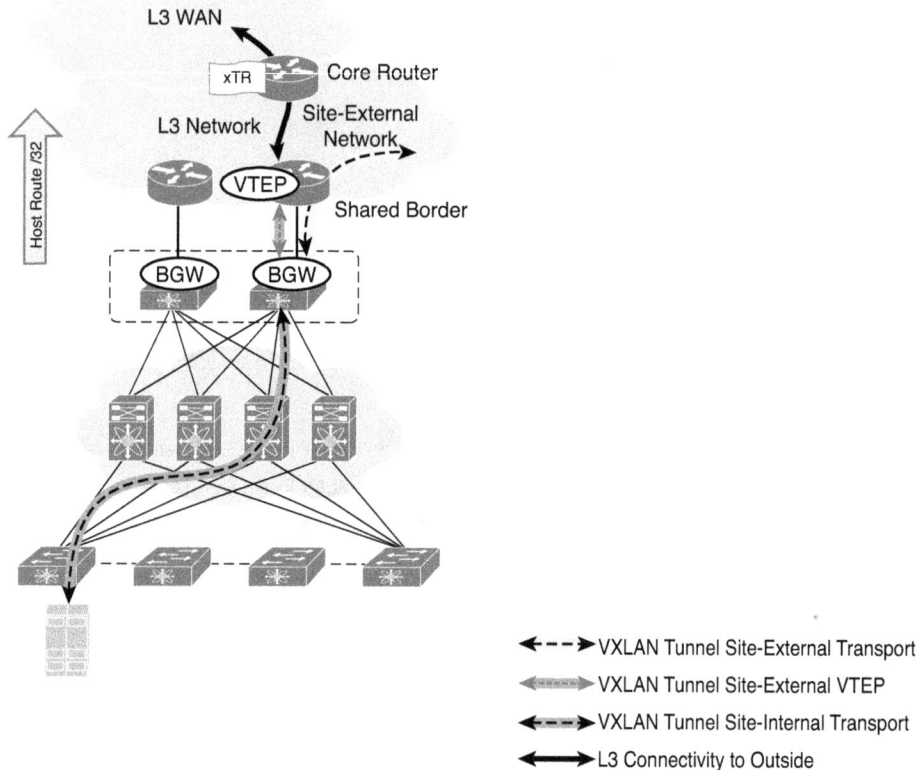

Figure 7-4 *Border Leaf and Border Gateway Roles from the Same Physical Nodes (Subcase 2)*

Another point about the boundary between the functions of LISP IP Mobility and the VXLAN EVPN fabric is that, technically, the LISP site gateway (SG) ingress/egress tunnel router (xTR) role could be initiated directly from the VXLAN fabric border nodes (that is, border leaf or border spine devices) using a Nexus 7000 series device. This option is not discussed in this chapter. Indeed, for security reasons, it is a best practice to insert network security services, such as firewalls, between the external WAN and the VXLAN EVPN fabric to inspect and secure the ingress traffic coming from outside. Having both functions running from the same physical device presents crucial challenges related to inserting a network service between the encapsulated LISP workflow and the VXLAN EVPN fabric.

To ease the understanding of the packet flow, this section uses separate physical devices for the functions of the LISP site gateway and the VXLAN EVPN border node, as depicted in Figure 7-4.

In a legacy data center network, the LISP first-hop router offers the LISP Multihop function, and it is also the default gateway of the roaming EID; this functionality is commonly enabled from the traditional aggregation layer. In the context of VXLAN EVPN, the function of LISP first-hop router is replaced by the function of host routes that the VXLAN EVPN border leaf node injects toward the Layer 3 domain, where the local LISP site gateways reside. The centralized routing block that supports default gateways is replaced by the distributed function of the Layer 3 anycast gateway. Multiple Layer 3 hops can exist between the VXLAN EVPN Multi-Site BGW and the LISP site gateway. Indeed, as just mentioned, non-LISP-capable devices such as firewalls and load balancers can be inserted seamlessly between the data center fabric and the WAN edge layer of the enterprise or the service provider's data center.

Figure 7-5 shows a physical separation between the VXLAN EVPN fabric and the LISP site gateways (xTRs), using the EVPN Multi-Site BGW. In this example, the EVPN Multi-Site BGW is also responsible for advertising the host route to the upstream Layer 3 router (LISP xTR in this case), using the subinterfaces connecting the VRF Lite networks.

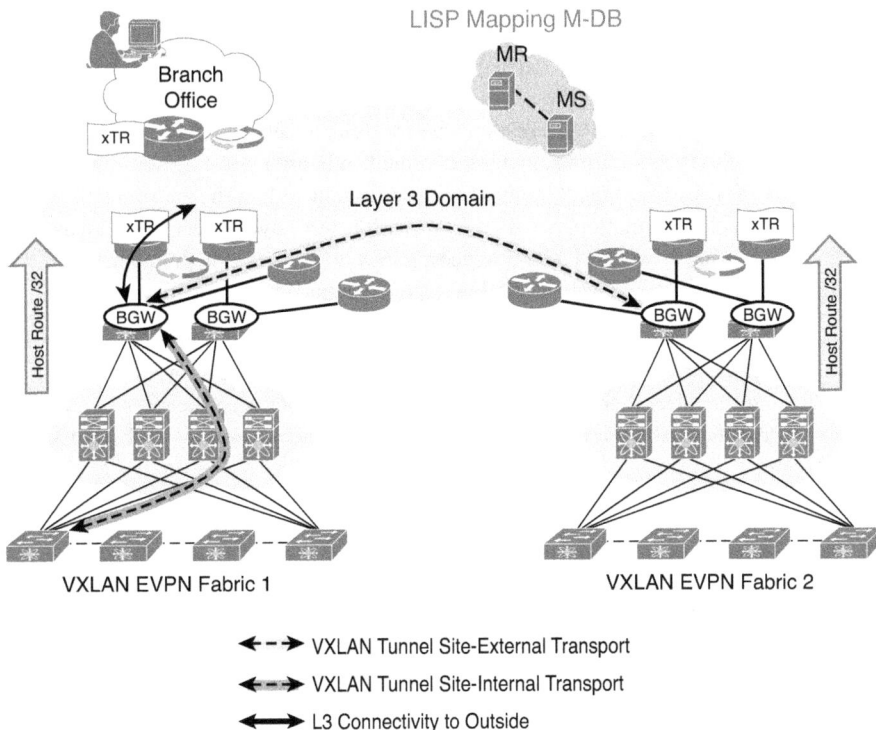

Figure 7-5 *VXLAN EVPN Multi-Site with LISP Mobility*

The following points summarize the roles and functions of the LISP infrastructure and the VXLAN EVPN fabrics:

- **LISP site gateways (xTRs):** From a control plane point of view, an xTR is responsible for notifying a LISP mapping database for new discovered EIDs. This dynamic EID registration is done with the LISP map server. From a data plane point of view, the xTR offers the function of an ITR, encapsulating the ingress traffic coming from its internal site interface and destined to a remote LISP router. It also provides the LISP ETR function for de-encapsulating the inbound traffic coming from the remote LISP router, also known as egress traffic, and destined to an endpoint inside the data center network, typically the dynamic EID. It is commonly called a LISP xTR because the same LISP site gateway can provide either the ingress or egress tunnel routing functions, either in the LISP site or in the LISP branch site.

- **LISP mapping database:** The mapping database provides the LISP map server (MS) function, in which the LISP site gateways from each site register their local EID prefixes. The MS stores the registered EID prefixes in a mapping database, where they are associated to RLOCs. The LISP mapping database also includes the LISP map resolver (MR) function, which resolves EID-to-RLOC mappings as soon as it receives a LISP map request query from a LISP ITR.

- **VXLAN MP BGP EVPN fabric:** The VXLAN data plane is responsible for encapsulating traditional Layer 2 frames from external connectivity into a VXLAN IP UDP header. The VXLAN overlay is carried from an ingress VTEP and sent toward an egress VTEP, also known as the next hop, to reach the destination endpoint. The control plane MP-BGP EVPN is responsible for dynamically discovering the endpoints as well as their locations, including immediately after a live move. It is also responsible for distributing all the network prefixes, including the endpoint MAC and IP-reachable information, across the fabric. It offers Layer 3 services such as intra-VRF routing as well as Layer 3 anycast gateway services distributed across all VXLAN edge devices, as well as VRF segmentation inside and outside the fabric.

- **VXLAN EVPN border gateway (BGW):** This is the gateway responsible for establishing the VXLAN EVPN interconnections between the VXLAN EVPN sites by stitching the Layer 2 and Layer 3 VXLAN segments between the site-internal network and the site-external network. It is the key element used by VXLAN EVPN Multi-Site.

VXLAN EVPN: Endpoint Discovery and Notification

With VXLAN EVPN fabrics, one of the key functions of the control plane is to detect and distribute endpoints' reachability information (IP and MAC address information) across the whole VXLAN EVPN fabric. Prefix networks, including host routes, are by default advertised outside the VXLAN EVPN fabric, as illustrated in Figure 7-6.

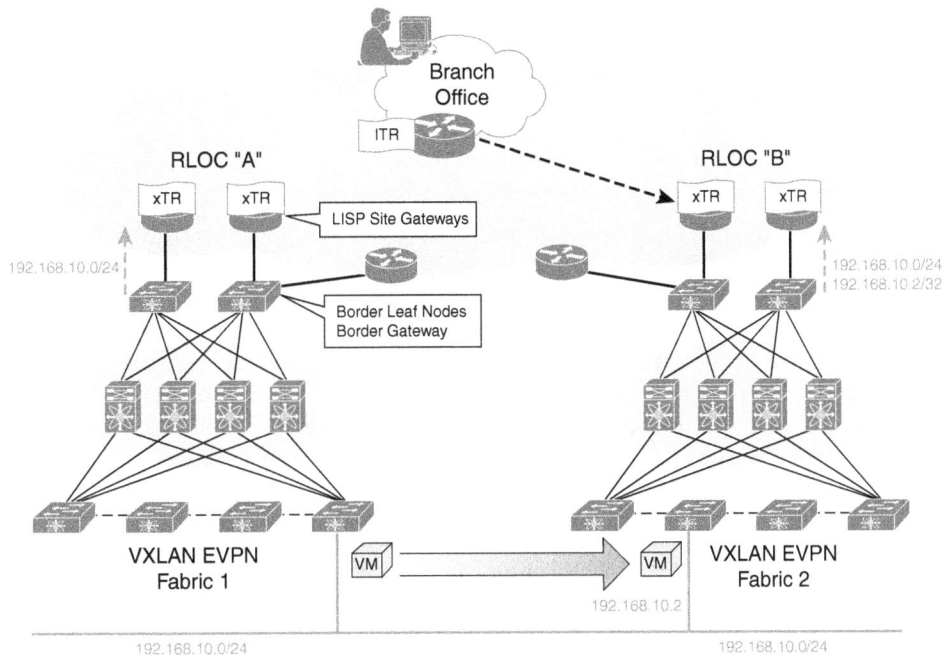

Figure 7-6 *Ingress Path Optimization with LISP Mobility*

When the local leaf node—typically the first-hop router—learns the MAC address and IP address of a new endpoint from its host mobility manager (HMM) process, it records it into its local host table and signals this new host reachability information with its location (next hop) to the rest of the fabric network by using the MP-BGP EVPN control plane. This notification includes a unique sequence number. The EVPN notification for the new location of the roamer increments the value for the sequence number attribute sent across the whole VXLAN EVPN fabric. The EVPN notification also hits the original leaf node from which the host moved, immediately withdrawing that particular host route from its local host table after checking. In the context of VXLAN EVPN Multi-Site, if a roaming endpoint lands in the new site, as illustrated in Figure 7-6, its reachability information (IP address and MAC address) is discovered and distributed across the fabric using BGP EVPN signaling, providing a dynamic update of all endpoints across the end-to-end multi-site VXLAN EVPN fabrics.

VXLAN EVPN: Host Route Advertisement

It is crucial to ensure optimal east–west communication between endpoints, whether they are virtual machines (VMs) or bare-metal nodes. As a result, most specific IP routes and host routes are exchanged across the VXLAN EVPN fabric between all edge devices (VTEPs) as well as the route reflectors (RRs). IP routes and host routes can also be exchanged across independent VXLAN EVPN fabrics (for optimal east–west traffic flow). VM mobility is supported using the same process of detecting new endpoint attachment as soon as a new MAC address/IP address is seen directly connected to the local switch. Its IP address and MAC address are provided to the rest of the fabric. This process of VM mobility discovery and notification is detailed step by step in the next section.

VXLAN EVPN: Configuration for Host Route Advertisement

To offer external connectivity for each particular tenant network of choice, the VXLAN BGP EVPN fabric must be extended to the external routed network by using a per-VRF IP routing transport. The approach used for extending the Layer 3 segmented network is traditionally referred to as *VRF Lite hand-off*. When configured with the Layer 3 subinterface associated with an individual VRF Lite connection toward the external upstream router, the border leaf node advertises the subnets and host routes associated with the concerned tenant (for northbound optimal traffic flow). By default, a VXLAN BGP EVPN fabric always advertises all known routes, including host routes.

For some particular scenarios, it might be desirable to not advertise some specific routes, including host routes, to the external network. To this end, a particular route filtering approach can be leveraged. Route filtering is beyond the scope of this book; see the "Cisco Programmable Fabric with VXLAN BGP EVPN Configuration Guide" for further details.

Figure 7-7 illustrates the physical topology of the fabric in DC 1 connected to the external network (core router). VRF Lite hand-offs occur at the border leaf nodes (BGW1 and BGW2), to be bound with the appropriate external segmentations using subinterfaces for north–south (N–S) traffic flow.

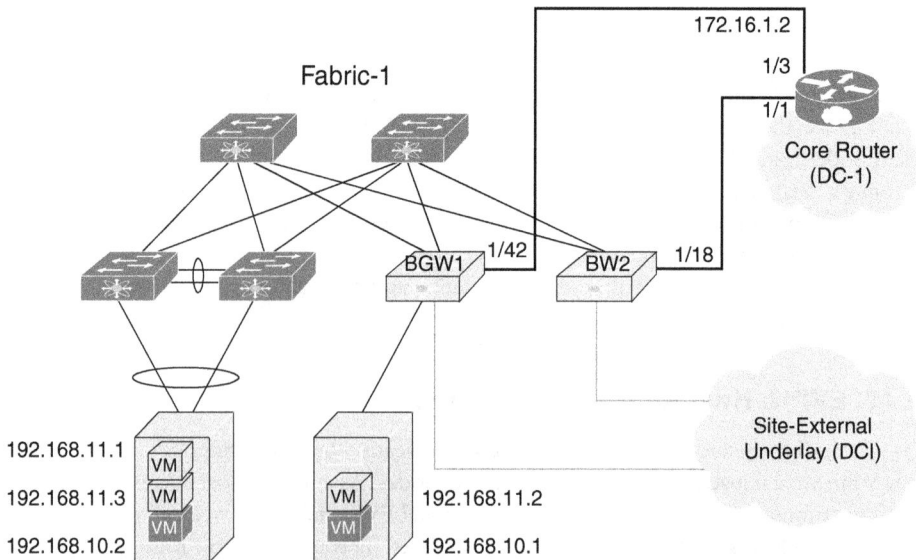

Figure 7-7   *VRF Lite Deployment for Fabric 1*

Example 7-1 details the VRF context configuration for Tenant-1.

Example 7-1 *BGW1: VRF Tenant-1 Configuration with BGP*

```
vrf context tenant-1
  vni 50000
  rd auto
  address-family ipv4 unicast
    route-target both auto
    route-target both auto evpn
  ip route 0.0.0.0/0 172.16.1.2
  address-family ipv6 unicast
    route-target both auto
    route-target both auto evpn
router bgp 65511
  vrf tenant-1
    address-family ipv4 unicast
      advertise l2vpn evpn
      redistribute direct route-map fabric-rmap-redist-subnet
```
(!) notice the direct route-map allows distribution for routes and host routes
learned via BGP (from other leaf nodes). To allow distribution of host route
locally connected to the same border leaf node connecting to the external routed
network, a route-map with redistribution of endpoints learned from hmm is required
```
      redistribute hmm route-map extcon-rmap-filter-allow-host
      maximum-paths ibgp 2
      network 0.0.0.0/0
    address-family ipv6 unicast
      advertise l2vpn evpn
      redistribute direct route-map fabric-rmap-redist-subnet
      redistribute hmm route-map extcon-rmap-filter-allow-host
      maximum-paths ibgp 2
    neighbor 172.16.1.2
      remote-as 65500
      address-family ipv4 unicast
        send-community both
        route-map extcon-rmap-filter-allow-host out
interface Ethernet1/42.2
```
(!) configuration of the sub-interface
```
  encapsulation dot1q 2
  vrf member tenant-1
  ip address 172.16.1.1/30
  no shutdown
```

If you look at the upstream core router, you can see the host route advertised from the
border leaf node (BGW1 in Example 7-2).

Example 7-2   *Host Routes Learned by the External Core Router*

```
Core-router-1# show ip route vrf tenant-1
IP Route Table for VRF "Tenant-1"
'*' denotes best ucast next-hop
'**' denotes best mcast next-hop
'[x/y]' denotes [preference/metric]

0.0.0.0/0, ubest/mbest: 1/0
    *via Null0, [1/0], 11w6d, static
21.1.1.0/30, ubest/mbest: 1/0, attached
    *via 21.1.1.2, Eth1/48.1, [0/0], 11w6d, direct
21.1.1.2/32, ubest/mbest: 1/0, attached
    *via 21.1.1.2, Eth1/48.1, [0/0], 11w6d, local
101.101.101.101/32, ubest/mbest: 2/0, attached
    *via 101.101.101.101, Lo100, [0/0], 11w6d, local
    *via 101.101.101.101, Lo100, [0/0], 11w6d, direct
172.16.1.0/30, ubest/mbest: 1/0, attached
    *via 172.16.1.2, Eth1/3.2, [0/0], 3w3d, direct
172.16.1.2/32, ubest/mbest: 1/0, attached
    *via 172.16.1.2, Eth1/3.2, [0/0], 3w3d, local
192.168.10.0/24, ubest/mbest: 1/0
    *via 172.16.1.1, [20/0], 1w2d, bgp-65500, external, tag 65511
192.168.10.1/32, ubest/mbest: 1/0
    *via 172.16.1.1, [20/0], 02:42:08, bgp-65500, external, tag 65511
192.168.10.2/32, ubest/mbest: 1/0
    *via 172.16.1.1, [20/0], 00:11:57, bgp-65500, external, tag 65511
192.168.11.0/24, ubest/mbest: 1/0
    *via 172.16.1.1, [20/0], 1w2d, bgp-65500, external, tag 65511
192.168.11.1/32, ubest/mbest: 1/0
    *via 172.16.1.1, [20/0], 1w2d, bgp-65500, external, tag 65511
192.168.11.2/32, ubest/mbest: 1/0
    *via 172.16.1.1, [20/0], 00:13:32, bgp-65500, external, tag 65511
192.168.11.3/32, ubest/mbest: 1/0
    *via 172.16.1.1, [20/0], 6d20h, bgp-65500, external, tag 65511
Core-router-1#
```

An easy way to configure the advertisement of routes, including the host route, is to use the Data Center Network Manager (DCNM) appliance, version 11.1 or later. Figure 7-8 shows a screen capture of the configuration of the VRF for Tenant-1.

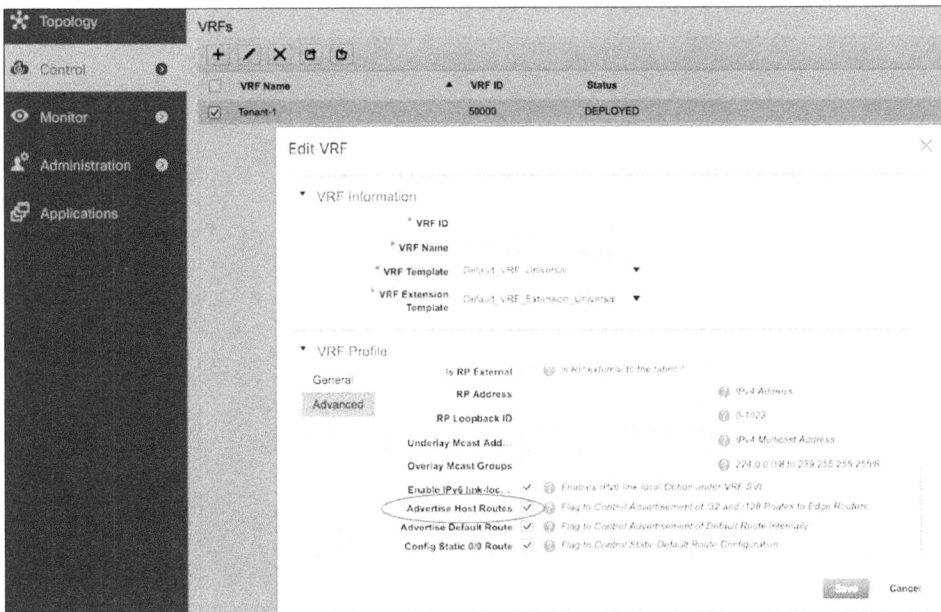

Figure 7-8 *Using the DCNM to Advertise Host Route Configuration*

VXLAN EVPN and Layer 3 Connectivity to the External Network

This section reviews the support for host mobility across multiple VXLAN EVPN fabrics. VXLAN EVPN Multi-Site is the recommended solution for interconnecting VXLAN Ethernet VPN (EVPN) fabrics, as elaborated in Chapter 6. In Figure 7-9, there are two VXLAN EVPN fabrics, named Fabric 1 and Fabric 2. Each VXLAN EVPN fabric is built with the recommended parameters with an Interior Gateway Protocol (IGP) for the underlay network and Interior Border Gateway Protocol (iBGP) for the overlay network. Each fabric runs its own autonomous system, and an overlay exterior BGP (eBGP) session is established between the two sites. A virtual machine 192.168.10.2 is going to move from Fabric 1 to Fabric 2.

Assume that before its migration, the roamer 192.168.10.2, which belongs to VLAN Green, is attached to Leaf 4 (L4) in Fabric 1. The virtual machine 192.168.10.2 belongs to the same Layer 2 segment Green. To capture only the main values for the purpose of this chapter, Figure 7-9 depicts the routing tables from different angles before the machine migrates.

In a production network, at least two BGWs per site must be deployed for resiliency and load-sharing purposes. At the time of writing this book, up to six anycast BGWs per site are supported (up to two BGWs per site when configured in virtual port channel [vPC] BGW mode).

This example assumes that the virtual machine VM2 (endpoint) was previously discovered, and its Layer 2 and 3 reachability information was announced across both sites.

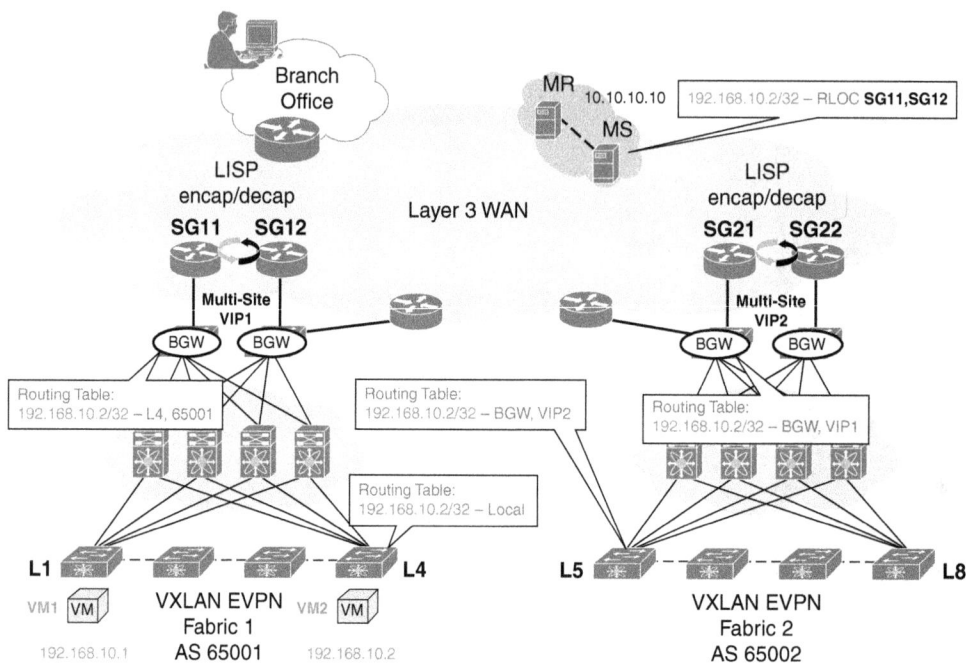

Figure 7-9 *VXLAN EVPN Multi-Site with LISP Mobility*

At this stage, Leaf 4 (L4) discovered the VM2 192.168.10.2 from its HMM process. The VXLAN EVPN BGWs are fully integrated in the VXLAN EVPN fabric. However, they can offer two main functions, as shown in Figure 7-9: The BGW nodes establish a VXLAN EVPN Multi-Site tunnel with the remote site to extend the Layer 2 and Layer 3 traffic over a unique VXLAN EVPN transport, which is its main role. Nonetheless, as mentioned earlier, if required, the BGW nodes can also support the role of border leaf node, providing Layer 3 connectivity to outside each data center, using a separate interface. The WAN edge routers that connect each data center to the Layer 3 WAN offer the function of LISP site gateways (named SG*xx* in Figure 7-9).

All leaf nodes within EVPN Fabric 1, including the BGW devices, know that the next hop to reach VM2 is the VTEP from L4.

From the leaf nodes in Fabric 2, the next hop to reach VM2 is the Multi-Site VIP2 deployed on all the local BGWs in Site 2. From the BGW devices in Fabric 2, the next hop to communicate with VM2 is the Multi-Site VIP1 in Fabric 1.

Figure 7-10 shows the process for maintaining communication between the virtual machines in a host mobility scenario. Let's look next at the distribution of the VXLAN EVPN signaling. For operational purposes, the virtual machine VM2 moves from Leaf 4 in Fabric 1 to Leaf 5 in Fabric 2, as depicted in Figure 7-10.

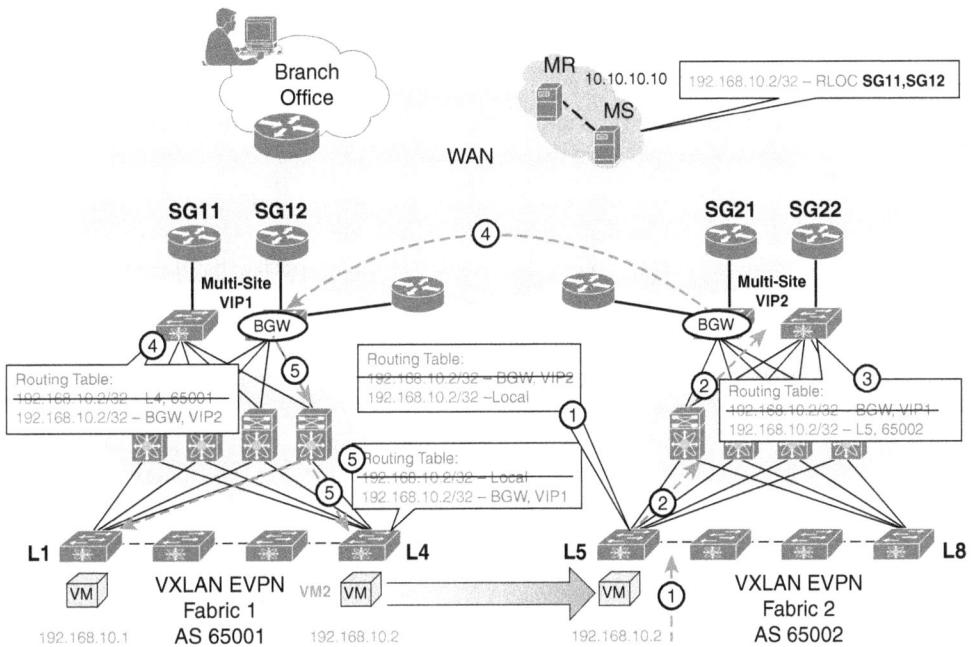

Figure 7-10   *VXLAN EVPN Multi-Site—EVPN Signaling*

The process shown in Figure 7-10 involves the following steps:

Step 1.   After the migration process is complete, VM2 is rediscovered in the new location. Consider these two different mechanisms to discover the endpoint reachability information:

- From the control plane with an ARP message, which triggers the learning process and records the host IP address

- From the data plane with data packets, which triggers the learning process and records the host MAC address

Note   VMware ESXi leverages Reverse Address Resolution Protocol (RARP). RARP frames do not contain any local host IP information in the payload, so they are used only to learn Layer 2 endpoint information and not the IP addresses. For other hypervisors, such as Microsoft Hyper-V or Citrix Xen, a Gratuitous Address Resolution Protocol (GARP) request is sent instead; it includes the source IP address of the sender in the payload. As a result, the procedure to learn the host IP address is slightly different with RARP messages.

Step 2.   Leaf 5 sends an MP-BGP EVPN **route-type-2** update in Fabric 2 with VM2's reachability information. When doing so, it increases the sequence number associated with this specific entry, specifying as the next hop to reach the roamer VM2 the VTEP IP address of Leaf 5. Because VM2 was already known in Fabric 2, Leaf 5 withdraws the previous known next hop of that roamer VM2 and sends an MP-BGP EVPN update. This procedure helps ensure that this information can be cleared from the forwarding tables of all the devices in Fabric 2.

Step 3.   The receiving devices update their forwarding tables with the new reachability information, including the two local BGW devices in Fabric 2.

Step 4.   The VM2 host route is distributed toward the original Fabric 1 across the eBGP session established between the two sites. As a result, the two BGW nodes in Fabric 1 update their routing tables to specify that the next hop for VM2 is the remote BGW devices in Site 2, identified as Multi-Site VIP2.

Step 5.   A BGP EVPN notification with the VM2 reachability information (MAC and IP addresses) is distributed across all the leaf nodes in Fabric 1 where the corresponding VRF is created, and the next hop to reach VM2 is Multi-Site VIP1 in Fabric 1. All leaf nodes update their respective local host tables. Leaf 4 updates its host table after checking that VM2 is no longer locally attached to prevent any false positive learning in case of duplicate address.

Now that we have had a high-level overview of the BGP EVPN discovery and distribution processes that occur inside and between VXLAN EVPN fabric, let's look at the LISP site gateway signaling (see Figure 7-11). It is assumed that prior to the migration of VM2, the LISP map server (MS) knows VM2 from the LISP map registry control plane message sent previously by SG11 and SG12 as the current locations (RLOCs).

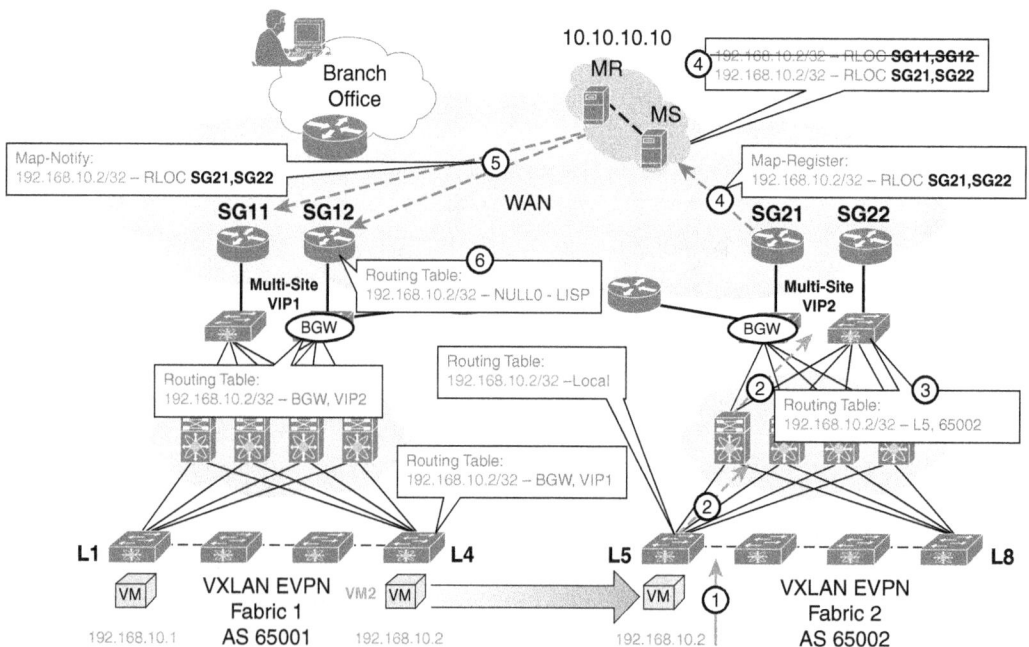

Figure 7-11   *VXLAM EVPN Multi-Site with LISP Mobility—LISP Signaling*

Steps 1 and 2 of the LISP signaling process are the same as the VXLAN EVPN notification steps discussed in relation to Figure 7-10. The border leaf is responsible for triggering the process to update the LISP mapping database, as detailed in the following steps:

Step 3. The BGWs receive the EVPN notification for VM2 and update their routing tables accordingly. Each EVPN border gateway advertises the host route toward its respective Layer 3 next hop, which is the two LISP site gateways (SG21 and SG22) for Fabric 2.

Step 4. Each local LISP site gateway registers the /32 prefix for VM2 with the LISP map server by sending a LISP map registry control plane message with SG21 and SG22 as the new locations (RLOCs) for VM2.

Step 5. The map server, in its turn, updates the last LISP site gateways belonging to the original data centers where the dynamic EID VM2 was initially active. This informs the last LISP routers about the new RLOC mapping for the particular EID, which now is located in Site 2 and identified by RLOCs SG21 and SG22.

Step 6. This map notification triggers, in parallel, a routing table update with a null route installed for the dynamic EID VM2 (/32). As described in Chapter 6, the purpose of configuring a static host route to Null0 is to make sure that traffic received on the concerned router destined to this host is dropped in order to prevent a black-hole condition for the next data packet for VM2 received in Fabric 1. Indeed, if the remote LISP router (ITR) that sources the traffic to VM2 has not been updated with the new RLOC of the latter, it sends the LISP-encapsulated packet to the RLOC retrieved from its local LISP map cache. The receiving LISP site gateway in Fabric 1 applies a Layer 3 lookup in its routing table and notices a Null0 entry for the EID of interest, VM2. This allows the traffic to be punted to the CPU and, hence, to be passed to the LISP process that generates the solicit map request (SMR) destined for the remote ITR.

The LISP site gateway of each data center and the LISP mapping database are updated appropriately with the new location of the roaming device. The last LISP component to be updated is the LISP ITR from the branch office.

For the purpose of the workflow, assume that the end user previously established a communication with VM 2. After the seamless hot live migration of the concerned machine, data packets from the workstation continue to be forwarded toward the application hosted by the roaming VM 2. While the LISP signaling process is running in the background and updating the LISP infrastructure components, the LISP router from the branch office, which has not yet been updated with the new location, needs to process the next user data packet.

The process is explained in the following steps:

Step 1. As shown in Figure 7-12, the LISP router in the branch office does a LISP lookup from its local map cache and finds the RLOCs SG11 and SG12 associated with the dynamic EID VM2. As a result, the LISP ITR encapsulates and sends the data packet to Fabric 1, destined to RLOC SG12. The election of RLOC is based on the hashing algorithm to distribute the load across locators with the same priority and equal weight values.

Note See RFC 6830 for more details on hashing.

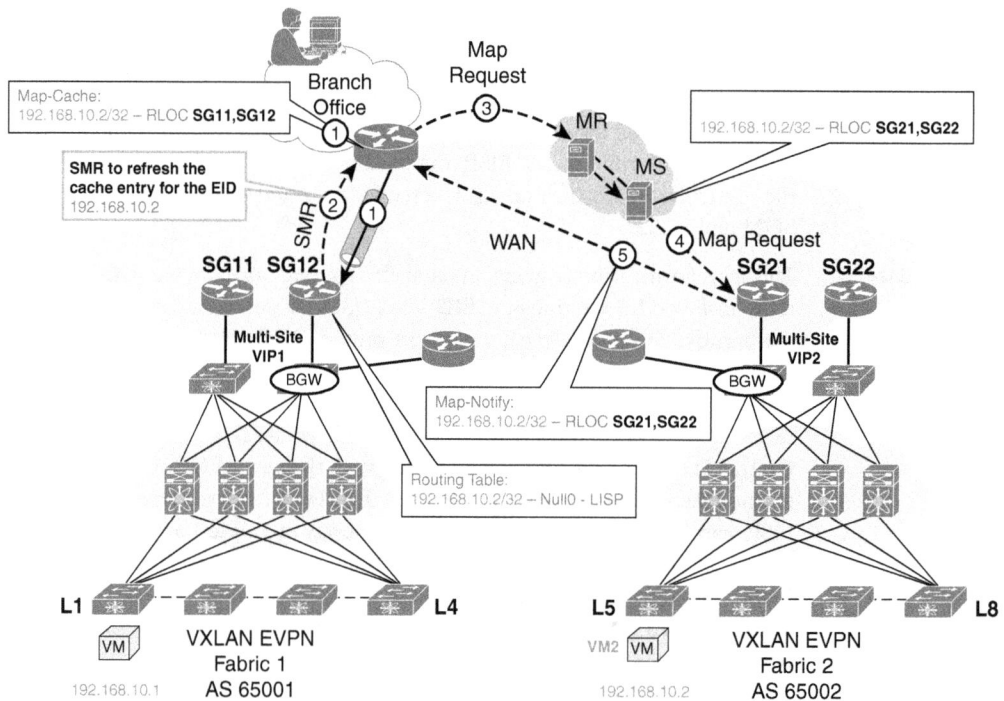

Figure 7-12 *Refreshing the Map Cache in the Branch Office*

Step 2. The receiving LISP ETR SG12 de-encapsulates the LISP IP packet and applies a Layer 3 lookup for the user data packet in its routing table and hits a Null0 route for the dynamic EID 192.168.10.2. The LISP router creates a control plane message called a solicit map request (SMR) and sends it toward the remote source ITR that generated the LISP IP packet. This handshake informs the remote LISP ITR that it should refresh its map cache.

Step 3. The LISP router from the remote branch office receives the SMR and sends a new map request to the map resolver to get the new location for the roaming device's IP address, 192.168.10.2. The map resolver then forwards the request to the map server engine.

Step 4.   The MS forwards the map request to the LISP site gateway in Fabric 2 that
last registered the 192.168.10.2/32 IP address for the migrated EID.

Step 5.   As shown in Figure 7-12, the elected LISP site gateway GS21 sends a map
reply with the updated mapping information for the EID VM2 directly to
the ITR that originated the LISP map request. The key reason for this direct
return reply is to guarantee that Layer 3 reachability is validated between the
destined RLOCs in the new location (Fabric 2) and the initial LISP ITR from
the branch office.

Step 6.   The remote LISP xTR from the branch office updates the new EID mapping
information in its map cache, replacing the last RLOCs, SG11 and SG12, with
the new RLOCs that result from the xTRs deployed in Fabric 2 (that is, SG21
and SG22), as shown in Figure 7-13.

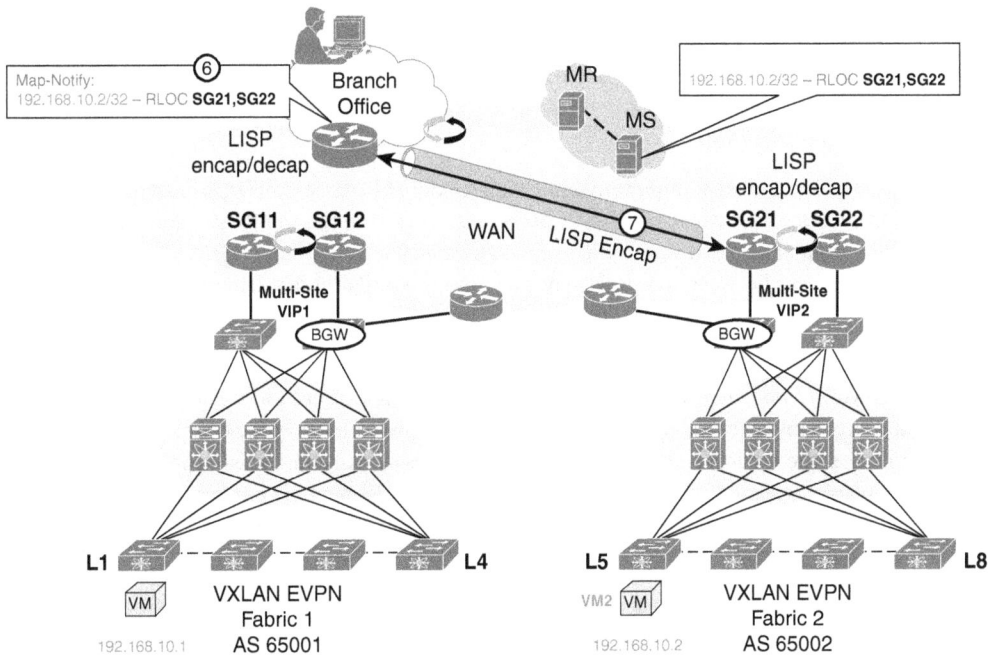

Figure 7-13   *LISP Mobility Optimizing the Ingress Path*

Step 7.   The LISP ITR from the branch office encapsulates the user data packets using
the destination to RLOC SG21 (LISP ETR) as the IP address. The traffic is
now optimally steered toward Site 2. This migration and ingress optimization
happen with almost no interruption for the applications.

ACI Multi-Pod with LISP IP Mobility

For further details on ACI Multi-Pod and ACI Multi-Site, see Chapter 6, which reviews the two main solutions for extending Layer 2 and/or Layer 3 segmentation between two or more ACI pods or ACI fabric.

The data plane and control plane packet walk elaborated in the first section of this chapter applies the same way for ACI Multi-Pod and ACI Multi-Site. Therefore, this section focuses on configuration and testing of a LISP deployment with an ACI domain.

ACI Multi-Pod and ACI Multi-Site

As a quick recap, today, there are two architecture models that provide tight Layer 2 and Layer 3 communications with consistent end-to-end policy enforcement between distant ACI domains: ACI Multi-Pod and ACI Multi-Site. These solutions offer highly reliable and integrated solutions for interconnecting either multiple ACI pods or multiple ACI domain fabrics. The deployment of ACI Multi-Pod and ACI Multi-Site enables extension of Layer 2 and Layer 3 transport communication between endpoints connected to separate locations.

The ACI Multi-Pod architecture relies on a single APIC cluster being spread across multiple locations where other ACI pods exist. As a result, a single ACI domain fabric exists from end to end across different sites managed by the same APIC SDN controller. The distances between the pods may vary, and the pods can be deployed within a metropolitan area or geographically across longer distances, with up to a maximum supported inter-pod latency of 50 ms RTT.

ACI Multi-Pod offers a separation for the control plane at each location. Every instance of a protocol delimited inside each pod runs independently from each other pod, reducing the failure domain to its single form. This approach increases the reliability of the whole extended infrastructure. This is a key requirement for extending Layer 2 segments beyond a single location, making ACI Multi-Pod the validated design for extending a distinct ACI domain across different locations.

Figure 7-14 illustrates physical inter-pod connectivity. The spine layer is connected to a Layer 3 domain called the Inter-Pod Network (IPN). The IPN is a pure routed network that requires multicast support with a larger maximum transmit unit (MTU) size dimensioned to support VXLAN encapsulation. A VXLAN tunnel is established between the remote pods.

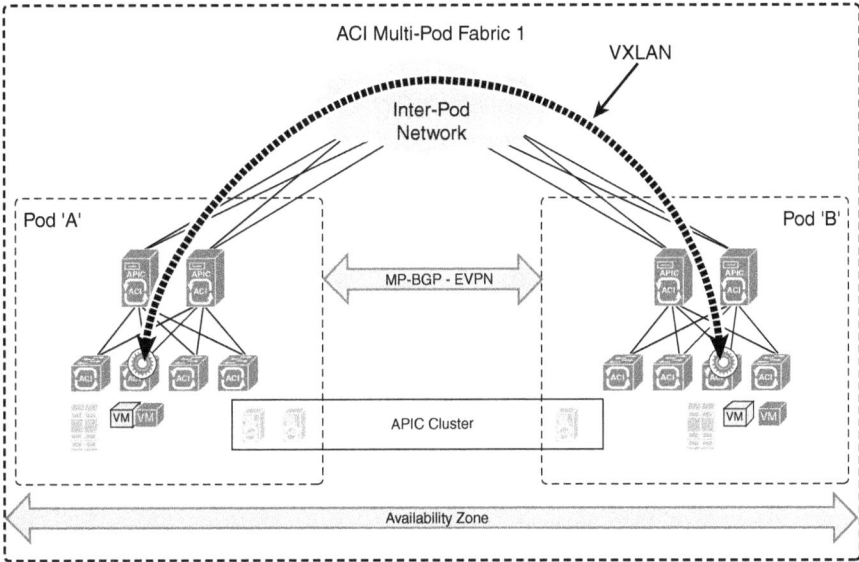

Figure 7-14 *ACI Multi-Pod Architecture*

The other validated infrastructure, depicted in Figure 7-15, is referenced as ACI Multi-Site. This model offers a solution architecture for interconnecting independent ACI domain fabrics for Layer 3 and/or Layer 2 extension and consistent end-to-end policy enforcement. Consequently, each ACI fabric belonging to a particular site runs its own Application Policy Infrastructure Controller (APIC) software-defined networking (SDN) controller. The Data plane and Control plane are contained within each individual Availability zone. Thus, every ACI domain is identified within its availability zone.

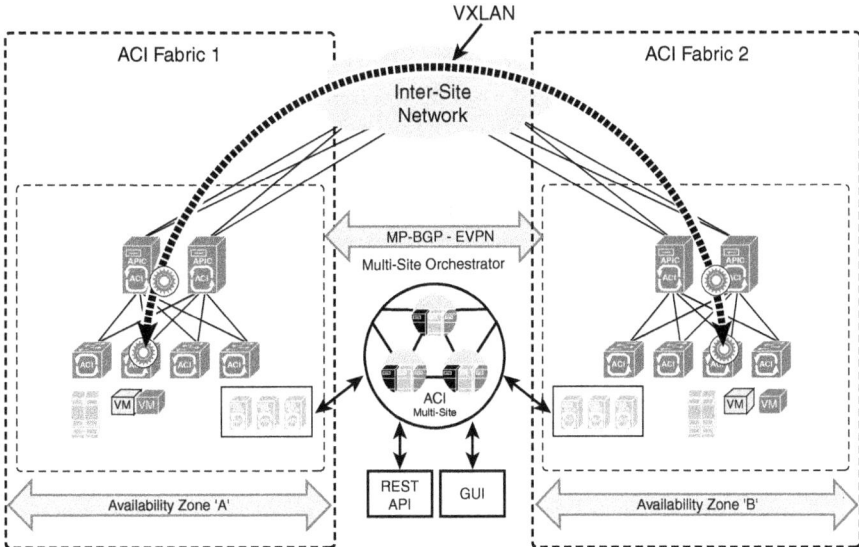

Figure 7-15 *ACI Multi-Site Architecture*

To simplify and accelerate the Day 1 and Day 2 operations across multiple ACI domains, ACI Multi-Site includes the multi-site orchestrator platform, which is responsible for deploying any policy change configurations across the sites of interest where an ACI fabric was deployed. Policy definitions and enforcement are provisioned from the centralized management platform to all or a part of selected sites.

As with ACI Multi-Pod, with ACI Multi-Site, the inter-site control plane exchanges the endpoint reachability information using the VXLAN MP-BGP EVPN control plane across sites. Layer 2 and Layer 3 communication between endpoints connected to different sites is accomplished by establishing a VXLAN overlay between ACI spine devices. The VXLAN tunnel is transported over an inter-site network (ISN) that interconnects the various ACI domains at Layer 3. The IP network has no specific functional requirements other than the capability to support routing. MTU size must be dimensioned based on the extra header for VXLAN encapsulation.

ACI Multi-Pod and LISP IP Mobility

For the purpose of LISP IP Mobility deployed in conjunction with ACI fabrics, this section relies on the ACI Multi-Pod scenario. From a LISP IP Mobility point of view, the workflow, the LISP signaling, and the LISP site gateway configuration are the same, regardless of whether the fabric is a VXLAN EVPN fabric, ACI Multi-Pod, or ACI Multi-Site. The common denominator for all these fabric models is that the Layer 2 domain is extended from one location to a remote location, and the host routes are injected from each data center fabric belonging to a different location toward the Layer 3 core network. Mobile subnets exist on all distant locations.

As mentioned in the introduction to this chapter, the role of the LISP FHR is replaced by the discovery and distribution signaling embedded within the fabric using the control plane.

Since ACI 4.0, host routes on a bridge domain (BD) are advertised directly from the ACI fabric to the external Layer 3 domain. Individual host routes of endpoints belonging to public subnets are injected toward the external Layer 3 network. These host route advertisements are performed from the local border leaf devices from each site (either from ACI pods or ACI domain fabrics), along with the subnet. Notice that the local endpoint host route is never advertised through remote border leaf nodes that belong on different locations.

From an ACI Multi-Pod point of view, when an endpoint is moved away from its local pod to another location, its route advertisement is immediately withdrawn from the local pod. Consequently, after a live migration of a VM from one data center to a different site, its prefix is revoked from the initial border leaf node while it is announced from the new location. This approach natively brings optimal performance for ingress communication to be directed to the right location dynamically when the enterprise owns the Layer 3 core, as traffic is steered to the most specific route.

However, as discussed previously with VXLAN EVPN, if the Layer 3 WAN domain is managed by a service provider (SP), it is not possible to inject the host route directly into the managed Layer 3 core routers. Hence, the alternative is to initiate a tunnel over the provider network by using a LISP-encapsulated overlay network.

The following discussion leverages host route advertisement, which has been available since ACI 4.0. Figure 7-16 shows a high-level view with an ACI Multi-Pod infrastructure.

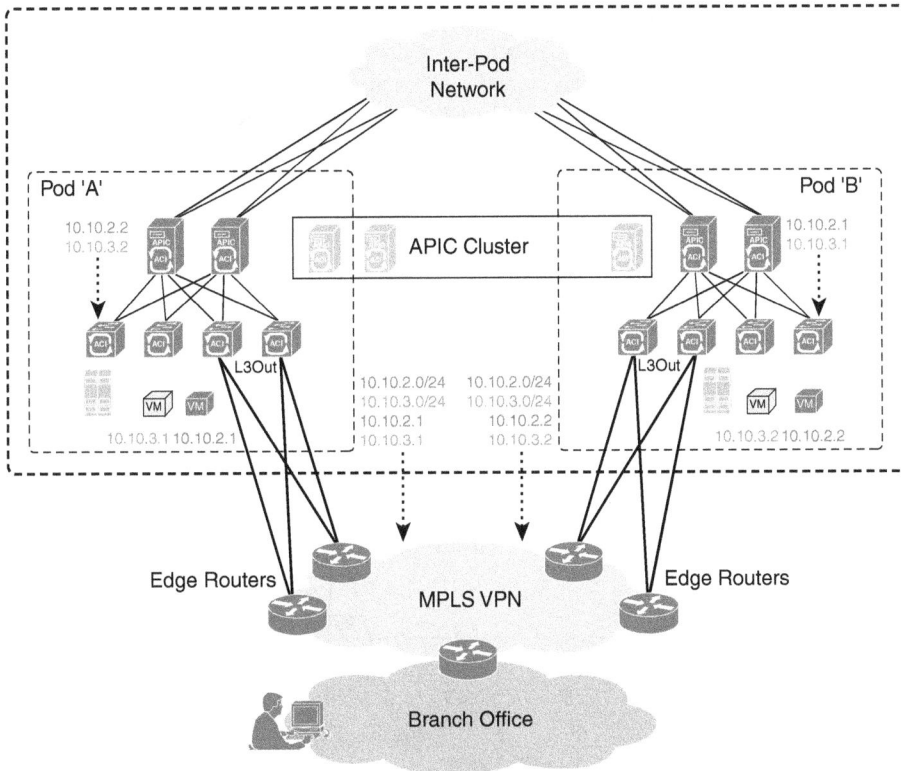

Figure 7-16 *ACI Multi-Pod and Layer 3 Outside Network Connection*

The communication between ACI pods is established through the spine devices connected to the inter-pod network.

The Layer 3 communication to outside the ACI fabric is established through the border leaf nodes from the pods. This Layer 3 interface connecting to the external core routers is formally referred to as *L3Out* in an ACI environment. The demarcation point can be an L3Out with OSPF, EIGRP, or BGP peering with the fabric.

Host route advertisement supports both bridge domain (BD)–to–L3Out association and explicit route map configuration. Note that explicit route map configuration allows greater control in selecting individuals or a range of host routes to configure.

East–west Layer 2 and Layer 3 communication between ACI sites happens across the inter-pod network, and each location knows the remote endpoint reachability information from its spine devices. However, for northbound Layer 2 communication, host route information for a locally discovered endpoint is never advertised through the L3Out connection defined on border leaf nodes that are part of a remote pod. The bridge domain subnet must have the Advertise Externally option enabled to advertise tenant subnets externally on L3Out (public subnets).

The next step is to leverage the host route advertisement in order to enable LISP IP Mobility. Depending on the enterprise infrastructure, edge routers or customer edge (CE) devices typically implement both LISP ITR and ETR functions at the same time. When this is the case, the device is referred to as a *LISP xTR router*. Figure 7-17 shows the placement of the LISP routers (xTRs) deployed in conjunction with host route advertisement through the border leaf nodes from the ACI multi-pod domain. In this scenario, the LISP xTR devices are distributed across the CE devices on both pods.

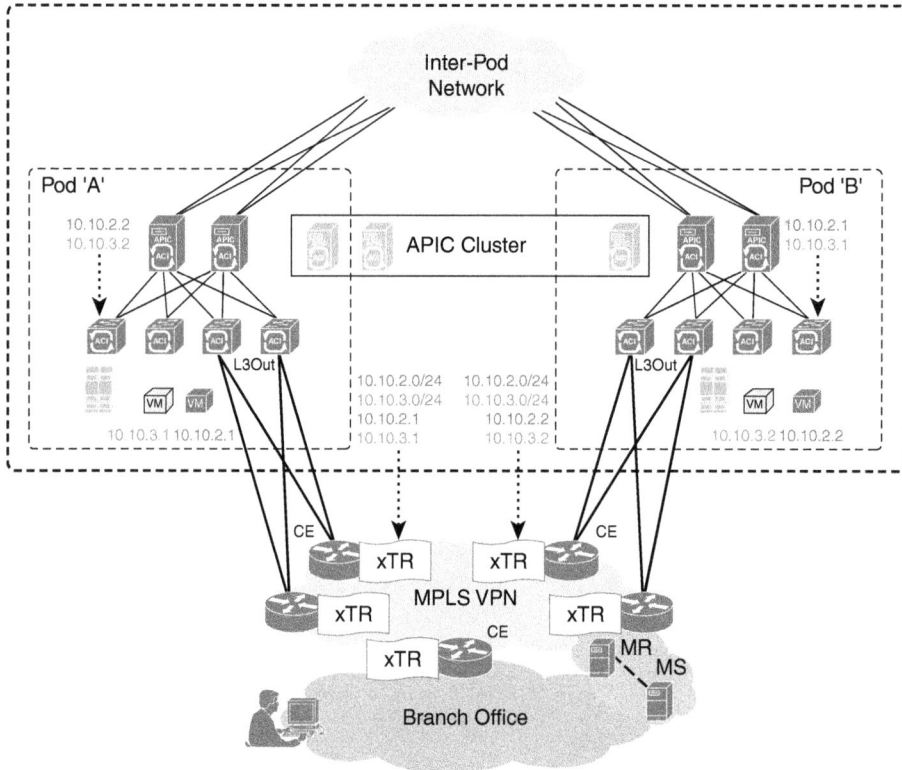

Figure 7-17   *ACI Multi-Pod Host Route Through L3Out and LISP IP Mobility*

Note   LISP site gateway can be enabled multiple Layer 3 hops away from each ACI pod; it doesn't have to be the next Layer 3 adjacent device from the border leaf switches. However, the host route advertisements must be routed up to the LISP site gateway to trigger the LISP notification and update the LISP map server accordingly.

ACI Multi-Pod Configuration for Host Route Advertisement

For simplicity in the configuration, we can reduce the infrastructure topology to its smallest form. In Figure 7-18, there is only a single LISP router for each site, including the branch office (referred to as *xTR*). The LISP map server and LISP map resolver are configured in the same device and share the same loopback address for both roles.

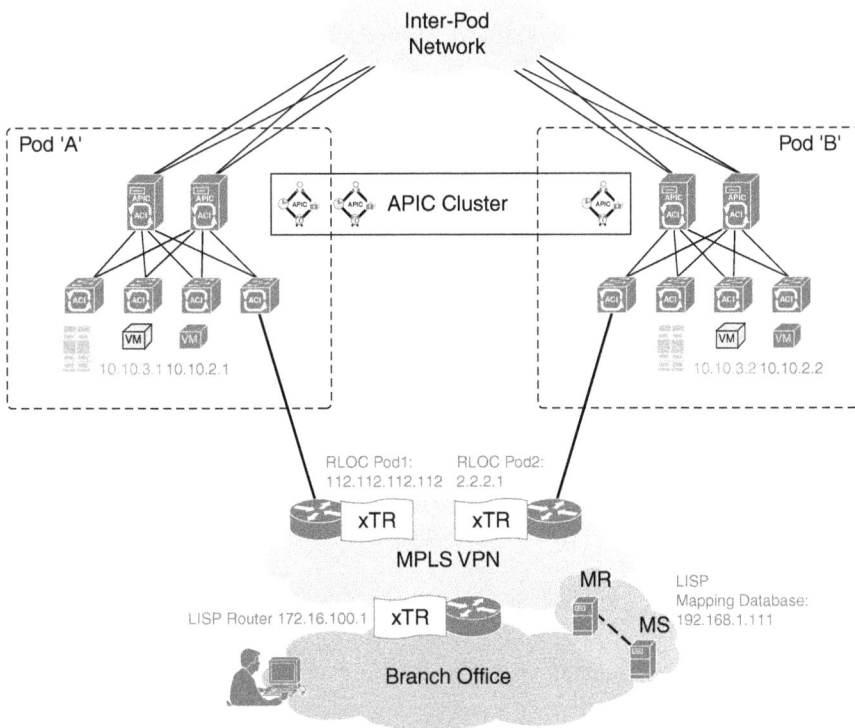

Figure 7-18   *Test Lab for ACI Host Route Advertisement with LISP Mobility*

In a production network, the strong recommendation is to either dedicate a cluster of servers to run the two functions of the LISP mapping database separately or configure them on different remote sites. Moreover, distinct devices might perform the roles of LISP map server and LISP map resolver. Traditionally, an anycast IP address is used on the devices supporting the map resolver function and for the map server; however, a unique IP address is used for each physical node. The LISP site gateways must be configured in a fully resilient fashion, using redundant routers.

This use-case focuses on only the elements that are required to be configured for successful communication between the host from each ACI pod: the host mobility across distant pods and the host route toward the LISP routers. You should be able to infer the configuration for a highly reliable deployment without any concerns. Some details are provided with the configuration samples in this section to help operate the redundant devices.

On the ACI fabric side, you need to configure the L3Out. Recall that there are three main approaches to deploying the ACI configuration: using the REST API, using the NX-OS-style CLI, or using the GUI. This example shows the configuration using the GUI. The same workflow and parameters apply to the configuration programming methods.

Prior to enabling L3Out, it is assumed you have already done the following:

■ Create the tenant and VRF environment associated with the host(s) supporting the application to be advertised outside

■ The application EPG where the front-end hosts reside must be advertised outside the fabric for public access

■ Create associated filters and contracts to allow communication between application EPG and external EPG

Note   For the full configuration details, see the "Cisco APIC Layer 3 Networking Configuration Guide," Release 4.0(1).

In this particular case, you need to configure L3Out on each pod. This example shows a slightly different L3Out configuration to help you understanding the flexibility and options that exist to allow subnets to be advertised to the external network.

Using the APIC GUI, for the concerned tenant, create a routed outside interface on the External Routed Outside tab. Select the VRF of choice—in this case T3-VRF1—and the external routed domain L3Out-Test. For this particular example of configuring L3Out, use Open Shortest Path First (OSPF) as the routing transport protocol to advertise network subnets toward the external first-hop router.

Figure 7-19 shows the L3Out interface configuration using the APIC graphical interface.

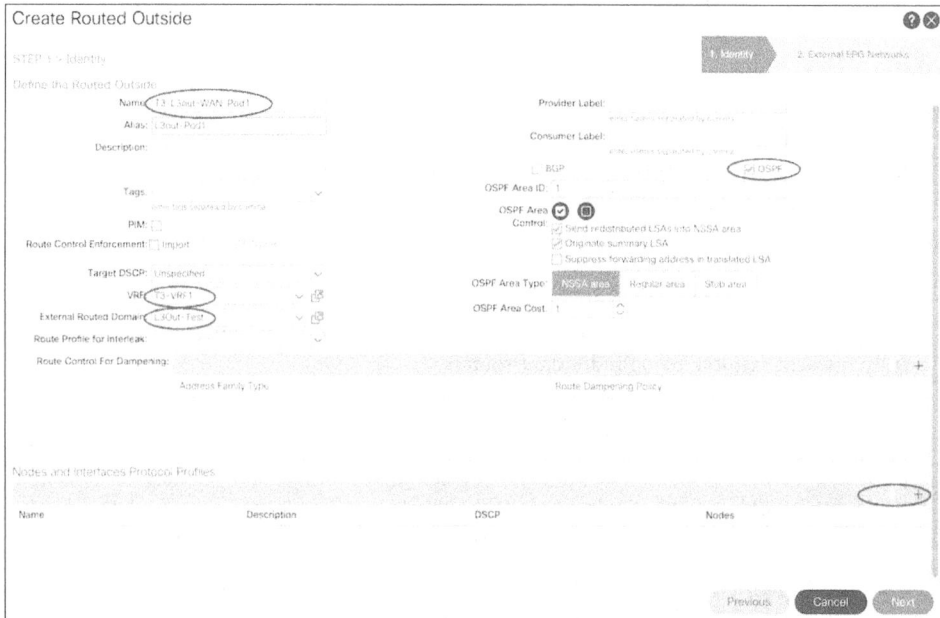

Figure 7-19   *ACI L3Out for Pod 1*

Under the L3Out just created for Pod 1, create the node and interfaces protocol profile. First, create the nodes profile to specify the border leaf nodes used for connecting to the outside network. Then, as part of this profile, define the new logical interface profile, which associates the L3Out with the physical interface from the border leaf node connecting with the external network, as shown in Figure 7-20.

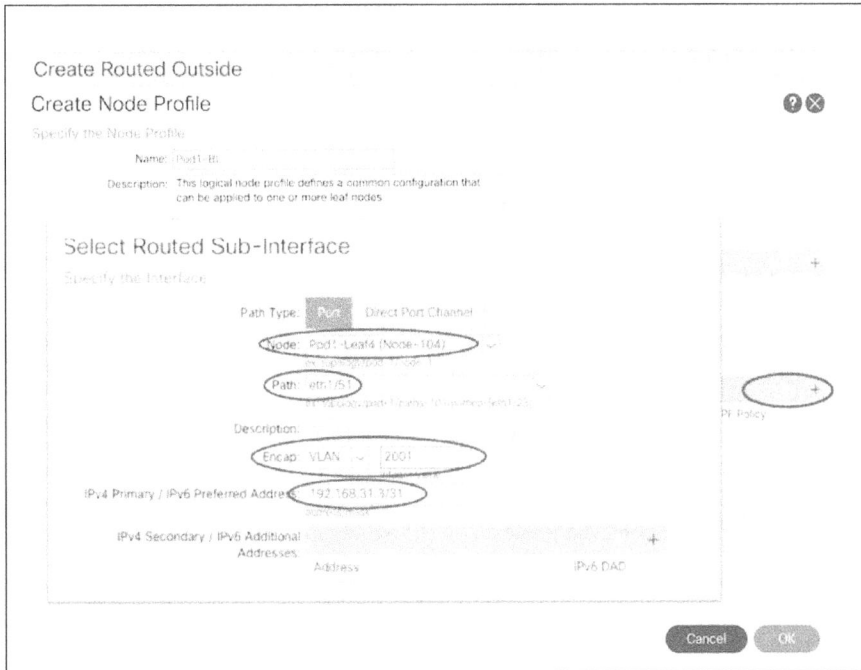

Figure 7-20 *ACI L3Out and Subinterface*

In today's modern data center, you also need to leverage the multi-tenancy-based infrastructure and maintain the Layer 3 segmentation to outside. This is very important as LISP IP Mobility is multi-tenant capable, and you want the LISP site gateways to control the mobile endpoints for each tenant VRF. As a result, the choice of routed interface can be a subinterface with the associated Dot1q VLAN.

Regarding the L3Out for the route profile, the ACI fabric supports two methods for enabling host route advertisements. Either the bridge domain can be directly associated to L3Out without granular control or an explicit configuration of the route map for selective prefix subnets can be enabled. It is recommended to use explicit route map configuration, which allows greater control in selecting an individual host route or a range of host routes to advertise.

The L3Out and Route Map for Selective Prefix Subnets

For the interface profile being associated with the logical node profile, you need to configure the explicit route maps for the L3Out for Pod 1. To do so, under the same L3Out as before, create a new route map/profile as shown in Figure 7-21: Select the default-export type to match the profile and routing policy. Then create a route control context for this route map.

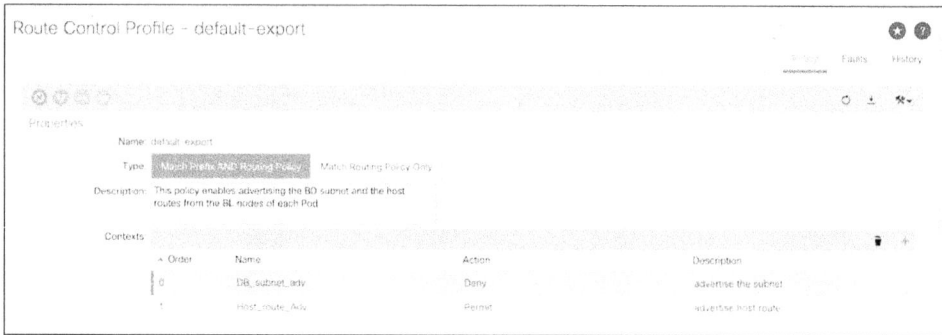

Figure 7-21 *L3Out with a Route Map*

Figure 7-21 illustrates the configuration of the route map policy required to deny the subnet of the bridge domain and to permit the host routes from the border leaf nodes of Pod 1. This route map needs to be replicated in Pod 2. In this scenario, say that you decide not to advertise the /24 subnet but just the host routes for the endpoints belonging to that particular subnet. As a result, the first route map policy explicitly denies the subnet 10.10.3.0/24, and the second policy permits host route advertisement. The way the subnet and host route are achieved depends on the aggregate mode chosen.

Figure 7-22 shows the rules associated with matching the prefix network. As you can see, the aggregate mode is set to False. This means that more specific prefixes belonging to this subnet, such as the host route, are ignored; only subnet /24 matches the condition, and the everything else is excluded.

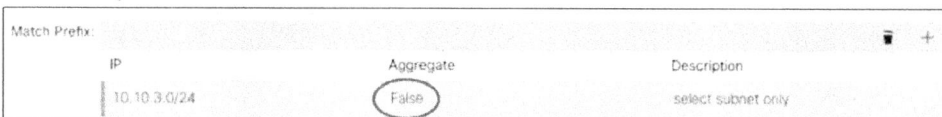

Figure 7-22 *L3Out Route Map Match Prefix: Permitting Only One Subnet*

You need to add another rule to match for the prefix of the host routes to be permitted. This is achieved by setting the aggregate condition to True for the same subnet, as shown in Figure 7-23.

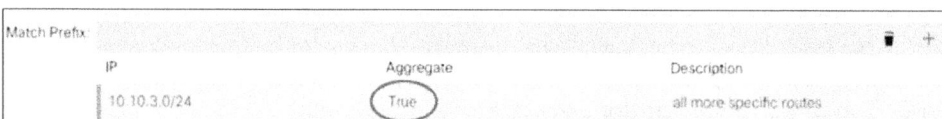

Figure 7-23 *L3Out Route Map Match Prefix: Permitting Host Routes*

As a result, from the route maps, subnet 10.10.3.0/24 is permitted, and all more specific routes are also permitted. The external router connecting to this L3Out receives the advertisement for prefix network 10.10.3.0/24 as well as the host routes from that particular subnet. As highlighted in this example, it is possible to deny the subnet /24 for all or for a particular pod maintaining the host route advertisements. This use case might be interesting in a situation in which only a few hosts are migrating to a secondary data center, but most of machines belonging to this particular subnet are located in the primary data center. For this purpose, you want to trigger the LISP signaling based on the discovering host routes, so the configuration doesn't change.

Next, you must advertise out the bridge domain subnet and the host route. This is achieved under the Layer 3 policy configuration for the particular bridge domain that hosts the machines to be advertised to outside. Thus, you need to create a bridge domain with the option Advertise Host Routes selected to enable advertisement to all deployed border leaf nodes. In addition, the VRF of interest previously created for that purpose must be chosen from the drop-down list, as shown in Figure 7-24.

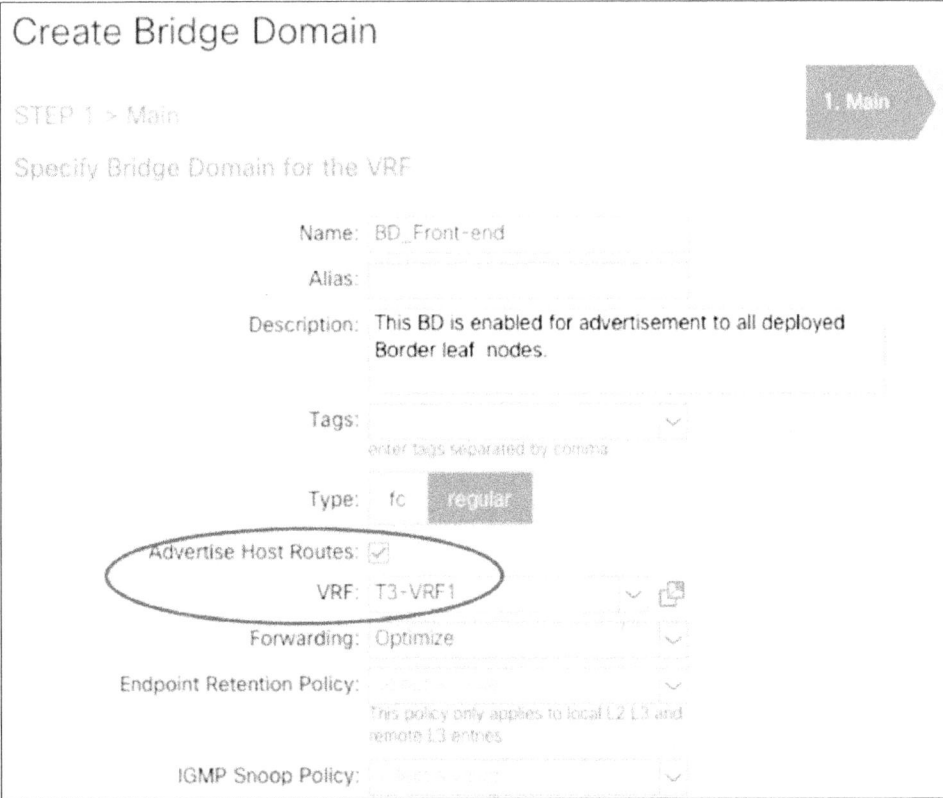

Figure 7-24 *ACI : Creation of a Bridge Domain*

Notice that the advertised host route process is tightly related to the public subnets concerned with the advertisement to the external network. This means host routes are advertised only for the specific subnets allowed to communicate with the external networks, as shown in Figure 7-25.

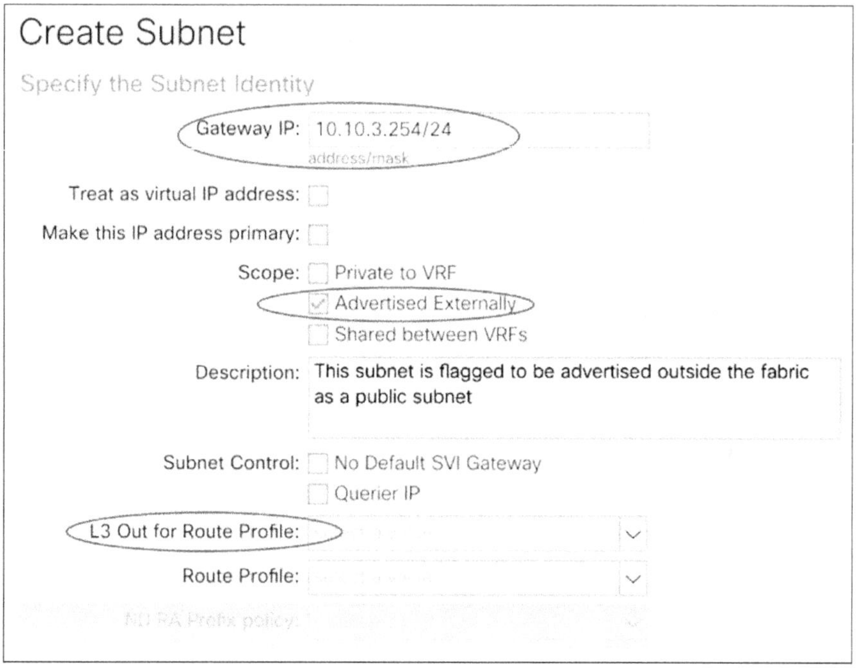

Create Subnet

Specify the Subnet Identity

Gateway IP: 10.10.3.254/24
address/mask

Treat as virtual IP address: ☐

Make this IP address primary: ☐

Scope: ☐ Private to VRF
☑ Advertised Externally
☐ Shared between VRFs

Description: This subnet is flagged to be advertised outside the fabric as a public subnet

Subnet Control: ☐ No Default SVI Gateway
☐ Querier IP

L3 Out for Route Profile: ⌄

Route Profile: ⌄

No RA Prefix policy ⌄

Figure 7-25   *ACI: Creation of a Public Subnet with the Gateway IP Address*

Next, you can select the next action to add the public subnet of interest. During this stage, the gateway IP address for that particular subnet must be specified. To advertise a host route from that subnet, the subnet must be flagged with the state Advertised Externally, as shown in Figure 7-25.

Bridge Domain Associated to a Particular L3Out

Now that you've seen the route map configuration with Pod 1 to inject host routes for an individual subnet into an external Layer 3 network, you are ready to see how a bridge domain can be directly associated to the L3Out as an alternative to advertising host routes for a specific bridge domain prefix. This configuration is achieved under the Layer 3 policy for the particular bridge domain that hosts the endpoints to be advertised to outside.

Figure 7-26 clarifies the association between the bridge domain and the L3Out from Pod 2. This configuration must be applied under the Bridge Domain section of the GUI.

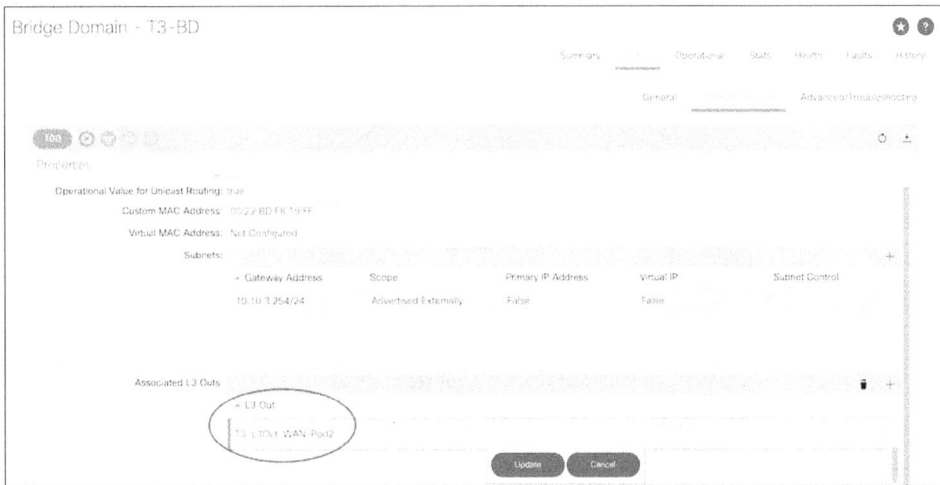

Figure 7-26 *ACI Bridge Domain Associated with L3Out*

You need to associate the bridge domain with the L3Out from Pod 2 in order to advertise the subnet and host route directly from there because there is no explicit route map defined for that L3Out for Pod 2. You need to add a new L3Out to be associated with that particular bridge domain and select the L3Out T3-L3Out-WAN-Pod2 for Pod 2 from the drop-down list.

As a result of advertising the prefix in two ways, you have now Pod 1 configured using route map policies to deny the subnet 10.10.3.0/24 and to advertise the host routes of that subnet, and you have Pod 2 configured to announce the subnet 10.10.3.0/24 with the associated host routes. Figure 7-27 summarizes the subnets and host routes announced by each pod.

You can now check on the external upstream router to capture how its routing table is filled with the prefix subnet and host route, as shown in the following snippet:

```
Pod1-XTR# show ip route vrf MP-T3 | include 10.10
10.10.3.1/32, ubest/mbest: 1/0
Pod1-XTR#
```

As you can see here, only the route for the host that is active in Pod 1 was advertised toward the edge router in Pod 1. The reason is that the route map takes precedence for L3Out in Pod 1, and hence the prefix subnet /24 for 10.10.3.0 is not advertised outside. As depicted in Figure 7-18, for that particular subnet, only host 10.10.3.1 is active in Pod 1.

If you look at the edge router attached to Pod 2, you can see that subnet 10.10.3.0/24 is advertised from ACI Pod 2, and so is the host route for 10.10.3.2, which is now located in Pod 2, as shown in Example 7-3.

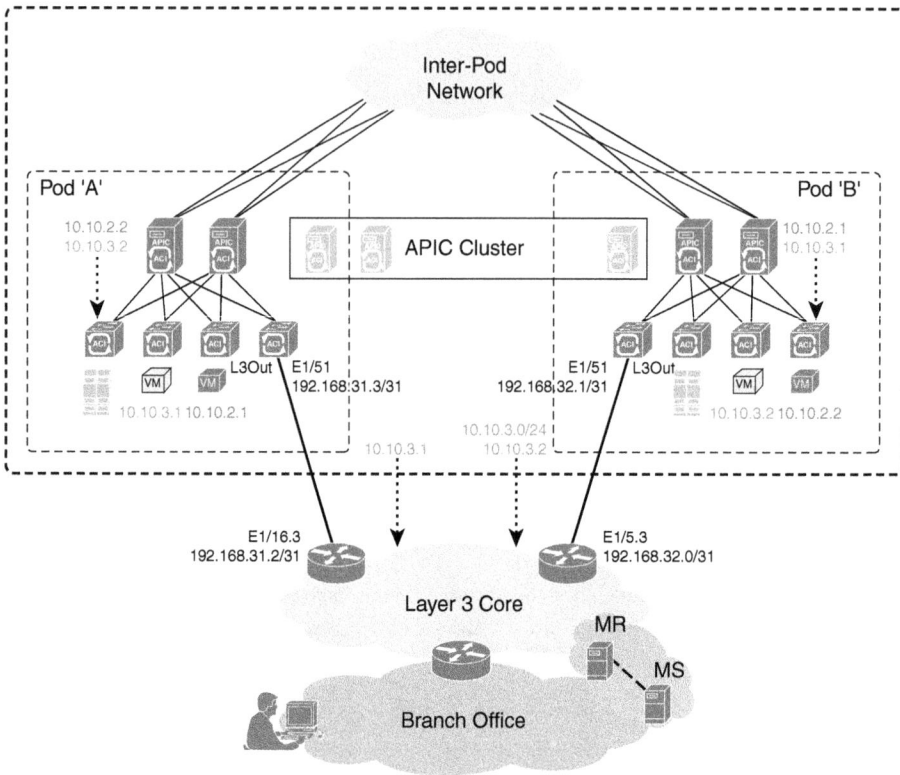

Figure 7-27 *ACI Multi-Pod Subnet and Host Route Advertisement*

Example 7-3 *List of Subnets Advertised from Pod 2*

```
Pod2-XTR# show ip route vrf MP-T3| include 10.10
10.10.3.0/24, ubest/mbest: 1/0
10.10.3.2/32, ubest/mbest: 1/0
Pod2-XTR#
```

Next, you can migrate the endpoint 10.10.3.2 and check that the routing table is updated dynamically and accordingly. As shown in Example 7-4, only the remaining subnet 10.10.3.0/24 is advertised in Pod 2, and both host routes in Pod 1 are advertised. This is exactly the information you expect with the host route advertisement.

Example 7-4   *Routing Table with Entries in Each Pod After Endpoint Migration*

```
Pod1-XTR# show ip route vrf MP-T3| include 10.10
10.10.3.1/32, ubest/mbest: 1/0
10.10.3.2/32, ubest/mbest: 1/0
Pod1-XTR#
..//..
Pod2-XTR# show ip route vrf MP-T3| include 10.10
10.10.3.0/24, ubest/mbest: 1/0
Pod2-XTR#
```

As mentioned earlier, LISP IP Mobility aims to leverage the dynamic advertisement of host routes to automatically trigger LISP signaling to notify the LISP mapping dataset.

The traditional data center used a separate LISP first-hop router function to notify dynamic EIDs using LISP signaling toward the LISP site gateways; this method is no longer appropriate with modern fabric. Because modern fabrics such as VXLAN EVPN or ACI fabrics offer the function of a first-hop router from the leaf nodes where the endpoints are directly attached, it is important for the LISP site gateway to trigger the mobility registration at the reception of traditional host routes. To achieve this association, the new LISP command **register-route-notifications** must be used to activate this LISP notification process. This is the main difference from the traditional LISP deployment, which simplifies the mobility semantic operations across ACI Multi-Pod or ACI Multi-Site.

Figure 7-28 highlights the additional LISP Multihop function required with a traditional data center network to discover and to notify the LISP site gateway with the local EIDs. With modern fabrics such as VXLAN EVPN or ACI, this function of discovery and notification is superseded by the control plane of the fabric. The default gateway for a particular subnet is distributed across all leaf nodes, becoming the first-hop router for the locally attached leaf node endpoints. Consequently, the border leaf nodes, populated with the reachability information of all the active endpoints, can subsequently advertise the host routes of the concerned subnets toward the upstream LISP router. Multiple Layer 3 hops may exist between the border leaf nodes and the LISP site gateway.

Another important difference—not in terms of new features but in terms of operational deployment—is the support for multi-tenancy. Indeed, VXLAN EVPN and ACI both natively offer Layer 3 segmentation (VRF IP routing), so LISP Mobility can also be configured per tenant, maintaining the Layer 3 segmentation from end to end.

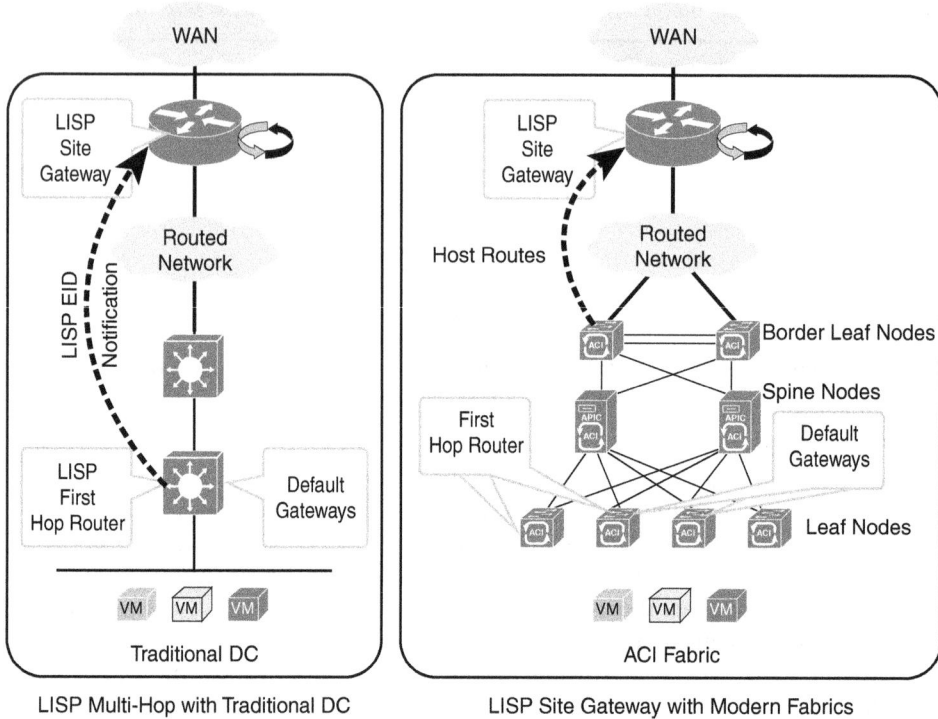

Figure 7-28   *LISP Multihop Versus a Simple LISP Site Gateway*

LISP IP Mobility Configuration with Host Route Advertisement

The testbed used for this section has an architecture comprising ACI Multi-Pod with two pods and one branch office, as shown in Figure 7-29.

The Layer 3 core interconnecting the branch office with the LISP sites is constructed with an MPLS VPN network managed by a service provider. Hence, the enterprise deploying LISP IP Mobility has no control of it. In this case, the LISP overlay network for data plane and control plane traffic flow is running transparently over the service provider network.

RLOCs rely on loopback—in this example, Loopback 10 for Pod 1 (112.112.112.112) and Loopback 10 for Pod 2 (2.2.2.2). The xTR in the branch office is reachable with Loopback 0 (172.16.100.1), as shown in Example 7-5.

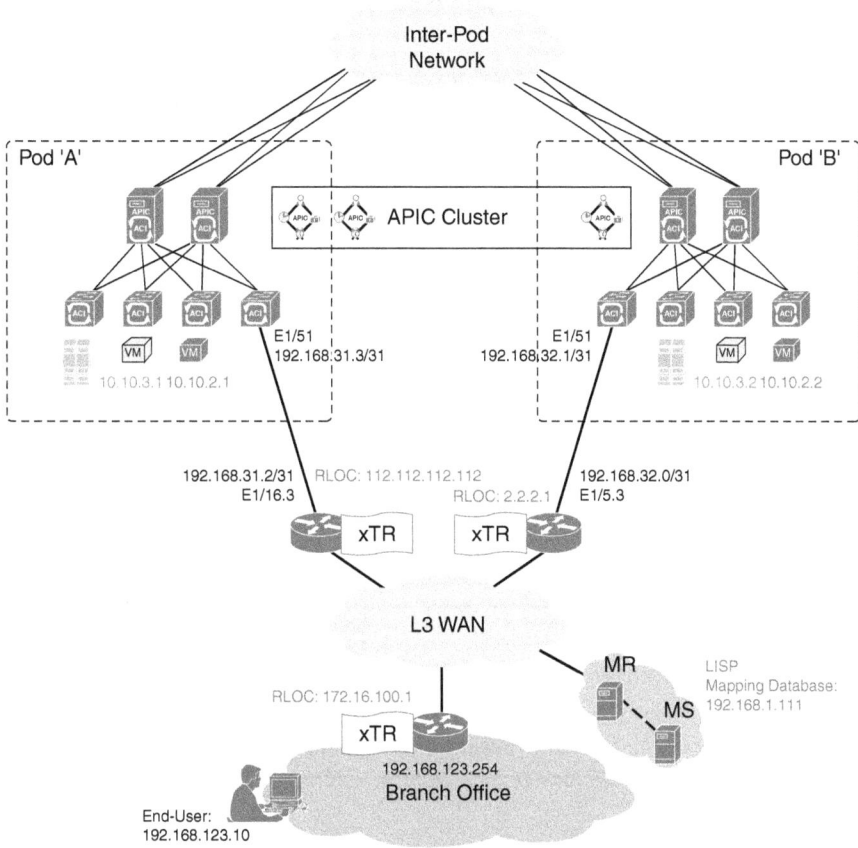

Figure 7-29 *LISP Mobility Configuration with ACI Multi-Pod*

Example 7-5 *LISP xTR in Pod 1: Interface Configuration*

```
interface loopback10
  description LISP XTR Pod 1
  ip address 112.112.112.112/32
!
..//..
!
interface Ethernet1/16.3
  description L3 to Pod1-Leaf4 (MP-T3)
  encapsulation dot1q 2003
  vrf member MP-T3
  ip address 192.168.31.2/31
  ip ospf network point-to-point
  ip ospf mtu-ignore
  ip router ospf 1 area 0.0.0.0
  no shutdown
```

Example 7-6 shows the configuration for the LISP xTR in Pod 2.

Example 7-6   *LISP xTR in Pod 2: Interface Configuration*

```
interface loopback10
  description LISP XTR Pod 1
  ip address 2.2.2.1/32
!
..//..
!
interface Ethernet1/5.3
  description L3 to Pod2-Leaf1 (MP-T3)
  encapsulation dot1Q 2003
  vrf member MP-T3
  ip address 192.168.32.0/31
  ip ospf network point-to-point
  ip ospf mtu-ignore
  ip router ospf 1 area 0.0.0.0
  no shutdown
```

Example 7-7 shows the configuration for the LISP xTR in the remote branch office.

Example 7-7   *LISP xTR in the Branch Office: Interface Configuration*

```
interface Loopback0
 description LISP XTR Branch Office
 ip address 172.16.100.1 255.255.255.255
!
..//..
!
interface GigabitEthernet3
 description Branch-Subnet-MP-T3
 ip address 192.168.123.254 255.255.255.0
 negotiation auto
!
```

For the purpose of this scenario, the tenant VRF instance named MP-T3 is used. Only roamers from the mobile subnet 10.10.3.0/24 are registered in the LISP database. Consequently, the configuration remains simple, as shown in the following sections.

LISP Mapping Database

For this particular assessment with ACI Multi-Pod and LISP Mobility infrastructure, the same IP reachable information for both functions is enabled for the map server and the map resolver. That doesn't change the concept of the mapping database or the behavior regarding the control plane signaling and notification and the data plane encapsulation and de-encapsulation. The LISP mapping database is deployed in a separate NX-OS device. The configuration shown in Example 7-8, which is trivial, can be deployed using a different IP address for each function. In a production network, the recommended deployment is a cluster of machines dedicated for the LISP mapping database from which a distinct group of nodes perform independently the roles of LISP map server and LISP map resolver. For a cluster deployment with multiple members, an anycast IP address is used on all nodes for the function of map resolver. Consequently, a map request originating from a LISP ITR device is sent to the closest map resolver from a routing metric point of view. For the map server, however, a unique IP address is used for each physical node. As a result, each LISP ETR registers its EID subnets with all devices that form the map server.

Example 7-8 *LISP Mapping Database Configuration*

```
interface loopback0
  description LISP MSMR
  ip address 192.168.1.111/32
!
ip lisp map-resolver
ip lisp map-server
!
lisp site BRANCH
  eid-prefix 192.168.123.0/24
  eid-prefix 192.168.123.0/24 instance-id 1
  authentication-key 0 thisisthepassword
!
lisp site DATA_CENTER
  eid-prefix 10.0.0.0/8 accept-more-specifics
  eid-prefix 10.0.0.0/8 instance-id 1 accept-more-specifics
  authentication-key 0 thisisthepassword
```

In this scenario, the LISP map resolver and map server functionalities must be enabled for the IPv4 address family. The second component concerns the LISP sites with their respective site configuration. The EID prefix becomes authoritative for the LISP site from which it is configured. For the LISP site where the dynamic EID map is configured—typically for the LISP ETR belonging to the LISP data centers—a more specific prefix flag must be specified. It is crucial to construct the map server with the prefix networks for the corresponding sites.

LISP Site Gateway, xTRs, and ACLs

In the following example, the LISP ETR function is initiated globally as well as per tenant VRF instance. Indeed, in the context of multi-tenancy, traffic is encapsulated from both the underlay (default) and the overlay (tenant) VRF instance and de-encapsulated from the underlay VRF instance. As shown in Figure 7-30, the encapsulated LISP traffic generated from the ITR located in the remote branch office reaches the local LISP site gateway xTR in the LISP data center.

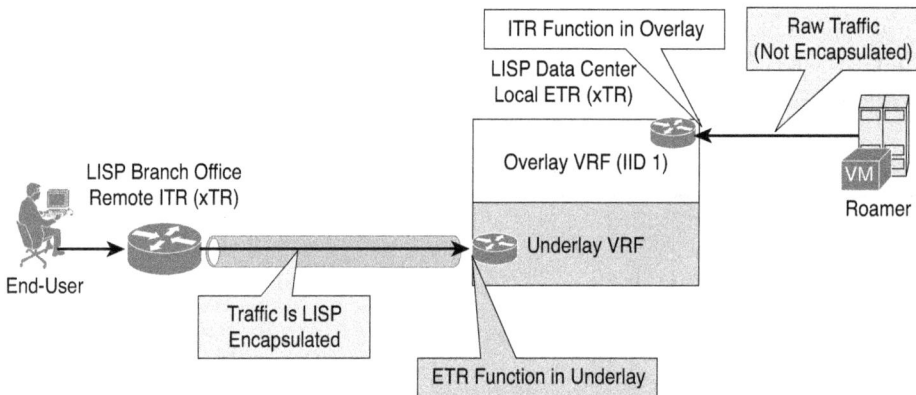

Figure 7-30   *LISP ITR, ETR, and ACL*

To de-encapsulate the ingress LISP traffic from the LISP ITR from the remote branch office destined to the ETR, data packets with UDP port 4341 must first be permitted. Thus, an ACL must be installed in the underlay VRF instance. It is the role of the ETR from the underlay VRF instance to apply the ACL based on receiving data plane traffic with destination port 4341. In addition, from a control plane standpoint, the ETR function is also required from the overlay VRF instance for the dynamic EID registration of that particular tenant VRF instance toward the LISP map server. To trigger the LISP map resolution, a **copy-to-sup** entry needs to be installed in the overlay VRF instance. The original raw data traffic received from the tenant's roamer destined to the remote LISP router xTR is encapsulated from the overlay VRF instance.

In this case, you want to enable the ETR function for both the default VRF instance and the tenant VRF instances, as shown in Example 7-9.

Example 7-9 *LISP xTR Functions Enabled for the Default and Tenant VRF Instances*

```
ip lisp etr (!) ETR functions must be configured in both Tenant VRF and underlay VRF
ip lisp itr map-resolver 192.168.2.111
ip lisp etr map-server 192.168.2.111 key 3 9125d59c18a9b015
!
vrf context MP-T3
   ip lisp itr
     ip lisp etr (!) ETR functions must be configured in both Tenant VRF and
                    underlay VRF
```

When both ITR and ETR functionalities are enabled on the same LISP router, the configuration can be simplified by using the unique command **ip lisp itr-etr**, as shown in the following snippet:

```
ip lisp etr
vrf context MP-T3
     ip lisp itr-etr
```

LISP Site Gateway in Pod 1

The configurations for some LISP components must be enabled globally. LISP must be configured in the default VRF. The LISP ETR role for de-encapsulating LISP traffic received from the Layer 3 domain must be initiated in the LISP site gateway router. As mentioned previously, the LISP ETR function must be configured under the global configuration (also known as the underlay, or default VRF instance) as well as under the tenant VRF context (overlay VRF instance). This is required if the LISP **locator-vrf** points to the default VRF. For ease and to prevent mistakes, the more global command **itr-etr**, which comprises both ETR and ITR roles, can be used, as shown in the configuration example in Example 7-10.

Example 7-10 *LISP Site Gateway in Pod 1: LISP xTR Configuration*

```
feature lisp
!
ip lisp itr-etr
!
ip lisp itr map-resolver 192.168.1.111
ip lisp etr map-server 192.168.1.111 key 0 thisisthepassword
!
```

In Example 7-10, the map server and map resolver are shared with all tenant VRF instances; you can configure them globally as well. Recall that the LISP map resolver is used by the LISP ITR role to update its LISP map cache with new EIDs or new locations of EIDs—for example, when it receives a solicitation request for a new mapping by the remote LISP ETR. The LISP xTR uses the LISP map server to register its dynamic EIDs into the LISP mapping database. In this example, the same loopback address is used for both MS and MR functions. As mentioned earlier, in a production network, distinct devices with their respective IP reachability information might independently perform the roles of LISP map server and LISP map resolver.

With multi-tenant fabrics such as ACI, it is ordinarily desirable to maintain the segregation of roamer registration for ingress path optimization for each tenant. Consequently, the LISP configuration for the dynamic EID should be done under the tenant VRF instance of interest. Example 7-11 illustrates VRF 1 and MP-T3, used for the mobile subnet 10.10.3.0/24.

It is critical to ensure that the prefixes specified under the dynamic EID are more specific than the ones listed here in the global **ip lisp database-mapping** section. Because the LISP **database-mapping** command is configured in the dynamic EID map configuration mode, the LISP ETR registers a /32 host prefix with the mapping system after a dynamic EID is detected in the configured range. If the site is assigned multiple dynamic EID prefix blocks, the database mapping is configured for each dynamic EID prefix block assigned to the site and for each locator from which the EID prefix block can be reached. In addition, the subnet associated with the dynamic EID prefixes must be more specific than the one used in the global database mapping configuration and the one used for the switch virtual interfaces (SVIs) on which the LISP map is applied. In Example 7-11, the mask /8 is associated with the prefix in the global mapping, and /24 is used as the mask for the IP subnet associated with the SVI. With the current configuration, the weight to balance the traffic is the same (mask, priority, and weight parameters) for both the RLOC in Pod 1 (112.112.112.112) and the one in Pod 2 (2.2.2.2). Some may prefer to steer all the traffic to a single location, in which case only RLOCs for one site are specified. This is the case if the enterprise deploys a primary/secondary data center model. Moreover, the amount of traffic distributed across the two sites relies on the policy defined by value of the weight. In Example 7-11, the balance is shared equally between the two locations.

Example 7-11   *LISP Site Gateway in Pod 1: LISP Database Mapping Configuration*

```
vrf context MP-T3
  ip lisp itr-etr
  ip lisp database-mapping 10.0.0.0/8 2.2.2.1 priority 1 weight 50
  ip lisp database-mapping 10.0.0.0/8 112.112.112.112 prio 1 weight 50
  lisp instance-id 1
  ip lisp locator-vrf default
  lisp dynamic-eid DC-Subnets
    database-mapping 10.10.3.0/24 112.112.112.112 priority 1 weight 100
    register-route-notifications
```

The dynamic EID prefix subnets must be configured for mapping the relationship between the unique IPv4 or IPv6 addresses of registered EIDs and their current locators (EID to RLOC) as well as the associated traffic policy (priority and weight). It needs to be more specific than the subnet mask configured on the Layer 3 interface where the dynamic EID mapping with its RLOC is applied. As mentioned earlier, in Example 7-11, the mask /8 is associated with the prefix in the global mapping, and /24 is used as the mask for the IP subnet associated with the SVI. Several prefix subnets can be configured under the VRF context, according to the mobile networks to which roamers belong. Theoretically, only public subnets associated with mobile endpoints are used for the dynamic EIDs. Beyond the prefix subnets configured in the database mapping, the other migrations are ignored for registration into the LISP database mapping. LISP IP Mobility optimizes the ingress traffic associated with the prefix subnets configured in the LISP database. Notice that when the database mapping is associated to a tenant VRF context, it is important that the IP prefix specified for the mobile prefix subnet (the prefix where dynamic EID can be registered with the **locator** argument) belong to a local interface that is a member of the same VRF. In this use case, the local interface that belongs to the same VRF context MP-T3 is the interface Ethernet1/16.3 (xTR in Pod 1) with the IP address 192.168.31.2/31 (xTR Pod 1, as specified).

The LISP instance ID must be associated with the VRF instance or the default VRF instance.

In a scenario where you want to maintain the Layer 3 segmentation with the LISP EID registration, the instance ID value is set to 1 for that particular VRF instance. The value of the instance ID configured on the site gateway xTR and the remote xTR must match. The default value is 0, and it is conventionally associated with the default VRF. It must be different from the other VRF in case multiple tenants are optimized using LISP mobility.

locator-vrf defines the routing domain (VRF instance) where you want to perform the lookup for the RLOC prefixes. In this example, the LISP mapping database is reachable through the RLOC VRF default.

It is crucial for the coexistence with host route advertisement from the modern fabrics that the **register-route-notifications** command be introduced under the VRF context to trigger the mobility registration on reception of host routes for the tenant of interest. Optionally, a tag can be configured in case different BGP autonomous system numbers (ASNs) are configured in each LISP data center. The tag in the route notification must match the BGP ASN used for the data center to which this LISP site gateway and the border leaf switches belong. The value of the tag can be verified with a **show** command, as illustrated later in this chapter, in the Example 7-20.

This tag option might be very useful when each site is configured with a different ASN. In the context of ACI Multi-Pod, the ASN is the same number across the whole ACI domain fabric. In the scenario discussed in this section, 65501 is the ASN of ACI Pod 1 and Pod 2. In the context of one ASN per site—for example, VXLAN EVPN Multi-Site—the ASN is unique for each site, and it is therefore required to specify the tag with the ASN.

LISP Site Gateway in Pod 2

The same configuration described in the previous section must be repeated for the LISP site gateway in Pod 2. Example 7-12 illustrates the LISP configuration for one of the LISP routers located in Pod 2.

Example 7-12   *LISP Site Gateway in Pod 2: LISP Configuration*

```
feature lisp
!
ip lisp itr-etr
!
ip lisp itr map-resolver 192.168.1.111
ip lisp etr map-server 192.168.1.111 key 0 thisisthepassword
!
vrf context MP-T3
  ip lisp itr-etr
  ip lisp database-mapping 10.0.0.0/8 2.2.2.1 priority 1 weight 50
  ip lisp database-mapping 10.0.0.0/8 112.112.112.112 prio 1 weight 50
  lisp instance-id 1
  ip lisp locator-vrf default
  lisp dynamic-eid DC-Subnets
    database-mapping 10.10.3.0/24 2.2.2.1 priority 1 weight 100
    register-route-notifications
```

In addition to the loopback and physical interfaces used to carry the tenant data, the difference from the configuration given earlier for the LISP site gateway in Pod 1 is the EID-to-RLOC mapping database association between the LISP router location (2.2.2.2 in Pod 2) and the EID prefix subnet with the related traffic policy for the LISP site.

LISP Site Gateway in the Branch Office

The branch office leverages the ASR 1000 series used as a WAN customer edge router for the LISP xTR router. The configuration differs marginally from that of the Nexus 7000 devices previously discussed. However, the logic remains the same.

As with most of the routing configuration with the ASR series, the LISP configuration is built under the **router lisp** function. Example 7-13 shows the LISP configuration for the LISP router located in the remote branch office. For this particular scenario use case, this LISP configuration applies to an ASR 1000 series router.

Example 7-13 *LISP Site Gateway in the Remote Branch Office: LISP Configuration*

```
interface LISP0
!
router lisp
 locator-table default
 locator-set Branch-office
  172.16.100.1 priority 10 weight 50
  exit
!
 eid-table vrf MP-T3 instance-id 1
  database-mapping 192.168.123.0/24 172.16.100.1 priority 1 weight 100
  ipv4 itr
  ipv4 etr
  exit
 !
 ipv4 locator reachability exclude-default
 ipv4 itr map-resolver 192.168.1.111
 ipv4 itr
 ipv4 etr map-server 192.168.1.111 key thisisthepassword
 ipv4 etr
 exit
!
```

The association between the VRF table and a LISP instance ID must be configured, with the EID table configuration as parameters. Thus, the mapping relationship and an associated traffic policy for the LISP VM mobility (dynamic EID) policy must be created.

The **locator reachability** command is used to configure the conditions that must be met for an RLOC to be treated as being reachable. More specifically, if a remote RLOC is reached via the default route, then it is treated as unreachable. In this particular example, the locator reachability command applies in the LISP address family IPv4 configuration mode.

You can enter the **limit dynamic value** keyword to control the number of discoverable dynamic EIDs.

The functions of LISP ITR and ETR must be specified under the VRF context. Finally, the LISP map resolver IP address to which this router sends the map request messages for EID-to-RLOC mapping resolutions must be configured. In addition, the LISP map server with the authentication key that the IPv4 LISP ETR uses to register with the LISP mapping system must be defined. The authentication key must be provided for the map server only.

In the scenario discussed throughout this section, because each xTR has only IPv4 RLOC connectivity, and for the purpose of this exercise, the map resolver and the map server are both reachable via the same IPv4 locator address. As mentioned in Chapter 6 and earlier, this doesn't change the understanding of the packet walk; however, in a production network, the recommendation is to provide a separate device for each function.

LISP IP Mobility Verification with Host Route Advertisement

As illustrated in Figure 7-31, the two roamers associated with the dynamic EID prefix subnet 10.10.3.0/24 are 10.10.3.1, belonging to Pod 1, and 10.10.3.2, currently active in Pod 2. For this particular scenario, both ACI pods have been configured to advertise the prefix subnet 10.10.30.0/24 concerned with the mobile EID. In addition, host routes for that specific subnet are also injected through the VRF Lite subinterface toward the Layer 3 WAN. These route advertisements are required for LISP IP Mobility to optimize the ingress workflows destined to the roamers. In this scenario, there are endpoints that belong to a different subnet, 10.10.2.0/24, which is not assigned as being a LISP dynamic EID prefix block. The database mapping is not configured for the dynamic EID prefix block 10.10.2.0/24; as a result, endpoints from that particular subnet are not being treated by LISP IP Mobility as dynamic EIDs. Only endpoints from 10.10.3.0/24 can be dynamically registered into the LISP mapping database with their respective RLOCs.

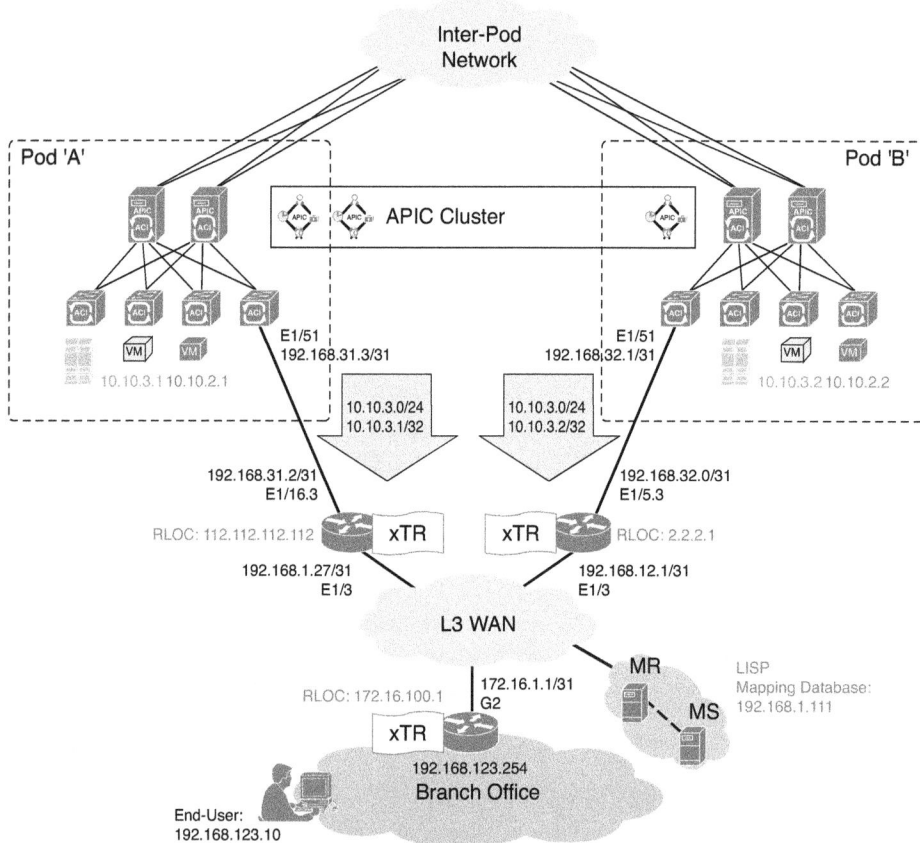

Figure 7-31 *ACI Multi-Pod with LISP Mobility Verification*

Different output monitoring and debug actions can be used to verified that the configuration conforms to the initial intent and also that the tables (routing, EID, locators) are correctly populated in real time. Finally, you need to verify that the LISP signaling (for example, map request, map notification, solicit map request) are triggered as expected.

Configuration Verification

This section shows the important commands needed to verify the status of the LISP IP Mobility infrastructure. As shown in Example 7-14, you can check the LISP database or the VRF MP-T3 for the LISP router in Pod 1 and verify that the result is in accordance with the initial intent.

Example 7-14 *LISP Site Gateway in Pod 1: Displaying the LISP Database*

```
Pod1-XTR# show ip lisp database vrf mp-t3
LISP ETR IP Mapping Database for VRF "MP-T3" (iid 1), global LSBs: 0x00000003

Local Database: 1
EID-prefix: 10.0.0.0/8,  instance-id: 1, LSBs:  0x00000003
  Producer: static , locator_set: Reserved-0, uptime: 2d22h
  Locator: 2.2.2.1, priority: 1, weight: 50
          Uptime: 2d22h, state: up
  Locator: 112.112.112.112, priority: 1, weight: 50
          Uptime: 2d22h, state: up, local
```

Example 7-15 shows how to display the LISP database for the LISP router xTR in Pod 2 for the VRF MP-T3.

Example 7-15 *LISP Site Gateway in Pod 2: Displaying the LISP Database*

```
Pod2-XTR# show ip lisp database vrf mp-t3
LISP ETR IP Mapping Database for VRF "MP-T3" (iid 1), global LSBs: 0x00000003

Local Database: 1
EID-prefix: 10.0.0.0/8,  instance-id: 1, LSBs:  0x00000003
  Producer: static , locator_set: Reserved-0, uptime: 2d17h
  Locator: 2.2.2.1, priority: 1, weight: 50
          Uptime: 2d17h, state: up, local
  Locator: 112.112.112.112, priority: 1, weight: 50
          Uptime: 2d17h, state: up
```

The two locations (RLOCs) are listed as per the configuration just given on the LISP site gateway from each data center.

Example 7-16 highlights a similar **show** LISP command for the ASR 1000 series. As with previous examples, it provides the mapping database configuration for the dynamic

EID—but this time for the end users that are located in the remote branch office. The LISP router located in the remote branch office is configured with the subnet of the end users associated with its locator. According to the xTR registration updated process in the data centers, this configuration is also exchanged with the map server.

Example 7-16 *LISP Router xTR in the Branch Office: Showing the LISP Database*

```
WAN-XTR# show ip lisp instance-id 1 database
LISP ETR IPv4 Mapping Database for EID-table vrf MP-T3 (IID 1), LSBs: 0x1, 1 entries

192.168.123.0/24
  Locator       Pri/Wgt  Source    State
  172.16.100.1   1/100   cfg-addr  site-self, reachable
```

Example 7-17 *LISP Mapping Database: Displaying the LISP Site*

```
MSMR# show lisp site
LISP Site Registration Information for VRF "default"
* = truncated IPv6 address, -x = more-specifics count

Site Name    Last       Actively   Who last          EID-prefix
             Registered Registered Registered
DATA_CENTER  00:00:10   yes        2.2.2.1        [1] 10.0.0.0/8-2
             00:00:10   yes        192.168.2.111  [2] 10.0.0.0/8-3
BRANCH       00:00:47   yes        172.16.1.1     [1] 192.168.123.0/24
             never      no         --             [2] 192.168.123.0/24
```

A refresh update is sent every 60 seconds, alternately by each LISP xTR using LISP control plane signaling. The purpose of these updates is to maintain the latest information concerning the registered EID prefix subnet and the dynamic EID registered with each locator. The **show lisp site detail** command provides more details for all registered elements or for a particular EID, as shown in Example 7-18.

Example 7-18 *LISP Mapping Database: Displaying LISP Site Information*

```
MSMR # show lisp site 10.10.3.1 instance-id 1 detail
LISP Site Registration Information for VRF "default"
* = truncated IPv6 address, -x = more-specifics count

Site name: "DATA_CENTER"
Description: none configured
Allowed configured locators: any
  Requested EID-prefix: 10.10.3.1/32, instance-id: 1
    Currently registered: yes, first/last registered: 01:44:19/00:00:30
```

```
   Who last registered: 192.168.1.27, authentication key-id: sha1
     Registered ttl: 3 mins, routing table tag: 0
     Merge requested: no, xTR site-id: 0, proxy-reply requested: no
     Wants Map-Notifications: yes, is mobile-node: no
   Registered locator-set:
     112.112.112.112 (up), priority: 1, weight: 100
   Registration errors:
     Authentication failures: 0
     Allowed locators mismatch: 0
```

The output in Example 7-18 confirms that the dynamic EID 10.10.3.1 is located in Pod 1 (registered locator set 112.112.112.112). The output in Example 7-19 confirms that the dynamic EID 10.10.3.2 is located in Pod 2 (registered locator set 2.2.2.1).

Example 7-19 *LISP Mapping Database: Locating a Dynamic EID*

```
MSMR# show lisp site 10.10.3.2 instance-id 1 detail
LISP Site Registration Information for VRF "default"
* = truncated IPv6 address, -x = more-specifics count

Site name: "DATA_CENTER"
Description: none configured
Allowed configured locators: any
  Requested EID-prefix: 10.10.3.2/32, instance-id: 1
    Currently registered: yes, first/last registered: 02:27:52/00:00:55
    Who last registered: 192.168.12.1, authentication key-id: sha1
      Registered ttl: 3 mins, routing table tag: 0
      Merge requested: no, xTR site-id: 0, proxy-reply requested: no
      Wants Map-Notifications: yes, is mobile-node: no
    Registered locator-set:
      2.2.2.1 (up), priority: 1, weight: 100
    Registration errors:
      Authentication failures: 0
      Allowed locators mismatch: 0
```

Routing Table Verification

The routing table for each LISP router must be verified with the accurate network prefixes and host routes being advertised from the ACI pods. Example 7-20 displays the list of IP routes for the VRF MP-T3.

Note   The output of some of the **show** commands in this section has been truncated for ease of reading.

Example 7-20 *LISP Site Gateway in Pod 1: Displaying the IP Routes*

```
Pod1-XTR# show ip route vrf mp-t3 detail
IP Route Table for VRF "MP-T3"
'*' denotes best ucast next-hop
'**' denotes best mcast next-hop
'[x/y]' denotes [preference/metric]
'%<string>' in via output denotes VRF <string>

..//..

10.10.3.0/24, ubest/mbest: 1/0
    *via 192.168.31.3, [20/0], 03:21:32, bgp-3, external, tag 65501
    client-specific data: 4
    recursive next hop: 192.168.31.3/32
    extended route information: BGP origin AS 65501 BGP peer AS 65501
10.10.3.1/32, ubest/mbest: 1/0
    *via 192.168.31.3, [20/0], 03:21:32, bgp-3, external, tag 65501
    client-specific data: 4
    recursive next hop: 192.168.31.3/32
    extended route information: BGP origin AS 65501 BGP peer AS 65501
10.10.3.2/32, ubest/mbest: 1/0
    *via 2.2.2.1%default, glt2, [240/1], 02:45:05, lisp, eid
    TLV length: 21
    Source Locator Identifier: 172.16.10.16
    Flags nonce: 0x970EFD88
    Repeat factor: 1
    Instance-ID/LSB: 0x03010000

    via 10.10.3.2, Null0, [241/0], 03:19:57, lisp, dyn-eid (shadow)
        client-specific data: 5593c754
```

As expected with the configured L3Out interface from ACI Pod 1, the prefix subnet 10.10.3.0/24 is advertised from Pod 1. In addition, host routes in the /32 subnet are advertised, as shown with 10.10.3.1/32 in the routing table of the LISP xTR in Pod 1.

Regarding the roaming EID 10.10.3.2 located in Pod 2, the routing table provides two distinct details. The glt2 interface (for the Generic LISP tunnel) is driven by the LISP map cache. The glt2 interface is the virtual tunnel interface that initiates the LISP-encapsulated flows. In NX-OS, LISP programs the map caches as routing entries.

With the **show ip route detail** command, the prefix 10.10.3.2 has a second next-hop entry with the **Null0** statement and the shadow flag. The entry with Null0 was triggered when this LISP site gateway in Pod 1 was notified by the LISP map server to add the entry Null0 for the host route 10.10.3.2/32. This entry allows the LISP xTR to return a solicit map request (SMR), signaling for any request it receives for remote LISP ITR destined to this migrated EID.

It is important to verify which EID was discovered and registered by the LISP site gateway. In Example 7-21, 10.10.3.1 was registered via the local interface associated to the tenant VRF MP-T3.

Example 7-21   *LISP Site Gateway in Pod 1: Displaying the LISP Dynamic EID*

```
Pod1-XTR# show lisp dynamic-eid summary vrf MP-T3
LISP Dynamic EID Summary for VRF "MP-T3"
* = Dyn-EID learned by site-based Map-Notify
! = Dyn-EID learned by routing protocol
^ = Dyn-EID learned by EID-Notify
Dyn-EID Name   Dynamic-EID      Interface      Uptime     Last       Pending
                                                          Packet     Ping Count

DC-Subnets     !10.10.3.1       Eth1/16.3      00:47:55   00:47:55   0
```

You can verify the same results with the LISP xTR in Pod 2, as shown in Example 7-22.

Example 7-22   *LISP Site Gateway xTR in Pod 2: Displaying the IP Route*

```
Pod2-XTR# show ip route vrf MP-T3 | include 10.10.3 next 1
10.10.3.0/24, ubest/mbest: 1/0
    *via 192.168.32.1, [20/0], 1d01h, bgp-3, external, tag 65501
10.10.3.1/32, ubest/mbest: 1/0, attached
    *via 10.10.3.1, Null0, [241/0], 00:03:19, lisp, dyn-eid

10.10.3.2/32, ubest/mbest: 1/0
    *via 192.168.32.1, [20/0], 00:04:03, bgp-3, external, tag 65501


Pod2-XTR# show ip route vrf mp-t3 detail
IP Route Table for VRF "MP-T3"
'*' denotes best ucast next-hop
'**' denotes best mcast next-hop
'[x/y]' denotes [preference/metric]
'%<string>' in via output denotes VRF <string>
..//..
10.10.3.0/24, ubest/mbest: 1/0
    *via 192.168.32.1, [20/0], 03:11:20, bgp-3, external, tag 65501
     client-specific data: 5
     recursive next hop: 192.168.32.1/32
     extended route information: BGP origin AS 65501 BGP peer AS 65501
10.10.3.1/32, ubest/mbest: 1/0, attached
    *via 10.10.3.1, Null0, [240/4], 03:06:47, lisp, dyn-eid (shadow)
     client-specific data: 5633de48
10.10.3.2/32, ubest/mbest: 1/0
    *via 192.168.32.1, [20/0], 03:11:20, bgp-3, external, tag 65501
     client-specific data: 5
     recursive next hop: 192.168.32.1/32
     extended route information: BGP origin AS 65501 BGP peer AS 65501
```

In Pod 2, in addition to the local host route 10.10.3.2/32, the prefix subnet 10.10.3.0/24 is advertised from the routed subinterface from which VRF Lite hands off to carry to outside the traffic for the tenant MP-T3 traffic. Notice the LISP site gateway was notified by the map server to withdraw the host route 10.10.3.1/32 for the local routing database (Null0).

Example 7-23 summarizes the dynamic EIDs discovered for the VRF MP-T3.

Example 7-23   *LISP Site Gateway xTR in Pod 2: Displaying Dynamic EIDs*

```
Pod2-XTR# show lisp dynamic-eid summary vrf MP-T3
LISP Dynamic EID Summary for VRF "MP-T3"
* = Dyn-EID learned by site-based Map-Notify
! = Dyn-EID learned by routing protocol
^ = Dyn-EID learned by EID-Notify
Dyn-EID Name   Dynamic-EID      Interface    Uptime     Last      Pending
                                                        Packet    Ping Count
DC-Subnets     !10.10.3.2       Eth1/5.3     00:51:27   00:51:27  0
```

You can verify which EID is discovered and registered by the LISP site gateway. In Example 7-23, you can see that the dynamic EID 10.10.3.2 was registered with the LISP site router in Pod 2 via the local interface associated to the tenant VRF MP-T3.

Example 7-24 shows the LISP mapping cache table from the LISP router xTR located in the remote branch office.

Example 7-24   *LISP Router xTR in the Branch Office: Displaying the LISP Map Cache*

```
WAN-XTR# show ip lisp instance-id 1 map-cache
LISP IPv4 Mapping Cache for EID-table vrf MP-T3 (IID 1), 3 entries

0.0.0.0/0, uptime: 07:57:18, expires: never, via static send map-request
  Negative cache entry, action: send-map-request
10.10.3.1/32, uptime: 07:57:17, expires: 16:02:42, via map-reply, complete
  Locator         Uptime    State     Pri/Wgt
  112.112.112.112 07:57:17  up           1/100

10.10.3.2/32, uptime: 07:56:51, expires: 16:39:03, via map-reply, complete
  Locator  Uptime    State     Pri/Wgt
  2.2.2.1  07:20:56  up           1/100
WAN-XTR#
```

The local map cache of the LISP ITR in the branch office knows the location to use as the destination for the encapsulated traffic destined to either 10.10.3.1 or 10.10.3.2.

LISP Map Request Verification

This section describes the LISP communication and notification established between the LISP site gateways and the LISP mapping database infrastructure.

To better understand the push model for LISP ITR to send traffic to the right location—in other words, to see step by step how the remote LISP ITR fills up its map cache—let's first clear the map-cache table, as shown in Example 7-25.

Example 7-25 *LISP Router xTR in the Branch Office: Map Request*

```
WAN-XTR# clear ip lisp instance-id 1 map-cache (!) clear the map-cache
!
!
WAN-XTR# show ip lisp instance-id 1 map-cache
LISP IPv4 Mapping Cache for EID-table vrf MP-T3 (IID 1), 1 entries

0.0.0.0/0, uptime: 00:00:08, expires: never, via static send map-request
  Negative cache entry, action: send-map-request
```

A series of pings is started from the end user located in the branch office to the dynamic EID 10.10.3.2. Notice that the log in Example 7-26 is sorted to show only the relevant information.

Example 7-26 *LISP Router xTR in the Branch Office: Debugging the LISP Control Plane*

```
WAN-XTR# debug lisp control-plane map-request
WAN-XTR# terminal monitor
WAN-XTR#
*Jan 21 17:10:29.144: LISP-0: Remote EID IID 1 prefix 10.10.3.2/32, Change state to
  incomplete (sources: <signal>, state: unknown, rlocs: 0). (!) the ITR looked for
  the destined EID, but it missed it
...


*Jan 21 17:10:29.208: LISP: Send map request for EID prefix IID 1 10.10.3.2/32
*Jan 21 17:10:29.208: LISP-0: Remote EID IID 1 prefix 10.10.3.2/32, Send map request (1)
  (sources: <signal>, state: incomplete, rlocs: 0).
*Jan 21 17:10:29.208: LISP-0: EID-AF IPv4, Sending map-request from 10.10.3.2 to
  10.10.3.2 for EID 10.10.3.2/32, ITR-RLOCs 1, nonce 0x7C6A0920-0x9715E9AB (encap
  src 172.16.1.1, dst 192.168.1.111).
(!) ITR sends a Map-request for the destined EID to its Map-server
..//..


*Jan 21 17:10:29.211: LISP: Received map reply nonce 0x7C6A0920-0x9715E9AB, records 1
*Jan 21 17:10:29.211: LISP: Processing Map-Reply mapping record for IID 1 10.10.3.2/32,
  ttl 1440, action none, authoritative, 1 locator
    2.2.2.1 pri/wei=1/100 LpR (!) the ITR receives the Map-reply for the EID 10.10.3.2
...
*Jan 21 17:10:29.211: LISP: RIB Watch Group default 2.2.2.1 , created.
*Jan 21 17:10:29.211: LISP: RIB Watch Group default 2.2.2.1 , scheduling RIB update.
  (!) the new entry is registered with its RLOC + RIB updated scheduled
...
```

The LISP ITR has no IP route for that destination. Consequently, according to the LISP configuration, the ITR needs to look up the destination in its LISP map cache. The map cache is initially empty following the map cache clearing done previously. The LISP ITR executes an EID prefix for 10.10.3.2 lookup but misses the EID entry. As a result, it sends a LISP map request to its LISP map server. The LISP map request (control plane) is sent from its interface facing the WAN toward the map server.

The LISP ITR receives the map reply from the LISP map server with the location and the policies for the EID 10.10.3.2. Subsequently, the new EID is registered into its map cache with its location (2.2.2.2) and the associated policies (priority and weight), as shown in Example 7-27.

Example 7-27   *LISP Router xTR in the Branch Office: Map Request*

```
WAN-XTR# sho ip lisp instance-id 1 map-cache
LISP IPv4 Mapping Cache for EID-table vrf MP-T3 (IID 1), 2 entries
(!) the new EID entry is registered in the map-cache
0.0.0.0/0, uptime: 00:15:40, expires: never, via static send map-request
  Negative cache entry, action: send-map-request
10.10.3.2/32, uptime: 00:00:05, expires: 23:59:54, via map-reply, complete
  Locator  Uptime    State     Pri/Wgt
  2.2.2.1  00:00:05  up            1/100
WAN-XTR#
```

When the end user sends a data packet to the other endpoint 10.10.3.1, located in ACI Pod 1, the same process is repeated, as shown in Example 7-28.

Example 7-28   *LISP Router xTR in the Branch Office: Debugging the LISP Control Plane*

```
WAN-XTR#
*Jan 23 12:03:06.513: LISP: Processing data signal for EID prefix IID 1 10.10.3.1/32
*Jan 23 12:03:06.513: LISP-0: Remote EID IID 1 prefix 10.10.3.1/32, Change state to
  incomplete (sources: <signal>, state: unknown, rlocs: 0). (!) this triggers a
  Map-request
..//..
*Jan 23 12:03:06.577: LISP: Send map request for EID prefix IID 1 10.10.3.1/32
  (!) sends the Map-request
..//..(encap src 172.16.1.1, dst 192.168.1.111). (!) to its Map-server
..//..
*Jan 23 12:03:06.581: LISP-0: Map Request IID 1 prefix 10.10.3.1/32 remote EID
  prefix[LL], Received reply with rtt 4ms.
..//..
*Jan 23 12:03:06.581: LISP-0: Remote EID IID 1 prefix 10.10.3.1/32, Change state to
  complete (sources: <map-rep>, state: reused, rlocs: 0).
*Jan 23 12:03:06.581: LISP: RIB Watch Group default 112.112.112.112 , created.
*Jan 23 12:03:06.581: LISP: RIB Watch Group default 112.112.112.112 , scheduling RIB
  update.
..//..
```

Now, in addition to the primary roamer 10.10.3.2, the dynamic EID 10.10.3.1 is registered in its map cache, as shown in Example 7-29.

Example 7-29   *LISP Router xTR in the Branch Office: Map Request*

```
WAN-XTR# sho ip lisp instance-id 1 map-cache
LISP IPv4 Mapping Cache for EID-table vrf MP-T3 (IID 1), 3 entries


0.0.0.0/0, uptime: 00:19:15, expires: never, via static send map-request
  Negative cache entry, action: send-map-request
10.10.3.1/32, uptime: 00:08:45, expires: 23:51:15, via map-reply, complete
  Locator          Uptime     State     Pri/Wgt
  112.112.112.112  00:08:45   up            1/100
10.10.3.2/32, uptime: 00:04:22, expires: 23:58:45, via map-reply, complete
  Locator          Uptime     State     Pri/Wgt
  2.2.2.1          00:01:14   up            1/100
WAN-XTR#
```

Roaming an EID Across Two Sites: Verification

In the scenario shown in Example 7-30, the dynamic EID 10.10.3.1 is roaming from Pod 1 to Pod 2, and data packets are sent to 10.10.3.1 from the end user located in the branch office.

Example 7-30   *LISP Site Gateway in Pod 2: Displaying IP Routes*

```
Pod2-XTR# show ip route vrf mp-t3 detail
IP Route Table for VRF "MP-T3"
'*' denotes best ucast next-hop
'**' denotes best mcast next-hop
'[x/y]' denotes [preference/metric]
'%<string>' in via output denotes VRF <string>


..//..
10.10.3.0/24, ubest/mbest: 1/0
    *via 192.168.32.1, [20/0], 11:42:48, bgp-3, external, tag 65501
     client-specific data: 5
     recursive next hop: 192.168.32.1/32
     extended route information: BGP origin AS 65501 BGP peer AS 65501
10.10.3.1/32, ubest/mbest: 1/0
    *via 192.168.32.1, [20/0], 00:19:29, bgp-3, external, tag 65501
     client-specific data: 5
     recursive next hop: 192.168.32.1/32
     extended route information: BGP origin AS 65501 BGP peer AS 65501
10.10.3.2/32, ubest/mbest: 1/0
    *via 192.168.32.1, [20/0], 04:00:27, bgp-3, external, tag 65501
     client-specific data: 5
     recursive next hop: 192.168.32.1/32
     extended route information: BGP origin AS 65501 BGP peer AS 65501
```

The LISP xTR router belonging to the landing Pod 2 discovers the roamer 10.10.3.1. The LISP ETR immediately sends a map register to the LISP map server, which stores in the LISP mapping database the locator of the dynamic EID 10.10.3.1, as shown in Example 7-31.

Example 7-31   *ISP Router xTR in the Branch Office: Debugging the LISP Control Plane*

```
MSMR#

2019 Jan 23 07:56:04.094702 lisp: <default> Received IPv4 Map-Register from ETR
  192.168.12.1, proxy-reply: 0, want-map-notify: 1, mobile-node: 0, use-ttl: 1,
  merge-request: 0

2019 Jan 23 07:56:04.094745 lisp: <default> EID-prefix 10.10.3.1/32 (iid 1) sha1
  authentication succeeded for site "DATA_CENTER", locator count: 1

2019 Jan 23 07:56:04.094779 lisp: <default>       Map-Register has locator 2.2.2.1,
  geo: none, encap port: 0, up/uw/mp/mw:: 1/100/255/0, cached state is reachable,
  lisp-sec not capable

2019 Jan 23 07:56:04.094810 lisp: <default>       Registration complete for EID-prefix
  10.10.3.1/32
```

The last registered LISP device for the EID 10.10.3.1 uses the interface 192.168.12.1, which is the interface facing the WAN of the ETR belonging to the landing site. Subsequently, the map server sends a LISP map notification to the initial ETR belonging to Pod 1 (112.112.112.112) to indicate that the roamer 10.10.3.1 was last registered with the new locator, 2.2.2.1.

Upon receiving the map notification from the map server, the ETR at the source site installs an away entry (LISP Null0 entry) for the roamer EID.

The ETRs from both Pod 1 and Pod 2 acknowledge the LISP map notification by using a map notify ack message sent back to the map server, as shown in Example 7-32.

Example 7-32   *LISP Router xTR in the Branch Office: Debugging the LISP Control Plane*

```
2019 Jan 23 07:56:04.094910 lisp: <default> Send notify: TRUE, unsolicited: FALSE,
  current_want_map_notify: TRUE, send_map_notify: TRUE, helper->want_map_notify:
  TRUE, (old-)want_map_notify: TRUE, parent_site_eid: 0x5d046554, helper->
  last_registerer: 192.168.12.1


../..

Send Map-Notify to ETR 192.168.1.27 using sha1 retransmit:TRUE

2019 Jan 23 07:56:04.095104 lisp: <default> Send Map-Notify to ETR 112.112.112.112
  using sha1 retransmit:TRUE

2019 Jan 23 07:56:04.095146 lisp: <default> Send parent notify, send_map_notify:
  TRUE, helper->last_registerer: 2.2.2.1


2019 Jan 23 07:56:04.097526 lisp: <default> Received Map-Notify-Ack from ETR 2.2.2.1,
  nonce: 0x7dc9f428-0x3761c97d

2019 Jan 23 07:56:04.097767 lisp: <default> Received Map-Notify-Ack from ETR
  112.112.112.112, nonce: 0x7dc9f428-0x3761c97d
```

The mapping database is updated with the new locator for the roamer 10.10.3.1, as shown in Example 7-33.

Example 7-33   *LISP Mapping Database: Displaying Dynamic EID Information*

```
MSMR# show lisp site 10.10.3.1 instance-id 1
LISP Site Registration Information for VRF "default"
* = truncated IPv6 address, -x = more-specifics count


Site name: "DATA_CENTER"
Description: none configured
Allowed configured locators: any
  Requested EID-prefix: 10.10.3.1/32, instance-id: 1
    Currently registered: yes, first/last registered: 02:17:34/00:00:20
    Who last registered: 192.168.12.1, authentication key-id: sha1
      Registered ttl: 3 mins, routing table tag: 0
      Merge requested: no, xTR site-id: 0, proxy-reply requested: no
      Wants Map-Notifications: yes, is mobile-node: no
    Registered locator-set:
      2.2.2.1 (up), priority: 1, weight: 100
    Registration errors:
      Authentication failures: 0
      Allowed locators mismatch: 0
```

The LISP ITR in the branch office believes from its map cache that the locator of 10.10.3.1 is still Pod 1 (112.112.112.112). As a result, it continues sending the encapsulated packets toward the ETR in Pod 1. This is expected as it was not updated with the LISP map notify. It is responsible for triggering the handshake mechanism to update its map cache. This allows it to verify that the communication is available between the LISP ITR from the branch office and the ETR in the new landing site. As a result, the LISP ETR in Pod 1 receives the LISP packet, strips off the encapsulated header, and does a Layer 3 lookup for 10.10.3.1. This Layer 3 lookup from the destination 10.10.3.1 drives the ETR to realize that this particular EID points to Null0, meaning it is away from that location. This allows the traffic destined to the roamer to be punted to the central processing unit (CPU). As a result, the request is relayed to the LISP process that generates a solicit map request message destined to the remote xTR in the branch office, as shown in Example 7-34.

Example 7-34   *LISP Router xTR in Pod 1: Displaying IP Routes*

```
Pod1-XTR# show ip route vrf mp-t3 detail
IP Route Table for VRF "MP-T3"
'*' denotes best ucast next-hop
'**' denotes best mcast next-hop
'[x/y]' denotes [preference/metric]
'%<string>' in via output denotes VRF <string>
```

```
../..

10.10.3.0/24, ubest/mbest: 1/0
    *via 192.168.31.3, [20/0], 00:16:07, bgp-3, external, tag 65501
     client-specific data: 5
     recursive next hop: 192.168.31.3/32
     extended route information: BGP origin AS 65501 BGP peer AS 65501
10.10.3.1/32, ubest/mbest: 1/0, attached
    *via 10.10.3.1, Null0, [240/4], 00:05:28, lisp, dyn-eid (shadow)
         client-specific data: 5633ea00
```

To better understand the map cache update process using the solicit map request, it is worth activating the LISP debugging control plane to capture the solicit map request notification, as shown in the following snippet:

```
WAN-XTR# debug lisp control-plane solicit-map-request
LISP Control plane solicit-map-request debugging is on
WAN-XTR# terminal monitor
```

Upon receiving the map notification from the map server, the LISP ETR in Pod 1 installs a Null0 entry in the routing table for the host route 10.10.3.1. Subsequently, upon receiving the next packet sent from the ITR located at the remote branch office, the LIST ETR de-encapsulates the LISP data packet. The Layer 3 lookup is activated for the destination 10.10.3.1, causing it to hit the Null0 pointing to this precise EID, punt the traffic to the CPU, and pass it to the LISP process. The Null0 triggers the ETR in Pod 1 to generate the solicit map request (SMR) toward to the ITR that sourced the initial data packet.

The LISP ITR from the branch office receives the SMR associated to the EID 10.10.3.1 from the LISP xTR in Pod 1 (112.112.112.112), as shown in Example 7-35.

Example 7-35   *LISP Router xTR in the Branch Office: Debugging the LISP Control Plane*

```
WAN-XTR#
*Jan 23 15:08:05.066: LISP: Processing received Map-Request(1) message on Giga-
  bitEthernet2 from 112.112.112.112:64175 to 172.16.1.1:4342
*Jan 23 15:08:05.066: LISP: Received map request for IID 1 192.168.123.10/32,
  source_eid IID 1 10.10.3.1, ITR-RLOCs: 112.112.112.112, records 1, nonce
  0xAFAA1A70-0x383DAAAF, SMR, DoNotReply
*Jan 23 15:08:05.066: LISP-0: AF IID 1 IPv4, Scheduling SMR trigger Map-Request for
  10.10.3.1/32 from 192.168.123.10.
*Jan 23 15:08:05.066: LISP-0: IID 1 SMR & D bit set, not replying to map-request.
```

As a result, the ITR in the branch office immediately triggers a map request for 10.10.3.1 toward its map resolver. Notice in Example 7-36 that the map resolver and the map server are sharing the same IP address, 192.168.1.111.

Example 7-36 *LISP Router xTR in the Branch Office: Debugging the LISP Control Plane*

```
WAN-XTR#
*Jan 23 15:08:05.130: LISP-0: IID 1 Request processing of SMR map requests to IPv4.
*Jan 23 15:08:05.130: LISP: Send map request type SMR
*Jan 23 15:08:05.130: LISP: Send map request for EID prefix IID 1 10.10.3.1/32
*Jan 23 15:08:05.130: LISP-0: AF IID 1 IPv4, Send SMR triggered map request for
  10.10.3.1/32 (1) from 192.168.123.10.
*Jan 23 15:08:05.130: LISP-0: EID-AF IPv4, Sending map-request from 10.10.3.1 to
  10.10.3.1 for EID 10.10.3.1/32, ITR-RLOCs 1, nonce 0x83D910FD-0xCBEB0032 (encap
  src 172.16.1.1, dst 192.168.1.111).
```

The map resolver forwards the request to the map server, which in turn forwards the LISP map request to the LISP site gateway that belongs to the landing Pod 2.

The ETR in Pod 2 sends a map reply directly to the ITR belonging to the branch office with the new location 2.2.2.1 for the roamer 10.10.3.1, as shown in Example 7-37.

Example 7-37 *LISP Router xTR in the Branch Office: Debugging the LISP Control Plane*

```
*Jan 23 15:08:05.134: LISP: Processing received Map-Reply(2) message on
  GigabitEthernet2 from 172.16.20.4:4342 to 172.16.100.1:4342
*Jan 23 15:08:05.134: LISP: Received map reply nonce 0x83D910FD-0xCBEB0032,
  records 1
*Jan 23 15:08:05.134: LISP: Processing Map-Reply mapping record for IID 1 10.10.3.1/32,
  ttl 1440, action none, authoritative, 1 locator
.    2.2.2.1 pri/wei=1/100 LpR
*Jan 23 15:08:05.134: LISP-0: Map Request IID 1 prefix 10.10.3.1/32 SMR[LL],
  Received reply with rtt 4ms.
```

The ITR from the branch office updates its map cache with the new locator for that EID and starts forwarding the encapsulated data packets toward the ETR that belongs to Pod 2. Consequently, as verified in the **show** output in Example 7-38, 10.10.3.1 is identified in its LISP map cache as being located at 2.2.2.1 (RLOC).

Example 7-38 *LISP Router xTR in the Branch Office: Displaying the LISP Mapping Cache*

```
WAN-XTR# sho ip lisp instance-id 1 map-cache
LISP IPv4 Mapping Cache for EID-table vrf MP-T3 (IID 1), 3 entries

0.0.0.0/0, uptime: 03:21:45, expires: never, via static send map-request
  Negative cache entry, action: send-map-request
10.10.3.1/32, uptime: 02:38:09, expires: 23:53:43, via map-reply, complete
  Locator  Uptime    State     Pri/Wgt
  2.2.2.1  00:06:16  up              1/100
10.10.3.2/32, uptime: 02:38:59, expires: 22:48:02, via map-reply, complete
  Locator         Uptime    State     Pri/Wgt
  2.2.2.1         01:11:57  up              1/100
```

LISP Mobility for ACI in Conjunction with a Silent Host

The previous analysis shows the LISP control plane and data plane step by step, capturing the efficient association between the LISP notification and the routing tables as well as LISP tables being dynamically updated. However, as noted earlier, data packets were continuously generated between the end user and the dynamic EID, leaving no chance for the roamer to become silent.

As most of network teams know, some servers become silent if they are not solicited. This status may black-hole some traffic if data does not wake up the destination. Furthermore, it's important to remember that LISP relies on the control plane and/or the data plane data issued by the dynamic EID discovering the concerned endpoint. This dynamic discovery process traditionally triggers immediately the signaling to notify the LISP infrastructure components.

However, for this mechanism to be efficient, the EID must be identified with its Layer 3 reachability information, and it must exist in the routing table and the LISP database.

Assume that a roamer is silent for the reason just mentioned, and no data packets are sent to and from that host. Now say that this machine requires a migration to another site, either an ACI pod or an ACI fabric. Finally, assume that the hypervisor framework deployed for that purpose relies on RARP packets to notify the upstream physical switch whenever there is a need to update the internal MAC address table, also known as the *content addressable memory* (CAM) table. This is the specific case, for example, generated with a vMotion from the VMware vSphere platform, and it results in a RARP notification being sent toward the upstream top-of-rack switch, which is also the first-hop router anycast gateway.

RARP frames do not contain any local host IP information in the payload, so they are used only to learn Layer 2 endpoint information, triggering a CAM table update but not providing the IP addresses of the roamer.

It is also important to keep in mind that with most of other main hypervisor platforms, such as Microsoft Hyper-V and Citrix Xen, a GARP message packet is sent instead, which includes the source IP address of the sender in the payload. As the IP address of the transmitter remains detectable, after a move, the "silent" host is discovered and registered with the control plane, based on GARP messages. Hence, after the migration stage, a "silent" host status should not happen with GARP message notifications because traditionally the destination host sends a control plane GARP message that includes the source IP address of the roamer. Consequently, the "silent" host situation should not be an issue with GARP messages.

The procedure to learn an endpoint IP address is slightly different with RARP messages. Unlike in a traditional network or fabric, ACI prevents black holes with a silent host by using a unique process named *silent host discovery*. To demonstrate this behavior, you can migrate a virtual machine by using the VMware vCenter. For example, you can move the same machine 10.10.3.1 that is now active in Pod 2 back to Pod 1. Example 7-39 shows the key output that provides the information to localize the EID of interest.

The command on the map server in Example 7-39 indicates the last registered locators for that particular endpoint. As mentioned earlier, the last element that registered 10.10.3.1 is 192.168.12.1, which is the core interface of the xTR belonging to Pod 2. This is validated with the registered locator 2.2.2.2, which includes the associated policies (priority and weight).

Example 7-39 *LISP Mapping Database: Displaying the LISP Dynamic EID*

```
MSMR# show lisp site 10.10.3.1 instance 1
LISP Site Registration Information for VRF "default"
* = truncated IPv6 address, -x = more-specifics count


Site name: "DATA_CENTER"
Description: none configured
Allowed configured locators: any
  Requested EID-prefix: 10.10.3.1/32, instance-id: 1
    Currently registered: yes, first/last registered: 05:46:44/00:00:31
    Who last registered: 192.168.12.1, authentication key-id: sha1
      Registered ttl: 3 mins, routing table tag: 0
      Merge requested: no, xTR site-id: 0, proxy-reply requested: no
      Wants Map-Notifications: yes, is mobile-node: no
    Registered locator-set:
      2.2.2.1 (up), priority: 1, weight: 100
    Registration errors:
      Authentication failures: 0
      Allowed locators mismatch: 0
```

On the xTR in Pod 1, 10.10.3.1 is flagged with Null0, which means that if a request destined to that particular host hits this local LISP xTR, the latter returns a solicit map request to the ITR that initiated that encapsulated packet.

Notice in Example 7-40 that the other VM 10.10.3.2 is local as the next hop; it is the L3Out interface of the ACI border leaf in Pod 1.

Example 7-40 *LISP Site Gateway in Pod 1: Displaying the Roamer's Host Route*

```
Pod1-XTR# show ip route vrf mp-t3 detail
IP Route Table for VRF "MP-T3"
..//..
10.10.3.1/32, ubest/mbest: 1/0, attached
   *via 10.10.3.1, Null0, [240/4], 00:30:53, lisp, dyn-eid (shadow)
    client-specific data: 5633ea00
10.10.3.2/32, ubest/mbest: 1/0
   *via 192.168.31.3, [20/0], 00:49:54, bgp-3, external, tag 65501
    client-specific data: 5
    recursive next hop: 192.168.31.3/32
    extended route information: BGP origin AS 65501 BGP peer AS 65501
```

The routing table from the xTR in Pod 2 shows that 10.10.3.1 is local, as expected. The next hop is 192.168.32.1, which indicates the L3Out interface reachability information of the border leaf deployed at ACI Pod 2, as shown in Example 7-41.

Example 7-41   *LISP Site Gateway in Pod 2: Displaying the Roamer's Host Route*

```
Pod2-XTR# show ip route vrf mp-t3 detail
IP Route Table for VRF "MP-T3"
..//..
10.10.3.1/32, ubest/mbest: 1/0
    *via 192.168.32.1, [20/0], 00:32:41, bgp-3, external, tag 65501
    client-specific data: 5
    recursive next hop: 192.168.32.1/32
    extended route information: BGP origin AS 65501 BGP peer AS 65501
..//..
```

Thus, Example 7-41 demonstrates that 10.10.3.1 is currently located in Pod 2, which can be confirmed with the command shown in Example 7-42.

Example 7-42   *LISP Site Gateway in Pod 2: Displaying the Dynamic EID*

```
Pod2-XTR# show lisp dynamic-eid summary vrf MP-T3
LISP Dynamic EID Summary for VRF "MP-T3"
* = Dyn-EID learned by site-based Map-Notify
! = Dyn-EID learned by routing protocol
^ = Dyn-EID learned by EID-Notify
Dyn-EID Name   Dynamic-EID     Interface     Uptime     Last       Pending
                                                        Packet     Ping Count
DC-Subnets     !10.10.3.1      Eth1/5.3      07:53:41   07:53:41   0
Pod2-XTR#
```

No data packet is sent to or from this EID. As a result, the machine 10.10.3.1 is currently silent. Some operating systems become silent if no data packets are sent to them.

The next step is to move 10.10.3.1 from Pod 2 to Pod 1, as shown in Figure 7-32.

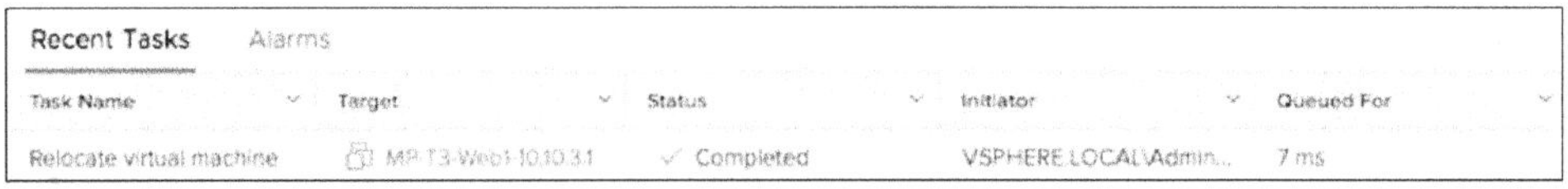

Recent Tasks	Alarms				
Task Name	Target	Status	Initiator	Queued For	
Relocate virtual machine	MP-T3-Web1-10.10.3.1	✓ Completed	VSPHERE.LOCAL\Admin...	7 ms	

Figure 7-32   *Migration Status of 10.10.3.1 from the Hypervisor*

After the successful migration of the roamer in Pod 1, the VMkernel of the target ESXi sent the RARP to the upstream switch. Because there is no source IP address in the RARP message, the discovery process to learn the EID couldn't be triggered from the control plane discovery process. As a result, if you look at the LISP mapping database, you see that the dynamic EID 10.10.3.1 still belongs to Pod 2.

In a traditional network, this could cause a black-hole situation or, in the best case, a non-optimal path to reach the destination. Indeed, although 10.10.3.1 is now physically located in Pod 1, the map server still refers to the locator set being Pod 2 (2.2.2.1). This is expected because the IP address 10.10.3.1 was not discovered yet in the new location Pod 1 due to its silent mode, as shown in Example 7-43.

Example 7-43   *LISP Mapping Database: Displaying the LISP Dynamic EID*

```
MSMR# show lisp site 10.10.3.1 instance 1
LISP Site Registration Information for VRF "default"
* = truncated IPv6 address, -x = more-specifics count


Site name: "DATA_CENTER"
Description: none configured
Allowed configured locators: any
  Requested EID-prefix: 10.10.3.1/32, instance-id: 1
    Currently registered: yes, first/last registered: 05:50:38/00:01:20
    Who last registered: 192.168.12.1, authentication key-id: sha1
      Registered ttl: 3 mins, routing table tag: 0
      Merge requested: no, xTR site-id: 0, proxy-reply requested: no
      Wants Map-Notifications: yes, is mobile-node: no
    Registered locator-set:
      2.2.2.1 (up), priority: 1, weight: 100
```

In the Layer 3 routing table of the xTR where the concerned EID just landed, you can see that the EID is pointing to Null0. Typically, if it receives a data packet destined to 10.10.3.1—theoretically detecting that the EID points to Null0—the local xTR should reply to the sender with an SMR LISP message, as shown in Example 7-44.

Example 7-44   *LISP Site Gateway in Pod 1: Displaying the IP Routes for VRF MP-T3*

```
Pod1-XTR# show ip route vrf mp-t3 detail
IP Route Table for VRF "MP-T3"
..//..
10.10.3.0/24, ubest/mbest: 1/0
    *via 192.168.31.3, [20/0], 09:07:37, bgp-3, external, tag 65501
     client-specific data: 5
     recursive next hop: 192.168.31.3/32
     extended route information: BGP origin AS 65501 BGP peer AS 65501
10.10.3.1/32, ubest/mbest: 1/0, attached
    *via 10.10.3.1, Null0, [240/4], 00:35:01, lisp, dyn-eid (shadow)
     client-specific data: 5633ea00
..//..
```

However, if you look at the LISP xTR Pod 2 from which the EID 10.10.3.1 comes, you see that the roamer disappeared from its routing table, as shown in Example 7-45.

Example 7-45   *LISP Site Gateway in Pod 2: Displaying the IP Routes for VRF MP-T3*

```
Pod2-XTR# show ip route vrf mp-t3 detail
IP Route Table for VRF "MP-T3"
..//..
10.10.3.0/24, ubest/mbest: 1/0
    *via 192.168.32.1, [20/0], 14:01:18, bgp-3, external, tag 65501
        client-specific data: 5
        recursive next hop: 192.168.32.1/32
        extended route information: BGP origin AS 65501 BGP peer AS 65501
10.10.3.2/32, ubest/mbest: 1/0, attached
    *via 10.10.3.2, Null0, [240/4], 00:53:47, lisp, dyn-eid (shadow)
        client-specific data: 5633de48
```

Actually, this is the expected result. When the ESXi host in Pod 1 sends the RARP message on behalf of the roamer, the ACI border leaf node in Pod 1 learns the MAC address of that machine. However, because of the RARP message format, its IP address is unknown. As a result, the border leaf node in Pod 1 sends a COOP update for the MAC address of the concerned roamer toward the local spine nodes (in Pod 1) to register the Layer 2 reachability information in the COOP database. This triggers an EVPN route type 2 advertisement to the ACI spine nodes in Pod 2. Only the MAC address is distributed.

As soon as the spine device in Pod 2 receives this EVPN route type 2 update, it notices that the location information for the original endpoint with the same MAC address changed. As a result, the ACI spine nodes in initial Pod 2 revoke the IP entry associated to that mobile machine from the COOP database and send a COOP message to the local border leaf node to stop advertising that IP address for that machine out of the L3Out connection. Hence, the /32 disappears from the Pod 2 XTR routing table.

Because the map server is not updated, the remote LISP router remains the same original locator in Pod 2 for the EID 10.10.3.1. Because no data packet is sent from the end user, there is no mechanism to trigger a new map notification, as shown in Example 7-46.

Example 7-46   *LISP Site Gateway in the Branch Office: Displaying the LISP EID for VRF Instance 1*

```
WAN-XTR# show ip lisp instance-id 1 map-cache
LISP IPv4 Mapping Cache for EID-table vrf MP-T3 (IID 1), 3 entries
 ..//..
0.0.0.0/0, uptime: 09:50:38, expires: never, via static send map-request
  Negative cache entry, action: send-map-request
10.10.3.1/32, uptime: 09:07:01, expires: 23:21:21, via map-reply, complete
  Locator  Uptime    State     Pri/Wgt
  2.2.2.1  00:38:38  up          1/100
 ..//..
```

After a couple minutes, the recorded roamer is removed from the mapping database, as shown in Example 7-47. This is expected with the LISP timer, which protects against endpoints being disconnected from the fabric.

Example 7-47   *LISP Mapping Database: Displaying the LISP EID for VRF Instance 1*

```
MSMR# show lisp site 10.10.3.1 instance 1
LISP Site Registration Information for VRF "default"
* = truncated IPv6 address, -x = more-specifics count


Site name: "DATA_CENTER"
Description: none configured
Allowed configured locators: any
  Requested EID-prefix: 10.0.0.0/8, instance-id: 1
    More-specifics registered: 1
    Currently registered: yes, first/last registered: 08:24:14/00:00:34
    Who last registered: 2.2.2.1, authentication key-id: sha1
      Registered ttl: 3 mins, routing table tag: 0
      Merge requested: no, xTR site-id: 0, proxy-reply requested: no
      Wants Map-Notifications: yes, is mobile-node: no
    Registered locator-set:
      2.2.2.1 (up), priority: 1, weight: 50
      112.112.112.112 (up), priority: 1, weight: 50
    Registration errors:
      Authentication failures: 0
      Allowed locators mismatch: 0
```

Sending Data Packets Toward a Silent Host

A first data packet (ping) destined to 10.10.3.1 is generated from the end user. This ping hits the LISP xTR in Pod 2 because this is the last registered locator for the remote LISP ITR. The LISP xTR has no entry for that host route, so it routes the data packet toward the next hop for the prefix subnet 10.10.30.0/24, which is advertised by the border leaf nodes in Pod 2 of the ACI fabric.

Because 10.10.3.1 is currently unknown inside the ACI fabric—you only know the Layer 2 reachability information, not the IP address—the silent host discovery process is started. To accomplish this discovery, ACI generates an ARP gleaning that is sent to all the edge interfaces belonging to that particular bridge domain. As a result, the endpoint receives an ARP request generated by the ACI fabric that originated from the default gateway on that bridge domain (in this example, 10.10.3.254). The ARP request is broadcast and hits the desired destination, as shown in Example 7-48, where **tcpdump** runs in the web server.

Example 7-48 *ARP Request from ARP Gleaning Hits the Endpoint*

```
root@MP-T3-Web1:~# tcpdump
tcpdump: verbose output suppressed, use -v or -vv for full protocol decode
  Listening on eth0, link-type EN10MB (Ethernet), capture size 65535 bytes
  00:45:04.893798 ARP, Request who-has 10.10.3.1 (Broadcast) tell 10.10.3.254,
  length 46 00:45:04.893831 ARP, Reply 10.10.3.1 is-at 00:50:56:b9:c9:ac (oui
  Unknown), length 28    ..//..
```

The endpoint replies to this ARP gleaning. As a result, its IP address is discovered, and consequently its status as a silent host disappears because the ACI fabric has forced the silent host to talk.

As a result of the discovery process, the IP address of the roamer is advertised out the L3Out interface in the border leaf node Pod 1 toward the LISP xTR belonging in the same pod (Pod 1), which sends a LISP map register message toward its LISP mapping database (map server).

The LISP map server sends a map notification to the original xTR in Pod 2 to inform it to update its routing table with the roamer pointing to Null0. Subsequently, the LISP xTR in Pod 1 updates its routing table appropriately, as shown in Example 7-49.

Example 7-49 *LISP Site Gateway in Pod 1: Displaying the IP Routes for VRF MP-T3 (Instance 1)*

```
Pod1-XTR# show ip route vrf mp-t3 detail
IP Route Table for VRF "MP-T3"
..//..
10.10.3.0/24, ubest/mbest: 1/0
    *via 192.168.31.3, [20/0], 09:14:32, bgp-3, external, tag 65501
        client-specific data: 5
        recursive next hop: 192.168.31.3/32
        extended route information: BGP origin AS 65501 BGP peer AS 65501
10.10.3.1/32, ubest/mbest: 1/0
    *via 192.168.31.3, [20/0], 00:01:13, bgp-3, external, tag 65501
    client-specific data: 5
    recursive next hop: 192.168.31.3/32
    extended route information: BGP origin AS 65501 BGP peer AS 65501
10.10.3.2/32, ubest/mbest: 1/0
    *via 192.168.31.3, [20/0], 01:00:57, bgp-3, external, tag 65501
    client-specific data: 5
    recursive next hop: 192.168.31.3/32
    extended route information: BGP origin AS 65501 BGP peer AS 65501
```

At this stage, the map server is updated with the new location for 10.10.3.1, as shown in Example 7-50.

Example 7-50 *LISP Mapping Database: Displaying the Dynamic EID for VRF Instance 1*

```
MSMR# show lisp site 10.10.3.1 instance 1
LISP Site Registration Information for VRF "default"
* = truncated IPv6 address, -x = more-specifics count


Site name: "DATA_CENTER"
Description: none configured
Allowed configured locators: any
  Requested EID-prefix: 10.10.3.1/32, instance-id: 1
    Currently registered: yes, first/last registered: 00:00:19/00:00:19
    Who last registered: 192.168.1.27, authentication key-id: sha1
      Registered ttl: 3 mins, routing table tag: 0
      Merge requested: no, xTR site-id: 0, proxy-reply requested: no
      Wants Map-Notifications: yes, is mobile-node: no
    Registered locator-set:
      112.112.112.112 (up), priority: 1, weight: 100
    Registration errors:
      Authentication failures: 0
      Allowed locators mismatch: 0
```

At the original LISP xTR in Pod 2, the location for the roamer 10.10.3.1 is known behind the RLOC (LISP xTR 112.112.112.112) in Pod 1 as a first choice and points to Null0, as the alternate option, as shown in Example 7-51.

Example 7-51 *LISP Site Gateway in Pod 2: Displaying IP Routes for VRF MP-T3 (Instance 1)*

```
Pod2-XTR# show ip route vrf mp-t3 detail
IP Route Table for VRF "MP-T3"
../...
10.10.3.0/24, ubest/mbest: 1/0
    *via 192.168.32.1, [20/0], 14:08:14, bgp-3, external, tag 65501
    client-specific data: 5
    recursive next hop: 192.168.32.1/32
    extended route information: BGP origin AS 65501 BGP peer AS 65501
10.10.3.1/32, ubest/mbest: 1/0
    *via 10.10.3.1, Null0, [240/4], 00:02:04, lisp, dyn-eid (shadow)
        client-specific data: 5633de48
10.10.3.2/32, ubest/mbest: 1/0, attached
    *via 10.10.3.2, Null0, [240/4], 01:00:43, lisp, dyn-eid (shadow)
    client-specific data: 5633de48
```

Nonetheless, the single data packet triggers the discovery process for the mapping database, driven by the ARP gleaning generated by the ACI fabric. All LISP components are updated with the new location, 112.112.112.112. However, the WAN xTR in the branch office has not yet been updated because the SMR message from the new xTR in Pod 1 hasn't started. From its map cache, the locator to reach 10.10.3.1 is still Pod 2 (2.2.2.1), as shown in Example 7-52.

Example 7-52 *LISP Site Gateway in the Branch Office: Displaying the Dynamic EID*

```
WAN-XTR# show ip lisp instance-id 1 map-cache
LISP IPv4 Mapping Cache for EID-table vrf MP-T3 (IID 1), 3 entries

0.0.0.0/0, uptime: 1d03h, expires: never, via static send map-request
  Negative cache entry, action: send-map-request
10.10.3.1/32, uptime: 1d02h, expires: 23:43:58, via map-reply, complete
  Locator  Uptime    State     Pri/Wgt
  2.2.2.1  00:16:01  up           1/100
10.10.3.2/32, uptime: 1d02h, expires: 23:44:04, via map-reply, complete
  Locator  Uptime    State     Pri/Wgt
  2.2.2.1  00:15:55  up           1/100
WAN-XTR#
```

The remote ITR has still the EID 10.10.3.1 recorded with the location in Pod 2.

A second data packet from the end user that is destined to 10.10.3.1 is encapsulated by the remote LISP ITR and sent toward the RLOC 2.2.2.1, which is the LISP ETR in Pod 2.

The LISP site gateway in Pod 2 strips off the LISP header and does a Layer 3 lookup in its routing table. It realizes that the host route 10.10.3.1 points to Null0. As a result, it sends a solicit map request (SMR) back to the remote ITR. The SMR informs the ITR to generate a map request for the EID 10.10.3.1 from 192.168.123.10, as shown in Example 7-53.

Example 7-53 *LISP Site Gateway in the Branch Office: Debugging the Control Plane; Map Request for 10.10.3.1*

```
WAN-XTR# debug lisp control-plane solicit-map-request
LISP Control plane solicit-map-request debugging is on
WAN-XTR# terminal monitor
WAN-XTR#
*Jan 24 15:28:59.560: LISP: Processing received Map-Request(1) message on
  GigabitEthernet2 from 2.2.2.1:63260 to 172.16.1.1:4342
*Jan 24 15:28:59.560: LISP: Received map request for IID 1 192.168.123.10/32,
  source_eid IID 1 10.10.3.1, ITR-RLOCs: 2.2.2.1, records 1, nonce 0x1CA61500-
  0x31D7A71C, SMR, DoNotReply
*Jan 24 15:28:59.560: LISP-0: AF IID 1 IPv4, Scheduling SMR trigger Map-Request
  for 10.10.3.1/32 from 192.168.123.10.
*Jan 24 15:28:59.560: LISP-0: IID 1 SMR & D bit set, not replying to map-request.
..//..
```

The remote xTR (172.16.1.1) sends the map request to its map server (192.168.1.111) for the last registered locator for the dynamic EID 10.10.3.1/32, as shown in Example 7-54.

Example 7-54 *LISP Site Gateway in the Branch Office: Debugging the Control Plane; Map Request to Map Server*

```
*Jan 24 15:28:59.624: LISP-0: AF IID 1 IPv4, Send SMR triggered map request for
  10.10.3.1/32 (1) from 192.168.123.10.
*Jan 24 15:28:59.624: LISP-0: EID-AF IPv4, Sending map-request from 10.10.3.1 to
  10.10.3.1 for EID 10.10.3.1/32, ITR-RLOCs 1, nonce 0x4AD84A43-0x052854A2
  (encap src 172.16.1.1, dst 192.168.1.111).
*Jan 24 15:28:59.627: LISP: Processing received Map-Reply(2) message on
  GigabitEthernet2 from 172.16.10.16:4342 to 172.16.100.1:4342
```

The map server replies with the new RLOC 112.112.112.112 for 10.10.3.1/32, with the policies associated to this registered EID, as shown in Example 7-55.

Example 7-55 *LISP Site Gateway in the Branch Office: Debugging the Control Plane; Map Reply from Map Server*

```
*Jan 24 15:28:59.627: LISP: Received map reply nonce 0x4AD84A43-0x052854A2,
  records 1
*Jan 24 15:28:59.627: LISP: Processing Map-Reply mapping record for IID 1
  10.10.3.1/32, ttl 1440, action none, authoritative, 1 locator
    112.112.112.112 pri/wei=1/100 LpR
*Jan 24 15:28:59.627: LISP-0: Map Request IID 1 prefix 10.10.3.1/32 SMR[LL],
  Received reply with rtt 3ms.
```

The map cache of the remote xTR is now updated properly with the last registered locator, as shown in Example 7-56.

Example 7-56 *LISP Site Gateway in the Branch Office: Displaying the IP Routes for VRF MP-T3 (Instance 1)*

```
WAN-XTR# show ip lisp instance-id 1 map-cache
LISP IPv4 Mapping Cache for EID-table vrf MP-T3 (IID 1), 3 entries

0.0.0.0/0, uptime: 1d03h, expires: never, via static send map-request
  Negative cache entry, action: send-map-request
10.10.3.1/32, uptime: 1d02h, expires: 23:59:35, via map-reply, complete
  Locator          Uptime    State      Pri/Wgt
    112.112.112.112 00:00:24  up            1/100
10.10.3.2/32, uptime: 1d02h, expires: 23:41:09, via map-reply, complete
  Locator  Uptime    State     Pri/Wgt
    2.2.2.1  00:18:50  up             1/100
```

Data packets can be sent using the optimal path toward Pod 1, where the roamer is currently active.

Note   It is worth noting that the ARP gleaning mechanism works both with ACI Multi-Pod and ACI Multi-Site. This is a special and unique functionality of ACI.

For a deployment of LISP IP Mobility in conjunction with an ACI SDN platform, it is possible to improve the business continuity with no disruption during a hot live migration.

There are two main options for achieving a migration without any interruption. First, ACI Multi-Pod or ACI Multi-Site must be configured with the Layer 2 network extended between distant locations. Second, the prefix subnet (10.10.3.0/24) must be advertising continuously from each pod or site. As a result, during the migration of the machine and before LISP updates occur across all the infrastructure components, the traffic continues to be sent toward the original xTR, known as the *initial locator*, before the roaming is completely achieved. The traffic destined for the mobile endpoint is therefore seamlessly routed inside the primary ACI pod, which advertises the concerned prefix domain. The traffic destined for a machine that landed in a remote location can be forwarded across the Layer 2 extension toward the final destination. In practice, this should not happen. However, it might be crucial to offer this alternate path if, for any reason, LISP IP Mobility has not yet registered the last locations in the mapping database and other remote xTRs—which might happen in the event of network disruption.

The second option discussed previously mitigates the risk of disruption. For example, a LISP cache miss might occur due to an interface network or link bouncing, and so the traffic might use inter-pod transit to reach the destination. Even if the transit across the ACI fabric is made for a short period of time, this guarantees the continuity of the active session without any interruption. As soon as LISP updates the dynamic EID and routing tables, the redirection uses the optimal path to the destination.

For this improvement to be totally efficient, it is necessary to advertise the prefix subnet /24 in addition to the host route /32 from all data center locations. In case of a network outage during a map notification for the migration of an EID, for example, it might appear to be an interruption until the next xTR registers its EID update toward the map server, which happens every 60 seconds.

Troubleshooting LISP IP Mobility with ACI or VXLAN Fabrics

There are many **show** and **debug** commands available to troubleshoot LISP IP Mobility with ACI or VXLAN fabrics. As demonstrated in this chapter, only a few of them are used to verify the configuration as well as the health of the LISP infrastructure.

In this particular host route advertisement, it is important to verify that all the mobile prefix networks and host routes of interest are injected properly into the routing table of the local ITR, as shown in the following snippet.

```
xTR NX-OS # show ip route vrf MP-T3 detail
```

The LISP xTR must have all the dynamic EIDs registered, as shown in the following snippet:

```
xTR NX-OS # show lisp dynamic-eid summary vrf <vrf_name>
xTR-NX-OS# show ip lisp map-cache vrf <vrf_name>
IOS XE# show ip lisp instance-id <id>  map-cache
```

LISP xTRs register their dynamic EIDs with the map server (LISP mapping database) every 60 seconds, as shown in the following snippet:

```
MS NX-OS# show lisp site details
MS NX-OS# show lisp site a.b.c.d instance <id>
```

To better follow the LISP notifications and update, it is useful to leverage the **debug** log events. In addition, it can be useful is to verify the map register events from both the xTRs and the MS, as shown in the following snippet:

```
xTR NX-OS# debug lisp mapping register
```

From the remote ITR, it is useful to capture the logs related to the roaming (that is, the solicit map request). From the ETR belonging to the original data center of the roamer:

```
xTR NX-OS# show lisp smr
IOS XE # debug lisp control-plane solicit-map-request
```

More generally, a debug of all events might also be useful to better isolate where a non-identified issue comes from, as shown in the following snippet:

```
xTR NX-OS# show lisp events
```

LISP and MTU Considerations

The LISP transport adds 36 extra bytes (IPv4) or 56 extra bytes (IPv6) to the original packet size when sending an encapsulated IP packet across the Layer 3 transport infrastructure. As with many other protocols that encapsulate or tunnel traffic—such as VXLAN, IP Security (IPsec), Ethernet over Multiprotocol Label Switching (EoMPLS), and generic routing encapsulation [GRE])—it is possible that the resulting encapsulated packets could exceed the allowed MTU size along the transit layer path.

LISP provides both stateful and stateless mechanisms for handling potential MTU issues, with the main goals being to prevent packets from being dropped and to prevent the need for ETRs to perform packet reassembly prior to LISP de-encapsulation. Those two mechanisms are described as follows in Section 5.4 of RFC 6830:

> This section proposes two mechanisms to deal with packets that exceed the path MTU between the ITR and ETR.

> It is left to the implementor to decide if the stateless or stateful mechanism should be implemented. Both or neither can be used because it is a local decision in the ITR regarding how to deal with MTU issues, and sites can interoperate with differing mechanisms.

Both stateless and stateful mechanisms also apply to Re-encapsulating and Recursive Tunneling, so any actions below referring to an ITR also apply to a TE-ITR.

Although LISP offers a mechanism to deal with packets that exceed the path MTU, it is a best practice and recommendation, if allowed to increase the MTU size to 1556 or more on service provider connections. Prior to the MTU change, it is recommended to verify the transmission of a 1500-byte packet between LISP routers with the don't fragment (DF) bit set.

If increasing the MTU of the access links is not possible, ensure that ICMP is not being filtered to allow path MTU discovery to take place. By default, **path-mtu-discovery** is enabled by the LISP router. It is possible (and optional) to configure the minimum and maximum MTU settings for the LISP router for **path-mtu-discovery**, as shown in the following snippet:

```
xTR NX-OS# { ip | ipv6 } lisp path-mtu-discovery { min lower-bound|
  max upper-bound}
```

It is not recommended to disable the use of **path-mtu-discovery**.

Another recommendation is to ensure that the enterprise is not filtering ICMP unreachable or time exceeded messages on a firewall or router.

Flowchart Depicting the Roaming Process

The flowchart shown in Figure 7-33 summarizes the various steps and associations between the LISP signaling and update processes used while an endpoint is migrating.

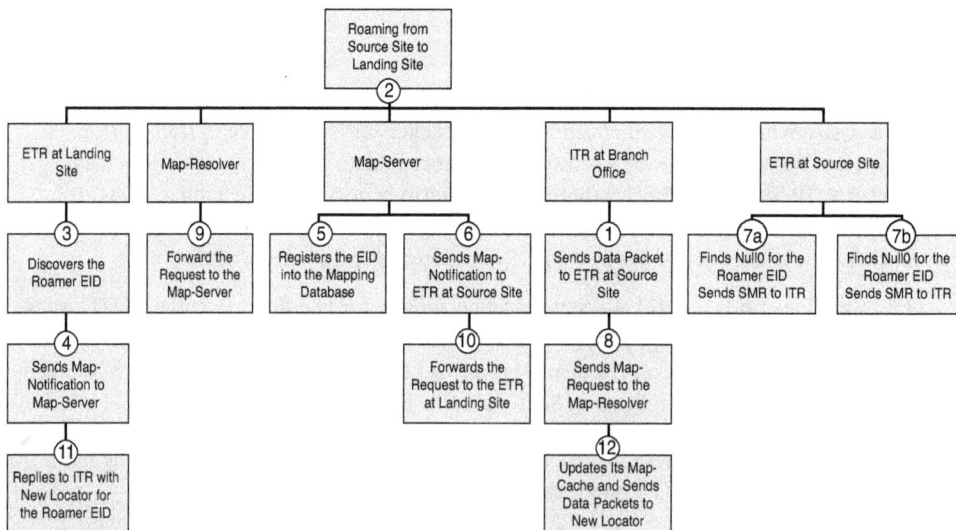

Figure 7-33 *Flowchart for the LISP Process*

The flowchart depicts the following steps that occur during a migration process with LISP:

Step 1. Before the migration of the roamer, the remote ITR continuously sends data packets to the original site.

Step 2. The roamer migrates from the source location to the landing site.

Step 3. The xTR at the landing site discovers the roaming EID, which it registers to its database.

Step 4. The xTR sends a map register to the map server.

Step 5. The map server receives the map register and stores the new location of the roaming EID in the mapping database.

Step 6. The map server sends a LISP map notify message to the original ETR belonging to the source site.

Step 7a. Upon receiving the map notification, the ETR at the source site installs an away entry (LISP Null0 entry) for the roamer EID.

Step 7b. In addition, when the original ETR belonging to the source site receives the next packet, it de-encapsulates it and runs a Layer 3 lookup for the destination. The lookup for the destination of interest hits the Null0 entry. This allows the traffic to be punted to the CPU and hence to be passed to the LISP process that generates the solicit map request (SMR) destined to the remote XTR.

Step 8. The remote ITR at the branch office receives the SMR for the roamer of interest. As a result, it sends a map request to the map resolver for that particular roamer EID.

Step 9. The map resolver forwards the request to the map server.

Step 10. The map server in turn forwards the map request to the LISP ETR that belongs to the landing site.

Step 11. The ETR at the landing site sends a LISP map reply to the ITR located at the branch office with the new location for the roamer.

Step 12. The ITR from the branch office updates its map cache with the new locator and immediately forwards the data packets to the ETR belonging to the landing site.

Summary

LISP IP Mobility triggers notifications and database mapping updates to redirect the traffic using the optimal path seamlessly within a few seconds. The source and destination endpoints are agnostic about LISP signaling and LISP encapsulation. The same statement applies to the Layer 3 core network, constructed with either a private routed network or an MPLS VPN managed network. A part from increasing the MTU size as discussed above, the Layer 3 core doesn't require any specific configuration to support the LISP overlay traffic. Finally, the fabric itself doesn't need to be LISP capable or to establish a link with the LISP routers using a particular LISP protocol, unlike in traditional data center networks (that is, the LISP FHR). LISP IP Mobility can leverage the embedded native function of host routing supported by VXLAN EVPN or ACI fabrics.

As discussed in Chapter 6, LISP Host Mobility offers two different deployment models, which are usually associated with different workload mobility scenarios and network designs; LISP IP Mobility with Extended Subnet Mode (ESM) in conjunction with Layer 2 networks/subnets extended across sites and LISP IP Mobility Across Subnet Mode (ASM) with Layer 3 routed network only between sites.

In the first scenario discussed in this chapter, LISP IP Mobility ESM is deployed in conjunction with a network solution extending the bridge domain and maintaining the Layer 2 adjacency between the source location and the target destination. The key concern that LISP addresses is managing the IP localization in real time for any movement of dynamic roamers, thus immediately establishing the most optimal path toward the mobile destination, wherever that is in a LISP data center. LISP IP Mobility in conjunction with modern fabrics such as VXLAN EVPN Multi-Site or ACI Multi-Pod or ACI Multi-Site offers ingress path optimization for hot live migration, which means there is no need to restart any running application or software process on the mobile machine. LISP takes the routed information (including the prefix subnet and host routes) from the fabric transparently, without the need to meticulously configure LISP parameters inside the fabric. In such a scenario, the virtual machine can migrate without traffic interruption from one place to a distant location, and the ingress traffic is dynamically redirected to the site of interest, reducing the latency to its lowest value.

LISP IP Mobility ASM can also be deployed across multiple locations, in which subnets are different between distant sites and with no Layer 2 extensions deployed across the data centers. This is typically the scenario used for disaster recovery planning or for extending resources to a cloud provider data center while managing cost containment. This model allows an endpoint to move to a different IP subnet while retaining its original IP address, as is commonly done in cold migration scenarios. In such a scenario, LISP provides both IP mobility and dynamic inbound traffic path optimization functionalities without any manual human action.

In summary, the LISP IP Mobility solution deployed with an ACI Multi-Pod, ACI Multi-Site, or VXLAN Multi-Site provides the following key benefits:

- LISP coexistence with host route advertisement natively supported by the fabric

- Automated move detection

- Dynamic EID discovery in multihomed sites

- Seamless ingress path optimization that avoids traffic triangulation problems

- Active connections maintained across move use cases, such as hot live migrations

- No routing re-convergence

- No DNS updates required

- Transparent to the endpoints and to the IP core

- Transparent to the fabrics (VXLAN or ACI fabrics)

- Guaranteed optimal shortest-path routing

- Seamless hot live migration (ESM) or cold migration (ASM)

- Support for any combination of IPv4 and IPv6 addressing

- Fine granular locations of endpoints

References

The following references provide more details on the topics discussed in this chapter:

RFC 6830, "The Locator/ID Separation Protocol (LISP)"

Cisco, "VXLAN EVPN Multi-Site Design and Deployment," http://www.cisco.com

Cisco, "ACI Multi-Pod," http://www.cisco.com

Cisco, "Cisco ACI Multi-Site Architecture," http://www.cisco.com

Cisco, "Optimizing Ingress Routing with LISP Across Multiple VXLAN/EVPN Sites," http://www.cisco.com

Cisco, "Cisco Programmable Fabric with VXLAN BGP EVPN Configuration Guide," http://www.cisco.com

Cisco, "Cisco APIC Layer 3 Networking Configuration Guide," Release 4.0(1), http://www.cisco.com

## Chapter 8

LISP Network Virtualization/ Multi-Tenancy

Any enterprise or service provider network today has multiple organizations sharing the same physical infrastructure to minimize capital and operating expenses. A service provider uses its infrastructure to host multiple customers and provides multiple types of services, ranging from Multiprotocol Label Switching (MPLS) virtual private networks (VPNs), Internet, transport service, voice, video, WAN links, and possibly cloud services. Enterprises also have various departments, such as human resources, finance, and engineering, that all utilize the same network infrastructure. This chapter shows how LISP allows logical segmentation in the network so multiple groups of users or types of services can share a common physical infrastructure. You will first learn about how LISP supports segmenting the network in the control plane and data plane through the LISP instance identifier (IID) field in LISP packets. This chapter covers the following topics in use cases:

- Multi-tenancy in the network

- LISP Instance Identifier and virtualization models

- Shared model virtualization

- Parallel model virtualization

Configuration examples are shown for each use case listed. Finally, the chapter ends by providing guidance on how to troubleshoot virtualized LISP networks.

Multi-tenancy in the Network

Virtualization basically involves abstracting, pooling, or partitioning the components of a physical device in software to optimize resource and isolate or improve the portability of an application or service. One common example of virtualization is server virtualization.

The VMware ESXi hypervisor is a popular server virtualization solution in the industry. In server virtualization solutions, the hypervisor abstracts the physical server components such as its storage, network, and input/output components into software objects, which any guest operating system installed on top of the hypervisor layer can consume without having to worry about the right firmware support. Each of these instances of guest operating systems installed on the hypervisor of each server is known as a *virtual machine* (*VM*). Multiple guest operating systems of various types and from a number of vendors can exist on the same physical server as virtual machines, each hosting different applications and services and eliminating the restriction of having one server for one operating system or application. Server virtualization technologies allow a server to have multiple tenants. In the case of the servers, the tenants are applications or operating systems for a particular organization.

If servers living in a network are hosting multiple tenants, each of these tenants is an independent operational unit that is part of a business function or group of users. The tenants should be identifiable in the network, and the communication between tenants should be controlled based on the organizational security framework and business and functional requirements of the IT infrastructure. The networking industry has addressed the multi-tenancy requirements of the network infrastructure through various network virtualization technologies.

A virtual local area network (VLAN) takes a physical switch with a single bridge table and allows it to create multiple bridge tables, each identified by a unique 12-bit IEEE 802.1Q identifier called a *VLAN number*. Each VLAN acts as an isolated LAN; as the media access control (MAC) forwarding tables are independent from each other inside the software of the switch, and no traffic flows from one VLAN to the other within the switch unless routing is enabled natively (for a multilayer switch) or through an external device such as a router that is a common point that has connectivity to both VLANs and can forward traffic between the VLANs. VLANs segment the network at the data link layer, or Layer 2, of the Open System Interconnection (OSI) model.

At Layer 3 of the OSI model, the network layer, virtual routing and forwarding (VRF) enables the creation of multiple routing tables apart from the default or global routing table in a router. Each routing table is completely isolated from the others. Routing protocols and interfaces are assigned to a VRF routing context, which determines which routes are populated inside the VRF instances and which interfaces packets can be received on and forwarded from. VLANs and VRF instances involve layers of segmentation that must work together to provide end-to-end network virtualization for control plane and data plane traffic.

Data plane traffic path isolation is achieved either through a single-hop or multihop method. Single-hop methods include techniques such as using VLAN and VRF instances that provide isolation at a device level from one device to its connected next hop and onward until the packet reaches its destination. At every hop, the same VLAN/VRF instance is configured to ensure path isolation from source to destination. The single-hop method is shown in Figure 8-1.

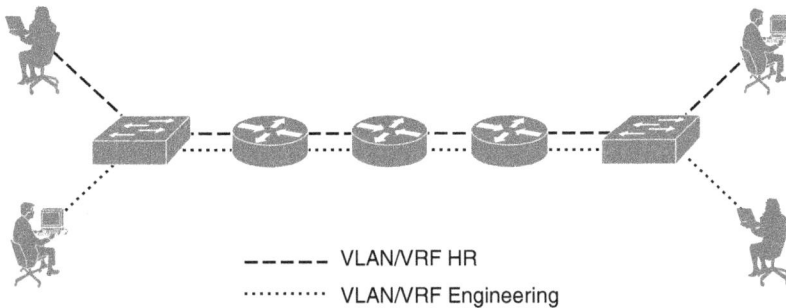

```
----- VLAN/VRF HR
.......... VLAN/VRF Engineering
```

Figure 8-1   *Single-Hop Path Isolation*

Every device in the path shown in Figure 8-1 is configured with both the Human Resources (HR) and Engineering VLANs and VRF instance to ensure path isolation end to end. Forwarding state information for both VLANs and VRF instances is also maintained end to end. This approach is a viable option in a small network, but as the number of tenants and network scale grow, this option becomes operationally painful and lacks scalability. Also, if you want to maintain tenancy across networks that are separated by the enterprise core, a service provider, a wide area network (WAN), or the Internet, how do you maintain multi-tenancy? You can use multihop path isolation with technologies such as MPLS VPNs, Generic Routing Encapsulation (GRE), Layer 2 Tunneling Protocol (L2TPv3), Virtual Extensible LAN (VXLAN), or LISP. Multihop path isolation is needed when organizations are separated by a WAN or Internet network, as shown in Figure 8-2, and there is a need to isolate these two organizations' networks from each other end to end.

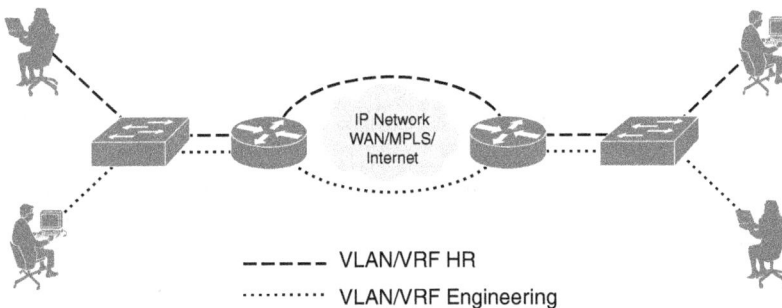

```
IP Network
WAN/MPLS/
Internet
```

```
----- VLAN/VRF HR
.......... VLAN/VRF Engineering
```

Figure 8-2   *Multihop Path Isolation*

Multihop path isolation is also seen in spine and leaf data center fabrics, where the spine adds the extra hop between the leafs to which tenants attach; in the case of service provider networks, the core routers are the hops to which tenant traffic attaches when edge router traffic must traverse to each remote provider edge router with members of the same tenant attached to it. MPLS VPNs and VXLAN Ethernet Virtual Private Network (EVPN) are overlay solutions that provide control plane and data plane network virtualization through packet header attributes and fields as packets are exchanged in the network. For example, in both the case of MPLS VPNs and VXLAN EVPNs, the Border Gateway Protocol (BGP) extended community attribute route target (RT) is used to control import and export of routing information into VRF tables. Each VRF table has a unique RT value associated with it, which defines the VPNs or tenancy in the network for IP routing. Route distinguishers are also used to convert overlapping routing native IP prefix entries across VPNs into BGP VPNv4 or VPNv6 address families by appending unique 64-bit BGP attributes, creating 96-bit VPNv4 and 192-bit VPNv6 prefixes. The VPNv4 and VPNv6 prefixes allow routers to differentiate the overlapping prefixes from each other as the prefixes for the VPNs are advertised through the core network. In MPLS networks, the data plane MPLS labels are used to define the unique transport path and the VPNs to which the data packet is forwarded from a certain source to a particular destination. In VXLAN EVPN networks, the VXLAN header has a virtual network identifier (VNID) field that defines the network segment the data traffic is part of. If the packet is being switched, the VNID value represents the Layer 2 segment or bridge domain the packet belongs to, and if the packet is being routed from source to destination, the VNID represents the VRF, assuming symmetric integrated routing and bridging. In the case of MPLS and VXLAN EVPN, the control plane protocol is BGP, and the data plane protocols are MPLS and VXLAN, respectively.

In the case of a LISP network, LISP is both the control plane protocol and the data plane protocol.

Note   It is not a requirement for LISP to be both the control plane protocol and the data plane protocol. In the case of Cisco Software Defined Access (SD-Access) enterprise networks, the LISP function is handled by the control plane, VXLAN is used in the data plane, and Security Group Tags (SGT) is used in the policy plane. One of the greatest strengths of LISP is the decoupling of the control plane and data plane, which allows engineers to use non-LISP data plane encapsulation such as VXLAN while using LISP to map a network address (identity) to its location.

The LISP protocol also ensures network segmentation both in the data plane and in the control plane, with one single LISP header field called the LISP instance identifier (IID). The LISP IID is referenced during control plane packet exchange between LISP device as well as when LISP-encapsulated data packets are forwarded to ensure proper processing of a packet within the correct virtual network. The next section defines in detail the LISP IID.

LISP Instance ID

The LISP IID is encoded inside LISP control plane messages based on the LISP Canonical Address Format standard in RFC 8060. The LISP address family identifier (AFI) that is reserved to encode the LISP IID prefix is AFI 16387 with type value 2 in the LISP control plane message header, as shown in Figure 8-3.

```
 0                   1                   2                   3
 0 1 2 3 4 5 6 7 8 9 0 1 2 3 4 5 6 7 8 9 0 1 2 3 4 5 6 7 8 9 0 1
```

AFI = 16387			Rsvd1	Flags
Type = 2	IID Mask-len		Length	
Instance ID				
AFI = x		Address …		

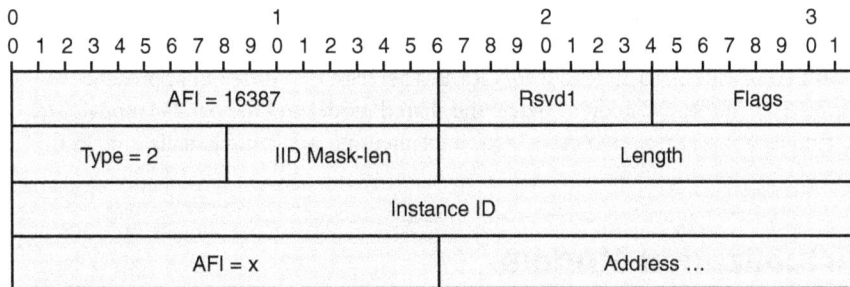

Figure 8-3 *LISP IID Encoding*

A map server uses a LISP IID to store addresses for a particular VPN site in its local database. The egress tunnel router (ETR) node registers an endpoint identifier (EID) prefix with the map server and uses the LISP IID to signal which VPN the EID prefix is a part of. The storing and signaling of IID with the EID prefix allows overlapping prefixes to be deployed across VPNs as long as the VPNs have unique IIDs. Cisco enforces the uniqueness of LISP IIDs mapped to VRF instances in a single LISP routing instance. Since LISP is a Layer 3 network overlay, and VRF creates unique instances of routing tables, segmentation through the LISP IID in a LISP network is mapped to a VRF instance.

The LISP data packets also encode LISP IIDs into the LISP header. The LISP instance bit (I-bit) in the LISP header flag indicates whether the IID is encoded in the packet. If the I-bit is set to 1, this means that out of the 32 bits allocated to the IID/locator-status-bit (LSB) field, the highest 24 bits have the IID encoded into it, while the lower-order 8 bits are for LSB, as shown in Figure 8-4.

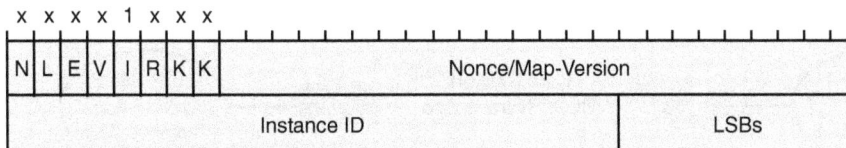

```
 x  x  x  x  1  x  x  x
```

N	L	E	V	I	R	K	K	Nonce/Map-Version
Instance ID								LSBs

Figure 8-4 *Data Packet LISP IID Encoding*

The EID address space represents the identity of the endpoints, the routing locator (RLOC) space represents the location of the EID, and the LISP IID represents the VPN the EID resides in. During registration of the EID from the ETR, the LISP IID always represents the EID prefix VPN, which maps to a VRF instance. In data packets, the LISP IID is the destination EID VPN, which can exist within the same VPN as the source or in a different VPN. LISP intranet communication occurs when endpoints in LISP networks communicate within the same VRF instance/VPN. LISP extranet communication occurs when endpoints in LISP networks communicate across VRF instances/VPNs.

LISP networks consist of two address spaces, EID and RLOC. The address spaces can be virtualized independently, and the ingress/egress tunnel routers (xTRs) register and resolve an EID in VRF A to an RLOC in VRF B. There are two different approaches to virtualizing EID and RLOC address space: the shared model and the parallel model. The next section examines these two models for implementing network virtualization in LISP networks.

LISP Virtualization Models

Any organization implementing LISP is not a monolithic organization but has various departments and institutions providing various services and housing various applications. A subset of users or tenants exists in each unique network segment, such as a VRF instance mapped to a LISP IID with an allocated EID address space. When implementing a VPN, there are two things to consider. First, will you dedicate an xTR node for each tenant, or will you share an xTR node among various tenants? Single-tenant configuration involves configuring a single VPN for each xTR as a LISP site with an EID prefix, as shown in Figure 8-5.

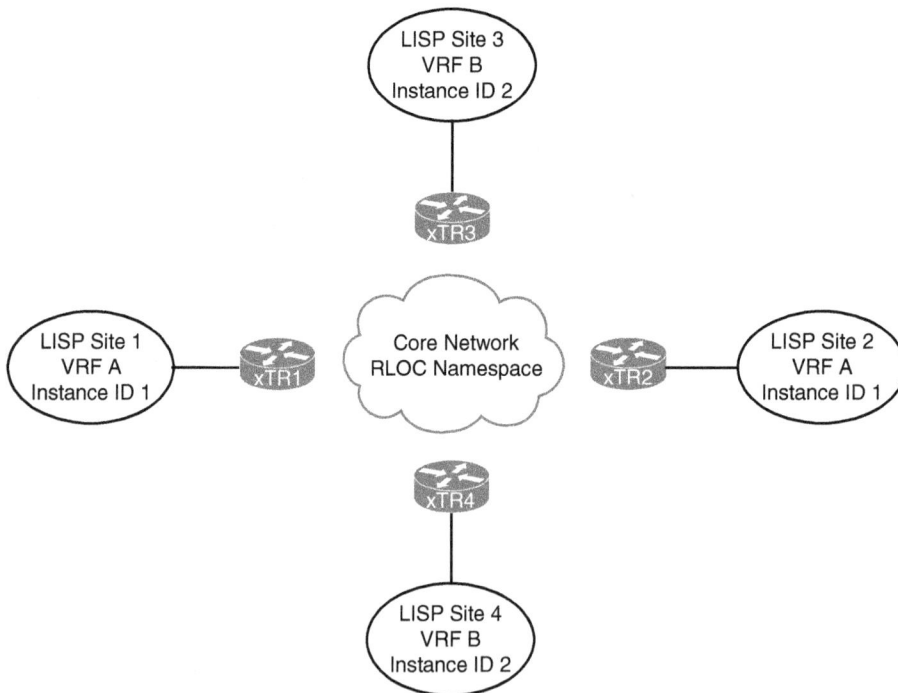

Figure 8-5   *LISP Virtualization Single-Tenant Configuration*

With a multi-tenant configuration, multiple VPNs are configured for each xTR, each with an EID prefix, as shown in Figure 8-6.

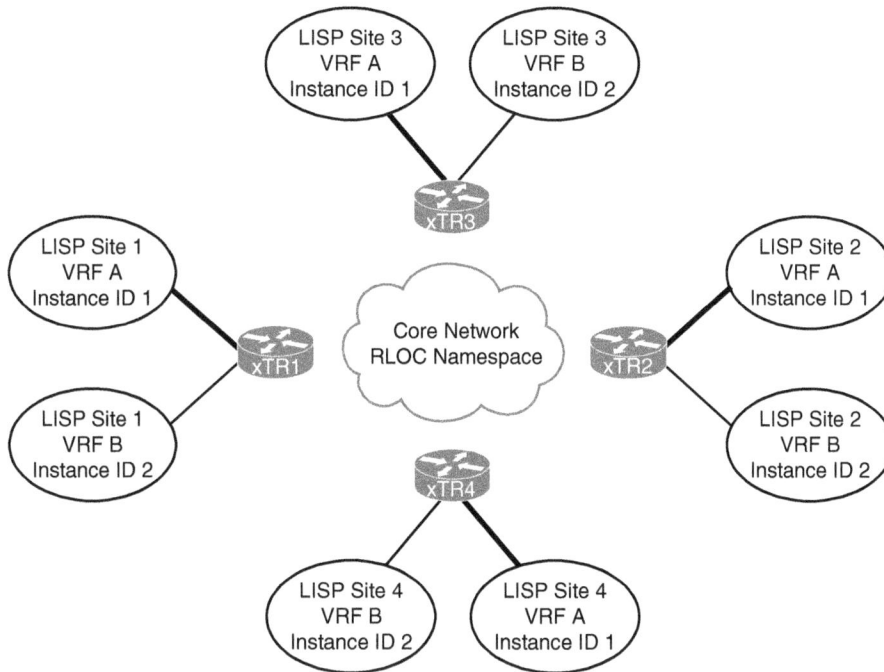

Figure 8-6 *LISP Virtualization Multi-Tenant Configuration*

The second consideration when implementing a VPN is whether you will share a common RLOC space across all the LISP site VPNs or whether each LISP site VPN will have a dedicated RLOC space. The following sections look more closely at the shared and parallel models of LISP virtualization.

Shared Model

With the LISP virtualization shared model, a common RLOC address space is shared among all the EID address space. The EID address space may be virtualized into different VRF instances mapped to a LISP IID, but all the EIDs resolve to a common locator address space. The locator address space can be the default/global VRF instance or a user-created VRF instance, but it is shared among all the LISP VPN sites/EID address spaces. Figure 8-7 shows the LISP virtualization shared model.

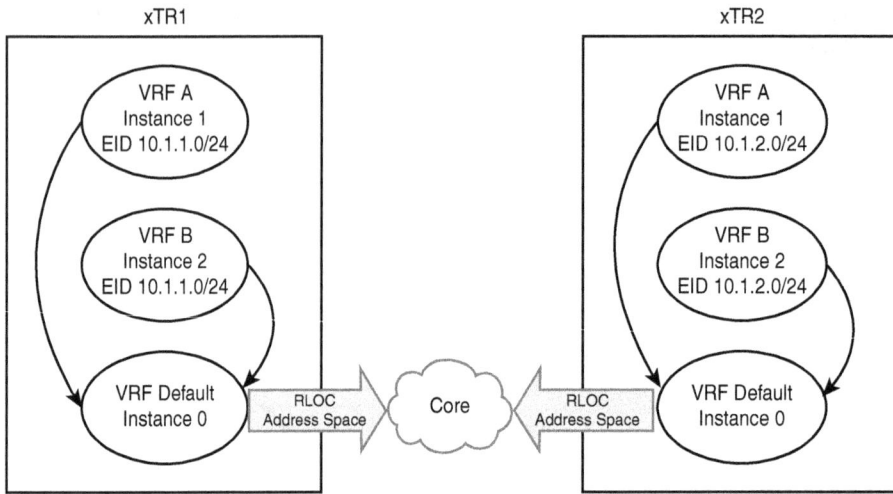

Figure 8-7   *LISP Virtualization Shared Model*

Notice that the two VRF instances, VRF A and VRF B, resolve to a single RLOC address space on the xTR node. There is basically an *N*:1 mapping, where *N* is the number of virtualized EID address spaces to 1 RLOC address space.

A common use case for the shared model is in an enterprise network where the network has been virtualized to support a multi-tenant environment but a common backbone enterprise core is managed by a single network administration team; in such a scenario, the backbone network does not need to be segmented, and it uses a single routing instance and table. Operationally, this model is simpler because the RLOC addresses all exist in a single VRF, and there is no configuration required to further segment the core network. A similar use case can also be applied to a service provider network providing LISP routing service to its various enterprise customers across a common backbone core, with each customer represented as a unique VPN with LISP IID and VRF instance.

The parallel model, discussed next, implements a 1:1 mapping between virtualized EID address space and virtualized RLOC address space.

Parallel Model

A common use case for the parallel model is a tier 1 service provider acting as a LISP VPN backbone carrier to smaller tier 2 and tier 3 carriers. With the parallel model, a smaller carrier uses the backbone carrier core infrastructure as an RLOC namespace, and the service carriers are isolated from each other. Every smaller carrier is a LISP site VPN customer of the backbone carrier with a dedicated VRF instance in the backbone carrier that acts as its transport network to interconnect the xTRs attached to each LISP site VPNs. Because each LISP VPN requires a dedicated VRF for its locater address space, the EID and the RLOC address space are both virtualized using VRF instances.

The EID and locater address space do not need to be in the same VRF. But for simplicity, Figure 8-8 shows parallel model LISP virtualization with each virtualized EID namespace mapped to an RLOC namespace in the same VRF instance.

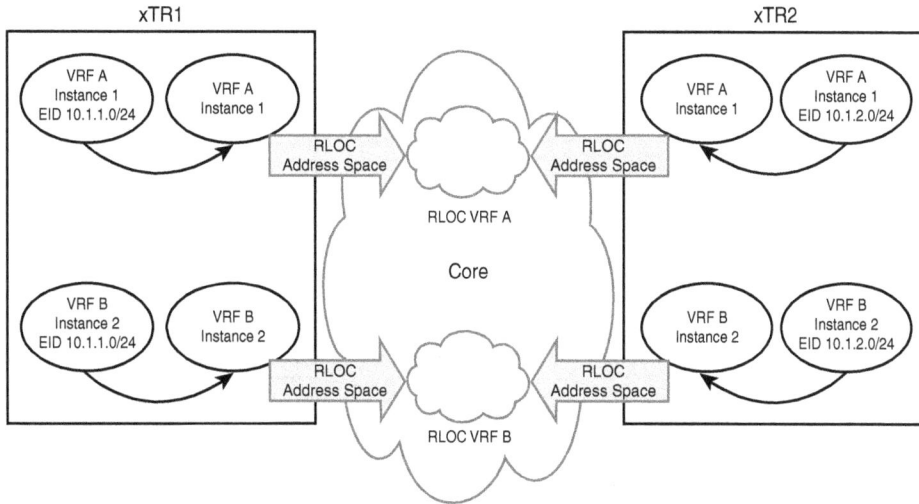

Figure 8-8 *LISP Virtualization Parallel Model*

In Figure 8-8, notice that VRF A is part of LISP Instance 1. LISP Instance 1 has EID prefix 10.1.1.0/24 in xTR1, which is a LISP VPN site. The LISP VPN site in VRF A resolves its locator address in VRF A, as indicated by the curved arrow. The locator address space VRF A is extended to the core network, where the RLOCs connect with each other for VRF A VPN sites. VRF A and VRF B are completely isolated from each other both in the LISP sites attached to the xTR and in the core, as shown by the separate clouds for the VRF locator address space in the core network. RLOCs in VRF A cannot ping RLOCs in VRF B because their routing tables are separate from each other.

Hybrid Model

The shared and parallel models of LISP virtualization can be combined to create a hybrid model. As you can guess, this is an *N*:1 mapping of virtualized EID to virtualized RLOC address space. Let's return to the previous example with the smaller carriers using the backbone carrier for LISP network service; the smaller carrier has its own customers, each in a virtualized LISP site. The customers of the smaller carrier also need to be isolated into virtualized EID namespace by being placed in their own VRF instances. The customers of the smaller carrier share the common virtualized locator address space, but it goes through the backbone carrier network. Figure 8-9 shows a hybrid model.

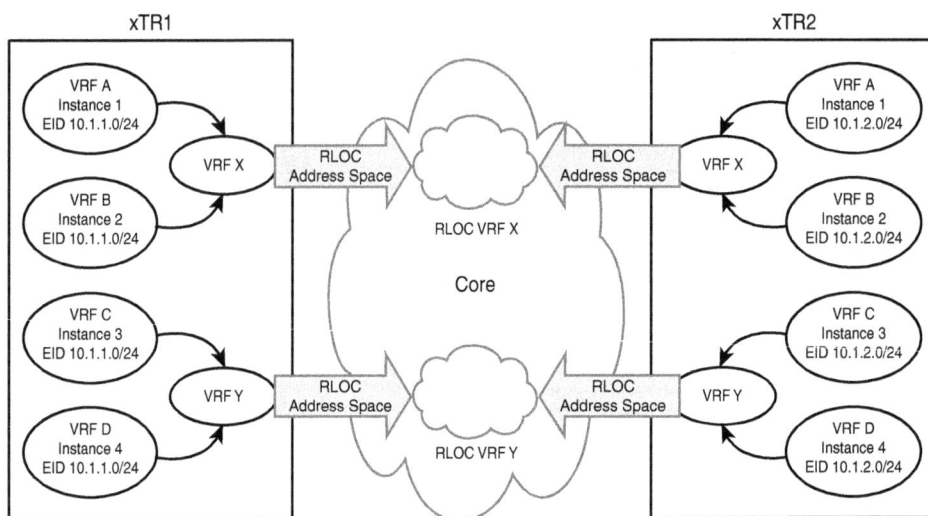

Figure 8-9 *LISP Virtualization Hybrid Model*

In Figure 8-9, VRF X and VRF Y represent two small carrier locator address spaces. VRF A and VRF B are VPN customers of one small carrier with locator addresses in VRF X. VRF C and VRF D are VPN customers of the second small carrier, with locator addresses in VRF Y. The core network represents the backbone carrier providing network transport service to each of its customers, which are the small carriers.

LISP Shared Model Virtualization Configuration

This section provides a LISP shared model implementation example to reinforce the concepts related to LISP virtualization models that have been explained so far in this chapter. Figure 8-10 is the sample topology used for the following configuration examples.

The steps to implement LISP virtualization are the same as the steps shown in earlier chapters. The main difference now is that you must consider the VRF and LISP IID according to the LISP virtualization model you are deploying. In the scenario shown in Figure 8-10, each xTR has two VRF instances named ComA and ComB. The xTR devices have routers with hostnames CE# attached to them. Each of the customer edge (CE) routers represents a LISP VPN site assigned to VRF ComA or ComB. xTR1 and xTR2 have CE routers attached to them in both VRF ComA and VRF ComB, assigned to LISP IID 1 and LISP IID 2, respectively. The CE nodes use a static default route pointing toward their directly attached xTRs. The core network is running Open Shortest Path First (OSPF) as the underlay Interior Gateway Protocol (IGP) for the purpose of advertising RLOC loopback addresses between the xTRs and the map server (MS) and map resolver (MR). The core network has a single instance of OSPF with all routing learning and forwarding information in the default or global VRF. The RLOC namespace default VRF is shared by all the LISP VPN sites in VRF ComA and ComB.

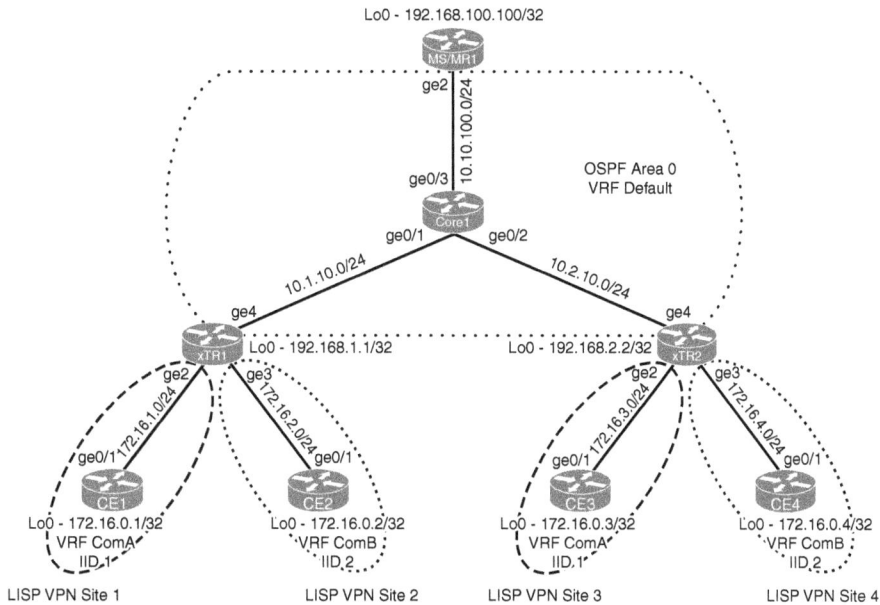

Figure 8-10 *LISP Virtualization Shared Model Topology*

Note A non-default VRF for the RLOC namespace could have been created for this example, but we kept it simple by using the default VRF.

The xTR LISP virtualization configuration must consider the VRF and LISP IID when specifying the EID prefix attached to the xTR. The RLOC locater table by default is associated to the default VRF. The command to create an EID prefix table and associate the table with a VRF instance and LISP IID is **eid-table** { **default** | **vrf** *vrf-name* } **instance-id iid**. The command to associate the locator address table to a VRF instance is **locator-table** { **default** | **vrf** *vrf-name* }.

Note For the sake of brevity, all the configuration examples in this chapter are for the IPv4 address family. IPv6 is, of course, supported, and similar configuration steps apply.

The configuration of the xTR1 device attached to LISP VPN Site 1 and Site 2 is shown in Example 8-1.

Example 8-1 *xTR1 LISP Shared Model Configuration*

```
!xTR1 IOS-XE LISP shared model configuration

 hostname xTR1

vrf definition ComA
 !
 address-family ipv4
 exit-address-family
!
vrf definition ComB
 !
 address-family ipv4
 exit-address-family

 interface Loopback0
 ip address 192.168.1.1 255.255.255.255
 ip ospf 1 area 0

 interface GigabitEthernet2
 vrf forwarding ComA
 ip address 172.16.1.1 255.255.255.0

!
interface GigabitEthernet3
 vrf forwarding ComB
 ip address 172.16.2.1 255.255.255.0

!
interface GigabitEthernet4
 ip address 10.1.10.2 255.255.255.0
 ip ospf 1 area 0

 router ospf 1
 router-id 192.168.1.1

!static routing between xTR and CE nodes.

ip route vrf ComA 172.16.0.1 255.255.255.255 172.16.1.2
ip route vrf ComB 172.16.0.2 255.255.255.255 172.16.2.2

router lisp

locator-table default
```

```
eid-table vrf ComA instance-id 1
  database-mapping 172.16.1.0/24 192.168.1.1 priority 1 weight 1
  database-mapping 172.16.0.1/32 192.168.1.1 priority 1 weight 1

 eid-table vrf ComB instance-id 2
  database-mapping 172.16.2.0/24 192.168.1.1 priority 1 weight 1
  database-mapping 172.16.0.2/32 192.168.1.1 priority 1 weight 1

 exit
 !
 ipv4 itr map-resolver 192.168.100.100
 ipv4 itr
 ipv4 etr map-server 192.168.100.100 key cisco
 ipv4 etr
 exit
```

Example 8-1 shows that VRF ComA maps to LISP IID 1, and VRF ComB maps to LISP IID 2. There is an EID table for each site attached to xTR1. Example 8-2 shows that the configuration for xTR2 is similar to the configuration for xTR1.

Example 8-2   *xTR2 LISP Shared Model Configuration*

```
hostname xTR2

vrf definition ComA
 !
 address-family ipv4
 exit-address-family
 !
vrf definition ComB
 !
 address-family ipv4
 exit-address-family

 interface Loopback0
 ip address 192.168.2.2 255.255.255.255
 ip ospf 1 area 0

 interface GigabitEthernet2
 vrf forwarding ComA
 ip address 172.16.3.1 255.255.255.0

 !
```

```
interface GigabitEthernet3
 vrf forwarding ComB
 ip address 172.16.4.1 255.255.255.0

 !
interface GigabitEthernet4
 ip address 10.2.10.2 255.255.255.0
 ip ospf 1 area 0

router ospf 1
 router-id 192.168.2.2

ip route vrf ComA 172.16.0.3 255.255.255.255 172.16.3.2
ip route vrf ComB 172.16.0.4 255.255.255.255 172.16.4.2

router lisp

locator-table default

 eid-table vrf ComA instance-id 1
  database-mapping 172.16.3.0/24 192.168.2.2 priority 1 weight 1
  database-mapping 172.16.0.3/32 192.168.2.2 priority 1 weight 1

 eid-table vrf ComB instance-id 2
  database-mapping 172.16.4.0/24 192.168.2.2 priority 1 weight 1
  database-mapping 172.16.0.4/32 192.168.2.2 priority 1 weight 1
 exit
 !
 ipv4 itr map-resolver 192.168.100.100
 ipv4 itr
 ipv4 etr map-server 192.168.100.100 key cisco
 ipv4 etr

exit
```

It is important to make sure the sites that fall within the same VPN map to the same LISP IID across the different xTRs. This is similar to how the different provider edge routers for the same VPNs have a common RT value. The sites within the same VRF instance (intranet VPNs) are only able to ping each other, as shown in Example 8-3.

Example 8-3 *LISP VPN Site-to-Site Connectivity Test*

```
!Quick observation of LISP map cache before first time communication on xTR1

xTR1# show ip lisp map-cache instance-id 1
LISP IPv4 Mapping Cache for EID-table vrf ComA (IID 1), 1 entries

0.0.0.0/0, uptime: 2d12h, expires: never, via static-send-map-request
  Negative cache entry, action: send-map-request

xTR1# show ip lisp map-cache instance-id 2
LISP IPv4 Mapping Cache for EID-table vrf ComB (IID 2), 1 entries

0.0.0.0/0, uptime: 2d12h, expires: never, via static-send-map-request
  Negative cache entry, action: send-map-request


!initiate ping within VRF ComA from CE1 to CE3

CE1# ping 172.16.0.3 source loopback 0
Type escape sequence to abort.
Sending 5, 100-byte ICMP Echos to 172.16.0.3, timeout is 2 seconds:
Packet sent with a source address of 172.16.0.1
!!!!!
Success rate is 100 percent (5/5), round-trip min/avg/max = 5/6/7 ms


!Trying to ping across VPNs fails from CE1 to CE2 or CE4.

CE1# ping 172.16.0.2 source loopback 0
Type escape sequence to abort.
Sending 5, 100-byte ICMP Echos to 172.16.0.2, timeout is 2 seconds:
Packet sent with a source address of 172.16.0.1
.U.U.
Success rate is 0 percent (0/5)


CE1# ping 172.16.0.4 source loopback 0
Type escape sequence to abort.
Sending 5, 100-byte ICMP Echos to 172.16.0.4, timeout is 2 seconds:
Packet sent with a source address of 172.16.0.1
.U.U.
Success rate is 0 percent (0/5)


!Verifying connectivity from CE2 to CE4 for VRF ComB.
```

```
CE2# ping 172.16.0.4 source loopback 0
Type escape sequence to abort.
Sending 5, 100-byte ICMP Echos to 172.16.0.4, timeout is 2 seconds:
Packet sent with a source address of 172.16.0.2
!!!!!
Success rate is 100 percent (5/5), round-trip min/avg/max = 5/5/7 ms


!state of lisp map cache on xTR1 post ping.


xTR1# show ip lisp map-cache instance-id 1
LISP IPv4 Mapping Cache for EID-table vrf ComA (IID 1), 4 entries


0.0.0.0/0, uptime: 2d13h, expires: never, via static-send-map-request
  Negative cache entry, action: send-map-request
172.16.0.2/32, uptime: 00:09:46, expires: 00:05:13, via map-reply, forward-native
  Negative cache entry, action: forward-native
172.16.0.3/32, uptime: 00:10:53, expires: 23:49:06, via map-reply, complete
  Locator      Uptime     State     Pri/Wgt      Encap-IID
  192.168.2.2  00:10:53   up          1/1           -

xTR1# show ip lisp map-cache instance-id 2
LISP IPv4 Mapping Cache for EID-table vrf ComB (IID 2), 2 entries


0.0.0.0/0, uptime: 2d13h, expires: never, via static-send-map-request
  Negative cache entry, action: send-map-request
172.16.0.4/32, uptime: 00:07:28, expires: 23:52:31, via map-reply, complete
  Locator      Uptime     State     Pri/Wgt      Encap-IID
  192.168.2.2  00:07:28   up          1/1           -
```

The ping output in Example 8-3 confirms that CE1 can only ping CE3, and CE2 can only ping CE4 because the two nodes exist in the same VRF instance, mapped to the same LISP IID. The LISP map cache on the xTR nodes is segmented according to the LISP IID created. Each virtualized instance of the LISP map cache only has entries for prefixes within the VRF instance mapped to the LISP IID. The MS/MR1 node must also properly build site databases, taking LISP IID as an attribute to consider when receiving registration from ETRs. The MS/MR1 in Example 8-4 does not also act as an xTR; therefore, there is no requirement to configure VRF instances as there are no interfaces attached to sites on the MS/MR1 node, which is a dedicated map server and map resolver device.

Example 8-4 *LISP MS/MR1 Shared Model Configuration*

```
!MS/MR1 IOSXE router shared model configuration

hostname MS/MR1

interface Loopback0
 ip address 192.168.100.100 255.255.255.255
 ip ospf 1 area 0

 interface GigabitEthernet2
 ip address 10.10.100.2 255.255.255.0
 ip ospf 1 area 0

!
router ospf 1
 router-id 192.168.100.100

 router lisp
  !
  locator-table default

  site LISP-VPN-Site-1
   authentication-key cisco
   eid-prefix instance-id 1 172.16.1.0/24
   eid-prefix instance-id 1 172.16.0.1/32
   exit
  !
  site LISP-VPN-Site-2
   authentication-key cisco
   eid-prefix instance-id 2 172.16.2.0/24
   eid-prefix instance-id 2 172.16.0.2/32
   exit

  site LISP-VPN-Site-3
   authentication-key cisco
   eid-prefix instance-id 1 172.16.3.0/24
   eid-prefix instance-id 1 172.16.0.3/32
   exit

  site LISP-VPN-Site-4
   authentication-key cisco
   eid-prefix instance-id 2 172.16.4.0/24
   eid-prefix instance-id 2 172.16.0.4/32
   exit

  !
  ipv4 map-server
  ipv4 map-resolver
```

In the MS/MR1 node, it is important to remember which LISP VPN site maps to which LISP IID. The EID prefix configured under each site is configured with its LISP IID. The MS/MR1 site configuration LISP IID, password, and EID prefix is verified against the LISP map register message received from the ETR nodes—in this example, xTR1 and xTR2. The LISP site registration information can be viewed globally for all sites, per site, or per IID, as shown in Example 8-5.

Example 8-5 *LISP Site Verification on MS/MR1*

```
!LISP site registration on MS/MR1 global view


MS/MR1# show lisp site
LISP Site Registration Information
* = Some locators are down or unreachable
# = Some registrations are sourced by reliable transport


Site Name        Last      Up    Who Last           Inst   EID Prefix
                 Register        Registered         ID
LISP-VPN-Site-1 2d14h      yes#  192.168.1.1:29029  1      172.16.0.1/32
                2d14h      yes#  192.168.1.1:29029  1      172.16.1.0/24
LISP-VPN-Site-2 2d14h      yes#  192.168.1.1:29029  2      172.16.0.2/32
                2d14h      yes#  192.168.1.1:29029  2      172.16.2.0/24
LISP-VPN-Site-3 2d14h      yes#  192.168.2.2:28550  1      172.16.0.3/32
                2d14h      yes#  192.168.2.2:28550  1      172.16.3.0/24
LISP-VPN-Site-4 2d14h      yes#  192.168.2.2:28550  2      172.16.0.4/32
                2d14h      yes#  192.168.2.2:28550  2      172.16.4.0/24


!LISP site registration on MS/MR1 detail per site view. Single example from VRF ComA
 and !VRF ComB


MS/MR1# show lisp site name LISP-VPN-Site-1
Site name: LISP-VPN-Site-1
Allowed configured locators: any
Allowed EID-prefixes:


  EID-prefix: 172.16.0.1/32 instance-id 1
    First registered:     2d14h
    Last registered:      2d14h
    Routing table tag:    0
    Origin:               Configuration
    Merge active:         No
    Proxy reply:          No
    TTL:                  1d00h
    State:                complete
    Registration errors:
```

```
           Authentication failures:   0
           Allowed locators mismatch: 0
        ETR 192.168.1.1:29029, last registered 2d14h, no proxy-reply, map-notify
                             TTL 1d00h, no merge, hash-function sha1, nonce
                                0x2BA48E38-0xD4475258
                             state complete, no security-capability
                             xTR-ID 0x28738D5D-0x6065A8BE-0xD6ACCB94-0xAFF4A437
                             site-ID unspecified
                             sourced by reliable transport
           Locator      Local  State      Pri/Wgt  Scope
           192.168.1.1  yes    up         1/1      IPv4 none


     EID-prefix: 172.16.1.0/24 instance-id 1
        First registered:     2d14h
        Last registered:      2d14h
        Routing table tag:    0
        Origin:               Configuration
        Merge active:         No
        Proxy reply:          No
        TTL:                  1d00h
        State:                complete
        Registration errors:
          Authentication failures:   0
          Allowed locators mismatch: 0
        ETR 192.168.1.1:29029, last registered 2d14h, no proxy-reply, map-notify
                             TTL 1d00h, no merge, hash-function sha1, nonce
                                0x2BA48E38-0xD4475258
                             state complete, no security-capability
                             xTR-ID 0x28738D5D-0x6065A8BE-0xD6ACCB94-0xAFF4A437
                             site-ID unspecified
                             sourced by reliable transport
           Locator      Local  State      Pri/Wgt  Scope
           192.168.1.1  yes    up         1/1      IPv4 none

MS/MR1# show lisp site name LISP-VPN-Site-2
Site name: LISP-VPN-Site-2
Allowed configured locators: any
Allowed EID-prefixes:

  EID-prefix: 172.16.0.2/32 instance-id 2
     First registered:     2d14h
     Last registered:      2d14h
     Routing table tag:    0
     Origin:               Configuration
     Merge active:         No
```

```
    Proxy reply:           No
    TTL:                   1d00h
    State:                 complete
    Registration errors:
      Authentication failures:   0
      Allowed locators mismatch: 0
    ETR 192.168.1.1:29029, last registered 2d14h, no proxy-reply, map-notify
                           TTL 1d00h, no merge, hash-function sha1, nonce
                             0x73EF6DC1-0x6AC1BCBD
                           state complete, no security-capability
                           xTR-ID 0x28738D5D-0x6065A8BE-0xD6ACCB94-0xAFF4A437
                           site-ID unspecified
                           sourced by reliable transport
      Locator       Local  State    Pri/Wgt  Scope
      192.168.1.1   yes    up       1/1      IPv4 none

  EID-prefix: 172.16.2.0/24 instance-id 2
    First registered:      2d14h
    Last registered:       2d14h
    Routing table tag:     0
    Origin:                Configuration
    Merge active:          No
    Proxy reply:           No
    TTL:                   1d00h
    State:                 complete
    Registration errors:
      Authentication failures:   0
      Allowed locators mismatch: 0
    ETR 192.168.1.1:29029, last registered 2d14h, no proxy-reply, map-notify
                           TTL 1d00h, no merge, hash-function sha1, nonce
                             0x73EF6DC1-0x6AC1BCBD
                           state complete, no security-capability
                           xTR-ID 0x28738D5D-0x6065A8BE-0xD6ACCB94-0xAFF4A437
                           site-ID unspecified
                           sourced by reliable transport
      Locator       Local  State    Pri/Wgt  Scope
      192.168.1.1   yes    up       1/1      IPv4 none

!LISP site registration on MS/MR1 per LISP IID view. Single example from VRF ComA
 !and VRF ComB

MS/MR1# show lisp site instance-id 1
LISP Site Registration Information
* = Some locators are down or unreachable
# = Some registrations are sourced by reliable transport
```

```
Site Name         Last      Up    Who Last              Inst   EID Prefix
                  Register        Registered            ID
LISP-VPN-Site-1   2d14h     yes#  192.168.1.1:29029     1      172.16.0.1/32
                  2d14h     yes#  192.168.1.1:29029     1      172.16.1.0/24
LISP-VPN-Site-3   2d14h     yes#  192.168.2.2:28550     1      172.16.0.3/32
                  2d14h     yes#  192.168.2.2:28550     1      172.16.3.0/24


MS/MR1# show lisp site instance-id 2
LISP Site Registration Information
* = Some locators are down or unreachable
# = Some registrations are sourced by reliable transport


Site Name         Last      Up    Who Last              Inst   EID Prefix
                  Register        Registered            ID
LISP-VPN-Site-2   2d14h     yes#  192.168.1.1:29029     2      172.16.0.2/32
                  2d14h     yes#  192.168.1.1:29029     2      172.16.2.0/24
LISP-VPN-Site-4   2d14h     yes#  192.168.2.2:28550     2      172.16.0.4/32
                  2d14h     yes#  192.168.2.2:28550     2      172.16.4.0/24
```

The **show lisp site** command output in Example 8-5 demonstrates how the MS/MR1 node stores LISP site EID prefix information according to the configured LISP site EID prefix entries mapped to LISP IID. As an example, xTR1 with RLOC address 192.168.1.1 registers the EID prefixes 172.16.2.0/24 and 172.16.0.2/32 with LISP IID value 2 under LISP-VPN-Site-2. xTR1 with RLOC address 192.168.1.1 registers EID prefixes 172.16.1.0/24 and 172.16.0.1/32 with LISP IID value 1 under LISP-VPN-Site-1. LISP-VPN-Site-1 and LISP-VPN-Site-3 are in the same VRF, ComA, so all their EID prefix entries are registered with the same LISP IID value on the MS/MR1 router.

This concludes the configuration example for LISP VPN shared model. Next we look at configuration of the LISP virtualization parallel model.

LISP Parallel Model Virtualization Configuration

In the LISP parallel model, you virtualize each LISP site and the mapping system, and you segment the core network to support the multiple LISP VPNs. Completely separate LISP logical infrastructure is shared on top of the same physical infrastructure. To implement parallel model LISP virtualization, perform the following steps:

Step 1.   Create the VRF instances in the core, the xTRs, and the MS/MR routers for the EID and for RLOC namespace. The RLOC namespace can be in the same VRF instance as the EID VRF, but each EID VRF must be unique for each LISP VPN.

Step 2.   Configure a unique instance of the LISP process for each LISP VPN.

Step 3.   Assign the interfaces to their appropriate VRF instances on the routers.

Step 4.   Configure unique VRF instances to provide underlay connectivity for each LISP VPN site in the core routers.

Step 5.   Associate the EID tables to their VRF instances and LISP IID under the LISP routing process for each LISP VPN in the xTR nodes.

Step 6.   In the MS/MR node, configure a LISP routing process for each LISP VPN, with their respective sites and EID prefix. Make sure to specify the VRF for the locator table also.

Figure 8-11 is a reference diagram for the network topology used for the LISP parallel model configuration examples that follow.

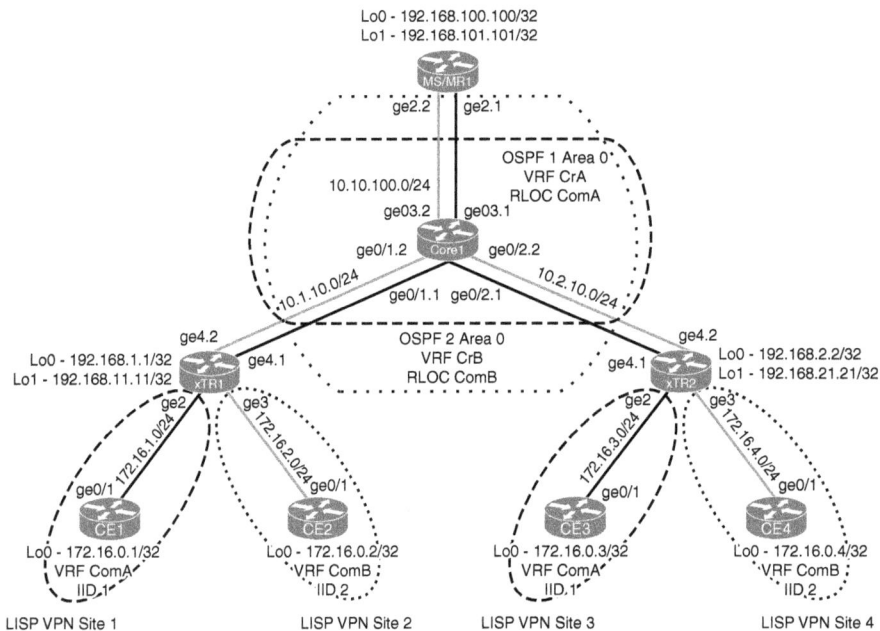

Figure 8-11   *LISP Virtualization Parallel Model Topology*

Notice in Figure 8-11 that there are four LISP VPN sites, called LISP VPN Site 1 through LISP VPN Site 4. LISP VPN Site 1 and LISP VPN Site 3 are part of the same VPN, which is in the VRF ComA. LISP VPN Site 2 and LISP VPN Site 4 belong to a separate VPN in the VRF ComB. LISP VPN Sites 1 and 2 are attached to xTR1, and LISP VPN Sites 3 and 4 are attached to xTR2. In the core of the network, VRF CrA and VRF CrB virtualize the RLOC namespace. The VRF ComA uses the VRF CrA RLOC namespace, while the VRF ComB uses the VRF CrB RLOC namespace to connect with LISP sites within its VPN. A unique OSPF routing instance is configured for each VRF instance in the core: OSPF process 1 for VRF CrA and OSPF process 2 for VRF CrB. A unique LISP routing instance is also created for each VPN, as each EID namespace in each VPN maps to a separate RLOC namespace; each RLOC namespace is in a unique VRF. In other words, the EID namespaces across the VRF instance are not sharing a common RLOC namespace in a common VRF. As a result, VRF ComA and VRF ComB are isolated from each other in the underlay and overlay, creating LISP intranet VPNs. CE nodes act as endpoints in each LISP site; they are directly attached to their local xTRs.

The xTR configuration in Example 8-6 is similar to what was shown earlier for the shared model example, but of course how the virtualized EID and RLOC namespace map to each other is different in the parallel model, as explained earlier. Example 8-6 shows the xTR1 configuration.

Example 8-6 *xTR1 LISP Parallel Model Configuration*

```
!xTR1 IOSXE LISP parallel model configuration

hostname xTR1

vrf definition ComA
 !
 address-family ipv4
 exit-address-family
!
vrf definition ComB
 !
 address-family ipv4
 exit-address-family

 vrf definition CrA
 !
 address-family ipv4
 exit-address-family
 !
vrf definition CrB
 !
 address-family ipv4
 exit-address-family

 interface Loopback0
 vrf forwarding CrA
 ip address 192.168.1.1 255.255.255.255
 ip ospf 1 area 0


 interface Loopback1
 vrf forwarding CrB
 ip address 192.168.11.11 255.255.255.255
 ip ospf 2 area 0
```

```
 interface GigabitEthernet2
 vrf forwarding ComA
 ip address 172.16.1.1 255.255.255.0

!
interface GigabitEthernet3
 vrf forwarding ComB
 ip address 172.16.2.1 255.255.255.0

!
interface GigabitEthernet4.1
 encapsulation dot1Q 1
 vrf forwarding CrA
 ip address 10.1.10.2 255.255.255.0
 ip ospf 1 area 0

 interface GigabitEthernet4.2
 encapsulation dot1Q 2
 vrf forwarding CrB
 ip address 10.1.10.2 255.255.255.0
 ip ospf 2 area 0

 router ospf 1 vrf CrA
 router-id 192.168.1.1

 router ospf 2 vrf CrB
 router-id 192.168.11.11

ip route vrf ComA 172.16.0.1 255.255.255.255 172.16.1.2
ip route vrf ComB 172.16.0.2 255.255.255.255 172.16.2.2

router lisp 1

locator-table vrf CrA

 eid-table vrf ComA instance-id 1
  database-mapping 172.16.1.0/24 192.168.1.1 priority 1 weight 1
  database-mapping 172.16.0.1/32 192.168.1.1 priority 1 weight 1

 exit
 !
 ipv4 itr map-resolver 192.168.100.100
 ipv4 itr
```

```
ipv4 etr map-server 192.168.100.100 key cisco
ipv4 etr


exit


router lisp 2


locator-table vrf CrB


eid-table vrf ComB instance-id 2
 database-mapping 172.16.2.0/24 192.168.11.11 priority 1 weight 1
 database-mapping 172.16.0.2/32 192.168.11.11 priority 1 weight 1


exit
!
ipv4 itr map-resolver 192.168.101.101
ipv4 itr
ipv4 etr map-server 192.168.101.101 key cisco
ipv4 etr
```

LISP Process 1 for VPN VRF ComA is using the VRF CrA routing table as its RLOC address space, and LISP Process 2 for VPN VRF ComB is using the VRF CrB routing table to resolve RLOC addresses. A global parameter under the LISP process defines the RLOC locator table VRF instance; if you have virtualized the RLOC namespace into different VRF instances, separate LISP instance must be created. Parallel instances of LISP are running in the network, hence the name *parallel model* for such implementations.

Note   Each instance of OSPF requires a unique router ID. Therefore, loopback1 is configured with a unique IP address to be used as the router ID for the OSPF process ID 2 for the VRF CrB in the core network.

The LISP VPN Site 1 on xTR1 consists of two EID prefixes, 172.16.0.1/32 and 172.16.1.0/24, in VRF ComA. LISP VPN Site 2 on xTR1 consists of two EID prefixes, 172.16.0.2/32 and 172.16.2.0/24, in VRF ComB. On xTR2, 172.16.3.0/24 and 172.16.0.3/32 are part of VRF ComA in LISP VPN Site 3. LISP VPN Site 4 is part of VRF ComB, with EID prefixes 172.16.4.0/24 and 172.16.0.4/32 attached to xTR2. LISP Site 1 and LISP Site 3 form one LISP intranet network, while LISP Site 2 and LISP Site 4 form the second LISP intranet network. Example 8-7 shows the configuration for xTR2.

Example 8-7   *xTR2 LISP Parallel Model Configuration*

```
!xTR2 IOSXE LISP parallel model configuration

hostname xTR2

vrf definition ComA
 !
 address-family ipv4
 exit-address-family
!
vrf definition ComB
 !
 address-family ipv4
 exit-address-family

 vrf definition CrA
 !
 address-family ipv4
 exit-address-family
!
vrf definition CrB
 !
 address-family ipv4
 exit-address-family

interface Loopback0
 vrf forwarding CrA
 ip address 192.168.2.2 255.255.255.255
 ip ospf 1 area 0

interface Loopback1
 vrf forwarding CrB
 ip address 192.168.21.21 255.255.255.255
 ip ospf 2 area 0

interface GigabitEthernet2
 vrf forwarding ComA
 ip address 172.16.3.1 255.255.255.0

 !
interface GigabitEthernet3
 vrf forwarding ComB
 ip address 172.16.4.1 255.255.255.0
```

```
!
 interface GigabitEthernet4.1
 encapsulation dot1Q 1
 vrf forwarding CrA
 ip address 10.2.10.2 255.255.255.0
 ip ospf 1 area 0

interface GigabitEthernet4.2
 encapsulation dot1Q 2
 vrf forwarding CrB
 ip address 10.2.10.2 255.255.255.0
 ip ospf 2 area 0

router ospf 1 vrf CrA
 router-id 192.168.2.2

router ospf 2 vrf CrB
 router-id 192.168.21.21

ip route vrf ComA 172.16.0.3 255.255.255.255 172.16.3.2
ip route vrf ComB 172.16.0.4 255.255.255.255 172.16.4.2

router lisp 1

locator-table vrf CrA

  eid-table vrf ComA instance-id 1
   database-mapping 172.16.3.0/24 192.168.2.2 priority 1 weight 1
   database-mapping 172.16.0.3/32 192.168.2.2 priority 1 weight 1

 exit
 !
 ipv4 itr map-resolver 192.168.100.100
 ipv4 itr
 ipv4 etr map-server 192.168.100.100 key cisco
 ipv4 etr

 exit

router lisp 2

  locator-table vrf CrB
```

```
eid-table vrf ComB instance-id 2
 database-mapping 172.16.4.0/24 192.168.21.21 priority 1 weight 1
 database-mapping 172.16.0.4/32 192.168.21.21 priority 1 weight 1

exit
!
ipv4 itr map-resolver 192.168.101.101
ipv4 itr
ipv4 etr map-server 192.168.101.101 key cisco
ipv4 etr
```

In the xTR1 and xTR2 configuration, the **eid-table** EID-to-RLOC database mapping entry for each LISP VPN maps to a unique RLOC address. Notice how for VRF ComA, LISP Instance 1 uses RLOC addresses 192.168.1.1 in xTR1 and 192.168.2.2 in xTR2, and for VRF ComB, LISP Instance 2 uses RLOC address 192.168.11.11 in xTR1 and 192.168.21.21 in xTR2. Because the RLOC address space is virtualized into two separate VRF instances, the RLOC addresses have to be separate. If the VRF instances are different for the different VPN RLOC address spaces, can't the RLOC IP be the same for both the VPNs? The answer is yes. But in this specific example, the loopback that is being used as the OSPF router ID is also being used as the LISP RLOC address for the xTR. OSPF requires a unique router ID for each OSPF context. If separate loopbacks were created—one for the OSPF router ID and one for xTR RLOC address—exactly the same RLOC IP address could be used for both LISP VPNs.

Let's now look at the MS/MR1 node where each of the xTR nodes will register its attached site EID prefixes for each instance of LISP running on the devices. In the shared model configuration explained earlier, the MS/MR1 router had only a single instance of LISP running because the RLOC address space was common for all virtualized EID address spaces across both VRF instances ComA and ComB. Now the RLOC address space has been virtualized into VRF CrA and VRF CrB, which means it follows a pattern similar to xTR node configurations; the MS/MR1 node must also run two instances of LISP, one for each LISP VPN site. Example 8-8 shows the LISP parallel mode virtualization site configuration on MS/MR1.

Example 8-8 *MS/MR1 LISP Parallel Model Configuration*

```
!MS/MR1 IOSXE LISP parallel model configuration
hostname MS/MR1

vrf definition CrA
 !
 address-family ipv4
 exit-address-family
 !
```

```
vrf definition CrB
 !
 address-family ipv4
 exit-address-family

interface Loopback0
 vrf forwarding CrA
 ip address 192.168.100.100 255.255.255.255
 ip ospf 1 area 0

interface Loopback1
 vrf forwarding CrB
 ip address 192.168.101.101 255.255.255.255
 ip ospf 2 area 0

interface GigabitEthernet2.1
 encapsulation dot1q 1
 vrf forwarding CrA
 ip address 10.10.100.2 255.255.255.0
 ip ospf 1 area 0

interface GigabitEthernet2.2
 encapsulation dot1q 2
 vrf forwarding CrB
 ip address 10.10.100.2 255.255.255.0
 ip ospf 2 area 0

 !
router ospf 1 vrf CrA
 router-id 192.168.100.100

router ospf 2 vrf CrB
 router-id 192.168.101.101

router lisp 1
  !
  locator-table vrf CrA

  site LISP-VPN-Site-1
   authentication-key cisco
   eid-prefix instance-id 1 172.16.1.0/24
   eid-prefix instance-id 1 172.16.0.1/32
   exit
  !
```

```
site LISP-VPN-Site-3
 authentication-key cisco
 eid-prefix instance-id 1 172.16.3.0/24
 eid-prefix instance-id 1 172.16.0.3/32
 exit


 !
ipv4 map-server
ipv4 map-resolver


router lisp 2
 !
locator-table vrf CrB


 !
site LISP-VPN-Site-2
 authentication-key cisco
 eid-prefix instance-id 2 172.16.2.0/24
 eid-prefix instance-id 2 172.16.0.2/32
 exit


site LISP-VPN-Site-4
 authentication-key cisco
 eid-prefix instance-id 2 172.16.4.0/24
 eid-prefix instance-id 2 172.16.0.4/32
 exit


 !
ipv4 map-server
ipv4 map-resolver
```

MS/MR1 is configured as a map server and map resolver. MS/MR1 is configured to refer to VRF CrA routing table for ETR RLOC IP addresses when receiving registration for EID prefixes with LISP IID 1 and when receiving registration for EID prefixes with LISP IID 2 refer to VRF CrB routing table. In short, the **locator-table** command under each LISP process specifies in which VRF instance the ETRs for each LISP sites configured exist. The VRF instances used to reach each of the LISP site xTRs is configured on the core devices, which provides the underlay routing or RLOC address spaces. Example 8-9 shows the configuration for the Core1 router, which acts as the underlay transport to interconnect the LISP VPN sites.

Example 8-9 *Core1 LISP Parallel Mode Configuration*

```
!Core1 IOSXE LISP parallel mode configuration

hostname Core1

vrf definition CrA
 !
 address-family ipv4
 exit-address-family
!
vrf definition CrB
 !
 address-family ipv4
 exit-address-family

interface Loopback0
 vrf forwarding CrA
 ip address 192.168.3.3 255.255.255.255
 ip ospf 1 area 0

 interface Loopback1
 vrf forwarding CrB
 ip address 192.168.31.31 255.255.255.255
 ip ospf 2 area 0

 interface GigabitEthernet0/1.1
 encapsulation dot1Q 1
 vrf forwarding CrA
 ip address 10.1.10.1 255.255.255.0
 ip ospf 1 area 0

 interface GigabitEthernet0/1.2
 encapsulation dot1Q 2
 vrf forwarding CrB
 ip address 10.1.10.1 255.255.255.0
 ip ospf 2 area 0

 !
interface GigabitEthernet0/2.1
 encapsulation dot1Q 1
 vrf forwarding CrA
 ip address 10.2.10.1 255.255.255.0
 ip ospf 1 area 0
```

```
interface GigabitEthernet0/2.2
encapsulation dot1Q 2
vrf forwarding CrB
ip address 10.2.10.1 255.255.255.0
ip ospf 2 area 0


!
interface GigabitEthernet0/3.1
encapsulation dot1Q 1
vrf forwarding CrA
ip address 10.10.100.1 255.255.255.0
ip ospf 1 area 0

interface GigabitEthernet0/3.2
encapsulation dot1Q 2
vrf forwarding CrB
ip address 10.10.100.1 255.255.255.0
ip ospf 2 area 0

router ospf 1 vrf CrA
router-id 192.168.3.3

router ospf 2 vrf CrB
router-id 192.168.31.31
```

Remember that the core devices in the RLOC address space act as the underlay routing devices; therefore, they do not require any LISP configuration. The only configuration required is the routing context configuration, which is based on the number of virtualized RLOC address spaces. In this example, VRF CrA and VRF CrB are two VRF instances, which create two separate RLOC address spaces in the core network. As discussed earlier, each of the RLOC address space VRF instances is mapped to a virtualized EID address space VRF instance. VRF CrA is the locator VRF instance for **eid-table** in VRF ComA, LISP IID 1, and VRF CrB is the locator VRF for **eid-table** in VRF ComB, LISP IID 2.

Next, we examine and verify the LISP control plane for each of the configured devices in this section. Example 8-10 starts with the xTR1 nodes.

Example 8-10 *xTR1 LISP Process Verification*

```
!xTR IOSXE LISP process verification

xTR1# show ip lisp 1 instance-id 1
  Instance ID:                          1
  Router-lisp ID:                       1
  Locator table:                        vrf CrA
  EID table:                            vrf ComA
  Ingress Tunnel Router (ITR):          enabled
  Egress Tunnel Router (ETR):           enabled
  Proxy-ITR Router (PITR):              disabled
  Proxy-ETR Router (PETR):              disabled
  NAT-traversal Router (NAT-RTR):       disabled
  Mobility First-Hop Router:            disabled
  Map Server (MS):                      disabled
  Map Resolver (MR):                    disabled
  Delegated Database Tree (DDT):        disabled
  Site Registration Limit:              0
  Map-Request source:                   derived from EID destination
  ITR Map-Resolver(s):                  192.168.100.100
  ETR Map-Server(s):                    192.168.100.100 (2d02h)
  xTR-ID:                               0x7AC5E2DF-0x891DEBB5-0xCF6BDE87-0x3B73482B
  site-ID:                              unspecified
  ITR local RLOC (last resort):         192.168.1.1
  ITR Solicit Map Request (SMR):        accept and process
    Max SMRs per map-cache entry:       8 more specifics
    Multiple SMR suppression time:      20 secs
  ETR accept mapping data:              disabled, verify disabled
  ETR map-cache TTL:                    1d00h
  Locator Status Algorithms:
    RLOC-probe algorithm:               disabled
    RLOC-probe on route change:         N/A (periodic probing disabled)
    RLOC-probe on member change:        disabled
    LSB reports:                        process
    IPv4 RLOC minimum mask length:      /0
    IPv6 RLOC minimum mask length:      /0
  Map-cache:
    Static mappings configured:         0
    Map-cache size/limit:               1/60000
    Imported route count/limit:         0/5000
    Map-cache activity check period:    60 secs
    Map-cache FIB updates:              established
    Persistent map-cache:               disabled
```

```
 Database:
    Total database mapping size:       2
    static database size/limit:        2/50000
    dynamic database size/limit:       0/50000
    route-import database size/limit:  0/5000
    import-site-reg database size/limit0/50000
    proxy database size:               0
    Inactive (deconfig/away) size:     0
    Encapsulation type:                lisp


xTR1# show lisp vrf *


===============================================
Output for router lisp vrf default
===============================================
default ID 0x0 UP users  EID
  Topology IPv4 UP, topoid 0x0, locks 0, RIB no
  Topology IPv6 DOWN, topoid 0x503316480, locks 0, RIB no


===============================================
Output for router lisp vrf CrB
===============================================
vrf CrB ID 0x4 UP users  RLOC
  Topology IPv4 UP, topoid 0x4, locks 12, RIB registered
    User RLOC, top ID 2, lock count 0, RIB watch count 6
  Topology IPv6 DOWN, topoid 0x65535, locks 0, RIB no
    User RLOC, top ID 2, lock count 0, RIB watch count 0


===============================================
Output for router lisp vrf CrA
===============================================
vrf CrA ID 0x3 UP users  RLOC
  Topology IPv4 UP, topoid 0x3, locks 12, RIB registered
    User RLOC, top ID 1, lock count 0, RIB watch count 6
  Topology IPv6 DOWN, topoid 0x65535, locks 0, RIB no
    User RLOC, top ID 1, lock count 0, RIB watch count 0


===============================================
Output for router lisp vrf ComB
===============================================
vrf ComB ID 0x2 UP users  EID
  Topology IPv4 UP, topoid 0x2, locks 5, RIB registered
    User EID, top ID 2, IID 2, lock count 5, RIB watch count 2
  Topology IPv6 DOWN, topoid 0x65535, locks 0, RIB no
```

```
===========================================
Output for router lisp vrf ComA
===========================================
vrf ComA ID 0x1 UP users  EID
  Topology IPv4 UP, topoid 0x1, locks 5, RIB registered
    User EID, top ID 1, IID 1, lock count 5, RIB watch count 2
  Topology IPv6 DOWN, topoid 0x65535, locks 0, RIB no


xTR1# show lisp 1 service ipv4 summary
Router-lisp ID:    1
Instance count:    1
Key: DB - Local EID Database entry count (@ - RLOC check pending
                                         * - RLOC consistency problem),
     DB no route - Local EID DB entries with no matching RIB route,
     Cache - Remote EID mapping cache size, IID - Instance ID,
     Role - Configured Role


                      Interface   DB  DB no  Cache Incom Cache
EID VRF name            (.IID)   size  route  size plete  Idle Role
ComA                   LISP1.1    2      0      1  0.0%    0% ITR-ETR


Number of eid-tables:                             1
Total number of database entries:                2 (inactive 0)
Maximum database entries:                     50000
EID-tables with inconsistent locators:            0
Total number of map-cache entries:                1
Maximum map-cache entries:                    60000
EID-tables with incomplete map-cache entries:     0
EID-tables pending map-cache update to FIB:       0
```

The xTR1 node is running two LISP process, process IDs 1 and 2, each configured with a unique LISP IID. It is important to understand that the LISP routing process number is the number that identifies the LISP routing process instance running in the operating system, and the LISP IID is the virtualized instance of LISP in a LISP routing process to segment the LISP network at Layer 3 of the OSI model. Within the LISP process, you can create multiple EID database mappings for specific LISP VPN sites mapped to a unique LISP IID, but within a LISP process globally, you share one common locator table, which may exist in the default VRF instance or in a user-created VRF instance. In the output shown in Example 8-9, notice the one-to-one mapping between the LISP routing process and LISP IID; this occurs because a unique LISP process was created for each LISP VPN site. Each LISP process also has a unique VRF created for the locator address. The output in Example 8-9 focuses on LISP process 1 and LISP IID 1 on xTR1. To complete the LISP control plane verification for the xTR devices, Example 8-11 shows the verification of LISP process 2 and LISP IID 2 on xTR2.

Example 8-11 *xTR2 LISP Process Verification*

```
!xTR2 IOSXE LISP process verification

xTR2# show ip lisp 2 instance-id 2
  Instance ID:                          2
  Router-lisp ID:                       2
  Locator table:                        vrf CrB
  EID table:                            vrf ComB
  Ingress Tunnel Router (ITR):          enabled
  Egress Tunnel Router (ETR):           enabled
  Proxy-ITR Router (PITR):              disabled
  Proxy-ETR Router (PETR):              disabled
  NAT-traversal Router (NAT-RTR):       disabled
  Mobility First-Hop Router:            disabled
  Map Server (MS):                      disabled
  Map Resolver (MR):                    disabled
  Delegated Database Tree (DDT):        disabled
  Site Registration Limit:              0
  Map-Request source:                   derived from EID destination
  ITR Map-Resolver(s):                  192.168.101.101
  ETR Map-Server(s):                    192.168.101.101 (2d02h)
  xTR-ID:                               0xA0382B3D-0x129A0C0D-0xD1CFFA28-0x7D379925
  site-ID:                              unspecified
  ITR local RLOC (last resort):         192.168.21.21
  ITR Solicit Map Request (SMR):        accept and process
    Max SMRs per map-cache entry:       8 more specifics
    Multiple SMR suppression time:      20 secs
  ETR accept mapping data:              disabled, verify disabled
  ETR map-cache TTL:                    1d00h
  Locator Status Algorithms:
    RLOC-probe algorithm:               disabled
    RLOC-probe on route change:         N/A (periodic probing disabled)
    RLOC-probe on member change:        disabled
    LSB reports:                        process
    IPv4 RLOC minimum mask length:      /0
    IPv6 RLOC minimum mask length:      /0
  Map-cache:
    Static mappings configured:         0
    Map-cache size/limit:               1/60000
    Imported route count/limit:         0/5000
    Map-cache activity check period:    60 secs
    Map-cache FIB updates:              established
    Persistent map-cache:               disabled
```

```
  Database:
    Total database mapping size:        2
    static database size/limit:         2/50000
    dynamic database size/limit:        0/50000
    route-import database size/limit:   0/5000
    import-site-reg database size/limit0/50000
    proxy database size:                0
    Inactive (deconfig/away) size:      0
  Encapsulation type:                   lisp


xTR2# show lisp vrf *


=============================================
Output for router lisp vrf CrB
=============================================
vrf CrB ID 0x4 UP users  RLOC
  Topology IPv4 UP, topoid 0x4, locks 12, RIB registered
    User RLOC, top ID 2, lock count 0, RIB watch count 6
  Topology IPv6 DOWN, topoid 0x65535, locks 0, RIB no
    User RLOC, top ID 2, lock count 0, RIB watch count 0


=============================================
Output for router lisp vrf CrA
=============================================
vrf CrA ID 0x3 UP users  RLOC
  Topology IPv4 UP, topoid 0x3, locks 12, RIB registered
    User RLOC, top ID 1, lock count 0, RIB watch count 6
  Topology IPv6 DOWN, topoid 0x65535, locks 0, RIB no
    User RLOC, top ID 1, lock count 0, RIB watch count 0


=============================================
Output for router lisp vrf ComB
=============================================
vrf ComB ID 0x2 UP users  EID
  Topology IPv4 UP, topoid 0x2, locks 5, RIB registered
    User EID, top ID 2, IID 2, lock count 5, RIB watch count 2
  Topology IPv6 DOWN, topoid 0x65535, locks 0, RIB no


=============================================
Output for router lisp vrf ComA
=============================================
vrf ComA ID 0x1 UP users  EID
  Topology IPv4 UP, topoid 0x1, locks 5, RIB registered
    User EID, top ID 1, IID 1, lock count 5, RIB watch count 2
  Topology IPv6 DOWN, topoid 0x65535, locks 0, RIB no
```

```
xTR2# show lisp 2 service ipv4 summary
Router-lisp ID:    2
Instance count:    1
Key: DB - Local EID Database entry count (@ - RLOC check pending
                                          * - RLOC consistency problem),
     DB no route - Local EID DB entries with no matching RIB route,
     Cache - Remote EID mapping cache size, IID - Instance ID,
     Role - Configured Role


                      Interface   DB  DB no  Cache Incom Cache
EID VRF name            (.IID)   size  route  size plete  Idle Role
ComB                   LISP2.2     2      0      1  0.0%    0% ITR-ETR


Number of eid-tables:                        1
Total number of database entries:            2 (inactive 0)
Maximum database entries:                50000
EID-tables with inconsistent locators:       0
Total number of map-cache entries:           1
Maximum map-cache entries:                60000
EID-tables with incomplete map-cache entries:    0
EID-tables pending map-cache update to FIB:      0
```

The MS/MR1 node is receiving EID prefix registration from both xTR1 and xTR2 for all the LISP VPN sites attached to them. The LISP process verification on MS/MR1 is shown in Example 8-12.

Example 8-12 *MS/MR1 LISP Process Verification*

```
!MS/MR1 IOSXE LISP process verification

MS/MR1# show ip lisp 1
Information applicable to all EID instances:
  Router-lisp ID:                  1
  Locator table:                   vrf CrA
  Ingress Tunnel Router (ITR):     disabled
  Egress Tunnel Router (ETR):      disabled
  Proxy-ITR Router (PITR):         disabled
  Proxy-ETR Router (PETR):         disabled
  NAT-traversal Router (NAT-RTR):  disabled
  Mobility First-Hop Router:       disabled
  Map Server (MS):                 enabled
  Map Resolver (MR):               enabled
```

```
Delegated Database Tree (DDT):            disabled
ITR local RLOC (last resort):             *** NOT FOUND ***
ITR Solicit Map Request (SMR):            accept and process
  Max SMRs per map-cache entry:           8 more specifics
  Multiple SMR suppression time:          20 secs
ETR accept mapping data:                  disabled, verify disabled
ETR map-cache TTL:                        1d00h
Locator Status Algorithms:
  RLOC-probe algorithm:                   disabled
  RLOC-probe on route change:             N/A (periodic probing disabled)
  RLOC-probe on member change:            disabled
  LSB reports:                            process
  IPv4 RLOC minimum mask length:          /0
  IPv6 RLOC minimum mask length:          /0
Map-cache:
  Map-cache limit:                        60000
  Map-cache activity check period:        60 secs
  Persistent map-cache:                   disabled
Database:
  Dynamic database mapping limit:         50000

MS/MR1# show ip lisp 2
Information applicable to all EID instances:
Router-lisp ID:                           2
Locator table:                            vrf CrB
Ingress Tunnel Router (ITR):              disabled
Egress Tunnel Router (ETR):               disabled
Proxy-ITR Router (PITR):                  disabled
Proxy-ETR Router (PETR):                  disabled
NAT-traversal Router (NAT-RTR):           disabled
Mobility First-Hop Router:                disabled
Map Server (MS):                          enabled
Map Resolver (MR):                        enabled
Delegated Database Tree (DDT):            disabled
ITR local RLOC (last resort):             *** NOT FOUND ***
ITR Solicit Map Request (SMR):            accept and process
  Max SMRs per map-cache entry:           8 more specifics
  Multiple SMR suppression time:          20 secs
ETR accept mapping data:                  disabled, verify disabled
ETR map-cache TTL:                        1d00h
Locator Status Algorithms:
  RLOC-probe algorithm:                   disabled
  RLOC-probe on route change:             N/A (periodic probing disabled)
  RLOC-probe on member change:            disabled
```

```
   LSB reports:                     process
   IPv4 RLOC minimum mask length:   /0
   IPv6 RLOC minimum mask length:   /0
 Map-cache:
   Map-cache limit:                 60000
   Map-cache activity check period: 60 secs
   Persistent map-cache:            disabled
 Database:
   Dynamic database mapping limit:  50000

MS/MR1# show lisp 1 site detail
LISP Site Registration Information

Site name: LISP-VPN-Site-1
Allowed configured locators: any
Allowed EID-prefixes:

  EID-prefix: 172.16.0.1/32 instance-id 1
    First registered:    2d03h
    Last registered:     2d03h
    Routing table tag:   0
    Origin:              Configuration
    Merge active:        No
    Proxy reply:         No
    TTL:                 1d00h
    State:               complete
    Registration errors:
      Authentication failures:   0
      Allowed locators mismatch: 0
    ETR 192.168.1.1:26279, last registered 2d03h, no proxy-reply, map-notify
                    TTL 1d00h, no merge, hash-function sha1, nonce
                      0x7DA94BE2-0x6AE46466
                    state complete, no security-capability
                    xTR-ID 0x7AC5E2DF-0x891DEBB5-0xCF6BDE87-0x3B73482B
                    site-ID unspecified
                    sourced by reliable transport
     Locator      Local  State    Pri/Wgt  Scope
     192.168.1.1  yes    up       1/1      IPv4 none

  EID-prefix: 172.16.1.0/24 instance-id 1
    First registered:    2d03h
    Last registered:     2d03h
    Routing table tag:   0
    Origin:              Configuration
```

```
    Merge active:          No
    Proxy reply:           No
    TTL:                   1d00h
    State:                 complete
    Registration errors:
      Authentication failures:   0
      Allowed locators mismatch: 0
    ETR 192.168.1.1:26279, last registered 2d03h, no proxy-reply, map-notify
                           TTL 1d00h, no merge, hash-function sha1, nonce
                             0x7DA94BE2-0x6AE46466
                           state complete, no security-capability
                           xTR-ID 0x7AC5E2DF-0x891DEBB5-0xCF6BDE87-0x3B73482B
                           site-ID unspecified
                           sourced by reliable transport
      Locator       Local  State     Pri/Wgt  Scope
      192.168.1.1   yes    up          1/1    IPv4 none
Site name: LISP-VPN-Site-3
Allowed configured locators: any
Allowed EID-prefixes:

  EID-prefix: 172.16.0.3/32 instance-id 1
    First registered:      2d03h
    Last registered:       2d03h
    Routing table tag:     0
    Origin:                Configuration
    Merge active:          No
    Proxy reply:           No
    TTL:                   1d00h
    State:                 complete
    Registration errors:
      Authentication failures:   0
      Allowed locators mismatch: 0
    ETR 192.168.2.2:17255, last registered 2d03h, no proxy-reply, map-notify
                           TTL 1d00h, no merge, hash-function sha1, nonce
                             0x3E963855-0xB2E03063
                           state complete, no security-capability
                           xTR-ID 0x320FE47D-0xD5A0AAB8-0x8C9129B1-0xC7D74959
                           site-ID unspecified
                           sourced by reliable transport
      Locator       Local  State     Pri/Wgt  Scope
      192.168.2.2   yes    up          1/1    IPv4 none

  EID-prefix: 172.16.3.0/24 instance-id 1
    First registered:      2d03h
    Last registered:       2d03h
```

```
Routing table tag:     0
Origin:                Configuration
Merge active:          No
Proxy reply:           No
TTL:                   1d00h
State:                 complete
Registration errors:
  Authentication failures:   0
  Allowed locators mismatch: 0
ETR 192.168.2.2:17255, last registered 2d03h, no proxy-reply, map-notify
                   TTL 1d00h, no merge, hash-function sha1, nonce
                     0x3E963855-0xB2E03063
                   state complete, no security-capability
                   xTR-ID 0x320FE47D-0xD5A0AAB8-0x8C9129B1-0xC7D74959
                   site-ID unspecified
                   sourced by reliable transport
    Locator      Local  State      Pri/Wgt  Scope
    192.168.2.2  yes    up           1/1    IPv4 none

MS/MR1# show lisp 2 site detail
LISP Site Registration Information

Site name: LISP-VPN-Site-2
Allowed configured locators: any
Allowed EID-prefixes:

  EID-prefix: 172.16.0.2/32 instance-id 2
    First registered:    2d03h
    Last registered:     2d03h
    Routing table tag:   0
    Origin:              Configuration
    Merge active:        No
    Proxy reply:         No
    TTL:                 1d00h
    State:               complete
    Registration errors:
      Authentication failures:   0
      Allowed locators mismatch: 0
    ETR 192.168.11.11:19432, last registered 2d03h, no proxy-reply, map-notify
                       TTL 1d00h, no merge, hash-function sha1, nonce
                         0x59947A18-0x2BEAF478
                       state complete, no security-capability
                       xTR-ID 0xA0C7E47A-0x1004C176-0x25539398-0xA11829DC
                       site-ID unspecified
                       sourced by reliable transport
```

```
       Locator         Local  State      Pri/Wgt  Scope
       192.168.11.11  yes     up          1/1     IPv4 none


   EID-prefix: 172.16.2.0/24 instance-id 2
     First registered:     2d03h
     Last registered:      2d03h
     Routing table tag:    0
     Origin:               Configuration
     Merge active:         No
     Proxy reply:          No
     TTL:                  1d00h
     State:                complete
     Registration errors:
       Authentication failures:   0
       Allowed locators mismatch: 0
     ETR 192.168.11.11:19432, last registered 2d03h, no proxy-reply, map-notify
                         TTL 1d00h, no merge, hash-function sha1, nonce
                           0x59947A18-0x2BEAF478
                         state complete, no security-capability
                         xTR-ID 0xA0C7E47A-0x1004C176-0x25539398-0xA11829DC
                         site-ID unspecified
                         sourced by reliable transport
       Locator         Local  State      Pri/Wgt  Scope
       192.168.11.11  yes     up          1/1     IPv4 none
Site name: LISP-VPN-Site-4
Allowed configured locators: any
Allowed EID-prefixes:


   EID-prefix: 172.16.0.4/32 instance-id 2
     First registered:     2d03h
     Last registered:      2d03h
     Routing table tag:    0
     Origin:               Configuration
     Merge active:         No
     Proxy reply:          No
     TTL:                  1d00h
     State:                complete
     Registration errors:
       Authentication failures:   0
       Allowed locators mismatch: 0
     ETR 192.168.21.21:46507, last registered 2d03h, no proxy-reply, map-notify
                         TTL 1d00h, no merge, hash-function sha1, nonce
                           0xF676DAEE-0x3F996F97
                         state complete, no security-capability
                         xTR-ID 0xA0382B3D-0x129A0C0D-0xD1CFFA28-0x7D379925
```

```
                         site-ID unspecified
                         sourced by reliable transport
         Locator      Local  State      Pri/Wgt  Scope
         192.168.21.21 yes    up         1/1    IPv4 none


  EID-prefix: 172.16.4.0/24 instance-id 2
    First registered:     2d03h
    Last registered:      2d03h
    Routing table tag:    0
    Origin:               Configuration
    Merge active:         No
    Proxy reply:          No
    TTL:                  1d00h
    State:                complete
    Registration errors:
      Authentication failures:  0
      Allowed locators mismatch: 0
    ETR 192.168.21.21:46507, last registered 2d03h, no proxy-reply, map-notify
                         TTL 1d00h, no merge, hash-function sha1, nonce
                           0xF676DAEE-0x3F996F97
                         state complete, no security-capability
                         xTR-ID 0xA0382B3D-0x129A0C0D-0xD1CFFA28-0x7D379925
                         site-ID unspecified
                         sourced by reliable transport
         Locator      Local  State      Pri/Wgt  Scope
         192.168.21.21 yes    up         1/1    IPv4 none


MS/MR1# show lisp 1 site summary
                   ----------- IPv4 ----------- ----------- IPv6 -----------
----------- MAC -----------
Site name    Configured Registered Incons Configured Registered Incons Configured Registered Incons
LISP-VPN-Site-1    2          2       0       0          0        0        0          0        0
LISP-VPN-Site-3    2          2       0       0          0        0        0          0        0


Site-registration limit for router lisp 1:      0
Site-registration count for router lisp 1:      0
Number of address-resolution entries:           0
Number of configured sites:                     2
Number of registered sites:                     2
Sites with inconsistent registrations:          0
```

```
IPv4
  Number of configured EID prefixes:              4
  Number of registered EID prefixes:              4
  Maximum MS entries allowed:                100000


MS/MR1# show lisp 2 site summary
                    ----------- IPv4 ----------- ----------- IPv6 -----------
        ----------- MAC -----------
Site name    Configured Registered Incons Configured Registered Incons Configured Registered Incons
LISP-VPN-Site-2       2           2      0          0          0      0          0          0      0
LISP-VPN-Site-4       2           2      0          0          0      0          0          0      0


Site-registration limit for router lisp 2:        0
Site-registration count for router lisp 2:        0
Number of address-resolution entries:             0
Number of configured sites:                       2
Number of registered sites:                       2
Sites with inconsistent registrations:            0
IPv4
  Number of configured EID prefixes:              4
  Number of registered EID prefixes:              4
  Maximum MS entries allowed:                100000


MS/MR1# show lisp vrf *


===============================================
Output for router lisp vrf CrB
===============================================
vrf CrB ID 0x2 UP users  RLOC
  Topology IPv4 UP, topoid 0x2, locks 10, RIB registered
    User RLOC, top ID 2, lock count 0, RIB watch count 8
  Topology IPv6 DOWN, topoid 0x65535, locks 0, RIB no
    User RLOC, top ID 2, lock count 0, RIB watch count 0


===============================================
Output for router lisp vrf CrA
===============================================
vrf CrA ID 0x1 UP users  RLOC
  Topology IPv4 UP, topoid 0x1, locks 10, RIB registered
    User RLOC, top ID 1, lock count 0, RIB watch count 8
  Topology IPv6 DOWN, topoid 0x65535, locks 0, RIB no
    User RLOC, top ID 1, lock count 0, RIB watch count 0
```

The output on the MS/MR1 node confirms that all the EID prefixes configured on the xTR nodes for all the LISP VPN sites successfully registered their EID prefixes with the MS/MR1 router. Notice that on MS/MR1, the site registration information is separated into different tables, according to the LISP routing process and LISP IID. The VRF CrA is the source of reachability information for the RLOC in the LISP VPN ComA, mapped to LISP IID 1, and VRF CrB is the routing table source for RLOC addresses in the LISP VPN ComB, mapped to LISP IID 2. LISP VPN Sites 1 and 3 belong to VRF ComA, and LISP VPN Sites 2 and 4 belong to VRF ComB.

As this parallel mode LISP VPN is configured to be an intranet-only VPN, it is expected that reachability will be only between endpoints within the same VRF instance. According to the configuration just presented, CE1 should only be able to ping CE3 because are both of these customer edge routers in VRF ComA are mapped to LISP IID 1. Similarly, CE2 should only be able to ping CE4 as these two routers belong to a common VRF ComB, mapped to LISP IID 2. Example 8-13 shows a reachability test within the sites being verified and path isolation between the LISP VPN sites being confirmed.

Example 8-13   *LISP Parallel Model VPN Connectivity Verification*

```
!CE1 to CE3 LISP VPN for VRF ComA connectivity verification


CE1# ping 172.16.0.3 source loopback 0
Type escape sequence to abort.
Sending 5, 100-byte ICMP Echos to 172.16.0.3, timeout is 2 seconds:
Packet sent with a source address of 172.16.0.1
..!!!
Success rate is 60 percent (3/5), round-trip min/avg/max = 5/5/7 ms


!The first few packets fail due to ARP and LISP resolution process. Next ping
  succeeds !100%.


CE1# ping 172.16.0.3 source loopback 0
Type escape sequence to abort.
Sending 5, 100-byte ICMP Echos to 172.16.0.3, timeout is 2 seconds:
Packet sent with a source address of 172.16.0.1
!!!!!
Success rate is 100 percent (5/5), round-trip min/avg/max = 5/5/7 ms


!CE2 to CE4 also succeeds as they both are part same LISP VPN and VRF ComB


CE2# ping 172.16.0.4 source loopback 0
Type escape sequence to abort.
Sending 5, 100-byte ICMP Echos to 172.16.0.4, timeout is 2 seconds:
Packet sent with a source address of 172.16.0.2
!!!!!
Success rate is 100 percent (5/5), round-trip min/avg/max = 5/6/8 ms


!Ping between CE1 to CE2 or CE4 will fail as they are part of separate LISP VPNs.
```

```
CE1# ping 172.16.0.2 source loopback 0
Type escape sequence to abort.
Sending 5, 100-byte ICMP Echos to 172.16.0.2, timeout is 2 seconds:
Packet sent with a source address of 172.16.0.1
.U.U.
Success rate is 0 percent (0/5)


CE1# ping 172.16.0.4 source loopback 0
Type escape sequence to abort.
Sending 5, 100-byte ICMP Echos to 172.16.0.4, timeout is 2 seconds:
Packet sent with a source address of 172.16.0.1
.U.U.
Success rate is 0 percent (0/5)
```

The map cache on the xTR nodes shown in Example 8-14 confirms successful resolution of the destination EIDs after executing a ping connectivity test within the LISP VPN sites.

Example 8-14 *xTR Node LISP Parallel Model Map Cache Entries*

```
!xTR1 LISP map cache entry per LISP VPN site.

xTR1# show ip lisp 1  map-cache instance-id 1
LISP IPv4 Mapping Cache for LISP 1 EID-table vrf ComA (IID 1), 2 entries

0.0.0.0/0, uptime: 2d06h, expires: never, via static-send-map-request
  Negative cache entry, action: send-map-request
172.16.0.3/32, uptime: 00:08:02, expires: 23:51:57, via map-reply, complete
  Locator      Uptime    State     Pri/Wgt      Encap-IID
  192.168.2.2  00:08:02  up           1/1         -


xTR1# show ip lisp 2  map-cache instance-id 2
LISP IPv4 Mapping Cache for LISP 2 EID-table vrf ComB (IID 2), 2 entries

0.0.0.0/0, uptime: 2d06h, expires: never, via static-send-map-request
  Negative cache entry, action: send-map-request
172.16.0.4/32, uptime: 00:04:18, expires: 23:55:42, via map-reply, complete
  Locator       Uptime    State     Pri/Wgt      Encap-IID
  192.168.21.21 00:04:18  up           1/1         -

!xTR2 LISP map cache entry per LISP VPN site.

xTR2# show ip lisp 1 map-cache instance-id 1
LISP IPv4 Mapping Cache for LISP 1 EID-table vrf ComA (IID 1), 2 entries
```

```
0.0.0.0/0, uptime: 2d04h, expires: never, via static-send-map-request
  Negative cache entry, action: send-map-request
172.16.0.1/32, uptime: 00:16:24, expires: 23:43:35, via map-reply, complete
  Locator      Uptime     State     Pri/Wgt      Encap-IID
  192.168.1.1  00:16:24   up          1/1          -

xTR2# show ip lisp 2 map-cache instance-id 2
LISP IPv4 Mapping Cache for LISP 2 EID-table vrf ComB (IID 2), 2 entries

0.0.0.0/0, uptime: 2d04h, expires: never, via static-send-map-request
  Negative cache entry, action: send-map-request
172.16.0.2/32, uptime: 00:12:42, expires: 23:47:17, via map-reply, complete
  Locator        Uptime     State     Pri/Wgt      Encap-IID
  192.168.11.11  00:12:42   up          1/1          -
```

The xTR nodes' map cache gets segmented for each LISP IID created under each LISP routing process. The xTR1 node has a map cache table for LISP IID 1 under LISP routing process 1 with EID prefix entries for VRF ComA. For VRF ComB, the EID prefixes are populated under LISP IID 2 in LISP Routing Process 2.

This concludes our practical example for LISP parallel model intranet VPNs.

LISP Virtualization Troubleshooting

The troubleshooting process for LISP virtualization involves the following high-level steps:

Step 1.   Verify the LISP configuration.

Step 2.   Check the LISP process and control plane state.

Step 3.   Verify the LISP forwarding state.

Note   The output for this troubleshooting section are based on the shared model scenario covered in the previous section. Refer to Figure 8-10.

To verify the LISP-related configuration on the IOS XE platform, you must filter the running configuration output, as shown in Example 8-15. The command **show running-config | section router lisp** applies to the xTR, PxTR, and MS/MR nodes.

Example 8-15 *xTR1 LISP Virtualization Configuration Verification*

```
!xTR1 LISP configuration verification.


xTR1# show running-config | section router lisp
router lisp
 locator-table default
 eid-table vrf ComA instance-id 1
  database-mapping 172.16.0.1/32 192.168.1.1 priority 1 weight 1
  database-mapping 172.16.1.0/24 192.168.1.1 priority 1 weight 1
  exit
 !
 eid-table vrf ComB instance-id 2
  database-mapping 172.16.0.2/32 192.168.1.1 priority 1 weight 1
  database-mapping 172.16.2.0/24 192.168.1.1 priority 1 weight 1
  exit
 !
 ipv4 itr map-resolver 192.168.100.100
 ipv4 itr
 ipv4 etr map-server 192.168.100.100 key cisco
 ipv4 etr
 exit
```

The command **show [ip | ipv6] lisp** helps verify the operational status of the LISP protocol running on the LISP router. This command applies to all types of LISP nodes. This command can be used with various options to verify different LISP protocol state information. For example, if you want to confirm whether an xTR node's LISP EID table was properly configured with the LISP instances and EID prefixes, you can use the command **show ip lisp eid-table summary** to see the number of EID tables created, the VRF instances for which the EID tables were created, the total number of EID database entries across all VRF instances, and the number of EID prefix entries per VRF. This gives the data center operator statistics on distribution of EID prefixes across the tenant VRF instances in the data center attached to each xTR. The command **show ip lisp eid-table vrf** *[vrf name]* provides EID table details for a specific VRF, including EID prefixes and whether they are reachable by the xTR node—to determine whether a router was properly configured as an xTR node and is able to reach the MS/MR routers. To determine the LISP process map cache parameters, such as total number of entries and TTL value for the map cache, the command **show ip lisp instance-id** *LISP IID* provides details on the state of the LISP process in a device according to the LISP function for which the device has been configured for a specific LISP instance. Examples of the **show** command output are shown in Example 8-16.

Example 8-16 *LISP Virtualization Protocol State Verification*

```
!xTR1 IOS-XE LISP protocol state verification


xTR1# show ip lisp eid-table summary
Router-lisp ID:   0
Instance count:   2
Key: DB - Local EID Database entry count (@ - RLOC check pending
                                          * - RLOC consistency problem),
     DB no route - Local EID DB entries with no matching RIB route,
     Cache - Remote EID mapping cache size, IID - Instance ID,
     Role - Configured Role


                      Interface   DB  DB no  Cache Incom Cache
EID VRF name          (.IID)    size  route   size plete  Idle Role
ComA                  LISP0.1      2      0      1  0.0%    0% ITR-ETR
ComB                  LISP0.2      2      0      1  0.0%    0% ITR-ETR


Number of eid-tables:                            2
Total number of database entries:               4 (inactive 0)
Maximum database entries:                    50000
EID-tables with inconsistent locators:           0
Total number of map-cache entries:               2
Maximum map-cache entries:                   60000
EID-tables with incomplete map-cache entries:    0
EID-tables pending map-cache update to FIB:      0


xTR1# show ip lisp instance-id 1
   Instance ID:                     1
   Router-lisp ID:                  0
   Locator table:                   default
   EID table:                       vrf ComA
   Ingress Tunnel Router (ITR):     enabled
   Egress Tunnel Router (ETR):      enabled
   Proxy-ITR Router (PITR):         disabled
   Proxy-ETR Router (PETR):         disabled
   NAT-traversal Router (NAT-RTR):  disabled
   Mobility First-Hop Router:       disabled
   Map Server (MS):                 disabled
   Map Resolver (MR):               disabled
   Delegated Database Tree (DDT):   disabled
   Site Registration Limit:         0
   Map-Request source:              derived from EID destination
   ITR Map-Resolver(s):             192.168.100.100
```

```
   ETR Map-Server(s):                 192.168.100.100 (00:14:19)
   xTR-ID:                            0x2AC9A653-0x59D65F42-0x20946F05-0x2271DFFC
   site-ID:                           unspecified
   ITR local RLOC (last resort):      192.168.1.1
   ITR Solicit Map Request (SMR):     accept and process
     Max SMRs per map-cache entry:    8 more specifics
     Multiple SMR suppression time:   20 secs
   ETR accept mapping data:           disabled, verify disabled
   ETR map-cache TTL:                 1d00h
   Locator Status Algorithms:
     RLOC-probe algorithm:            disabled
     RLOC-probe on route change:      N/A (periodic probing disabled)
     RLOC-probe on member change:     disabled
     LSB reports:                     process
     IPv4 RLOC minimum mask length:   /0
     IPv6 RLOC minimum mask length:   /0
   Map-cache:
     Static mappings configured:      0
     Map-cache size/limit:            1/60000
     Imported route count/limit:      0/5000
     Map-cache activity check period: 60 secs
     Map-cache FIB updates:           established
     Persistent map-cache:            disabled
   Database:
     Total database mapping size:     2
     static database size/limit:      2/50000
     dynamic database size/limit:     0/50000
     route-import database size/limit: 0/5000
     import-site-reg database size/limit0/50000
     proxy database size:             0
     Inactive (deconfig/away) size:   0
   Encapsulation type:                lisp


!xTR1 IOSXE LISP database mapping verification

xTR1# show ip lisp database eid-table vrf ComA
LISP ETR IPv4 Mapping Database for EID-table vrf ComA (IID 1), LSBs: 0x1
Entries total 2, no-route 0, inactive 0


172.16.0.1/32
  Locator       Pri/Wgt  Source     State
  192.168.1.1    1/1     cfg-addr   site-self, reachable
172.16.1.0/24
  Locator       Pri/Wgt  Source     State
  192.168.1.1    1/1     cfg-addr   site-self, reachable
```

To verify the operational status of the LISP map cache for particular VRF on the xTR and PxTR devices, use the command **show [ip | ipv6] lisp map-cache eid-table vrf** *vrf-name*, as shown in Example 8-17.

Example 8-17　*LISP Virtualization Map Cache Verification*

```
!xTR1 IOSXE node LISP map cache verification

xTR1# show ip lisp map-cache eid-table vrf ComA
LISP IPv4 Mapping Cache for EID-table vrf ComA (IID 1), 2 entries

0.0.0.0/0, uptime: 00:23:16, expires: never, via static-send-map-request
  Negative cache entry, action: send-map-request
172.16.0.3/32, uptime: 00:00:44, expires: 23:59:15, via map-reply, complete
  Locator      Uptime    State    Pri/Wgt      Encap-IID
  192.168.2.2  00:00:44  up         1/1          -

xTR1# show ip lisp map-cache eid-table vrf ComB
LISP IPv4 Mapping Cache for EID-table vrf ComB (IID 2), 2 entries

0.0.0.0/0, uptime: 00:23:23, expires: never, via static-send-map-request
  Negative cache entry, action: send-map-request
172.16.0.4/32, uptime: 00:00:18, expires: 23:59:42, via map-reply, complete
  Locator      Uptime    State    Pri/Wgt      Encap-IID
  192.168.2.2  00:00:18  up         1/1          -
```

On the map server, verify the LISP site configuration and the operational state of the site with the commands **show running-config | section router lisp** and **show lisp site**, as shown in Example 8-18.

Example 8-18　*MS/MR Node LISP Virtualization Site Verification*

```
!MS/MR1 IOSXE LISP site verification

MS/MR1# show running-config | section router lisp
router lisp
 locator-table default
 site LISP-VPN-Site-1
  authentication-key cisco
  eid-prefix instance-id 1 172.16.0.1/32
  eid-prefix instance-id 1 172.16.1.0/24
  exit
 !
```

```
site LISP-VPN-Site-2
  authentication-key cisco
  eid-prefix instance-id 2 172.16.0.2/32
  eid-prefix instance-id 2 172.16.2.0/24
  exit
 !
 site LISP-VPN-Site-3
  authentication-key cisco
  eid-prefix instance-id 1 172.16.0.3/32
  eid-prefix instance-id 1 172.16.3.0/24
  exit
 !
 site LISP-VPN-Site-4
  authentication-key cisco
  eid-prefix instance-id 2 172.16.0.4/32
  eid-prefix instance-id 2 172.16.4.0/24
  exit
 !
 ipv4 map-server
 ipv4 map-resolver
 exit


MS/MR1# show lisp site instance-id 1
LISP Site Registration Information
* = Some locators are down or unreachable
# = Some registrations are sourced by reliable transport


Site Name       Last     Up    Who Last          Inst   EID Prefix
                Register       Registered        ID
LISP-VPN-Site-1 00:32:21 yes#  192.168.1.1:22255  1     172.16.0.1/32
                00:32:21 yes#  192.168.1.1:22255  1     172.16.1.0/24
LISP-VPN-Site-3 00:32:21 yes#  192.168.2.2:21882  1     172.16.0.3/32
                00:32:21 yes#  192.168.2.2:21882  1     172.16.3.0/24


MS/MR1# show lisp site rloc members instance-id 1
LISP RLOC Membership for router lisp 0 IID 1
Entries: 2 valid / 2 total, Distribution disabled


RLOC                            Origin              Valid
192.168.1.1                     Registration        Yes
192.168.2.2                     Registration        Yes


!Verifying LISP IID 1 at site 1 on MS/MR1
```

```
MS/MR1# show lisp site name LISP-VPN-Site-1 instance-id 1
Site name: LISP-VPN-Site-1
Allowed configured locators: any
Allowed EID-prefixes:

  EID-prefix: 172.16.0.1/32 instance-id 1
    First registered:      00:42:16
    Last registered:       00:42:02
    Routing table tag:     0
    Origin:                Configuration
    Merge active:          No
    Proxy reply:           No
    TTL:                   1d00h
    State:                 complete
    Registration errors:
      Authentication failures:   0
      Allowed locators mismatch: 0
    ETR 192.168.1.1:22255, last registered 00:42:02, no proxy-reply, map-notify
                        TTL 1d00h, no merge, hash-function sha1, nonce
                          0x72CD1374-0x7CC616BC
                        state complete, no security-capability
                        xTR-ID 0x2AC9A653-0x59D65F42-0x20946F05-0x2271DFFC
                        site-ID unspecified
                        sourced by reliable transport
      Locator      Local State      Pri/Wgt  Scope
      192.168.1.1  yes   up          1/1     IPv4 none

  EID-prefix: 172.16.1.0/24 instance-id 1
    First registered:      00:42:16
    Last registered:       00:42:02
    Routing table tag:     0
    Origin:                Configuration
    Merge active:          No
    Proxy reply:           No
    TTL:                   1d00h
    State:                 complete
    Registration errors:
      Authentication failures:   0
      Allowed locators mismatch: 0
    ETR 192.168.1.1:22255, last registered 00:42:02, no proxy-reply, map-notify
                        TTL 1d00h, no merge, hash-function sha1, nonce
                          0x72CD1374-0x7CC616BC
                        state complete, no security-capability
                        xTR-ID 0x2AC9A653-0x59D65F42-0x20946F05-0x2271DFFC
                        site-ID unspecified
                        sourced by reliable transport
```

```
          Locator       Local  State      Pri/Wgt  Scope
          192.168.1.1   yes    up           1/1    IPv4 none


!Verifying LISP IID 1 now at Site 3 on MS/MR1


MS/MR1# show lisp site name LISP-VPN-Site-3 instance-id 1
Site name: LISP-VPN-Site-3
Allowed configured locators: any
Allowed EID-prefixes:

  EID-prefix: 172.16.0.3/32 instance-id 1
    First registered:     00:45:03
    Last registered:      00:44:49
    Routing table tag:    0
    Origin:               Configuration
    Merge active:         No
    Proxy reply:          No
    TTL:                  1d00h
    State:                complete
    Registration errors:
      Authentication failures:   0
      Allowed locators mismatch: 0
    ETR 192.168.2.2:21882, last registered 00:44:49, no proxy-reply, map-notify
                      TTL 1d00h, no merge, hash-function sha1, nonce
                        0xF909D6C7-0x443F823E
                      state complete, no security-capability
                      xTR-ID 0x8C3EECD2-0x45CF392A-0x33FE8E68-0xDFB43684
                      site-ID unspecified
                      sourced by reliable transport
          Locator       Local  State      Pri/Wgt  Scope
          192.168.2.2   yes    up           1/1    IPv4 none


  EID-prefix: 172.16.3.0/24 instance-id 1
    First registered:     00:45:03
    Last registered:      00:44:49
    Routing table tag:    0
    Origin:               Configuration
    Merge active:         No
    Proxy reply:          No
    TTL:                  1d00h
    State:                complete
    Registration errors:
      Authentication failures:   0
      Allowed locators mismatch: 0
```

```
    ETR 192.168.2.2:21882, last registered 00:44:49, no proxy-reply, map-notify
                    TTL 1d00h, no merge, hash-function sha1, nonce
                      0xF909D6C7-0x443F823E
                    state complete, no security-capability
                    xTR-ID 0x8C3EECD2-0x45CF392A-0x33FE8E68-0xDFB43684
                    site-ID unspecified
                    sourced by reliable transport
      Locator      Local  State     Pri/Wgt  Scope
      192.168.2.2  yes    up          1/1    IPv4 none
```

The command **lig** {[**self** {**ipv4** | **ipv6**}] | {*hostname* | *destination-EID*} is very useful for testing whether a particular destination EID or a local EID prefix is registered with the LISP map server. The registration of an EID prefix in the map server is confirmed by sending a LISP map request message to the map server to test proper resolution of EID to RLOC. The **lig** command (which is the LISP Internet Groper) has two use cases. The first is for querying the mapping database for a particular EID. The second use case is for verifying whether a site has registered successfully with map server. The **lig** command applies to PxTR and xTR nodes, as shown in Example 8-19.

Example 8-19 *LISP Registration Verification Using lig*

```
!xTR1 verifying LISP registration using lig


xTR1# lig instance-id 1 172.16.0.3
Mapping information for EID 172.16.0.3 from 10.2.10.2 with RTT 6 msecs
172.16.0.3/32, uptime: 00:35:29, expires: 23:59:59, via map-reply, complete
  Locator      Uptime    State    Pri/Wgt      Encap-IID
  192.168.2.2  00:35:29  up         1/1          -


xTR1# lig eid-table vrf ComB 172.16.0.4
Mapping information for EID 172.16.0.4 from 10.2.10.2 with RTT 7 msecs
172.16.0.4/32, uptime: 00:35:55, expires: 23:59:59, via map-reply, complete
  Locator      Uptime    State    Pri/Wgt      Encap-IID
  192.168.2.2  00:35:55  up         1/1          -


xTR1# lig self instance-id 1
Mapping information for EID 172.16.0.1 from 192.168.1.1 with RTT 5 msecs
172.16.0.1/32, uptime: 00:00:00, expires: 23:59:59, via map-reply, self, complete
  Locator      Uptime    State    Pri/Wgt      Encap-IID
  192.168.1.1  00:00:00  up, self   1/1          -
```

The verification of the ETR registration to the map server can be further analyzed with certain **debug** commands. Use **debug** commands cautiously—and preferably with the help of Cisco Technical Assistance Center (TAC). In Example 8-20, the LISP-VPN-SITE-1

EID prefix registration entries are cleared to trigger a re-registration to the MS/MR1 node; therefore, you see a clearing of the existing entries and then registration messages. Remember that LISP-VPN-SITE-1 is attached to xTR1. The command **debug lisp control-plane map-server-registration** is used to observe in real time LISP registration message exchanges between ETR and MS nodes.

Note   As of IOS XE release 16.10.1, the **debug lisp filter** command allows you to enter the command up to four times. As shown in Example 8-20, the **debug lisp filter** command provides a mechanism to reduce the debug output displayed on the terminal by matching only the parameters of interest, such as a specific EID, RLOC, or LISP instance identifier (IID). Refer to the "Cisco IOS XE LISP Configuration Guide" for further details.

Example 8-20   *LISP Registration Verification Using the **debug** Command*

```
!MS/MR1 IOSXE LISP EID Prefix registration verification


MS/MR1# debug lisp control-plane map-server-registration


MS/MR1# clear lisp site  LISP-VPN-Site-1
*Jan 13 20:57:51.140: [MS]  LISP-0: MS registration IID 1 prefix 172.16.0.1/32
  192.168.1.1 SVC_IP_IAF_IPv4 site LISP-VPN-Site-1, Deleting due to forced clear.
*Jan 13 20:57:51.141: [MS]  LISP-0: MS registration IID 1 prefix 172.16.1.0/24
  192.168.1.1 SVC_IP_IAF_IPv4 site LISP-VPN-Site-1, Deleting due to forced clear.
*Jan 13 20:57:51.145: [MS]  LISP: Session VRF default, Local 192.168.100.100, Peer
  192.168.1.1:49050, Role: Passive, State: Up, Received reliable registration
  message registration for IID 1  EID 172.16.1.0/24  (RX 0, TX 0).
*Jan 13 20:57:51.145: [MS]  LISP-0: MS registration IID 1 prefix 172.16.1.0/24
  192.168.1.1 SVC_IP_IAF_IPv4 site LISP-VPN-Site-1, Created new registration.
*Jan 13 20:57:51.145: [MS]  LISP: Session VRF default, Local 192.168.100.100, Peer
  192.168.1.1:49050, Role: Passive, State: Up, Received reliable registration
  message registration for IID 1  EID 172.16.0.1/32  (RX 0, TX 0).
*Jan 13 20:57:51.145: [MS]  LISP-0: MS registration IID 1 prefix 172.16.0.1/32
  192.168.1.1 SVC_IP_IAF_IPv4 site LISP-VPN-Site-1, Created new registration.

!XTR1 IOSXE LISP EID prefix registration verification


xTR1# debug lisp control-plane map-server-registration
LISP control plane map-server registration debugging is on

*Jan 13 20:57:51.140: [MS]  LISP: Session VRF default, Local 192.168.1.1, Peer
  192.168.100.100:4342, Role: Active, State: Up, Received reliable registration
  message registration-refresh for IID 1  EID 172.16.0.1/32 , Refresh Rejected:
  FALSE, Scope: specific prefix/4, EID AFI: IPv4/1 (RX 0, TX 0).
*Jan 13 20:57:51.140: [MS]  LISP: Session VRF default, Local 192.168.1.1, Peer
  192.168.100.100:4342, Role: Active, State: Up, Received reliable registration
  message registration-refresh for IID 1  EID 172.16.1.0/24 , Refresh Rejected:
  FALSE, Scope: specific prefix/4, EID AFI: IPv4/1 (RX 0, TX 0).
```

```
*Jan 13 20:57:51.145: [MS]  LISP: Session VRF default, Local 192.168.1.1, Peer
   192.168.100.100:4342, Role: Active, State: Up, Received reliable registration
   message registration-ack for IID 1  EID 172.16.1.0/24  (RX 0, TX 0).
*Jan 13 20:57:51.145: [MS]  LISP: Session VRF default, Local 192.168.1.1, Peer
   192.168.100.100:4342, Role: Active, State: Up, Received reliable registration
   message registration-ack for IID 1  EID 172.16.0.1/32  (RX 0, TX 0).
*Jan 13 20:57:51.145: [MS]  LISP: Session VRF default, Local 192.168.1.1, Peer
   192.168.100.100:4342, Role: Active, State: Up, Received reliable registration
   message mapping-notification for IID 1  EID 172.16.1.0/24  (RX 0, TX 0).
*Jan 13 20:57:51.145: [MS]  LISP: Session VRF default, Local 192.168.1.1, Peer
   192.168.100.100:4342, Role: Active, State: Up, Received reliable registration
   message mapping-notification for IID 1  EID 172.16.0.1/32  (RX 0, TX 0).
```

Control plane packets are also encoded with LISP IIDs. Figure 8-12 shows a packet capture of a map register message sent from the ETR xTR1 to the map server MS/MR1 to register EID prefix 172.16.0.2 in VRF ComB.

```
No.    Time        Source          Destination       Protocol  Length  Info
  1 0.000000    10.1.10.2       192.168.100.100   LISP      182 Map-Register
  2 0.000029    10.1.10.2       192.168.100.100   LISP      182 Map-Register
  3 0.002990    192.168.100.100 10.1.10.2         LISP      182 Map-Notify
  4 0.003301    192.168.100.100 10.1.10.2         LISP      182 Map-Notify
  5 4.247150    192.168.100.100 10.1.10.2         LISP      262 Map-Notify

▶ Frame 2: 182 bytes on wire (1456 bits), 182 bytes captured (1456 bits)
▶ Ethernet II, Src: fa:16:3e:c2:2e:7a (fa:16:3e:c2:2e:7a), Dst: fa:16:3e:76:21:4a (fa:16:3e:76:21:4a)
▶ Internet Protocol Version 4, Src: 10.1.10.2, Dst: 192.168.100.100
▶ User Datagram Protocol, Src Port: 4342, Dst Port: 4342
▼ Locator/ID Separation Protocol
    0011 .... .... .... .... .... = Type: Map-Register (3)
    .... 0... .... .... .... .... = P bit (Proxy-Map-Reply): Not set
    .... .0.. .... .... .... .... = S bit (LISP-SEC capable): Not set
    .... ..1. .... .... .... .... = I bit (xTR-ID present): Set ◀──
    .... ...0 .... .... .... .... = R bit (Built for an RTR): Not set
    .... .... 0000 0000 0000 000. = Reserved bits: 0x0000
    .... .... .... .... .... ...1 = M bit (Want-Map-Notify): Set
    Record Count: 2
    Nonce: 0x30b8ded63971e629
    Key ID: 0x0001
    Authentication Data Length: 20
    Authentication Data: d54f9e3b03c8008ef82a0e012865bb93206a6ddb
  ▶ Mapping Record 1, EID Prefix: [2] 172.16.2.0/24, TTL: 1440, Action: No-Action, Authoritative
  ▼ Mapping Record 2, EID Prefix: [2] 172.16.0.2/32, TTL: 1440, Action: No-Action, Authoritative
      Record TTL: 1440
      Locator Count: 1
      EID Mask Length: 32
      000. .... .... .... = Action: No-Action (0)
      ...1 .... .... .... = Authoritative bit: Set
      .... .000 0000 0000 = Reserved: 0x000
      0000 .... .... .... = Reserved: 0x0
      .... 0000 0000 0000 = Mapping Version: 0
      EID Prefix AFI: LISP Canonical Address Format (LCAF) (16387)
    ▼ EID Prefix: [2] 172.16.0.2
      ▶ LCAF: Instance ID: 2, Address: 172.16.0.2 ◀──
    ▶ Locator Record 1, Local RLOC: 192.168.1.1, Reachable, Priority/Weight: 1/1, Multicast Priority/Weight: 1/1
    xTR-ID: 2ac9a65359d65f4220946f052271dffc
    Site-ID: 0000000000000000
```

Figure 8-12 *LISP Control Plane Packet Capture with LISP IID Encoded*

Now that the LISP control plane has been verified to have knowledge of the EID, and the mapping database has the appropriate information to reach the remote xTR, we can examine the data plane communication. Because this example uses case a non-default

VRF, LISP is configured to include the IID in the data packets, which provide information to the xTR about on which VRF the packets should be placed after the LISP header is removed. The packet capture in Figure 8-13 shows how the LISP IID is encoded in the LISP header of a LISP data plane packet. A ping packet is sent from CE2 attached to xTR1 to CE4 attached to xTR2 in LISP VPN VRF ComB, mapped to LISP IID 2.

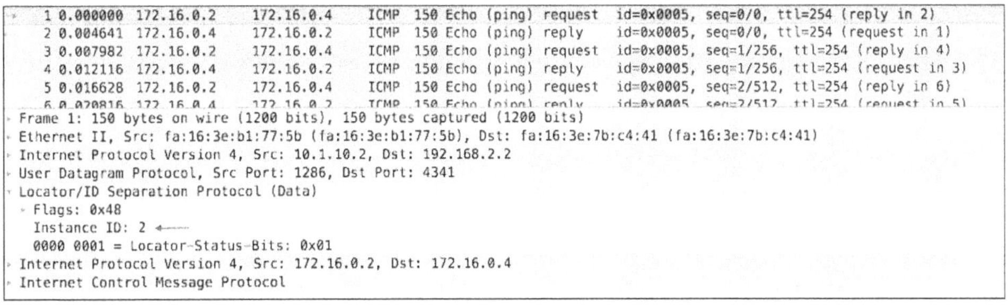

```
    1 0.000000 172.16.0.2    172.16.0.4    ICMP 150 Echo (ping) request  id=0x0005, seq=0/0, ttl=254 (reply in 2)
    2 0.004641 172.16.0.4    172.16.0.2    ICMP 150 Echo (ping) reply    id=0x0005, seq=0/0, ttl=254 (request in 1)
    3 0.007982 172.16.0.2    172.16.0.4    ICMP 150 Echo (ping) request  id=0x0005, seq=1/256, ttl=254 (reply in 4)
    4 0.012116 172.16.0.4    172.16.0.2    ICMP 150 Echo (ping) reply    id=0x0005, seq=1/256, ttl=254 (request in 3)
    5 0.016628 172.16.0.2    172.16.0.4    ICMP 150 Echo (ping) request  id=0x0005, seq=2/512, ttl=254 (reply in 6)
    6 0.020816 172.16.0.4    172.16.0.2    ICMP 150 Echo (ping) reply    id=0x0005, seq=2/512, ttl=254 (request in 5)
- Frame 1: 150 bytes on wire (1200 bits), 150 bytes captured (1200 bits)
- Ethernet II, Src: fa:16:3e:b1:77:5b (fa:16:3e:b1:77:5b), Dst: fa:16:3e:7b:c4:41 (fa:16:3e:7b:c4:41)
- Internet Protocol Version 4, Src: 10.1.10.2, Dst: 192.168.2.2
- User Datagram Protocol, Src Port: 1286, Dst Port: 4341
- Locator/ID Separation Protocol (Data)
  - Flags: 0x48
    Instance ID: 2  ←----
    0000 0001 = Locator-Status-Bits: 0x01
- Internet Protocol Version 4, Src: 172.16.0.2, Dst: 172.16.0.4
- Internet Control Message Protocol
```

Figure 8-13 *LISP Data Packet Capture with LISP IID Encoded*

The capture in Figure 8-13 confirms the proper exchange of both LISP control plane packets and data plane packets for the particular LISP VPN site.

Troubleshooting LISP requires verification of the control plane and data plane. Control plane troubleshooting requires verifying the following:

- The LISP process state on each node

- The LISP EID mapping database entries on the ETR nodes

- The LISP EID prefix registration entries on the map server

- The successful resolution of EID-to-RLOC for local and remote EID prefixes on xTR nodes (using the lig command)

- The LISP control plane message exchanges between xTR nodes and the mapping system to determine the root cause of control plane failures (using **debug** commands)

The data plane troubleshooting includes verifying the LISP map cache entries on each xTR node for both local and remote EID prefixes. Existence of map cache entries for the locally attached EID prefix entries confirms reachability to locally attached endpoints, and remote map cache entries confirm proper control plane operation in resolving remote endpoint addresses. If LISP map cache entries exist for source and destination EIDs but communication still fails, you need to verify whether the end-to-end path between the ITR and ETR nodes is configured for the right maximum transmission unit (MTU). Extended **ping** commands can be used with the data size and do-not-fragment (DF) bit option to test the sending of ICMP packets with various byte sizes. If the MTU is configured properly in the underlay to support LISP packet encapsulation, you can verify whether any ACL or security appliance in the path is blocking LISP port ranges. If after these basic verifications LISP packets continue to drop, depending on the platform, you can cautiously execute certain **debug lisp forwarding** or **debug lisp packet** commands with the assistance of Cisco TAC to determine the root cause of any hardware or software issues that may be causing encapsulation or decapsulation failures on the xTR nodes.

Summary

LISP VPNs provide the same level of isolation in the control plane and data plane as many other existing technologies, such as MPLS Layer3 VPNs, but they do so using a simpler approach of encoding a single attribute called the LISP instance identifier (IID). The LISP IID field in the LISP header is encoded with the LISP IID value, which maps to a particular VRF instance both for control plane and data plane LISP packets.

The LISP architecture creates the ability to virtualize both the EID and RLOC address spaces. The two models to virtualize EID and RLOC address space are the shared and parallel models. In addition, a hybrid model borrows characteristics of both the shared and parallel models. The shared model of LISP virtualization maps multiple virtualized EID prefix address spaces or VRF instances to a single virtualized RLOC address space or VRF (that is, a many-to-one mapping). The parallel model maps each virtualized EID prefix address space in a VRF instance to its own unique virtualized RLOC address space (that is, a one-to-one mapping). In the parallel model, the number of VRF instances in the RLOC address space is equal to the number of VRF instances in the EID prefix address space. In the hybrid model, you can have multiple RLOC address spaces, each in its own VRF instance, map to a group of virtualized EID prefix address spaces, each in its own VRF instance.

References

The following references provide more details on the topics discussed in this chapter:

Internet Draft, "LISP Virtual Private Networks (VPNs) RFC," draft-ietf-lisp-vpn-04

RFC 6835, "The Locator/ID Separation Protocol Internet Groper (LIG)"

RFC 8060, "LISP Canonical Address Format (LCAF)"

Cisco, "Cisco Nexus 7000 Series NX-OS LISP Configuration Guide,"
   http://www.cisco.com

Cisco, "Cisco IOS XE LISP Configuration Guide," http://www.cisco.com

## Chapter 9

LISP in the Enterprise Multihome Internet/WAN Edge

The edge of the network is where network components internal to an organization interface with a device that connects the internal infrastructure to some outside network. The outside network can be a remote data center, a campus, a branch location, or the Internet. There are many architectures in edge network design. When it comes to environments with large scale, high availability, and granular traffic engineering control, Border Gateway Protocol (BGP) is the preferred protocol choice for many engineers. LISP has also gained popularity in enterprise edge routing mainly due to its operational simplicity. Customer-side ingress/egress tunneling router (xTR) routing configuration can simply involve a default route to a service provider router to reach remote routing locator (RLOC) addresses instead of exchanging routes through a dynamic routing protocol such as BGP. LISP simplifies the traffic engineering configuration on the edge devices tremendously and is a very good option at the edge of a network. The traffic engineering attributes of LISP are briefly discussed in Chapter 2, "LISP Architecture." This chapter covers the following topics:

- How to use the traffic engineering capabilities of LISP at the enterprise edge

- LISP explicit locator path (ELP) concepts and applications for understanding how to traffic engineer data packets across a WAN network

- The common use cases of LISP in the enterprise edge and how to implement them

- How to use LISP to interconnect different routing domains with each other, using the LISP Disjoint RLOC Domains feature

LISP at the Enterprise Edge

WAN edge connectivity offers many design options. The decision of which one to use depends on the level of redundancy required to support the technical and business requirements of the organization. These are the basic questions you need to answer when designing WAN edge connectivity:

- Do you need a single router or dual routers at the edge of your network?

■ Which WAN connection type should you use—Internet or WAN technologies such as Multiprotocol Label Switching (MPLS), Frame Relay, Metro Ethernet, or something else?

■ Will you connect to a single service provider or two different service providers for each of your edge connections?

■ Which routes will you learn from your service provider—the default route only, some customer-specific routes, or a complete Internet table?

■ Do you need redundant connections for failover from primary to secondary paths, for load balancing traffic, or for both?

■ Which routing protocol should you use to achieve the WAN edge connectivity redundancy requirements?

Figure 9-1 shows some of the WAN edge connectivity options that are available for enterprises.

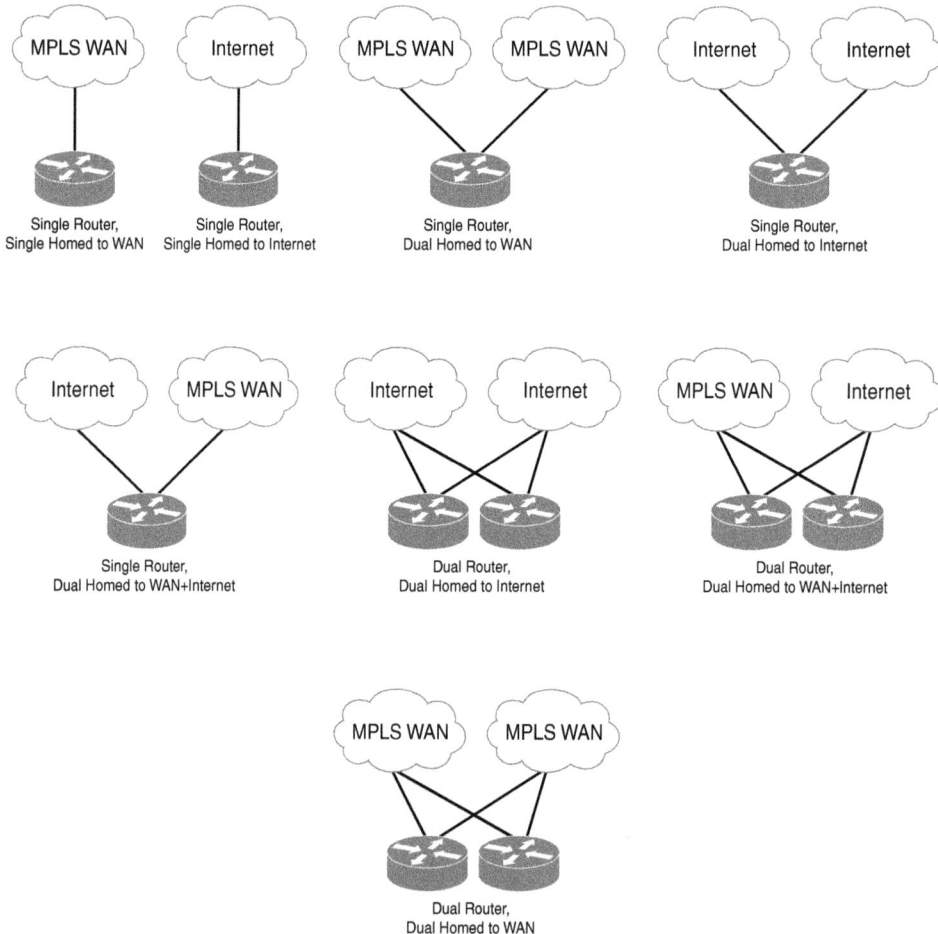

Figure 9-1 *WAN Edge Connectivity Options*

The two major connectivity options are single-homed and dual-homed. In the dual-homed option, the WAN device may connect to a single service provider or two different service providers. The dual-homed, or multihomed, option provides more redundancy, resiliency, and provider diversity, which, in turn, gives customer leverage to negotiate service-level agreements and contract rates.

Multihoming forces customers into a situation where they must decide to use provider-assigned (PA) or provider-independent (PI) address space. The PI option forces service providers to advertise the customer address space without aggregating as the site prefix is independent of the service provider address space. The lack of aggregation by service providers' off-site prefixes with PI address space increases the size of the Internet routing table. Sites with PI address space are able to change service providers without having to renumber. Besides avoiding technical complexities in migration, another major reason to choose PI over PA is to have more control of the paths traffic takes to enter or leave a site.

A router forwards IP packets by looking at the destination IP address and then referencing the routing table to find the prefix with the longest matching prefix length. The longest prefix length match rule supersedes any other criteria, such as metric or administrative distance. Only when the router has two routing sources of the same prefix length does the administrative distance become the tie breaker, and if the administrative distance is also equal, the router compares the metric. Knowing this, the customer can use this fundamental IP routing rule to engineer traffic coming into or leaving the customer site. The customer site divides its site prefix into two or more parts to attract traffic for certain prefixes toward a particular edge router. To steer traffic out a particular path from the customer site, the customer chooses to manipulate metric prefixes learned from the services providers.

A customer peering BGP with a service provider receives only the default route, the default route plus customer-specific routes, or the default route plus the complete Internet routes. Based on the redundancy, load balancing, or load sharing requirements for outbound traffic, the customer site chooses which routes to learn and how to manipulate metrics using inbound policy on the edge routers. The options available to engineer traffic using BGP include the following:

- **Local preference:** Used to influence outbound traffic flow within a BGP site.

- **Weight:** A Cisco-proprietary BGP attribute used to influence outbound traffic flow local to a router.

- **AS-PATH prepending:** Commonly used to influence inbound traffic flow but can easily be overridden by an upstream provider using communities and local preference. AS-PATH prepending can also be used to influence outbound traffic.

- **Community values:** Used with the three previously listed attributes to influence both inbound and outbound traffic within a BGP site or across to a peer site.

- **Prefix splitting:** Splitting a local site prefix into multiple chunks of equal size, such as two halves or four quarters. This option is most commonly used by customer BGP sites for traffic engineering related to ingress traffic flows. Figure 9-2 shows a simple prefix splitting example for controlling ingress traffic to a site.

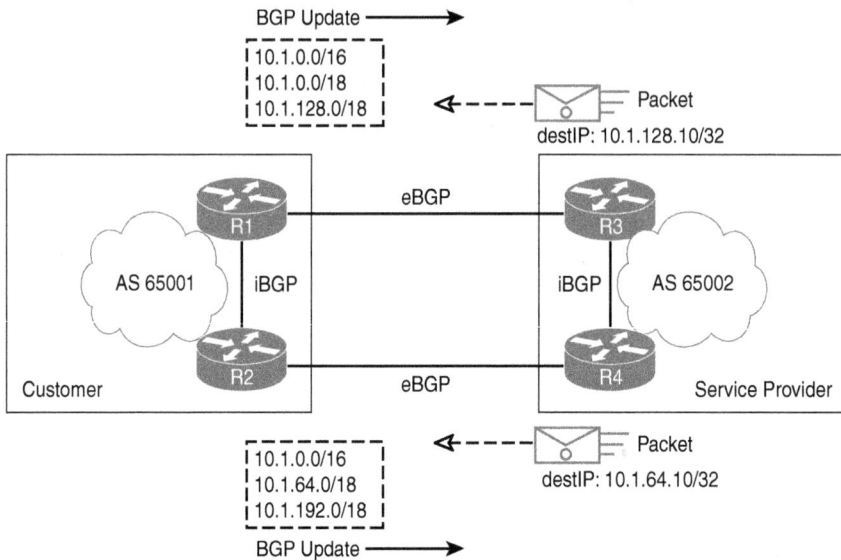

Figure 9-2   *Prefix Splitting for ingress traffic engineering*

Note   Figure 9-2 uses private Internet Protocol (IP) address and autonomous system (AS) numbers to explain the concept. Private IP address space and AS numbers are not used in the Internet.

In Figure 9-2, notice that both the R1 and R2 nodes advertise the aggregate prefix address 10.1.0.0/16 to the service provider routers R3 and R4, respectively. The purpose of the aggregate prefix is to ensure that if there is any failure in any specific path due to node or link failure, the other path is still available. With the aggregate prefix, each edge router at the customer site advertises a unique set of prefixes, which are essentially subnets under the aggregate prefix. The 10.1.128.0/18 prefix is advertised by R1 toward the service provider router R3, which then causes all traffic destined to the 10.1.128.0/18 network to come inbound to R1 from R3. Similarly, R2 advertises the 10.1.64.0/18 network to R4, which steers any data packets destined to any host in the 10.1.64.0/18 network inbound toward R2.

This has been a very brief primer on how to do traffic engineering on WAN edge routers using BGP. This summary should give you an idea about how complex traffic engineering can become when using BGP due to the various design considerations and knobs available to tweak BGP routing policies. A network architect needs to evaluate several factors before determining which approach to take. Fortunately, LISP helps you achieve redundancy, load sharing, and load balancing, using a much simpler approach, especially when it comes to ingress traffic engineering.

LISP removes the following complexities when designing multihoming in the edge:

- LISP eliminates the need to configure complex routing policy and use BGP attributes to steer traffic toward a customer LISP site destined to a specific prefix. In simple cases of LISP-to-LISP network communication, LISP uses priority and weight to communicate the preferred RLOC for reaching an EID prefix.

- LISP eliminates the need to advertise PI address space outside the customer site as the EID prefix is not meant to be routed in the Internet (at least in a LISP network). Only the RLOC address space is routable on the Internet, and as a result, LISP removes requirements for edge routers to the learn default route, the default route plus the customer networks, or the complete Internet routing table because all this information is stored in the mapping system. The xTR nodes in LISP networks only cache to EID prefix destinations with which it has active conversations, which helps improve scale while ensuring reachability. Only routing information for remote xTR RLOC addresses exists in the routing table. When communicating to a non-LISP site in the Internet, reachability to the PETR node gets the packets from the LISP site to the non-LISP sites. This also simplifies traffic engineering between LISP and non-LISP sites.

- LISP eliminates the customer edge router requirement to run BGP for routing to the Internet or a WAN simply for traffic engineering, which lowers the resource requirements on the customer edge router.

We do not mean to imply that LISP eliminates BGP from the edge. BGP is the standard protocol on the Internet for routing update exchange between various ASs, regardless of the address family. With LISP networks, BGP is the protocol that provides RLOC reachability in the default free zone or Internet. Of course, organizations will continue to run BGP within a LISP site also. LISP helps make the BGP Internet architecture more scalable and introduces new applications, as explained throughout the various chapters in this book. LISP is not meant to replace BGP but to complement it to help improve scale, efficient mobility, traffic engineering, and much more.

The next section presents a practical example of how to deploy LISP in the WAN edge with multihoming to dual service providers with two xTR devices at a LISP site.

Configuring LISP at the Enterprise Edge

The WAN connectivity options shown in Figure 9-1 may also apply to LISP routers installed at the edge of the LISP network—of course, with specific LISP configuration requirements to ensure reachability to RLOC and MS/MR addresses for the nodes that are part of the common LISP network communication exchange. For brevity, this chapter does not discuss every single option. The focus of this section is on a single scenario with dual LISP routers attached to dual service providers across two LISP sites, as shown in Figure 9-3.

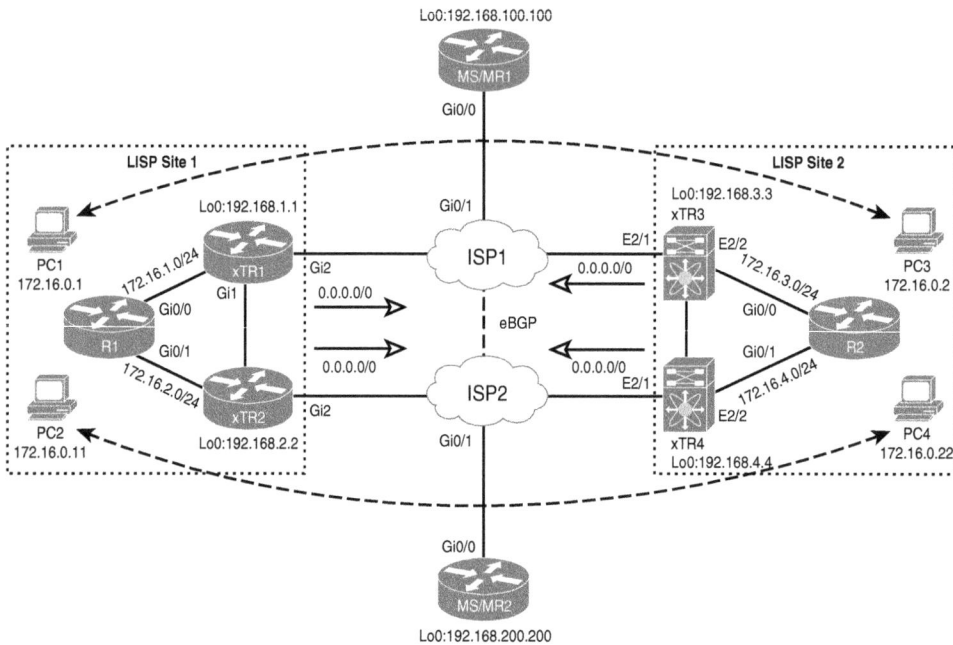

Figure 9-3   *LISP WAN Edge Dual Router, Dual Service Provider*

In this scenario, there are two LISP sites, each with dual xTRs, with each xTR connecting to a separate service provider. The service providers have eBGP peering with each other to exchange routing information, including their common customer RLOC and MS/MR IP addresses. The xTRs in LISP Site 1 are IOS XE routers, and the xTRs in LISP Site 2 are NX-OS routers. The xTR is connecting to the Internet service provider (ISP) using static routing only; there is no dynamic routing protocol configuration between the service provider (SP) and the xTRs. The ISP routers ensure the reachability to the xTR RLOC address across its network; this is the only key traffic engineering connectivity requirement to steer traffic into a LISP site using two basic attributes, the priority and weight of each EID-to-RLOC address mapping advertise by the egress tunnel router (ETR) to the map server.

Suppose your traffic engineering requirement is that for all users who want to communicate with PC1 with IP address 172.16.0.1/32, the preferred path should be through xTR1, and for users who want to communicate with PC2 with IP address 172.16.0.11/32, the primary path should be through xTR2. Similarly, in LISP Site 2, the preferred path to reach PC3 with IP address 172.16.0.2/32 is through xTR3, and to reach PC4 with IP address 172.16.0.22/32 is through xTR4. As shown with the curved arrows in Figure 9-3, when PC1 communicates with PC3, the path taken in both directions is only through ISP1. When PC2 and PC4 communicate, the path taken for the traffic is only through ISP2.

To achieve the described traffic requirements, the xTR must be configured to advertise itself as the primary RLOC to the mapping system for the specific EID prefix. Example 9-1 shows the LISP-related configuration for xTR1 in LISP Site 1.

Example 9-1 *xTR1 LISP WAN Edge Routing Configuration*

```
!xTR1 IOSXE LISP WAN edge routing configuration

interface Loopback0
 ip address 192.168.1.1 255.255.255.255
!
!
interface GigabitEthernet1
 ip address 172.16.1.1 255.255.255.0
 ip ospf 1 area 0


!
interface GigabitEthernet2
 ip address 10.1.1.2 255.255.255.0

router lisp
 database-mapping 172.16.0.1/32 192.168.1.1 priority 1 weight 50
 database-mapping 172.16.0.1/32 192.168.2.2 priority 50 weight 50
 database-mapping 172.16.0.11/32 192.168.1.1 priority 50 weight 50
 database-mapping 172.16.0.11/32 192.168.2.2 priority 1 weight 50
 database-mapping 172.16.1.0/24 192.168.1.1 priority 1 weight 50
 database-mapping 172.16.1.0/24 192.168.2.2 priority 50 weight 50
 database-mapping 172.16.2.0/24 192.168.1.1 priority 50 weight 50
 database-mapping 172.16.2.0/24 192.168.2.2 priority 1 weight 50
 ipv4 itr map-resolver 192.168.100.100
 ipv4 itr map-resolver 192.168.200.200
 ipv4 itr
 ipv4 etr map-server 192.168.100.100 key cisco
 ipv4 etr map-server 192.168.200.200 key cisco
 ipv4 etr
 ipv4 map-request-source 192.168.1.1
 exit

router ospf 1
 router-id 192.168.1.1

ip route 0.0.0.0 0.0.0.0 10.1.1.1
```

From the LISP configuration on xTR1, notice the weight and priority values set for each database mapping entry. The preferred RLOC is chosen for an EID based first on the entry with the lowest priority value. If the priority values are equal, then traffic is load balanced to the RLOC based on the weight value. In the LISP database mapping entries for both xTRs, the priority value 1 is set for the xTRs that are the preferred nodes to ingress a LISP site destined to an EID prefix. In Example 9-1, priority is equal to 1 for

172.16.0.1/32 mapped to xTR1 with RLOC address 192.168.1.1 because xTR1 is the preferred xTR to reach PC1. Notice that the value for xTR2 is the default value of 50, which is a higher value than 1 and so is a less preferred RLOC in the mapping system to reach PC1. The xTRs in each site register their connected site EID prefixes to the MS/MR in both ISPs for high availability. The node xTR2 has the same LISP configuration as xTR1.

As shown in Example 9-2, in LISP Site 2, the LISP configuration for the xTRs looks similar to the configuration for LISP Site 1.

Example 9-2   *xTR3 LISP WAN Edge Routing Configuration*

```
!xTR3 NXOS LISP WAN edge routing configuration

feature lisp

interface loopback0
  ip address 192.168.3.3/32
  ip router ospf 1 area 0.0.0.0

interface Ethernet2/1
  no switchport
  ip address 10.3.1.1/24
  no shutdown

interface Ethernet2/2
  no switchport
  ip address 172.16.3.1/24
  ip router ospf 1 area 0.0.0.0
  no shutdown


ip route 0.0.0.0/0 10.3.1.2

ip lisp itr
ip lisp etr
ip lisp database-mapping 172.16.0.2/32 192.168.3.3 priority 1 weight 100
ip lisp database-mapping 172.16.0.2/32 192.168.4.4 priority 50 weight 100
ip lisp database-mapping 172.16.0.22/32 192.168.3.3 priority 50 weight 100
ip lisp database-mapping 172.16.0.22/32 192.168.4.4 priority 1 weight 100
ip lisp database-mapping 172.16.3.0/24 192.168.3.3 priority 1 weight 100
ip lisp database-mapping 172.16.3.0/24 192.168.4.4 priority 50 weight 100
ip lisp database-mapping 172.16.4.0/24 192.168.3.3 priority 50 weight 100
ip lisp database-mapping 172.16.4.0/24 192.168.4.4 priority 1 weight 100
ip lisp itr map-resolver 192.168.100.100
ip lisp itr map-resolver 192.168.200.200
ip lisp etr map-server 192.168.100.100 key 3 9125d59c18a9b015
ip lisp etr map-server 192.168.200.200 key 3 9125d59c18a9b015
```

In this configuration, xTR3 is advertising its own loopback0 IP address 192.168.3.3 as the preferred RLOC (priority 1) for the EID prefixes 172.16.0.2/32 and 172.16.3.0/24 making it the preferred entry point into the LISP site. xTR3 must also advertise prefixes xTR4 is the preferred RLOC for with a higher priority value of 50, making it less preferred entry point into the LISP site to reach the EID prefixes 172.16.0.22/32 and 172.16.4.0/24. xTR4 is advertising its loopback0 IP address 192.168.4.4 as the preferred RLOC (priority 1) for the prefixes 172.16.0.22/32 and 172.16.4.0/24, making xTR4 the preferred entry point to reach the LISP site. The LISP configurations for xTR3 and xTR4 are the same because they connect to a common LISP site.

The MS/MR node configuration is what you saw in previous chapters with each node configured for the map server and/or map resolver function. After you enable the map server or map resolver function, you specify the EID prefix for each site. The two MS/MR nodes have similar LISP configuration. Example 9-3 shows the configuration for the MS/MR node in ISP 1.

Example 9-3 *MS/MR1 LISP Site Configuration*

```
!IOS XE MS/MR1 LISP site configurations

interface Loopback0
 ip address 192.168.100.100 255.255.255.255
 ip ospf 2 area 0
!
interface GigabitEthernet0/0
 ip address 10.1.100.2 255.255.255.0
 ip ospf 2 area 0

router lisp

 site Site-1
  authentication-key cisco
  eid-prefix 172.16.0.1/32
  eid-prefix 172.16.0.11/32
  eid-prefix 172.16.1.0/24
  eid-prefix 172.16.2.0/24
  exit
 !
 site Site-2
  authentication-key cisco
  eid-prefix 172.16.0.2/32
  eid-prefix 172.16.0.22/32
  eid-prefix 172.16.3.0/24
  eid-prefix 172.16.4.0/24
  exit
```

```
 !
 ipv4 map-server
 ipv4 map-resolver
 exit
 !
 router ospf 2
 !
```

The confirmation of the LISP site registration for a specific EID prefix from each site is shown in the MS/MR1 node in Example 9-4.

Example 9-4   *MS/M1 LISP Site Registration*

```
!MS/MR1 LISP site registration

MS/MR1# show lisp site 172.16.0.1/32
LISP Site Registration Information

Site name: Site-1
Allowed configured locators: any
Requested EID-prefix:
  EID-prefix: 172.16.0.1/32
    First registered:    00:07:51
    Last registered:     00:00:55
    Routing table tag:   0
    Origin:              Configuration
    Merge active:        No
    Proxy reply:         No
    TTL:                 1d00h
    State:               complete
    Registration errors:
      Authentication failures:   0
      Allowed locators mismatch: 0
    ETR 10.1.2.2, last registered 00:00:55, no proxy-reply, map-notify
                 TTL 1d00h, no merge, hash-function sha1, nonce 0x9FC0A53F-0x2AFC57F0
                 state complete, no security-capability
                 xTR-ID 0x628EB628-0x17FCD972-0x75E4A3A7-0x4ECE2449
                 site-ID unspecified
    Locator      Local  State     Pri/Wgt  Scope
    192.168.1.1  no     up          1/50   IPv4 none
    192.168.2.2  yes    up         50/50   IPv4 none
    ETR 10.1.1.2, last registered 00:00:58, no proxy-reply, map-notify
                 TTL 1d00h, no merge, hash-function sha1, nonce 0x18CA7EFE-0xB61CD464
                 state complete, no security-capability
                 xTR-ID 0xAEF298D2-0x24D5549F-0x1C36736B-0x6C3013EB
```

```
                     site-ID unspecified
        Locator      Local  State      Pri/Wgt  Scope
        192.168.1.1  yes    up             1/50  IPv4 none
        192.168.2.2  no     up            50/50  IPv4 none

MS/MR1# show lisp site 172.16.0.2/32
LISP Site Registration Information

Site name: Site-2
Allowed configured locators: any
Requested EID-prefix:
  EID-prefix: 172.16.0.2/32
    First registered:     00:09:06
    Last registered:      00:00:10
    Routing table tag:    0
    Origin:               Configuration
    Merge active:         No
    Proxy reply:          No
    TTL:                  00:03:00
    State:                complete
    Registration errors:
      Authentication failures:   0
      Allowed locators mismatch: 0
    ETR 192.168.4.4, last registered 00:00:10, no proxy-reply, no map-notify
                    TTL 00:03:00, no merge, hash-function sha1, nonce
                      0x00000000-0x00000000
                    state complete, no security-capability
                    xTR-ID N/A
                    site-ID N/A
      Locator      Local  State      Pri/Wgt  Scope
      192.168.3.3  no     up             1/100  IPv4 none
      192.168.4.4  yes    up            50/100  IPv4 none
    ETR 192.168.3.3, last registered 00:00:50, no proxy-reply, no map-notify
                    TTL 00:03:00, no merge, hash-function sha1, nonce
                      0x00000000-0x00000000
                    state complete, no security-capability
                    xTR-ID N/A
                    site-ID N/A
      Locator      Local  State      Pri/Wgt  Scope
      192.168.3.3  yes    up             1/100  IPv4 none
      192.168.4.4  no     up            50/100  IPv4 none

!debug lisp capture for EID prefix 172.16.0.1/32 and 172.16.0.2/32
```

```
MS/MR1# debug lisp control-plane map-server-registration
*Mar 13 03:14:39.196: LISP: Processing received Map-Register(3) message on
   GigabitEthernet0/0 from 10.1.2.2:4342 to 192.168.100.100:4342
*Mar 13 03:14:39.196: LISP: Processing Map-Register no proxy, map-notify, no merge,
   no security, no mobile-node, not to-RTR, no fast-map-register, no EID-notify,
   ID-included, 4 records, nonce 0xAAA54EFF-0x26C62FB1, key-id 1, auth-data-len 20,
   hash-function sha1, xTR-ID 0xFAD79A9D-0xA99AB7E2-0x37AB3661-0x524C9067, site-ID
   unspecified
*Mar 13 03:14:39.196: LISP: Processing Map-Register mapping record for IID 0
   172.16.0.1/32, ttl 1440, action none, authoritative, 2 locators
     192.168.1.1 pri/wei=1/50 lpR
     192.168.2.2 pri/wei=50/50 LpR
*Mar 13 03:14:39.196: LISP-0: MS registration IID 0 prefix 172.16.0.1/32 10.1.2.2
   site Site-1, Updating.
<SNIP>
*Mar 13 03:17:09.255: LISP: Processing received Map-Register(3) message on
   GigabitEthernet0/0 from 192.168.4.4:65365 to 192.168.100.100:4342
*Mar 13 03:17:09.255: LISP: Processing Map-Register no proxy, no map-notify, no
   merge, no security, no mobile-node, not to-RTR, fast-map-register, no EID-notify,
   no ID-included, 4 records, nonce 0x00000000-0x00000000, key-id 1, auth-data-len
   20, hash-function sha1
*Mar 13 03:17:09.255: LISP: Processing Map-Register mapping record for IID 0
   172.16.0.2/32, ttl 3, action none, authoritative, 2 locators
     192.168.3.3 pri/wei=1/100 lpr
     192.168.4.4 pri/wei=50/100 LpR
*Mar 13 03:17:09.255: LISP-0: MS registration IID 0 prefix 172.16.0.2/32 192.168.4.4
   site Site-2, Updating.
```

The output in Example 9-4 shows that in Site 1, both the ETRs with RLOC IP addresses 192.168.1.1 and 192.168.2.2 registered the 172.16.0.1/32 EID prefix. In Site 2, the ETRs with RLOC IP addresses 192.168.3.3 and 192.168.4.4 both registered 172.16.0.2/32. The preferred xTR sends a registration message with the lowest priority value of 1.

The next section focuses on troubleshooting this example with an emphasis on packet forwarding on the LISP nodes.

Troubleshooting LISP at the Enterprise Edge

In this section, we continue with the dual-router, dual-SP example from the previous section. The **show lisp site** command output already confirmed that the EID prefixes are successfully registering with the MS/MR nodes.

To verify whether there is connectivity between the LISP sites, pings are initiated from PC1 to PC3 and from PC2 to PC4, as shown in Example 9-5.

Note   In Example 9-5, the R1 router's loopback0 is assigned the PC1 IP address 172.16.0.1, and R1 router's loopback1 is assigned the PC2 IP address 172.16.0.2. The R2 node is also configured with loopback0 assigned to the PC3 IP address 172.16.0.3 and loopback1 assigned to the PC4 IP address 172.16.0.4. Two separate logical interfaces are created on the routers in each LISP site to simulate host IP addresses.

Example 9-5 *LISP Site-to-Site Connectivity Test*

```
R1# ping 172.16.0.2 source loopback 0
Type escape sequence to abort.
Sending 5, 100-byte ICMP Echos to 172.16.0.2, timeout is 2 seconds:
Packet sent with a source address of 172.16.0.1
!!!!!
Success rate is 100 percent (5/5), round-trip min/avg/max = 2/2/3 ms

R1# ping 172.16.0.22 source loopback 1
Type escape sequence to abort.
Sending 5, 100-byte ICMP Echos to 172.16.0.22, timeout is 2 seconds:
Packet sent with a source address of 172.16.0.11
!!!!!
```

The ping is successful—but which path did the packets actually take to reach the destination site? According to the traffic engineering requirement, when PC1 is communicating with PC2, packets should go to xTR1 and then route to xTR3 to reach PC2 and then take the symmetric path back. This is achieved by lowering the priority value to 1 in the LISP database mapping entry for EID prefix 172.16.0.2 mapped to the RLOC IP address of xTR3, 192.168.3.3, on xTR3. On xTR1, the priority of 1 is assigned to the EID prefix entry for 172.16.0.1 mapped to the RLOC IP address of xTR1. 192.168.1.1. xTR1 and xTR3 communicate the EID-to-RLOC mapping entry with the priority value set to the map server using the LISP map register control plane message. When xTR3 tries to resolve the 172.16.0.1 EID address from the mapping system, it receives xTR1 as the RLOC to reach EID prefix 172.160.1. Similarly, when xTR1 tries to resolve the 172.160.2 EID address from the mapping system, it receives xTR3 as the RLOC to reach 172.16.0.2. xTR1 has the lower priority value to become the preferred node to enter LISP Site 1 to reach PC1 IP address 172.16.0.1, while xTR3 becomes the preferred node to enter LISP Site 2. The output in Example 9-6 confirms that the path taken by the LISP packet is as per the traffic engineering requirements for PC1 and PC2.

Example 9-6 *PC1-to-PC2 LISP Forwarding Verification*

```
! xTR1 LISP map cache only shows entry for 172.16.0.2/32 post ping test.

xTR1# show ip lisp map-cache
LISP IPv4 Mapping Cache for EID-table default (IID 0), 2 entries

0.0.0.0/0, uptime: 00:50:37, expires: never, via static-send-map-request
  Negative cache entry, action: send-map-request
172.16.0.2/32, uptime: 00:00:39, expires: 23:59:20, via map-reply, complete
  Locator      Uptime    State    Pri/Wgt     Encap-IID
  192.168.3.3  00:00:39  up          1/100    -
  192.168.4.4  00:00:39  down       50/100    -
```

```
!xTR3 receiving the 5 ping packet from PC1 to PC2 and decapsulating it.

xTR3# debug ip lisp packet decap
xTR3# 2019 Mar 13 03:54:16.197165 netstack: liblisp [4115] <default> LISP decap-
   sulate packet, outer: 10.1.1.2 -> 192.168.3.3, inner: 172.16.0.1 -> 172.16.0.2,
   header: [nLevi-0x00000000-0x00000003]

2019 Mar 13 03:54:16.199990 netstack: liblisp [4115] <default> LISP decapsulate
   packet, outer: 10.1.1.2 -> 192.168.3.3, inner: 172.16.0.1 -> 172.16.0.2, header:
   [nLevi-0x00000000-0x00000003]

2019 Mar 13 03:54:16.202665 netstack: liblisp [4115] <default> LISP decapsulate
   packet, outer: 10.1.1.2 -> 192.168.3.3, inner: 172.16.0.1 -> 172.16.0.2, header:
   [nLevi-0x00000000-0x00000003]

2019 Mar 13 03:54:16.205324 netstack: liblisp [4115] <default> LISP decapsulate
   packet, outer: 10.1.1.2 -> 192.168.3.3, inner: 172.16.0.1 -> 172.16.0.2, header:
   [nLevi-0x00000000-0x00000003]

2019 Mar 13 03:54:16.208462 netstack: liblisp [4115] <default> LISP decapsulate
   packet, outer: 10.1.1.2 -> 192.168.3.3, inner: 172.16.0.1 -> 172.16.0.2, header:
   [nLevi-0x00000000-0x00000003]


!xTR3 PC2 response to PC1 packet path.

xTR3# show ip lisp locator-hash 172.16.0.2 172.16.0.1
LISP Locator Hashing for VRF "default"


EIDs 172.16.0.2 -> 172.16.0.1 yields:
   RLOCs 10.3.1.1 -> 192.168.1.1 (Ethernet2/1)
   Address hash: 0x03 [(3), hash bucket: 3, RLOC index: 0


!xTR3 LISP map cache

xTR3# show ip lisp map-cache
LISP IP Mapping Cache for VRF "default" (iid 0), 3 entries

0.0.0.0/1, uptime: 00:02:45, expires: 00:12:14, via map-reply
   Negative cache entry, action: forward-native

172.16.0.1/32, uptime: 00:05:19, expires: 23:54:40, via map-reply, auth
   Locator      Uptime    State     Priority/  Data      Control     MTU
                                    Weight     in/out    in/out
   192.168.1.1  00:05:19  up        1/50       0/11      1/1         1500
   192.168.2.2  00:05:19  up        50/50      0/0       0/0         1500
```

This output confirms that when a ping is sent from PC1, IP address 172.16.0.1/32, to PC2, IP address 172.16.0.2/32, the R1 router forwards it to xTR1 because it is the only xTR node that has the map cache for the 172.16.0.2/32 EID prefix entry resolved from the map server. xTR3 receives it, as confirmed by the **debug ip lisp packet decap** output, which shows ping packets received from RLOC IP source address 10.1.1.2, which is the outbound interface Gi2 of xTR1, connecting to ISP1. The xTR3 LISP map cache shows that the echo request that was sent back from PC2 to PC1 was received only on xTR3 because it is the node with the map cache entry for EID prefix 172.16.0.1/32.

Example 9-7 shows the confirmation of the traffic path PC2 and PC4 are using to communicate with each other.

Example 9-7 *PC4 LISP Forwarding Verification*

```
!xTR2 LISP map cache only has entry for 172.16.0.22/32 post ping test.


xTR2# show ip lisp map-cache
LISP IPv4 Mapping Cache for EID-table default (IID 0), 2 entries


0.0.0.0/0, uptime: 00:54:45, expires: never, via static-send-map-request
  Negative cache entry, action: send-map-request
172.16.0.22/32, uptime: 00:04:30, expires: 23:55:38, via map-reply, complete
  Locator      Uptime    State    Pri/Wgt      Encap-IID
  192.168.3.3  00:04:30  up        50/100      -
  192.168.4.4  00:04:30  up         1/100      -


!xTR4 NXOS LISP map cache


xTR4# show ip lisp  map-cache
LISP IP Mapping Cache for VRF "default" (iid 0), 2 entries


172.16.0.11/32, uptime: 00:07:47, expires: 23:52:12, via map-reply, auth
  Locator      Uptime    State    Priority/  Data     Control    MTU
                                  Weight     in/out   in/out
  192.168.1.1  00:07:47  up        50/50     0/0      0/0        1500
  192.168.2.2  00:07:47  up         1/50     0/8      0/0        1500


!xTR4 outbound interface LISP hash


xTR4# show ip lisp locator-hash 172.16.0.22 172.16.0.11
LISP Locator Hashing for VRF "default"


EIDs 172.16.0.22 -> 172.16.0.11 yields:
  RLOCs 10.3.2.1 -> 192.168.2.2 (Ethernet2/1)
  Address hash: 0x1d [(29), hash bucket: 4, RLOC index: 1


!xTR4 PC4 to PC2 LISP packet encapsulation
```

```
xTR4# debug ip lisp packet encap
2019 Mar 13 03:56:26.911602 netstack: liblisp [4115] <default> LISP encapsulate
  packet, outer: 10.3.2.1 -> 192.168.2.2, inner: 172.16.0.22 -> 172.16.0.11,
  header: [NLevi-0x005536af-0x00000002]

2019 Mar 13 03:56:26.914591 netstack: liblisp [4115] <default> LISP encapsulate
  packet, outer: 10.3.2.1 -> 192.168.2.2, inner: 172.16.0.22 -> 172.16.0.11,
  header: [NLevi-0x0082d96b-0x00000002]

2019 Mar 13 03:56:26.917455 netstack: liblisp [4115] <default> LISP encapsulate
  packet, outer: 10.3.2.1 -> 192.168.2.2, inner: 172.16.0.22 -> 172.16.0.11,
  header: [NLevi-0x00ae9c7e-0x00000002]

2019 Mar 13 03:56:26.920447 netstack: liblisp [4115] <default> LISP encapsulate
  packet, outer: 10.3.2.1 -> 192.168.2.2, inner: 172.16.0.22 -> 172.16.0.11,
  header: [NLevi-0x00dc638f-0x00000002]

2019 Mar 13 03:56:26.923715 netstack: liblisp [4115] <default> LISP encapsulate
  packet, outer: 10.3.2.1 -> 192.168.2.2, inner: 172.16.0.22 -> 172.16.0.11,
  header: [NLevi-0x000e3d8f-0x00000002]
```

The output confirms the following:

- On xTR2, the map cache entry is learned for 172.16.0.22/32 because it was the xTR in LISP Site 1 that received the ping packet sent from PC2 to PC4.

- xTR4 received the echo response from PC4 to PC2, which is confirmed by the map cache entry for 172.16.0.11/32 in the router. The **debug ip lisp packet encap** command output shows the encapsulation of the echo reply packet from PC4 to PC2 into a LISP packet with an outer RLOC destination address of the xTR2 IP address 192.168.2.2.

Traffic Engineering with LISP Explicit Locator Path

Much as with driving a car on a road, the path that traffic in a network takes can be defined dynamically, statically, or dynamically with some constraints. The need for controlling the traffic path is predicated on application or business requirements. There is commonly an application requirement for voice/video traffic to take certain paths from point A to point B in the network with minimal congestion and round-trip time (RTT) delay to ensure voice/video Quality of Service requirements. Businesses that invest in multiple WAN or Internet connections may want links to carry traffic according to their capacity. An organization might have a satellite link with a 2 Gigabit Ethernet connection and a 1 Gigabit Ethernet Dense Wavelength Division Multiplexing (DWDM) connection between two sites. When Open Shortest Path First (OSPF) calculates the best path, it considers cost, which is inversely proportional to the bandwidth of the outbound interface. OSPF uses the satellite link as its preferred path simply because the satellite link has a higher bandwidth. However, you would probably want to avoid sending the VoIP traffic on the 2 Gigabit Ethernet satellite link because although it has a higher bandwidth, it has much higher latency. Sending data traffic through the satellite link might make more sense to save the higher-bandwidth path for applications that are not sensitive to latency.

Can standard destination-based routing achieve such routing requirements for applications today? The answer is a resounding no! The only factor any dynamic routing protocol takes into consideration is the metrics it understands and uses to calculate the optimal path. The optimal path calculation is set on a fixed set of parameters and equations. In a network with quickly changing business and application requirements, more sophisticated mechanisms need to be introduced into the network to forward traffic, considering the application, link utilization, source of packets, and the Quality of Service requirement of the packets, and so on. The popular solution to meet the requirements of controlling traffic path based on application or business constraints has been predominantly Multiprotocol Label Switching (MPLS) Traffic Engineering (MPLS TE), particularly in service provider and large enterprise backbone networks. MPLS TE is a successful technology, but it requires you to have a label switching protocol, particularly the extended flavor of Resource Reservation Protocol (RSVP-TE RFC 3209), which supports label extensions or Constraint-Based Label Distribution Protocol (C-LDP RFC 3212). Then it also requires Multiprotocol Border Gateway Protocol (MP-BGP) in an MPLS Layer3 VPN or an MPLS Layer2 VPN deployment to distribute virtual private network (VPN) labels and next-hop information from ingress to egress provider edge routers. In a multi-tenant network hosting various services and users, VPNs are a requirement to ensure separation of control plane and data plane traffic, which is the primary function of MP-BGP. Where MPLS TE gets even more complicated is when you want to traffic engineer application packets from one autonomous system to another—that is, inter-AS MPLS TE. Some solutions require organizations to build a level of trust to allow certain routing information to leak across from one autonomous system to the other to allow the signaling and establish the end-to-end label switch path. This introduces operational complexity and requires experienced engineers to design, deploy, operate, and implement such networks. Finally, for unicast traffic, MPLS TE label-switched paths (LSPs) terminate at a single egress node. If a particular site has multiple edge routers acting as egress nodes for traffic sourced from another site that is trying to reach an address sourced from edge routers at the egress site, two individual MPLS TE tunnels must be provisioned to each of the egress routers at the destination site as the tail end. Prior to even provisioning the MPLS TE tunnels, you must ensure that BGP considers both egress routers as best next hops to the destination, which requires the BGP attribute and routing policy manipulation so a single best path is not chosen by BGP, as is done by default.

MPLS TE obviously requires an MPLS transport network. LISP performs traffic engineering without the need for MPLS or BGP. In comparison to other IP traffic engineering techniques, such as policy-based routing, LISP is easier to operate and flexible in terms of scale and applications. The next section dives further into traffic engineering applications of LISP in WAN networks.

Explicit Locator Path

The LISP packet encapsulated at the ingress tunnel router (ITR) takes a direct best path route determined by the underlay Interior Gateway Protocol (IGP) to the ETR RLOC address of preference. As explained in earlier chapters, the EID is associated with a set of RLOCs. Each RLOC is assigned a priority and weight. The priority defines the preferred RLOC to reach the EID. The ITR selects the RLOC with the highest priority as the ETR to which to send the packet destined to the EID. Priority field provides the option to have primary and secondary paths into a LISP site. In the event that the RLOC with the highest priority fails, the RLOC with the second highest priority takes over as the ETR for reaching the EID. If the LISP site wants to load share the traffic between the ETRs, the RLOCs for the ETR are set with equal priority but different weight values. The weight values determine the distribution of traffic the ITR sends to each ETR. Regardless of which ETR the LISP packet is sent to, the LISP packet is routed directly through various routers and link types, based on the outer LISP header with the RLOC address from the ITR (source RLOC) to the ETR (destination RLOC). At every hop, each router forwards based on its best path to the destination RLOC address, regardless of what type of data the LISP packet is carrying. If the ITR and ETR are nodes existing on two opposite ends of the service provider network with various media types and multiple hops of routers in between, then it is important to consider that the path a LISP packet takes is based on what type of application is inside the payload. So, as with a trip in a car, the trip a LISP packet takes from the ITR to the ETR has to be explicitly defined, based on various requirements of the application data. IGP is not dependable in this situation because the underlay routing protocol does not understand the network condition or the business or application requirements. LISP packets need to be traffic engineered from ITR to ETR, with the ability to define which intermediary nodes to traverse through.

The explicit locator path (ELP) in LISP provides a mechanism to define which RLOCs on the path to the ETR or PETR the LISP packet should traverse. It is very similar to an MPLS TE explicit path, where you define hop by hop which next-hop IP address the traffic should be switched to next. An MPLS TE explicit path is configured either in strict mode or loose mode. The "Cisco NX-OS Configuration Guide" defines loose and strict as follows:

> Loose specifies that the previous address (if any) in the explicit path does not need to be directly connected to the next IP address, and that the router is free to determine the path from the previous address (if any) to the next IP address.

> Strict specifies that the previous address (if any) in the explicit path must be directly connected to the next IP address.

The LISP ELP is similar to the loose MPLS TE explicit path. The ELP has a strict list of RLOCs that the packet must visit in the specific sequence; however, each path between RLOCs can consist of intermediary devices, and the IGP determines the best path as the packet travels from one RLOC to the next RLOC in the ELP. An MPLS TE explicit path defines a list of next-hop IP addresses, and LISP ELP defines a list of RLOC destination addresses in sequence. The destination address of the IP MPLS TE labeled packet remains the same, but the MPLS labels are swapped, directing the IP packet to its next-hop IP address, as defined by the explicit path. The destination RLOC address in the outer LISP IP packet header changes at each RLOC on the path to the destination ETR. Does this mean intermediary devices between the ITR and ETR must also have RLOC addresses? Yes, it does, and such devices have the role of re-encapsulating tunnel routers (RTRs), as explained in detail in the next section.

Figure 9-4 shows that the path between the two LISP sites diverges at RTR-B.

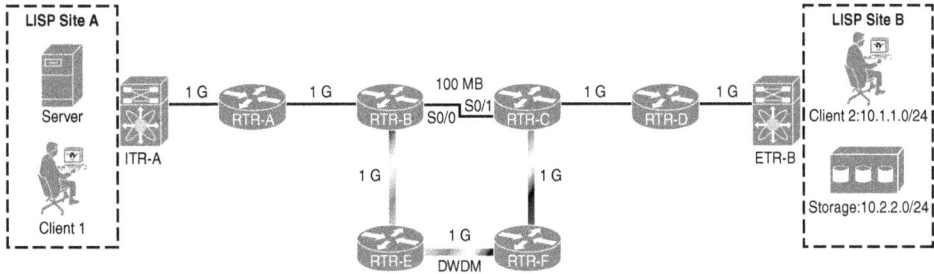

Figure 9-4 *LISP ELP*

Note RTR here stands for *re-encapsulating tunnel router*; it is not a short form for *router*.

RTR-B has a serial 0/0 link with bandwidth of 100 MB and a DWDM Ethernet link going south toward RTR-E with 1 Gigabit Ethernet bandwidth. ITR-A is encapsulating LISP packets and sending them to ETR-B, which hosts two EIDs, with prefixes 10.1.1.0/24 and 10.2.2.0/24. The 10.1.1.0/24 prefix simply has clients using day-to-day work applications such as web-based applications with some collaboration tools. The 10.2.2.0/24 prefix is where the storage devices are located, with all the backup and critical application data for the entire enterprise. The server in Site A regularly performs incremental backups of all the data to the storage device in Site B. The bandwidth requirement for backups usually is around 250+ Mbps. Thus, forwarding the traffic from the server to the storage via the WAN link would choke the link, causing severe packet drops. The solution is to create two ELPs: one for client-to-client traffic and one for server-to-storage traffic. The Client 1 to Client 2 communication should take this path:

ITR-A → RTR-A → RTR-B → RTR-C → RTR-D → ETR-B

The server-to-storage traffic should take this path:

ITR-A → RTR-A → RTR-B → RTR-E → RTR-F → RTR-C → RTR-D → ETR-B

The format for ELP is defined in the Internet Draft "LISP Canonical Address Format (LCAF)." The general notation for a formatted ELP is (a,b,etr). The letters a and b represent RTRs through which a packet should travel to reach the ETR, which is the final router behind which the EID is hosted. The ELP for each EID is stored in the mapping database. An ELP mapping entry for a particular EID prefix might look like this:

```
EID-prefix: 172.16.0.0/16
Locator-set: (a,b, ETR-A): priority 1, weight 50
             (c,d, ETR-B): priority 1,  weight 50
```

The EID prefix 172.16.0.0/16 is reachable via two ETRs with equal priority and equal weight. Thus, LISP packets are sent to both ETR-A and ETR-B to reach prefix

172.16.0.0/16, but half of the LISP packets go through RTR a and then to RTR b, and the other half go through RTR c and then to RTR d.

Flow-based sharing across multiple paths to the same ETR ELP mapping entry in the mapping database looks as follows:

```
EID-prefix: 192.168.1.0/24
Locator-set: (a,b, ETR-B): priority 1, weight 75
                 (x,y, ETR-B): priority 1, weight 25
```

According to the policy in place, the ITR sends 75% of the load of traffic to the (a,b,ETR-B) path and 25% of the traffic to the (x,y,ETR-B) path. If any of the paths go down—for example, if RTR a were to fail—then 100% of the traffic would take the (x,y,ETR-B) path. This would be a dynamic operation. ETR-B would notify the mapping database to withdraw the entry with the failed path.

Refer to Figure 9-4 and assume that the host is in network 172.16.1.0/24 in LISP Site A. A LISP ELP can be defined based on different classes of service, taking the source into consideration, as shown in the following example:

```
EID-prefix: (172.16.1.0/24, 10.2.2.0/24)
Locator-set: (a,b,e,f,c,d ETR-B): priority 1, weight 100
 EID-prefix: (0.0.0.0, 10.2.2.0/24)
Locator-set: (a,b,c,d, ETR-B): priority 1, weight 100
```

The mapping entries result in traffic from 172.16.1.0/24 to the 10.2.2.0/24 EID prefix taking the DWDM path, while traffic from any other source—for example, Client 1 backing up a small file on the remote storage device—takes the WAN path to reach the same 10.2.2.0/24 EID prefix where the storage device sits.

The ELP RTRs can be proxy ITRs (PITRs) and ETRs (PETRs). As explained in Chapter 3, "LISP IPv4 Unicast Routing," PITRs and PETRs allow LISP and non-LISP sites to talk to each other. A PITR also allows internetworking between IPv4 and IPv6 sites. Consider that the PITR and PETR can act as RTRs and can be listed in the ELP. This implies the ability to traffic engineer LISP packets across routing domains with different address families. The RLOCs appearing in the ELP can be a mix of IPv4 or IPv6. Figure 9-5 shows a use case.

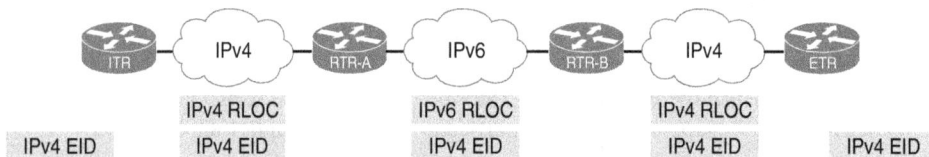

Figure 9-5 *LISP ELP Internetworking*

In Figure 9-5, the ITR and ETR are separated by multiple networks, and one of the networks in the path from the ITR to the ETR is an IPv6 network, while both the ITR and ETR are part of an IPv4 network. There might have been an alternative path through an IPv4-only network, but due to some requirement, the best path for particular traffic might have been determined to be the one through an IPv6 network—perhaps because that path has fewer hops or better network resources (such as bandwidth) available. The ELP looks like (RTR-A, RTR-B, ETR). A packet is encapsulated with an IPv4 RLOC from the ITR to RTR-A, with the source RLOC address of the ITR and a destination RLOC of the RTR-A IPv4 RLOC address. RTR-A then re-encapsulates the packet with a source IPv6 RLOC address of its own IPv6 RLOC address and destination of the IPv6 RLOC address of RTR-B. RTR-B searches in the ELP and learns that the next RLOC address to send to is the ETR. RTR-B re-encapsulates with source IPv4 address its own IPv4 RLOC and the destination IPv4 RLOC address of the ETR.

LISP ELPs can be applied in multicast environments, as in the earlier example where RTRs are used to interconnect networks of different address families. The RTR at each hop in the ELP can take a multicast packet from a particular source with a destination multicast group EID address and re-encapsulate the multicast packet with a unicast RLOC address. This provides the ability to interconnect two discontinuous multicast networks through a unicast network. This is a plausible scenario a customer or service provider might face where certain parts of the service provider network do not support multicast natively in the core.

If the traffic is a multicast packet, instead of resolving a destination EID prefix to RLOC, the ITR resolves an (S,G) entry in the mapping database. The S is the source EID unicast address, and the G is the destination multicast address. The ELP entry in the mapping database may look like this:

```
Multicast EID key: (10.1.1.1, 239.0.0.1)
Locator-set:
        (RTR-1, RTR-2, ETR-A): priority 1, weight 50
        (RTR-3, 239.0.0.2, RTR-4, ETR-B): priority 1, weight 50
```

Remember that any of the RTRs can be from any address family. Figure 9-6 is an interesting use case to help understand the versatility of LISP ELPs in steering multicast packets between LISP sites.

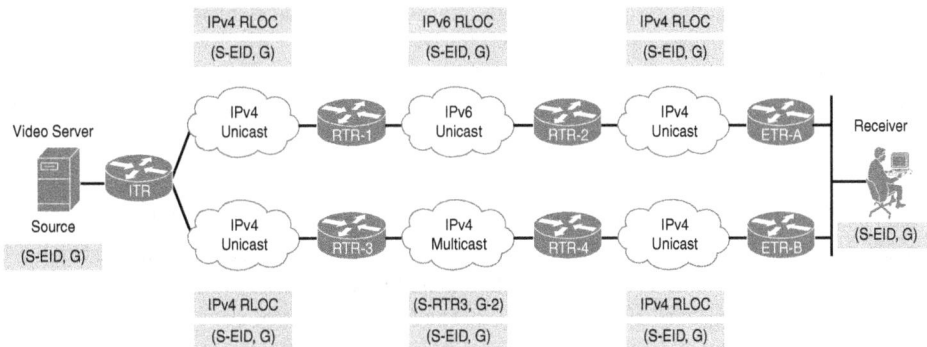

Figure 9-6 *LISP ELP in a Multicast Environment*

On the left side of Figure 9-6, a video server sends a stream of traffic with a unicast source EID IPv4 address of the video server and a destination multicast address for the video stream. As per the ELP in this example, the source can be 10.1.1.1/24 and the destination address can be 239.0.0.1. The ITR acts as the first-hop multicast router connected to the source. The right side of the diagram shows a receiver that has subscribed to the multicast address 239.0.0.1 through a multicast application on its desktop. The receiver LISP site has two ETRs, ETR-A and ETR-B, both acting as last-hop multicast routers connected to the receiver. Two paths of equal preference exist between the source and receiver. The network architect has a few challenges to address. First, the intermediary network hops do not all natively support multicast or were not enabled for multicast routing. How do you get multicast traffic through a non-multicast routing domain? The second challenge to overcome is the multiple address family network domains in between the source and the receiver for the multicast stream. How do you send IPv4 multicast traffic through a IPv6 unicast routing network domain? The final challenge is the ability to load balance traffic across the two paths, equally or unequally. Without LISP, such a task is quite challenging to implement and manage—although it is possible. A LISP ELP solution addresses all the challenges using a dynamic mapping system that reconverges from any unexpected failures in the intermediate networks between the source and receiver.

The first ELP is defined by the locator set (RTR-1, RTR-2, ETR-A), and the ITR encapsulates the multicast packet inside the LISP packet with the RLOC IPv4 unicast address of RTR-1 as the destination address and the ITR RLOC IPv4 unicast address as the source address—essentially encapsulating multicast into a unicast packet. Once RTR-1 receives the LISP packet, RTR-1 re-encapsulates the LISP packet with the source IPv6 RLOC address of itself and the IPv6 RLOC address of RTR-2 as the destination address. On receiving the LISP packet, RTR-2 refers to its ELP entry and learns that it needs to forward the packet on to the ETR with the IPv4 RLOC address. Finally, when the ETR receives the LISP packet, it de-encapsulates the packet by removing the outer IP RLOC header, the User Datagram Protocol (UDP) header, and the LISP header and forwards the native IP packet with the source address of the video server (S-EID) and the destination multicast EID address 239.0.0.1. The receiver eventually receives the packet because it subscribed to the multicast group through Internet Group Management Protocol (IGMP), and Protocol Independent Multicast (PIM) builds the multicast tree rooted at either the first-hop router attached to the source in the case of the PIM shortest path tree or Rendezvous Point (RP) in the case of a shared tree. The multicast tree extends down to all the last-hop routers attached to receivers subscribed to the multicast group.

The second ELP, which from the mapping entry is of equal priority and weight to the first, equals distribution of multicast traffic sent to ETR-A and ETR-B from the ITR. The ITR encapsulates the multicast stream into LISP unicast packets with source and destination IPv4 RLOC addresses to RTR-3. RTR-3 refers to its ELP entry in its local cache to determine which RLOC address to send it to next. The RLOC address is not a unicast address but a multicast group address G-2. G-2 is a multicast group that exists in the routing domain of the network between RTR-3 and RTR-4. RTR-4, which is a member node in the multicast domain, also receives traffic destined to multicast group G-2 simply because RTR-4 also has a host interested in multicast group G-2. Multicast G-2 is 239.0.0.2, and RTR-3 re-encapsulates the LISP packet with the source RLOC unicast IPv4 address of RTR-3 and the multicast address 239.0.0.2 as the destination RLOC address. At this stage, RTR-3 has re-encapsulated the IPv4 multicast packet inside another multicast packet to route the traffic through a separate multicast routing domain. Once RTR-4 receives the LISP multicast packet, it re-encapsulates the packet and forwards it toward the ETR with IPv4 unicast addresses both for the source and destination RLOCs. The beauty of this entire process is that the receiver and source are completely oblivious to what routing domain the packet went through, and the packet is received by the user as sent by the sender, in its original format. There is no translation mechanism required or redistribution of one routing protocol into another. LISP makes it possible to interconnect two end hosts through many different types of heterogeneous networks, and this is all possible through the mapping information provided by the mapping system to each of the LISP nodes and the separation of address into two namespaces: one specifying the location and the other the endpoint identifier. Each ELP RLOC address is simply a location in the network to get to an end-point. The packet hops from one location to the next location to route through the nearest location to the endpoint. The RTR nodes are placed in the explicitly defined path to control the path of the LISP packet. A closer look at RTR and its function is required now.

Re-encapsulating Tunnel Routers

Any sort of traffic needs some entity to control the direction of traffic. RTRs are landing points, where decisions are made about where to send packets next. RTRs use ELPs to control the path of traffic through the network. So what is unique about an RTR? It de-encapsulates LISP packets destined to itself and then re-encapsulates the LISP packets and sends them on to the next RLOC defined in the ELP. So the RTR acts as an ETR because it de-encapsulates LISP packets and then uses the ITR function to build a new LISP header to the next ETR/RTR in the forwarding path. The new LISP header destination RLOC address is what defines the direction of the traffic, without the overhead of an additional header. The entire process in which each RTR uses ELP is dynamic. Every RTR also learns the ELP for a particular EID prefix entry dynamically through the mapping system. The ETR registers to the mapping system which RTRs a LISP packet traverses to get to a destination EID. The ETR defines the RTRs in ELP by using message mechanisms similar to those explained in Chapter 3.

The following steps outline the life of a LISP packet as it goes from an ITR to an ETR using ELP (a,b,etr):

Step 1.   The ITR receives a packet with a source EID address and a destination EID address. The ITR with LISP enabled, in the Cisco implementation, first refers to its local routing table to verify whether it has a match for the destination EID. The destination EID, by definition, should not exist in the global routing table, and the router refers to the LISP map cache. The Cisco implementation also verifies whether the source EID is configured as a local EID prefix. It assumes that the ITR has already resolved the mapping entry for the destination EID prefix and in return retrieved the ELP from the mapping database, following a control plane mechanism similar to that explained in Chapter 3. Prior to using the ELP for packet forwarding, the ITR ensures that no RLOC address appears twice in the ELP to prevent the looping of the LISP packet; this is a simple but effective loop prevention mechanism. Because the LISP packet is an IP packet, it also has time-to-live (TTL) copying procedures to prevent loops.

Step 2.   The ELP is processed from left to right, and the ITR proceeds to encapsulate the LISP packet, leaving the original packet intact, with itself as the source RLOC and the IP address of RTR a as the destination RLOC address.

Step 3.   RTR a receives the LISP packet and de-encapsulates it because it sees its own RLOC address as the destination RLOC address. RTR a inspects the inner packet and performs a lookup for the destination EID in the inner header into its local cache for the ELP entry, which instructs RTR a to send the packet on to the RTR b RLOC IP address. Therefore, the packet is once again encapsulated by RTR a and sent to the next RTR defined in the ELP with RLOC b.

Step 4.   RTR b, with RLOC b, now receives the packet and de-encapsulates it. RTR b refers to the inner IP header and performs a lookup in its local mapping database for the destination EID. The ETR refers to the ELP entry for the EID prefix, which instructs it now to forward it to an ETR with RLOC etr. RTR b encapsulates the LISP packet again, now with its own RLOC address in the source RLOC field and the destination RLOC address etr of the ETR.

Step 5.   When the ETR receives the LISP packet, it de-encapsulates the packet and sends it to the interface to the next hop of the EID prefix.

The RTR LISP packet's encapsulation and de-encapsulation capability allows it to act as a transit node to direct traffic down specific paths by referencing the ELP field in the LISP packet for instructions about which RTR or ETR to send the packet to next. This same capability allows the RTR to act as a border device between two routing domains. The next section looks into another use case for RTRs—in LISP WAN networks.

LISP Disjoint RLOC Domains

The LISP Disjoint RLOC Domains feature supports sites being connected to locator spaces that have no connectivity to each other. For example, the IPv4 Internet and IPv6 Internet are disjointed RLOC spaces. Relative to a node in the IPv4 Internet, the IPv6 Internet is not globally routable and vice versa. Establishing communication between two hosts in two separate routing domains can be quite complex. There has to exist a device that can stitch together the path between the two routing domains for end-to-end host communication. This device in LISP networks is the RTR.

The RTR node has one RLOC interface address in all the domains. It acts as a gateway to interconnect the LISP sites in different routing domains. An RTR de-encapsulates packets that are sent to it by stripping off the outer IP header with RLOC addressing information; then it does a map cache lookup and re-encapsulates and forwards the packet toward the destination routing domain ETR device in another locator scope. We can compare an RTR with an airport. Imagine that you are travelling through airports and have to recheck your luggage at the airline counter for your next destination. The ground crew removes your old baggage tag (de-encapsulates) and sticks on a new baggage tag (re-encapsulates) that has the information to transport your luggage to your next destination. The old tag could be from an incoming flight with Air Canada, and the new tag could be for the next departing flight on United Airlines. Two different airlines are like two different namespaces, with different tags identifying each carrier. The RTR must have presence in all the RLOC domains to encapsulate and de-encapsulate packets from one domain to another. Thus, the RTR must have RLOCs in all the domains, and because it performs similar functions to the PITR and PETR, the RTR must have both PITR and PETR features enabled on the node acting as the RTR.

The RTR takes care of the data plane to interconnect two disjointed routing domains. If any ITR in a LISP network in Routing Domain A is to communicate with an ETR in Routing Domain B, a common map server must exist that knows that the two routing domains need to communicate with each other and that is able to direct traffic to the RTR that can stitch together the two routing domains. An RTR has one interface that is reachable in both routing domains, and the same is true of the map server, to ensure that ITRs can send map requests to resolve the RLOCs for the destination EIDs in another routing domain. It is important to note that the ITR and ETR in the entire LISP communication process are not even aware that packets are traversing heterogenous network domains.

The Disjoint RLOC Domains feature supports the following common use cases:

■ Across address families (AFs) with IPv4/IPv6 locators, as shown in Figure 9-7

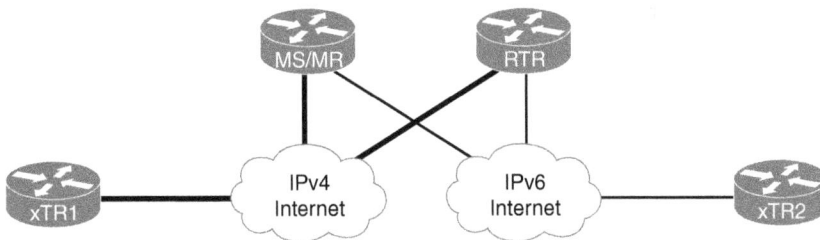

Figure 9-7   *LISP Disjoint RLOC Domains Across Address Families*

■ Across distinct IPv4 or IPv6 cores—for example, two MPLS VPN providers, as shown in Figure 9-8

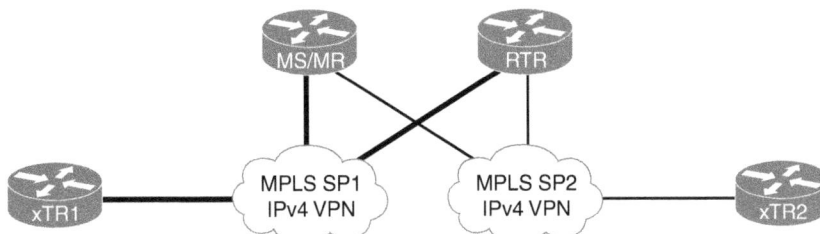

Figure 9-8   *Disjoint RLOC Domains Across Distinct Service Provider Cores*

Summary

WAN router integration with external networks is a complex part of network to design. Routing design gets tricky when a particular enterprise wants to control data traffic paths both in the ingress and egress directions. Traffic engineering with routing protocols requires advanced knowledge and expertise in the protocol attributes and packet types to determine traffic paths for data traffic in the network. History has shown that solving a complex problem with a complex solution adds to operational complexity, which increases the chances of network incidents. LISP provides a simple and scalable approach to traffic engineering that complements existing routing infrastructure protocols commonly used in WANs today. LISP does not replace these protocols but complements them with its versatility to address the same use cases with few operational changes and little complexity. LISP accomplishes traffic engineering through the priority and weight attributes to achieve equal- and unequal-cost load balancing. A LISP RTR using the ELP field steers traffic down specific paths. ELP defines multiple hops of RTRs through which a LISP packet must transit between two LISP xTRs. RTRs are also used for transit between two routing domains that are part of different address families or MPLS service provider networks.

References

The following references provide more details on the topics discussed in this chapter:

Internet Draft, "LISP Traffic Engineering Use-Cases," draft-ietf-lisp-te-04

Internet Draft, "LISP Canonical Address Format (LCAF)," draft-ietf-lisp-lcaf

Cisco, "Locator/ID Separation Protocol (LISP)," http://lisp.cisco.com

Cisco, "IP Routing: LISP Configuration Guide IOS XE," http://www.cisco.com

## Chapter 10

LISP Security

As the use of LISP has advanced in the Internet of Things (IoT) space along with the enterprise and data center, security has become a major concern that keeps network architects and network engineers up at night. The number of connected IoT devices is increasing rapidly and poses a huge security threat to the network infrastructure. There are two main aspects of any LISP deployment: the control plane and the data plane. LISP provides support for features to secure both the control plane and the data plane. This chapter elaborates on securing the LISP control plane as well as the LISP data plane.

This chapter covers the following topics:

- Securing the LISP control plane using LISP-SEC

- Securing the LISP data plane

- LISP with GETVPN encryption

Securing the LISP Control Plane Using LISP-SEC

As defined in RFC 6830, the LISP specification includes a basic mechanism for implementing security for LISP control plane traffic. The two-way LISP header nonce exchange provides a basic level of security by preventing ingress tunnel router (ITR) from spoofing attacks. When an ITR sends a map request, a nonce key (which is a 64-bit field present in every LISP control plane message) is sent in the LISP header of the map request. The map reply must include a matching nonce key for the ITR to validate a matching response for its map request. If the validation fails, the map reply is ignored and dropped. This mechanism makes it difficult for off-path attackers to create a spoofing attack within the LISP network as they do not have the correct nonce value.

Preventing other denial of service (DoS) attacks in a LISP network involves implementing rate limiters for the number of allowed map requests and map replies. However, such mechanisms do not provide protection against man-in-the-middle attacks as they do not help validate the origin of a map reply on the ITR. Thus, just the nonce mechanism alone is not very useful in this case. To overcome such attacks, the nonce mechanism can be supplemented with another security mechanism, known as LISP-Security (LISP-SEC).

The LISP-SEC mechanism helps authenticate the origin and integrity of LISP control plane messages. LISP-SEC enables a LISP network with antireplay protection capability for the endpoint identifier–to–routing locator (EID-to-RLOC) mapping data shared in a map reply message. It also enables the verification of authorization on EID prefix in the map reply messages.

The LISP-SEC mechanism involves a few simple steps.

Step 1.   The ITR generates a one-time-key (OTK) known as the ITR-OTK. The ITR then caches the ITR-OTK, which is used for the map reply verification process. The ITR then builds a map request message, embeds the ITR-OTK in the LISP control header, and sets the S bit. When the map request message is built, the ITR sends the map request toward the map resolver (MR). Note that the map request is sent for the EID prefix residing on the egress tunnel router (ETR) along with the nonce value and ITR-OTK.

Step 2.   The MR resolves the EID prefix and forwards the map request to the map server (MS).

Step 3.   The MS extracts the ITR-OTK from the incoming LISP control header. The MS uses the ITR-OTK to compute the map server OTK (MS-OTK) by applying the hash-based message authentication code (HMAC)–based key derivative function (HKDF) on the ITR-OTK (that is, MS-OTK = HKDF(ITR-OTK)).

The MS builds the map request message as follows:

  ■ It uses the X EID prefix from the MS configuration.

  ■ It uses the ITR-OTK to compute the HMAC hash (that is, EID-HMAC).

  ■ It embeds the MS-OTK.

  ■ It embeds the EID authentication data (EID-AD) in the LISP control header.

  ■ It sets the S bit.

The MS then sends the map request to the registered ETR.

Step 4.   When the ETR receives the map request, it extracts the MS-OTK and EID-AD from the LISP control header and builds a map reply message that includes the following fields:

  ■ The ETR-supplied EID-to-RLOC mapping

  ■ A copy of the EID-AD from the map request message

  ■ The MS-OTK used in a computation of the HMAC hash, known as packet-HMAC (PKT-HMAC) over the entire map reply packet (that is, HMACITR-OTK[{EID Prefix}])

■ The packet authentication data (PKT-AD) embedded in the map reply

■ The S bit

The ETR then sends the map reply toward the ITR.

Step 5. When the ITR receives the map reply, it extracts the PKT-AD and EID-AD. The ITR uses the cached ITR-OTK to recompute the HMAC across the EID-AD. The ITR compares this HMAC with the EID-HMAC and drops the map reply if the value does not match. The MS-OTK is calculated using the same HKDF used for the MS on the ITR-OTK.

To verify the PKT-AD, the ITR uses the MS-OTK to recompute the HMAC hash across the entire map reply, which is then compared with the PKT-HMAC. If the values match, the map-reply is processed; otherwise, the map-reply is dropped.

Figure 10-1 shows all the steps involved in LISP control plane security.

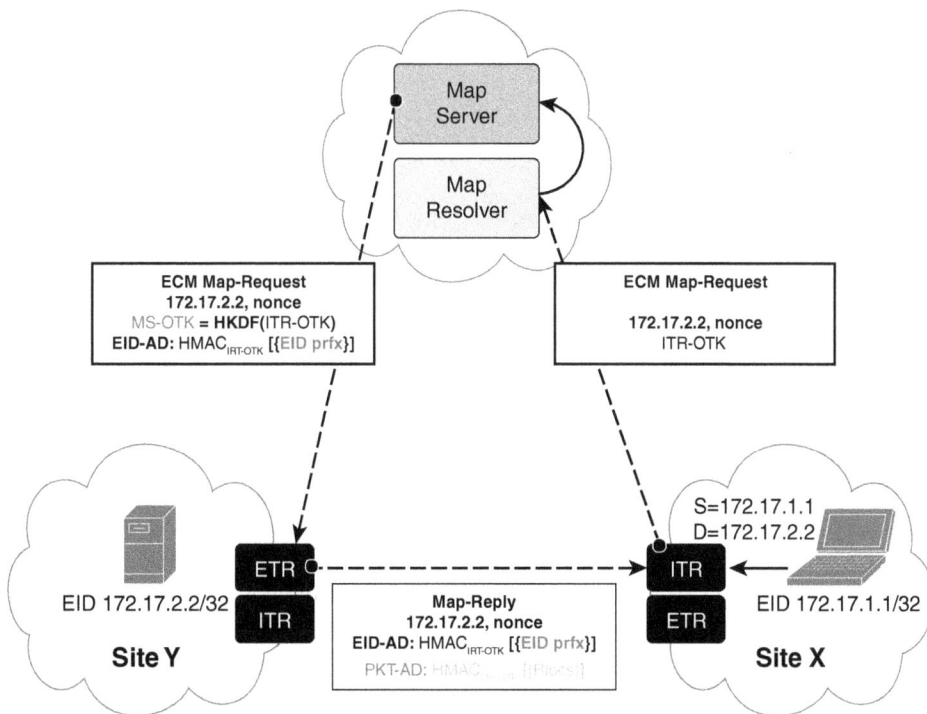

Figure 10-1 *LISP Control Plane Security*

Configuring and Verifying LISP-SEC

Figure 10-2 illustrates how LISP-SEC works. In this figure, there are three LISP-enabled sites, with an xTR router at each site. xTR1 is running IOS-XE, xTR2 is running IOS-XR, and xTR3 is running NX-OS. The MR/MS node does not necessarily need to be enabled with LISP-SEC but should be running software that supports LISP-SEC. The LISP-SEC feature is not supported on IOS-XR. Thus, the xTR2 node in Figure 10-2 is a non-LISP-SEC-capable xTR, whereas xTR1 and xTR3 are LISP-SEC-enabled xTRs.

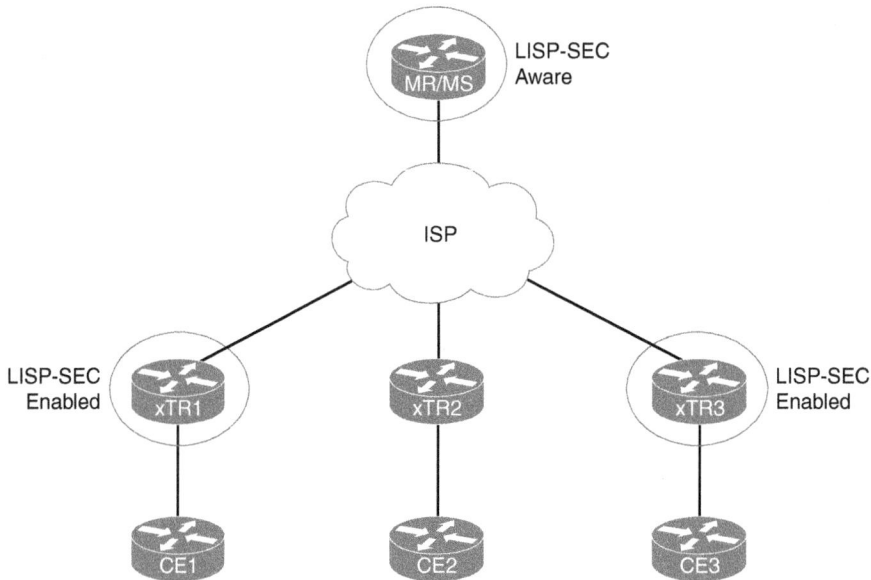

Figure 10-2 *Topology for LISP-SEC*

LISP-SEC is enabled using the command **security [strong]**, which is configured under the router lisp configuration mode on IOS/IOS-XE and using the command **lisp security [strong]** on NX-OS. If the **strong** keyword is not used, LISP security is configured in loose mode. Example 10-1 illustrates the configuration on xTR1 and xTR3 for enabling LISP-SEC. In this example, xTR1 is enabled with loose security, and xTR3 is enabled with strong security. The main difference between the two is that the xTR node with strong security does not accept map replies from a node that is not enabled with LISP-SEC, whereas the xTR with loose security accepts the map replies from both LISP-SEC and non-LISP-SEC xTRs. Having loose security enabled is useful when migrating a LISP-enabled network from being non-LISP-SEC capable to being a LISP-SEC-enabled network.

Example 10-1 *Configuring LISP-SEC*

```
xTR1 (IOS-XE)
xTR1(config)# router lisp
xTR1(config-router-lisp)# security
```
```
xTR3 (NX-OS)
xTR3(config)# lisp security strong
```

When the xTR is configured for LISP-SEC, the ETR advertises the LISP-SEC capability to the MS, along with its map register message. You can verify this information on the MS by using the command **show lisp site name** *site-name* **instance-id** *instance-id*. Example 10-2 shows the site prefix information for both site AS64001 and site AS64002. Notice in this example that the EID prefix from site AS64001 (xTR1) is advertised with the security capability, whereas the EID prefix from site AS64002 (xTR2) is not advertised with this capability.

Example 10-2   *Verifying LISP-SEC Capability on the MS/MR*

```
! Output for LISP-SEC enabled site
MR-MS-1# show lisp site name AS64001 instance-id 1
Site name: AS64001
Allowed configured locators: any
Allowed EID-prefixes:

  EID-prefix: 172.16.1.0/24 instance-id 1
    First registered:     20:11:22
    Last registered:      16:51:36
    Routing table tag:    0
    Origin:               Configuration
    Merge active:         No
    Proxy reply:          No
    TTL:                  1d00h
    State:                complete
    Registration errors:
      Authentication failures:   0
      Allowed locators mismatch: 0
    ETR 192.168.1.1:20239, last registered 16:51:36, no proxy-reply, map-notify
                      TTL 1d00h, no merge, hash-function sha1, nonce
                        0x66533E3A-0xEEDB86D8
                      state complete, security-capability
                      xTR-ID 0x8732DAD0-0x7617B5C9-0x711D1127-0x4CAF9B24
                      site-ID unspecified
                      sourced by reliable transport
      Locator      Local  State    Pri/Wgt  Scope
      192.168.1.1  yes    up        1/100   IPv4 none

  EID-prefix: 172.17.1.1/32 instance-id 1
! Output omitted for brevity
! Output for Non LISP-SEC site
MR-MS-1# show lisp site name AS64002 instance-id 1
Site name: AS64002
Allowed configured locators: any
```

```
Allowed EID-prefixes:
 EID-prefix: 172.16.2.0/24 instance-id 1
    First registered:      20:11:54
    Last registered:       00:00:20
    Routing table tag:     0
    Origin:                Configuration
    Merge active:          No
    Proxy reply:           No
    TTL:                   1d00h
    State:                 complete
    Registration errors:
      Authentication failures:    0
      Allowed locators mismatch: 0
    ETR 192.168.2.2, last registered 00:00:20, no proxy-reply, map-notify
                    TTL 1d00h, no merge, hash-function sha1, nonce 0xAA467CE7-
                       0x86279BD8
                    state complete, no security-capability
                    xTR-ID 0x97728DDB-0xA05017E9-0x5D8ABD2E-0xB1926851
                    site-ID unspecified
      Locator      Local  State   Pri/Wgt  Scope
      192.168.2.2  yes    up       1/100   IPv4 none
```

Because xTR1 is enabled with loose security and xTR3 is enabled with strong security capability, control plane traffic from xTR2 (the non-LISP-SEC-enabled site) is dropped by xTR3 and accepted by xTR1. Example 10-3 shows this behavior by initiating Internet Control Message Protocol (ICMP) traffic from the host behind xTR1 and xTR3 toward the host behind xTR2. In this example, the map reply from xTR2 is accepted only by xTR1 and not by xTR3.

Example 10-3   *Verifying Map Cache Entries with LISP-SEC Enabled*

```
CE1
CE1# ping 172.17.2.2 source loopback0
Type escape sequence to abort.
Sending 5, 100-byte ICMP Echos to 172.17.2.2, timeout is 2 seconds:
Packet sent with a source address of 172.17.1.1
..!!!
Success rate is 60 percent (3/5), round-trip min/avg/max = 4/4/5 ms
xTR1 (IOS-XE)
xTR1# show ip lisp map-cache instance-id 1
LISP IPv4 Mapping Cache for EID-table default (IID 1), 3 entries

0.0.0.0/0, uptime: 00:00:22, expires: never, via static-send-map-request
  Negative cache entry, action: send-map-request
```

```
172.17.2.2/32, uptime: 00:00:15, expires: 23:59:45, via map-reply, complete
  Locator       Uptime    State     Pri/Wgt      Encap-IID
  192.168.2.2  00:00:15  up            1/100       -
CE3
CE3# ping 172.17.2.2 source loopback0
Type escape sequence to abort.
Sending 5, 100-byte ICMP Echos to 172.17.2.2, timeout is 2 seconds:
Packet sent with a source address of 172.17.3.3
.....
Success rate is 0 percent (0/5)
xTR3 (NX-OS)


! Notice the map-cache entry missing for 172.17.2.2
xTR3# show ip lisp map-cache
LISP IP Mapping Cache for VRF "default" (iid 1), 1 entries


172.16.1.0/24, uptime: 00:00:15, expires: 23:59:44, via map-reply, auth
  Locator       Uptime    State     Priority/  Data       Control      MTU
                                    Weight     in/out     in/out
  192.168.1.1  00:00:15  up           1/100      0/0        1/0        1500
```

When the migration is complete and LISP-SEC is enabled on all sites, map replies from non-LISP-SEC-enabled sites are not allowed and are thus not installed in the LISP map cache. Only map replies from LISP-SEC-enabled sites are installed in the map cache table. To see how this works, you can enable strong security on the xTR1 site using the command **security strong**. After you clear the map cache entries on xTR1, CE1 is only able to reach CE3 and not the CE2 router, as illustrated in Example 10-4. This is because CE2 is connected to a non-LISP-SEC-enabled site.

Example 10-4 *Verifying Map Cache Entries with LISP-SEC Enabled*

```
CE1
! Ping to host being non-LISP-SEC enabled xTR - xTR2
CE1# ping 172.17.2.2 source lo0
Type escape sequence to abort.
Sending 5, 100-byte ICMP Echos to 172.17.2.2, timeout is 2 seconds:
Packet sent with a source address of 172.17.1.1
.....
Success rate is 0 percent (0/5)


! Ping to host being LISP-SEC enabled xTR - xTR3
CE1# ping 172.17.3.3 source lo0
Type escape sequence to abort.
Sending 5, 100-byte ICMP Echos to 172.17.3.3, timeout is 2 seconds:
Packet sent with a source address of 172.17.1.1
.!!!!
```

```
Success rate is 80 percent (4/5), round-trip min/avg/max = 3/3/4 ms
xTR1 (IOS-XE)
xTR1# show ip lisp map-cache instance-id 1
LISP IPv4 Mapping Cache for EID-table default (IID 1), 3 entries

0.0.0.0/0, uptime: 1d21h, expires: never, via static-send-map-request
  Negative cache entry, action: send-map-request
172.16.1.0/24, uptime: 21:02:15, expires: 02:57:44, via map-reply, self, complete
  Locator      Uptime     State       Pri/Wgt     Encap-IID
  192.168.1.1  21:02:15   up, self    1/100       -
172.17.3.3/32, uptime: 00:00:27, expires: 23:59:32, via map-reply, complete
  Locator      Uptime     State       Pri/Wgt     Encap-IID
  192.168.3.3  00:00:27   up          1/100       -
```

You can verify security on the xTRs by enabling debugs. On IOS-XE, use the command **debug lisp control-plane all** to view the processing of the control plane messages. On NX-OS, use the command **debug ip lisp mapping control** *eid-prefix*, which allows you to view all the control plane message exchange information for the specified EID prefix. Example 10-5 shows the use of **debug** commands on both xTR1 and xTR3 to view the control plane message exchange. In this example, notice that xTR1 drops the map request for prefix 172.17.2.2/32 from xTR2 because it fails the security check, and it accepts the map request for 172.17.3.3/32 and initiates a map reply toward xTR3. Similarly, **debug** on xTR3 shows that LISP-SEC is present for the prefix 172.17.1.1/32.

Example 10-5 *LISP Control Plane Debugging*

```
xTR1 (XE)
xTR1# debug lisp control-plane all
All LISP control debugging is on
05:04:45.017: LISP: Processing data signal for EID prefix IID 1 172.17.2.2/32
05:04:45.017: LISP-0: Remote EID IID 1 prefix 172.17.2.2/32, Change state to
  incomplete (sources: <signal>, state: unknown, rlocs: 0).
05:04:45.017: LISP-0: Remote EID IID 1 prefix 172.17.2.2/32, [incomplete] Scheduling
  map requests delay 00:00:00 min_elapsed 00:00:01 (sources: <signal>, state:
  incomplete, rlocs: 0).
05:04:45.151: LISP-0: IID 1 Request processing of remote EID prefix map requests to
  IPv4.
05:04:45.151: LISP: Send map request type remote EID prefix
05:04:45.151: LISP: Send map request for EID prefix IID 1 172.17.2.2/32
05:04:45.151: LISP-0: Remote EID IID 1 prefix 172.17.2.2/32, Send map request (1)
  (sources: <signal>, state: incomplete, rlocs: 0).
05:04:45.151: LISP-0: EID-AF IPv4, Sending authenticated map-request from
    192.168.1.1 to 172.17.2.2 for EID 172.17.2.2/32, ITR-RLOCs 1, nonce
    0x7C7DC495-0xA1FA7A30 (encap src 192.168.1.1, dst 192.168.100.100).
```

```
05:04:45.157: LISP: Processing received Map-Reply(2) message on GigabitEthernet2
  from 192.168.2.2:4342 to 192.168.1.1:4342

05:04:45.157: LISP: Received map reply nonce 0x7C7DC495-0xA1FA7A30, records 1

05:04:45.157: LISP-0: Map Request IID 1 prefix 172.17.2.2/32 remote EID prefix[LL],
  Map-reply verification failed due to lack of security info.

05:04:45.158: LISP-0: Map Request IID 1 prefix 172.17.2.2/32 remote EID prefix[LL],
  Map-reply failed security verification, dropping.


06:23:43.292: LISP: Processing data signal for EID prefix IID 1 172.17.3.3/32

06:23:43.292: LISP-0: Remote EID IID 1 prefix 172.17.3.3/32, Change state to
  incomplete (sources: <signal>, state: unknown, rlocs: 0).

06:23:43.292: LISP-0: Remote EID IID 1 prefix 172.17.3.3/32, [incomplete] Scheduling
  map requests delay 00:00:00 min_elapsed 00:00:01 (sources: <signal>, state:
  incomplete, rlocs: 0).

06:23:43.425: LISP-0: IID 1 Request processing of remote EID prefix map requests to
  IPv4.

06:23:43.425: LISP: Send map request type remote EID prefix

06:23:43.425: LISP: Send map request for EID prefix IID 1 172.17.3.3/32

06:23:43.425: LISP-0: Remote EID IID 1 prefix 172.17.3.3/32, Send map request (1)
  (sources: <signal>, state: incomplete, rlocs: 0).

06:23:43.425: LISP-0: EID-AF IPv4, Sending authenticated map-request from
  192.168.1.1 to 172.17.3.3 for EID 172.17.3.3/32, ITR-RLOCs 1, nonce 0xB145CD86-
  0xBA6ED827 (encap src 192.168.1.1, dst 192.168.100.100).

06:23:43.430: LISP: Processing received Map-Reply(2) message on GigabitEthernet2
  from 10.3.10.3:4342 to 192.168.1.1:4342

06:23:43.430: LISP: Received authenticated map reply nonce 0xB145CD86-0xBA6ED827,
  records 1

06:23:43.430: LISP: Processing Map-Reply mapping record for IID 1 SVC_IP_IAF_IPv4
  172.17.3.3/32 LCAF 2, ttl 1440, action none, authoritative, 1 locator
          192.168.3.3 pri/wei=1/100 LpR

06:23:43.430: LISP-0: Map Request IID 1 prefix 172.17.3.3/32 remote EID prefix[LL],
  Received reply with rtt 5ms.

06:23:43.430: LISP: Processing mapping information for EID prefix IID 1
  172.17.3.3/32

06:23:43.430: LISP-0: Remote EID IID 1 prefix 172.17.3.3/32, Change state to reused
  (sources: <map-rep>, state: incomplete, rlocs: 0).

06:23:43.430: LISP-0: Remote EID IID 1 prefix 172.17.3.3/32, Starting idle timer
  (delay 00:02:30) (sources: <map-rep>, state: reused, rlocs: 0).

06:23:43.430: LISP-0: IAF IID 1 SVC_IP_IAF_IPv4, Persistent db: ignore writing
  request, disabled.

06:23:43.430: LISP-0: Remote EID IID 1 prefix 172.17.3.3/32, Change state to
  complete (sources: <map-rep>, state: reused, rlocs: 0).

06:23:43.430: LISP-0: Remote EID IID 1 prefix 172.17.3.3/32, Recalculated RLOC
  status bits from 0x0 to 0x1 (sources: <map-rep>, state: complete, rlocs: 1).
```

```
XTR3 (NX-OS)
xTR3# debug logfile lisp
xTR3# debug ip lisp mapping control 172.17.1.1/32
xTR3# show debug logfile lisp
```

```
19:23:48.335037 lisp: <default> Setting mtu of interface: Ethernet2/1, local:1
19:23:48.336688 lisp: <default> Process URIB route notification for DB EID
  192.168.1.1/32
19:23:48.336739 lisp: <default> Process URIB route notification for locator
  192.168.1.1
19:23:48.337190 lisp: <default> Process URIB route notification for DB EID
  192.168.1.1/32
19:23:48.337214 lisp: <default> Process URIB route notification for locator
  192.168.1.1
19:24:07.229015 lisp: <default> Build LISP Map-Request for 172.17.1.1/32 (iid 1),
  source-EID: 172.16.3.0, nonce: 0x42b35b12-0x0d43b342, ITR-RLOCs:
19:24:07.229063 lisp: <default>   AFI: 0x0001, RLOC address: 192.168.3.3
19:24:07.229115 lisp: <default> Encapsulate LISP IP Map-Request from 192.168.3.3 to
  configured map-resolver 192.168.100.100, lisp-sec present
19:24:07.233905 lisp: <default> lisp_process_add_mapping: Processing EID:
  172.17.1.1/32 cache_state: complete
19:24:07.233929 lisp: <default> lisp_process_add_mapping: Adding EID: 172.17.1.1/32
  to map cache cache_state: complete
19:24:07.233946 lisp: <default> lisp_add_mapping: Invoked for EID: 172.17.1.1/32
  cache_state: complete
19:24:07.233974 lisp: <default> Send Add: 172.17.1.1/32 RNH to URIB
19:24:07.234045 lisp: <default> Setting mtu of interface: Ethernet2/1, local:1
19:24:07.234236 lisp: <default> Add mapping, EID: 172.17.1.1/32 (iid 1), state:
  complete, ttl: 1440 mins, locator: 192.168.1.1, port: 0, loc-state: up, up/uw/mp/
  mw: 1/100/1/100, source: 192.168.1.1, protocol-source: map-reply, a: 1
19:24:07.234410 lisp: <default> Recalculation of RLOC hash indexes for
  172.17.1.1/32:
19:24:07.234431 lisp: <default>   Current indexes: [*****-*****-*****-*****-*****]
19:24:07.234455 lisp: <default>   New indexes: [00000-00000-00000-00000-00000]
```

Securing the LISP Data Plane

LISP shared mode virtualization provides EID space segmentation over a shared
RLOC core. The LISP EID instance ID is used to identify tenant EID networks both in
LISP control plane messages and in LISP-encapsulated data packets. Even though the
segmentation is done, external traffic can still enter the segmented LISP VPN space,
causing a security breach. This is easily done by spoofing the destination instance
IDs (IIDs), RLOC address, and EID in the LISP-encapsulated traffic; tunnel routers,
thinking the traffic is legitimate, may then authenticate the traffic and de-encapsulate
the packets (see Figure 10-3). To prevent such security breaches, you need to secure data
plane traffic in the LISP VPN network.

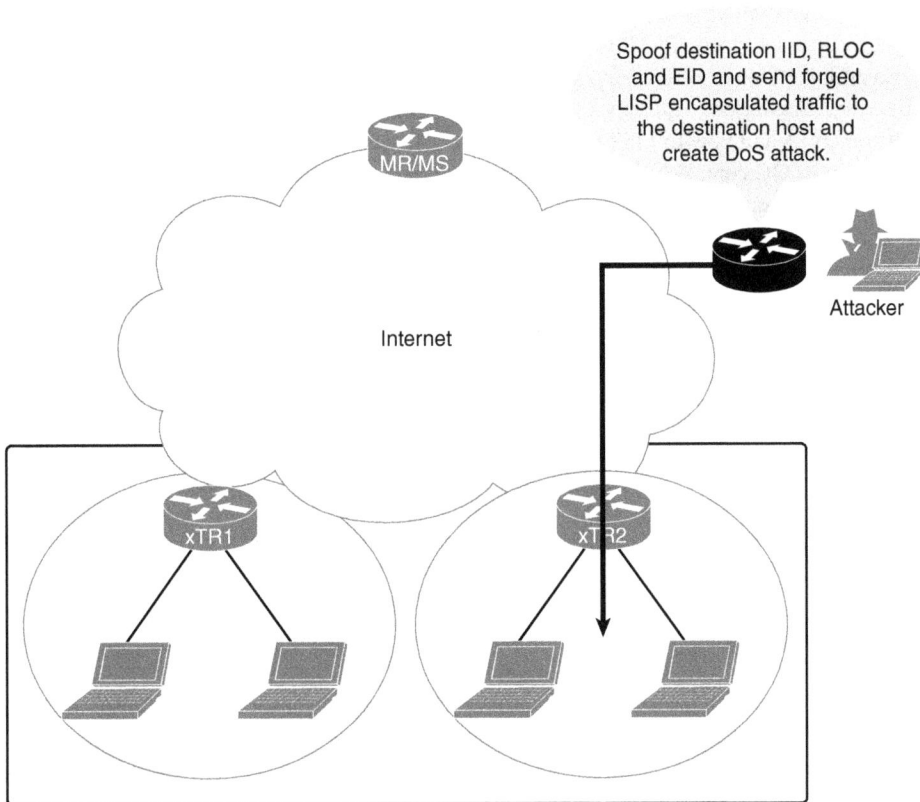

Figure 10-3 *A DoS Attack in a LISP Network*

You can easily prevent such DoS attacks in traditional routing domains by using a unicast reverse path forwarding (uRPF) check. The same concept can be applied in a LISP environment for LISP-encapsulated packets. In a LISP virtual private network (VPN) environment, uRPF checking is enabled to validate whether the LISP-encapsulated traffic is coming from a legitimate source xTR and not from a rogue device. This method reduces the overhead of authentication and encryption but still achieves tenant segmentation without compromising security. This mechanism is known as *LISP de-encapsulation source RLOC filtering*.

Note   GETVPN with shared mode virtualization is discussed later in this chapter, in the section "LISP and GETVPN."

Source RLOC Decapsulation Filtering

Source RLOC decapsulation filtering requires total control of the RLOC network and leverages the uRPF mechanism. Source RLOC de-encapsulation filtering enhances LISP security by monitoring the data packets during the de-encapsulation phase—that is, when the traffic is sent from (P)ITR to (P)ETR. It prevents traffic injections from external sources into a LISP VPN. To better understand the concept of source RLOC de-encapsulation filtering, examine the topology shown in Figure 10-4. In this topology, there are two customers, A and B, with LISP EID instance ID (IID) 10 and 20, respectively, over a shared common RLOC core. When the traffic comes in from the shared RLOC core, the (P)xTR validates the packets carrying the instance ID 10 having a source RLOC in the encapsulation header of either A1, A2, or A3. Similarly, the (P)xTR can validate that the source RLOC is B1, B2, or B3 (for instance, ID 20). Any LISP-encapsulated packet that does not carry a valid source RLOC is dropped. The combination of RLOC space uRPF enforcement and source RLOC–based de-encapsulation filtering guarantees that it is not possible for a source that is not a member of a tenant VPN to inject traffic into the VPN.

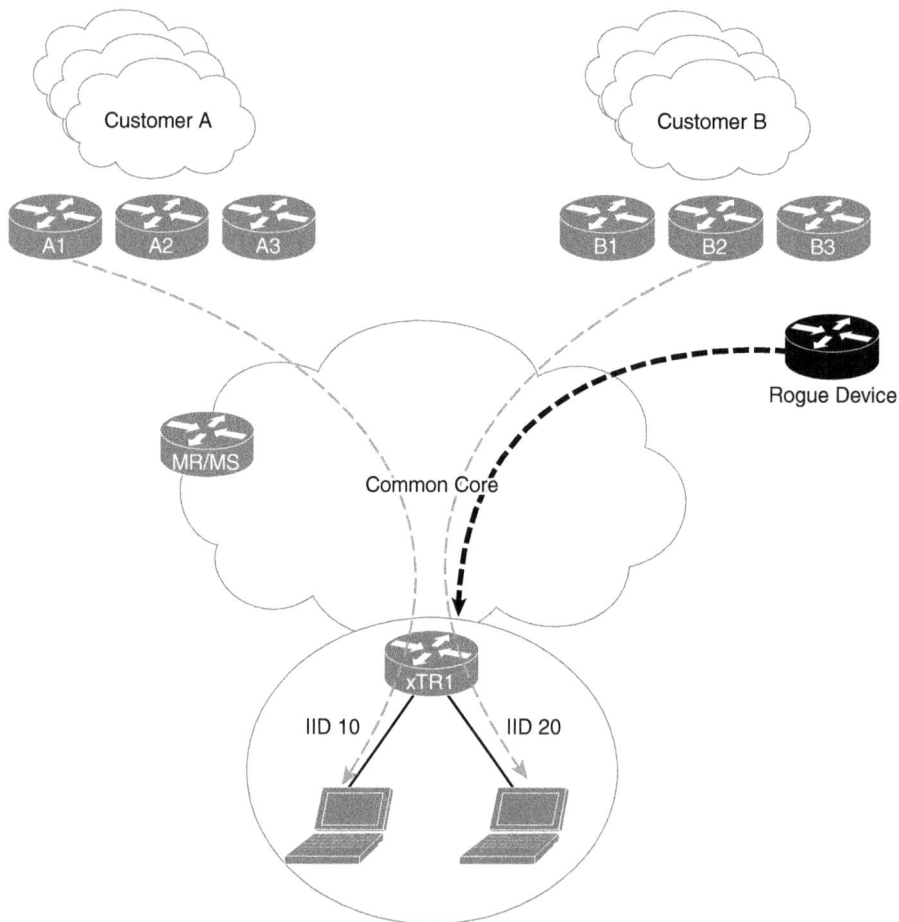

Figure 10-4 *Source RLOC Decapsulation Filtering*

LISP xTRs validate the source addresses of the incoming LISP packets with the dynamically distributed set of RLOC addresses corresponding to valid LISP VPN sites. The map servers construct an EID instance ID RLOC membership list using the RLOC information in the mapping records received in the map register messages. The complete list is then pushed out to all the xTRs and PxTRs that will participate in the de-encapsulation of traffic for the VPN sites identified by EID instance IDs.

Examine the EID membership distribution mechanism illustrated in Figure 10-5. In this figure, the MR/MS pushes the locator list for each IID to all the xTRs. If a rogue xTR tries to become part of the LISP network but its information is not present on the xTR, it does not receive the distribution list from the MR/MS, and thus it is unable to de-encapsulate the LISP-encapsulated traffic.

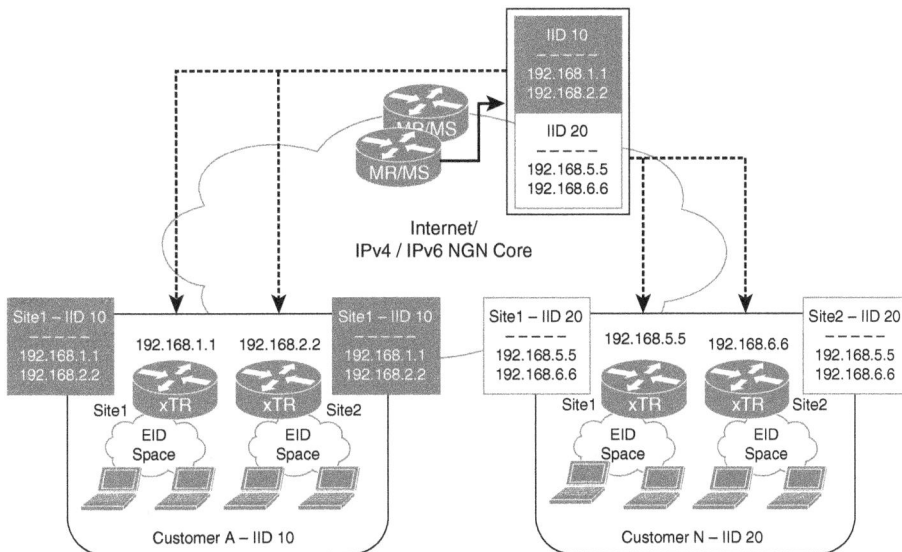

Figure 10-5 *EID Membership Distribution*

LISP Reliable Transport

In a LISP-enabled network, the communication channel between the LISP xTRs and map servers is based on unreliable User Datagram Protocol (UDP) message exchange. The map register messages are retransmitted every minute by an ETR or xTR. While registering multiple EID prefixes, the ETR includes multiple mapping records in the message that are split across multiple map register messages if the number of EID prefixes is more than what can be packed in a single map register message. The map server, on the other hand, updates the corresponding registration state and builds and transmits matching map notify messages. The map server times out its state if the state is not refreshed for three successive periods.

Such aggressive periodic message exchange between the xTR and the map server, especially in use cases where the xTRs have large EID prefix sets, such as with LISP mobility, database replication and redistribution and overlapping prefixes in the LISP network can cause a huge amount of overload on the xTRs as well as the map servers. Along with this existing load, the EID instance membership mechanism introduces an additional load on the xTRs as well as the map servers.

To reduce the load on the xTRs and map servers, a single reliable transport session is established between a pair of LISP peers. The EID instance membership distribution mechanism uses this reliable transport mechanism over which the membership list can be communicated to the xTRs. Note that the existing map register and map notify messages still leverage the existing UDP-based transport mechanism.

The use of Transmission Control Protocol (TCP) to implement reliable transport sessions introduces some limitations:

- The number of xTRs for which a map server can cater is limited by the number of TCP sessions that a platform can handle. This also determines the number of VPN customers that a map server can host. Horizontal scaling is achieved by dividing VPN customers between multiple map servers.

- All the xTRs belonging to the same VPN must register with the same map server. Thus, you cannot have VPNs with a larger number of xTRs than the map server TCP session scale limit.

On Cisco IOS/IOS-XE and IOS-XR platforms, a reliable TCP session is established by default with a map server. The TCP session is established on a well-known TCP port 4342 that was assigned to LISP. You can validated this by using the command **show lisp session**, and you can validate the TCP connections in the TCP table by using the command **show tcp brief**. Example 10-6 shows the LISP sessions established between xTR1, xTR2, and MR-MS-1.

Example 10-6   *Verifying a LISP Session and TCP Connection*

```
xTR1 - IOS-XE
xTR1# show lisp session

  ʼ
Sessions for VRF default, total: 1, established: 1
Peer                         State      Up/Down        In/Out      Users
192.168.100.100:4342         Up         4d12h           9/7        3


xTR1# show tcp brief
TCB            Local Address             Foreign Address            (state)
7FF156E759B8   192.168.1.1.17966         192.168.100.100.4342       ESTAB
7FF162BD2248   10.1.20.1.29060           10.1.20.20.179             ESTAB
7FF0F5163000   10.1.10.1.15286           10.1.10.10.179             ESTAB
xTR2 - IOS-XR
```

```
RP/0/0/CPU0:xTR2# show lisp session
Sessions for VRF default, total: 1, established: 1
Peer                       State     Up/Down      In/Out    Users
192.168.100.100            Up        4d12h        2435/2433 2


RP/0/0/CPU0:xTR2# show tcp brief
   PCB      VRF-ID      Recv-Q Send-Q Local Address       Foreign Address         State
0x1215eacc 0x60000000      0      0  :::179               :::0                   LISTEN
0x1215b088 0x00000000      0      0  :::179               :::0                   LISTEN
0x121515d4 0x60000000      0      0  :::4342              :::0                   LISTEN
0x1214de1c 0x00000000      0      0  :::4342              :::0                   LISTEN
0x1215ec9c 0x60000000      0      0  10.2.10.2:179        10.2.10.10:32658       ESTAB
0x12163ed8 0x60000000      0      0  10.2.20.2:34045      10.2.20.20:179         ESTAB
0x1213b4ec 0x60000000      0      0  192.168.2.2:43931    192.168.100.100:4342   ESTAB
MR-MS-1
MR-MS-1# show lisp session

Sessions for VRF default, total: 5, established: 2
Peer                       State     Up/Down      In/Out    Users
192.168.1.1:17966          Up        4d12h        7/9       3
192.168.2.2:43931          Up        4d12h        2434/2436 1


MR-MS-1# show tcp brief numeric
TCB            Local Address          Foreign Address         (state)
7F7AAA0C8970   192.168.100.100.4342   192.168.1.1.17966       ESTAB
7F7AABC54060   192.168.100.100.4342   192.168.2.2.43931       ESTAB
```

Configuring Source RLOC Decapsulation Filtering

When enabling LISP source RLOC decapsulation filtering in a LISP-enabled network, the configuration is broken down into two simple steps:

Step 1. Enable the RLOC membership distribution mechanism on the MR/MS.

Step 2. Enable source RLOC decapsulation filtering on the xTRs.

As the first step, you enable the RLOC membership distribution mechanism on the MR/MS device by using the command **map-server rloc members distribute**. This command enables the distribution of the list of EID prefixes to xTRs. This command distributes the entire list of EID prefixes for the given VPN. You can further filter these prefixes on the MR/MS to prevent them from being sent to xTRs by using the command

map-server rloc members modify-discovered [add | override] locator-set
locator-set-name under the LISP EID table configuration mode.

To demonstrate LISP source RLOC decapsulation filtering, look again at the topology
shown in Figure 10-2. In this topology, xTR1 (running IOS-XE) and xTR2 (running
IOS-XR) are the devices capable of performing LISP source RLOC de-encapsulation filtering, whereas xTR3 (running NX-OS) does not support this feature. Example 10-7 illustrates the configuration of an MR/MS. MR-MS-1 in this example is configured with the
default RLOC distribution, which implies that MR-MS-1 will not perform any filtering on
the distribution list.

Example 10-7 *Configuring an MR/MS for RLOC Membership Distribution*

```
MR-MS-1
router lisp
map-server rloc members distribute
!
exit-router-lisp
```

After MR-MS-1 is configured, you configure the xTR devices to perform the de-encapsulation
filtering on the received RLOC distribution list. You do this by using the command
decapsulation filter rloc source member under the instance-id configuration mode.
Example 10-8 shows the configuration on xTR1 (IOS-XE) and xTR2 (IOS-XR).

Example 10-8 *Configuring (P)xTRs for Source De-encapsulation Filtering*

```
xTR1 - IOS-XE
router lisp
!
! Output omitted for brevity
!
instance-id 1
  decapsulation filter rloc source member
  service ipv4
    eid-table default
    database-mapping 172.16.1.0/24 192.168.1.1 priority 1 weight 100
    database-mapping 172.17.1.1/32 192.168.1.1 priority 1 weight 100
    map-request-source 192.168.1.1
    exit-service-ipv4
  !
!
  decapsulation filter rloc source member
 exit-router-lisp
xTR2 - IOS-XR
router lisp
!
```

```
eid-table default instance-id 1
  address-family ipv4 unicast
   database-mapping 172.16.2.0/24 192.168.2.2 priority 1 weight 100
   database-mapping 172.17.2.2/32 192.168.2.2 priority 1 weight 100
   !
  decapsulation filter rloc source member
 !
 !
```

This is the basic configuration that is required to enable source RLOC de-encapsulation filtering. When the configuration is complete, you can check to determine whether each MS is configured for membership distribution by using the command **show lisp service ipv4**, which shows whether the membership distribution capability is in the enabled or disabled state. If the membership distribution capability is enabled, you can validate the RLOC members for each instance ID by using the command **show lisp instance-id** *instance-id* **site rloc members**. This command displays all the RLOC members who registered their EID prefixes for the given IID. Example 10-9 shows the output from MR-MS-1 for membership distribution and the site RLOC members for IID 1.

Example 10-9 *Verification on the MS/MR for LISP Membership Distribution*

```
MR-MS-1
MR-MS-1# show lisp service ipv4
Information applicable to all EID instances:
  Router-lisp ID:                     0
  Locator table:                      default
  Ingress Tunnel Router (ITR):        disabled
  Egress Tunnel Router (ETR):         disabled
  Proxy-ITR Router (PITR):            disabled
  Proxy-ETR Router (PETR):            disabled
  NAT-traversal Router (NAT-RTR):     disabled
  Mobility First-Hop Router:          disabled
  Map Server (MS):                    enabled
    Membership distribution:          enabled
  Map Resolver (MR):                  enabled
  Delegated Database Tree (DDT):      disabled
  ITR local RLOC (last resort):       *** NOT FOUND ***
  ITR Solicit Map Request (SMR):      accept and process
    Max SMRs per map-cache entry:     8 more specifics
    Multiple SMR suppression time:    20 secs
  ETR accept mapping data:            disabled, verify disabled
  ETR map-cache TTL:                  1d00h
  Locator Status Algorithms:
    RLOC-probe algorithm:             disabled
    RLOC-probe on route change:       N/A (periodic probing disabled)
```

```
     RLOC-probe on member change:       disabled
     LSB reports:                       process
     IPv4 RLOC minimum mask length:     /0
     IPv6 RLOC minimum mask length:     /0
  Map-cache:
     Map-cache limit:                   1000
     Map-cache activity check period:   60 secs
     Persistent map-cache:              disabled
  Database:
     Dynamic database mapping limit:    1000


MR-MS-1# show lisp instance-id 1 site rloc members
LISP RLOC Membership for router lisp 0 (default) IID 1
Entries: 3 valid / 3 total, Distribution enabled


RLOC                          Origin                    Valid
192.168.1.1                   Registration              Yes
192.168.2.2                   Registration              Yes
192.168.3.3                   Registration              Yes
```

On xTR routers, you use the command **show lisp decapsulation filter instance-id**
instance-id on IOS-XE or use the command **show lisp instance-id** *instance-id* **decapsulation filter** on IOS-XR to verify the received RLOC membership list received from
the mapping server. This list varies between the mapping server and xTR if there is a
filter applied on the mapping server. Along with verifying the source RLOC distribution
list, you can use the command **show cef source-filter table** to view the packet counts
for any packets forwarded or dropped due to the uRPF check of the source RLOC
de-encapsulation filter. This command displays the counters on a per-IID basis. On
IOS-XR, use the command **show cef lisp decapsulation instance-id** *instance-id* [detail]
to verify the action on the payload, such as whether the IPv4 or IPv6 payload is supposed to be de-encapsulated or dropped. Example 10-10 shows the output of the noted
commands on xTR1 and xTR2.

Example 10-10   *Verifying Source De-encapsulation Filtering on (P)xTRs*

```
xTR1
xTR1# show lisp decapsulation filter instance-id 1
LISP decapsulation filter for EID table default (IID 1), 3 entries
Source RLOC                          Added by
192.168.1.1                          MS 192.168.100.100
192.168.2.2                          MS 192.168.100.100
192.168.3.3                          MS 192.168.100.100
```

```
xTR1# show cef source-filter table
[lisp:0:1:IPv4] state [enabled, active], 3 entries, refcount 4, flags [],
    action [drop]
Database epoch 0
Hits 0, misses 0, fwd 0, drop 0


[lisp:0:101:IPv4] state [enabled, active], 3 entries, refcount 4, flags [],
    action [drop]
Database epoch 0
Hits 0, misses 0, fwd 0, drop 0
xTR2
RP/0/0/CPU0:xTR2# show lisp instance-id 1 decapsulation filter


LISP decapsulation filter for EID table default (IID 1), 3 entries
Source RLOC                             Added by
192.168.1.1                             MS 192.168.100.100
192.168.2.2                             MS 192.168.100.100
192.168.3.3                             MS 192.168.100.100


RP/0/0/CPU0:xTR2# show cef lisp decapsulation instance-id 1 detail
Sat Feb  9 07:51:05.334 UTC


Number of EID tables handling LISP payload received in this table: 2


Transport LISP ipv4 packets received in VRF: default, Instance ID: 1
        Payload IPv4 is         : decapsulated
        Payload IPv6 is         : dropped
        Payload switched in VRF : default (0xe0000000/0x00000000)
        H/W driver signalled    : active
        Binding in retry        : no


Source RLOC Prefix Filter       : disabled
```

Now, if the xTR receives a LISP-encapsulated packet sourcing from an RLOC IP that is not distributed by the map server, even if the RLOC is a valid RLOC, the receiving xTR drops the packet, and an ICMP unreachable message is sent toward the next hop because the source RLOC is not found in the distributed RLOC filter list. Figure 10-6 shows a Wireshark capture of this. In this figure, notice that the LISP-encapsulated packet is being received with the source IP address 10.2.10.2, which is the interface IP xTR2, but xTR1 is only supposed to accept the packet when the source IP address is coming from 192.168.2.2 because that is the only IP address distributed by MS.

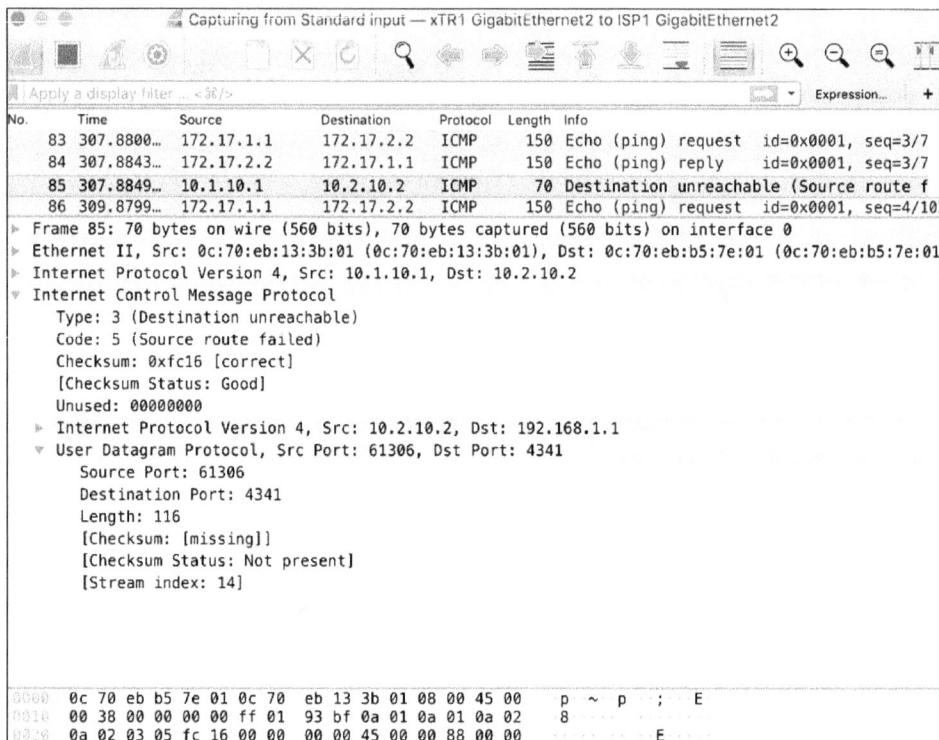

Figure 10-6   *Packet Capture Showing an ICMP Unreachable Message from the xTR*

This problem is easily resolved by modifying the membership distribution list on the MS by using filters. To modify the membership distribution list, you first define a locator set, which consists of the RLOC addresses and the priority and weight of each one. After you define the locator set, you can either modify the RLOC membership distribution list by adding members to it, or you can override the distribution with a completely new RLOC membership list, as defined in the locator set. To modify the distribution list, use the command **map-server rloc members modify-discovered [add | override] locator-set** *locator-set-name*. Example 10-11 shows the configuration on MR-MS-1, where the membership distribution list is being modified by the addition of an RLOC address 10.2.10.2 defined in the locator set INST-1-LSET. After modifying the RLOC membership distribution list, you can validate the xTRs for the updated RLOC membership distribution list as received from MR-MS-1.

Example 10-11   *Modifying RLOC Membership Distribution*

```
MR-MS-1
router lisp
 locator-set INST-1-LSET
  10.2.10.2 priority 1 weight 1
  exit-locator-set
 !
```

```
instance-id 1
  map-server rloc members modify-discovered add locator-set INST-1-LSET
  !
  exit-instance-id
 !
exit-router-lisp
```

xTR1

```
xTR1# show lisp decapsulation filter instance-id 1
LISP decapsulation filter for EID table default (IID 1), 4 entries
Source RLOC                          Added by
10.2.10.2                            MS 192.168.100.100
192.168.1.1                          MS 192.168.100.100
192.168.2.2                          MS 192.168.100.100
192.168.3.3                          MS 192.168.100.100
```

xTR2

```
RP/0/0/CPU0:xTR2# show lisp instance-id 1 decapsulation filter
Sun Feb 10 06:00:40.169 UTC


LISP decapsulation filter for EID table default (IID 1), 4 entries
Source RLOC                          Added by
10.2.10.2                            MS 192.168.100.100
192.168.1.1                          MS 192.168.100.100
192.168.2.2                          MS 192.168.100.100
192.168.3.3                          MS 192.168.100.100
```

After you verify the membership distribution list, the hosts behind the xTR1 should now be able to reach the host behind xTR2 but not the host behind xTR3, where the traffic is entering xTR1 with source IP address 10.3.10.3, and thus you could notice drop counters incrementing. Example 10-12 shows the verification of reachability between xTR1 and xTR2 as well as xTR1 and xTR3 and the respective forward and drop counters.

Example 10-12 *Modifying RLOC Membership Distribution*

```
CE1
! Ping towards host connected on xTR2 - 10.2.10.2
CE1# ping 172.17.2.2 source lo0
Type escape sequence to abort.
Sending 5, 100-byte ICMP Echos to 172.17.2.2, timeout is 2 seconds:
Packet sent with a source address of 172.17.1.1
!!!!!
Success rate is 100 percent (5/5), round-trip min/avg/max = 3/4/7 ms


! Ping towards host connected on xTR3 - 10.3.10.3
CE1# ping 172.17.3.3 source lo0
```

```
Type escape sequence to abort.

Sending 5, 100-byte ICMP Echos to 172.17.3.3, timeout is 2 seconds:

Packet sent with a source address of 172.17.1.1

.....

Success rate is 0 percent (0/5)

xTR1

xTR1# show cef source-filter table

[lisp:0:1:IPv4] state [enabled, active], 4 entries, refcount 4, flags [], action
  [drop]

Database epoch 0

Hits 8, misses 5, fwd 8, drop 5


[lisp:0:101:IPv4] state [enabled, active], 3 entries, refcount 4, flags [], action
  [drop]

Database epoch 0

Hits 0, misses 0, fwd 0, drop 0
```

You can verify the RLOC membership distribution pushed onto the xTRs by the MS by using the traces on both the IOS-XE and IOS-XR platforms. On IOS-XE, use the command **show monitor event-trace lisp all**. This command displays the RLOC filter prefix event history (showing, for example, when the RLOC filter list is deleted or updated). Similarly, on IOS-XR, use the command **show lisp os trace verbose**. This command displays the list of source RLOC filters for the instance IDs. Example 10-13 shows the output of these commands on both xTR1 and xTR2.

Example 10-13 *LISP Event Traces*

```
xTR1

xTR1# show monitor event-trace lisp all


lisp_forwarding:
*Feb 10 06:38:53.424: RLOC fltr pfx  delete      [0/0:1:IPv4] 10.2.10.2/32 [OK]
*Feb 10 06:38:53.427: RLOC fltr pfx  delete      [0/0:1:IPv4] 192.168.1.1/32 [OK]
*Feb 10 06:38:53.427: RLOC fltr pfx  delete      [0/0:1:IPv4] 192.168.2.2/32 [OK]
*Feb 10 06:38:53.428: RLOC fltr pfx  delete      [0/0:1:IPv4] 192.168.3.3/32 [OK]


*Feb 10 06:44:41.470: RLOC fltr pfx  update      [0/0:1:IPv4] 192.168.1.1/32
                      forward [OK]
*Feb 10 06:44:41.471: RLOC fltr pfx  update      [0/0:1:IPv4] 192.168.3.3/32
                      forward [OK]
*Feb 10 06:44:41.472: RLOC fltr pfx  update      [0/0:1:IPv4] 192.168.2.2/32
                      forward [OK]
*Feb 10 06:44:41.473: RLOC fltr pfx  update      [0/0:1:IPv4] 10.2.10.2/32
                      forward [OK]
```

```
xTR2
RP/0/0/CPU0:xTR2# show lisp os trace verbose last 100
open /dev/shmem/ltrace/lisp_os
open /dev/shmem/ltrace/lisp_os_b1_ob911d
open /dev/shmem/ltrace/lisp_os_b2_o10b911d
428 wrapping entries (10304 possible, 576 allocated, 0 filtered, 428 total)


! Output omitted for brevity

06:45:38.655 lisp_os 0/0/CPU0 t7   rib:[ok] tbl 0xe0000000/IPv4: rloc src filter:
  IID 1:...
06:45:38.655 lisp_os 0/0/CPU0 t7   rib:[ok] tbl 0xe0000000/IPv4: 192.168.1.1/32:
  RSF upd
06:45:38.655 lisp_os 0/0/CPU0 t7   rib:[ok] tbl 0xe0000000/IPv4: rloc src filter:
  IID 1:...
06:45:38.655 lisp_os 0/0/CPU0 t7   rib:[ok] tbl 0xe0000000/IPv4: 192.168.3.3/32:
  RSF upd
06:45:38.655 lisp_os 0/0/CPU0 t7   rib:[ok] tbl 0xe0000000/IPv4: rloc src filter:
  IID 1:...
06:45:38.655 lisp_os 0/0/CPU0 t7   rib:[ok] tbl 0xe0000000/IPv4: 192.168.2.2/32:
  RSF upd
06:45:38.655 lisp_os 0/0/CPU0 t7   rib:[ok] tbl 0xe0000000/IPv4: rloc src filter:
  IID 1:...
06:45:38.655 lisp_os 0/0/CPU0 t7   rib:[ok] tbl 0xe0000000/IPv4: 10.2.10.2/32:
  RSF upd
```

LISP and GETVPN

Group Encrypted Transport Virtual Private Network (GETVPN) is one of the most scalable VPN solutions deployed over many Multiprotocol Label Switching (MPLS) service provider networks today. With GETVPN, VPN gateways use group keys to encrypt the traffic and tunnel the IP packets. These keys are provided to these VPN gateways through the Group Domain of Interpretation (GDOI) key server defined in RFC 6407. A GETVPN protected network uses IP Encapsulating Security Payload (ESP) to protect the traffic. With GETVPN, the crypto engine copies the IP address from the innermost IP address to the outermost IP header. However, this functionality of GETVPN alone poses a security challenge of enterprise address hiding as the customers do not want an observer to know which enterprise addresses are in use.

LISP provides a peer-discovery mechanism along with tunnel encapsulation. LISP allows dynamic peer VPN gateway discoveries, is highly scalable, and provides the state of the peers to the VPN gateways. Thus, both LISP and GETVPN can be used to build encrypted VPNs.

In LISP with GETVPN deployment, GDOI is used to add encryption. GDOI is a group key management protocol used to create and distribute cryptographic keys and policies to a group of devices, thus creating a trusted group and eliminating the need for point-to-point IPsec associations. In this deployment, redundant key servers are usually set up. The key servers perform the following tasks:

- Validate the group members

- Manage the security policy (by using an access control list [ACL])

- Create group keys

- Distribute the policy and keys to the group members

Group members (GMs) are encryption devices to which the policies are pushed by the key servers. The group members are usually the xTRs and hub routers. All GMs share a common security association (SA), enabling all GMs to decrypt traffic that was encrypted by another GM. In LISP and GETVPN solutions, a crypto map is applied on the lisp0.x virtual interface created as part of the LISP shared model virtualization, thus providing the capability for applying unique security policies for each individual VPN environment. In this model, the GETVPN encryption occurs first, followed by LISP encapsulation. Figure 10-7 illustrates what the packet looks like in a GETVPN plus LISP deployment.

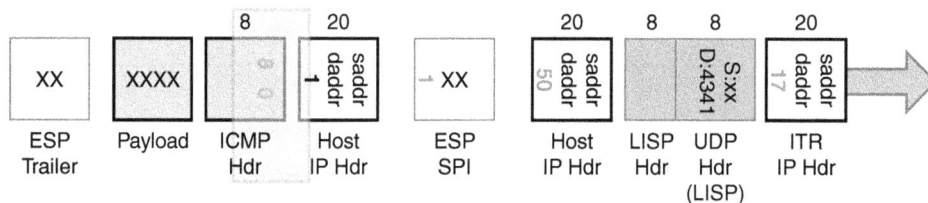

Figure 10-7 *GETVPN and LISP Packet Structure*

Configuring and Verifying LISP over GETVPN

To understand the working behavior of LISP over GETVPN, examine the topology shown in Figure 10-8. In this topology, there are two hub routers: Hub1-xTR and Hub2-xTR. There are also three branch site xTR routers: Site1-xTR, Site2-xTR, and Site3-xTR. The hub routers are acting as both MRs/MSs and xTRs for providing connectivity for the nodes sitting behind the hub routers. There are two separate redundant key servers, KS-1 and KS-2, deployed to provide the keying mechanism for the LISP network.

When deploying the LISP over GETVPN network, the first step is to establish connectivity between all the hub routers, key servers, and site xTR routers. When that connectivity is established, the next step is to enable LISP on the hub routers and the site xTR routers. Example 10-14 shows the configuration of the Hub1-xTR and Site1-xTR devices.

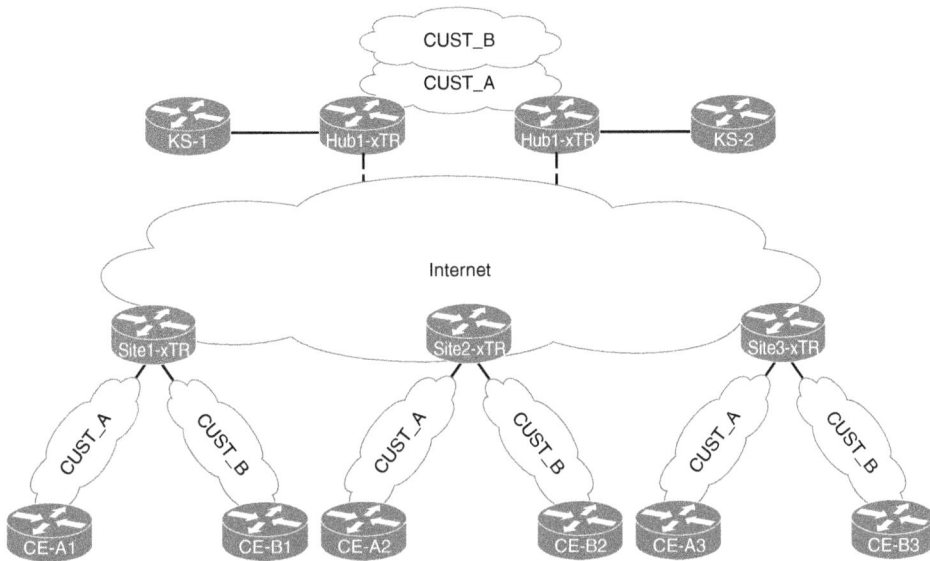

Figure 10-8 *LISP over GETVPN Topology*

Example 10-14 *Enabling LISP on Hub and Site xTR Devices*

```
Hub1-xTR
router lisp
 locator-table default
 locator-set HQ-RLOC
  10.11.10.11 priority 1 weight 50
  10.12.10.12 priority 1 weight 50
  exit
 !
 eid-table vrf Cust_A instance-id 1
  database-mapping 172.16.11.0/24 locator-set HQ-RLOC
  database-mapping 2002:172:16:11::/64 locator-set HQ-RLOC
  ipv4 map-request-source 192.168.11.11
  exit
 !
 eid-table vrf Cust_B instance-id 2
  database-mapping 172.16.11.0/24 locator-set HQ-RLOC
  database-mapping 2002:172:16:11::/64 locator-set HQ-RLOC
  exit
 !
```

```
site HQ
 authentication-key cisco
 eid-prefix instance-id 1 172.16.11.0/24
 eid-prefix instance-id 1 2002:172:16:11::/64
 eid-prefix instance-id 2 172.16.11.0/24
 eid-prefix instance-id 2 2002:172:16:11::/64
 exit
 !
site Site1
 authentication-key cisco
 eid-prefix instance-id 1 172.16.1.0/24
 eid-prefix instance-id 1 172.17.1.1/32
 eid-prefix instance-id 1 2002:172:16:1::/64
 eid-prefix instance-id 2 172.16.101.0/24
 eid-prefix instance-id 2 172.17.101.101/32
 eid-prefix instance-id 2 2002:172:16:101::/64
 exit
 !
site Site2
 authentication-key cisco
 eid-prefix instance-id 1 172.16.2.0/24
 eid-prefix instance-id 1 172.17.2.2/32
 eid-prefix instance-id 1 2002:172:16:2::/64
 eid-prefix instance-id 2 172.16.102.0/24
 eid-prefix instance-id 2 172.17.102.102/32
 eid-prefix instance-id 2 2002:172:16:102::/64
 exit
 !
site Site3
 authentication-key cisco
 eid-prefix instance-id 1 172.16.3.0/24
 eid-prefix instance-id 1 172.17.3.3/32
 eid-prefix instance-id 1 2002:172:16:3::/64
 eid-prefix instance-id 2 172.16.103.0/24
 eid-prefix instance-id 2 172.17.103.103/32
 eid-prefix instance-id 2 2002:172:16:103::/64
 exit
 !
ipv4 map-server
ipv4 map-resolver
ipv4 itr map-resolver 192.168.11.11
ipv4 itr map-resolver 192.168.12.12
ipv4 itr
ipv4 etr map-server 192.168.11.11 key cisco
```

```
 ipv4 etr map-server 192.168.12.12 key cisco
 ipv4 etr
 ipv6 map-server
 ipv6 map-resolver
 ipv6 itr map-resolver 192.168.11.11
 ipv6 itr map-resolver 192.168.12.12
 ipv6 itr
 ipv6 etr map-server 192.168.11.11 key cisco
 ipv6 etr map-server 192.168.12.12 key cisco
 ipv6 etr
 exit
Site1-xTR
router lisp
 locator-table default
 locator-set Site1-RLOC
  IPv4-interface GigabitEthernet1 priority 1 weight 1
  exit
 !
 eid-table vrf Cust_A instance-id 1
  database-mapping 172.16.1.0/24 locator-set Site1-RLOC
  database-mapping 172.17.1.1/32 locator-set Site1-RLOC
  database-mapping 2002:172:16:1::/64 locator-set Site1-RLOC
  ipv4 map-request-source 192.168.1.1
  exit
 !
 eid-table vrf Cust_B instance-id 2
  database-mapping 172.16.101.0/24 locator-set Site1-RLOC
  database-mapping 172.17.101.101/32 locator-set Site1-RLOC
  database-mapping 2002:172:16:101::/64 locator-set Site1-RLOC
  ipv4 map-request-source 192.168.1.1
  exit
 !
 ipv4 itr map-resolver 192.168.11.11
 ipv4 itr map-resolver 192.168.12.12
 ipv4 itr
 ipv4 etr map-server 192.168.11.11 key cisco
 ipv4 etr map-server 192.168.12.12 key cisco
 ipv4 etr
 ipv6 itr map-resolver 192.168.11.11
 ipv6 itr map-resolver 192.168.12.12
 ipv6 itr
 ipv6 etr map-server 192.168.11.11 key cisco
 ipv6 etr map-server 192.168.12.12 key cisco
 ipv6 etr
 exit
```

> **Note**   The Hub2 router has a configuration similar to that of the Hub1 router, and
> Site2-xTR and Site3-xTR are configured much like the Site1-xTR router shown in
> Example 10-14.

Another way to configure the LISP network is by enabling reachability between the
loopback addresses of the hub and site xTR devices and ensuring that the key servers are
reachable over the LISP network. The loopbacks and the key server subnet can be advertised as EID prefixes, and the reachability between them can be established over LISP
instance-id 0. If you use this method, you find that each GM uses LISP encapsulation to
reach the GETVPN key servers, thereby allowing the key servers to run in IPv4 LISP EID
space, even if the core is an IPv6-only network. Example 10-15 illustrates the configuring
of LISP devices to enable reachability of loopback addresses and key servers over LISP
infrastructure.

Example 10-15   *Loopback and Key Server Reachability over LISP Infrastructure*

```
Hub1-XTR
router lisp
 locator-table default
 locator-set HQ-RLOC
  10.11.10.11 priority 1 weight 50
  10.12.10.12 priority 1 weight 50
  exit
 !
 eid-table vrf default instance-id 0
  database-mapping 192.168.11.11/32 locator-set HQ-RLOC
  database-mapping 10.11.13.0/24 locator-set HQ-RLOC
  exit
Site-xTR
router lisp
 locator-table default
 locator-set Site1-RLOC
  IPv4-interface GigabitEthernet1 priority 1 weight 1
  exit
 !
 eid-table vrf default instance-id 0
  database-mapping 192.168.1.1/32 locator-set Site1-RLOC
  exit
```

When LISP is enabled and both the hub site and the branch sites are configured, you
can verify the connectivity between the sites. You can also verify the connectivity
between the xTR loopback addresses and the key servers in case the connectivity is
being established using the LISP EID space. Example 10-16 shows how to verify the
connectivity between the branch and hub site hosts.

Example 10-16 *Verifying Connectivity Between the Sites over LISP*

```
CE1
CE1# ping 172.17.3.3 source loopback0
Type escape sequence to abort.
Sending 5, 100-byte ICMP Echos to 172.17.3.3, timeout is 2 seconds:
Packet sent with a source address of 172.17.1.1
..!!!
Success rate is 60 percent (3/5), round-trip min/avg/max = 1/1/2 ms


CE1# ping 172.16.11.2 source loopback0
Type escape sequence to abort.
Sending 5, 100-byte ICMP Echos to 172.16.11.2, timeout is 2 seconds:
Packet sent with a source address of 172.17.1.1
..!!!
Success rate is 60 percent (3/5), round-trip min/avg/max = 1/1/2 ms
```

After verifying the LISP connectivity, you can deploy the key servers. Before proceeding with the key server configuration, however, it is important to generate RSA keys to be used during the configuration. To generate the RSA keys, use the command **crypto key generate rsa general-keys label** *name*. For this command you must enter the number of bits in the modulus, which defaults to 512 bits. Example 10-17 shows how to generate RSA keys.

Example 10-17 *Generating RSA Keys*

```
KS-1 & KS-2
KS-1(config)# crypto key generate rsa general-keys label CISCO-KEY
The name for the keys will be: CISCO-KEY
Choose the size of the key modulus in the range of 360 to 4096 for your
  General Purpose Keys. Choosing a key modulus greater than 512 may take
  a few minutes.

How many bits in the modulus [512]:
% Generating 512 bit RSA keys, keys will be non-exportable...
[OK] (elapsed time was 0 seconds)
```

After you generate the RSA keys, you configure the key server with the crypto configuration, which is broken down into a few simple steps:

Step 1.   Create an isakmp policy.

Step 2.   Configure the IPsec transform set.

Step 3.   Define GDOI profiles.

Step 4.   Define GDOI groups.

For a given key server, a single Internet Key Exchange (IKE) (isakmp) policy must be configured. You can configure multiple IPsec transform sets or configure a single transform set that can be used in multiple places. The next step is to define GDOI profiles. A single GDOI profile can be deployed in a multi-VPN deployment, but multiple GDOI profiles can be configured and are needed if additional IPsec transform sets are being used. After you configure the GDOI profiles, you need to create multiple GDOI groups for the individual VPNs or IIDs. A GDOI group creates a binding between a GDOI profile, key server properties, and an access list of interesting traffic. Multiple GDOI groups allow you to create a custom policy for each VPN and each address family. Example 10-18 shows how to configure key server KS-1. A similar configuration is required on key server KS-2. Note that KS-1 and KS-2 are redundant key servers to each other.

Example 10-18 *Configuring Key Servers*

```
KS-1
crypto isakmp policy 10
 encr aes 256
 authentication pre-share
 group 16
crypto isakmp key cisco address 0.0.0.0
crypto isakmp keepalive 15 periodic
crypto ipsec transform-set GDOI-TSET esp-aes 256 esp-sha512-hmac
 mode tunnel
crypto ipsec profile GDOI-PROFILE
 set transform-set GDOI-TSET
crypto gdoi group V4GROUP-1
 identity number 101
 server local
  rekey retransmit 60 number 2
  rekey authentication mypubkey rsa CISCO-KEY
  rekey transport unicast
  sa ipsec 1
   profile GDOI-PROFILE
   match address ipv4 GETVPN-1
   replay time window-size 5
   no tag
  address ipv4 10.11.13.13
  redundancy
   local priority 100
   peer address ipv4 10.12.14.14
crypto gdoi group V4GROUP-2
 identity number 102
 server local
  rekey retransmit 60 number 2
  rekey authentication mypubkey rsa CISCO-KEY
```

```
   rekey transport unicast
   sa ipsec 1
    profile GDOI-PROFILE
    match address ipv4 GETVPN-2
    replay time window-size 5
    no tag
   address ipv4 10.11.13.13
   redundancy
    local priority 100
    peer address ipv4 10.12.14.14
 !
ip access-list extended GETVPN-1
 permit ip any any
ip access-list extended GETVPN-2
 permit ip any any
```

After configuring the key server, you need to configure crypto maps on GMs. This is a cookie-cutter process because all the GMs have the same configuration. When configuring crypto maps, you first configure IKE (isakmp) policy. Users then create GDOI groups with the same identity number as the key server, the server addresses, and the local registration interface. Each GDOI group is then bound to the respective crypto maps on the GMs. Example 10-19 shows how to configure the crypto maps on all GMs.

Example 10-19 *Configuring GM Crypto Maps*

```
Hub-xTR and Site xTR Routers
crypto isakmp policy 10
 encr aes 256
 authentication pre-share
 group 16
 !
crypto isakmp key cisco address 10.11.13.13
crypto isakmp key cisco address 10.12.14.14
 !
crypto gdoi group V4GROUP-1
 identity number 101
 server address ipv4 10.11.13.13
 server address ipv4 10.12.14.14
 client registration interface Loopback0
 !
```

```
crypto gdoi group V4GROUP-2
 identity number 102
 server address ipv4 10.11.13.13
 server address ipv4 10.12.14.14
 client registration interface Loopback0
!
crypto map MAP-V4-1 10 gdoi
 set group V4GROUP-1
!
crypto map MAP-V4-2 10 gdoi
 set group V4GROUP-2
```

Next, you apply the crypto maps to the LISP0.x interface for the respective VPNs. The *x* in LISP0.x indicates the IID. You apply a crypto map by using the command **crypto map** *crypto-map-name*. Example 10-20 shows how to apply crypto maps to the LISP0.1 and LISP0.2 interfaces on all GM routers.

Example 10-20 *Applying Crypto Maps on GM Routers*

```
Hub and Site xTR Routers
interface LISP0.1
 ip mtu 1456
 ipv6 mtu 1436
 crypto map MAP-V4-1
!
interface LISP0.2
 ip mtu 1456
 ipv6 mtu 1436
 crypto map MAP-V4-2
```

As soon as the crypto maps are applied to the LISP virtual interfaces, the registration process starts between the GMs and the key servers. If the configuration is correct, then the keys and policies are installed on the GMs from the key servers. Example 10-21 shows the registration logs on all GMs after crypto maps are applied on LISP virtual interfaces.

Example 10-21 *Crypto Registration Logs on GMs*

```
Hub1-xTR
05:22:38.797: %CRYPTO-5-GM_REGSTER: Start registration to KS 10.12.14.14 for group
  V4GROUP-1 using address 192.168.11.11 fvrf default ivrf default
05:22:38.797: %CRYPTO-5-GM_REGSTER: Start registration to KS 10.12.14.14 for group
  V4GROUP-2 using address 192.168.11.11 fvrf default ivrf default
05:22:39.068: %GDOI-5-SA_TEK_UPDATED: SA TEK was updated
05:22:39.074: %GDOI-5-SA_KEK_UPDATED: SA KEK was updated
  0x87865D9D840263AD3D3A8BA99CFD1591
```

```
05:22:39.079: %GDOI-5-GM_REGS_COMPL: Registration to KS 10.12.14.14 complete for
  group V4GROUP-1 using address 192.168.11.11 fvrf default ivrf default
05:22:39.142: %GDOI-5-GM_REGS_COMPL: Registration to KS 10.12.14.14 complete for
  group V4GROUP-2 using address 192.168.11.11 fvrf default ivrf default
05:22:39.365: %GDOI-5-GM_INSTALL_POLICIES_SUCCESS: SUCCESS: Installation of Reg/
  Rekey policies from KS 10.12.14.14 for group V4GROUP-1 & gm identity 192.168.11.11
  fvrf default ivrf default
05:22:39.365: %GDOI-5-GM_INSTALL_POLICIES_SUCCESS: SUCCESS: Installation of Reg/
  Rekey policies from KS 10.12.14.14 for group V4GROUP-2 & gm identity 192.168.11.11
  fvrf default ivrf default
05:22:39.633: %GDOI-5-GM_REGS_COMPL: Registration to KS 10.11.13.13 complete for
  group V4GROUP-1 using address 192.168.11.11 fvrf default ivrf default
05:22:39.639: %GDOI-5-GM_INSTALL_POLICIES_SUCCESS: SUCCESS: Installation of Reg/
  Rekey policies from KS 10.11.13.13 for group V4GROUP-1 & gm identity 192.168.11.11
  fvrf default ivrf default
05:22:39.642: %GDOI-5-GM_REGS_COMPL: Registration to KS 10.11.13.13 complete for
  group V4GROUP-2 using address 192.168.11.11 fvrf default ivrf default
05:22:39.647: %GDOI-5-GM_INSTALL_POLICIES_SUCCESS: SUCCESS: Installation of Reg/
  Rekey policies from KS 10.11.13.13 for group V4GROUP-2 & gm identity 192.168.11.11
  fvrf default ivrf default
```

As soon as the GMs register themselves with the key servers, you can validate the member information on the key servers by using the command **show crypto gdoi ks members.** Example 10-22 shows all the GMs (Hub-xTR and Site-xTR devices) that registered with key servers KS-1 and KS-2.

Example 10-22 *Verifying the GM Registration on Key Servers*

```
KS-1 and KS-2
KS-1# show crypto gdoi ks members | in Group
Group Member Information :
Group Member ID    : 192.168.12.12      GM Version: 1.0.16
 Group ID          : 101
 Group Name        : V4GROUP-1
 Group Type        : GDOI (ISAKMP)
Group Member ID    : 192.168.1.1        GM Version: 1.0.16
 Group ID          : 101
 Group Name        : V4GROUP-1
 Group Type        : GDOI (ISAKMP)
Group Member ID    : 192.168.2.2        GM Version: 1.0.16
 Group ID          : 101
 Group Name        : V4GROUP-1
 Group Type        : GDOI (ISAKMP)
Group Member ID    : 192.168.3.3        GM Version: 1.0.16
 Group ID          : 101
 Group Name        : V4GROUP-1
 Group Type        : GDOI (ISAKMP)
```

```
Group Member ID      : 192.168.11.11      GM Version: 1.0.16
 Group ID            : 101
 Group Name          : V4GROUP-1
 Group Type          : GDOI (ISAKMP)
Group Member ID      : 192.168.12.12      GM Version: 1.0.16
 Group ID            : 102
Group Member Information :
 Group Name          : V4GROUP-2
 Group Type          : GDOI (ISAKMP)
Group Member ID      : 192.168.1.1        GM Version: 1.0.16
 Group ID            : 102
 Group Name          : V4GROUP-2
 Group Type          : GDOI (ISAKMP)
Group Member ID      : 192.168.2.2        GM Version: 1.0.16
 Group ID            : 102
 Group Name          : V4GROUP-2
 Group Type          : GDOI (ISAKMP)
Group Member ID      : 192.168.3.3        GM Version: 1.0.16
 Group ID            : 102
 Group Name          : V4GROUP-2
 Group Type          : GDOI (ISAKMP)
Group Member ID      : 192.168.11.11      GM Version: 1.0.16
 Group ID            : 102
 Group Name          : V4GROUP-2
 Group Type          : GDOI (ISAKMP)
```

Note It is recommended that you perform connectivity checks in both the underlay and the overlay in case the key servers are reachable through LISP. To perform the connectivity checks, refer to Chapter 3, "LISP IPv4 Unicast Routing."

Because the key servers are redundant, one of the key servers functions as the primary server, and the others are secondary servers. Use the command **show crypto gdoi group** *group-name* to view the status of a key server, its profile information, and the status of its peer. Example 10-23 shows the output of the command **show crypto gdoi group** *group-name* on key server KS-2, which is selected as the primary key server. The same command on GM routers displays the profile and other details, such as rekey time and IPsec SA information. If there is a problem with the message exchange between the GMs and the key servers, you can use the command **show crypto gdoi ks coop detail** to view the number of messages exchanged or any messages that were dropped.

Example 10-23 *GDOI Information on Key Servers and GM Routers*

```
KS-2
KS-2# show crypto gdoi group V4GROUP-1
GROUP INFORMATION

    Group Name                 : V4GROUP-1 (Unicast)
    Re-auth on new CRL         : Disabled
    Group Identity             : 101
    Group Type                 : GDOI (ISAKMP)
    Crypto Path                : ipv4
    Key Management Path        : ipv4
    Group Members              : 5
    IPSec SA Direction         : Both
    IP D3P Window              : Disabled
    Split Resiliency Factor    : 0
    CKM status                 : Disabled
    Redundancy                 : Configured
        Local Address          : 10.12.14.14
        Local Priority         : 100
        Local KS Status        : Alive
        Local KS Role          : Primary
        Local KS Version       : 1.0.18
        Local COOP Version     : 1.0.8
    Group Rekey Lifetime       : 86400 secs
    Group Rekey
        Remaining Lifetime     : 83587 secs
        Time to Rekey          : 40387 secs
        Acknowledgement Cfg    : Cisco
    Rekey Retransmit Period    : 60 secs
    Rekey Retransmit Attempts: 2
    Group Retransmit
        Remaining Lifetime     : 0 secs

      IPSec SA Number          : 1
      IPSec SA Rekey Lifetime: 3600 secs
      Profile Name             : GDOI-PROFILE
      Replay method            : Time Based
      Replay Window Size       : 5
      Tagging method           : Disabled
      SA Rekey
         Remaining Lifetime    : 788 secs
         Time to Rekey         : 302 secs
      ACL Configured           : access-list GETVPN-1

    Group Server list          : Local
```

```
KS-2# show crypto gdoi ks coop detail
Crypto Gdoi Group Name :V4GROUP-1
        Group handle: 2147483650, Local Key Server handle: 2147483650

        Local Address: 10.12.14.14
        Local Priority: 100
        Local KS Role: Primary   , Local KS Status: Alive
        Local KS version: 1.0.18
        Local COOP version: 1.0.8
        Primary Timers:
                Primary Refresh Policy Time: 20
                Remaining Time: 11
                Per-user timer remaining time: 0
                Antireplay Sequence Number: 817
        Peer Sessions:
        Session 1:
                Server handle: 2147483651
                Peer Address: 10.11.13.13
                Peer Version: 1.0.18
                Peer COOP version: 1.0.8
                COOP Protocol: base
                Peer Priority: 100
                Peer KS Role: Secondary , Peer KS Status: Alive
                Antireplay Sequence Number: 5

                IKE status: Established
                Counters:
                    Ann msgs sent: 815
                    Ann msgs sent with reply request: 1
                    Ann msgs recv: 4
                    Ann msgs recv with reply request: 1
                    Packet sent drops: 1
                    Packet Recv drops: 0
                    Total bytes sent: 561139
                    Total bytes recv: 1957

! Output omitted for brevity
Hub-1
Hub1-xTR# show crypto gdoi group V4GROUP-1
    Group Name            : V4GROUP-1
    Group Identity        : 101
    Group Type            : GDOI (ISAKMP)
    Crypto Path           : ipv4
    Key Management Path    : ipv4
```

```
    Rekeys received        : 1
    IPSec SA Direction     : Both

     Group Server list     : 10.11.13.13
                             10.12.14.14

Group Member Information For Group V4GROUP-1:
    IPSec SA Direction     : Both
    ACL Received From KS    : gdoi_group_V4GROUP-1_temp_acl

    Group member           : 192.168.11.11   vrf: None
       Local addr/port     : 192.168.11.11/848
       Remote addr/port    : 10.12.14.14/848
       fvrf/ivrf           : None/None
       Version             : 1.0.16
       Registration status  : Registered
       Registered with     : 10.12.14.14
       Re-registers in     : 3032 sec
       Succeeded registration: 2
       Attempted registration: 2
       Last rekey from     : 10.12.14.14
       Last rekey seq num   : 1
       Unicast rekey received: 1
       Rekey ACKs sent     : 1
       Rekey Rcvd(hh:mm:ss) : 00:06:05
       DP Error Monitoring  : OFF
       IPSEC init reg executed   : 0
       IPSEC init reg postponed  : 0
       Active TEK Number    : 2
       SA Track (OID/status) : disabled

       allowable rekey cipher: any
       allowable rekey hash  : any
       allowable transformtag: any ESP

     Rekeys cumulative
       Total received      : 1
       After latest register : 1
       Rekey Acks sents    : 1

 ACL Downloaded From KS 10.12.14.14:
   access-list   permit ip any any
```

```
KEK POLICY:

    Rekey Transport Type     : Unicast
    Lifetime (secs)          : 82917
    Encrypt Algorithm        : 3DES
    Key Size                 : 192
    Sig Hash Algorithm       : HMAC_AUTH_SHA
    Sig Key Length (bits)    : 752


TEK POLICY for the current KS-Policy ACEs Downloaded:
  LISP0.1:
    IPsec SA:
        spi: 0x6653721C(1716744732)
        transform: esp-256-aes esp-sha512-hmac
        sa timing:remaining key lifetime (sec): (3234)
        Anti-Replay(Time Based) : 5 sec interval
        tag method : disabled
        alg key size: 32 (bytes)
        sig key size: 64 (bytes)
        encaps: ENCAPS_TUNNEL


    IPsec SA:
        spi: 0x1AC835A1(449328545)
        transform: esp-256-aes esp-sha512-hmac
        sa timing:remaining key lifetime (sec): (119)
        Anti-Replay(Time Based) : 5 sec interval
        tag method : disabled
        alg key size: 32 (bytes)
        sig key size: 64 (bytes)
        encaps: ENCAPS_TUNNEL



KGS POLICY:
  REG_GM: local_addr 192.168.11.11 (client_reg enabled)


P2P POLICY:
  REG_GM: local_addr 192.168.11.11 (client_reg enabled)
```

After you perform all the verifications, you can determine connectivity between the end hosts. Example 10-24 verifies the connectivity from the host behind Site1-xTR to the host behind Site3-xTR and the host behind Hub1-xTR.

Example 10-24 *Verifying Connectivity Between Sites over LISP*

```
CE1
CE1# ping 172.17.3.3 source loopback0
Type escape sequence to abort.
Sending 5, 100-byte ICMP Echos to 172.17.3.3, timeout is 2 seconds:
Packet sent with a source address of 172.17.1.1
..!!!
Success rate is 60 percent (3/5), round-trip min/avg/max = 1/1/2 ms

CE1# ping 172.16.11.2 source loopback0
Type escape sequence to abort.
Sending 5, 100-byte ICMP Echos to 172.16.11.2, timeout is 2 seconds:
Packet sent with a source address of 172.17.1.1
..!!!
Success rate is 60 percent (3/5), round-trip min/avg/max = 1/1/2 ms
```

Summary

Every modern-day network requires enhanced security for both its control plane and data plane traffic. LISP provides seamless yet scalable and easy-to-deploy methods for implementing security in both the control plane and the data plane.

LISP leverages both the nonce field inside the LISP header and the LISP-SEC mechanism for securing control plane messages. The LISP-SEC mechanism works based on one-time-keys (OTKs) and series of hashes that are used to ensure that the control plane message is coming from a legitimate source and not from an attacker. It prevents man-in-the-middle attacks, which is very critical in an enterprise environment.

To secure the data plane without the extra costs of IPsec and other cryptographic techniques, LISP performs uRPF checks against the RLOC membership list that is distributed by the mapping server. This method, known as *source RLOC decapsulation filtering*, ensures that the data plane traffic is coming from a valid source and only allows the packets to be de-encapsulated.

LISP also can work in conjunction with GETVPN technology to ensure that the control plane and data plane traffic is encrypted with ESP and then forwarded out toward the service provider to reach the remote RLOC.

References

RFC 7835, "Locator/ID Separation Protocol (LISP) Threat Analysis"

RFC 8061, "Locator/ID Separation Protocol (LISP) Data-Plane Confidentiality"

Internet Draft, "LISP-Security (LISP-SEC)," draft-ietf-lisp-sec-17

Index

Symbols

H

I

J-K

L

O

P

Q-R